Large Scale and Big Data

Processing and Management

Large Scale and Big Data

Processing and Management

Edited by

Sherif Sakr

Cairo University, Egypt and
University of New South Wales, Australia

Mohamed Medhat Gaber

School of Computing Science and Digital Media
Robert Gordon University

CRC Press
Taylor & Francis Group
Boca Raton London New York

CRC Press is an imprint of the
Taylor & Francis Group, an **Informa** business
AN AUERBACH BOOK

CRC Press
Taylor & Francis Group
6000 Broken Sound Parkway NW, Suite 300
Boca Raton, FL 33487-2742

© 2014 by Taylor & Francis Group, LLC
CRC Press is an imprint of Taylor & Francis Group, an Informa business

No claim to original U.S. Government works

Printed on acid-free paper
Version Date: 20140721

International Standard Book Number-13: 978-1-4665-8150-0 (Hardback)

Library of Congress Cataloging-in-Publication Data

Large scale and big data : processing and management / editors, Sherif Sakr, Mohamed Medhat Gaber.
       pages cm
Includes bibliographical references and index.
ISBN 978-1-4665-8150-0 (hardback)
   1. Database management. 2. Big data. I. Sakr, Sherif, 1979- II. Gaber, Mohamed Medhat.

QA76.9.D3L3667 2014
005.7--dc23   2014002749

Visit the Taylor & Francis Web site at
http://www.taylorandfrancis.com

and the CRC Press Web site at
http://www.crcpress.com

Contents

Preface

Information from multiple sources is growing at a staggering rate. The number of Internet users reached 2.27 billion in 2012. Every day, Twitter generates more than 12 TB of tweets, Facebook generates more than 25 TB of log data, and the New York Stock Exchange captures 1 TB of trade information. About 30 billion radio-frequency identification (RFID) tags are created every day. Add to this mix the data generated by the hundreds of millions of GPS devices sold every year, and the more than 30 million networked sensors currently in use (and growing at a rate faster than 30% per year). These data volumes are expected to double every two years over the next decade. On the other hand, many companies can generate up to petabytes of information in the course of a year: web pages, blogs, clickstreams, search indices, social media forums, instant messages, text messages, email, documents, consumer demographics, sensor data from active and passive systems, and more. By many estimates, as much as 80% of this data is semistructured or unstructured. Companies are always seeking to become more nimble in their operations and more innovative with their data analysis and decision-making processes, and they are realizing that time lost in these processes can lead to missed business opportunities. In principle, the core of the Big Data challenge is for companies to gain the ability to analyze and understand Internet-scale information just as easily as they can now analyze and understand smaller volumes of structured information. In particular, the characteristics of these overwhelming flows of data, which are produced at multiple sources are currently subsumed under the notion of Big Data with 3Vs (volume, velocity, and variety). *Volume* refers to the scale of data, from terabytes to zettabytes, *velocity* reflects streaming data and large-volume data movements, and *variety* refers to the complexity of data in many different structures, ranging from relational to logs to raw text.

Cloud computing technology is a relatively new technology that simplifies the time-consuming processes of hardware provisioning, hardware purchasing, and software deployment, therefore, it revolutionizes the way computational resources and services are commercialized and delivered to customers. In particular, it shifts the location of this infrastructure to the network to reduce the costs associated with the management of hardware and software resources. This means that the cloud represents the long-held dream of envisioning computing as a utility, a dream in which the economy of scale principles help to effectively drive down the cost of the computing infrastructure.

This book approaches the challenges associated with Big Data-processing techniques and tools on cloud computing environments from different but integrated perspectives; it connects the dots. The book is designed for studying various fundamental challenges of storing and processing Big Data. In addition, it discusses the applications of Big Data processing in various domains. In particular, the book is divided into three main sections. The first section discusses the basic concepts and tools of large-scale big-data processing and cloud computing. It also provides an overview of different programming models and cloud-based deployment models. The second section focuses on presenting the usage of advanced Big Data-processing techniques in different practical domains such as semantic web, graph processing, and stream processing. The third section further discusses advanced topics of Big Data processing such as consistency management, privacy, and security.

In a nutshell, the book provides a comprehensive summary from both of the research and the applied perspectives. It will provide the reader with a better understanding of how Big Data-processing techniques and tools can be effectively utilized in different application domains.

Sherif Sakr
Mohamed Medhat Gaber

MATLAB® is a registered trademark of The MathWorks, Inc. For product information, please contact:

The MathWorks, Inc.
3 Apple Hill Drive
Natick, MA 01760-2098 USA
Tel: 508 647 7000
Fax: 508-647-7001
E-mail: info@mathworks.com
Web: www.mathworks.com

Editors

Dr. Sherif Sakr is a Senior Researcher National ICT Australia (NICTA), Sydney, Australia. He is also a Conjoint Senior Lecturer at University of New South Wales (UNSW). He received his PhD degree in Computer and Information Science from Konstanz University, Germany in 2007. He received his BSc and MSc degrees in Computer Science from Cairo University, Egypt, in 2000 and 2003 respectively. In 2011, Sherif held a Visiting Researcher position at the eXtreme Computing Group, Microsoft Research, USA. In 2012, he held a Research MTS position in Alcatel-Lucent Bell Labs. Dr. Sakr has published more than 60 refereed research publications in international journals and conferences such as the *IEEE TSC, ACM CSUR, JCSS, IEEE COMST, VLDB, SIGMOD, ICDE, WWW,* and *CIKM*. He has served in the organizing and program committees of numerous conferences and workshops.

Dr. Mohamed Medhat Gaber is a reader in the School of Computing Science and Digital Media of Robert Gordon University, UK. Mohamed received his PhD from Monash University, Australia, in 2006. He then held appointments with the University of Sydney, CSIRO, Monash University, and the University of Portsmouth. He has published over 100 papers, coauthored one monograph-style book, and edited/coedited four books on data mining, and knowledge discovery. Mohamed has served in the program committees of major conferences related to data mining, including *ICDM, PAKDD, ECML/PKDD,* and *ICML*. He has also been a member of the organizing committees of numerous conferences and workshops.

Contributors

Umut A. Acar
Carnegie Mellon University
Pittsburgh, Pennsylvania

Gabriel Antoniu
INRIA Rennes - Bretagne Atlantique
Rennes, France

Kemafor Anyanwu
North Carolina State University
Raleigh, North Carolina

Jagannath Aryal
University of Tasmania
Hobart, Tasmania, Australia

Pramod Bhatotia
MPI-SWS
Saarbrucken, Germany

Keke Chen
Wright State University
Dayton, Ohio

Rishan Chen
University of California San Diego
La Jolla, California

Meenal Chhabra
Virginia Tech
Blacksburg, Virginia

Byron Choi
Hong Kong Baptist University
Kowloon Tong, Hong Kong

Ritaban Dutta
CSIRO
Hobart, Tasmania, Australia

Sourav Dutta
IBM Research Lab
New Delhi, India

Houssem-Eddine Chihoub
INRIA Rennes - Bretagne Atlantique
Rennes, France

Radwa Elshawi
NICTA
and
University of Sydney
Sydney, New South Wales, Australia

Ayman G. Fayoumi
King Abdulaziz University
Jeddah, Saudi Arabia

Lixin Gao
University of Massachusetts Amherst
Amherst, Massachusetts

Qixin Gao
Northeastern University
Qinhuangdao, China

Rahul Ghosh
IBM
Durham, North Carolina

Shumin Guo
Wright State University
Dayton, Ohio

Mohammad Hammoud
Carnegie Mellon University
Doha, Qatar

Ragib Hasan
University of Alabama at Birmingham
Birmingham, Alabama

Bingsheng He
Nanyang Technological University
Singapore

Thomas Hornung
University of Freiburg
Freiburg, Germany

Shadi Ibrahim
INRIA Rennes - Bretagne Atlantique
Rennes, France

HyeongSik Kim
North Carolina State University
Raleigh, North Carolina

Georg Lausen
University of Freiburg
Freiburg, Germany

Anna Liu
NICTA
and
University of New South Wales
Sydney, New South Wales, Australia

Francesco Longo
Università degli Studi di Messina
Messina, Italy

Ahmed Metwally
Google
Mountain View, California

Ahsan Morshed
CSIRO
Hobart, Tasmania, Australia

Ankur Narang
IBM Research Lab
New Delhi, India

Matt Paduano
Google
Mountain View, California

Maria S. Perez
Universidad Politecnica de Madrid
Madrid, Spain

James Powers
Wright State University
Dayton, Ohio

Martin Przyjaciel-Zablocki
University of Freiburg
Freiburg, Germany

Padmashree Ravindra
North Carolina State University
Raleigh, North Carolina

Rodrigo Rodrigues
Nova University of Lisbon
Caparica, Portugal

Majd F. Sakr
Carnegie Mellon University
Doha, Qatar

Sherif Sakr
Cairo University
Cairo, Egypt

and

NICTA
and
University of New South Wales
Sydney, New South Wales, Australia

Alexander Schätzle
University of Freiburg
Freiburg, Germany

Fabio Soldo
Google
Mountain View, California

Fengguang Tian
Wright State University
Dayton, Ohio

Kishor S. Trivedi
Duke University
Durham, North Carolina

Charalampos E. Tsourakakis
Carnegie Mellon University
Pittsburgh, Pennsylvania

Cuirong Wang
Northeastern University
Qinhuangdao, China

Xuetian Weng
Stony Brook University
Stony Brook, New York

Alexander Wieder
MPI-SWS
Saarbrucken, Germany

Mao Yang
Microsoft Research Asia
Beijing, China

Yanfeng Zhang
Northeastern University
Shenyang, China

Liang Zhao
NICTA
and
University of New South Wales
Sydney, New South Wales, Australia

1 Distributed Programming for the Cloud
Models, Challenges, and Analytics Engines

Mohammad Hammoud and Majd F. Sakr

CONTENTS

1.1 INTRODUCTION

The effectiveness of cloud programs hinges on the manner in which they are designed, implemented, and executed. Designing and implementing programs for the cloud requires several considerations. First, they involve specifying the underlying programming model, whether message passing or shared memory. Second, they entail developing synchronous or asynchronous computation model. Third,

1

cloud programs can be tailored for graph or data parallelism, which require employing either data striping and distribution or graph partitioning and mapping. Lastly, from architectural and management perspectives, a cloud program can be typically organized in two ways, master/slave or peer-to-peer. Such organizations define the program's complexity, efficiency, and scalability.

Added to the above design considerations, when constructing cloud programs, special attention must be paid to various challenges like scalability, communication, heterogeneity, synchronization, fault tolerance, and scheduling. First, scalability is hard to achieve in large-scale systems (e.g., clouds) due to several reasons such as the inability of parallelizing all parts of algorithms, the high probability of load imbalance, and the inevitability of synchronization and communication overheads. Second, exploiting locality and minimizing network traffic are not easy to accomplish on (public) clouds since network topologies are usually unexposed. Third, heterogeneity caused by two common realities on clouds, virtualization environments and variety in datacenter components, impose difficulties in scheduling tasks and masking hardware and software differences across cloud nodes. Fourth, synchronization mechanisms must guarantee mutual exclusive accesses as well as properties like avoiding deadlocks and transitive closures, which are highly likely in distributed settings. Fifth, fault-tolerance mechanisms, including task resiliency, distributed checkpointing and message logging should be incorporated since the likelihood of failures increases on large-scale (public) clouds. Finally, task locality, high parallelism, task elasticity, and service level objectives (SLOs) need to be addressed in task and job schedulers for effective programs' executions.

Although designing, addressing, and implementing the requirements and challenges of cloud programs are crucial, they are difficult, require time and resource investments, and pose correctness and performance issues. Recently, distributed analytics engines such as MapReduce, Pregel, and GraphLab were developed to relieve programmers from worrying about most of the needs to construct cloud programs and focus mainly on the sequential parts of their algorithms. Typically, these analytics engines automatically parallelize sequential algorithms provided by users in high-level programming languages like Java and C++, synchronize and schedule constituent tasks and jobs, and handle failures, *all* without any involvement from users/developers. In this chapter, we first define some common terms in the theory of distributed programming, draw a requisite relationship between distributed systems and clouds, and discuss the main requirements and challenges for building distributed programs for clouds. While discussing the main requirements for building cloud programs, we indicate how MapReduce, Pregel, and GraphLab address each requirement. Finally, we close up with a summary on the chapter and a comparison among MapReduce, Pregel, and GraphLab.

1.2 TAXONOMY OF PROGRAMS

A computer program consists of variable declarations, variable assignments, expressions, and flow control statements written typically using a high-level programming language such as Java or C++. Computer programs are compiled before executed on machines. After compilation, they are converted to a machine instructions/code that run over computer processors either *sequentially* or *concurrently* in an in-order or out-of-order manner, respectively. A **sequential program** is a program that runs in the *program order*. The program order is the original order of statements in a program as specified by a programmer. A **concurrent program** is a set of sequential programs that *share in time* a certain processor when executed. Sharing in time (or timesharing) allows sequential programs to take turns in using a certain resource component. For instance, with a single CPU and multiple sequential programs, the operating system (OS) can allocate the CPU to each program for a specific time interval; given that only one program can run at a time on the CPU. This can be achieved using a specific CPU scheduler such as the round-robin scheduler [69].

Programs, being sequential or concurrent, are often named interchangeably as applications. A different term that is also frequently used alongside concurrent programs is **parallel programs**. Parallel programs are technically different than concurrent programs. A parallel program is a set of sequential programs that overlap in time by running on separate CPUs. In multiprocessor systems such as chip multicore machines, related sequential programs that are executed at different cores represent a parallel program, while related sequential programs that share the same CPU in time represent a concurrent program. To this end, we refer to a parallel program with multiple sequential programs that run on different networked machines (not on different cores at the same machine) as **distributed program**. Consequently, a distributed program can essentially include all types of programs. In particular, a distributed program can consist of multiple parallel programs, which in return can consist of multiple concurrent programs, which in return can consist of multiple sequential programs. For example, assume a set S that includes 4 sequential programs, P_1, P_2, P_3, and P_4 (i.e., $S = \{P_1, P_2, P_3, P_4\}$). A concurrent program, P', can encompass P_1 and P_2 (i.e., $P' = \{P_1, P_2\}$), whereby P_1 and P_2 share in time a single core. Furthermore, a parallel program, P'', can encompass P' and P_3 (i.e., $P'' = \{P', P_3\}$), whereby P' and P_3 overlap in time over multiple cores on the same machine. Lastly, a distributed program, P''', can encompass P'' and P_4 (i.e., $P''' = \{P'', P_4\}$), whereby P'' runs on different cores on the same machine and P_4 runs on a different machine as opposed to P''. In this chapter, we are mostly concerned with distributed programs. Figure 1.1 shows our program taxonomy.

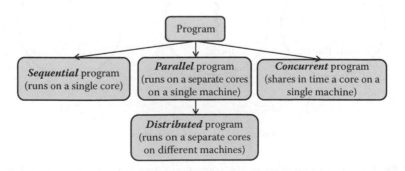

FIGURE 1.1 Our taxonomy of programs.

1.3   TASKS AND JOBS IN DISTRIBUTED PROGRAMS

Another common term in the theory of parallel/distributed programming is *multi-tasking*. Multitasking is referred to overlapping the computation of one program with that of another. Multitasking is central to all modern operating systems (OSs), whereby an OS can overlap computations of multiple programs by means of a scheduler. Multitasking has become so useful that almost all modern programming languages are now supporting multitasking via providing constructs for *multithreading*. A thread of execution is the smallest sequence of instructions that an OS canmanage through its scheduler. The term thread was popularized by Pthreads (POSIX threads [59]), a specification of concurrency constructs that has been widely adopted, especially in UNIX systems [8]. A technical distinction is often made between **processes** and **threads**. A process runs using its own address space while a thread runs within the address space of a process (i.e., threads are parts of processes and not *standalone* sequences of instructions). A process can contain one or many threads. In principle, processes do not share address spaces among each other, while the threads in a process do share the process's address space. The term **task** is also used to refer to a small unit of work. In this chapter, we use the term task to denote a process, which can include multiple threads. In addition, we refer to a group of tasks (which can only be one task) that belong to the same program/application as a **job**. An application can encompass multiple jobs. For instance, a fluid dynamics application typically consists of three jobs, one responsible for structural analysis, one for fluid analysis, and one for thermal analysis. Each of these jobs can in return have multiple tasks to carry on the pertaining analysis. Figure 1.2 demonstrates the concepts of processes, threads, tasks, jobs, and applications.

1.4   MOTIVATIONS FOR DISTRIBUTED PROGRAMMING

In principle, every sequential program can be parallelized by identifying sources of parallelism in it. Various analysis techniques at the algorithm and code levels can be applied to identify parallelism in sequential programs [67]. Once sources of parallelism are detected, a program can be split into *serial* and *parallel* parts as shown in

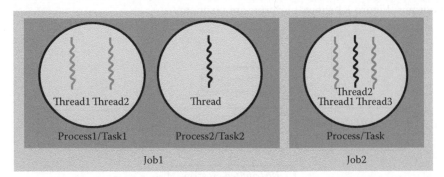

Distributed application/program

FIGURE 1.2   A demonstration of the concepts of processes, threads, tasks, jobs, and applications.

Figure 1.3. The parallel parts of a program can be run either concurrently or in parallel on a single machine, or in a distributed fashion across machines. Programmers parallelize their sequential programs primarily to run them faster and/or achieve higher throughput (e.g., number of data blocks read per hour). Specifically, in an ideal world, what programmers expect is that by parallelizing a sequential program into an n-way distributed program, an n-fold decrease in execution time is obtained. Using distributed programs as opposed to sequential ones is crucial for multiple domains, especially for science. For instance, simulating a single protein folding can take years if performed sequentially, while it only takes days if executed in a distributed manner [67]. Indeed, the pace of scientific discovery is contingent on how fast some certain scientific problems can be solved. Furthermore, some programs have real time constraints by which if computation is not performed fast enough, the whole program might turn out to be useless. For example, predicting the direction of hurricanes and tornados using weather modeling must be done in a timely manner or the whole prediction will be unusable. In actuality, scientists and engineers have relied on distributed programs for decades to solve important and complex scientific problems such as quantum mechanics, physical simulations, weather forecasting, oil and gas exploration, and molecular modeling, to mention a few. We expect this trend to continue, at least for the foreseeable future.

Distributed programs have also found a broader audience outside science, such as serving search engines, Web servers, and databases. For instance, much of the success of Google can be traced back to the effectiveness of its algorithms such as PageRank [42]. PageRank is a distributed program that is run within Google's search engine over thousands of machines to rank web pages. Without parallelization, PageRank cannot achieve its goals effectively. Parallelization allows also leveraging available resources effectively. For example, running a Hadoop MapReduce [27] program over a single Amazon EC2 instance will not be as effective as running it over a large-scale cluster of EC2 instances. Of course, committing jobs earlier on the cloud leads to fewer dollar costs, a key objective for cloud users. Lastly, distributed programs can further serve greatly in alleviating subsystem bottlenecks. For instance, I/O devices such as disks and

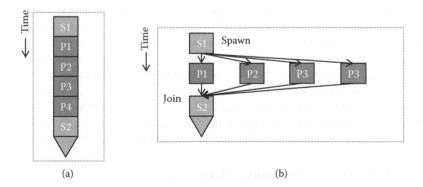

(a) (b)

FIGURE 1.3 (a) A sequential program with serial (S_i) and parallel (P_i) parts. (b) A parallel/distributed program that corresponds to the sequential program in (a), whereby the parallel parts can be either distributed across machines or run concurrently on a single machine.

network card interfaces typically represent major bottlenecks in terms of bandwidth, performance, and/or throughput. By distributing work across machines, data can be serviced from multiple disks simultaneously, thus offering an increasingly aggregate I/O bandwidth, improving performance, and maximizing throughput. In summary, distributed programs play a critical role in rapidly solving various computing problems and effectively mitigating resource bottlenecks. This subsequently improves performances, increases throughput and reduces costs, especially on the cloud.

1.5 MODELS OF DISTRIBUTED PROGRAMS

Distributed programs are run on distributed systems, which consist of networked computers. The cloud is a special distributed system. In this section, we first define distributed systems and draw a relationship between clouds and distributed systems. Second, in an attempt to answer the question of how to program the cloud, we present two traditional distributed programming models, which can be used for that sake, the **shared-memory** and the **message-passing** programming models. Third, we discuss the computation models that cloud programs can employ. Specifically, we describe the **synchronous** and **asynchronous** computation models. Fourth, we present the two main parallelism categories of distributed programs intended for clouds, **data parallelism** and **graph parallelism**. Lastly, we end the discussion with the architectural models that cloud programs can typically utilize, **master/slave** and **peer-to-peer** architectures.

1.5.1 DISTRIBUTED SYSTEMS AND THE CLOUD

Networks of computers are ubiquitous. The Internet, high-performance computing (HPC) clusters, mobile phone, and in-car networks, among others, are common examples of networked computers. Many networks of computers are deemed as distributed systems. We define a distributed system as one in which networked computers communicate using message passing and/or shared memory and coordinate their actions to solve a certain problem or offer a specific service. One significant consequence of our definition pertains to clouds. Specifically, since a cloud is defined as a set of Internet-based software, platform and infrastructure services offered through a cluster of networked computers (i.e., a datacenter), it becomes a distributed system. Another consequence of our definition is that distributed programs will be the norm in distributed systems such as the cloud. In particular, we defined distributed programs in Section 1.1 as a set of sequential programs that run on separate processors at different machines. Thus, the only way for tasks in distributed programs to interact over a distributed system is to either send and receive messages explicitly or read and write from/to a shared distributed memory supported by the underlying distributed system. We next discuss these two possible ways of enabling distributed tasks to interact over distributed systems.

1.5.2 TRADITIONAL PROGRAMMING MODELS AND
DISTRIBUTED ANALYTICS ENGINES

A distributed programming model is an abstraction provided to programmers so that they can translate their algorithms into distributed programs that can execute over distributed systems (e.g., the cloud). A distributed programming model defines how easily and efficiently algorithms can be specified as distributed programs. For instance, a distributed programming model that highly abstracts architectural/ hardware details, automatically parallelizes and distributes computation, and transparently supports fault tolerance is deemed an easy-to-use programming model. The efficiency of the model, however, depends on the effectiveness of the techniques that underlie the model. There are two classical distributed programming models that are in wide use, **shared memory** and **message passing**. The two models fulfill different needs and suit different circumstances. Nonetheless, they are elementary in a sense that they only provide a basic interaction model for distributed tasks and lack any facility to automatically parallelize and distribute tasks or tolerate faults. Recently, there have been other advanced models that address the inefficiencies and challenges posed by the shared-memory and the message-passing models, especially upon porting them to the cloud. Among these models are MapReduce [17], Pregel [49], and GraphLab [47]. These models are built upon the shared-memory and the message-passing programming paradigms, yet are more involved and offer various properties that are essential for the cloud. As these models highly differ from the traditional ones, we refer to them as **distributed analytics engines**.

1.5.2.1 The Shared-Memory Programming Model

In the shared-memory programming model, tasks can communicate by reading and writing to shared memory (or disk) locations. Thus, the abstraction provided by the shared-memory model is that tasks can access any location in the distributed memories/disks. This is similar to threads of a single process in operating systems, whereby all threads share the process address space and communicate by reading and writing to that space (see Figure 1.4). Therefore, with shared-memory, data is not explicitly communicated but implicitly exchanged via sharing. Due to sharing, the shared-memory programming model entails the usage of **synchronization** mechanisms within distributed programs. Synchronization is needed to control the order in which read/write operations are performed by various tasks. In particular, what is required is that distributed tasks are prevented from simultaneously writing to a shared data, so as to avoid corrupting the data or making it inconsistent. This can be typically achieved using **semaphores**, **locks**, and/or **barriers**. A semaphore is a point-to-point synchronization mechanism that involves two parallel/distributed

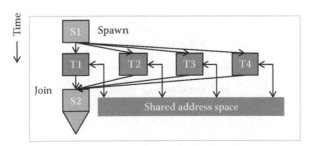

FIGURE 1.4 Tasks running in parallel and sharing an address space through which they can communicate.

tasks. Semaphores use two operations, post and wait. The post operation acts like depositing a token, signaling that data has been produced. The wait operation blocks until signaled by the post operation that it can proceed with consuming data. Locks protect **critical sections** or regions that at most one task can access (typically write) at a time. Locks involve two operations, lock and unlock for acquiring and releasing a lock associated with a critical section, respectively. A lock can be held by only one task at a time, and other tasks cannot acquire it until released. Lastly, a barrier defines a point at which a task is not allowed to proceed until every other task reaches that point. The efficiency of semaphores, locks, and barriers is a critical and challenging goal in developing distributed/parallel programs for the shared-memory programming model (details on the challenges that pertain to synchronization are provided in Section 1.5.4).

Figure 1.5 shows an example that transforms a simple sequential program into a distributed program using the shared-memory programming model. The sequential program adds up the elements of two arrays *b* and *c* and stores the resultant elements in array *a*. Afterward, if any element in *a* is found to be greater than 0, it is added to a grand sum. The corresponding distributed version assumes only two tasks and splits the work evenly across them. For every task, start and end variables are specified to correctly index the (shared) arrays, obtain data, and apply the given algorithm. Clearly, the grand sum is a critical section; hence, a lock is used to protect it. In addition, no task can print the grand sum before every other task has finished its part, thus a barrier is utilized prior to the printing statement. As shown in the program, the communication between the two tasks is implicit (via reads and writes to shared

```
for (i=0; i<8; i++)
  a[i] = b[i] + c[i];
sum = 0;
for (i=0; i<8; i++)
  if (a[i] > 0)
    sum = sum + a[i];
Print sum;
```

(a)

```
begin parallel // spawn a child thread
private int start_iter, end_iter, i;
shared int local_iter=4, sum=0;
shared double sum=0.0, a[], b[], c[];
shared lock_type mylock;

start_iter = getid() * local_iter;
end_iter = start_iter + local_iter;
for (i=start_iter; i<end_iter; i++)
  a[i] = b[i] + c[i];
barrier;

for (i=start_iter; i<end_iter; i++)
  if (a[i] > 0) {
    lock(mylock);
      sum = sum + a[i];
    unlock(mylock);
  }
barrier;     // necessary

end parallel // kill the child thread
Print sum;
```

(b)

FIGURE 1.5 (a) A sequential program that sums up elements of two arrays and computes a grand sum on results that are greater than zero. (b) A distributed version of the program in (a) coded using the shared-memory programming model.

arrays and variables) and synchronization is explicit (via locks and barriers). Lastly, as pointed out earlier, sharing of data has to be offered by the underlying distributed system. Specifically, the underlying distributed system should provide an illusion that all memories/disks of the computers in the system form a single shared space addressable by all tasks. A common example of systems that offer such an underlying shared (virtual) address space on a cluster of computers (connected by a LAN) is denoted as *distributed shared memory* (DSM) [44,45,70]. A common programing language that can be used on DSMs and other distributed shared systems is OpenMP [55].

Other modern examples that employ a shared-memory view/abstraction are MapReduce and GraphLab. To summarize, the shared-memory programming model entails two main criteria: (1) developers need not explicitly encode functions that send/receive messages in their programs, and (2) the underlying storage layer provides a shared view to all tasks (i.e., tasks can transparently access any location in the underlying storage). Clearly, MapReduce satisfies the two criteria. In particular, MapReduce developers write only two sequential functions known as the map and the reduce functions (i.e., no functions are written or called that explicitly send and receive messages). In return, MapReduce breaks down the user-defined map and reduce functions into multiple tasks denoted as map and reduce tasks. All map tasks are encapsulated in what is known as the map phase, and all reduce tasks are encompassed in what is called the reduce phase. Subsequently, all communications occur only between the map and the reduce phases and under the full control of the engine itself. In addition, any required synchronization is also handled by the MapReduce engine. For instance, in MapReduce, the user-defined reduce function cannot be applied before all the map phase output (or intermediate output) are shuffled, merged, and sorted. Obviously, this requires a barrier between the map and the reduce phases, which the MapReduce engine internally incorporates. Second, MapReduce uses the Hadoop Distributed File System (HDFS) [27] as an underlying storage layer. As any typical distributed file system, HDFS provides a shared abstraction for all tasks, whereby any task can transparently access any location in HDFS (i.e., as if accesses are local). Therefore, MapReduce is deemed to offer a shared-memory abstraction provided internally by Hadoop (i.e., the MapReduce engine and HDFS).

Similar to MapReduce, GraphLab offers a shared-memory abstraction [24,47]. In particular, GraphLab eliminates the need for users to explicitly send/receive messages in update functions (which represent the user-defined computations in it) and provides a shared view among vertices in a graph. To elaborate, GraphLab allows **scopes** of vertices to overlap and vertices to read and write from and to their scopes. The scope of a vertex v (denoted as Sv) is the data stored in v and in all v's adjacent edges and vertices. Clearly, this poses potential read–write and write–write conflicts between vertices sharing scopes. The GraphLab engine (and not the users) synchronizes accesses to shared scopes and ensures consistent parallel execution via supporting three levels of consistency settings, **full consistency**, **edge consistency**, and **vertex consistency**. Under full consistency, the update function at each vertex has an exclusive read–write access to its vertex, adjacent edges, and adjacent vertices. While this guarantees strong consistency and full correctness, it limits parallelism and consequently performance. Under edge consistency, the update function at a vertex has an exclusive read–write access to its vertex and adjacent edges, but only a read access to adjacent vertices. Clearly, this relaxes consistency and enables a superior leverage of parallelism. Finally, under vertex consistency, the update function at a vertex has an exclusive write access to only its vertex, hence, allowing all update functions at all vertices to run simultaneously. Obviously, this provides the maximum possible parallelism but, in return, the most relaxed consistency. GraphLab allows users to choose whatever consistency model they find convenient for their applications.

1.5.2.2 The Message-Passing Programming Model

In the message-passing programming model, distributed tasks communicate by sending and receiving messages. In other words, distributed tasks do not share an address space at which they can access each other's memories (see Figure 1.6). Accordingly, the abstraction provided by the message-passing programming model is similar to that of processes (and not threads) in operating systems. The message-passing programming model incurs communication overheads (e.g., variable network latency, potentially excessive data transfers) for explicitly sending and receiving messages that contain data. Nonetheless, the explicit sends and receives of messages serve in implicitly synchronizing the sequence of operations imposed by the communicating tasks. Figure 1.7 demonstrates an example that transforms the same sequential program shown in Figure 1.5a into a distributed program using message passing. Initially, it is assumed that only a main task with id = 0 has access to arrays *b* and *c*. Thus, assuming the existence of only two tasks, the main task first sends parts of the arrays to the other task (using an explicit send operation) to evenly split the work among the two tasks. The other task receives the required data (using an explicit receive operation) and performs a local sum. When done, it sends back its local sum to the main task. Likewise, the main task performs a local sum on its part of data and collects the local sum of the other task before aggregating and printing a grand sum.

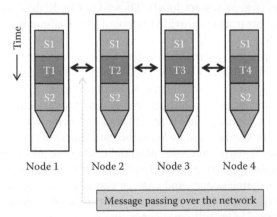

FIGURE 1.6 Tasks running in parallel using the message-passing programming model whereby the interactions happen only via sending and receiving messages over the network.

```
id = getpid();
local_iter = 4;
start_iter = id * local_iter;
end_iter = start_iter + local_iter;

if (id == 0)
  send_msg (P1, b[4..7], c[4..7]);
else
  recv_msg (P0, b[4..7], c[4..7]);

for (i=start_iter; i<end_iter; i++)
  a[i] = b[i] + c[i];

local_sum = 0;
for (i=start_iter; i<end_iter; i++)
  if (a[i] > 0)
    local_sum = local_sum + a[i];
if (id == 0) {
  recv_msg (P1, &local_sum1);
  sum = local_sum + local_sum1;
  Print sum;
}
else
  send_msg (P0, local_sum);
```

FIGURE 1.7 A distributed program that corresponds to the sequential program in Figure 1.5a coded using the message-passing programming model.

As shown, for every send operation, there is a corresponding receive operation. No explicit synchronization is needed.

Clearly, the message-passing programming model does not necessitate any support from the underlying distributed system due to relying on explicit messages. Specifically, no illusion for a single shared address space is required from the distributed system in order for the tasks to interact. A popular example of a message-passing programming model is provided by the Message Passing Interface (MPI) [50]. MPI is a message passing, industry-standard library (more precisely, a specification of what a library can do) for writing message-passing programs. A popular high-performance and widely portable implementation of MPI is MPICH [52]. A common analytics engine that employs the message-passing programming model is Pregel. In Pregel, vertices can communicate only by sending and receiving messages, which should be explicitly encoded by users/developers.

To this end, Table 1.1 compares between the shared-memory and the message-passing programming models in terms of five aspects, *communication, synchronization, hardware support, development effort,* and *tuning effort.* Shared-memory programs are easier to develop at the outset because programmers need not worry about how data is laid out or communicated. Furthermore, the code structure of a shared-memory program is often not much different than its respective sequential one. Typically, only additional directives are added by programmers to specify parallel/distributed tasks, scope of variables, and synchronization points. In contrast, message-passing programs require a switch in the programmer's thinking,

TABLE 1.1

A Comparison between the Shared-Memory and the Message-Passing Programming Models

Aspect	The Shared-Memory Model	The Message-Passing Model
Communication	Implicit	Explicit
Synchronization	Explicit	Implicit
Hardware support	Usually required	Not required
Initial development effort	Lower	Higher
Tuning effort upon scaling up	Higher	Lower

wherein the programmer needs to think a priori about how to partition data across tasks, collect data, and communicate and aggregate results using explicit messaging. Alongside, scaling up the system entails less tuning (denoted as tuning effort in Table 1.1) of message-passing programs as opposed to shared-memory ones. Specifically, when using a shared-memory model, how data is laid out, and where it is stored start to affect performance significantly. To elaborate, large-scale distributed systems like the cloud imply non-uniform access latencies (e.g., accessing remote data takes more time than accessing local data), thus enforces programmers to lay out data close to relevant tasks. While message-passing programmers think about partitioning data across tasks during pre-development time, shared memory programmers do not. Hence, shared memory programmers need (most of the time) to address the issue during post-development time (e.g., through data migration or replication). Clearly, this might dictate a greater post-development tuning effort as compared with the message-passing case. Finally, synchronization points might further become performance bottlenecks in large-scale systems. In particular, as the number of users that attempt to access critical sections increases, delays, and waits on such sections also increase. More on synchronization and other challenges involved in programming the cloud are presented in Section 1.5.

1.5.3 SYNCHRONOUS AND ASYNCHRONOUS DISTRIBUTED PROGRAMS

Apart from programming models, distributed programs, being shared-memory or message-passing based, can be specified as either **synchronous** or **asynchronous** programs. A distributed program is synchronous if and only if the distributed tasks operate in a *lock-step mode*. That is, if there is some constant $c \geq 1$ and any task has taken $c + 1$ steps, every other task should have taken at least 1 step [71]. Clearly, this entails a coordination mechanism through which the activities of tasks can be synchronized and the lock-step mode be accordingly enforced. Such a mechanism usually has an important effect on performance. Typically, in synchronous programs, distributed tasks must wait at predetermined points for the completion of certain computations or for the arrival of certain data [9]. A distributed program that is not synchronous is referred to as asynchronous. Asynchronous programs expose no requirements for waiting at predetermined points and/or for the arrival of specific data. Obviously, this has less effect on performance but implies that the correctness/ validity of the program must be assessed. In short, the distinction between synchronous and asynchronous distributed programs refers to the presence or absence of a (global) coordination mechanism that synchronizes the operations of tasks and imposes a lock-step mode. As specific examples, MapReduce and Pregel programs are synchronous, while GraphLab ones are asynchronous.

One synchronous model that is commonly employed for effectively implementing distributed programs is the **bulk synchronous parallel** (BSP) model [74] (see Figure 1.8). The Pregel programs follow particularly the BSP model. BSP is defined as a combination of three attributes, *components*, a *router*, and a *synchronization* method. A component in BSP consists of a processor attached with data stored in local memory. BSP, however, does not exclude other arrangements such as holding data in remote memories. BSP is neutral about the number of processors, be it two or millions. BSP programs can be written for v virtual distributed processors to run on p physical distributed processors, where v is larger than p. BSP is based on the message-passing programming model, whereby components can only communicate by sending and receiving messages. This is achieved through a router which in principle can only pass messages point to point between pairs of components (i.e., no broadcasting facilities are available, though it can be implemented using multiple point-to-point communications). Finally, as being a synchronous model, BSP splits every computation into a sequence of steps called **super-steps**. In every super-step, S, each component is assigned a task encompassing (local) computation. Besides, components in super-step S are allowed to send messages to components in super-step $S + 1$, and are (implicitly) allowed to receive messages from components in super-step $S - 1$. Tasks within every super-step operate simultaneously and do not communicate with each other. Tasks across super-steps move in a lock-step mode as suggested by any synchronous model. Specifically, no task in super-step $S + 1$ is allowed to start before every task in super-step S commits. To satisfy this condition, BSP applies a global barrier-style synchronization mechanism as shown in Figure 1.8.

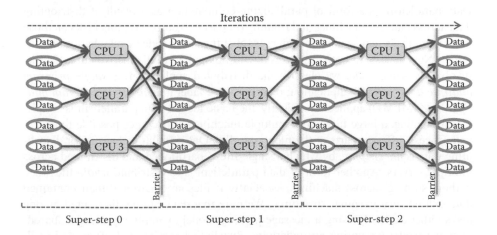

FIGURE 1.8 The bulk synchronous parallel (BSP) model.

BSP does not suggest simultaneous accesses to the same memory location, hence, precludes the requirement for a synchronization mechanism other than barriers. Another primary concern in a distributed setting is to allocate data in a way that computation will not be slowed down by non-uniform memory access latencies or uneven loads among individual tasks. BSP promotes uniform access latencies via enforcing local data accesses. In particular, data are communicated across super-steps before triggering actual task computations. As such, BSP carefully segregates computation from communication. Such a segregation entails that no particular network topology is favored beyond the requirement that high throughput is delivered. Butterfly, hypercube, and optical crossbar topologies can all be employed with BSP. With respect to task loads, data can still vary across tasks within a super-step. This typically depends on: (1) the responsibilities that the distributed program imposes on its constituent tasks, and (2) the characteristics of the underlying cluster nodes (more on this in Section 1.5.1). As a consequence, tasks that are lightly loaded (or are run on fast machines) will potentially finish earlier than tasks that are heavily loaded (or are run on slow machines). Subsequently, the time required to finish a super-step becomes bound by the slowest task in the super-step (i.e., a super-step cannot commit before the slowest task commits). This presents a major challenge for the BSP model as it might create load imbalance, which usually degrades performance. Finally, it is worth noting that while BSP suggests several design choices, it does not make their use obligatory. Indeed, BSP leaves many design choices open (e.g., barrier-based synchronization can be implemented at a finer granularity or completely switched off–if it is acceptable by the given application).

1.5.4 DATA PARALLEL AND GRAPH PARALLEL COMPUTATIONS

As distributed programs can be constructed using either the shared-memory or the message-passing programming models as well as specified as being synchronous or asynchronous, they can be tailored for different parallelism types. Specifically, distributed programs can either incorporate **data parallelism** or **graph parallelism**. Data parallelism is a form of parallelizing computation as a result of distributing data across multiple machines and running (in parallel) corresponding tasks on those machines. Tasks across machines may involve the same code or may be totally different. Nonetheless, in both cases, tasks will be applied to distinctive data. If tasks involve the same code, we classify the distributed application as *single program multiple data* (SPMD) application; otherwise, we label it as *multiple program multiple data* (MPMD) application. Clearly, the basic idea of data parallelism is simple; by distributing, a large file across multiple machines, it becomes possible to access and process different parts of the file in parallel. One popular technique for distributing data is *file striping*, by which a single file is partitioned and distributed across multiple servers. Another form of data parallelism is to distribute *whole* files (i.e., without striping) across machines, especially if files are small and their contained data exhibit very irregular structures. We note that data can be distributed among tasks either explicitly using a message-passing model or implicitly using a shared-memory model (assuming an underlying distributed system that offers a shared-memory abstraction).

Data parallelism is achieved when each machine runs one or many tasks over different partitions of data. As a specific example, assume array A is shared among three machines in a distributed shared memory system. Consider also a distributed program that simply adds all elements of array A. It is possible to charge machines 1, 2, and 3 to run the addition task, each on 1/3 of A, or 50 elements, as shown in Figure 1.9. The data can be allocated across tasks using the shared-memory programming model, which requires a synchronization mechanism. Clearly, such a program is SPMD. In contrast, array A can also be partitioned evenly and distributed across three machines using the message-passing model as shown in Figure 1.10. Each machine will run the addition task independently; nonetheless, summation results will have to be eventually aggregated at one main task to generate a grand total. In such a scenario, every task is similar in a sense that it is performing the same addition operation, yet on a different part of A. The main task, however, is further aggregating summation results, thus making it a little different than the other two tasks. Obviously, this makes the program MPMD.

As a real example, MapReduce uses data parallelism. In particular, input data sets are partitioned by HDFS into blocks (by default, 64 MB per block) allowing MapReduce to effectively exploit data parallelism via running a map task per one or many blocks (by default, each map task processes only one HDFS block). Furthermore, as map tasks operate on HDFS blocks, reduce tasks operate on the output of map tasks denoted as **intermediate output** or **partitions**. In principle, each reduce task can process one or many partitions. As a consequence, the data processed by map and reduce tasks become different. Moreover, map and reduce tasks are inherently dissimilar (i.e., the map and the reduce functions incorporate different binary codes). Therefore, MapReduce jobs lie under the MPMD category.

Graph parallelism contrasts with data parallelism. Graph parallelism is another form of parallelism that focuses more on distributing graphs as opposed to data. Indeed, most distributed programs fall somewhere on a continuum between data

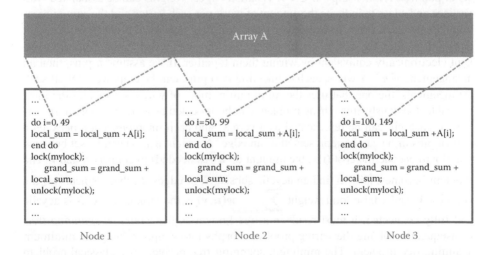

FIGURE 1.9   An SPMD distributed program using the shared-memory programming model.

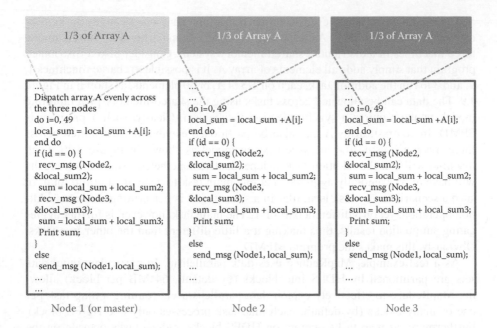

| 1/3 of Array A | 1/3 of Array A | 1/3 of Array A |

```
...
Dispatch array A evenly across
the three nodes
do i=0, 49
local_sum = local_sum +A[i];
end do
if (id == 0) {
  recv_msg (Node2,
&local_sum2);
  sum = local_sum + local_sum2;
  recv_msg (Node3,
&local_sum3);
  sum = local_sum + local_sum3;
  Print sum;
}
else
  send_msg (Node1, local_sum);
...
...
```

```
...
...
do i=0, 49
local_sum = local_sum +A[i];
end do
if (id == 0) {
  recv_msg (Node2,
&local_sum2);
  sum = local_sum + local_sum2;
  recv_msg (Node3,
&local_sum3);
  sum = local_sum + local_sum3;
  Print sum;
}
else
  send_msg (Node1, local_sum);
...
...
```

```
...
...
do i=0, 49
local_sum = local_sum +A[i];
end do
if (id == 0) {
  recv_msg (Node2,
&local_sum2);
  sum = local_sum + local_sum2;
  recv_msg (Node3,
&local_sum3);
  sum = local_sum + local_sum3;
  Print sum;
}
else
  send_msg (Node1, local_sum);
...
...
```

Node 1 (or master)   Node 2   Node 3

FIGURE 1.10 An MPMD distributed program using the message-passing programming model.

parallelism and graph parallelism. Graph parallelism is widely used in many domains such as machine learning, data mining, physics, and electronic circuit designs, among others. Many problems in these domains can be modeled as *graphs* in which *vertices* represent computations and edges encode data dependencies or communications. Recall that a graph *G* is a pair (*V*, *E*), where *V* is a finite set of vertices and *E* is a finite set of pairwise relationships, $E \subset V \times V$, called edges. Weights can be associated with vertices and edges to indicate the amount of work per each vertex and the communication data per each edge. To exemplify, let us consider a classical problem from circuit design. It is often the case in circuit design that pins of several components are to be kept electronically equivalent by wiring them together. If we assume *n* pins, then an arrangement of *n* − 1 wires, each connecting two pins, can be employed. Of all such arrangements, the one that uses the minimum number of wires is normally the most desirable. Obviously, this wiring problem can be modeled as a graph problem. In particular, each pin can be represented as a vertex, and each interconnection between a pair of pins (*u*, *v*) can be represented as an edge. A weight *w*(*u*, *v*) can be set between *u* and *v* to encode the cost (i.e., the amount of wires needed) to connect *u* and *v*. The problem becomes, how to find an acyclic subset, *S*, of edges, *E*, that connects all the vertices, *V*, and whose total weight $\sum_{(u,v) \in s} w(u,v)$ is the *minimum*. As *S* is acyclic and fully connected, it must result in a tree known as the *minimum spanning tree*. Consequently, solving the wiring problem morphs into simply solving the minimum spanning tree problem. The minimum spanning tree problem is a classical problem and can be solved using Kruskal's or Prim's algorithms, to mention a few [15].

Once a problem is modeled as a graph, it can be distributed over machines in a distributed system using a **graph partitioning technique**. Graph partitioning implies dividing the work (i.e., the vertices) over distributed nodes for efficient distributed computation. As is the case with data parallelism, the basic idea is simple; by distributing a large graph across multiple machines, it becomes possible to process different parts of the graph in parallel. As such, graph partitioning enables what we refer to as *graph parallelism*. The standard objective of graph partitioning is to uniformly distribute the work over p processors by partitioning the vertices into p equally weighted partitions, while minimizing inter-node communication reflected by edges. Such an objective is typically referred to as the standard **edge cut metric** [34]. The graph partitioning problem is NP-hard [21], yet heuristics can be implemented to achieve near optimal solutions [34,35,39]. As a specific example, Figure 1.11 demonstrates three partitions, P_1, P_2, and P_3 at which vertices $v_1,..., v_8$ are divided using the edge cut metric. Each edge has a weight of 2 corresponding to 1 unit of data being communicated in each direction. Consequently, the total weight of the shown edge cut is 10. Other cuts will result in more communication traffic. Clearly, for communication-intensive applications, graph partitioning is very critical and can play a dramatic role in dictating the overall application performance. We discuss some of the challenges pertaining to graph partitioning in Section 1.5.3.

As real examples, both Pregel and GraphLab employ graph partitioning. Specifically, in Pregel each vertex in a graph is assigned a unique ID, and partitioning of the graph is accomplished via using a *hash(ID) mod N* function, where N is the number of partitions. The hash function is customizable and can be altered by users. After partitioning the graph, partitions are mapped to cluster machines using a mapping function of a user choice. For example, a user can define a mapping function for a Web graph that attempts to exploit locality by co-locating vertices of the same Web site (a vertex in this case represents a Web page). In contrast to Pregel, GraphLab utilizes a *two-phase partitioning* strategy. In the first phase, the input

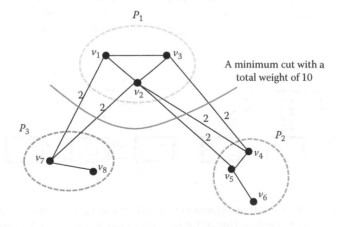

FIGURE 1.11   A graph partitioned using the edge cut metric.

graph is partitioned into k partitions using a hash-based random algorithm [47], with k being much larger than the number of cluster machines. A partition in GraphLab is called an **atom**. GraphLab does not store the actual vertices and edges in atoms, but *commands* to generate them. In addition to commands, GraphLab maintains in each atom some information about the atom's neighboring vertices and edges. This is denoted in GraphLab as **ghosts**. Ghosts are used as a caching capability for efficient adjacent data accessibility. In the second phase of the two-phase partitioning strategy, GraphLab stores the connectivity structure and the locations of atoms in an **atom index file** referred to as **metagraph**. The atom index file encompasses k vertices (with each vertex corresponding to an atom) and edges encoding connectivity among atoms. The atom index file is split uniformly across the cluster machines. Afterward, atoms are loaded by cluster machines and each machine constructs its partitions by executing the commands in each of its assigned atoms. By generating partitions via executing commands in atoms (and *not* directly mapping partitions to cluster machines), GraphLab allows future changes to graphs to be simply appended as additional commands in atoms without needing to repartition the entire graphs. Furthermore, the same graph atoms can be reused for different sizes of clusters by simply re-dividing the corresponding atom index file and re-executing atom commands (i.e., only the second phase of the two-phase partitioning strategy is repeated). In fact, GraphLab has adopted such a graph partitioning strategy with the *elasticity* of clouds being in mind. Clearly, this improves upon the *direct* and *non-elastic* hash-based partitioning strategy adopted by Pregel. Specifically, in Pregel, if graphs or cluster sizes are altered after partitioning, the entire graphs need to be repartitioned prior to processing.

1.5.5 SYMMETRICAL AND ASYMMETRICAL ARCHITECTURAL MODELS

From architectural and management perspectives, a distributed program can be typically organized in two ways, **master/slave** (or **asymmetrical**) and **peer-to-peer** (or **symmetrical**) (see Figure 1.12). There are other organizations, such as hybrids of asymmetrical and symmetrical, which do exist in literature [71]. For the purpose of our chapter, we are only concerned with the master/slave and peer-to-peer organizations. In a master/slave organization, a central process known as the *master* handles

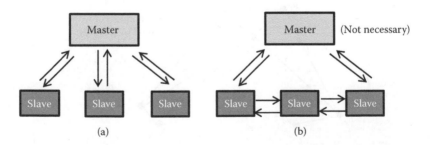

FIGURE 1.12 (a) A master/slave organization. (b) A peer-to-peer organization. The master in such an organization is optional (usually employed for monitoring the system and/or injecting administrative commands).

all the logic and controls. All other processes are denoted as *slave* processes. As such, the interaction between processes is asymmetrical, whereby bidirectional connections are established between the master and all the slaves, and no interconnection is permitted between any two slaves (see Figure 1.12a). This requires that the master keeps track of every slave's network location within what is referred to as a *metadata* structure. In addition, this entails that each slave is always capable of identifying and locating the master.

The master in master/slave organizations can distribute the work among the slaves using one of two protocols, **push-based or pull-based**. In the push-based protocol, the master assigns work to the slaves without the slaves asking for that. Clearly, this might allow the master to apply fairness over the slaves via distributing the work equally among them. In contrast, this could also overwhelm/congest slaves that are currently experiencing some slowness/failures and are unable to keep up with work. Consequently, load imbalance might occur, which usually leads to performance degradation. Nevertheless, smart strategies can be implemented by the master. In particular, the master can assign work to a slave if and only if the slave is *observed* to be *ready* for that. For this to happen, the master has to continuously monitor the slaves and apply some certain logic (usually complex) to accurately determine ready slaves. The master has also to decide upon the amount of work to assign to a ready slave so as fairness is maintained and performance is not degraded. In clouds, the probability of faulty and slow processes increases due to heterogeneity, performance unpredictability, and scalability (see Section 1.5 for details on that). This might make the push-based protocol somehow inefficient on the cloud.

Unlike the push-based protocol, in the pull-based protocol, the master assigns work to the slaves only if they ask for that. This highly reduces complexity and potentially avoids load imbalance, since the decision of whether a certain slave is ready to receive work or not is delegated to the slave itself. Nonetheless, the master still needs to monitor the slaves, usually to track the progresses of tasks at slaves and/or apply fault-tolerance mechanisms (e.g., to effectively address faulty and slow tasks, commonly present in large-scale clouds).

To this end, we note that the master/slave organization suffers from a single point of failure (SPOF). Specifically, if the master fails, the entire distributed program comes to a grinding halt. Furthermore, having a central process (i.e., the master) for controlling and managing everything might not scale well beyond a few hundred slaves, unless efficient strategies are applied to reduce the contention on the master (e.g., caching metadata at the slaves so as to avoid accessing the master upon each request). In contrary, using a master/slave organization simplifies decision making (e.g., allow a write transaction on a certain shared data). In particular, the master is always the sole entity that controls everything and can make any decision single-handedly without bothering anyone else. This averts the employment of **voting mechanisms** [23,71,72], typically needed when only a *group* of entities (not a single entity) have to make decisions. The basic idea of voting mechanisms is to require a task to request and acquire the permission for a certain action from at least half of the tasks plus one (a majority). Voting mechanisms usually complicate implementations of distributed programs. Lastly, as specific examples, Hadoop MapReduce and Pregel adopt master/slave organizations and apply the pull-based and the push-based protocols, respectively. We note, however, that recently, Hadoop has undergone a major overhaul to address several inherent technical deficiencies, including the reliability and availability of the JobTracker, among others. The outcome is a new version referred to as **Yet Another Resource Negotiator** (YARN) [53]. To elaborate, YARN still adopts a master/slave topology but with various enhancements. First, the resource management module, which is responsible for task and job scheduling as well as resource allocation, has been entirely detached from the master (or the JobTracker in Hadoop's parlance) and defined as a separate entity entitled as resource manager (RM). RM has been further sliced into two main components, the scheduler (S) and the applications manager (AsM). Second, instead of having a single master for all applications, which was the JobTracker, YARN has defined a master per application, referred to as application master (AM). AMs can be distributed across cluster nodes so as to avoid application SPOFs and potential performance degradations. Finally, the slaves (or what is known in Hadoop as TaskTrackers) have remained effectively the same but are now called Node Managers (NMs).

In a peer-to-peer organization, logic, control, and work are distributed evenly among tasks. That is, all tasks are equal (i.e., they all have the same capability) and no one is a boss. This makes peer-to-peer organizations symmetrical. Specifically, each task can communicate directly with tasks around it, without having to contact a master process (see Figure 1.12b). A master may be adopted, however, but only for purposes like monitoring the system and/or injecting administrative commands. In other words, as opposed to a master/slave organization, the presence of a master in a peer-to-peer organization is not requisite for the peer tasks to function correctly. Moreover, although tasks communicate with one another, their work can be totally independent and could even be unrelated. Peer-to-peer organizations eliminate the potential for SPOF and bandwidth bottlenecks, thus typically exhibit good scalability and robust fault-tolerance. In contrary, making decisions in peer-to-peer organizations has to be carried out collectively using usually voting mechanisms. This typically implies increased implementation complexity as well as more communication overhead and latency, especially in large-scale systems such as the cloud. As a specific example, GraphLab employs a peer-to-peer organization. Specifically, when GraphLab is launched on a cluster, one instance of its engine is started on each machine. All engine instances in GraphLab are symmetric. Moreover, they all communicate directly with each other using a customized asynchronous remote procedure call (RPC) protocol over TCP/IP. The first triggered engine instance, however, will have an additional responsibility of being a monitoring/master engine. The other engine instances across machines will still work and communicate directly without having to be coordinated by the master engine. Consequently, GraphLab satisfies the criteria to be a peer-to-peer system.

1.6   MAIN CHALLENGES IN BUILDING CLOUD PROGRAMS

Designing and implementing a distributed program for the cloud involves more than just sending and receiving messages and deciding upon the computational and architectural models. While all these are extremely important, they do not reflect the whole story of developing programs for the cloud. In particular, there are various challenges that a designer needs to pay careful attention to and address before developing a cloud program. We next discuss **heterogeneity**, **scalability**, **communication**, **synchronization**, **fault-tolerance**, and **scheduling** challenges exhibited in building cloud programs.

1.6.1 HETEROGENEITY

The cloud datacenters are composed of various collections of components including computers, networks, operating systems (OSs), libraries, and programming languages. In principle, if there is variety and difference in datacenter components, the cloud is referred to as a **heterogeneous cloud**. Otherwise, the cloud is denoted as a **homogenous cloud**. In practice, homogeneity does not always hold. This is mainly due to two major reasons. First, cloud providers typically keep multiple generations of IT resources purchased over different timeframes. Second, cloud providers are increasingly applying the virtualization technology on their clouds for server consolidation, enhanced system utilization, and simplified management. Public clouds are primarily virtualized datacenters. Even on private clouds, it is expected that virtualized environments will become the norm [83]. Heterogeneity is a direct cause of virtualized environments. For example, co-locating virtual machines (VMs) on similar physical machines may cause heterogeneity. Specifically, if we suppose two identical physical machines **A** and **B**, placing 1 VMover machine **A** and 10 VMs over machine **B** will stress machine **B** way more than machine **A**, assuming all VMs are identical and running the same programs. Having dissimilar VMs and diverse demanding programs are even more probable on the cloud. An especially compelling setting is Amazon EC2. Amazon EC2 offers 17 VM types [1] (as of March 4, 2013) for millions of users with different programs. Clearly, this creates even more heterogeneity. In short, heterogeneity is already, and will continue to be, the norm on the cloud.

Heterogeneity poses multiple challenges for running distributed programs on the cloud. First, distributed programs must be designed in a way that masks the heterogeneity of the underlying hardware, networks, OSs, and the programming languages. This is a necessity for distributed tasks to communicate, or otherwise, the whole concept of distributed programs will not hold (recall that what defines distributed programs is passing messages). To elaborate, messages exchanged between tasks would usually contain primitive data types such as integers. Unfortunately, not all computers store integers in the same order. In particular, some computers might use the so-called big-endian order, in which the most significant byte comes first, while others might use the so-called little-endian order, in which the most significant byte comes last. The floating-point numbers can also differ across computer architectures. Another issue is the set of codes used to represent characters. Some systems use ASCII characters, while others use the Unicode standard. In a word, distributed programs have to work out such heterogeneity so as to exist. The part that can be incorporated in distributed programs to work out heterogeneity is commonly referred to as **middleware**. Fortunately, most middleware are implemented over the Internet protocols, which themselves mask the differences in the underlying networks. The Simple Object Access Protocol (SOAP) [16] is an example of a middleware. SOAP defines a scheme for using Extensible Markup Language (XML), a textual self-describing format, to represent contents of messages and allow distributed tasks at diverse machines to interact.

In general, code suitable for one machine might not be suitable for another machine on the cloud, especially when instruction set architectures (ISAs) vary across machines. Ironically, the virtualization technology, which induces heterogeneity, can effectively serve in solving such a problem. Same VMs can be initiated for a user cluster and mapped to physical machines with different underlying ISAs. Afterward, the virtualization hypervisor will take care of emulating any difference between the ISAs of the provisioned VMs and the underlying physical machines (if any). From a user's perspective, all emulations occur transparently. Lastly, users can always install their own OSs and libraries on system VMs, like Amazon EC2 instances, thus ensuring homogeneity at the OS and library levels.

Another serious problem that requires a great deal of attention from distributed programmers is **performance variation** [20,60] on the cloud. Performance variation entails that running the same distributed program on the same cluster twice can result in largely different execution times. It has been observed that execution times can vary by a factor of 5 for the same application on the same private cluster [60]. Performance variation is mostly caused by the heterogeneity of clouds imposed by virtualized environments and resource demand spikes and lulls typically experienced over time. As a consequence, VMs on clouds rarely carry work at the same speed, preventing thereby tasks from making progress at (roughly) constant rates. Clearly, this can create tricky load imbalance and subsequently degrade overall performance. As pointed out earlier, load imbalance makes a program's performance contingent on its slowest task. Distributed programs can attempt to tackle slow tasks by detecting them and scheduling corresponding *speculative* tasks on fast VMs so as they finish earlier. Specifically, two tasks with the same responsibility can compete by running at two different VMs, with the one that finishes earlier getting committed and the other getting killed. For instance, Hadoop MapReduce follows a similar strategy for solving the same problem, known as **speculative execution** (see Section 1.5.5). Unfortunately, distinguishing between slow and fast tasks/VMs is very challenging on the cloud. It could happen that a certain VM running a task is temporarily passing through a demand spike, or it could be the case that the VM is simply faulty. In theory, not any detectably slow node is faulty and differentiating between faulty and slow nodes is hard [71]. Because of that, speculative execution in Hadoop MapReduce does not perform very well in heterogeneous environments [11,26,73].

1.6.2 SCALABILITY

The issue of scalability is a dominant subject in distributed computing. A distributed program is said to be scalable if it remains effective when the quantities of users, data and resources are increased significantly. To get a sense of the problem scope at hand, as per users, in cloud computing, most popular applications and platforms are currently offered as Internet-based services with *millions* of users. As per data, in the time of Big Data, or *the Era of Tera* as denoted by Intel [13], distributed programs typically cope with Web-scale data in the order of hundreds and thousands of gigabytes, terabytes, or petabytes. Also, Internet services such as e-commerce and social networks deal with sheer volumes of data generated by millions of users every day [83]. As per resources, cloud datacenters already host tens and hundreds of thousands of machines (e.g., Amazon EC2 is estimated to host almost half a million machines [46]), and projections for scaling up machine counts to extra folds have already been set forth.

As pointed out in Section 1.3, upon scaling up the number of machines, what programmers/users expect is escalated performance. Specifically, programmers expect from distributed execution of their programs on n nodes, vs. on a single node, an n-fold improvement in performance. Unfortunately, this never happens in reality due to several reasons. First, as shown in Figure 1.13, parts of programs can never be parallelized (e.g., initialization parts). Second, load imbalance among tasks is highly likely, especially in distributed systems like clouds. One of the reasons for load imbalance is the heterogeneity of the cloud as discussed in the previous section. As depicted in Figure 1.13b, load imbalance usually delays programs, wherein a program becomes bound to the slowest task. Particularly, even if all tasks in a program finish, the program cannot commit before the last task finishes (which might greatly linger!). Lastly, other serious overheads such as communication and synchronization can highly impede scalability. Such overheads are significantly important when measuring speedups obtained by distributed programs compared with sequential ones. A standard law that allows measuring speedups attained by distributed programs and, additionally, accounting for various overheads is known as **Amdahl's law**.

For the purpose of describing Amdahl's law we assume that a sequential version of a program P takes T_s time units, while a parallel/distributed version takes T_p time units using a cluster of n nodes. In addition, we suppose that s fraction of the program is not parallelizable. Clearly, this makes $1 - s$ fraction of the program parallelizable. According to Amdahl's law, the speedup of the parallel/distributed execution of P vs. the sequential one can be defined as follows:

$$Speedup_p = T_s/T_p = T_s/(T_s \times s + T_s \times (1 - s)/n) = 1/(s + (1 - s)/n).$$

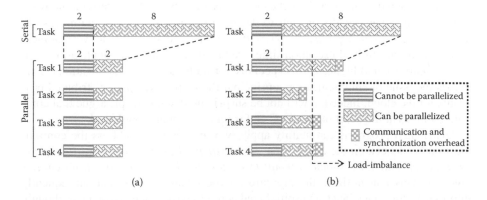

(a)   (b)

FIGURE 1.13 Parallel speedup. (a) Ideal case. (b) Real case.

While the formula is apparently simple, it exhibits a crucial implication. In particular, if we assume a cluster with an unlimited number of machines and a constant s, we can use the formula to express the maximum speedup that can be achieved by simply computing the $\lim_{n \to \infty} Speedup_p$ as follows:

$$\lim_{n \to \infty} Speedup_p = \lim_{n \to \infty} 1/(s + (1 - s)/n) = 1/s.$$

To understand the essentiality of the formula's implication, let us assume a serial fraction s of only 2%. Applying the formula with an assumingly unlimited number of machines will result in a maximum speedup of only 50. Reducing s to 0.5% would result in a maximum speedup of 200. Consequently, we realize that attaining scalability in distributed systems is quite challenging, as it requires s to be almost 0, let alone the effects of load imbalance, synchronization, and communication overheads. In practice, synchronization overheads (e.g., performing *barrier* synchronization and acquiring locks) increase with an increasing number of machines, often superlinearly [67]. Communication overheads also grow dramatically since machines in large-scale distributed systems cannot be interconnected with very short physical distances. Load imbalance becomes a big factor in heterogeneous environments as explained shortly. While this is truly challenging, we point out that with Webscale input data, the overheads of synchronization and communication can be highly reduced if they contribute way less toward the overall execution time as compared with computation. Fortunately, this is the case with many Big Data applications.

1.6.3 COMMUNICATION

As defined in Section 1.4.1, distributed systems are composed of networked computers that can communicate by explicitly passing messages or implicitly accessing shared memories. Even with distributed shared memory systems, messages are internally passed between machines, yet in a manner that is totally transparent to users. Hence, it all boils down essentially to passing messages. Consequently, it can be argued that the only way for distributed systems to communicate is by passing messages. In fact, Coulouris et al. [16] adopts such a definition for distributed systems. Distributed systems such as the cloud rely heavily on the underlying network to deliver messages rapidly enough to destination entities for three main reasons, *performance*, *cost*, and *quality of service* (QoS). Specifically, faster delivery of messages entails minimized execution times, reduced costs (as cloud applications can commit earlier), and higher QoS, especially for audio and video applications. This makes the issue of communication a principal theme in developing distributed programs for the cloud. Indeed, it will not be surprising if some people argue that communication is at the heart of the cloud and is one of its major bottlenecks.

Distributed programs can mainly apply two techniques to address the communication bottleneck on the cloud. First, *the strategy of distributing/partitioning the work across machines should attempt to co-locate highly communicating entities together.* This can mitigate the pressure on the cloud network and subsequently improve performance. Such an aspired goal is not as easy as it might appear, though. For instance, the standard edge cut strategy seeks to partition graph vertices into *p* equally weighted partitions over p processors so that the total weight of the edges crossing between partitions is minimized (see Section 1.4.4). Unfortunately, by carefully inspecting such a strategy, we realize a serious shortcoming that directly impacts communication. To exemplify, Figure 1.11 in Section 1.4.4 shows that the minimum cut resulted from the edge cut metric overlooks the fact that some edges may represent the same information flow. In particular, v_2 at P_1 in the figure sends the same message twice to P_2 (specifically to v_4 and v_5 at P_2), while it suffices to communicate the message only once, since v_4 and v_5 will exist on the same machine. Likewise, v_4 and v_7 can communicate messages to P_1 only once but they do it twice. Therefore, the standard edge cut metric causes an over-count of the true volume of communication and consequently incurs superfluous network traffic. As an outcome, interconnection bandwidth can be potentially stressed and performance degraded. Even if the total communication volume (or the number of messages) is minimized more effectively, load imbalance can render the bottleneck. In particular, it might happen that while the communication volume is minimized, some machines receive heavier partitions (i.e., partitions with more vertices) than others. An ideal, yet a challenging approach, is to minimize communication overheads while circumventing computation skew among machines. To summarize, this technique strives for *effective partitioning of work across machines so as highly communicating entities are co-located together.*

The second technique is *effective mapping of partitions*. Specifically, the mapping strategy of partitions to machines, whether graph or data partitions, should be done in a way that is totally aware of the underlying network topology. This dictates the number of switches that a message will hit before it reaches its destination. As a specific example, Figure 1.14 demonstrates the same graph shown previously in Figure 1.11 and a simplified cluster with a tree-style network and six machines. The cluster network consists of two rack switches (RSs), each connecting three machines, and a core switch (CS) connecting the two RSs. A salient point is that the bandwidth

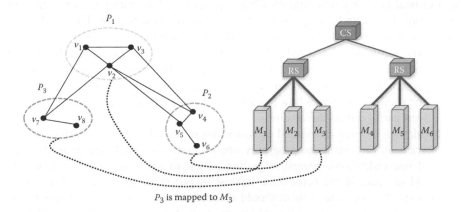

P_3 is mapped to M_3

FIGURE 1.14   Effective mapping of graph partitions to cluster machines. A mapping of P_1 to the other rack while P_2 and P_3 remain on the same rack causes more network traffic and potentially degraded performance.

between two machines is dependent on their relative locations in the network topology. For instance, machines that are on the same rack have higher bandwidth between them as opposed to machines that are off-rack. As such, it pays to minimize network traffic across racks. If P_1, P_2, and P_3 are mapped to M_1, M_2, and M_3, respectively, less network latency will be incurred when P_1, P_2, and P_3 communicate vs. if they are mapped across the two racks. More precisely, for P_1 to communicate with P_2 on the same rack, only one hop is incurred to route a message from P_1 to P_2. In contrast, for P_1 to communicate with P_2 on different racks, two hops are incurred per each message. Clearly, a less number of hops results in a better network latency and improved overall performance. Unfortunately, this is not as easy as it might appear to achieve on clouds, especially on public clouds, for one main reason. That is, clouds such as Amazon EC2 do not expose their network topologies. Nevertheless, the network topology can still be learned (though not very effectively) using a benchmark like Netperf [54] to measure point-to-point TCP stream bandwidths between all pairs of cluster nodes [32]. This enables estimating the relative locality of nodes and arriving at a reasonable inference regarding the rack topology of the cluster.

1.6.4   SYNCHRONIZATION

Distributed tasks should be allowed to simultaneously operate on shared data without corrupting data or causing any inconsistency. For instance, GraphLab allows multiple tasks to operate on different vertices of the same graph simultaneously. This might lead to race-conditions whereby two tasks might try to modify data on a shared edge at the same time, resulting in a corrupted value. Consequently, *synchronization* solutions for providing distributed *mutual exclusive accesses* by tasks will be required. Synchronization acts as a mechanism through which programmers can control the sequence of operations (reads and writes) that are performed by tasks. As discussed in Section 1.4.2.1, there are three types of synchronization methods that are in wide use, semaphores, locks, and barriers. The efficiency of such methods is a critical goal in developing distributed programs. For instance, as pointed out in Section 1.4.2.1 and exemplified by the BSP model (see Section 1.4.3), a barrier defines a point at which no task is allowed to continue unless all other tasks reach that point. While this is easy to implement, the whole execution time of a distributed program becomes dependent on the slowest task. In distributed systems such as the cloud, where heterogeneity is the norm, this can cause serious performance degradation. The challenge becomes how to apply synchronization methods and at the same time avert performance degradation.

In addition to ensuring mutual exclusion, there are other properties that need to be guaranteed for distributed programs when it comes to synchronization. To start with, if one task shows interest in getting access to a critical section, eventually it should succeed. If two tasks show interest in getting access to a critical section simultaneously, only one of them should succeed. This is denoted as the ***deadlock-free*** property and has to be delivered by any mutual exclusion mechanism. Things, however, might not go always as expected. For instance, if task *A* succeeds in acquiring lock1 and, at about the same time, task *B* succeeds in acquiring lock2; then if task *A* attempts to acquire lock2 and task *B* attempts to acquire lock1, we end up with what is known as a *deadlock*. Avoiding deadlocks is a real challenge in developing distributed programs, especially when the number of tasks is scaled up. To build upon the example of tasks *A* and *B*, let us assume a larger set of tasks *A*, *B*, *C*, *Z*. In ensuring mutual exclusion, task *A* might *wait on* task *B*, if *B* is holding a lock required by *A*. In return, task *B* might wait on task *C*, if *C* is holding a lock required by *B*. The "wait on" sequence can carry on all the way up to task *Z*. Specifically, task *C* might wait on task *D*, and task *D* might wait on task *E*, all the way until task *Y*, which might also wait on task *Z*. Such a "wait on" chain is usually referred to as *transitive closure*. When a transitive closure occurs, a circular wait is said to arise. Circular waits lead normally to stark deadlocks that might bring the whole distributed programs/systems to grinding halts. Lastly, we note that the "wait on" relation is at the heart of every mutual exclusion mechanism. In particular, no mutual exclusion protocol can preclude it; no matter how clever it is [36]. In normal scenarios, a task expects to "wait on" for a limited (reasonable) amount of time. But what if a task that is holding a lock/token crashes? This suggests another major challenge that distributed programs need to address, that is, *fault tolerance*.

1.6.5 FAULT TOLERANCE

A basic feature that distinguishes distributed systems such as the cloud fromuniprocessor systems is the concept of **partial failures**. Specifically, in distributed systems if a node or component fails, the whole system can continue functioning. On the other hand, if one component (e.g., the RAM) fails in a uniprocessor system, the whole system will fail. A crucial objective in designing distributed systems/programs is to construct them in a way that they can automatically tolerate partial failures without seriously affecting performance. A key technique for masking faults in distributed systems is to use hardware redundancy such as the RAID technology [56]. In most cases, however, distributed programs cannot only depend on the underlying hardware fault-tolerance techniques of distributed systems. Thus, they usually apply their own fault-tolerance techniques. Among these techniques is **software redundancy**.

A common type of software redundancy is **task redundancy** (or **resiliency** or **replication**). Task replication is applied as a protection against task failures. In particular, tasks can be replicated as **flat or hierarchical groups**, exemplified in Figure 1.15. In flat groups (see Figure 1.15a), all tasks are identical in a sense that they all carry the same work. Eventually, only the result of one task is considered and the other results are discarded. Obviously, flat groups are symmetrical and preclude single point of failures (SPOFs). Particularly, if one task crashes, the application will stay in business, yet the group will become smaller until recovered. However, if for some applications, a decision is to be made (e.g., acquiring a lock), a voting mechanism might be required. As discussed earlier, voting mechanisms incur implementation complexity, communication delays, and performance overheads.

A hierarchical group (see Figure 1.15b) usually employs a coordinator task and specifies the rest of the tasks as workers. In this model, when a user request is made, it first gets forwarded to the coordinator who, in return, decides which worker is best suited to fulfill it. Clearly, hierarchical groups reflect opposite properties as compared with flat ones. In particular, the coordinator is an SPOF and a potential

A flat group   A hierarchical group

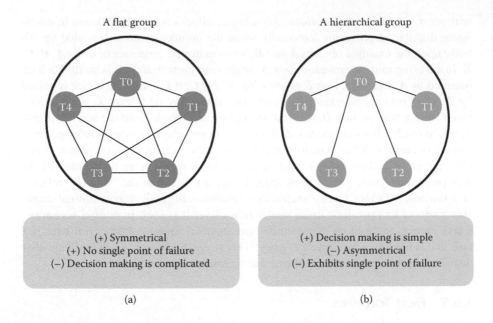

(+) Symmetrical	(+) Decision making is simple
(+) No single point of failure	(−) Asymmetrical
(−) Decision making is complicated	(−) Exhibits single point of failure

(a)   (b)

FIGURE 1.15   Two classical ways to employ task redundancy. (a) A flat group of tasks. (b) A hierarchical group of tasks with a central process (i.e., T0, whereby Ti stands for task i.).

performance bottleneck (especially in large-scale systems with millions of users). In contrast, as long as the coordinator is protected, the whole group remains functional. Furthermore, decisions can be easily made, solely by the coordinator without bothering any worker or incurring communication delays and performance overheads.

As a real example, Hadoop MapReduce applies task resiliency to recover from task failures and mitigate the effects of slow tasks. Specifically, Hadoop MapReduce suggests monitoring and *replicating* tasks in an attempt to detect and treat slow/faulty ones. To detect slow/faulty tasks, Hadoop MapReduce depends on what is denoted as the **heartbeat mechanism**. As pointed out earlier, MapReduce adopts a master/slave architecture. Slaves (or TaskTrackers) send their heartbeats every 3 seconds (by default) to the master (or the JobTracker). The JobTracker employs an *expiry thread* that checks these heartbeats and decides whether tasks at TaskTrackers are *dead* or *alive*. If the expiry thread does not receive heartbeats from a task in 10 minutes (by default), the task is deemed dead. Otherwise, the task is marked alive. Alive tasks can be slow (referred interchangeably to as **stragglers**) or *not-slow*. To measure the slowness of tasks, the JobTracker calculates task progresses using a *progress score* per each task between 0 and 1. The progress scores of map and reduce tasks are computed differently. For a map task, the progress score is a function of the input HDFS block read so far. For a reduce task the progress score is more involved. To elaborate, the execution of a reduce task is split into three main stages, the *Shuffle*, the *Merge and Sort*, and the reduce stages. Hadoop MapReduce assumes that each of these stages accounts for one third of a reduce task's score. Per each stage, the score is the fraction of data processed so far. For instance, a reduce task halfway through the Shuffle stage will have a progress score of $1/3 \times 1/2 = 1/6$. On the other hand, a reduce task halfway through the Merge and Sort stage will have a progress score of $1/3 + (1/2 \times 1/3) = 1/2$. Finally, a reduce task halfway through the reduce stage will have a progress score of $1/3 + 1/3 + (1/3 \times 1/2) = 5/6$. After slow tasks are detected, corresponding backup (or *speculative*) tasks are run simultaneously. Hadoop allows a maximum of one speculative task per an original slow task. The speculative tasks compete with the original ones and optimistically finish earlier. The tasks that finish earlier, being speculative or original, are committed while the others are killed. This type of task resiliency is known in Hadoop MapReduce as **speculative execution**. Speculative execution is turned on by default in Hadoop, but can be enabled or disabled independently for map and reduce tasks, on a cluster-wide basis or on a per-job basis. To this end, we indicate two points: (1) speculative tasks are identical due to running the same function on the same data, and (2) no coordinator task is specified among the speculative tasks, yet a coordinator is still used, but not from among the tasks (i.e., the JobTracker). As such, we refer to the strategy adopted by Hadoop MapReduce as a hybrid of flat and hierarchical task groups.

Fault tolerance in distributed programs is not only concerned with tolerating faults, but further with recovering from failures. The basic idea of **failure recovery** is to replace a flawed state with a flaw-free state. One way to achieve this is by using backward recovery. Backward recovery requires that the distributed program/system is brought from its present flawed state to a previously correct state. This can be accomplished by recording the state at each process from time to time. Once a failure occurs, recovery can be started from the last recorded correct state, typically denoted as the recovery line. Every time the state is recorded at a process, a checkpoint is said to be obtained. The checkpoints of a distributed program at different processes in a distributed system are known as a **distributed checkpoint**. The process of capturing a distributed checkpoint is not easy for one main reason. Specifically, a distributed checkpoint needs to maintain a *consistent global state*. More precisely, a distributed checkpoint should maintain the property that if a process P has recorded the receipt of a message, m, then there should be another process Q that has recorded the sending of m. After all, m should have been sent from somewhere. Figure 1.16 demonstrates two distributed checkpoints, D_1, which maintains a consistent global state and D_2, which does not maintain a consistent global state. The D_1's checkpoint at Q indicates that Q has received a message m_1, and the D_1's checkpoint at P indicates that P has sent m_1, hence, making D_1 consistent. In contrary, the D_2's checkpoint at Q indicates that message m_2 has been received, and the D_2's checkpoint at P does not indicate that m_2 has been sent from P. Therefore, D_2 cannot be treated as a recovery line due to being inconsistent.

The distributed program/system can inspect whether a certain distributed checkpoint is consistent or not by *rolling back* each process to its most recently saved state. When local states jointly form a consistent global state, a recovery line is said to be discovered. For instance, after a failure, the system exemplified in Figure 1.16 will roll back until hitting D_1. As D_1 reflects a global consistent state, a recovery line is said to be discovered. Unfortunately, the process of cascaded rollbacks is challenging since it might lead to what is called the **domino effect**. As a specific example, Figure 1.17 exhibits a case where a recovery line cannot be found. In particular, every

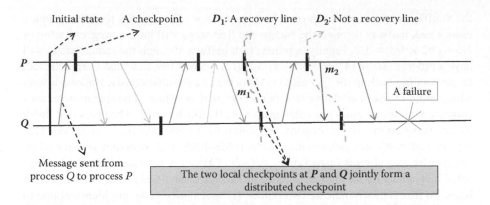

FIGURE 1.16 Demonstrating distributed checkpointing. D_1 is a valid distributed check-point while D_2 is not, due to being inconsistent. Specifically, D_2's checkpoint at Q indicates that m_2 has been received, while D_2's checkpoint at P does not indicate that m_2 has been sent.

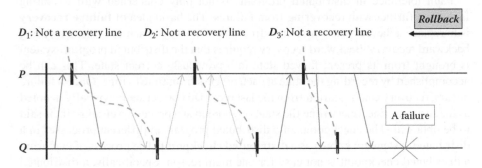

FIGURE 1.17 The domino effect that might result from rolling back each process (e.g., processes P and Q) to a saved local checkpoint in order to locate a recovery line. Neither D_1, D_2, nor D_3 are recovery lines because they exhibit inconsistent global states.

distributed checkpoint in Figure 1.17 is indeed inconsistent. This makes distributed checkpointing a costly operation, which might not converge to an acceptable recovery solution. Accordingly, many fault-tolerant distributed systems combine check-pointing with **message logging**. One way to achieve that is by logging messages of a process before sending them off and after a checkpoint has been taken. Obviously, this solves the problem of D_2 at Figure 1.16, for example. In particular, after the D_2's checkpoint at P is taken, the send of m_2 will be marked in a log message at P, which if merged with D_2's checkpoint at Q, can form a global consistent state. Apart from distributed analytics engines, Hadoop Distributed File System (HDFS) combines distributed checkpointing (i.e., the *image file*) and message logging (i.e., the *edit file*) to recover slave (or NameNode in HDFS's parlance) failures [27]. As examples from analytics engines, distributed checkpointing alone is adopted by GraphLab, while message logging and distributed checkpointing combined together are employed by Pregel.

1.6.6 SCHEDULING

The effectiveness of a distributed program hinges on the manner in which its constituent tasks are scheduled over distributed machines. Scheduling in distributed programs is usually categorized into two main classes, **task scheduling** and **job scheduling**. To start with, as defined in Section 1.2, a job can encompass one or many tasks. Tasks are the finest unit of granularity for execution. Many jobs from many users can be submitted simultaneously for execution on a cluster. Job schedulers decide on which job should go next. For instance, Hadoop MapReduce adopts a *first in, first out* (FIFO) job scheduler, whereby jobs are run according to the order of which they have been received. With FIFO, *running* jobs cannot be preempted so as to allow *waiting* jobs to proceed and, consequently, achieve certain objectives (e.g., avoiding job starvations and/or sharing resources effectively). As a result, simultaneous sharing of cluster resources is greatly limited. In particular, as long as a job occupies the *whole* cluster resources, no other job is allowed to carry on. That is, the next job in the FIFO work queue is not allowed to start up unless some resources become free and the currently running job has no more tasks to execute. Clearly, this might lead to a fairness issue wherein a very long job can block the whole cluster for a very long time starving all small jobs. Hadoop MapReduce, however, employs multiple other job schedulers besides FIFO (e.g., Capacity [28] and Fair [29] schedulers). After a job is granted the cluster, the decision morphs into how the job's tasks should be scheduled. Tasks can be scheduled either close to the data that they are supposed to process or *anywhere*. When tasks are scheduled nearby their data, *locality* is said to be exploited. For example, Hadoop MapReduce schedules map tasks in the vicinity of their uniform-sized input HDFS blocks and reduce tasks at *any* cluster nodes, irrespective of the locations of their input data. As opposed to MapReduce, Pregel, and GraphLab do not exploit any locality when scheduling tasks/vertices.

Task schedulers must account for the heterogeneity of the underlying cloud or, otherwise, performance might degrade significantly. To elaborate, similar tasks that belong to the same job can be scheduled at nodes of variant speeds in a heterogeneous cloud. As reiterated in Sections 1.4.3 and 1.5.1, this can create load imbalance and make jobs move at the pace of their slowest tasks. Strategies such as speculative execution in Hadoop MapReduce can (minimally) address such a challenge (see Section 1.5.5). In addition to considering heterogeneity, task schedulers must seek to enhance system utilization and improve task parallelism. Specifically, tasks should be uniformly distributed across cluster machines in a way that fairly utilizes the available cluster resources and effectively increases parallelism. Obviously, this presents some contradictory objectives. To begin with, by evenly distributing tasks across cluster machines, locality might be affected. For instance, machines in a Hadoop cluster can contain different numbers of HDFS blocks. If at one machine, a larger number of HDFS blocks exist as opposed to others, locality would entail scheduling all respective map tasks at that machine. This might make other machines less loaded and utilized. In addition, this can reduce task parallelism as a consequence of accumulating many tasks on the same machine. If locality is relaxed a little bit, however, utilization can be enhanced, loads across machines can be balanced, and task parallelism can be increased. Nonetheless, this would necessitate moving data toward tasks, which if done injudiciously, might increase communication overhead, impede scalability, and potentially degrade performance. In fact, with datacenters hosting thousands of machines, moving data frequently toward distant tasks might become one of the major bottlenecks. As such, an optimal task scheduler would strike a balance among system utilization, load balancing, task parallelism, communication overhead, and scalability so as performance is improved and costs are reduced. Unfortunately, in practice, this is very hard to accomplish. In reality, most task schedulers attempt to optimize one objective and overlook the others.

Another major challenge when scheduling jobs and tasks is to meet what is known as **service-level objectives** (SLOs). SLOs reflect the performance expectations of end-users. Amazon, Google, and Microsoft have identified SLO violations as a major cause of user dissatisfaction [31,64,79]. For example, SLO can be expressed as a maximum latency for allocating the desired set of resources to a job, a soft/hard deadline to finish a job, or GPU preferences of some tasks, among others. In multi-tenant heterogeneous clusters, SLOs are hard to achieve, especially upon the arrival of new jobs while others are executing. This might require *suspending* currently running tasks to allow the newly arrived ones to proceed and, subsequently, meet their specified SLOs. The capability of suspending and resuming tasks is referred to as **task elasticity**. Unfortunately, most distributed analytics engines at the moment; including Hadoop MapReduce, Pregel, and GraphLab do not support task elasticity. Making tasks elastic is quite challenging. It demands identifying *safe* points where a task can be suspended. A safe point in a task is a point at which the correctness of the task is not affected, and its committed work is not *all* repeated when it is suspended then resumed. In summary, meeting SLOs, enhancing system utilization, balancing load, increasing parallelism, reducing communication traffic, and facilitating scalability are among the objectives that make job and task scheduling one of the major challenges in developing distributed programs for the cloud.

1.7 SUMMARY

To this end, we conclude our discussion on distributed programming for the cloud. As a recap, we commenced our treatment for the topic with a brief background on the theory of distributed programming. Specifically, we categorized programs into sequential, parallel, concurrent, and distributed programs and recognized the difference among processes, threads, tasks, and jobs. Second, we motivated the case for distributed programming and explained why cloud programs (a special type of distributed programs) are important for solving complex computing problems. Third, we defined distributed systems and indicated the relationship between distributed systems and clouds. Fourth, we delved into the details of the models that cloud programs can adopt. In particular, we presented the distributed programming (i.e., shared memory or message passing), the computation (i.e., synchronous or asynchronous), the parallelism (i.e., graph-parallel or data-parallel), and the architectural (i.e., master/slave or peer-to-peer) models in detail. Lastly, we discussed the challenges with heterogeneity, scalability, communication, synchronization, fault tolerance, and scheduling, which are encountered when constructing cloud programs.

Throughout our discussion on distributed programming for the cloud, we also indicated that it is extremely advantageous to relieve programmers from worrying about specifying and implementing the distributed programming model, the computation model, the architectural model, the graph or data partitioning algorithm (e.g., file striping or edge cut metric), the fault-tolerance mechanism (i.e., task resiliency and/or distributed checkpointing and/or message logging), the low level synchronization methods (e.g., semaphores, locks, and/or barriers) and properties (e.g., avoiding deadlocks and transitive closures), and the job and task scheduling algorithms (e.g., FIFO, locality-aware, and elastic schedulers). Designing, developing, verifying, and debugging all (or some of) these requirements might induce tremendous correctness and performance hurdles, let alone the time and resources that need to be invested and the inherent difficulty involved. As a consequence, we presented Hadoop MapReduce, Pregel, and GraphLab as being easy-to-use, effective, and popular distributed analytics engines for building cloud programs.

Hadoop MapReduce, Pregel, and GraphLab were created to remove the burdens of creating and managing distributed programs from the shoulders of users/developers and delegate all that to the analytics engines themselves. Specifically, such engines eliminate the need for users to (1) design and implement the programming model and overcome all its associated synchronization and consistency issues, (2) develop the computation model, (3) specify the parallelism model and encode the accompanying partitioning and mapping algorithms, (4) architect the underlying organization (i.e., master/slave or peer-to-peer), and (5) apply the task/vertex scheduling strategy (i.e., push-based or pull-based). With respect to all these aspects, Table 1.2 compares Hadoop MapReduce, Pregel, and GraphLab. In short, Hadoop MapReduce is regarded as a data-parallel engine, while Pregel and GraphLab are characterized as graph-parallel engines. Furthermore, while both MapReduce and Pregel suggest synchronous computation models, GraphLab promotes an asynchronous model. MapReduce suits more loosely connected/embarrassingly parallel applications (i.e., applications with no or little dependency/communication between the parallel tasks), which involve vast volumes of data and non-iterative computations. On the other hand, Pregel and GraphLab suit more strongly connected applications (i.e., applications with high degrees of dependency between parallel tasks/vertices), which involve iterative computations and little data per a task/vertex. Asynchronous computation can lead to theoretical and empirical gains in algorithms and system performance. Thus, for graph and iterative oriented applications that do not converge

TABLE 1.2

A Comparison among the Hadoop MapReduce, the Pregel, and the GraphLab Analytics Engines

Aspect	Hadoop MapReduce	Pregel	GraphLab
Programming model	Shared memory	Message passing	Shared memory
Computation model	Synchronous	Bulk-synchronous	Asynchronous
Parallelism model	Data-parallel	Graph-parallel	Graph-parallel
Architectural model	Master/slave	Master/slave	Peer-to-peer
Task/vertex scheduling model	Pull-based	Push-based	Push-based

synchronously (e.g., greedy graph coloring) or converge way faster when executed asynchronously (e.g., dynamic PageRank), GraphLab becomes a superior option as opposed to Pregel. Finally, for graph and iterative oriented applications that converge faster if serializability (which entails that for every parallel/distributed execution, there is an equivalent sequential execution) is ensured or even necessitate serializability for correctness (e.g., Gibbs sampling, a very common algorithm in machine learning and data mining problems), GraphLab remains a supreme alternative vs. Pregel.

REFERENCES

1. Amazon Elastic Compute Cloud, http://aws.amazon.com/ec2/.
2. Amazon Elastic MapReduce, http://aws.amazon.com/elasticmapreduce/.
3. Amazon Simple Storage Service, http://aws.amazon.com/s3/.
4. Amazon, Amazon Web Services: Overview of Security Processes, *Amazon Whitepaper*, May 2011.
5. M. Bailey, The Economics of Virtualization: Moving Toward an Application-Based Cost Model, *VMware Sponsored Whitepaper*, 2009.
6. P. Barham, B. Dragovic, K. Fraser, S. Hand, T. Harris, A. Ho, R. Neugebauer, I. Pratt and A. Warfield, Xen and the Art of Virtualization, *SOSP*, October 2003.
7. J.R. Bell, Threaded Code, *Communications of the ACM*, 1973.
8. M. Ben-Ari, *Principles of Concurrent and Distributed Programming*, Addison-Wesley, Second Edition, March 6, 2006.
9. D.P. Bertsekas and J.N. Tsitsiklis, *Parallel and Distributed Computation: Numerical Methods*, Athena Scientific, First Edition, January 1, 1997.
10. C. Boulton, Novell, Microsoft Outline Virtual Collaboration, *Serverwatch*, 2007.
11. T.D. Braun, H.J. Siegel, N. Beck, L.L. Blni, M. Maheswaran, A.I. Reuther, J.P. Robertson, M.D. Theys, B. Yao, D. Hensgen and R.F. Freund, A Comparison of Eleven Static Heuristics for Mapping a Class of Independent Tasks onto Heterogeneous Distributed Computing Systems, *JPDC*, June 2001.
12. P.M. Chen and B.D. Nobel, When Virtual Is Better Than Real, *HOTOS*, May 2001.
13. S. Chen and S.W. Schlosser, MapReduce Meets Wider Varieties of Applications, *IRP-TR-08-05, Intel Research*, 2008.
14. D. Chisnall, *The Definitive Guide to the Xen Hypervisor*, Prentice Hall, 1st Edition, November 2007.
15. T.H. Cormen, C.E. Leiserson, R.L. Rivest and C. Stein, *Introduction to Algorithms*, The MIT Press, Third Edition, July 31, 2009.
16. G. Coulouris, J. Dollimore, T. Kindberg and G. Blair, *Distributed Systems: Concepts and Design*, Addison-Wesley, 5th Edition, May 2011.
17. J. Dean and S. Ghemawat, MapReduce: Simplified Data Processing on Large Clusters, *OSDI*, December 2004.
18. R.B.K. Dewar, Indirect Threaded Code, *Communications of the ACM*, June 1975.
19. T.W. Doeppner, *Operating Systems In Depth: Design and Programming*, Wiley, 1st Edition, November 2010.
20. B. Farley, V. Varadarajan, K. Bowers, A. Juels, T. Ristenpart and M. Swift, More for Your Money: Exploiting Performance Heterogeneity in Public Clouds, *SOCC*, 2012.
21. M.R. Garey, D.S. Johnson and L. Stockmeyer, Some Simplified NP-Complete Graph Problems, *Theoretical Computer Science*, 1976.
22. S. Ghemawat, H. Gobioff and S.T. Leung, The Google File System, *SOSP*, October 2003.

23. D.K. Gifford, Weighted Voting for Replicated Data, in *Proceedings of the Seventh ACM Symposium on Operating Systems Principles*, December 1979.
24. J.E. Gonzalez, Y. Low, H. Gu, D. Bickson and C. Guestrin, PowerGraph: Distributed Graph-Parallel Computation on Natural Graphs, *OSDI*, 2012.
25. M. Gschwind, E.R. Altman, S. Sathaye, P. Ledak and D. Appenzeller, Dynamic and Transparent Binary Translation, *IEEE Computer*, 2000.
26. Z. Guo and G. Fox, Improving MapReduce Performance in Heterogeneous Network Environments and Resource Utilization, in *Proceedings of the 2012 12th IEEE/ACM International Symposium on Cluster, Cloud and Grid Computing (CCGRID 2012)*, May 2012.
27. Hadoop. http://hadoop.apache.org/.
28. Hadoop Capacity Scheduler. http://hadoop.apache.org/docs/stable/capacity scheduler.html.
29. Hadoop Fair Scheduler. http://hadoop.apache.org/docs/r1.1.2/fair scheduler.html.
30. Hadoop Tutorial. http://developer.yahoo.com/hadoop/tutorial/.
31. J. Hamilton, The Cost of Latency, http://perspectives.mvdirona.com/2009/10/31/The CostOfLatency.aspx.
32. M. Hammoud, M.S. Rehman and M.F. Sakr, Center-of-Gravity Reduce Task Scheduling to Lower MapReduce Network Traffic, *CLOUD*, 2012.
33. M. Hammoud and M.F. Sakr, Locality-Aware Reduce Task Scheduling for MapReduce, *CloudComm*, 2011.
34. B. Hendrickson and T.G. Kolda, Graph Partitioning Models for Parallel Computing, *Parallel Computing*, 2000.
35. B. Hendrickson and R. Leland, *The Chaco User's Guide Version 2.0*, *Technical Report SAND95-2344*, Sandia National Laboratories, 1995.
36. M. Herlihy and N. Shavit, *The Art of Multiprocessor Programming*, Morgan Kaufmann, First Edition, March 14, 2008.
37. H. Herodotou, H. Lim, G. Luo, N. Borisov, L. Dong, F.B. Cetin and S. Babu, Starfish: A Self-Tuning System for Big Data Analytics, *CIDR*, 2011.
38. S. Ibrahim, H. Jin, L. Lu, S. Wu, B. He and L. Qi, LEEN: Locality/Fairness-Aware Key Partitioning for MapReduce in the Cloud, *CloudComm*, December 2010.
39. G. Karypis and V. Kumar, A Fast and High Quality Multilevel Scheme for Partitioning Irregular Graphs, *SIAM Journal on Scientific Computing*, 1998.
40. P. Klint, Interpretation Techniques, *Software Practice and Experience*, 1981.
41. P.M. Kogge, An Architecture Trail to Threaded-Code Systems, *IEEE Computer*, March 1982.
42. A.N. Langville and C.D. Meyer, *Google's PageRank and Beyond: The Science of Search Engine Rankings*, Princeton University Press, February 6, 2012.
43. Learn About Java Technology, http://www.java.com/en/about/.
44. K. Li, *Shared Virtual Memory on Loosely Coupled Multiprocessors*, Yale University, New Haven, CT (USA), 1986.
45. K. Li and P. Hudak, Memory Coherence in Shared Virtual Memory Systems, *Transactions on Computer Systems (TOCS)*, 1989.
46. H. Liu, Amazon Data Center Size, http://huanliu.wordpress.com/2012/03/13/amazon-data-center-size/, March 2012.
47. Y. Low, D. Bickson, J. Gonzalez, C. Guestrin, A. Kyrola and J.M. Hellerstein, Distributed GraphLab: A Framework for Machine Learning and Data Mining in the Cloud, in *Proceedings of the VLDB Endowment*, 2012.
48. P. Magnusson and D. Samuelsson, *A Compact Intermediate Format for SIMICS*, Swedish Institute of Computer Science, *Technical Report R94:17*, September 1994.
49. G. Malewicz, M.H. Austern, A.J. Bik, J.C. Dehnert, I. Horn, N. Leiser and G. Czajkowski, Pregel: A System for Large-Scale Graph Processing, in *Proceedings of the 2010 ACM SIGMOD International Conference on Management of Data*, June 2010.

50. Message Passing Interface, http://www.mcs.anl.gov/research/projects/mpi/.
51. Microsoft Corporation, ECMA C# and Common Language Infrastructure Standards, October 2009.
52. MPICH, http://www.mpich.org/.
53. A.C. Murthy, C. Douglas, M. Konar, O. O'Malley, S. Radia, S. Agarwal and K.V. Vinod, Architecture of Next Generation Apache Hadoop MapReduce Framework, *Apache Jira*, 2011.
54. Netperf, http://www.netperf.org/.
55. OpenMP, http://openmp.org/wp/.
56. D. Patterson, G. Gibson and R. Katz, A Case for Redundant Arrays of Inexpensive Disks (RAID), *ACM, Volume 17*, 1988.
57. I. Pratt, K. Fraser, S. Hand, Limpach, A. Warfield, Magenheimer, Nakajima and Mallick, Xen 3.0 and the Art of Virtualization, in *Proceedings of the Linux Symposium (Volume 2)*, July 2005.
58. G.J. Popek and R.P. Goldberg, Formal Requirements for Virtualizable Third Generation Architectures, *Communications of the ACM*, July 1974.
59. POSIX Threads Programming, https://computing.llnl.gov/tutorials/pthreads/.
60. M.S. Rehman and M.F. Sakr, Initial Findings for Provisioning Variation in Cloud Computing, *CloudCom*, November 2010.
61. Java RMI, http://www.oracle.com/technetwork/java/javase/tech/index-jsp-138781.html.
62. T.H. Romer, D. Lee, G.M. Voelker, A. Wolman, W.A. Wong, J.-L. Baer, B.N. Bershad and H.M. Levy, The Structure and Performance of Interpreters, *ASPLOS*, 1996.
63. N.B. Rizvandi, A.Y. Zomaya, A.J. Boloori and J. Taheri, *Preliminary Results: Modeling Relation between Total Execution Time of MapReduce Applications and Number of Mappers/Reducers, Technical Report 679*, The University of Sydney, 2011.
64. E. Schurman and J. Brutlag, The User and Business Impact of Server Delays, Additional Bytes, and Http Chunking in Web Search, in *Velocity Conference*, 2009.
65. R.L. Sites, A. Chernoff, M.B. Kirk, M.P. Marks and S.G. Robinson, Binary Translation, *Communications of the ACM*, February 1993.
66. J.E. Smith and R. Nair, *Virtual Machines: Versatile Platforms for Systems and Processes*, Morgan Kaufmann, 2005.
67. Y. Solihin, *Fundamentals of Parallel Computer Architecture*, Solihin Books, 2009.
68. S. Soltesz, H. Potz, M.E. Fiuczynski, A. Bavier and L. Peterson, Container-Based Operating System Virtualization: A Scalable, High-Performance Alternative to Hypervisors, *EuroSys*, March 2007.
69. A.S. Tanenbaum, *Modern Operating Systems*, Prentice Hall, Third Edition, December 21, 2007.
70. A.S. Tanenbaum, *Distributed Operating Systems*, Prentice Hall, First Edition, September 4, 1994.
71. A.S. Tanenbaum and M.V. Steen, *Distributed Systems: Principles and Paradigms*, Prentice Hall, Second Edition, October 12, 2006.
72. R.H. Thomas, A Majority Consensus Approach to Concurrency Control for Multiple Copy Databases, *ACM Transactions on Database Systems (TODS)*, 1979.
73. M. Tsugawa and J.A.B. Fortes, A Virtual Network (ViNe) Architecture for Grid Computing, in *IPDPS'06*, 2006.
74. L.G. Valiant, A Bridging Model for Parallel Computation, *Communications of the ACM*, 1990.
75. VMWare, http://www.vmware.com.
76. VMWare, Understanding Full Virtualization, Paravirtualization, and Hardware Assist, *VMware Whitepaper*, November 2007.
77. VMWare, VMware vSphere: The CPU Scheduler in VMware ESX 4.1, *VMware Whitepaper*, 2010.

78. VMWare, Understanding Memory Resource Management in VMware ESX Server, *VMware Whitepaper*, 2009.
79. A. Wang, S. Venkataraman, S. Alspaugh, R. Katz and I. Stoica, Cake: Enabling High-level SLOs on Shared Storage Systems, *SOCC*, 2012.
80. Xen Open Source Community, http://www.xen.org.
81. Xen 4.0 Release Notes, http://wiki.xen.org/wiki/Xen 4.0 Release Notes.
82. Xen 4.1 Release Notes, http://wiki.xen.org/wiki/Xen 4.1 Release Notes.
83. M. Zaharia, A. Konwinski, A. Joseph, R. Katz and I. Stoica, Improving Mapreduce Performance in Heterogeneous Environments, *OSDI*, 2008.
84. F. Zhou, M. Goel, P. Desnoyers and R. Sundaram, Scheduler Vulnerabilities and Attacks in Cloud Computing, *arXiv:1103.0759v1 [cs.DC]*, March 2011.

2 MapReduce Family of Large-Scale Data-Processing Systems

Sherif Sakr, Anna Liu, and Ayman G. Fayoumi

CONTENTS

In the last two decades, the continuous increase of computational power has produced an overwhelming flow of data, which has called for a paradigm shift in the computing architecture and large-scale data-processing mechanisms. MapReduce is a simple and powerful programming model that enables easy development of scalable parallel applications to process vast amounts of data on large clusters of commodity machines. It isolates the application from the details of running a distributed program such as issues on data distribution, scheduling, and fault tolerance. However, the original implementation of the MapReduce framework had some limitations that have been tackled by many research efforts in several follow-up works after its introduction. This chapter provides a comprehensive survey for a *family* of approaches and mechanisms of large-scale data-processing mechanisms that have been implemented based on the original idea of the MapReduce framework and are currently gaining a lot of momentum in both research and industrial communities. We also cover a set of systems that have been implemented to provide declarative programming interfaces on top of the MapReduce framework. In addition, we discuss a set of MapReduce-based approaches for processing massive data sets of different data models (e.g., XML, RDF, Graphs) and computationally expensive data-intensive operations. In addition, we review several large-scale data-processing systems that resemble some of the ideas of the MapReduce framework for different purposes and application scenarios. Finally, we discuss some of the future research directions for implementing the next generation of MapReduce-like solutions.

2.1 INTRODUCTION

We live in the era of *Big Data* where we are witnessing a continuous increase on the computational power that produces an overwhelming flow of data, which has called for a *paradigm shift* in the computing architecture and large-scale data-processing mechanisms. Powerful telescopes in astronomy, particle accelerators in physics, and genome sequencers in biology are putting massive volumes of data into the hands of scientists. For example, the Large Synoptic Survey Telescope [1] generates on the order of 30 TB of data every day. Many enterprises continuously collect large data sets that record customer interactions, product sales, results from advertising campaigns on the Web, and other types of information. For example, Facebook collects 15 TB of data each day into a petabyte-scale data warehouse [123]. Jim Gray, called the shift a "fourth paradigm" [69]. The first three paradigms were *experimental, theoretical* and, more recently, *computational science*. Gray argued that the only way to cope with this paradigm is to develop a new generation of computing tools to manage, visualize, and analyze the data flood. In general, current computer architectures are increasingly imbalanced where the latency gap between multicore CPUs and mechanical hard disks is growing every year, which makes the challenges of data-intensive computing much harder to overcome [17]. Hence, there is a crucial need for a systematic and generic approach to tackle these problems with an architecture that can also scale into the foreseeable future. In response, Gray argued that the new trend should instead focus on supporting cheaper clusters of computers to manage and process all this data instead of focusing on having the biggest and fastest single computer.

In general, the growing demand for large-scale data mining and data analysis applications has spurred the development of novel solutions from both the industry (e.g., web-data analysis, click-stream analysis, network-monitoring log analysis) and the sciences (e.g., analysis of data produced by massive-scale simulations, sensor deployments, high-throughput lab equipment). Although parallel database systems [46] serve some of these data analysis applications (e.g., Teradata,* SQL Server PDW,† Vertica,‡ Greenplum,§ ParAccel,¶ Netezza**), they are expensive, difficult to administer and lack fault tolerance for long-running queries [113]. MapReduce [43] is a framework that is introduced by Google for programming commodity computer clusters to perform large-scale data processing in a single pass. The framework is designed such that a MapReduce cluster can scale to thousands of nodes in a fault-tolerant manner. One of the main advantages of this framework is its reliance on a simple and powerful programming model. In addition, it isolates the application developer from all the complex details of running a distributed program such as: issues on data distribution, scheduling, and fault tolerance [112].

Recently, there has been a great deal of hype about cloud computing [11]. In principle, cloud computing is associated with a new paradigm for the provisioning of computing infrastructure. This paradigm shifts the location of this infrastructure to more centralized and larger-scale datacenters to reduce the costs associated with the management of hardware and software resources. In particular, cloud computing has promised a number of advantages for hosting the deployments of data-intensive applications such as

- Reduced time-to-market by removing or simplifying the time-consuming hardware provisioning, purchasing, and deployment processes
- Reduced monetary cost by following a *pay-as-you-go* business model
- Unlimited (virtually) throughput by adding servers if the workload increases

In principle, the success of many enterprises often rely on their ability to analyze expansive volumes of data. In general, cost-effective processing of large data sets is a nontrivial undertaking. Fortunately, MapReduce frameworks and cloud computing have made it easier than ever for everyone to step into the world of Big Data. This technology combination has enabled even small companies to collect and analyze terabytes of data to gain a competitive edge. For example, the Amazon Elastic Compute Cloud (EC2)†† is offered as a commodity that can be purchased and utilized. In addition, Amazon has also provided the Amazon Elastic MapReduce‡‡ as an online service to easily and cost-effectively process vast amounts of data without the need to worry about time-consuming setup, management, or tuning of computing

---

* http://teradata.com/.
† http://www.microsoft.com/sqlserver/en/us/solutions-technologies/data-warehousing/pdw.aspx.
‡ http://www.vertica.com/.
§ http://www.greenplum.com/.
¶ http://www.paraccel.com/.
** http://www-01.ibm.com/software/data/netezza/.
†† http://aws.amazon.com/ec2/.
‡‡ http://aws.amazon.com/elasticmapreduce/.

clusters or the compute capacity upon which they sit. Hence, such services enable third parties to perform their analytical queries on massive data sets with minimum effort and cost by abstracting the complexity entailed in building and maintaining computer clusters.

The implementation of the basic MapReduce architecture has had some limitations. Therefore, several research efforts have been triggered to tackle these limitations by introducing several advancements in the basic architecture to improve its performance. This chapter provides a comprehensive survey for a *family* of approaches and mechanisms of large-scale data analysis mechanisms that have been implemented based on the original idea of the MapReduce framework and are currently gaining a lot of momentum in both research and industrial communities. In particular, the remainder of this chapter is organized as follows. Section 2.2 describes the basic architecture of the MapReduce framework. Section 2.3 discusses several techniques that have been proposed to improve the performance and capabilities of the MapReduce framework from different perspectives. Section 2.4 covers several systems that support a high level SQL-like interface for the MapReduce framework, while Section 2.5 provides an overview of several research efforts of developing MapReduce-based solutions for data-intensive applications for different data models and different computationally expensive operations. Section 2.6 reviews several large-scale data-processing systems that resemble some of the ideas of the MapReduce framework, without sharing its architecture or infrastructure, for different purposes and application scenarios. In Section 2.7, we conclude the chapter and discuss some of the future research directions for implementing the next generation of MapReduce/Hadoop-like solutions.

2.2 MapReduce FRAMEWORK: BASIC ARCHITECTURE

The MapReduce framework is introduced as a simple and powerful programming model that enables easy development of scalable parallel applications to process vast amounts of data on large clusters of commodity machines [43,44]. In particular, the implementation described in the original paper is mainly designed to achieve high performance on large clusters of commodity PCs. One of the main advantages of this approach is that it isolates the application from the details of running a distributed program, such as issues on data distribution, scheduling, and fault tolerance. In this model, the computation takes a set of key/value pairs input and produces a set of key/value pairs as output. The user of the MapReduce framework expresses the computation using two functions: *map* and *reduce*. The map function takes an input pair and produces a set of intermediate key/value pairs. The MapReduce framework groups together all intermediate values associated with the same intermediate key I and passes them to the reduce function. The reduce function receives an intermediate key I with its set of values and merges them together. Typically, just zero or one output value is produced per reduce invocation. The main advantage of this model is that it allows large computations to be easily parallelized and re-executed to be used as the primary mechanism for fault tolerance. Figure 2.1 illustrates an example MapReduce program expressed in pseudo-code for counting the number of occurrences of each word in a collection of documents. In this example, the map function

map(String key, String value):	reduce(String key, Iterator values):
//key: document name	//key: a word
//value: document contents	//values: a list of counts
for each word w in value:	int result = 0;
EmitIntermediate(w, "1");	for each v in values:
	result += ParseInt(v);
	Emit(AsString(result));

FIGURE 2.1 An example MapReduce program. (From J. Dean and S. Ghemawat, MapReduce: Simplified data processing on large clusters, in: *OSDI*, pp. 137–150, 2004.)

emits each word plus an associated count of occurrences while the reduce function sums together all counts emitted for a particular word. In principle, the design of the MapReduce framework has considered the following main principles [36]:

- *Low-cost unreliable commodity hardware*: Instead of using expensive, high-performance, reliable symmetric multiprocessing (SMP) or massively parallel processing (MPP) machines equipped with high-end network and storage subsystems, the MapReduce framework is designed to run on large clusters of commodity hardware. This hardware is managed and powered by open-source operating systems and utilities so that the cost is low.
- *Extremely Scalable RAIN Cluster*: Instead of using centralized RAID-based SAN or NAS storage systems, every MapReduce node has its own local off-the-shelf hard drives. These nodes are loosely coupled where they are placed in racks that can be connected with standard networking hardware connections. These nodes can be taken out of service with almost no impact to still-running MapReduce jobs. These clusters are called redundant array of independent (and inexpensive) nodes (RAIN).
- *Fault-Tolerant yet Easy to Administer*: MapReduce jobs can run on clusters with thousands of nodes or even more. These nodes are not very reliable as at any point in time, a certain percentage of these commodity nodes or hard drives will be out of order. Hence, the MapReduce framework applies straightforward mechanisms to replicate data and launch backup tasks so as to keep still-running processes going. To handle crashed nodes, system administrators simply take crashed hardware off-line. New nodes can be plugged in at any time without much administrative hassle. There is no complicated backup, restore, and recovery configurations like those that can be seen in many DBMS.
- *Highly Parallel yet Abstracted*: The most important contribution of the MapReduce framework is its ability to automatically support the parallelization of task executions. Hence, it allows developers to focus mainly on the problem at hand rather than worrying about the low level implementation details such as memory management, file allocation, parallel, multithreaded, or network programming. Moreover, MapReduce's shared-nothing architecture [120] makes it much more scalable and ready for parallelization.

Hadoop* is an open-source Java library [131] that supports data-intensive distributed applications by realizing the implementation of the MapReduce framework.[†] It has been widely used by a large number of business companies for production purposes.[‡] On the implementation level, the map invocations of a MapReduce job are distributed across multiple machines by automatically partitioning the input data into a set of M splits. The input splits can be processed in parallel by different machines. Reduce invocations are distributed by partitioning the intermediate key space into R pieces using a partitioning function (e.g., hash[key] mod R). The number of partitions (R) and the partitioning function are specified by the user. Figure 2.2 illustrates an example of the overall flow of a MapReduce operation that goes through the following sequence of actions:

1. The input data of the MapReduce program is split into M pieces and starts up many instances of the program on a cluster of machines.
2. One of the instances of the program is elected to be the *master* copy while the rest are considered as *workers* that are assigned their work by the master copy. In particular, there are M map tasks and R reduce tasks to assign. The master picks idle workers and assigns each one or more map tasks and/or reduce tasks.
3. A worker who is assigned a map task processes the contents of the corresponding input split and generates key/value pairs from the input data and passes each pair to the user-defined map function. The intermediate key/value pairs produced by the map function are buffered in memory.
4. Periodically, the buffered pairs are written to local disk and partitioned into R regions by the partitioning function. The locations of these buffered pairs on the local disk are passed back to the master, who is responsible for forwarding these locations to the reduce workers.
5. When a reduce worker is notified by the master about these locations, it reads the buffered data from the local disks of the map workers that is then sorted by the intermediate keys so that all occurrences of the same key are grouped together. The sorting operation is needed because typically many different keys map to the same reduce task.
6. The reduce worker passes the key and the corresponding set of intermediate values to the user's reduce function. The output of the reduce function is appended to a final output file for this reduce partition.
7. When all map tasks and reduce tasks have been completed, the master program wakes up the user program. At this point, the MapReduce invocation in the user program returns the program control back to the user code.

During the execution process, the master pings every worker periodically. If no response is received from a worker within a certain amount of time, the master marks the worker as *failed*. Any map tasks marked *completed* or *in progress* by the worker are reset back to their initial idle state and therefore become eligible for scheduling

---

* http://hadoop.apache.org/.
† In the rest of this chapter, we use the two names: MapReduce and Hadoop, interchangeably.
‡ http://wiki.apache.org/hadoop/PoweredBy.

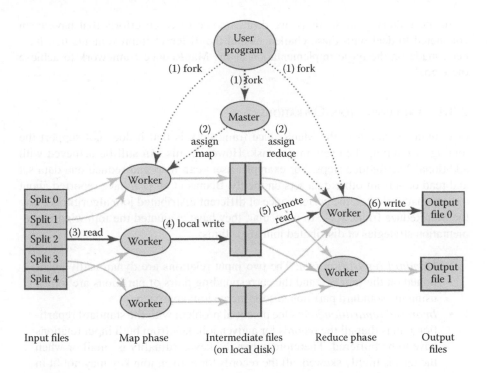

FIGURE 2.2   An overview of the flow of execution a MapReduce Operation. (From J. Dean and S. Ghemawat, MapReduce: Simplified data processing on large clusters, in *OSDI*, pp. 137–150, 2004.)

by other workers. Completed map tasks are re-executed on a task failure because their output is stored on the local disk(s) of the failed machine and is therefore inaccessible. Completed reduce tasks do not need to be re-executed since their output is stored in a global file system.

2.3   EXTENSIONS AND ENHANCEMENTS OF THE MapReduce FRAMEWORK

In practice, the basic implementation of the MapReduce is very useful for handling data processing and data loading in a heterogeneous system with many different storage systems. Moreover, it provides a flexible framework for the execution of more complicated functions than that can be directly supported in SQL. However, this basic architecture suffers from some limitations. Dean and Ghemawa [45] reported about some possible improvements that can be incorporated into the MapReduce framework. Examples of these possible improvements include the following:

- MapReduce should take advantage of natural indices whenever possible.
- Most MapReduce output can be left unmerged since there is no benefit of merging them if the next consumer is just another MapReduce program.
- MapReduce users should avoid using inefficient textual formats.

In the following subsections, we discuss some research efforts that have been conducted to deal with these challenges and the different improvements that have been made on the basic implementation of the MapReduce framework to achieve these goals.

2.3.1 PROCESSING JOIN OPERATIONS

One main limitation of the MapReduce framework is that it does not support the joining of multiple data sets in one task. However, this can still be achieved with additional MapReduce steps. For example, users can map and reduce one data set and read data from other data sets on the fly. Blanas et al. [20] have reported about a study that evaluated the performance of different distributed join algorithms using the MapReduce framework. In particular, they have evaluated the following implementation strategies of distributed join algorithms:

*   *Standard repartition join*: The two input relations are dynamically partitioned on the join key and the corresponding pairs of partitions are joined using the standard partitioned sort–merge join approach.
*   *Improved repartition join*: One potential problem with the standard repartition join is that all the records for a given join key from both input relations have to be buffered. Therefore, when the key cardinality is small or when the data is highly skewed, all the records for a given join key may not fit in memory. The improved repartition join strategy fixes the buffering problem by introducing the following key changes:
    *   In the map function, the output key is changed to a composite of the join key and the table tag. The table tags are generated in a way that ensures records from one input relation will be sorted ahead of those from the other input relation on a given join key.
    *   The partitioning function is customized so that the hashcode is computed from just the join key part of the composite key. This way records with the same join key are still assigned to the same reduce task.
    *   As records from the smaller input are guaranteed to be ahead of those from L for a given join key, only the records from the smaller input are buffered and the records of the larger input are streamed to generate the join output.
*   *Broadcast join*: Instead of moving both input relations across the network as in the repartition-based joins, the broadcast join approach moves only the smaller input relation so that it avoids the preprocessing sorting requirement of both input relations and more importantly avoids the network overhead for moving the larger relation.
*   *Semi-join*: This join approach tries to avoid the problem of the broadcast join approach where it is possible to send many records of the smaller input relation across the network while they may not be actually referenced by any records in the other relation. It achieves this goal at the cost of an extra scan of the smaller input relation where it determines the set of unique join keys in the smaller relation, send them to the other relation to specify

the list of the actual referenced join keys and then send only these records across the network for executing the real execution of the join operation.

- *Per-split semi-join*: This join approach tries to improve the semi-join approach with a further step to address the fact that not every record in the filtered version of the smaller relation will join with a particular split of the larger relation. Therefore, an extra process step is executed to determine the target split(s) of each filtered join key.

Figure 2.3 illustrates a decision tree that summarizes the tradeoffs of the studied join strategies according to the results of that study. Based on statistics, such as the relative data size and the fraction of the join key referenced, this decision tree tries to determine what is the right join strategy for a given circumstance. If data is not pre-processed, the right join strategy depends on the size of the data transferred via the network. If the network cost of broadcasting an input relation R to every node is less expensive than transferring both R and projected L, then the broadcast join algorithm should be used. When preprocessing is allowed, semi-join, per-split semi-join, and directed join with sufficient partitions are the best choices. Semi-join and per-split semi-join offer further flexibility since their preprocessing steps are insensitive to how the log table is organized and thus suitable for any number of reference tables. In addition, the preprocessing steps of these two algorithms are cheaper since there is no shuffling of the log data.

To tackle the limitation of the extra processing requirements for performing join operations in the MapReduce framework, the *map–reduce–merge* model [36] have been introduced to enable the processing of multiple data sets. Figure 2.4 illustrates the framework of this model where the map phase transforms an input key/value

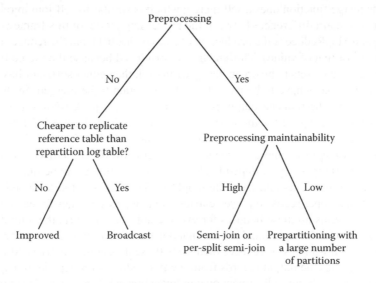

FIGURE 2.3 Decision tree for choosing between various join strategies on the MapReduce framework. (From S. Blanas et al., A comparison of join algorithms for log processing in mapreduce, in *SIGMOD*, pp. 975–986, 2010.)

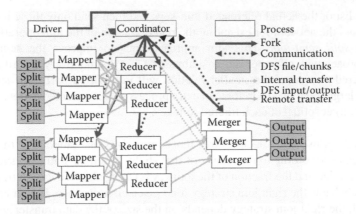

FIGURE 2.4   An overview of the map–reduce–merge framework. (From H. C. Yang et al., Map–reduce–merge: Simplified relational data processing on large clusters, in *SIGMOD*, pp. 1029–1040, 2007.)

pair ($k1$, $v1$) into a list of intermediate key/value pairs [($k2$, $v2$)]. The reduce function aggregates the list of values [$v2$] associated with $k2$ and produces a list of values [$v3$] that are also associated with $k2$. Note that inputs and outputs of both functions belong to the same lineage (α). Another pair of map and reduce functions produce the intermediate output ($k3$, [$v4$]) from another lineage (β). Based on keys $k2$ and $k3$, the merge function combines the two reduced outputs from different lineages into a list of key/value outputs [($k4$, $v5$)]. This final output becomes a new lineage (γ). If $\alpha = \beta$, then this merge function does a self-merge, which is similar to self-join in relational algebra. The main differences between the processing model of this framework and the original MapReduce is the production of a key/value list from the reduce function instead of just that of values. This change is introduced because the merge function requires input data sets to be organized (partitioned, then either sorted or hashed) by keys and these keys have to be passed into the function to be merged. In the original framework, the reduced output is final. Hence, users pack whatever is needed in [$v3$] while passing $k2$ for the next stage is not required. Figure 2.5 illustrates a sample execution of the map–reduce–merge framework. In this example, there are two data sets *employee* and *department*, where employee's key attribute is **emp-id** and the department's key is **dept-id**. The execution of this example query aims to join these two data sets and compute employee bonuses. On the left-hand side of Figure 2.5, a mapper reads employee entries and computes a bonus for each entry. A reducer then sums up these bonuses for every employee and sorts them by **dept-id**, then **emp-id**. On the right-hand side, a mapper reads department entries and computes bonus adjustments. A reducer then sorts these department entries. At the end, a merger matches the output records from the two reducers on **dept-id** and applies a department-based bonus adjustment on employee bonuses. Yang et al. [37] have also proposed an approach for improving the map–reduce–merge framework by adding a new primitive called *traverse*. This primitive can process index file entries

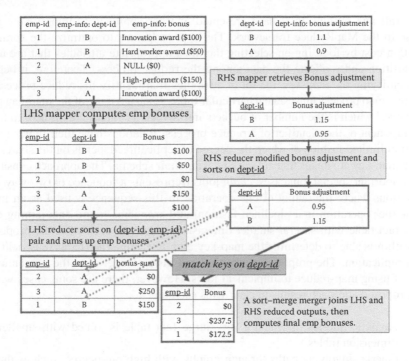

FIGURE 2.5 A sample execution of the map–reduce–merge framework. (From H. C. Yang et al., Map–reduce–merge: Simplified relational data processing on large clusters, in *SIGMOD*, pp. 1029–1040, 2007.)

recursively, select data partitions based on query conditions, and feed only selected partitions to other primitives.

The *map–join–reduce* [76] represents another approach that has been introduced with a filtering–join–aggregation programming model as an extension of the standard MapReduce's filtering–aggregation programming model. In particular, in addition to the standard mapper and reducer operation of the standard MapReduce framework, they introduce a third operation, join (called joiner), to the framework. Hence, to join multiple data sets for aggregation, users specify a set of *join*() functions and the join order between them. Then, the runtime system automatically joins the multiple input data sets according to the join order and invoke *join*() functions to process the joined records. They have also introduced a one-to-many shuffling strategy that shuffles each intermediate key/value pair to many joiners at one time. Using a tailored parti-tion strategy, they can utilize the one-to-many shuffling scheme to join multiple data sets in one phase instead of a sequence of MapReduce jobs. The runtime system for executing a map–join–reduce job launches two kinds of processes: *MapTask* and *ReduceTask*. Mappers run inside the MapTask process, whereas joiners and reducers are invoked inside the ReduceTask process. Therefore, map–join–reduce's process model allows for the pipelining of intermediate results between joiners and reducers since joiners and reducers are run inside the same ReduceTask process.

Afrati and Ullman [6,7] have presented another approach to improve the join phase in the MapReduce framework. The approach aims to optimize the communication cost by focusing on selecting the most appropriate attributes that are used to partition and replicate the data among the reduce process. Therefore, it begins by identifying the *map-key*, the set of attributes that identify the reduce process to which a map process must send a particular tuple. Each attribute of the map-key gets a *"share,"* which is the number of buckets into which its values are hashed, to form a component of the identifier of a reduce process. Relations have their tuples replicated in limited fashion of which the degree of replication depends on the shares for those map-key attributes that are missing from their schema. The approach considers two important special join cases: *chain* joins (represents a sequence of two-way join operations where the output of one operation in this sequence is used as an input to another operation in a pipelined fashion) and *star* joins (represents joining of a large fact table with several smaller dimension tables). In each case, the proposed algorithm is able to determine the map-key and determine the shares that yield the least replication. The proposed approach is not always superior to the conventional way of using map-reduce to implement joins. However, there are some cases where the proposed approach results in clear wins such as

- Analytic queries in which a very large fact table is joined with smaller dimension tables
- Queries involving paths through graphs with high out-degree, such as the Web or a social network

Li et al. [90] have proposed a data analysis platform, based on MapReduce, that is geared for *incremental* one-pass analytics. In particular, they replace the sort–merge implementation in the standard MapReduce framework with a purely hash-based framework, which is designed to address the computational and I/O bottlenecks as well as the blocking behavior of the sort–merge algorithm. Therefore, they devised two hash techniques to suit different user reduce functions, depending on whether the reduce function permits incremental processing. Besides eliminating the sorting cost from the map tasks, these hash techniques enable fast in-memory processing of the reduce function when the memory reaches a sufficient size as determined by the workload and algorithm. In addition, to bring the benefits of fast in-memory processing to workloads that require a large key-state space that far exceeds available memory, they presented a special technique to identify frequent keys and then update their states using a full in-memory processing path, both saving I/Os and also enabling early answers for these keys.

2.3.2 SUPPORTING ITERATIVE PROCESSING

Many data analysis techniques (e.g., PageRank algorithm, recursive relational queries, social network analysis) require iterative computations. These techniques have a common requirement, which is that data are processed iteratively until the computation satisfies a convergence or stopping condition. The basic MapReduce framework does not directly support these iterative data analysis applications. Instead, programmers must implement iterative programs by manually issuing multiple MapReduce jobs and orchestrating their execution using a driver program. In practice, there are two key problems with manually orchestrating an iterative program in MapReduce:

- Even though much of the data may be unchanged from iteration to iteration, the data must be reloaded and reprocessed at each iteration, wasting I/O, network bandwidth, and CPU resources.
- The termination condition may involve the detection of when a fixpoint has been reached. This condition may itself require an extra MapReduce job on each iteration, again incurring overhead in terms of scheduling extra tasks, reading extra data from disk, and moving data across the network.

The *HaLoop* system [25,26] is designed to support iterative processing on the MapReduce framework by extending the basic MapReduce framework with two main functionalities:

1. Caching the invariant data in the first iteration and then reusing them in later iterations.
2. Caching the reducer outputs, which makes checking for a fixpoint more efficient, without an extra MapReduce job.

Figure 2.6 illustrates the architecture of HaLoop as a modified version of the basic MapReduce framework. To accommodate the requirements of iterative data

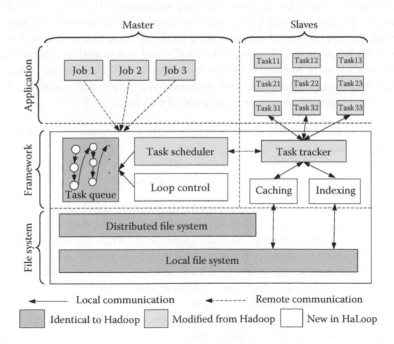

FIGURE 2.6 An overview of HaLoop architecture. (From Y. Bu et al., *PVLDB*, 3(1), 285–296, 2010.)

analysis applications, HaLoop has incorporated the following changes to the basic Hadoop MapReduce framework:

- It exposes a new application programming interface to users that simplifies the expression of iterative MapReduce programs.
- HaLoop's master node contains a new loop control module that repeatedly starts new map-reduce steps that compose the loop body until a user-specified stopping condition is met.
- It uses a new task scheduler that leverages data locality.
- It caches and indices application data on slave nodes. In principle, the task tracker not only manages task execution but also manages caches and indices on the slave node and redirects each task's cache and index accesses to local file system.

In principle, HaLoop relies on the same file system and has the same task queue structure as Hadoop but the task scheduler and task tracker modules are modified, and the loop control, caching, and indexing modules are newly introduced to the architecture. The task tracker not only manages task execution but also manages caches and indices on the slave node, and redirects each task's cache and index accesses to the local file system.

In the MapReduce framework, each map or reduce task contains its portion of the input data and the task runs by performing the map/reduce function on its input data records where the life cycle of the task ends when finishing the processing of all the input data records has been completed. The *iMapReduce* framework [138] supports the feature of iterative processing by keeping alive each map and reduce task during the whole iterative process. In particular, when all of the input data of a persistent task are parsed and processed, the task becomes dormant, waiting for the new updated input data. For a map task, it waits for the results from the reduce tasks and is activated to work on the new input records when the required data from the reduce tasks arrive. For the reduce tasks, they wait for the map tasks' output and are activated synchronously as in MapReduce. Jobs can terminate their iterative process in one of two ways:

1. *Defining fixed number of iterations*: Iterative algorithm stops after it iterates *n* times.
2. *Bounding the distance between two consecutive iterations*: Iterative algorithm stops when the distance is less than a threshold.

The iMapReduce runtime system does the termination check after each iteration. To terminate the iterations by a fixed number of iterations, the persistent map/reduce task records its iteration number and terminates itself when the number exceeds a threshold. To bound the distance between the output from two consecutive iterations, the reduce tasks can save the output from two consecutive iterations and compute the distance. If the termination condition is satisfied, the master will notify all the map and reduce tasks to terminate their execution.

Other projects have been implemented for supporting iterative processing on the MapReduce framework. For example, *Twister** is a MapReduce runtime with an

---

* http://www.iterativemapreduce.org/.

extended programming model that supports iterative MapReduce computations efficiently [48]. It uses a publish/subscribe messaging infrastructure for communication and data transfers and supports long running map/reduce tasks. In particular, it provides programming extensions to MapReduce with broadcast and scatter-type data transfers. Microsoft has also developed a project that provides an iterative MapReduce runtime for Windows Azure called *Daytona*.*

2.3.3 DATA AND PROCESS SHARING

With the emergence of cloud computing, the use of an analytical query-processing infrastructure (e.g., Amazon EC2) can be directly mapped to *monetary* value. Taking into account that different MapReduce jobs can perform similar work, there could be many opportunities for sharing the execution of their work. Thus, this sharing can reduce the overall amount of work, which consequently leads to the reduction of the monetary charges incurred while utilizing the resources of the processing infrastructure. The *MRShare* system [107] have been presented as a sharing framework that is tailored to transform a batch of queries into a new batch that will be executed more efficiently by merging jobs into groups and evaluating each group as a single query. Based on a defined cost model, they described an optimization problem that aims to derive the optimal grouping of queries to avoid performing redundant work and thus resulting in significant savings on both processing time and money. In particular, the approach considers exploiting the following sharing opportunities:

- *Sharing Scans.* To share scans between two mapping pipelines M_i and M_j, the input data must be the same. In addition, the key/value pairs should be of the same type. Given that, it becomes possible to merge the two pipelines into a single pipeline and scan the input data only once. However, it should be noted that such combined mapping will produce two streams of output tuples (one for each mapping pipeline M_i and M_j). To distinguish the streams at the reducer stage, each tuple is tagged with a $\texttt{tag()}$ part. This tagging part is used to indicate the origin mapping pipeline during the reduce phase.
- *Sharing Map Output.* If the map output key and value types are the same for two mapping pipelines M_i and M_j, then the map output streams for M_i and M_j can be shared. In particular, if Map_i and Map_j are applied to each input tuple, then the map output tuples coming only from Map_i are tagged with $\texttt{tag(i)}$ only. If a map output tuple was produced from an input tuple by both Map_i and Map_j, it is then tagged by $\texttt{tag(i)+tag(j)}$. Therefore, any overlapping parts of the map output will be shared. In principle, producing a smaller map output leads to savings on sorting and copying intermediate data over the network.
- *Sharing Map Functions.* Sometimes the map functions are identical, and thus, they can be executed once. At the end of the map stage, two streams are produced where each is tagged with its job tag. If the map output is

---

* http://research.microsoft.com/en-us/projects/daytona/.

shared, then clearly only one stream needs to be generated. Even if only some filters are common in both jobs, it is possible to share parts of the map functions.

In practice, sharing scans and sharing map-output yield I/O savings while sharing map functions (or parts of them) would yield additional CPU savings.

While the *MRShare* system focus on sharing the processing between queries that are executed concurrently, the *ReStore* system [49,50] has been introduced so that it can enable the queries that are submitted at different times to share the intermediate results of previously executed jobs and reusing them for future submitted jobs to the system. In particular, each MapReduce job produces output that is stored in the distributed file system used by the MapReduce system (e.g., HDFS). These intermediate results are kept (for a defined period) and managed so that it can be used as input by subsequent jobs. ReStore can make use of whole jobs or sub-jobs reuse opportunities. To achieve this goal, the ReStore consists of two main components:

- *Repository of MapReduce job outputs*: It stores the outputs of previously executed MapReduce jobs and the physical plans of these jobs.
- *Plan matcher and rewriter*: Its aim is to find physical plans in the repository that can be used to rewrite the input jobs using the available matching intermediate results.

In principle, the approach of the *ReStore* system can be viewed as analogous to the steps of building and using materialized views for relational databases [62].

2.3.4 SUPPORT OF DATA INDICES AND COLUMN STORAGE

One of the main limitations of the original implementation of the MapReduce framework is that it is designed in a way that the jobs can only scan the input data in a sequential-oriented fashion. Hence, the query processing performance of the MapReduce framework is unable to match the performance of a well-configured parallel DBMS [113]. To tackle this challenge, Dittrich et al. [47] have presented the *Hadoop++* system, which aims to boost the query performance of the Hadoop system without changing any of the system internals. They achieved this goal by injecting their changes through user-defined function (UDFs), which only affect the Hadoop system from inside without any external effect. In particular, they introduce the following main changes:

- *Trojan Index*: The original Hadoop implementation does not provide index access due to the lack of a priori knowledge of schema and the MapReduce jobs being executed. Hence, the Hadoop++ system is based on the assumption that if we know the schema and the anticipated MapReduce jobs, then we can create appropriate indices for the Hadoop tasks. In particular, Trojan index is an approach to integrate indexing capability into Hadoop in a non-invasive way. These indices are created during the data-loading time and thus have no penalty at query time. Each Trojan index provides an optional index access path, which can be used for selective MapReduce jobs. The scan access path can still be used for other MapReduce jobs. These indices are created by injecting appropriate UDFs inside the Hadoop implementation. Specifically, the main features of Trojan indices can be summarized as follows:

- *No external library or engine*: Trojan indices integrate indexing capability natively into the Hadoop framework without imposing a distributed SQL query engine on top of it.
- *Noninvasive*: They do not change the existing Hadoop framework. The index structure is implemented by providing the right UDFs.
- *Optional access path*: They provide an optional index access path that can be used for selective MapReduce jobs. However, the scan access path can still be used for other MapReduce jobs.
- *Seamless splitting*: Data indexing adds an index overhead for each data split. Therefore, the logical split includes the data as well as the index, as it automatically splits the indexed data at logical split boundaries.
- *Partial index*: Trojan index need not be built on the entire split. However, it can be built on any contiguous subset of the split as well.
- *Multiple indexes*: Several Trojan indexes can be built on the same split. However, only one of them can be the primary index. During query processing, an appropriate index can be chosen for data access based on the logical query plan and the cost model.
- *Trojan Join*: Similar to the idea of the Trojan index, the Hadoop++ system assumes that if we know the schema and the expected workload, then we can co-partition the input data during the loading time. In particular, given any two input relations, they apply the same partitioning function on the join attributes of both the relations at data loading time and place the co-group pairs, having the same join key from the two relations, on the same split and, hence, on the same node. As a result, join operations can be then processed locally within each node at query time. Implementing the Trojan joins do not require any changes to be made to the existing implementation of the Hadoop framework. The only changes are made on the internal management of the data splitting process. In addition, Trojan indices can be freely combined with Trojan joins.

The design and implementation of a column-oriented and binary backend storage format for Hadoop has been presented in [54]. In general, a straightforward way to implement a column-oriented storage format for Hadoop is to store each column of the input data set in a separate file. However, this raises two main challenges:

- It requires generating roughly equal sized splits so that a job can be effectively parallelized over the cluster.
- It needs to ensure that the corresponding values from different columns in the data set are co-located on the same node running the map task.

The first challenge can be tackled by horizontally partitioning the data set and storing each partition in a separate subdirectory. The second challenge is harder to tackle because of the default three-way block-level replication strategy of HDFS that provides fault tolerance on commodity servers but does not provide any colocation guarantees. Floratou et al. [54] tackle this challenge by implementing a modified HDFS block placement policy that guarantees that the files corresponding to the different columns of a split are always co-located across replicas. Hence, when reading a data set, the column input format can actually assign one or more split directories to a single split and the column files of a split directory are scanned sequentially and the records are reassembled using values from corresponding positions in the files. A lazy record construction technique is used to mitigate the deserialization overhead in Hadoop, as well as eliminate unnecessary disk I/O. The basic idea behind lazy record construction is to deserialize only those columns of a record that are actually accessed in a map function. Each column of the input data set can be compressed using one of the following compression schemes:

1. *Compressed blocks*: This scheme uses a standard compression algorithm to compress a block of contiguous column values. Multiple compressed blocks may fit into a single HDFS block. A header indicates the number of records in a compressed block and the block's size. This allows the block to be skipped if no values are accessed in it. However, when a value in the block is accessed, the entire block needs to be decompressed.
2. *Dictionary compressed skip list*: This scheme is tailored for map-typed columns. It takes advantage of the fact that the keys used in maps are often strings that are drawn from a limited universe. Such strings are well suited for dictionary compression. A dictionary is built of keys for each block of map values and store the compressed keys in a map using a skip list format. The main advantage of this scheme is that a value can be accessed without having to decompress an entire block of values.

One advantage of this approach is that adding a column to a data set is not an expensive operation. This can be done by simply placing an additional file for the new column in each of the split directories. However, a potential disadvantage of this approach is that the available parallelism may be limited for smaller data sets. Maximum parallelism is achieved for a MapReduce job when the number of splits is at least equal to the number of map tasks.

The *Llama* system [93] have introduced another approach of providing column storage support for the MapReduce framework. In this approach, each imported table is transformed into column groups where each group contains a set of files representing one or more columns. Llama introduced a column-wise format for Hadoop, called *CFile*, where each file can contain multiple data blocks, and each block of the file contains a fixed number of records (Figure 2.7). However, the size of each logical block may vary since records can be variable-sized. Each file includes a block index, which is stored after all data blocks, stores the offset of each block and is used to locate a specific block. To achieve storage efficiency, Llama uses block-level compression using any of the well-known compression schemes. To improve the query processing and the performance of join operations, Llama columns are formed into correlation groups to provide the basis for the vertical partitioning of tables. In particular, it creates multiple vertical groups where each group is defined by a collection

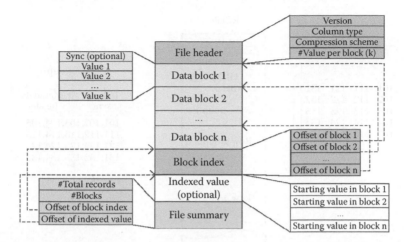

FIGURE 2.7   An example structure of *CFile*. (From Y. Lin et al., Llama: Leveraging columnar storage for scalable join processing in the MapReduce framework, in *SIGMOD Conference*, pp. 961–972, 2011.)

of columns, one of them is specified as the sorting column. Initially, when a new table is imported into the system, a basic vertical group is created, which contains all the columns of the table and sorted by the table's primary key by default. In addition, based on statistics of query patterns, some auxiliary groups are dynamically created or discarded to improve the query performance. The *Clydesdale* system [13,79], a system that has been implemented for targeting workloads where the data fits a star schema, uses *CFile* for storing its fact tables. It also relies on tailored join plans and block iteration mechanism [140] for optimizing the execution of its target workloads.

RCFile [63] (Record Columnar File) is another data placement structure that provides column-wise storage for Hadoop file system (HDFS). In RCFile, each table is first stored as horizontally partitioned into multiple row groups where each row group is then vertically partitioned so that each column is stored independently (Figure 2.8). In particular, each table can have multiple HDFS blocks where each block organizes records with the basic unit of a row group. Depending on the row group size and the HDFS block size, an HDFS block can have only one or multiple row groups. In particular, a row group contains the following three sections:

1. The *sync marker*, which is placed in the beginning of the row group and mainly used to separate two continuous row groups in an HDFS block.
2. A metadata header, which stores the information items on how many records are in this row group, how many bytes are in each column and how many bytes are in each field in a column.
3. The table data section, which is actually a column-store where all the fields in the same column are stored continuously together.

RCFile utilizes a column-wise data compression within each row group and provides a lazy decompression technique to avoid unnecessary column decompression

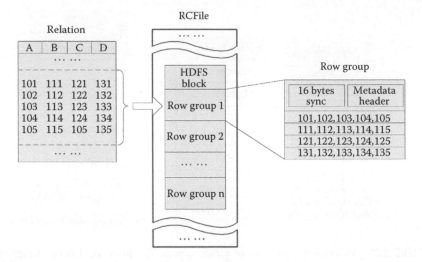

FIGURE 2.8   An example structure of *RCFile*. (From Y. He et al., RCFile: A fast and space-efficient data placement structure in MapReduce-based warehouse systems, in *ICDE*, pp. 1199–1208, 2011.)

during query execution. In particular, the metadata header section is compressed using the *RLE* (Run Length Encoding) algorithm. The table data section is not compressed as a whole unit. However, each column is independently compressed with the *Gzip* compression algorithm. When processing a row group, RCFile does not need to fully read the whole content of the row group into memory. It only reads the metadata header and the needed columns in the row group for a given query, and thus, it can skip unnecessary columns and gain the I/O advantages of a column-store. The metadata header is always decompressed and held in memory until RCFile processes the next row group. However, RCFile does not decompress all the loaded columns and uses a lazy decompression technique where a column will not be decompressed in memory until RCFile has determined that the data in the column will be really useful for query execution.

The notion of *Trojan data layout* has been coined in [78], which exploits the existing data block replication in HDFS to create different Trojan layouts on a per-replica basis. This means that rather than keeping all data block replicas in the same layout, it uses *different* Trojan layouts for each replica, which is optimized for a different subclass of queries. As a result, every incoming query can be scheduled to the most suitable data block replica. In particular, Trojan layouts change the internal organization of a data block and not among data blocks. They co-locate attributes together according to query workloads by applying a column grouping algorithm that uses an interestingness measure that denotes how well a set of attributes speeds up most or all queries in a workload. The column groups are then packed to maximize the total interestingness of data blocks. At query time, an incoming MapReduce job is transparently adapted to query the data block replica that minimizes the data access time. The map tasks are then routed of the MapReduce job to the data nodes storing such data block replicas.

2.3.5 EFFECTIVE DATA PLACEMENT

In the basic implementation of the Hadoop project, the objective of the data place-ment policy is to achieve good load balance by distributing the data evenly across the data servers, independently of the intended use of the data. This simple data placement policy works well with most Hadoop applications that access just a *single* file. However, there are some other applications that process data from *multiple* files, which can get a significant boost in performance with customized strategies. In these applications, the absence of data colocation increases the data-shuffling costs, increases the network overhead, and reduces the effectiveness of data parti-tioning. For example, log processing is a very common usage scenario for Hadoop framework. In this scenario, data are accumulated in batches from event logs such as: clickstreams, phone call records, application logs, or a sequences of transactions. Each batch of data is ingested into Hadoop and stored in one or more HDFS files at regular intervals. Two of the most common operations in log analysis of these applications are (1) joining the log data with some reference data and (2) sessioniza-tion, that is, computing user sessions. The performance of such operations can be significantly improved if they utilize the benefits of data colocation. *CoHadoop* [51] is a lightweight extension to Hadoop, which is designed to enable colocating related files at the file system level while at the same time retaining the good load balancing and fault tolerance properties. It introduces a new file property to identify related data files and modify the data placement policy of Hadoop to colocate copies of those related files in the same server. These changes are designed in a way to retain the benefits of Hadoop, including load balancing and fault tolerance. In principle, CoHadoop provides a generic mechanism that allows applications to control data placement at the file-system level. In particular, a new file-level property called a *locator* is introduced, and the Hadoop's data placement policy is modified so that it makes use of this locator property. Each locator is represented by a unique value (ID) where each file in HDFS is assigned to at most one locator and many files can be assigned to the same locator. Files with the same locator are placed on the same set of datanodes, whereas files with no locator are placed via Hadoop's default strategy. It should be noted that this colocation process involves all data blocks, including replicas. Figure 2.9 shows an example of colocating two files, A and B, via a common locator. All of A's two HDFS blocks and B's three blocks are stored on the same set of datanodes. To manage the locator information and keep track of co-located files, CoHadoop introduces a new data structure, the *locator table*, which stores a map-ping of locators to the list of files that share this locator. In practice, the CoHadoop extension enables a wide variety of applications to exploit data colocation by simply specifying related files such as: colocating log files with reference files for joins, colocating partitions for grouping and aggregation, colocating index files with their data files and colocating columns of a table.

2.3.6 PIPELINING AND STREAMING OPERATIONS

The original implementation of the MapReduce framework has been designed in a way that the entire output of each map and reduce task to be *materialized* into a local

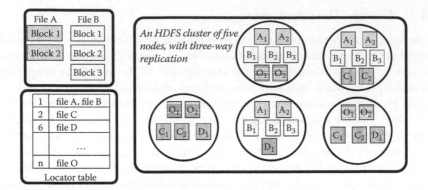

FIGURE 2.9 Example file colocation in CoHadoop. (From M. Y. Eltabakh et al., *PVLDB*, 4(9), 575–585, 2011.)

file before it can be consumed by the next stage. This materialization step allows for the implementation of a simple and elegant checkpoint/restart fault tolerance mechanism. The *MapReduce Online* approach [39,40] has been proposed as a modified architecture of the MapReduce framework in which intermediate data is *pipelined* between operators while preserving the programming interfaces and fault tolerance models of previous MapReduce frameworks. This pipelining approach provides important advantages to the MapReduce framework such as

- The reducers can begin their processing of the data as soon as it is produced by mappers. Therefore, they can generate and refine an approximation of their final answer during the course of execution. In addition, they can provide initial estimates of the results several orders of magnitude faster than the final results.
- It widens the domain of problems to which MapReduce can be applied. For example, it facilitates the ability to design MapReduce jobs that run continuously, accepting new data as it arrives and analyzing it immediately (continuous queries). This allows MapReduce to be used for applications such as event monitoring and stream processing.
- Pipelining delivers data to downstream operators more promptly, which can increase opportunities for parallelism, improve utilization, and reduce response time.

In this approach, each reduce task contacts every map task upon initiation of the job and opens a TCP socket that will be used to pipeline the output of the map function. As each map output record is produced, the mapper determines which partition (reduce task) the record should be sent to, and immediately sends it via the appropriate socket. A reduce task accepts the pipelined data it receives from each map task and stores it in an in-memory buffer. Once the reduce task learns that every map task has completed, it performs a final merge of all the sorted runs. In addition, the reduce tasks of one job can optionally pipeline their output directly to the map tasks of the next job, sidestepping the need for expensive fault-tolerant storage in HDFS for what amounts to a temporary file. However, the computation of the reduce function from the previous job and the map function of the next job cannot be overlapped as the final result of the reduce step cannot be produced until all map tasks have completed, which prevents effective pipelining. Therefore, the reducer treats the output of a pipelined map task as *tentative* until the *JobTracker* informs the reducer that the map task has committed successfully. The reducer can merge together spill files generated by the same uncommitted mapper, but will not combine those spill files with the output of other map tasks until it has been notified that the map task has committed. Thus, if a map task fails, each reduce task can ignore any tentative spill files produced by the failed map attempt. The *JobTracker* will take care of scheduling a new map task attempt, as in standard Hadoop. In principle, the main limitation of the *MapReduce Online* approach is that it is based on HDFS. Therefore, it is not suitable for streaming applications, in which data streams have to be processed without any disk involvement. A similar approach has been presented by Logothetis and Yocum [94], which defines an *incremental* MapReduce job as one that processes data in large batches of tuples and runs continuously according to a specific window range and slide of increment. In particular, it produces a MapReduce result that includes all data within a window (of time or data size) of every slide and considers landmark MapReduce jobs where the trailing edge of the window is fixed and the system incorporates new data into the existing result. Map functions are trivially continuous and process data on a tuple-by-tuple basis. However, before the reduce function may process the mapped data, the data must be partitioned across the reduce operators and sorted. When the map operator first receives a new key-value pair, it calls the map function and inserts the result into the latest increment in the map results. The operator then assigns output key-value pairs to reduce tasks, grouping them according to the partition function. Continuous reduce operators participate in the sort as well, grouping values by their keys before calling the reduce function.

The *Incoop* system [19] has been introduced as a MapReduce implementation that has been adapted for incremental computations, which detects the changes on the input dat sets and enables the automatic update of the outputs of the MapReduce jobs by employing a fine-grained result reuse mechanism. In particular, it allows MapReduce programs that are not designed for incremental processing to be executed transparently in an incremental manner. To achieve this goal, the design of Incoop introduces new techniques that are incorporated into the Hadoop MapReduce framework. For example, instead of relying on HDFS to store the input to MapReduce jobs, Incoop devises a file system called *Inc-HDFS* (Incremental HDFS) that provides mechanisms to identify similarities in the input data of consecutive job runs. In particular, Inc-HDFS splits the input into chunks whose boundaries depend on the file contents so that small changes to input do not change all chunk boundaries. Therefore, this partitioning mechanism can maximize the opportunities for reusing results from previous computations, while preserving compatibility with HDFS by offering the same interface and semantics. In addition, Incoop controls the granularity of tasks so that large tasks can be divided into smaller subtasks that can be re-used even when the large tasks cannot. Therefore, it introduces a new *Contraction phase* that leverages *Combiner* functions to reduce the network traffic by anticipating a small part of the processing done by the Reducer tasks and control their granularity. Furthermore, Incoop improves the effectiveness of memoization by implementing an affinity-based scheduler that applies a work-stealing algorithm to minimize the amount of data movement across machines. This modified scheduler strikes a balance between exploiting the locality of previously computed results and executing tasks on any available machine to prevent straggling effects. On the runtime, instances of incremental Map tasks take advantage of previously stored results by querying the memoization server. If they find that the result has already been computed, they fetch the result from the location of their memoized output and conclude. Similarly, the results of a reduce task are remembered by storing them persistently and locally where a mapping from a collision-resistant hash of the input to the location of the output is inserted in the memoization server.

Since a reduce task receives input from n map tasks, the key stored in the memoization server consists of the hashes of the outputs from all n map task that collectively form the input to the reduce task. Therefore, when executing a reduce task, instead of immediately copying the output from the map tasks, the reduce task consults map tasks for their respective hashes to determine if the reduce task has already been computed in previous run. If so, that output is directly fetched from the location stored in the memoization server, which avoids the re-execution of that task.

The M^3 system [10] has been proposed to support the answering of continuous queries over streams of data bypassing the HDFS so that data gets processed only through a main-memory-only data path and totally avoids any disk access. In this approach, mappers and reducers never terminate where there is only one MapReduce job per query operator that is continuously executing. In M^3, query processing is incremental where only the new input is processed, and the change in the query answer is represented by three sets of inserted (+ve), deleted (−ve), and updated (u) tuples. The query issuer receives as output a stream that represents the deltas (incremental changes) to the answer. Whenever an input tuple is received, it is transformed into a modify operation (+ve, −ve, or u) that is propagated in the query execution pipeline, producing the corresponding set of modify operations in the answer. Supporting incremental query evaluation requires that some intermediate state be kept at the various operators of the query execution pipeline. Therefore, mappers and reducers run continuously without termination, and hence, can maintain main-memory state throughout the execution. In contrast to splitting the input data based on its size as in Hadoops input split functionality, M^3 splits the streamed data based on arrival rates where the rate split layer, between the main-memory buffers and the mappers, is responsible for balancing the stream rates among the mappers. This layer periodically receives rate statistics from the mappers and accordingly redistributes the load of processing amongst mappers. For instance, a fast stream that can overflow one mapper should be distributed among two or more mappers. In contrast, a group of slow streams that would underflow their corresponding mappers should be combined to feed into only one Mapper. To support fault tolerance, input data is replicated inside the main memory buffers and an input split is not overwritten until the corresponding mapper commits. When a mapper fails, it re-reads its corresponding input split from any of the replica inside the buffers. A mapper writes its intermediate key-value pairs in its own main memory and does not overwrite a set of key-value pairs until the corresponding reducer commits. When a reducer fails, it rereads its corresponding sets of intermediate key-value pairs from the mappers.

The *DEDUCE* system [84] has been presented as a middleware that attempts to combine real-time stream processing with the capabilities of a large-scale data analysis framework like MapReduce. In particular, it extends the *IBM's System S* stream processing engine and augments its capabilities with those of the MapReduce framework. In this approach, the input data set to the MapReduce operator can be either prespecified at compilation time or could be provided at runtime as a punctuated list of files or directories. Once the input data is available, the MapReduce operator spawns a MapReduce job and produces a list of punctuated list of files or directories, which point to the output data. Therefore, a MapReduce operator can potentially spawn multiple MapReduce jobs over the application lifespan but such jobs are spawned only when the preceding job (if any) has completed its execution. Hence, multiple jobs can be cascaded together to create a data-flow of MapReduce operators where the output from the MapReduce operators can be read to provide updates to the stream processing operators.

2.3.7 SYSTEM OPTIMIZATIONS

Several studies have been conducted to evaluate the performance characteristics of the MapReduce framework. For example, Gu and Grossman [61] have reported the following lessons that they have learned from their experiments with the MapReduce framework:

- *The importance of data locality.* Locality is a key factor especially when relying on inexpensive commodity hardware.
- *Load balancing and the importance of identifying hot spots.* With poor load balancing, the entire system can be waiting for a single node. It is important to eliminate any "hot spots," which can be caused by data access (accessing data from a single node) or network I/O (transferring data into or out of a single node).
- *Fault tolerance comes with a price.* In some cases, fault tolerance introduces extra overhead to replicate the intermediate results. For example, in the cases of running on small to medium sized clusters, it might be reasonable to favor performance and rerun any failed intermediate task when necessary.
- *Streams are important.* Streaming is important to reduce the total running time of MapReduce jobs.

Jiang et al. [77] have conducted an in-depth performance study of MapReduce using its open-source implementation, Hadoop. As an outcome of this study, they identified some factors that can have significant performance impact on the MapReduce framework. These factors are described as follows:

- Although MapReduce is independent of the underlying storage system, it still requires the storage system to provide efficient I/O modes for scanning data. The experiments of the study on HDFS show that direct I/O outperforms streaming I/O by 10%–15%.
- The MapReduce can utilize three kinds of indices (range indices, block-level indices, and database-indexed tables) in a straightforward way. The

experiments of the study show that the range index improves the performance of MapReduce by a factor of 2 in the selection task and a factor of 10
in the join task when selectivity is high.

- There are two kinds of decoders for parsing the input records: mutable
  decoders and immutable decoders. The study claims that only immutable
  decoders introduce performance bottleneck. To handle database-like workloads, MapReduce users should strictly use mutable decoders. A mutable
  decoder is faster than an immutable decoder by a factor of 10 and improves
  the performance of selection by a factor of 2. Using a mutable decoder, even
  parsing the text record is efficient.
- Map-side sorting exerts negative performance effect on large aggregation tasks that require nontrivial key comparisons and produce millions of
  groups. Therefore, fingerprinting-based sort can significantly improve the
  performance of MapReduce on such aggregation tasks. The experiments
  show that fingerprinting-based sort outperforms direct sort by a factor of 4
  to 5, and improves overall performance of the job by 20%–25%.
- Scheduling strategy affects the performance of MapReduce as it can be
  sensitive to the processing speed of slave nodes, and slows down the execution time of the entire job by 25%–35%.

The experiments of the study show that with proper engineering for these factors, the performance of MapReduce can be improved by a factor of 2.5 to 3.5 and
approaches the performance of parallel databases. Therefore, several low-level system optimization techniques have been introduced to improve the performance of
the MapReduce framework.

In general, running a single program in a MapReduce framework may require
tuning a number of parameters by users or system administrators. The settings of
these parameters control various aspects of job behavior during execution such as
memory allocation and usage, concurrency, I/O optimization, and network bandwidth usage. The submitter of a Hadoop job has the option to set these parameters
either using a program-level interface or through XML configuration files. For any
parameter whose value is not specified explicitly during job submission, default values, either shipped along with the system or specified by the system administrator,
are used [12]. Users can run into performance problems because they do not know
how to set these parameters correctly, or because they do not even know that these
parameters exist. Herodotou and Babu [66] have focused on the optimization opportunities presented by the large space of configuration parameters for these programs.
They introduced a *Profiler* component to collect detailed statistical information from
unmodified MapReduce programs and a *what-if* engine for fine-grained cost estimation. In particular, the profiler component is responsible for the following two main
aspects:

1. Capturing information at the fine granularity of phases within the map and
   reduce tasks of a MapReduce job execution. This information is crucial to
   the accuracy of decisions made by the what-if engine and the cost-based
   optimizer components.

2. Using dynamic instrumentation to collect run-time monitoring information from unmodified MapReduce programs. The dynamic nature means that monitoring can be turned on or off on demand.

The what-if engine's accuracy come from how it uses a mix of simulation and model-based estimation at the phase level of the MapReduce job execution [65,67,68]. For a given MapReduce program, the role of the cost-based optimizer component is to enumerate and search efficiently through the high dimensional space of configuration parameter settings, making appropriate calls to the what-if engine. For the program to find a good configuration setting, it clusters parameters into lower-dimensional subspaces such that the globally optimal parameter setting in the high-dimensional space can be generated by composing the optimal settings found for the subspaces. Stubby [91] has been presented as a cost-based optimizer for MapReduce workflows that searches through the subspace of the full plan space that can be enumerated correctly and costed based on the information available in any given setting. Stubby enumerates the plan space based on plan-to-plan transformations and an efficient search algorithm.

The *Manimal* system [27,75] is designed as a static analysis-style mechanism for detecting opportunities for applying relational style optimizations in MapReduce programs. Like most programming-language optimizers, it is a best-effort system where it does not guarantee that it will find every possible optimization and it only indicates an optimization when it is entirely safe to do so. In particular, the analyzer component of the system is responsible for examining the MapReduce program and sends the resulting optimization descriptor to the optimizer component. In addition, the analyzer also emits an index generation program that can yield a B+ tree of the input file. The optimizer uses the optimization descriptor, plus a catalog of precomputed indexes, to choose an optimized execution plan, called an execution descriptor. This descriptor, plus a potentially modified copy of the user's original program, is then sent for execution on the Hadoop cluster. These steps are performed transparently from the user where the submitted program does not need to be modified by the programmer in any way. In particular, the main task of the analyzer is to produce a set of optimization descriptors that enable the system to carry out a phase roughly akin to logical rewriting of query plans in a relational database. The descriptors characterize a set of potential modifications that remain logically identical to the original plan. The catalog is a simple mapping from a filename to zero or more (X, O) pairs, where X is an index file and O is an optimization descriptor. The optimizer examines the catalog to see if there is any entry for input file. If not, then it simply indicates that Manimal should run the unchanged user program without any optimization. If there is at least one entry for the input file, and a catalog-associated optimization descriptor is compatible with analyzer output, then the optimizer can choose an execution plan that takes advantage of the associated index file.

A key feature of MapReduce is that it automatically handles failures, hiding the complexity of fault tolerance from the programmer. In particular, if a node crashes, MapReduce automatically restarts the execution of its tasks. In addition, if a node is available but is performing poorly, MapReduce runs a speculative copy of its task (backup task) on another machine to finish the computation faster. Without this mechanism of speculative execution, a job would be as slow as the misbehaving task. This situation can arise for many reasons, including faulty hardware and system misconfiguration. Meanwhile, launching too many speculative tasks may take away resources from useful tasks. Therefore, the accuracy in estimating the progress and time remaining long-running jobs is an important challenge for a runtime environment like the MapReduce framework. In particular, this information can play an important role in improving resource allocation, enhancing the task scheduling, enabling query debugging or tuning the cluster configuration. The *ParaTimer* system [103,104] has been proposed to tackle this challenge. In particular, ParaTimer provides techniques for handling several challenges including failures and data skew. To handle unexpected changes in query execution times such as those due to failures, ParaTimer provides users with a set of time-remaining estimates that correspond to the predicted query execution times in different scenarios (i.e., a single worst-case failure or data skew at an operator). Each of these indicators can be annotated with the scenario to which it corresponds, giving users a detailed picture of possible expected behaviors. To achieve this goal, ParaTimer estimates time remaining by breaking queries into pipelines where the time remaining for each pipeline is estimated by considering the work to be done and the speed at which that work will be performed, taking (time-varying) parallelism into account. To get processing speeds, ParaTimer relies on earlier debug runs of the same query on input data samples generated by the user. In addition, ParaTimer identifies the critical path in a query plan where it then estimates progress along that path, effectively ignoring other paths. Zaharia et al. [137] have presented an approach to estimate the progress of MapReduce tasks within environments of clusters with heterogeneous hardware configurations. In these environments, choosing the node on which to run a speculative task is as important as choosing the task. They proposed an algorithm for speculative execution called *LATE* (Longest Approximate Time to End) which is based on three principles: prioritizing tasks to speculate, selecting fast nodes on which to run, and capping speculative tasks to prevent thrashing. In particular, the algorithm speculatively execute the task that it suspects will finish farthest into the future, because this task provides the greatest opportunity for a speculative copy to overtake the original and reduce the job's response time. To get the best chance of beating the original task with the speculative task, the algorithm only launches speculative tasks on fast nodes (and not the first available node). The *RAFT* (Recovery Algorithms for Fast-Tracking) system [115,116] has been introduced, as a part of the *Hadoop++* system [47], for tracking and recovering MapReduce jobs under task or node failures. In particular, RAFT uses two main checkpointing mechanisms: *local checkpointing* and *query metadata checkpointing*. On the one hand, the main idea of local checkpointing is to utilize intermediate results, which are by default persisted by Hadoop, as checkpoints of ongoing task progress computation. In general, map tasks spill buffered intermediate results to local disk whenever the output buffer is on the verge to overflow. RAFT exploits this spilling phase to piggyback checkpointing metadata on the latest spill of each map task. For each checkpoint, RAFT stores a triplet of metadata that includes the *tasked*, which represents a unique task identifier, *spillID*, which represents the local path to the spilled data and *offset*, which specifies the last byte of input data that was processed in that spill. To recover from a task failure, the RAFT scheduler reallocates the failed task to the same node that was running the task. Then, the node resumes the task from the last checkpoint and reuses the spills previously produced for the same task. This simulates a situation where previous spills appear as if they were just produced by the task. In case that there is no local checkpoint available, the node recomputes the task from the beginning. On the other hand, the idea behind query metadata checkpointing is to push intermediate results to reducers as soon as map tasks are completed and to keep track of those incoming key-value pairs that produce local partitions and hence that are not shipped to another node for processing. Therefore, in case of a node failure, the RAFT scheduler can recompute local partitions.

In general, energy consumption and cooling are large components of the operational cost of datacenters [14]. Therefore, the cluster-level energy management of MapReduce framework is another interesting system optimization aspect. In principle, the energy efficiency of a cluster can be improved in two ways [89]:

1. By matching the number of active nodes to the current needs of the workload and placing the remaining nodes in low-power standby modes.
2. By engineering the compute and storage features of each node to match its workload and avoid energy wastage due to oversized components.

Lang and Patel [86] have investigated the approach to power down (and power up) nodes of a MapReduce cluster to save energy during periods of low utilization. In particular, they compared between the following two strategies for MapReduce energy management:

1. Covering Set (CS) strategy that keeps only a small fraction of the nodes powered up during periods of low utilization.
2. All-In Strategy (AIS) that uses all the nodes in the cluster to run a workload and then powers down the entire cluster.

The results from this comparison show that there are two crucial factors that affect the effectiveness of these two methods:

• The computational complexity of the workload.
• The time taken to transition nodes to and from a low power (deep hibernation) state to a high performance state.

The evaluation shows that *CS* is more effective than *AIS* only when the computational complexity of the workload is low (e.g., linear), and the time it takes for the hardware to transition a node to and from a low-power state is a relatively large fraction of the overall workload time (i.e., the workload execution time is small). In all other cases, the *AIS* shows better performance over *CS* in terms of energy savings and response time performance.

2.4   SYSTEMS OF DECLARATIVE INTERFACES FOR THE MapReduce FRAMEWORK

For programmers, a key appealing feature in the MapReduce framework is that there are only two main high-level declarative primitives (*map* and *reduce*) that can be written in any programming language of choice and without worrying about the details of their parallel execution. However, the MapReduce programming model has its own limitations such as

- Its one-input data format (key/value pairs) and two-stage data flow is extremely rigid. As we have previously discussed, to perform tasks that have a different data flow (e.g., joins or *n* stages) would require inelegant workarounds.
- Custom code has to be written for even the most common operations (e.g., projection and filtering), which leads to the fact that the code is usually difficult to reuse and maintain unless the users build and maintain their own libraries with the common functions they use for processing their data.

Moreover, many programmers could be unfamiliar with the MapReduce framework and they would prefer to use SQL (in which they are more proficient) as a high-level declarative language to express their task while leaving all of the execution optimization details to the backend engine. In addition, it is beyond doubt that high-level language abstractions enable the underlying system to perform automatic optimization. In the following subsection we discuss research efforts that have been proposed to tackle these problems and add SQL-like interfaces on top of the MapReduce framework.

2.4.1 Sawzall

Sawzall [114] is a scripting language used at Google on top of MapReduce. A Sawzall program defines the operations to be performed on a single record of the data. There is nothing in the language to enable examining multiple input records simultaneously, or even to have the contents of one input record influence the processing of another. The only output primitive in the language is the *emit* statement, which sends data to an external aggregator (e.g., sum, average, maximum, minimum) that gathers the results from each record after which the results are then correlated and processed. The authors argue that aggregation is done outside the language for a couple of reasons: (1) A more traditional language can use the language to correlate results but some of the aggregation algorithms are sophisticated and are best implemented in a native language and packaged in some form. (2) Drawing an explicit line between filtering and aggregation enables a high degree of parallelism and hides the parallelism from the language itself.

Figure 2.10 depicts an example Sawzall program where the first three lines declare the aggregators *count*, *total*, and *sum of squares*. The keyword *table* introduces an aggregator type that are called tables in Sawzall even though they may be singletons. These particular tables are *sum* tables that add up the values emitted to them, *ints* or *floats* as appropriate. The Sawzall language is implemented as a conventional compiler, written in C++, whose target language is an interpreted instruction set, or byte-code. The compiler and the byte-code interpreter are part of the same binary, so the user presents source code to Sawzall and the system executes it directly. It is structured as a library with an external interface that accepts source code, which

```
count: table sum of int;
total: table sum of float;
sum_of_squares: table sum of float;
x: float = input;
emit count <- 1;
emit total <- x;
emit sum_of_squares <- x * x;
```

FIGURE 2.10   An example Sawzall program. (From R. Pike et al., *Scientific Programming*, 13(4), 277–298, 2005.)

is then compiled and executed, along with bindings to connect to externally provided aggregators. The data sets of Sawzall programs are often stored in Google File System (GFS) [58]. The business of scheduling a job to run on a cluster of machines is handled by a software called *Workqueue*, which creates a large-scale time sharing system out of an array of computers and their disks. It schedules jobs, allocates resources, reports status, and collects the results.

Google has also developed *FlumeJava* [30], a Java library for developing and running data-parallel pipelines on top of MapReduce. FlumeJava is centered around a few classes that represent parallel collections. Parallel collections support a modest number of parallel operations that are composed to implement data-parallel computations where an entire pipeline, or even multiple pipelines, can be translated into a single Java program using the FlumeJava abstractions. To achieve good performance, FlumeJava internally implements parallel operations using *deferred* evaluation. The invocation of a parallel operation does not actually run the operation, but instead simply records the operation and its arguments in an internal execution plan graph structure. Once the execution plan for the whole computation has been constructed, FlumeJava optimizes the execution plan and then runs the optimized execution plan. When running the execution plan, FlumeJava chooses which strategy to use to implement each operation (e.g., local sequential loop vs. remote parallel MapReduce) based in part on the size of the data being processed, places remote computations near the data on which they operate and performs independent operations in parallel.

2.4.2   PIG LATIN

Olston et al. [109] have presented a language called *Pig Latin* that takes a *middle* position between expressing task using the high-level declarative querying model in the spirit of SQL and the low-level/procedural programming model using MapReduce. Pig Latin is implemented in the scope of the *Apache Pig* project* and is used by programmers at Yahoo! for developing data analysis tasks. Writing a Pig Latin program is similar to specifying a query execution plan (e.g., a data flow graph). To experienced programmers, this method is more appealing than encoding their task as an SQL query and then coercing the system to choose the desired plan through

---

* http://incubator.apache.org/pig.

optimizer hints. In general, automatic query optimization has its limits especially with uncatalogued data, prevalent user-defined functions, and parallel execution, which are all features of the data analysis tasks targeted by the MapReduce framework. Figure 2.11 shows an example SQL query and its equivalent Pig Latin program. Given a *URL* table with the structure (*url, category, pagerank*), the task of the SQL query is to find each large category and its average pagerank of high-pagerank URLs (> 0.2). A Pig Latin program is described as a sequence of steps where each step represents a single data transformation. This characteristic is appealing to many programmers. At the same time, the transformation steps are described using high-level primitives (e.g., filtering, grouping, aggregation) much like in SQL.

Pig Latin has several other features that are important for casual ad hoc data analysis tasks. These features include support for a flexible, fully nested data model, extensive support for user-defined functions and the ability to operate over plain input files without any schema information [56]. In particular, Pig Latin has a simple data model consisting of the following four types:

1. *Atom*: An atom contains a simple atomic value such as a string or a number, for example, "alice."
2. *Tuple*: A tuple is a sequence of fields, each of which can be any of the data types, for example, ("alice," "lakers").
3. *Bag*: A bag is a collection of tuples with possible duplicates. The schema of the constituent tuples is flexible where not all tuples in a bag need to have the same number and type of fields

$$\text{for example,} \left\{ \begin{array}{c} (\text{"alice," "lakers"}) \\ (\text{"alice," ("iPod," "apple"}))\end{array}\right\}$$

4. *Map*: A map is a collection of data items, where each item has an associated key through which it can be looked up. As with bags, the schema of the constituent data items is flexible. However, the keys are required to be data atoms,

$$\text{for example,} \left\{ \begin{array}{c} \text{"k1"} \rightarrow (\text{"alice," "lakers"}) \\ \text{"k2"} \rightarrow \text{"20"} \end{array}\right\}$$

SQL	Pig Latin
SELECT category, **AVG**(pagerank)	good_urls = **FILTER** urls **BY** pagerank > 0.2;
FROM urls	groups = **GROUP** good_urls **BY** category;
WHERE pagerank > 0.2	big_groups = **FILTER** groups **BY** COUNT(good_urls)>10^6;
GROUP BY category	output = **FOREACH** big_groups **GENERATE**
HAVING COUNT(*) > 10^6	category, **AVG**(good_urls.pagerank);

FIGURE 2.11   An example SQL query and its equivalent Pig Latin program. (From A. Gates et al., *PVLDB*, 2(2), 1414–1425, 2009.)

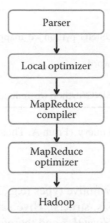

FIGURE 2.12 Pig compilation and execution steps. (From C. Olston et al., Pig latin: A not-so-foreign language for data processing, in *SIGMOD*, pp. 1099–1110, 2008.)

To accommodate specialized data-processing tasks, Pig Latin has extensive support for user-defined functions (UDFs). The input and output of UDFs in Pig Latin follow its fully nested data model. Pig Latin is architected such that the parsing of the Pig Latin program and the logical plan construction is independent of the execution platform. Only the compilation of the logical plan into a physical plan depends on the specific execution platform chosen. Currently, Pig Latin programs are compiled into sequences of MapReduce jobs that are executed using the Hadoop MapReduce environment. In particular, a Pig Latin program goes through a series of transformation steps [109] before being executed as depicted in Figure 2.12. The parsing steps verifies that the program is syntactically correct and that all referenced variables are defined. The output of the parser is a canonical logical plan with a one-to-one correspondence between Pig Latin statements and logical operators that are arranged in a directed acyclic graph (DAG). The logical plan generated by the parser is passed through a logical optimizer. In this stage, logical optimizations such as projection pushdown are carried out. The optimized logical plan is then compiled into a series of MapReduce jobs that are then passed through another optimization phase. The DAG of optimized MapReduce jobs is then topologically sorted and jobs are submitted to Hadoop for execution.

2.4.3 HIVE

The *Hive* project* is an open-source data warehousing solution that has been built by the Facebook Data Infrastructure Team on top of the Hadoop environment [123]. The main goal of this project is to bring the familiar relational database concepts (e.g., tables, columns, partitions) and a subset of SQL to the unstructured world of Hadoop while still maintaining the extensibility and flexibility that Hadoop provides.

---

* http://hadoop.apache.org/hive/.

```
FROM (
        MAP doctext USING 'python wc_mapper.py' AS (word, cnt)
        FROM docs
        CLUSTER BY word
) a
REDUCE word, cnt USING 'python wc_reduce.py';
```

FIGURE 2.13 An example HiveQl query. (From A. Thusoo et al., *PVLDB*, 2(2), 1626–1629, 2009.)

Thus, it supports all the major primitive types (e.g., integers, floats, strings) as well as complex types (e.g., maps, lists, structs). Hive supports queries expressed in an SQL-like declarative language, *HiveQL*,* and therefore can be easily understood by anyone who is familiar with SQL. These queries are compiled into MapReduce jobs that are executed using Hadoop. In addition, HiveQL enables users to plug in custom MapReduce scripts into queries [125]. For example, the canonical MapReduce word count example on a table of documents (Figure 2.1) can be expressed in HiveQL as depicted in Figure 2.13 where the *MAP* clause indicates how the input columns (*doctext*) can be transformed using a user program ('python wc_mapper.py') into output columns (*word* and *cnt*). The *REDUCE* clause specifies the user program to invoke ('python wc_reduce.py') on the output columns of the subquery.

HiveQL supports Data Definition Language (DDL) statements, which can be used to create, drop, and alter tables in a database [124]. It allows users to load data from external sources and insert query results into Hive tables via the load and insert Data Manipulation Language (DML) statements, respectively. However, HiveQL currently does not support the update and deletion of rows in existing tables (in particular, INSERT INTO, UPDATE, and DELETE statements), which allows the use of very simple mechanisms to deal with concurrent read and write operations without implementing complex locking protocols. The metastore component is the Hive's system catalog, which stores metadata about the underlying table. This metadata is specified during table creation and reused every time the table is referenced in HiveQL. The metastore distinguishes Hive as a traditional warehousing solution when compared with similar data-processing systems that are built on top of MapReduce-like architectures like Pig Latin [109].

2.4.4 TENZING

The *Tenzing* system [33] has been presented by Google as an SQL query execution engine which is built on top of MapReduce and provides a comprehensive SQL92 implementation with some SQL99 extensions (e.g., ROLLUP() and CUBE() OLAP extensions). Tenzing also supports querying data in different formats such as: row stores (e.g., MySQL database), column stores, *Bigtable* (Google's built in

---

* http://wiki.apache.org/hadoop/Hive/LanguageManual.

key-value store) [31,32], *GFS* (Google File System) [58], text, and protocol buffers. In particular, the Tenzing system has four major components:

- *The distributed worker pool*: represents the execution system that takes a query execution plan and executes the MapReduce jobs. The pool consists of master and worker nodes plus an overall gatekeeper called the master watcher. The workers manipulate the data for all the tables defined in the metadata layer.
- *The query server*: serves as the gateway between the client and the pool. The query server parses the query, applies different optimization mechanisms and sends the plan to the master for execution. In principle, the Tenzing optimizer applies some basic rule and cost-based optimizations to create an optimal execution plan.
- *Client interfaces*: Tenzing has several client interfaces including a command line client (CLI) and a Web UI. The CLI is a more powerful interface that supports complex scripting while the Web UI supports easier-to-use features such as query and table browsers tools. There is also an API to directly execute queries on the pool and a standalone binary, which does not need any server side components but rather can launch its own MapReduce jobs.
- *The metadata server*: provides an API to store and fetch metadata such as table names and schemas and pointers to the underlying data.

A typical Tenzing query is submitted to the query server (through the Web UI, CLI, or API), which is responsible for parsing the query into an intermediate parse tree and fetching the required metadata from the metadata server. The query optimizer goes through the intermediate format, applies various optimizations and generates a query execution plan that consists of one or more MapReduce jobs. For each MapReduce, the query server finds an available master using the master watcher and submits the query to it. At this stage, the execution is physically partitioned into multiple units of work where idle workers poll the masters for available work. The query server monitors the generated intermediate results, gathers them as they arrive and streams the output back to the client. To increase throughput, decrease latency and execute SQL operators more efficiently, Tenzing has enhanced the MapReduce implementation with some main changes:

- *Streaming and in-memory chaining*: The implementation of Tenzing does not serialize the intermediate results of MapReduce jobs to GFS. Instead, it streams the intermediate results between the map and reduce tasks using the network and uses GFS only for backup purposes. In addition, it uses a memory chaining mechanism where the reducer and the mapper of the same intermediate results are colocated in the same process.
- *Sort avoidance*: Certain operators such as hash join and hash aggregation require shuffling but not sorting. The MapReduce API was enhanced to automatically turn off sorting for these operations, when possible, so that the mapper feeds data to the reducer, which automatically bypasses the

intermediate sorting step. Tenzing also implements a block-based shuffle mechanism that combines many small rows into compressed blocks, which is treated as one row to avoid reducer side sorting and avoid some of the overhead associated with row serialization and deserialization in the underlying MapReduce framework code.

2.4.5 CHEETAH

The *Cheetah* system [35] has been introduced as a custom data warehouse solution that has been built on top of the MapReduce framework. In particular, it defines a virtual view on top of the common star or snowflake data warehouse schema and applies a stack of optimization techniques on top of the MapReduce framework including: data compression, optimized access methods, multiquery optimization, and the exploiting materialized views. Cheetah provides an SQL-like and a non-SQL interface for applications to directly access the raw data, which enables seamless integration of MapReduce and Data Warehouse tools so that the developers can take full advantage of the power of both worlds. For example, it has a JDBC interface such that a user program can submit query and iterate through the output results. If the query results are too big for a single program to consume, the user can write a MapReduce job to analyze the query output files that are stored on HDFS.

Cheetah stores data in the compressed columnar format. The choice of compression type for each column set is dynamically determined based on the data in each cell. During the *ETL* (extract–transfer–load) phase of a data warehousing project, the statistics of each column is maintained and the best compression method is chosen. During the query execution, Cheetah applies different optimization techniques. For example, the map phase uses a *shared scanner* that shares the scan of the fact tables and joins to the dimension tables where a selection pushup approach is applied to share the joins among multiple queries. Each scanner attaches a *query ID* to each output row, indicating which query this row qualifies. The reduce phase splits the input rows based on their query IDs and then sends them to the corresponding query operators. Cheetah also makes use of materialized view and applies a straightforward view-matching and query-rewriting process where the query must refer the virtual view that corresponds to the same fact table upon which the materialized view is defined. The nonaggregate columns referred in the SELECT and WHERE clauses in the query must be a subset of the materialized view's group by columns.

2.4.6 YSMART

The *YSmart* system [88] has been presented as a correlation aware SQL-to-MapReduce translator that attempts to optimize complex queries without modification to the MapReduce framework and the underlying system. It applies a set of rules to use the minimal number of MapReduce jobs to execute multiple correlated operations in a complex query with the aim of reducing redundant computations, I/O operations, and overhead of network transfers. The YSmart translator is used on the Facebook production environment to achieve these goals. In particular, YSmart batch-processes multiple correlated query operations within a query and applies a set of optimization rules to merge multiple jobs, which otherwise would have been run independently without YSmart, into a common job. Therefore, it provides a Common MapReduce Framework (CMF) that allows multiple types of jobs (e.g., a join job and an aggregation job) to be executed in a common job. In a query plan tree, YSmart detects three type of intraquery correlations that is defined based on the key/value pair model of the MapReduce framework:

1. *Input correlation*: Multiple nodes have input correlation if their input relation sets are not disjoint.
2. *Transit correlation*: Multiple nodes have transit correlation if they have the input correlation and the same partition key.
3. *Job flow correlation*: A node has job flow correlation with one of its child nodes if it has the same partition key as that child node.

On the other hand, the *HadoopToSQL* system [74] has been presented as an SQL translator for MapReduce jobs. It relies on a static analysis component that uses symbolic execution to analyze the Java code of a MapReduce query and transforms queries to make use of SQL's indexing, aggregation, and grouping features. In particular, HadoopToSQL applies two algorithms that generate SQL code from MapReduce queries. The first algorithm can extract input set restrictions from MapReduce queries and the other can translate entire MapReduce queries into equivalent SQL queries. Both algorithms function by finding all control flow paths through map and reduce functions, using symbolic execution to determine the behavior of each path, and then mapping this behavior onto possible SQL queries. This information is then used either to generate input restrictions, which avoid scanning the entire data set, or to generate equivalent SQL queries, which take advantage of SQL grouping and aggregation features. However, HadoopToSQL has reported some difficulties on the ability of analyzing MapReduce programs with loops and unknown method calls. It also unable to analyze across multiple MapReduce instances.

2.4.7 SQL/MAPREDUCE

In general, a user-defined function (UDF) is a powerful database feature that allows users to customize database functionality. Friedman et al. [55] introduced the SQL/MapReduce (SQL/MR) UDF framework which is designed to facilitate parallel computation of procedural functions across hundreds of servers working together as a single relational database. The framework is implemented as part of the *Aster Data Systems** nCluster shared-nothing relational database. The framework leverages ideas from the MapReduce programming paradigm to provide users with a straightforward API through which they can implement a UDF in the language of their choice. Moreover, it allows maximum flexibility as the output schema of the UDF is specified by the function itself at query plan-time. This means that a SQL/MR function is polymorphic as it can process arbitrary input because its behavior as well as output schema are dynamically determined by information available at query

---

* http://www.asterdata.com/.

```
SELECT ...
FROM functionname(
    ON table-or-query
    [PARTITION BY expr, ...]
    [ORDER BY expr, ...]
    [clausename(arg, ...) ...]
    )
...
```

FIGURE 2.14 Basic syntax of SQL/MR query function. (From E. Friedman et al., *PVLDB*, 2(2), 1402–1413, 2009.)

plan-time. This also increases reusability as the same SQL/MR function can be used on inputs with many different schemas or with different user-specified parameters. In particular, SQL/MR allows the user to write custom-defined functions in any programming language and insert them into queries that leverage traditional SQL functionality. A SQL/MR function is defined in a manner that is similar to MapReduce's map and reduce functions.

The syntax for using a SQL/MR function is depicted in Figure 2.14 where the SQL/MR function invocation appears in the SQL *FROM* clause and consists of the function name followed by a set of clauses that are enclosed in parentheses. The *ON* clause specifies the input to the invocation of the SQL/MR function. It is important to note that the input schema to the SQL/MR function is specified implicitly at query plan-time in the form of the output schema for the query used in the ON clause.

In practice, a SQL/MR function can be either a mapper (*Row* function) or a reducer (*Partition* function). The definitions of row and partition functions ensure that they can be executed in parallel in a scalable manner. In the *Row Function*, each row from the input table or query will be operated on by exactly one instance of the SQL/MR function. Semantically, each row is processed independently, allowing the execution engine to control parallelism. For each input row, the row function may emit zero or more rows. In the *Partition Function*, each group of rows as defined by the *PARTITION BY* clause will be operated on by exactly one instance of the SQL/MR function. If the *ORDER BY* clause is provided, the rows within each partition are provided to the function instance in the specified sort order. Semantically, each partition is processed independently, allowing parallelization by the execution engine at the level of a partition. For each input partition, the SQL/MR partition function may output zero or more rows.

2.4.8 HADOOPDB

Parallel database systems have been commercially available for nearly two decades and there are now about a dozen of different implementations in the marketplace (e.g., Teradata,* Aster Data,† Netezza,‡ Vertica,§ ParAccel,¶ Greenplum**). The

---

* http://www.teradata.com/.
† http://www.asterdata.com/.
‡ http://www.netezza.com/.
§ http://www.vertica.com/.
¶ http://www.paraccel.com/.
** http://www.greenplum.com/.

main aim of these systems is to improve performance through the parallelization of various operations such as loading data, building indices, and evaluating queries. These systems are usually designed to run on top of a shared-nothing architecture [120] where data may be stored in a distributed fashion and input/output speeds are improved using multiple CPUs and disks in parallel. On the other hand, there are some key reasons that make MapReduce a more preferable approach over a parallel RDBMS in some scenarios such as [20]

- Formatting and loading a huge amount of data into a parallel RDBMS in a timely manner is a challenging and time-consuming task.
- The input data records may not always follow the same schema. Developers often want the flexibility to add and drop attributes and the interpretation of an input data record may also change over time.
- Large-scale data processing can be very time consuming, and therefore, it is important to keep the analysis job going even in the event of failures. While most parallel RDBMSs have fault tolerance support, a query usually has to be restarted from scratch even if just one node in the cluster fails. In contrast, MapReduce deals with failures in a more graceful manner and can redo only the part of the computation that was lost due to the failure.

There has been a long debate on the comparison between the MapReduce framework and parallel database systems* [121]. Pavlo et al. [113] have conducted a large-scale comparison between the Hadoop implementation of MapReduce framework and parallel SQL database management systems in terms of performance and development complexity. The results of this comparison have shown that parallel database systems displayed a significant performance advantage over MapReduce in executing a variety of data-intensive analysis tasks. On the other hand, the Hadoop implementation was very much easier and more straightforward to set up and use in comparison to that of the parallel database systems. MapReduce have also shown to have superior performance in minimizing the amount of work that is lost when a hardware failure occurs. In addition, MapReduce (with its open-source implementations) represents a very cheap solution in comparison to the very financially expensive parallel DBMS solutions (the price of an installation of a parallel DBMS cluster usually consists of seven figures of U.S. dollars) [121].

The *HadoopDB* project† is a hybrid system that tries to combine the scalability advantages of MapReduce with the performance and efficiency advantages of parallel databases [3]. The basic idea behind HadoopDB is to connect multiple single-node database systems (Post-greSQL) using Hadoop as the task coordinator and network communication layer. Queries are expressed in SQL but their execution are parallelized across nodes using the MapReduce framework, however, as much of the single-node query work as possible is pushed inside of the corresponding node databases. Thus, HadoopDB tries to achieve fault tolerance and the ability to operate in heterogeneous environments by inheriting the scheduling and job-tracking implementation

---

* http://databasecolumn.vertica.com/database-innovation/mapreduce-a-major-step-backwards/.
† http://db.cs.yale.edu/hadoopdb/hadoopdb.html.

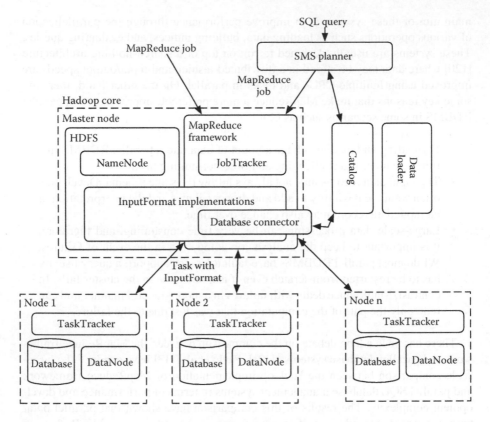

FIGURE 2.15 The architecture of HadoopDB. (From A. Abouzeid et al., *PVLDB*, 2(1), 922–933, 2009.)

from Hadoop. In parallel, it tries to achieve the performance of parallel databases by doing most of the query processing inside the database engine. Figure 2.15 illustrates the architecture of HadoopDB, which consists of two layers: (1) a data storage layer or the Hadoop Distributed File System* (HDFS) and (2) a data-processing layer or the MapReduce framework. In this architecture, HDFS is a block-structured file system managed by a central *NameNode*. Individual files are broken into blocks of a fixed size and distributed across multiple *DataNodes* in the cluster. The NameNode maintains metadata about the size and location of blocks and their replicas. The MapReduce Framework follows a simple master–slave architecture. The master is a single *JobTracker* and the slaves or worker nodes are *TaskTrackers*. The *JobTracker* handles the runtime scheduling of MapReduce jobs and maintains information on each TaskTracker's load and available resources. The *Database Connector* is the interface between independent database systems residing on nodes in the cluster and TaskTrackers. The Connector connects to the database, executes the SQL query, and

---

* http://hadoop.apache.org/hdfs/.

returns results as key-value pairs. The *Catalog* component maintains metadata about the databases, their location, replica locations, and data-partitioning properties. The *Data Loader* component is responsible for globally repartitioning data on a given partition key upon loading and breaking apart single-node data into multiple smaller partitions or chunks. The *SMS planner* extends the HiveQL translator [123] (Section 1.4.3) and transforms SQL into MapReduce jobs that connect to tables stored as files in HDFS. Abouzeid et al. [4] have demonstrated HadoopDB in action running the following two different application types:

1. A semantic web application that provides biological data analysis of protein sequences.
2. A classical business data warehouse.

2.4.9 JAQL

Jaql* is a query language that is designed for Javascript Object Notation (JSON),† a data format that has become popular because of its simplicity and modeling flexibility. JSON is a simple, yet flexible way to represent data that ranges from flat, relational data to semistructured, XML data. Jaql is primarily used to analyze large-scale semistructured data. It is a functional, declarative query language that rewrites high-level queries when appropriate into a low-level query consisting of map–reduce jobs that are evaluated using the Apache Hadoop project. Core features include user extensibility and parallelism. Jaql consists of a scripting language and compiler as well as a runtime component [18]. It is able to process data with no schema or only with a partial schema. However, Jaql can also exploit rigid schema information when it is available, for both type checking and improved performance.

Jaql uses a very simple data model; a *JDM value* is an atom, an array, or a record. Most common atomic types are supported, including strings, numbers, nulls, and dates. Arrays and records are compound types that can be arbitrarily nested. In more detail, an array is an ordered collection of values and can be used to model data structures such as vectors, lists, sets, or bags. A record is an unordered collection of name-value pairs and can model structs, dictionaries, and maps. Despite its simplicity, JDM is very flexible. It allows Jaql to operate with a variety of different data representations for both input and output, including delimited text files, JSON files, binary files, Hadoop's sequence files, relational databases, key-value stores, or XML documents. Functions are first-class values in Jaql. They can be assigned to a variable and are high order in that they can be passed as parameters or used as a return value. Functions are the key ingredient for reusability as any Jaql expression can be encapsulated in a function, and a function can be parameterized in powerful ways. Figure 2.16 depicts an example of a Jaql script that consists of a sequence of operators. The read operator loads raw data, in this case, from Hadoops Distributed File System (HDFS), and converts it into Jaql values. These values are processed by the countFields subflow, which extracts field names and computes their frequencies.

---

* http://code.google.com/p/jaql/.
† http://www.json.org/.

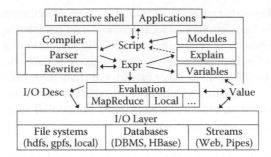

FIGURE 2.16   Jaql system architecture. (From K. S. Beyer et al., *PVLDB*, 4(12), 1272–1283, 2011.)

Finally, the write operator stores the result back into HDFS. In general, the core expressions of the Jaql scripting language include

1. *Transform*: The transform expression applies a function (or projection) to every element of an array to produce a new array. It has the form `e1->transform e2`, where `e1` is an expression that describes the input array and `e2` is applied to each element of `e1`.

2. *Expand*: The expand expression is most often used to unnest its input array. It differs from transform in two primary ways: (1) `e2` must produce a value v that is an array type and (2) each of the elements of v is returned to the output array, thereby removing one level of nesting.

3. *Group by*: Similar to SQL's GROUP BY, Jaql's group by expression partitions its input on a grouping expression and applies an aggregation expression to each group.

4. *Filter*: The filter expression, `e->filter p`, retains input values from e for which predicate p evaluates to true.

5. *Join*: The join expression supports equijoin of 2 or more inputs. All of the options for inner and outer joins are also supported.

6. *Union*: The union expression is a Jaql function that merges multiple input arrays into a single output array. It has the form: `union(e_1,...)` where each e_i is an array.

7. *Control-flow*: The two most commonly used control-flow expressions in Jaql are `if-then-else` and block expressions. The `if-then-else` expression is similar to conditional expressions found in most scripting and programming languages. A block establishes a local scope where zero or more local variables can be declared and the last statement provides the return value of the block.

At a high level, the Jaql architecture depicted in Figure 2.17 is similar to most database systems. Scripts are passed into the system from the interpreter or an application, compiled by the parser and rewrite engine, and either explained or evaluated over data from the I/O layer. The storage layer is similar to a federated database. It provides an API to access data of different systems including local or distributed file

```
1. import myrecord;
2.
3. countFields = fn(records) (
4.   records
5.   -> transform myrecord::names($)
6.   -> expand
7.   -> group by fName = $ as occurrences
8.   into { name: fName, num: count(occurrences) }
9. );
10.
11. read(hdfs("docs.dat"))
12. -> countFields()
13. -> write(hdfs("fields.dat"));
```

FIGURE 2.17 Sample Jaql script. (From K. S. Beyer et al., *PVLDB*, 4(12), 1272–1283, 2011.)

systems (e.g., Hadoop's HDFS), database systems (e.g., DB2, Netezza, HBase), or from streamed sources like the Web. Unlike federated databases, however, most of the accessed data is stored within the same cluster and the I/O API describes data partitioning, which enables parallelism with data affinity during evaluation. Jaql derives much of this flexibility from Hadoop's I/O API. It reads and writes many common file formats (e.g., delimited files, JSON text, Hadoop sequence files). Custom adapters are easily written to map a data set to or from Jaql's data model. The input can even simply be values constructed in the script itself. The Jaql interpreter evaluates the script locally on the computer that compiled the script, but spawns interpreters on remote nodes using MapReduce. The Jaql compiler automatically detects parallelization opportunities in a Jaql script and translates it to a set of MapReduce jobs.

2.5 SAMPLE MapReduce-BASED APPLICATIONS

MapReduce-based systems are increasingly being used for large-scale data analysis. There are several reasons for this such as [77]

- *The interface of MapReduce is simple yet expressive.* Although MapReduce only involves two functions map and reduce, a number of data analytical tasks including traditional SQL query, data mining, machine learning, and graph processing can be expressed with a set of MapReduce jobs.
- *MapReduce is flexible.* It is designed to be independent of storage systems and is able to analyze various kinds of data, structured, and unstructured.
- *MapReduce is scalable.* Installation of MapReduce can run over thousands of nodes on a shared-nothing cluster while keeping to provide fine-grain fault tolerance whereby only tasks on failed nodes need to be restarted.

These main advantages have triggered several research efforts with the aim of applying the MapReduce framework for solving challenging data-processing problems on large-scale data sets in different domains. For example, [53] have proposed an SQL-like query language for large-scale analysis of XML data on a MapReduce platform, called *MRQL* (the *Map–Reduce Query Language*). The evaluation system of MRQL leverages the relational query optimization techniques and compiles

MRQL queries to an algebra that is then translated to physical plans using cost-based optimizations. In particular, the query plans are represented trees that are evaluated using a plan interpreter where each physical operator is implemented with a single MapReduce job that is parameterized by the functional parameters of the physical operator. The data fragmentation technique of MRQL is built on top of the general Hadoop XML input format, which is based on a single XML tag name. Hence, given a data split of an XML document, Hadoop's input format allows reading the document as a stream of string fragments, so that each string will contain a single complete element that has the requested XML tag name. *ChuQL* [80] is another language that has been proposed to support distributed XML processing using the MapReduce framework. It presents a MapReduce-based extension for the syntax, grammar, and semantics of *XQuery* [21], the standard W3C language for querying XML documents. In particular, the ChuQL implementation takes care of distributing the computation to multiple XQuery engines running in Hadoop nodes, as described by one or more ChuQL MapReduce expressions. Figure 2.18 illustrates the representation of the *word count* example program in the ChuQL language using its extended expressions where the *MapReduce* expression is used to describe a MapReduce job. The *input* and *output* clauses are, respectively, used to read and write onto HDFS. The *rr* and *rw* clauses are, respectively, used for describing the record reader and writer. The *map* and *reduce* clauses represent the standard map and reduce phases of the framework where they process XML values or key/value pairs of XML values to match the MapReduce model, which are specified using XQuery expressions.

Some research efforts have been proposed for achieving scalable RDF processing using the MapReduce framework. *PigSPARQL* [118] is a system that has been introduced to process SPARQL queries using the MapReduce framework by translating them into *Pig Latin* programs where each Pig Latin program is executed by a series of MapReduce jobs on a Hadoop cluster. Myung et al. [105] have presented a preliminary algorithm for SPARQL graph pattern matching by adopting the traditional multiway join of the RDF triples and selecting a good join-key to avoid unnecessary iterations. Husain et al. [72] have described a storage scheme for RDF data using HDFS where the input data are partitioned into multiple files using two main steps: (1) The *Predicate Split*, which partitions the RDF triples according to their predicates. (2) The *Predicate Object Split* (POS), which uses the explicit type information in the RDF triples to denote that a resource is an instance of a specific class while the remaining predicate files are partitioned according to the type of their objects. Using summary statistics for estimating the selectivities of join operations, the authors

```
1    mapreduce {
2      input { fn:collection("hdfs://input/") }
3      rr { for $line at $i in $in//line return { key: $i, val: $line } }
4      map { for $word in fn:tokenize($in=>val, "␣")
5            return { key: $word, val: 1 } }
6      reduce { { key: $in=>key, val: fn:count($in=>val) } }
7      rw { <word text="{$in=>key}" count="{$in=>val}"/> }
8      output { fn:put($in,"hdfs://output/") }
9    }
```

FIGURE 2.18 The word count example program in ChuQL. (From S. Khatchadourian et al., Having a ChuQL at XML on the cloud, in *AMW*, 2011.)

proposed an algorithm that generates a query plan whose cost is bounded by the log of the total number of variables in the given SPARQL query. An approach for optimizing RDF graph pattern matching by reinterpreting certain join tree structures as grouping operations have been presented in [81,117]. The proposed approach represents the intermediate results as sets of groups of triples called *TripleGroups* and uses *Nested TripleGroup Algebra* for manipulating them. Abouzied et al. [4] have demonstrated an approach for storing and querying RDF data using the *HadoopDB* system in conjunction with a column-oriented database [2] that can provide a promising solution for supporting efficient and scalable semantic web applications. A similar approach has been presented in [71] where it replaced the column-oriented backend database with the state-of-the-art of RDF query processors, *RDF-3X* [106].

Surfer [34] is a large-scale graph-processing engine that is designed to provide two basic primitives for programmers: *MapReduce* and *Propagation*. In this engine, MapReduce processes different key value pairs in parallel, and propagation is an iterative computational pattern that transfers information along the edges from a vertex to its neighbors in the graph. In principle, these two primitives are complementary in graph processing where MapReduce is suitable for processing flat data structures (e.g., vertex-oriented tasks) while propagation is optimized for edge-oriented tasks on partitioned graphs. Lattanzi et al. [87] presented a set of MapReduce-based algorithms for a variety of fundamental graph problems such as minimum spanning trees, maximal matchings, approximate weighted matchings, approximate vertex and edge covers, and minimum cuts. All of the presented algorithms are parameterized by the amount of memory available on the machines that are used to determine the number of MapReduce rounds.

In general, graph algorithms can be written as a series of chained MapReduce invocations that requires passing the entire state of the graph from one stage to the next. However, this approach is ill-suited for graph processing and can lead to suboptimal performance due to the additional communication and associated serialization overhead in addition to the need of coordinating the steps of a chained MapReduce. The *Pregel* system [98] has been introduced by Google as scalable platform for implementing graph algorithms. It relies on a vertex-centric approach, which is inspired by the Bulk Synchronous Parallel model (BSP) [127], where programs are expressed as a sequence of iterations, in each of which a vertex can receive messages sent in the previous iteration, send messages to other vertices, and modify its own state as well as that of its outgoing edges or mutate graph topology. In particular, Pregel computations consist of a sequence of iterations, called *supersteps*. During a superstep the framework invokes a user-defined function for each vertex, conceptually in parallel, which specifies the behavior at a single vertex V and a single superstep S. It can read messages sent to V in superstep $S - 1$, send messages to other vertices that will be received at superstep $S + 1$, and modify the state of V and its outgoing edges. Messages are typically sent along outgoing edges, but a message may be sent to any vertex whose identifier is known (Figure 2.19). Similar to the MapReduce framework, Pregel has been designed to be an efficient, scalable, and fault-tolerant implementation on clusters of thousands of commodity computers where the distribution-related details are hidden behind an abstract. It keeps vertices and edges on the machine that performs computation and uses network transfers only for messages. Hence, the

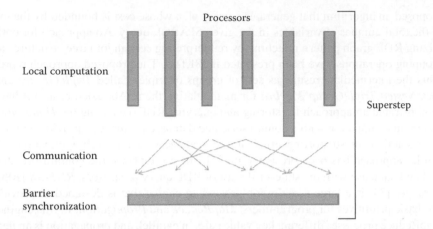

FIGURE 2.19 BSP programming model.

model is well suited for distributed implementations as it doesn't expose any mechanism for detecting order of execution within a superstep, and all communication is from superstep S to superstep $S + 1$. The ideas of Pregel have been cloned by many open-source projects such as *GoldenOrb,** *Apache Hama,†* and *Apache Giraph.‡* Both of Hama and Giraph are implemented to be launched as a typical Hadoop job that can leverage the Hadoop infrastructure. Other large-scale graph processing systems that have been introduced that neither follow the MapReduce model nor leverage the Hadoop infrastructure include *GRACE* [130], *GraphLab* [96,97], and *Signal/Collect* [122].

The *Dedoop* system (*De*duplication with Ha*doop*) [82,83] has been presented as an entity resolution framework based on MapReduce. It supports the ability to define complex entity resolution workflows that can include different matching steps and/ or apply machine learning mechanisms for the automatic generation of match classifiers. The defined workflows are then automatically translated into MapReduce jobs for parallel execution on Hadoop clusters. The *MapDupReducer* [129] is another system that has been proposed as a MapReduce-based solution, which is developed for supporting the problem of near duplicate detection over massive data sets using the *PPJoin* (*P*ositional and *P*refix filtering) algorithm [132].

An approach to efficiently perform set-similarity joins in parallel using the MapReduce framework has been proposed by Vernica et al. [128]. In particular, they propose a three-stage approach for end-to-end set-similarity joins. The approach takes as input a set of records and outputs a set of joined records based on a set-similarity condition. It partitions the data across nodes to balance the workload and minimize the need for replication. J. Lin [92] has presented three MapReduce algorithms for computing pairwise similarity on document collections. The first

---

* http://goldenorbos.org/.
† http://hama.apache.org/.
‡ http://giraph.apache.org/.

algorithm is based on brute force, the second algorithm treats the problem as a large-scale ad hoc retrieval and the third algorithm is based on the Cartesian product of postings lists. *V-SMART-Join* [101] is a MapReduce-based framework for discovering all pairs of similar entities, which is applicable to sets, multisets, and vectors. It presents a family of two-stage algorithms where the first stage computes and joins the partial results, and the second stage computes the similarity exactly for all candidate pairs. Afrati et al. [5] have provided a theoretical analysis of various MapReduce-based similarity join algorithms in terms of various parameters including map and reduce costs, number of reducers, and communication cost.

The *DisCo* (*Di*stributed *Co*-clustering) framework [111] has been introduced as an approach for distributed data preprocessing and co-clustering from the raw data to the end clusters using the MapReduce framework. Cordeiro et al. [41] have presented an approach for finding subspace clusters in very large moderate-to-high dimensional data that is having typically more than 5 axes. Ene et al. [52] described the design and the MapReduce-based implementations of the *k*-median and *k*-center clustering algorithms. *PLANET* (*P*arallel *L*earner for *A*ssembling *N*umerous *E*nsemble *T*rees) is a distributed framework for learning tree models over large data sets. It defines tree learning as a series of distributed computations and implements, each one using the MapReduce model [110]. The *SystemML* [60] provides a framework for expressing machine learning algorithms using a declarative higher-level language. The algorithms expressed in SystemML are then automatically compiled and optimized into a set of MapReduce jobs that can run on a cluster of machines. *NIMBLE* [59] provides an infrastructure that has been specifically designed to enable the rapid implementation of parallel machine learning and data mining algorithms. The infrastructure allows its users to compose parallel machine learning algorithms using reusable (serial and parallel) building blocks that can be efficiently executed using the MapReduce framework. *Mahout** is an Apache project with the aim of building scalable machine learning libraries using the MapReduce framework. *Ricardo* [42] is presented as a scalable platform for applying sophisticated statistical methods over huge data repositories. It is designed to facilitate the *trading* between *R* (a famous statistical software packages[†]) and Hadoop where each trading partner performs the tasks that it does best. In particular, this trading is done in a way where *R* sends aggregation-processing queries to Hadoop while Hadoop sends aggregated data to *R* for advanced statistical processing or visualization. Cary et al. [28] presented an approach for applying the MapReduce model in the domain of spatial data management. In particular, they focus on the bulk construction of R-Trees and aerial image quality computation which involves vector and raster data. Morales et al. [102] have presented two matching algorithms, *GreedyMR* and *StackMR*, which are geared for the MapReduce paradigm with the aim of distributing content from information suppliers to information consumers on social media applications. In particular, they seek to maximize the overall relevance of the matched content from suppliers to consumers while regulating the overall activity.

---

* http://mahout.apache.org/.
† http://www.r-project.org/.

2.6 RELATED LARGE-SCALE DATA-PROCESSING SYSTEMS

In this section, we give an overview of several large-scale data-processing systems that resemble some of the ideas of the MapReduce framework for different purposes and application scenarios. It must be noted, however, that the design architectures and the implementations of these systems do not follow the architecture of the MapReduce framework, and thus, they do not utilize nor are they related to the infrastructure of the framework's open-source implementations such as Hadoop.

2.6.1 SCOPE

SCOPE (Structured Computations Optimized for Parallel Execution) is a scripting language that is targeted for large-scale data analysis and is used daily for a variety of data analysis and data mining applications inside Microsoft [29]. SCOPE is a declarative language. It allows users to focus on the data transformations required to solve the problem at hand and hides the complexity of the underlying platform and implementation details. The SCOPE compiler and optimizer are responsible for generating an efficient execution plan and the runtime for executing the plan with minimal overhead.

Like SQL, data is modeled as sets of rows composed of typed columns. SCOPE is highly extensible. Users can easily define their own functions and implement their own versions of operators: extractors (parsing and constructing rows from a file), processors (row-wise processing), reducers (group-wise processing), and combiners (combining rows from two inputs). This flexibility greatly extends the scope of the language and allows users to solve problems that cannot be easily expressed in traditional SQL. SCOPE provides a functionality that is similar to that of SQL views. This feature enhances modularity and code reusability. It is also used to restrict access to sensitive data. SCOPE supports writing a program using traditional SQL expressions or as a series of simple data transformations. Figure 2.20 illustrates two equivalent scripts in the two different styles (SQL-like and MapReduce-like) to find from the search log the popular queries that have been requested at least 1000 times. In the MapReduce-like style, the *EXTRACT* command extracts all query string from the log file. The first *SELECT* command counts the number of occurrences of each query string. The second *SELECT* command retains only rows with a count

SQL-Like	MapReduce-Like

SELECT query,
          COUNT(*) AS count
FROM "search.log"
USING LogExtractor
GROUP BY query
HAVING count > 1000
ORDER BY count DESC;
OUTPUT TO "qcount.result";
	e = EXTRACT query
	     FROM "search.log" USING LogExtractor;
	s1 = SELECT query, COUNT(*) as count FROM e
	     GROUP BY query;
	s2 = SELECT query, count FROM s1
	     WHERE count > 1000;
	s3 = SELECT query, count FROM s2
	     ORDER BY count DESC;
	OUTPUT s3 TO "qcount.result";

FIGURE 2.20 Two equivalent SCOPE scripts in SQL-like style and MapReduce-like style. (From R. Chaiken et al., *PVLDB*, 1(2), 1265–1276, 2008.)

greater than 1000. The third *SELECT* command sorts the rows on count. Finally, the *OUTPUT* command writes the result to the file *"qcount.result."*

Microsoft has developed a distributed computing platform, called *Cosmos*, for storing and analyzing massive data sets. Cosmos is designed to run on large clusters consisting of thousands of commodity servers. Figure 2.21 shows the main components of the Cosmos platform, which is described as follows:

- *Cosmos storage*: a distributed storage subsystem designed to reliably and efficiently store extremely large sequential files.
- *Cosmos execution environment*: an environment for deploying, executing, and debugging distributed applications.
- *SCOPE*: a high-level scripting language for writing data analysis jobs. The SCOPE compiler and optimizer translate scripts to efficient parallel execution plans.

The Cosmos Storage System is an append-only file system that reliably stores petabytes of data. The system is optimized for large sequential I/O. All writes are append-only and concurrent writers are serialized by the system. Data is distributed and replicated for fault tolerance and compressed to save storage and increase I/O throughput. In Cosmos, an application is modeled as a dataflow graph: a directed acyclic graph (DAG) with vertices representing processes and edges representing data flows. The runtime component of the execution engine is called the Job Manager, which represents the central and coordinating process for all processing vertices within an application.

The SCOPE scripting language resembles SQL but with C# expressions. Thus, it reduces the learning curve for users and eases the porting of existing SQL scripts

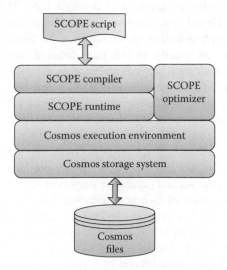

FIGURE 2.21 SCOPE/Cosmos execution platform. (From R. Chaiken et al., *PVLDB*, 1(2), 1265–1276, 2008.)

into SCOPE. Moreover, SCOPE expressions can use C# libraries where custom C# classes can compute functions of scalar values, or manipulate whole rowsets. A SCOPE script consists of a sequence of commands that are data transformation operators that take one or more rowsets as input, perform some operation on the data and output a rowset. Every rowset has a well-defined schema to which all its rows must adhere. The SCOPE compiler parses the script, checks the syntax and resolves names. The result of the compilation is an internal parse tree, which is then translated to a physical execution plan. A physical execution plan is a specification of Cosmos job, which describes a data flow DAG where each vertex is a program and each edge represents a data channel. The translation into an execution plan is performed by traversing the parse tree in a bottom-up manner. For each operator, SCOPE has an associated default implementation rule. Many of the traditional optimization rules from database systems are clearly also applicable in this new context, for example, removing unnecessary columns, pushing down selection predicates and pre-aggregating when possible. However, the highly distributed execution environment offers new opportunities and challenges, making it necessary to explicitly consider the effects of large-scale parallelism during optimization. For example, choosing the right partition scheme and deciding when to partition are crucial for finding an optimal plan. It is also important to correctly reason about partitioning, grouping, and sorting properties and their interaction to avoid unnecessary computations [139].

2.6.2   DRYAD/DRYADLINQ

Dryad is a general-purpose distributed execution engine introduced by Microsoft for coarse-grain data-parallel applications [73]. A Dryad application combines computational *vertices* with communication *channels* to form a dataflow graph. Dryad runs the application by executing the vertices of this graph on a set of available computers, communicating as appropriate through files, TCP pipes and shared-memory FIFOs. The Dryad system allows the developer fine-grained control over the communication graph as well as the subroutines that live at its vertices. A Dryad application developer can specify an arbitrary directed acyclic graph to describe the applications communication patterns and express the data transport mechanisms (files, TCP pipes, and shared-memory FIFOs) between the computation vertices. This direct specification of the graph gives the developer greater flexibility to easily compose basic common operations, leading to a distributed analogue of *piping* together traditional Unix utilities such as grep, sort, and head.

Dryad is notable for allowing graph vertices (and computations in general) to use an arbitrary number of inputs and outputs, while MapReduce restricts all computations to take a single input set and generate a single output set. The overall structure of a Dryad job is determined by its communication flow. A job is a directed acyclic graph where each vertex is a program and edges represent data channels. It is a logical computation graph that is automatically mapped onto physical resources by the runtime. At runtime each channel is used to transport a finite sequence of structured items. A Dryad job is coordinated by a process called the *job manager* that runs either within the cluster or on a user's workstation with network access to the cluster. The job manager contains the application-specific code to construct the job's communication graph along with library code to schedule the work across the available resources. All data is sent directly between vertices, and thus, the job manager is only responsible for control decisions and is not a bottleneck for any data transfers. Therefore, much of the simplicity of the Dryad scheduler and fault-tolerance model come from the assumption that vertices are deterministic.

Dryad has its own high-level language called *DryadLINQ* [133]. It generalizes execution environments such as SQL and MapReduce in two ways: (1) adopting an expressive data model of strongly typed .NET objects and (2) supporting general-purpose imperative and declarative operations on data sets within a traditional high-level programming language. DryadLINQ* exploits LINQ (Language INtegrated Query,† a set of .NET constructs for programming with data sets) to provide a powerful hybrid of declarative and imperative programming. The system is designed to provide flexible and efficient distributed computation in any LINQ-enabled programming language including C#, VB, and F#.‡ Objects in DryadLINQ data sets can be of any .NET type, making it easy to compute with data such as image patches, vectors, and matrices. In practice, a DryadLINQ program is a sequential program composed of LINQ expressions that perform arbitrary side-effect-free transformations on data sets and can be written and debugged using standard .NET development tools. The DryadLINQ system automatically translates the data-parallel portions of the program into a distributed execution plan, which is then passed to the Dryad execution platform. Figure 2.22 illustrates the flow of execution of a DryadLINQ program according to the following steps:

1. When a .NET user application runs, it creates a DryadLINQ expression object.
2. The application triggers a data-parallel execution where the expression object is handed to DryadLINQ.
3. DryadLINQ compiles the LINQ expression into a distributed Dryad execution plan. In particular, it performs the following tasks:
   a. Decomposing the expression into subexpressions where each expression can to be assigned to run in a separate Dryad vertex
   b. Generating the code and static data for the remote Dryad vertices
   c. Generating the serialization code for the required data types
4. DryadLINQ invokes a custom Dryad job manager.
5. The job manager creates the job graph and schedules the vertices as resources become available.
6. Each Dryad vertex executes a vertex-specific program as created in Step 3(b).
7. When the Dryad job completes successfully it writes the data to the output table(s).
8. The job manager process terminates and returns control back to DryadLINQ, which creates objects encapsulating the outputs of the execution. These objects may be used as inputs to subsequent expressions in the user program.

---

* http://research.microsoft.com/en-us/projects/dryadlinq/.
† http://msdn.microsoft.com/en-us/netframework/aa904594.aspx.
‡ http://research.microsoft.com/en-us/um/cambridge/projects/fsharp/.

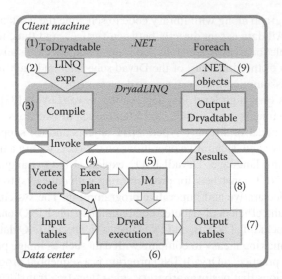

FIGURE 2.22 LINQ-expression execution in DryadLINQ. (From Y. Yu et al., DryadLINQ: A system for general-purpose distributed data-parallel computing using a high-level language, in *OSDI*, pp. 1–14, 2008.)

9. Control returns to the user application. The iterator interface over a Dryad table allows the user to read its contents as .NET objects.
10. The application may generate subsequent DryadLINQ expressions that can be executed by a repetition of Steps 2 to 9.

A commercial implementation of Dryad and DryadLINQ was released in 2011 under the name *LINQ to HPC.**

2.6.3 SPARK

The *Spark* system [135,136] has been proposed to support the applications that need to reuse a working set of data across multiple parallel operations (e.g., iterative machine learning algorithms and interactive data analytic) while retaining the scalability and fault tolerance of MapReduce. To achieve these goals, Spark introduces an abstraction called *resilient distributed data sets* (RDDs). An RDD is a read-only collection of objects partitioned across a set of machines that can be rebuilt if a partition is lost. Therefore, users can explicitly cache an RDD in memory across machines and reuse it in multiple MapReduce-like parallel operations. RDDs do not need to be materialized at all times. RDDs achieve fault tolerance through a notion of *lineage*. In particular, each RDD object contains a pointer to its parent and information about how the parent was transformed. Hence, if a partition of an RDD is lost, the RDD has sufficient information about how it was derived from other RDDs to be able to rebuild just that partition.

---

* http://msdn.microsoft.com/en-us/library/hh378101.aspx.

Spark is implemented in the Scala programming language* [108]. It is built on top of *Mesos* [70], a cluster operating system that lets multiple parallel frameworks share a cluster in a fine-grained manner and provides an API for applications to launch tasks on a cluster. It provides isolation and efficient resource sharing across frameworks running on the same cluster while giving each framework freedom to implement its own programming model and fully control the execution of its jobs. Mesos uses two main abstractions: *tasks* and *slots*. A task represents a unit of work. A slot represents a computing resource in which a framework may run a task, such as a core and some associated memory on a multicore machine. It employs the two-level scheduling mechanism. At the first level, Mesos allocates slots between frameworks using fair sharing. At the second level, each framework is responsible for dividing its work into tasks, selecting which tasks to run in each slot. This lets frameworks perform application-specific optimizations. For example, Spark's scheduler tries to send each task to one of its preferred locations using a technique called *delay scheduling* [134].

To use Spark, developers need to write a driver program that implements the high-level control flow of their application and launches various operations in parallel. Spark provides two main abstractions for parallel programming: resilient distributed data sets and parallel operations on these data sets (invoked by passing a function to apply on a data set). In particular, each RDD is represented by a Scala object, which can be constructed in different ways:

- From a file in a shared file system (e.g., HDFS).
- By parallelizing a Scala collection (e.g., an array) in the driver program, which means dividing it into a number of slices that will be sent to multiple nodes.
- By transforming an existing RDD. A data set with elements of type *A* can be transformed into a data set with elements of type *B* using an operation called *flatMap*.
- By changing the persistence of an existing RDD. A user can alter the persistence of an RDD through two actions:
  The cache action leaves the data set lazy but hints that it should be kept in memory after the first time it is computed because it will be reused.
  The save action evaluates the data set and writes it to a distributed filesystem such as HDFS. The saved version is used in future operations on it.

Different parallel operations can be performed on RDDs:

- The *reduce* operation, which combines data set elements using an associative function to produce a result at the driver program
- The *collect* operation, which sends all elements of the data set to the driver program
- The *foreach* operation, which passes each element through a user provided function

---

* http://www.scala-lang.org/.

Spark does not currently support a grouped reduce operation as in MapReduce. The results of reduce operations are only collected at the driver process. In addition, Spark supports two restricted types of shared variables to support two simple but common usage patterns:

- *Broadcast variables*: An object that wraps the value and ensures that it is only copied to each worker once.
- *Accumulators*: These are variables that workers can only *add* to using an associative operation and that only the driver can read.

It should be noted that Spark can also be used interactively from a modified version of the Scala interpreter that allows the user to define RDDs, functions, variables, and classes and use them in parallel operations on a cluster.

2.6.4   NEPHLE/PACT

The *Nephele/PACT* system [8,15] has been presented as a parallel data processor centered around a programming model of so-called *Parallelization Contracts* (PACTs) and the scalable parallel execution engine *Nephele*. The PACT programming model is a generalization of map/reduce as it is based on a key/value data model and the concept of *Parallelization Contracts* (PACTs). A PACT consists of exactly one second-order function, which is called *Input Contract* and an optional *Output Contract*. An Input Contract takes a first-order function with task-specific user code and one or more data sets as input parameters. The Input Contract invokes its associated first-order function with independent subsets of its input data in a data-parallel fashion. In this context, the two functions of *map* and *reduce* are just examples of the Input Contracts. Other example of Input Contracts include

- The *Cross* contract, which operates on multiple inputs and builds a distributed Cartesian product over its input sets.
- The *CoGroup* contract partitions each of its multiple inputs along the key. Independent subsets are built by combining equal keys of all inputs.
- The *Match* contract operates on multiple inputs. It matches key/value pairs from all input data sets with the same key (equivalent to the inner join operation).

An Output Contract is an optional component of a PACT and gives guarantees about the data that is generated by the assigned user function. The set of Output Contracts include

- The *Same-Key* contract where each key/value pair that is generated by the function has the same key as the key/value pair(s) from which it was generated. This means the function will preserve any partitioning and order property on the keys.
- The *Super-Key* where each key/value pair that is generated by the function has a superkey of the key/value pair(s) from which it was generated. This

means the function will preserve a partitioning and partial order on the keys.

- The *Unique-Key* where each key/value pair that is produced has a unique key. The key must be unique across all parallel instances. Any produced data is therefore partitioned and grouped by the key.
- The *Partitioned-by-Key* where key/value pairs are partitioned by key. This contract has similar implications as the Super-Key contract, specifically that a partitioning by the keys is given, but there is no order inside the partitions.

Figure 2.23 illustrate the system architecture of Nephele/PACT where a PACT program is submitted to the PACT Compiler, which translates the program into a data flow execution plan, which is then handed to the Nephele system for parallel execution. The Hadoop distributed filesystem (HDFS) is used for storing both the input and the output data.

The incoming jobs of Nephele are represented as data flow graphs where vertices represent subtasks and edges represent communication channels between these sub-tasks. Each subtask is a sequential program that reads data from its input channels and writes to its output channels. Prior execution, Nephele generates the parallel data flow graph by spanning the received DAG. Hence, vertices are multiplied to the desired degree of parallelism. Connection patterns that are attached to channels define how the multiplied vertices are rewired after spanning. During execution, the Nephele system takes care of resource scheduling, task distribution, communication as well as synchronization issues. Moreover, Nephele's fault-tolerance mechanisms help to mitigate the impact of hardware outages. Nephele also offers the ability to annotate the input jobs with a rich set of parameters that could influence the physical execution. For example, it is possible to set the desired degree of data parallelism for each subtask, assign particular sets of subtasks to particular sets of compute nodes, or explicitly specify the type of communication channels between subtasks. Nephele also supports three different types of communication channels:

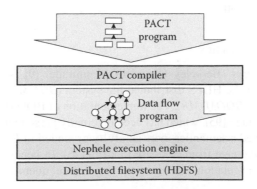

FIGURE 2.23 The Nephele/PACT system architecture. (From A. Alexandrov et al., *PVLDB*, 3(2), 1625–1628, 2010.)

network, in-memory, and file channels. The network and in-memory channels allow the PACT compiler to construct low-latency execution pipelines in which one task can immediately consume the output of another. The file channels collect the entire output of a task in a temporary file before passing its content on to the next task. Therefore, file channels can be considered check points, which help to recover from execution failures.

Due to the declarative character of the PACT programming model, the PACT compiler can apply different optimization mechanisms and select from several execution plans with varying costs for a single PACT program. For example, the *Match* contract can be satisfied using either a repartition strategy that partitions all inputs by keys or a broadcast strategy that fully replicates one input to every partition of the other input. Choosing the right strategy can dramatically reduce network traffic and execution time. Therefore, the PACT compiler applies standard SQL optimization techniques [119] where it exploits information provided by the Output Contracts and apply different cost-based optimization techniques. In particular, the optimizer generates a set of candidate execution plans in a bottom-up fashion (starting from the data sources) where the more expensive plans are pruned using a set of *interesting properties* for the operators. These properties are also used to spare plans from pruning that come with an additional property that may amortize their cost overhead later.

Heise et al. [64] have presented *Sopremo*, a semantically rich operator model, and *Meteor*, an extensible query language that is grounded in Sopremo. Sopremo provides a programming framework that allows users to define custom packages, the respective operators and their instantiations. Meteor's syntax is operator-oriented and uses a Json-like data model to support applications that analyze semistructured and unstructured data. Meteor queries are then translated into data flow programs of operator instantiations that represent concrete implementations of the involved Sopremo operators. A main advantage of this approach is that the operator's semantics can be accessed at compile time and potentially be used for data flow optimization, or for detecting syntactically correct, but semantically erroneous queries. Meteor and Sopremo have been implemented within Stratosphere,* a system for parallel data analysis, which comprises the Pact programming model and the Nephele execution engine as well.

2.6.5   BOOM Analytics

The *BOOM Analytics* (Berkeley Orders of Magnitude) [9] is an API-compliant reimplementation of the HDFS distributed file system (*BOOM-FS*) and the Hadoop MapReduce engine (*BOOM-MR*). The implementation of BOOM Analytics uses the *Overlog* logic language [95], which has been originally presented as an event-driven language and evolved a semantics more carefully grounded in *Datalog*, the standard deductive query language from database theory [126]. In general, the Datalog language is defined over relational tables as a purely logical query language that makes

---

* https://stratosphere.eu/.

no changes to the stored tables. Overlog extends Datalog with the following three main features [38]:

1. It adds notation to specify the location of data.
2. It provides some SQL-style extensions such as primary keys and aggregation.
3. It defines a model for processing and generating changes to tables.

When Overlog tuples arrive at a node, either through rule evaluation or external events, they are handled in an atomic local Datalog *timestep*. Within a timestep, each node sees only locally stored tuples. Communication between Datalog and the rest of the system (Java code, networks, and clocks) is modeled using events corresponding to insertions or deletions of tuples in Datalog tables. BOOM Analytics uses a Java-based Overlog runtime called *JOL*, which compiles Overlog programs into pipelined dataflow graphs of operators. In particular, JOL provides metaprogramming support where each Overlog program is compiled into a representation that is captured in rows of tables. In BOOM Analytics, *everything* is data. This includes traditional persistent information like file system metadata, runtime state like TaskTracker status, summary statistics like those used by the JobTracker's scheduling policy, communication messages, system events, and execution state of the system.

The BOOM-FS component represents the file system metadata as a collection of relations (*file, fqpath, fchunk, datanode, hbchunk*) where file system operations are implemented by writing queries over these tables. The *file* relation contains a row for each file or directory stored in BOOM-FS. The set of chunks in a file is identified by the corresponding rows in the *fchunk* relation. The *datanode* and hbchunk relations contain the set of live DataNodes and the chunks stored by each DataNode, respectively. The NameNode updates these relations as new heartbeats arrive. If the NameNode does not receive a heartbeat from a DataNode within a configurable amount of time, it assumes that the DataNode has failed and removes the corresponding rows from these tables. Since a file system is naturally hierarchical, the file system queries needed to traverse it are recursive. Therefore, the parent–child relationship of files is used to compute the transitive closure of each file and store its fully qualified path in the *fqpath* relation. Because path information is accessed frequently, the *fqpath* relation is configured to be cached after it is computed. Overlog will automatically update *fqpath* when the file is changed, using standard relational view maintenance logic [126]. BOOM-FS also defines several views to compute derived file system metadata such as the total size of each file and the contents of each directory. The materialization of each view can be changed via simple Overlog table definition statements without altering the semantics of the program. In general, HDFS uses three different communication protocols: the *metadata protocol*, which is used by clients and NameNodes to exchange file metadata, the *heartbeat protocol*, which is used by the DataNodes to notify the NameNode about chunk locations and DataNode liveness, and the *data protocol*, which is used by the clients and DataNodes used to exchange chunks. BOOM-FS reimplemented these three protocols using a set of Overlog rules. BOOM-FS also achieves the high availability failover mechanism using Overlog to implement the *hot standby* NameNodes feature using Lamport's Paxos algorithm [85].

BOOM-MR re-implements the MapReduce framework by replacing Hadoop's core scheduling logic with Overlog. The *JobTracker* tracks the ongoing status of the system and transient state in the form of messages sent and received by the *JobTracker* by capturing this information in four Overlog tables: *job, task, taskAttempt,* and *taskTracker.* The *job* relation contains a single row for each job submitted to the *JobTracker.* The *task* relation identifies each task within a job. The attributes of this relation identify the task type (map or reduce), the input partition (a chunk for map tasks, a bucket for reduce tasks), and the current running status. The *taskAttempt* relation maintains the state of each task attempt (a task may be attempted more than once due to speculation or if the initial execution attempt failed). The *taskTracker* relation identifies each TaskTracker in the cluster with a unique name. Overlog rules are used to update the *JobTracker's* tables by converting inbound messages into tuples of the four Overlog tables. Scheduling decisions are encoded in the *taskAttempt* table that assigns tasks to *TaskTrackers.* A scheduling policy is simply a set of rules that join against the *taskTracker* relation to find *TaskTrackers* with unassigned slots and schedules tasks by inserting tuples into *taskAttempt.* This architecture allows new scheduling policies to be defined easily.

2.6.6 HYRACKS/ASTERIX

Hyracks is presented as a partitioned-parallel dataflow execution platform that runs on shared-nothing clusters of computers [23]. Large collections of data items are stored as local partitions that are distributed across the nodes of the cluster. A Hyracks job submitted by a client is processed as one or more collections of data to produce one or more output collections (partitions). Hyracks provides a programming model and an accompanying infrastructure to efficiently divide computations on large data collections (spanning multiple machines) into computations that work on each partition of the data separately. Every Hyracks cluster is managed by a *Cluster Controller* process. The Cluster Controller accepts job execution requests from clients, plans their evaluation strategies, and then schedules the jobs' tasks to run on selected machines in the cluster. In addition, it is responsible for monitoring the state of the cluster to keep track of the resource loads at the various worker machines. The Cluster Controller is also responsible for re-planning and re-executing some or all of the tasks of a job in the event of a failure. On the task execution side, each worker machine that participates in a Hyracks cluster runs a *Node Controller* process. The Node Controller accepts task execution requests from the Cluster Controller and also reports on its health via a heartbeat mechanism.

In Hyracks, data flows between operators over connectors in the form of records that can have an arbitrary number of fields. Hyracks provides support for expressing data-type-specific operations such as comparisons and hash functions. The way Hyracks uses a record as the carrier of data is a generalization of the (key, value) concept of MapReduce. Hyracks strongly promotes the construction of reusable operators and connectors that end users can use to build their jobs. The basic set of Hyracks operators include

- The *File Readers/Writers* operators are used to read and write files in various formats from/to local file systems and the HDFS.

- The *Mappers* are used to evaluate a user-defined function on each item in the input.
- The *Sorters* are used to sort input records using user-provided comparator functions.
- The *Joiners* are binary-input operators that perform equi-joins.
- The *Aggregators* are used to perform aggregation using a user-defined aggregation function.

The Hyracks connectors are used to distribute data produced by a set of sender operators to a set of receiver operators. The basic set of Hyracks connectors include

- The *M:N Hash-Partitioner* hashes every tuple produced by senders to generate the receiver number to which the tuple is sent. Tuples produced by the same sender keep their initial order on the receiver side.
- The *M:N Hash-Partitioning Merger* takes as input sorted streams of data and hashes each tuple to find the receiver. On the receiver side, it merges streams coming from different senders based on a given comparator and thus producing ordered partitions.
- The *M:N Range-Partitioner* partitions data using a specified field in the input and a range-vector.
- The *M:N Replicator* copies the data produced by every sender to every receiver operator.
- The 1:1 Connector connects exactly one sender to one receiver operator.

In principle, Hyracks has been designed with the goal of being a runtime platform where users can create their jobs and also to serve as an efficient target for the compilers of higher-level programming languages such as Pig, Hive, or Jaql. The *ASTERIX* project [16,22] uses this feature for building a scalable information management system that supports the storage, querying, and analysis of large collections of semistructured nested data objects. The ASTERIX data storage and query processing are based on its own semistructured model called the *ASTERIX Data Model* (ADM). Each individual ADM data instance is typed and self-describing. All data instances live in *data sets* (the ASTERIX analogy to tables) and data sets can be indexed, partitioned, and possibly replicated to achieve the scalability and availability goals. External data sets that reside in files that are not under ASTERIX control are also supported. An instance of the ASTERIX data model can either be a primitive type (e.g., integer, string, time) or a derived type, which may include

- *Enum*: An enumeration type, whose domain is defined by listing the sequence of possible values.
- *Record*: A set of fields where each field is described by its name and type. A record can be either an open record where it contains fields that are not part of the type definition, or a closed record, which cannot be opened.
- *Ordered list*: A sequence of values for which the order is determined by the creation or insertion time.

- *Unordered list*: An unordered sequence of values, which is similar to bags in SQL.
- *Union*: Describes a choice between a finite set of types.

A data set is a target for AQL queries and updates and is also the attachment point for indexes. A collection of data sets related to an application are grouped into a namespace called a *dataverse*, which is analogous to a database in the relational world. In particular, data is accessed and manipulated through the use of the *ASTERIX Query Language* (AQL), which is designed to cleanly match and handle the data structuring constructs of ADM. It borrows from *XQuery* and *Jaql* their programmer-friendly declarative syntax that describes bulk operations such as iteration, filtering, and sorting. Therefore, AQL is comparable to those languages in terms of expressive power. The major difference with respect to XQuery is AQL's focus on data-centric use cases at the expense of built-in support for mixed content for document-centric use cases. In ASTERIX, there is no notion of document order or node identity for data instances. Differences between AQL and Jaql stem from the usage of the languages. While ASTERIX data is stored in and managed by the ASTERIX system, Jaql runs against data stored externally in Hadoop files or in the local file system. Figure 2.24 presents an overview of the ASTERIX system architecture. AQL requests are compiled into jobs for the ASTERIX execution layer, Hyracks. ASTERIX concerns itself with the data details of AQL and ADM, turning AQL requests into Hyracks jobs, while Hyracks determines and oversees the utilization of parallelism based on information and constraints associated with the resulting jobs' operators as well as on the runtime state of the cluster.

Another system that relies on a nested model of data representation is *Dremel* [99, 100], developed at Google, which is designed to support interactive analysis of very large data sets (stored on *GSF* [58] or *Bigtable* [32]) over shared clusters of commodity machines. Dremel uses a column-striped storage representation, which is adopted to store *nested* data models. Dremel provides a high-level SQL-like language to

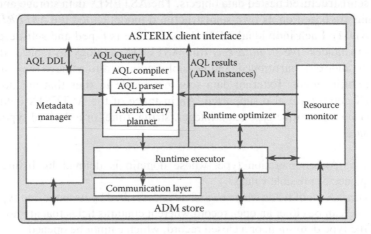

FIGURE 2.24 The ASTERIX system architecture. (From A. Behm et al., *Distributed and Parallel Databases*, 29(3), 185–216, 2011.)

express ad hoc queries. In contrast to other systems such as *Pig* [109] or *Hive* [123], it executes queries natively without translating them into MapReduce jobs. In particular, Dremel is designed to execute many queries that would ordinarily require a sequence of MapReduce jobs.

2.7 CONCLUSIONS

The database community has always been focusing on dealing with the challenges of *Big Data* management, although the meaning of *"big"* has been evolving continuously to represent different scales over the time [24]. According to IBM, we are currently creating 2.5 quintillion bytes of data, every day. This data comes from many different sources and in different formats including digital pictures, videos, posts to social media sites, intelligent sensors, purchase transaction records, and cell phone GPS signals. This is a new scale of *Big Data*, which is attracting a huge interest from both the industrial and research communities with the aim of creating the best means to process and analyze this data to make the best use of it. In the last decade, the MapReduce framework has emerged as a popular mechanism to harness the power of large clusters of computers. It allows programmers to think in a *data-centric* fashion where they can focus on applying transformations to sets of data records, while the details of distributed execution and fault tolerance are transparently managed by the MapReduce framework.

In this chapter, we presented a survey of the MapReduce family of approaches for developing scalable data-processing systems and solutions. In general, we notice that although the MapReduce framework and its open-source implementation of Hadoop are now considered to be sufficiently mature such that they are widely used for developing many solutions by academia and industry in different application domains, we believe that it is unlikely that MapReduce will completely replace database systems even for data warehousing applications. We expect that they will always coexist and complement each others in different scenarios. We are also convinced that there is still room for further optimization and advancement in different directions on the spectrum of the MapReduce framework that is required to bring forward the vision of providing large-scale data analysis as a commodity for novice end-users. For example, energy efficiency in the MapReduce is an important problem, which has not attracted sufficient attention from the research community, yet. The traditional challenge of debugging large-scale computations on distributed systems has not been given sufficient consideration by the MapReduce research community. Related with the issue of the power of expressiveness of the programming model, we feel that this is an area that requires more investigation. We also noticed that the over simplicity of the MapReduce programming model have raised some key challenges on dealing with complex data models (e.g., nested models, XML and hierarchical model, RDF, and graphs) efficiently. This limitation has called for the need of next generation of Big Data architectures and systems that can provide the required scale and performance attributes for these domain. For example, Google has created the *Dremel* system [99], commercialized under the name *of BigQuery*,* to support interactive analysis

---

* https://developers.google.com/bigquery/.

of nested data. Google has also presented the *Pregel* system [98], open-sourced by *Apache Giraph* and *Apache Hama* projects, which uses a BSP-based programming model for efficient and scalable processing of massive graphs on distributed cluster of commodity machines. Recently, Twitter has announced the release of the *Storm** system as a distributed and fault-tolerant platform for implementing continuous and real-time processing applications of streamed data. We believe that more of these domain-specific systems will be introduced in the future to form the new generation of Big Data systems. Defining the right and most convenient programming abstractions and declarative interfaces of these domain-specific Big Data systems is another important research direction that will need to be deeply investigated.

REFERENCES

1. Large synoptic survey. http://www.lsst.org/.
2. Daniel J. Abadi, Adam Marcus, Samuel Madden, and Kate Hollenbach. SW-Store: A vertically partitioned DBMS for semantic web data management. *VLDB Journal*, 18(2):385–406, 2009.
3. Azza Abouzeid, Kamil Bajda-Pawlikowski, Daniel J. Abadi, Alexander Rasin, and Avi Silberschatz. HadoopDB: An architectural hybrid of MapReduce and DBMS technologies for analytical workloads. *PVLDB*, 2(1):922–933, 2009.
4. Azza Abouzied, Kamil Bajda-Pawlikowski, Jiewen Huang, Daniel J. Abadi, and Avi Silberschatz. HadoopDB in action: Building real world applications. In *SIGMOD*, 2010.
5. Foto N. Afrati, Anish Das Sarma, David Menestrina, Aditya G. Parameswaran, and Jeffrey D. Ullman. Fuzzy joins using MapReduce. In *ICDE*, pp. 498–509, 2012.
6. Foto N. Afrati and Jeffrey D. Ullman. Optimizing joins in a map-reduce environment. In *EDBT*, pp. 99–110, 2010.
7. Foto N. Afrati and Jeffrey D. Ullman. Optimizing multiway joins in a map-reduce environment. *IEEE TKDE*, 23(9):1282–1298, 2011.
8. Alexander Alexandrov, Dominic Battré, Stephan Ewen, Max Heimel, Fabian Hueske, Odej Kao, Volker Markl, Erik Nijkamp, and Daniel Warneke. Massively parallel data analysis with PACTs on Nephele. *PVLDB*, 3(2):1625–1628, 2010.
9. Peter Alvaro, Tyson Condie, Neil Conway, Khaled Elmeleegy, Joseph M. Hellerstein, and Russell Sears. Boom analytics: Exploring data-centric, declarative programming for the cloud. In *EuroSys*, pp. 223–236, 2010.
10. Ahmed M. Aly, Asmaa Sallam, Bala M. Gnanasekaran, Long-Van Nguyen-Dinh, Walid G. Aref, Mourad Ouzzaniy, and Arif Ghafoor. M³: Stream processing on main-memory MapReduce. In *ICDE*, 2012.
11. Michael Armbrust, Armando Fox, Rean Griffith, Anthony D. Joseph, Randy H. Katz, Andrew Konwinski, Gunho Lee, David A. Patterson, Ariel Rabkin, Ion Stoica, and Matei Zaharia. Above the clouds: A Berkeley view of cloud computing, February 2009.
12. Shivnath Babu. Towards automatic optimization of MapReduce programs. In *SoCC*, pp. 137–142, 2010.
13. Andrey Balmin, Tim Kaldewey, and Sandeep Tata. Clydesdale: Structured data processing on hadoop. In *SIGMOD Conference*, pp. 705–708, 2012.
14. Luiz André Barroso and Urs Hölzle. The case for energy-proportional computing. *IEEE Computer*, 40(12):33–37, 2007.

---

* https://github.com/nathanmarz/storm/.

15. Dominic Battré, Stephan Ewen, Fabian Hueske, Odej Kao, Volker Markl, and Daniel Warneke. Nephele/PACTs: A programming model and execution framework for web-scale analytical processing. In *SoCC*, pp. 119–130, 2010.
16. Alexander Behm, Vinayak R. Borkar, Michael J. Carey, Raman Grover, Chen Li, Nicola Onose, Rares Vernica, Alin Deutsch, Yannis Papakonstantinou, and Vassilis J. Tsotras. ASTERIX: Towards a scalable, semistructured data platform for evolving-world models. *Distributed and Parallel Databases*, 29(3):185–216, 2011.
17. Gordon Bell, Jim Gray, and Alexander S. Szalay. Petascale computational systems. *IEEE Computer*, 39(1):110–112, 2006.
18. Kevin S. Beyer, Vuk Ercegovac, Rainer Gemulla, Andrey Balmin, Mohamed Y. Eltabakh, Carl-Christian Kanne, Fatma Özcan, and Eugene J. Shekita. Jaql: A scripting language for large scale semistructured data analysis. *PVLDB*, 4(12):1272–1283, 2011.
19. Pramod Bhatotia, Alexander Wieder, Rodrigo Rodrigues, Umut A. Acar, and Rafael Pasquini. Incoop: MapReduce for incremental computations. In *SOCC*, 2011.
20. Spyros Blanas, Jignesh M. Patel, Vuk Ercegovac, Jun Rao, Eugene J. Shekita, and Yuanyuan Tian. A comparison of join algorithms for log processing in mapreduce. In *SIGMOD*, pp. 975–986, 2010.
21. Scott Boag, Don Chamberlin, Mary F. Fernández, Daniela Florescu, Jonathan Robie, and Jérôme Siméon. XQuery 1.0: An XML query language, December 2010. http://www.w3.org/TR/xquery.
22. Vinayak Borkar, Sattam Alsubaiee, Yasser Altowim, Hotham Altwaijry, Alexander Behm, Yingyi Bu, Michael Carey, Raman Grover, Zachary Heilbron, Young-Seok Kim, Chen Li, Pouria Pirzadeh, Nicola Onose, Rares Vernica, and Jian Wen. ASTERIX: An open source system for big data management and analysis. *PVLDB*, 5(2), 2012.
23. Vinayak R. Borkar, Michael J. Carey, Raman Grover, Nicola Onose, and Rares Vernica. Hyracks: A flexible and extensible foundation for data-intensive computing. In *ICDE*, pp. 1151–1162, 2011.
24. Vinayak R. Borkar, Michael J. Carey, and Chen Li. Inside "Big Data management": Ogres, onions, or parfaits? In *EDBT*, pp. 3–14, 2012.
25. Yingyi Bu, Bill Howe, Magdalena Balazinska, and Michael D. Ernst. HaLoop: Efficient iterative data processing on large clusters. *PVLDB*, 3(1):285–296, 2010.
26. Yingyi Bu, Bill Howe, Magdalena Balazinska, and Michael D. Ernst. The HaLoop approach to large-scale iterative data analysis. *VLDB Journal*, 21(2):169–190, 2012.
27. Michael J. Cafarella and Christopher Ré. Manimal: Relational optimization for data-intensive programs. In *WebDB*, 2010.
28. Ariel Cary, Zhengguo Sun, Vagelis Hristidis, and Naphtali Rishe. Experiences on processing spatial data with MapReduce. In *SSDBM*, pp. 302–319, 2009.
29. Ronnie Chaiken, Bob Jenkins, Per-Åke Larson, Bill Ramsey, Darren Shakib, Simon Weaver, and Jingren Zhou. SCOPE: Easy and efficient parallel processing of massive data sets. *PVLDB*, 1(2):1265–1276, 2008.
30. Craig Chambers, Ashish Raniwala, Frances Perry, Stephen Adams, Robert R. Henry, Robert Bradshaw, and Nathan Weizenbaum. FlumeJava: Easy, efficient data-parallel pipelines. In *PLDI*, pp. 363–375, 2010.
31. Fay Chang, Jeffrey Dean, Sanjay Ghemawat, Wilson C. Hsieh, Deborah A. Wallach, Michael Burrows, Tushar Chandra, Andrew Fikes, and Robert Gruber. Bigtable: A distributed storage system for structured data. In *OSDI*, pp. 205–218, 2006.
32. Fay Chang, Jeffrey Dean, Sanjay Ghemawat, Wilson C. Hsieh, Deborah A. Wallach, Michael Burrows, Tushar Chandra, Andrew Fikes, and Robert E. Gruber. Bigtable: A distributed storage system for structured data. *ACM Transactions on Computing Systems*, 26(2), 2008.
33. Biswapesh Chattopadhyay, Liang Lin, Weiran Liu, Sagar Mittal, Prathyusha Aragonda, Vera Lychagina, Younghee Kwon, and Michael Wong. Tenzing a SQL implementation on the MapReduce framework. *PVLDB*, 4(12):1318–1327, 2011.

34. Rishan Chen, Xuetian Weng, Bingsheng He, and Mao Yang. Large graph processing in the cloud. In *SIGMOD*, pp. 1123–1126, 2010.
35. Songting Chen. Cheetah: A high performance, custom data warehouse on top of MapReduce. *PVLDB*, 3(2):1459–1468, 2010.
36. Hung Chih Yang, Ali Dasdan, Ruey-Lung Hsiao, and Douglas Stott Parker Jr. Map-reduce-merge: Simplified relational data processing on large clusters. In *SIGMOD*, pp. 1029–1040, 2007.
37. Hung Chih Yang and D. Stott Parker. Traverse: Simplified indexing on large map-reduce-merge clusters. In *DASFAA*, pp. 308–322, 2009.
38. Tyson Condie, David Chu, Joseph M. Hellerstein, and Petros Maniatis. Evita raced: Metacompilation for declarative networks. *PVLDB*, 1(1):1153–1165, 2008.
39. Tyson Condie, Neil Conway, Peter Alvaro, Joseph M. Hellerstein, Khaled Elmeleegy, and Russell Sears. MapReduce online. In *NSDI*, pp. 313–328, 2010.
40. Tyson Condie, Neil Conway, Peter Alvaro, Joseph M. Hellerstein, John Gerth, Justin Talbot, Khaled Elmeleegy, and Russell Sears. Online aggregation and continuous query support in MapReduce. In *SIGMOD Conference*, pp. 1115–1118, 2010.
41. Robson Leonardo Ferreira Cordeiro, Caetano Traina Jr., Agma Juci Machado Traina, Julio López, U. Kang, and Christos Faloutsos. Clustering very large multi-dimensional data sets with MapReduce. In *KDD*, pp. 690–698, 2011.
42. Sudipto Das, Yannis Sismanis, Kevin S. Beyer, Rainer Gemulla, Peter J. Haas, and John McPherson. Ricardo: Integrating R and Hadoop. In *SIGMOD*, pp. 987–998, 2010.
43. Jeffrey Dean and Sanjay Ghemawat. MapReduce: Simplified data processing on large clusters. In *OSDI*, pp. 137–150, 2004.
44. Jeffrey Dean and Sanjay Ghemawat. MapReduce: Simplified data processing on large clusters. *Communications of the ACM*, 51(1):107–113, 2008.
45. Jeffrey Dean and Sanjay Ghemawat. MapReduce: A flexible data processing tool. *Communications of the ACM*, 53(1):72–77, 2010.
46. David J. DeWitt and Jim Gray. Parallel database systems: The future of high performance database systems. *Communications of the ACM*, 35(6):85–98, 1992.
47. Jens Dittrich, Jorge-Arnulfo Quiané-Ruiz, Alekh Jindal, Yagiz Kargin, Vinay Setty, and Jörg Schad. Hadoop++: Making a yellow elephant run like a cheetah (without it even noticing). *PVLDB*, 3(1):518–529, 2010.
48. Jaliya Ekanayake, Hui Li, Bingjing Zhang, Thilina Gunarathne, Seung-Hee Bae, Judy Qiu, and Geoffrey Fox. Twister: A runtime for iterative MapReduce. In *HPDC*, pp. 810–818, 2010.
49. Iman Elghandour and Ashraf Aboulnaga. ReStore: Reusing results of MapReduce jobs. *PVLDB*, 5(6):586–597, 2012.
50. Iman Elghandour and Ashraf Aboulnaga. ReStore: Reusing results of MapReduce jobs in pig. In *SIGMOD Conference*, pp. 701–704, 2012.
51. Mohamed Y. Eltabakh, Yuanyuan Tian, Fatma Özcan, Rainer Gemulla, Aljoscha Krettek, and John McPherson. CoHadoop: Flexible data placement and its exploitation in Hadoop. *PVLDB*, 4(9):575–585, 2011.
52. Alina Ene, Sungjin Im, and Benjamin Moseley. Fast clustering using MapReduce. In *KDD*, pp. 681–689, 2011.
53. Leonidas Fegaras, Chengkai Li, Upa Gupta, and Jijo Philip. XML query optimization in Map-Reduce. In *WebDB*, 2011.
54. Avrilia Floratou, Jignesh M. Patel, Eugene J. Shekita, and Sandeep Tata. Column-oriented storage techniques for MapReduce. *PVLDB*, 4(7):419–429, 2011.
55. Eric Friedman, Peter M. Pawlowski, and John Cieslewicz. SQL/MapReduce: A practical approach to self-describing, polymorphic, and parallelizable user-defined functions. *PVLDB*, 2(2):1402–1413, 2009.
56. Alan Gates. *Programming Pig*. O'Reilly Media, 2011.

57. Alan Gates, Olga Natkovich, Shubham Chopra, Pradeep Kamath, Shravan Narayanam, Christopher Olston, Benjamin Reed, Santhosh Srinivasan, and Utkarsh Srivastava. Building a HighLevel Dataflow System on top of MapReduce: The Pig experience. *PVLDB*, 2(2):1414–1425, 2009.
58. Sanjay Ghemawat, Howard Gobioff, and Shun-Tak Leung. The Google file system. In *SOSP*, pp. 29–43, 2003.
59. Amol Ghoting, Prabhanjan Kambadur, Edwin P. D. Pednault, and Ramakrishnan Kannan. NIMBLE: A toolkit for the implementation of parallel data mining and machine learning algorithms on mapreduce. In *KDD*, pp. 334–342, 2011.
60. Amol Ghoting, Rajasekar Krishnamurthy, Edwin P. D. Pednault, Berthold Reinwald, Vikas Sindhwani, Shirish Tatikonda, Yuanyuan Tian, and Shivakumar Vaithyanathan. SystemML: Declarative machine learning on MapReduce. In *ICDE*, pp. 231–242, 2011.
61. Yunhong Gu and Robert L. Grossman. Lessons learned from a year's worth of benchmarks of large data clouds. In *SC-MTAGS*, 2009.
62. Alon Y. Halevy. Answering queries using views: A survey. *VLDB Journal*, 10(4):270–294, 2001.
63. Yongqiang He, Rubao Lee, Yin Huai, Zheng Shao, Namit Jain, Xiaodong Zhang, and Zhiwei Xu. RCFile: A fast and space-efficient data placement structure in MapReduce-based warehouse systems. In *ICDE*, pp. 1199–1208, 2011.
64. Arvid Heise, Astrid Rheinlaender, Marcus Leich, Ulf Leser, and Felix Naumann. Meteor/Sopremo: An extensible query language and operator model. In *BigData*, 2012.
65. Herodotos Herodotou. Hadoop performance models. *CoRR*, abs/1106.0940, 2011.
66. Herodotos Herodotou and Shivnath Babu. Profiling, What-if Analysis, and Cost-based Optimization of MapReduce Programs. *PVLDB*, 4(11):1111–1122, 2011.
67. Herodotos Herodotou, Fei Dong, and Shivnath Babu. MapReduce programming and cost-based optimization? Crossing THIS CHASM with Starfish. *PVLDB*, 4(12):1446–1449, 2011.
68. Herodotos Herodotou, Harold Lim, Gang Luo, Nedyalko Borisov, Liang Dong, Fatma Bilgen Cetin, and Shivnath Babu. Starfish: A self-tuning system for big data analytics. In *CIDR*, pp. 261–272, 2011.
69. Tony Hey, Stewart Tansley, and Kristin Tolle, editors. *The Fourth Paradigm: Data-Intensive Scientific Discovery*. Microsoft Research, October 2009.
70. Benjamin Hindman, Andy Konwinski, Matei Zaharia, and Ion Stoica. A common substrate for cluster computing. In *HotCloud, USENIX Workshop*, 2009.
71. Jiewen Huang, Daniel J. Abadi, and Kun Ren. Scalable SPARQL querying of large RDF Graphs. *PVLDB*, 4(11):1123–1134, 2011.
72. Mohammad Farhan Husain, James P. McGlothlin, Mohammad M. Masud, Latifur R. Khan, and Bhavani M. Thuraisingham. Heuristics-based query processing for large RDF graphs using cloud computing. *IEEE TKDE*, 23(9):1312–1327, 2011.
73. Michael Isard, Mihai Budiu, Yuan Yu, Andrew Birrell, and Dennis Fetterly. Dryad: Distributed data-parallel programs from sequential building blocks. In *EuroSys*, pp. 59–72, 2007.
74. Ming-Yee Iu and Willy Zwaenepoel. HadoopToSQL: A MapReduce query optimizer. In *EuroSys*, pp. 251–264, 2010.
75. Eaman Jahani, Michael J. Cafarella, and Christopher Ré. Automatic optimization for MapReduce programs. *PVLDB*, 4(6):385–396, 2011.
76. David Jiang, Anthony K. H. Tung, and Gang Chen. MAP-JOIN-REDUCE: Toward scalable and efficient data analysis on large clusters. *IEEE TKDE*, 23(9):1299–1311, 2011.
77. Dawei Jiang, Beng Chin Ooi, Lei Shi, and Sai Wu. The performance of MapReduce: An in-depth study. *PVLDB*, 3(1):472–483, 2010.
78. Alekh Jindal, Jorge-Arnulfo Quiane-Ruiz, and Jens Dittrich. Trojan data layouts: Right shoes for a running elephant. In *SoCC*, 2011.

79. Tim Kaldewey, Eugene J. Shekita, and Sandeep Tata. Clydesdale: Structured data processing on MapReduce. In *EDBT*, pp. 15–25, 2012.

80. Shahan Khatchadourian, Mariano P. Consens, and Jérôme Siméon. Having a ChuQL at XML on the Cloud. In *AMW*, 2011.

81. HyeongSik Kim, Padmashree Ravindra, and Kemafor Anyanwu. From SPARQL to MapReduce: The journey using a nested TripleGroup algebra. *PVLDB*, 4(12):1426–1429, 2011.

82. Lars Kolb, Andreas Thor, and Erhard Rahm. Dedoop: Efficient deduplication with Hadoop. *PVLDB*, 5(12), 2012.

83. Lars Kolb, Andreas Thor, and Erhard Rahm. Load balancing for MapReduce-based entity resolution. In *ICDE*, pp. 618–629, 2012.

84. Vibhore Kumar, Henrique Andrade, Bugra Gedik, and Kun-Lung Wu. DEDUCE: At the intersection of MapReduce and stream processing. In *EDBT*, pp. 657–662, 2010.

85. Leslie Lamport. The part-time parliament. *ACM Transactions on Computing Systems*, 16(2):133–169, 1998.

86. Willis Lang and Jignesh M. Patel. Energy management for MapReduce Clusters. *PVLDB*, 3(1):129–139, 2010.

87. Silvio Lattanzi, Benjamin Moseley, Siddharth Suri, and Sergei Vassilvitskii. Filtering: A method for solving graph problems in MapReduce. In *SPAA*, pp. 85–94, 2011.

88. Rubao Lee, Tian Luo, Yin Huai, Fusheng Wang, Yongqiang He, and Xiaodong Zhang. YSmart: Yet another SQL-to-MapReduce translator. In *ICDCS*, pp. 25–36, 2011.

89. Jacob Leverich and Christos Kozyrakis. On the energy (in)efficiency of Hadoop clusters. *Operating Systems Review*, 44(1):61–65, 2010.

90. Boduo Li, Edward Mazur, Yanlei Diao, Andrew McGregor, and Prashant J. Shenoy. A platform for scalable one-pass analytics using MapReduce. In *SIGMOD Conference*, pp. 985–996, 2011.

91. Harold Lim, Herodotos Herodotou, and Shivnath Babu. Stubby: A transformation-based optimizer for MapReduce workflows. *PVLDB*, 5(12), 2012.

92. Jimmy J. Lin. Brute force and indexed approaches to pairwise document similarity comparisons with MapReduce. In *SIGIR*, pp. 155–162, 2009.

93. Yuting Lin, Divyakant Agrawal, Chun Chen, Beng Chin Ooi, and Sai Wu. Llama: Leveraging columnar storage for scalable join processing in the MapReduce framework. In *SIGMOD Conference*, pp. 961–972, 2011.

94. Dionysios Logothetis and Ken Yocum. Ad-hoc data processing in the cloud. *PVLDB*, 1(2):1472–1475, 2008.

95. Boon Thau Loo, Tyson Condie, Joseph M. Hellerstein, Petros Maniatis, Timothy Roscoe, and Ion Stoica. Implementing declarative overlays. In *SOSP*, pp. 75–90, 2005.

96. Yucheng Low, Joseph Gonzalez, Aapo Kyrola, Danny Bickson, Carlos Guestrin, and Joseph M. Hellerstein. GraphLab: A new framework for parallel machine learning. In *UAI*, pp. 340–349, 2010.

97. Yucheng Low, Joseph Gonzalez, Aapo Kyrola, Danny Bickson, Carlos Guestrin, and Joseph M. Hellerstein. Distributed GraphLab: A framework for machine learning in the cloud. *PVLDB*, 5(8):716–727, 2012.

98. Grzegorz Malewicz, Matthew H. Austern, Aart J. C. Bik, James C. Dehnert, Ilan Horn, Naty Leiser, and Grzegorz Czajkowski. Pregel: A system for large-scale graph processing. In *SIGMOD*, pp. 135–146, 2010.

99. Sergey Melnik, Andrey Gubarev, Jing Jing Long, Geoffrey Romer, Shiva Shivakumar, Matt Tolton, and Theo Vassilakis. Dremel: Interactive analysis of web-scale data sets. *PVLDB*, 3(1):330–339, 2010.

100. Sergey Melnik, Andrey Gubarev, Jing Jing Long, Geoffrey Romer, Shiva Shivakumar, Matt Tolton, and Theo Vassilakis. Dremel: Interactive analysis of web-scale data sets. *Communications of the ACM*, 54(6):114–123, 2011.

101. Ahmed Metwally and Christos Faloutsos. V-SMART-Join: A scalable MapReduce framework for all-pair similarity joins of multisets and vectors. *PVLDB*, 5(8):704–715, 2012.

102. Gianmarco De Francisci Morales, Aristides Gionis, and Mauro Sozio. Social content matching in MapReduce. *PVLDB*, 4(7):460–469, 2011.

103. Kristi Morton, Magdalena Balazinska, and Dan Grossman. ParaTimer: A progress indicator for MapReduce DAGs. In *SIGMOD Conference*, pp. 507–518, 2010.

104. Kristi Morton, Abram Friesen, Magdalena Balazinska, and Dan Grossman. Estimating the progress of MapReduce pipelines. In *ICDE*, pp. 681–684, 2010.

105. Jaeseok Myung, Jongheum Yeon, and Sang Goo Lee. SPARQL basic graph pattern processing with iterative MapReduce. In *MDAC*, 2010.

106. Thomas Neumann and Gerhard Weikum. RDF-3X: A RISC-style engine for RDF. *PVLDB*, 1(1), 2008.

107. Tomasz Nykiel, Michalis Potamias, Chaitanya Mishra, George Kollios, and Nick Koudas. MRShare: Sharing across multiple queries in MapReduce. *PVLDB*, 3(1):494–505, 2010.

108. Martin Odersky, Lex Spoon, and Bill Venners. *Programming in Scala: A Comprehensive Step-by-Step Guide*. Artima, 2011.

109. Christopher Olston, Benjamin Reed, Utkarsh Srivastava, Ravi Kumar, and Andrew Tomkins. Pig latin: A not-so-foreign language for data processing. In *SIGMOD*, pp. 1099–1110, 2008.

110. Biswanath Panda, Joshua Herbach, Sugato Basu, and Roberto J. Bayardo. PLANET: Massively parallel learning of tree ensembles with MapReduce. *PVLDB*, 2(2):1426–1437, 2009.

111. Spiros Papadimitriou and Jimeng Sun. DisCo: Distributed co-clustering with Map-Reduce: A case study towards petabyte-scale end-to-end mining. In *ICDM*, pp. 512–521, 2008.

112. David A. Patterson. Technical perspective: The data center is the computer. *Communications of the ACM*, 51(1):105, 2008.

113. Andrew Pavlo, Erik Paulson, Alexander Rasin, Daniel J. Abadi, David J. DeWitt, Samuel Madden, and Michael Stonebraker. A comparison of approaches to large-scale data analysis. In *SIGMOD*, pp. 165–178, 2009.

114. Rob Pike, Sean Dorward, Robert Griesemer, and Sean Quinlan. Interpreting the data: Parallel analysis with Sawzall. *Scientific Programming*, 13(4):277–298, 2005.

115. Jorge-Arnulfo Quiané-Ruiz, Christoph Pinkel, Jörg Schad, and Jens Dittrich. RAFT at work: Speeding-up mapreduce applications under task and node failures. In *SIGMOD Conference*, pp. 1225–1228, 2011.

116. Jorge-Arnulfo Quiané-Ruiz, Christoph Pinkel, Jörg Schad, and Jens Dittrich. RAFTing MapReduce: Fast recovery on the RAFT. In *ICDE*, pp. 589–600, 2011.

117. Padmashree Ravindra, HyeongSik Kim, and Kemafor Anyanwu. An intermediate algebra for optimizing RDF graph pattern matching on MapReduce. In *ESWC (2)*, pp. 46–61, 2011.

118. Alexander Schätzle, Martin Przyjaciel-Zablocki, Thomas Hornung, and Georg Lausen. PigSPARQL: Mapping SPARQL to Pig Latin. In *SWIM*, pp. 65–84, 2011.

119. Patricia G. Selinger, Morton M. Astrahan, Donald D. Chamberlin, Raymond A. Lorie, and Thomas G. Price. Access path selection in a relational database management system. In *SIGMOD Conference*, pp. 23–34, 1979.

120. Michael Stonebraker. The case for shared nothing. *IEEE Database Engineering Bulletin*, 9(1):4–9, 1986.

121. Michael Stonebraker, Daniel J. Abadi, David J. DeWitt, Samuel Madden, Erik Paulson, Andrew Pavlo, and Alexander Rasin. MapReduce and parallel DBMSs: Friends or foes? *Communications of the ACM*, 53(1):64–71, 2010.

122. Philip Stutz, Abraham Bernstein, and William W. Cohen. Signal/Collect: Graph Algorithms for the (Semantic) Web. In *International Semantic Web Conference (1)*, pp. 764–780, 2010.

123. Ashish Thusoo, Joydeep Sen Sarma, Namit Jain, Zheng Shao, Prasad Chakka, Suresh Anthony, Hao Liu, Pete Wyckoff, and Raghotham Murthy. Hive – A warehousing solution over a map–reduce framework. *PVLDB*, 2(2):1626–1629, 2009.

124. Ashish Thusoo, Joydeep Sen Sarma, Namit Jain, Zheng Shao, Prasad Chakka, Ning Zhang, Suresh Anthony, Hao Liu, and Raghotham Murthy. Hive – A petabyte scale data warehouse using Hadoop. In *ICDE*, pp. 996–1005, 2010.

125. Ashish Thusoo, Zheng Shao, Suresh Anthony, Dhruba Borthakur, Namit Jain, Joy-deep Sen Sarma, Raghotham Murthy, and Hao Liu. Data warehousing and analytics infrastructure at facebook. In *SIGMOD Conference*, pp. 1013–1020, 2010.

126. Jeffrey D. Ullman. *Principles of Database and Knowledge-Base Systems: Volume II: The New Technologies*. W. H. Freeman & Co., New York, NY, USA, 1990.

127. Leslie G. Valiant. A bridging model for parallel computation. *Communications of the ACM*, 33(8):103–111, 1990.

128. Rares Vernica, Michael J. Carey, and Chen Li. Efficient parallel set-similarity joins using MapReduce. In *SIGMOD*, pp. 495–506, 2010.

129. Chaokun Wang, Jianmin Wang, Xuemin Lin, Wei Wang, Haixun Wang, Hongsong Li, Wanpeng Tian, Jun Xu, and Rui Li. MapDupReducer: Detecting near duplicates over massive data sets. In *SIGMOD*, pp. 1119–1122, 2010.

130. Guozhang Wang, Wenlei Xie, Alan Demers, and Johannes Gehrke. Asynchronous Large-Scale Graph Processing Made Easy. In *CIDR*, 2013.

131. Tom White. *Hadoop: The Definitive Guide*. O'Reilly Media, 2012.

132. Chuan Xiao, Wei Wang, Xuemin Lin, Jeffrey Xu Yu, and Guoren Wang. Efficient similarity joins for near-duplicate detection. *ACM Transactions on Database Systems*, 36(3):15, 2011.

133. Yuan Yu, Michael Isard, Dennis Fetterly, Mihai Budiu, Úlfar Erlingsson, Pradeep Kumar Gunda, and Jon Currey. DryadLINQ: A system for general-purpose distributed data-parallel computing using a high-level language. In *OSDI*, pp. 1–14, 2008.

134. Matei Zaharia, Dhruba Borthakur, Joy-deep Sen Sarma, Khaled Elmeleegy, Scott Shenker, and Ion Stoica. Delay scheduling: A simple technique for achieving locality and fairness in cluster scheduling. In *EuroSys*, pp. 265–278, 2010.

135. Matei Zaharia, Mosharaf Chowdhury, Tathagata Das, Ankur Dave, Justin Ma, Murphy McCauley, Michael J. Franklin, Scott Shenker, and Ion Stoica. Resilient distributed data sets: A fault-tolerant abstraction for in-memory cluster computing. In *NSDI*, 2012.

136. Matei Zaharia, Mosharaf Chowdhury, Michael J. Franklin, Scott Shenker, and Ion Stoica. Spark: Cluster computing with working sets. In *HotCloud*, 2010.

137. Matei Zaharia, Andy Konwinski, Anthony D. Joseph, Randy H. Katz, and Ion Stoica. Improving MapReduce performance in heterogeneous environments. In *OSDI*, pp. 29–42, 2008.

138. Yanfeng Zhang, Qinxin Gao, Lixin Gao, and Cuirong Wang. iMapReduce: A distributed computing framework for iterative computation. *Journal of Grid Computing*, 10(1):47–68, 2012.

139. Jingren Zhou, Per-Åke Larson, and Ronnie Chaiken. Incorporating partitioning and parallel plans into the SCOPE optimizer. In *ICDE*, pp. 1060–1071, 2010.

140. Marcin Zukowski, Peter A. Boncz, Niels Nes, and Sándor Héman. MonetDB/X100 – A DBMS in the CPU cache. *IEEE Data Engineering Bulletin*, 28(2):17–22, 2005.

3 iMapReduce
Extending MapReduce for Iterative Processing

Yanfeng Zhang, Qixin Gao,
Lixin Gao, and Cuirong Wang

CONTENTS

To use Big Data to serve our daily life, data scientists have explored a flurry of data mining and machine learning algorithms to make sense of these data. Many of these data analysis algorithms require iterative processing. For example, the well-known PageRank algorithm parses the web linkage graph iteratively for deriving ranking scores for web pages, and the K-means algorithm iteratively refines the cluster centroids for grouping data points.

To analyze the massive data sets, a distributed computing framework is needed on top of a cluster of servers. MapReduce is a framework proposed for Big Data processing in a large-scale distributed environment. Since its introduction, MapReduce, in particular its open-source implementation, Hadoop,* has become extremely popular for analyzing large data sets. It provides a simple programming model and takes care of the distributed execution, data exchanging, and fault tolerance, which enables programmers with no experience on distributed systems to exploit a large cluster of commodity machines to perform data-intensive computation.

However, Hadoop MapReduce is designed for a batch-oriented computation such as log analysis and text processing. It lacks the built-in support for iterative processing. In this chapter, we introduce iMapReduce that extends Hadoop to support iterative processing. iMapReduce follows the programming paradigm of MapReduce. Existing applications implemented in Hadoop or MapReduce can be easily adapted into iMapReduce, and can benefit from the iterative processing support provided by iMapReduce.

3.1 ITERATIVE ALGORITHMS IN MapReduce

Many data mining algorithms have an iterative process to operate data recursively. We first briefly introduce MapReduce. Then, we provide three examples of iterative algorithms and describe their MapReduce implementations. Through these examples, we summarize some observations of writing iterative algorithms in MapReduce. Then we summarize the performance penalties of iterative computations in Hadoop MapReduce.

3.1.1 MAPREDUCE OVERVIEW

MapReduce is the most popular distributed framework for Big Data processing. MapReduce integrates distributed file system (DFS) for scalable and reliable storage. A MapReduce job reads the input data from DFS and writes the output data to DFS. On DFS, a big file is divided into multiple blocks, which are distributed in the cluster. Each file block has several copies that are stored on different nodes for fault tolerance. In Hadoop ecosystem, Hadoop Distributed FileSystem (HDFS) is an open-source implementation of DFS.

MapReduce exploits a batch-processing model with three main phases called map, shuffle, and reduce. The input data on DFS is first divided into several splits. The input data is expressed as a set of key-value pairs (KVs) for MapReduce processing.

---

* http://hadoop.apache.org/.

The map tasks scheduled on the cluster nodes will then process these splits in a distributed manner. A map task with a map function processes a set of KVs, produces a new set of intermediate KVs, and ends its life cycle when its assigned input KVs are processed. In the shuffle phase, the map tasks send their output KVs to the reduce tasks. An all-to-all communication between map tasks and reduce tasks is performed. Finally, in the reduce phase, each reduce task with a reduce function integrates the received intermediate KVs, produces the final result KVs, and ends its life cycle when its received intermediate KVs are processed. A MapReduce job returns when all the map tasks and reduce tasks have completed. The final output data containing the result KVs is written to DFS, which can be accessed by users.

3.1.2 Examples of Implementing Iterative Algorithms in MapReduce

To implement iterative computations in MapReduce, users have to submit a series of MapReduce jobs. One iteration corresponds to one or more MapReduce jobs. The previous iteration job's output is feed to the next iteration job as input. In this section, three iterative algorithm examples and their MapReduce implementations are provided.

3.1.2.1 PageRank

PageRank [1] is a popular algorithm initially proposed for ranking web pages. Later on, it has been used in a wide range of applications, such as link prediction and recommendation systems.

The PageRank vector R is defined over a directed graph $G = (V, E)$. Each node v in the graph is associated with a PageRank score $R(v)$. The initial rank of each node is $\frac{1}{|V|}$. Each node v updates its rank score iteratively as follows:

$$R^{(k+1)}(v) = \frac{1-d}{|V|} + \sum_{u \in N^-(v)} \frac{dR^{(k)}(u)}{|N^+(u)|}, \tag{1.1}$$

where $N^-(v)$ is the set of nodes pointing to node v, $N^+(v)$ is the set of nodes that v points to, k is the iteration number, and d is a constant representing the damping factor. This iterative process continues for a fixed number of iterations or until the difference between the resulting PageRank scores of two consecutive iterations is smaller than a threshold.

In MapReduce, the map function is applied on each node u, where the input key is the node id and the input value contains node u's ranking score $R(u)$ as well as node u's outbound neighbors set $N^+(u)$. The mapper on node u derives the partial ranking score of v, $v \in N^+(u)$, that is, $d\frac{R(u)}{|N^+(u)|}$, that will be shuffled to node v. Meanwhile, the retained PageRank score $\frac{1-d}{|V|}$ and the outbound neighbors set $N^+(u)$ are shuffled to itself. The reducer on node v accumulates these partial ranking scores and the retained ranking score to produce a new ranking score of v. The updated ranking score of v along with the outbound neighbors set is written to DFS for feeding the next iteration MapReduce job. To stop the iterative process, users have to perform another MapReduce job after each iteration to measure the difference from the result of the last iteration.

The map and reduce operations can be described as follows.

PageRank Map: For each node u, output KVs $\left\langle v, d \dfrac{R(u)}{|N^+(u)|} \right\rangle$, where $v \in N^+(u)$,

and output the retained ranking score and its outbound neighbors set,

$$\left\langle u, \left[\frac{1-d}{|V|}, N^+(u) \right] \right\rangle.$$

PageRank Reduce: For each node v, add the retained rank score $\dfrac{1-d}{|V|}$ and

the values received from any u $d \dfrac{R(u)}{|N^+(u)|}$ to update $R(v)$, and output KV $\langle v,$

$[R(v), N^+(v)] \rangle$.

3.1.2.2 K-means

K-means [11] is a commonly used clustering algorithm, which partitions n nodes into k clusters so that the nodes in the same cluster are more similar than those in other clusters. We describe the algorithm briefly as follows. (1) Start with selecting k random nodes as cluster centroids. (2) Assign each node to the nearest cluster centroid. (3) Update the k cluster centroids by "averaging" the nodes belonging to the same cluster centroid. Repeat steps (2) and (3) until convergence has been reached. The algorithm has converged when the assignments no longer change.

The map and reduce operations for the K-means algorithm can be described as follows.

K-Means Map: For each key *nid* (node id), compute the distance from the node to any cluster centroid, and output the closest cluster id *cid* along with the node coordinate information *ncoord*, that is, output KV $\langle cid, ncoord \rangle$.

K-Means Reduce: For each key *cid* (cluster id), update the cluster centroid coordinate by averaging all the nodes' coordinates that belong to *cid*, and output *cid* along with the cluster's updated centroid coordinate *ccoord*, that is, output KV $\langle cid, ncoord \rangle$.

3.1.2.3 Matrix Power Iteration

Square matrices can be multiplied by themselves repeatedly. This repeated multiplication can be described as a power of the matrix, that is, $M^k = \prod_1^k M$. This iterative process is called *matrix power iteration* (MPI). The operation of each iteration is matrix multiplication, that is, $M^k = M \times N$, where $N = M^{k-1}$. If M is a matrix with element m_{ij} in row i and column j, and N is a matrix with element n_{jk} in row j and column k, then the product $P = MN$ is the matrix P with element p_{ik} in row i and column k, where $p_{ik} = \sum_j m_{ij} n_{jk}$.

In the MapReduce framework, we use two map–reduce phases to perform the matrix multiplication,* which forms each iteration. In the first phase, the map extracts the columns of M and the rows of N, and the reduce joins column j of M and row j of N together. In the second phase, the map multiplies a column vector with the joined row vector to obtain a matrix, and the reduce sums these matrices to obtain the final result matrix. The map and reduce operations in each iteration are described as follows.

MPI Map 1: For each key (i, j), send each matrix element m_{ij} of M to the KV $\langle j, (M, i, m_{ij}) \rangle$. For each key (j, k), send each matrix element n_{jk} of N to the KV $\langle j, (N, k, n_{jk}) \rangle$.

MPI Reduce 1: For each key j, collect its list of associated values
$$\left\langle j, \left[\left(M, i_1, m_{i_1 j} \right), \left(M, i_2, m_{i_2 j} \right), \ldots, \left(N, k_1, n_{jk_1} \right), \left(N, k_2, n_{jk_2} \right), \ldots \right] \right\rangle.$$

MPI Map 2: Take the output KV of Reduce 1. For each value that comes from M, say (M, i, m_{ij}), and each value that comes from N, say (N, k, n_{jk}), produce the KV $\langle (i, k), m_{ij} n_{jk} \rangle$. It will output all the permutations $\left\langle (i_1, k_1), m_{i_1 j} n_{jk_1} \right\rangle$, $\left\langle (i_1, k_2), m_{i_1 j} n_{jk_2} \right\rangle, \ldots, \left\langle (i_2, k_1), m_{i_2 j} n_{jk_1} \right\rangle, \ldots$

MPI Reduce 2: For each key (i, k), produce the sum of the list of values associated with this key. The result KV is $\langle (i, k), p_{ik} \rangle$, where $p_{ik} = \sum_j m_{ij} n_{jk}$.

3.1.3 PROPERTIES OF ITERATIVE COMPUTATIONS IN MAPREDUCE

Through these examples, we have several observations about writing iterative algorithms in Hadoop MapReduce.

- **Iterative Data Flow.** MapReduce exploits a batched processing model. By using MapReduce to implement an iterative algorithm, the iterative loop is missing. On the other hand, to emulate an iterative data flow, an iterative algorithm is implemented by a series of MapReduce jobs. Each iteration corresponds to one or more jobs. The next job's input is the previous job's output. The map/reduce operations in all iterations are the same.

- **Dynamic State Data vs. Static Structure Data.** Iterative computation involves two kinds of data, the *state data* and the *structure data*. During the iterative computation, the state data is iteratively updated (e.g., the PageRank scores in PageRank, the centroids in K-means, or the matrix multiplier $N = M^{k-1}$ in MPI), while the structure data is iteration-invariant (e.g., the Web linkage graph in PageRank, the point coordinates in K-means, or the basic matrix M in MPI). To process these data in MapReduce, both the dynamic state data and the static structure data are represented by KVs (i.e., state KVs and structure

---

* http://infolab.stanford.edu/ullman/mmds/book.pdf.

KVs). Then, a series of MapReduce jobs update the state KVs based on the structure KVs.

- **Use of State/Structure KVs.** In each iteration, a mapper operating on a structure KV produces intermediate KVs based the state KVs, and a reducer updates a state KV. For example, in PageRank, the mapper operating on each node needs a node's PageRank score (state KV) and its outgoing neighbors (structure KV), and the reducer updates a node's PageRank score (state KV); In K-means, the mapper operating on each point needs the coordinates of all centroids (state KVs) and its own coordinate (structure KV), and the reducer updates a centroid's coordinate (state KV); In MPI, the mapper 2 operating on each column of M needs the jth column of N (state KV) and the jth column of M (structure KV), and the reducer 2 updates a column of N (state KV).

- **Mappings between Reducers and Mappers.** The map function operates on a structure KV and produces intermediate results based on one or more state KVs. Accordingly, a structure KV has different mappings with the state KVs. For example, in PageRank, the mapper operates on a node's PageRank score and the same node's outgoing neighbors, which is "one-to-one" mapping. In K-means, the mapper operates on a point and all centroids, which is "one-to-all" mapping. In MPI, the mapper 1 operates on an entry (i, j) of M and the entries of the jth row of N, which is "one-to-more" mapping. To sum up, a mapper operates on a structure KV, and a reducer updates a state KV. That is, the mappings between a reducer of the ith job and the mappers of the $(i + 1)$th job can be different.

These observations reflect the properties of iterative computations in MapReduce, which are very helpful. Programmers can first find the state/structure KVs and then define the iterative data flow to design the MapReduce programs. Moreover, these properties are useful for us to design an efficient programming model for iterative computations. iMapReduce is proposed based on these properties.

3.1.4 Limited Support of Iterative Computations by MapReduce

As described above, MapReduce can be used to implement iterative algorithms. However, MapReduce has limited support for iterative computations. We list three performance penalties of implementing iterative algorithms in Hadoop MapReduce.

1. The operations in all iterations are the same. Nevertheless, MapReduce implementation starts one/more new job(s) for each iteration, which involves repeated task initializations and cleanups. Moreover, these jobs have to load the input data from DFS and dump the output data to DFS repeatedly. It is known that Hadoop usually has around 20 seconds of start-up overhead [7]. A series of jobs might result in the unnecessary **job startup overhead**.

2. The map tasks in an iteration cannot start before finishing all the reduce tasks in the previous iteration. The main loop in the MapReduce implementation requires the completion of the previous iteration job before starting the next iteration job. However, the map tasks should be started as soon as

their input data are available. This limitation results in the unnecessary **synchronization overhead**.

3. MapReduce framework cannot separate the state data from the structure data. The structure data is shuffled in each iteration between map and reduce, despite the fact that it remains the same across all iterations. This results in the unnecessary **communication overhead**.

The synchronization overhead and the static data communication overhead have been studied and measured in [21]. iMapReduce aims to address these limitations and provides an efficient distributed computing framework for implementing iterative algorithms.

3.2 PROGRAMMING MODEL

Based on the observations and analysis, we are aware of the limitations of implementing iterative algorithms in Hadoop MapReduce. To overcome these performance penalties, iMapReduce is proposed. The design goals of iMapReduce are as follows:

- **Goal 1: Supporting iterative processing in one job.** In the MapReduce implementations, a series of MapReduce jobs consisting of map tasks and reduce tasks are scheduled. Figure 3.1a shows the data flow in the MapReduce implementation. Each MapReduce job has to load the input data from DFS before the map operation and dump the output data to DFS after the reduce operation. In the next iteration, the map function loads the iterated data from DFS again

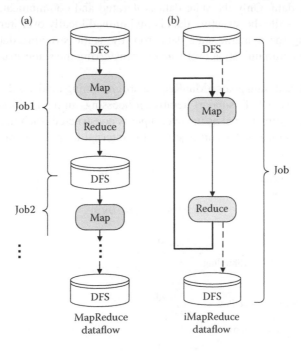

FIGURE 3.1   Data flow of (a) MapReduce and (b) iMapReduce.

and repeats the process. However, one design goal of iMapReduce is to support iterative processing in a single job. That is, the reduce output is fed to the map for next round iteration, and the map/reduce operations are kept executing till the iteration is terminated. Figure 3.1b shows the data flow in iMapReduce. Only one job is scheduled. The dashed line indicates that the data loading from DFS happens only once in the initialization stage, and the output data are written to DFS only once when the iteration terminates. By supporting iterative processing in one job, we can avoid the job startup overhead.

- **Goal 2: Executing map tasks asynchronously.** In MapReduce implementations, two synchronization barriers exist, during map-to-reduce shuffles and between MapReduce jobs, respectively. Due to the synchronization barrier between jobs, the map tasks of the next iteration job cannot start before the completion of the previous iteration job, which requires the completion of all reduce tasks. However, a map task is fed with a reduce task. The map task can start its execution as soon as its input from a reduce task is ready, rather than waiting for the completion of all reduce tasks. iMapReduce schedules the execution of map tasks asynchronously. By enabling the asynchronous execution of the map tasks, we can avoid the synchronization overhead.

- **Goal 3: Separating dynamic state data from static structure data.** Even though the structure data is unchanged from iteration to iteration, the MapReduce implementations reload and reshuffle the unchanged structure data in each iteration, which poses considerable communication overhead. iMapReduce differentiates the iteratively updated state data from the static structure data. Only the state data is iterated and communicated in each iteration, while the structure data is maintained locally over iterations. By separating the dynamic state data from the static structure data, we can avoid the communication overhead on transferring the static structure data.

Based on these design goals, iMapReduce programming model is designed, which is shown in Figure 3.2. To support iterative processing, an internal loop that makes the reduce output directly fed as the map input is constructed, such that the data can be iterated automatically. By constructing this internal loop, the iterative algorithm

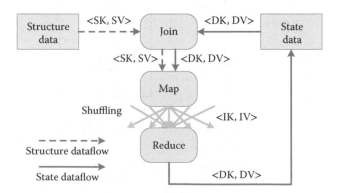

FIGURE 3.2   iMapReduce programming model.

can be implemented in a single job. Moreover, the map operation of the next iteration can start without the synchronization barriers between jobs. Thus, Goal 1 and Goal 2 are achieved. Additionally, to achieve Goal 3, the iterated state data is separated from the static structure data. The read-only structure data is queried in each iteration but never changed, while the state data is updated in each iteration. Correspondingly, two data flows, the state data flow (composed of state KVs) and the structure data flow (composed of structure KVs), are existing in iMapReduce.

Except for the user defined functions (UDF) map and reduce, users have to implement join in iMapReduce. The UDF join is used for users to specify the mapping rules between the reducers and the mappers, based on which iMapReduce combines the state data flow and the structure data flow before map operation.

3.3 SYSTEM DESIGN

iMapReduce is designed and implemented by modifying Hadoop MapReduce. Hadoop MapReduce framework is changed for iterative processing. The iterated state data and the static structure data are separated with the built-in framework support. Besides, iteration termination, fault tolerance, and load balancing are supported in iMapReduce.

3.3.1 OVERVIEW

Figure 3.3 shows the system overview of iMapReduce. An iMapReduce job will launch multiple map tasks and reduce tasks. Note that, the number of map tasks and

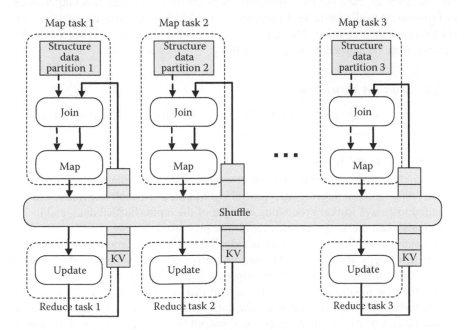

FIGURE 3.3 System overview.

the number of reduce tasks should be equal. The join operation and the map operation are performed in map tasks. The reduce operation is performed in reduce tasks. A reduce task is connected to a local map task correspondingly for iterative processing. The paired map task and reduce task are refereed as a *MRPair*. These map/reduce tasks are persistent tasks that keep alive during the entire iterative process.

An application's structure data is partitioned and distributed to map tasks before iterative processing. These structure data partitions are maintained locally in each map task. Each structure data partition contains a set of structure KVs. As we know, the structure KVs combined with the state KVs will be used for map operation. Each structure KV can be mapped to one or more state KVs based on a mapping rule (specified by join operation, i.e., "one-to-one," "one-to-all," or "one-to-more"). As the structure KVs are distributed, the problem is, given a set of structure KVs (i.e., structure data partition) located in a map task, how to send their corresponding state KVs to that map task, where they will be combined for the map operation.

Suppose the structure KVs are partitioned according to a hash function F. That is, a structure KV with key SK is assigned to a partition according to $p = F(SK, n)$, where p is the partition id and n is the total number of partitions. Map task p is assigned for processing partition p. Since reduce task p is connected to map task p, the output of reduce task p should contain the state KVs corresponding to the structure KVs maintained in map task p. The output of reduce task is determined by the reduce input, which is generated in the shuffling phase. iMapReduce carefully picks the partition function in the shuffling phase, such that the map output KVs are shuffled to the correct reduce task, where these map output KVs are converted to the state KVs that correspond to the local maintained structure KVs in the paired map task. This approach works for the "one-to-one" case and the "one-to-more" case. For the "one-to-all" mapping case, the reduce task output should be broadcasted to all map tasks. In summary, each MRPair performs the iterative computation on a data partition. The necessary information exchanged between MRPairs occurs during the mappers-to-reducers shuffling.

3.3.2   Iterative Processing

To support iterative processing in iMapReduce, a few changes to the original Hadoop framework are made.

3.3.2.1   Persistent Tasks

A map/reduce task is a computing process with a specified map/reduce operation applied on a subset of data records. In Hadoop MapReduce, each map/reduce task is assigned to a slave worker processing a subset of the input/shuffled data, and its life cycle ends when the assigned data records are processed.

In contrast, each map/reduce task in iMapReduce is persistent. A persistent map/reduce task keeps alive during the entire iterative process. When all the assigned data records of a persistent task are processed, the task becomes dormant, waiting for the new input/shuffled data. For a map task, it waits for the results from the reduce tasks, and is reactivated when the data from the reduce task arrives. For the reduce task, it waits for all the map tasks' output and is reactivated synchronously as in MapReduce.

To implement persistent tasks, there should be enough *available task slots*. The number of available map/reduce task slots is the number of map/reduce tasks that the framework can accommodate (allows to be executed) simultaneously. In Hadoop MapReduce, the master splits a job into many small map/reduce tasks, the number of map/reduce tasks executed simultaneously cannot be larger than the number of the available map/reduce task slots (the default number in Hadoop is 2 per slave worker). Once a slave worker completes an assigned task, it requests another one from the master. iMapReduce requires to guarantee that there are sufficient available task slots for all the persistent tasks to start at the beginning. This means that the task granularity should be set coarser to have fewer tasks. Clearly, this might make load balancing challenging. iMapReduce addresses this issue with a load balancing scheme, which will be introduced later.

3.3.2.2 Passing State Data from Reduce to Map

In MapReduce, the output of a reduce task is written to DFS and might be used later in the next MapReduce job. In contrast, iMapReduce allows the state data to be passed from the reduce task to the map task directly, so as to trigger the join operation with the structure data and to start the map execution for the next iteration. To do so, iMapReduce builds persistent socket connections from the reduce tasks to the map tasks.

3.3.2.3 Joining State Data with Structure Data

iMapReduce differentiates the structure data from the state data and processes them separately. iMapReduce will combine them before using them in the map operation. By specifying the partition of the structure data and customizing the shuffling of the state data correspondingly, a reduce task's output state KVs and their corresponding structure KVs are always in the same map task. In each iteration, before executing the map operation, for each state KV, a join operation that extracts its corresponding structure KV is performed. Then they are used together in the map operation.

iMapReduce achieves automatic join by leveraging sorted files. With the support of MapReduce framework, the state KVs from reduce task to map task are sorted in the order of their keys. Suppose a structure key is SK and its corresponding state key is $cord(SK)$, iMapReduce sorts the structure KVs of each structure data partition in the order of $cord(SK)$. Therefore, given the sorted state data flow, by sequentially parsing the structure data partition file once, all the corresponding state KVs and structure KVs are extracted. The joined state KV and structure KV are provided to map operation as the input parameters. Users can concentrate on implementing the map operation, without worrying about the maintenance of the structure data in their iterative algorithm implementations.

3.3.2.4 Asynchronous Execution of Map Tasks

In MapReduce iterative algorithm implementations, there are two synchronization barriers in each iteration; one is between mappers and reducers and another one is between MapReduce jobs. Due to the synchronization barrier between jobs, the map tasks of the next iteration job cannot start before the completion of the previous iteration job, which requires the completion of all reduce tasks. However, since the map task needs only the state data from its corresponding reduce task, a map task can start its execution as soon as its input state data arrives, without waiting for the other reduce tasks' completion. iMapReduce schedules the execution of map tasks asynchronously. By enabling the asynchronous execution, the synchronization barriers between MapReduce jobs are eliminated, which can further speed up the iterative process.

To implement the asynchronous execution, iMapReduce builds a persistent socket connection from a reduce task to its paired map task. In a naive implementation, as soon as the reduce task produces a state KV, it is immediately sent back to its paired map task. Upon receipt of the data from the reduce task, the map task performs the map operation on the data immediately. However, the eager triggering in the native implementation will result in frequent context switches that impact performance. Thus, a buffer is designed in each reduce task. As the buffer size grows larger than a threshold, the buffered state KVs are sent to the paired map task.

3.3.3 ITERATION TERMINATION

Iterative algorithm typically stops when a termination condition is met. Users terminate an iterative process in two ways: (1) fixed number of iterations: iterative algorithm stops after a fixed number of iterations; (2) bounding the distance between two consecutive iterations: iterative algorithm stops when the difference between two consecutive iterations is less than a threshold.

iMapReduce performs termination check after each iteration. To terminate the iterative computation by a fixed number of iterations, it is straightforward to record the iteration number in each task and terminate it when the number exceeds a threshold. To bound the distance between two consecutive iterations, the reduce tasks save the output from two consecutive iterations and calculate the distance. Users should specify the distance measurement method, for example, Euclidean distance, Manhattan distance, etc. To obtain a global distance value from all reduce tasks, the local distance values from the reduce tasks are merged by the master. The master then checks the termination condition to decide whether to terminate or not. If the termination condition is satisfied, the master will notify all the persistent map/reduce tasks to terminate their executions.

3.3.4 FAULT TOLERANCE

Fault tolerance is important in a server cluster environment. MapReduce splits a job into multiple fine-grained tasks. Whenever a task failure is detected, the failed task is rescheduled. Moreover, MapReduce provides speculative execution [19] that is designed on clusters of heterogeneous hardware. Speculative execution starts another concurrent task to process the same data block if extra resources are available, where the first completed task's output is preferred.

iMapReduce relies on checkpointing mechanism for fault tolerance. For each map task, the structure data block has several replicas on DFS. For each reduce task, the output state data as the checkpoint are dumped to DFS every few iterations. In case there is a failure, iMapReduce recovers from the most recent checkpoint, instead of starting the iterative process from scratch. Since the state data are relatively small, it is expected to consume little time for dumping these data to DFS (i.e., make several copies on several other machines for data redundancy). Note that the checkpointing process is performed in parallel with the iterative processing.

3.3.5   LOAD BALANCING

In MapReduce, the master decomposes a submitted job into multiple tasks. The slave worker completes one task followed by requesting another one from the master. This "complete-and-then-feed" task scheduling mechanism makes good use of computing resources. In iMapReduce, all tasks are assigned to slave workers in the beginning at one time, since tasks are persistent in iMapReduce. This one-time assignment conflicts with MapReduce's task scheduling strategy, so that iMapReduce cannot confer the benefit from the original MapReduce framework.

Lack of load balancing support may lead to several problems: (1) Even though the initial input data are evenly partitioned among workers, it does not necessarily mean that the computation workload is evenly distributed due to the skewed degree distribution. (2) Even though the computation workload is evenly distributed among workers, it still cannot guarantee the best utilization of computing resources, since a large cluster might consist of heterogeneous servers [19].

To address these problems, iMapReduce performs *task migration* when the workload is unbalanced among workers. After each iteration, each reduce task sends an iteration completion report to the master, which contains the reduce task id, the iteration number, and the processing time of that iteration. Upon receipt of all the reduce tasks' reports, the master calculates the average processing time. Based on the average time, the master calculates the time deviation of each worker and identifies the slower workers and the faster workers. If the time deviation is larger than a threshold, a MRPair in the slowest worker is migrated to the fastest worker in the following three steps. The master (1) kills an MRPair in the slow worker, (2) launches a new MRPair in the fast worker, and (3) sends a rollback command to the other map/reduce tasks. All the map/reduce tasks that receive the rollback command skip their current processing. The rolled back map tasks reload the latest checkpointed state data from DFS and proceed. The new launched map tasks load not only the state data but also the corresponding structure data from DFS.

3.4   ALGORITHM IMPLEMENTATION

iMapReduce supports the implementation of iterative algorithms and is compatible with traditional Hadoop MapReduce. Users can turn on iterative processing functionalities for implementing iterative algorithms or turn them off for implementing Hadoop MapReduce jobs as usual.

3.4.1   IMAPREDUCE API

To implement an iterative algorithm in iMapReduce, users should implement the following interfaces, which is slightly changed from Hadoop API (written in Java):

- `StateK join(StructureK)`.
  The join interface is used to specify the mapping rules between state KVs and structure KVs. Given a structure key, a corresponding state key is returned.
- `void map(StateK, StateV, StructureV)`.
  The map interface in iMapReduce has one input key StateK and two input values: the state data value StateV and the structure data value StructureV. iMapReduce framework joins the state KVs and the structure KVs automatically. The StateV and the StructureV are the joined state value and structure value.
- `void reduce(IK, [IV])`.
  The reduce interface in iMapReduce is the same as that in MapReduce, with an input key IK and a list of input values [IV]. Note that the input value only contains state data information but no structure data information. It will output a state KV.
- `float distance(StateK, PrevStateV, CurrStateV)`.
  Users implement the distance interface to specify the distance measurement using a state key's previous state value PrevStateV and its current state value CurrStateV. The returned float values for different keys are accumulated to obtain the distance value between two consecutive iterations' results. For example, Manhattan distance and Euclidean distance can be used to quantify the difference.

In addition, iMapReduce provides the following job parameters (i.e., JobConf's parameters) to help users specify an iterative computation:

- `job.set("mapred.iterjob.state.path," path)`.
  Set the DFS path of the initial state data.
- `job.set("mapred.iterjob.structure.path," path)`.
  Set the DFS path of the structure data.
- `job.setInt("mapred.iterjob.maxiter," n)`.
  Set the maximum iteration number n to terminate an iterative computation.
- `job.setFloat("mapred.iterjob.disthresh," d)`.
  Set the distance threshold as d, which is used to terminate an iterative computation.

3.4.2 PageRank Implementation Example

To show how to implement iterative algorithms in iMapReduce, an example of PageRank algorithm implementation code is given in Figure 3.4. In PageRank, the state KVs and the structure KVs have "one-to-one" mapping. Each node has a PageRank score as the state value and its neighbors set as the structure value. The join interface specifies that node n's structure data corresponds node n's state data (Line 1). In the map function (Line 2–5), each node's PageRank score is evenly distributed to its neighbors and retaining $\dfrac{(1-d)}{N}$ by itself, where N is the total number

StateK=Join(StructureK)
Input: StructureK *n*
  1: return n;

Map(StateK, StateV, StructureV)
Input: StateK *n*, StateV *R* (*n*), StructureV *adj* (*n*)
  2: **for** link in *adj* (*n*) **do**
  3:     output(link.endnode, (d × *R* (*n*))/|*adj* (*n*)|);
  4: **end for**
  5: output(*n*, (1-d)/N);

Reduce(IK, [IV])
Input: Key *n*, Set [*values*]
  6: output(*n*, sum([*values*]));

float=Distance(StateK, PrevStateV, CurrStateV)
Input: StateK *n*, PrevStateV *R1* (*n*), CurrStateV *R2* (*n*)
  7: return abs(*R1* (*n*) - *R2* (*n*));

Main
  8: Job job = new Job();
  9: job.setJoin(Join);
  10: job.setMap(Map);
  11: job.setReduce(Reduce);
  12: job.setDistance(Distance);
  13: job.set("mapred.iterjob.state.path", "hdfs://.../initRankings");
  14: job.set("mapred.iterjob.structure.path", "hdfs://.../adjacencylists");
  15: job.setFloat("mapred.iterjob.disthresh", 0.01);
  16: job.submit();

FIGURE 3.4   PageRank implementation in iMapReduce.

of nodes in the graph. In the reduce function (Line 6), for each node, it updates its PageRank score by combining the partial PageRank scores from its incoming neighbors and its own retained score. For the distance measurement, the distance function calculates the Manhattan distance (Line 7). Additionally, users should specify the location of the initial state data (Line 13), as well as the location of the structure data (Line 14). iMapReduce supports automatically structure data partition for a few input data formats (including weighted and unweighted graphs). Users can first format their input data file in our supported formats. By using the distance-based termination check method, the iterative computation will terminate when the distance is smaller than 0.01 (Line 15).

3.5   PERFORMANCE

iMapReduce has much better performance than Hadoop on iterative computations. Some experiments have been conducted. Four iterative algorithms, Single Source Shortest Path (SSSP), PageRank, K-means, and MPI, are considered for comparing iMapReduce with Hadoop. The description of the detailed experiment environment and the data sets can be found in [21].

With 20 EC2 m1.small instances, SSSP and PageRank are performed on different-size graphs. SSSP is executed with 10 iterations on the three synthetic graphs SSSP-s, SSSP-m, SSSP-l. Figure 3.5a shows the results of SSSP. The iMap-Reduce implementation reduces running time to 23.2%, 37.0%, and 38.6% of Hadoop MapReduce implementations for data set SSSP-s, SSSP-m, and SSSP-l, respectively. Similarly, PageRank is executed with 10 iterations on the three synthetic graphs PageRank-s, PageRank-m, and PageRank-l. The results are shown in Figure 3.5b.

Figure 3.6a shows the K-means running time limited in 10 iterations, which are performed on Last.FM data set and on local cluster with 4 nodes. iMapReduce achieves about 1.2× speedup over Hadoop. The improvement is less significant than that is achieved for SSSP or PageRank. Nevertheless, this is under expectation since the implementation of K-means needs to shuffle static structure data and has to execute map operations synchronously. Figure 3.6b shows the MPI running time on local cluster with 4 nodes. MPI is performed on a synthetic matrix (1000 × 1000) for 5 iterations. As shown, iMapReduce can achieve about 10% speedup over Hadoop.

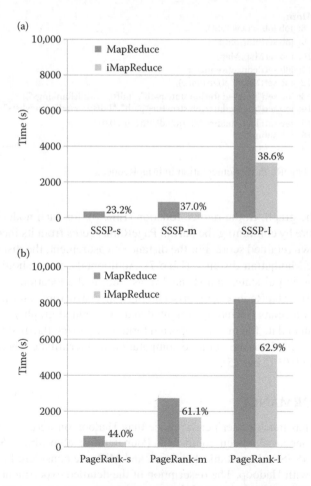

FIGURE 3.5   The running time of SSSP (a) and PageRank (b) on different-size graphs.

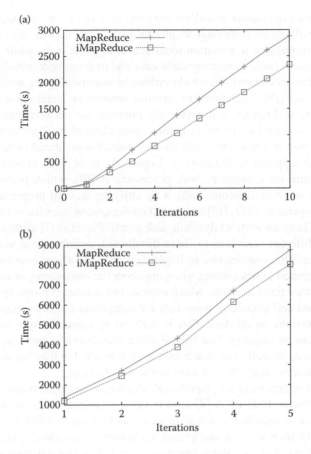

FIGURE 3.6 The running time of K-means (a) and MPI (b).

3.6 RELATED WORK

MapReduce, as a popular distributed framework for data-intensive computation, has gained considerable attention over the past few years [4]. The framework has been extended for diverse application requirements. MapReduce Online [3] pipelines map/reduce operations and performs online aggregation to support efficient online queries, which directly inspires our work.

To support implementing large-scale iterative algorithms, there are a number of studies proposing new distributed computing frameworks for iterative processing [2,5,8–10,13,14,16,17,20].

A class of these efforts targets on managing static data efficiently. Design patterns for running efficient graph algorithms in MapReduce have been introduced in [10]. They partition the static graph adjacency list into *n* parts and pre-store them on DFS. However, since the MapReduce framework arbitrarily assigns reduce tasks to workers, accessing the graph adjacency list can involve remote reads. This cannot guarantee local access to the static data. HaLoop [2] is proposed aiming at iterative processing on a large cluster. It realizes the join of the static data and the state data by explicitly specifying an additional MapReduce job, and relies on the task scheduler and caching techniques to maintain local access to static data, while iMapReduce relies on persistent tasks to manage static data and to avoid task initialization.

Some studies accelerate iterative algorithms by maintaining the iterated state data in memory. Spark [18] is developed to optimize iterative and interactive computation. It uses caching techniques to dramatically improve the performance for repeated operations. The main idea in Spark is the construction of *resilient distributed data set* (RDD), which is a read-only collection of objects maintained in memory across iterations and supports fault recovery. Logothetis et al. [12] presents a generalized architecture for continuous bulk processing (CBP), which performs iterative computations in an incremental fashion by unifying stateful programming with a data-parallel operator. CIEL [15] supports data-dependent iterative or recursive algorithms by building an abstract dynamic task graph. Piccolo [17] allows computation running on different machines to share distributed, mutable state via a key-value table interface. This enables one to implement iterative algorithms that access in-memory distributed tables without worrying about the consistency of the data. Priter [22] enables prioritized iteration, which exploits the dominant property of some portion of the data and schedules them first for computation, rather than blindly performs computations on all data. This is realized by maintaining a state table and a priority queue in memory. Our iMapReduce framework is built on Hadoop, the iterated state data as well as the static data are maintained in files but not in memory. Therefore, it is more scalable and more resilient to failures.

Some other efforts focus on graph-based iterative algorithms, an important class of iterative algorithms. PEGASUS [9] models those seemingly different graph iterative algorithms as a generalization of matrix-vector multiplication (GIM-V). By exploring matrix property, such as block multiplication, clustered edges and diagonal block iteration, it can achieve 5 times faster performance over the regular job. Pregel [13] chooses a pure message passing model to process graphs. In each iteration, a vertex can, independently of other vertices, receive messages sent to it in the previous iteration, send messages to other vertices, modify its own and its outgoing edges' states, and mutate the graph's topology. Using this model, processing large graphs is expressive and easy to program. iMapReduce exploits the property that the map and reduce functions operate on the same type of keys, that is, node id, to accelerate graph-based iterative algorithms.

The most relevant work is that of Ekanayake et al., who proposed Twister [5,6], which employs stream-based MapReduce implementation that supports iterative applications. Twister employs novel ideas of loading the input data only once in the initialization stage and performing iterative map–reduce processing by long running map/reduce daemons. iMapReduce differs from Twister mainly on that Twister stores intermediate data in memory, while iMapReduce stores intermediate data in files. Twister loads all data in distributed memory for fast data access and grounds on the assumption that data sets and intermediate data can fit into the distributed memory of the computing infrastructure. iMapReduce aims at providing a MapReduce based iterative computing framework running on a cluster of commodity machines where each node has limited memory resources. In iMapReduce, the intermediate data, including the intermediate results, the shuffled data between map and reduce, and the static data, are all stored in files. This key difference results in different implementation mechanisms, including different data transfers and different joining techniques of static data and state data. Furthermore, iMapReduce supports asynchronous map execution, which further improves performance. Besides, iMapReduce is implemented based on Hadoop MapReduce. The iterative applications in Hadoop can be easily modified to run on iMapReduce.

3.7 SUMMARY

Hadoop MapReduce exploiting batched processing model has a few limitations on supporting iterative computations. iMapReduce extends MapReduce framework, which aims at improving the performance of iterative computations under a large cluster environment. iMapReduce extracts the common features of iterative algorithms and provides the built-in support for iterative processing. In particular, iMapReduce (1) builds an internal loop from reduce to map within a job to avoid the job startup overhead, (2) allows asynchronous map task execution to avoid the synchronization overhead, and (3) separates the iterated state data from the static structure data to avoid the communication overhead. Accordingly, the system performance is greatly improved through these optimizations.

ACKNOWLEDGMENTS

This work was partially supported by U.S. NSF grants (CCF-1018114, CNS-1217284), National Natural Science Foundation of China (61300023), and Fundamental Research Funds for the Central Universities (N120416001, N120816001).

REFERENCES

1. Sergey Brin and Lawrence Page. The anatomy of a large-scale hypertextual web search engine. *Computer Networks and ISDN Systems*, 30:107–117, 1998.
2. Yingyi Bu, Bill Howe, Magdalena Balazinska, and Michael D. Ernst. Haloop: Efficient iterative data processing on large clusters. *Proceedings of International Conference on Very Large Database (VLDB'10)*, 3:285–296, September 2010.
3. Tyson Condie, Neil Conway, Peter Alvaro, Joseph M. Hellerstein, Khaled Elmeleegy, and Russell Sears. Mapreduce online. In *Proceedings of the 7th USENIX Conference on Networked Systems Design and Implementation (NSDI'10)*, pages 21–21, 2010.
4. Jeffrey Dean and Sanjay Ghemawat. MapReduce: Simplified data processing on large clusters. *Communications of the ACM*, 51:107–113, January 2008.
5. Jaliya Ekanayake, Hui Li, Bingjing Zhang, Thilina Gunarathne, Seung-Hee Bae, Judy Qiu, and Geoffrey Fox. Twister: A runtime for iterative MapReduce. In *Proceedings of the 1st International Workshop on MapReduce and its Applications (MAPREDUCE'10)*, pages 810–818, 2010.
6. Jaliya Ekanayake, Shrideep Pallickara, and Geoffrey Fox. MapReduce for data intensive scientific analyses. In *Proceedings of the 4th IEEE International Conference on eScience (eScience'08)*, pages 277–284, 2008.
7. Jiewen Huang, Daniel J. Abadi, and Kun Ren. Scalable SPARQL querying of large rdf graphs. In *VLDB'2011: Proceedings of the 37th International Conference on Very Large Data Bases*. VLDB Endowment, 2011.

8. Karthik Kambatla, Naresh Rapolu, Suresh Jagannathan, and Ananth Grama. Asynchronous algorithms in mapreduce. In *Proceedings of the 2010 IEEE International Conference on Cluster Computing (Cluster'10)*, pages 245–254, 2010.

9. U Kang, Charalampos E. Tsourakakis, and Christos Faloutsos. Pegasus: A peta-scale graph mining system implementation and observations. In *Proceedings of the 9th IEEE International Conference on Data Mining (ICDM'09)*, pages 229–238, 2009.

10. Jimmy Lin and Michael Schatz. Design patterns for efficient graph algorithms in mapreduce. In *Proceedings of the 8th Workshop on Mining and Learning with Graphs (MLG'10)*, pages 78–85, 2010.

11. Stuart P. Lloyd. Least squares quantization in pcm. *IEEE Transactions on Information Theory*, 28:129–136, 1982.

12. Dionysios Logothetis, Christopher Olston, Benjamin Reed, Kevin C. Webb, and Ken Yocum. Stateful bulk processing for incremental analytics. In *Proceedings of the 1st ACM Symposium on Cloud Computing (SOCC'10)*, pages 51–62, 2010.

13. Grzegorz Malewicz, Matthew H. Austern, Aart J.C. Bik, James C. Dehnert, Ilan Horn, Naty Leiser, and Grzegorz Czajkowski. Pregel: A system for large-scale graph processing. In *Proceedings of the 28th ACM Symposium on Principles of Distributed Computing (PODC'09)*, pages 6–146, 2009.

14. Derek G. Murray and Steven Hand. Scripting the cloud with skywriting. In *Proceedings of the 2nd USENIX Conference on Hot Topics in Cloud Computing (HotCloud'10)*, pages 12–12, 2010.

15. Derek G. Murray, Malte Schwarzkopf, Christopher Smowton, Steven Smith, Anil Madhavapeddy, and Steven Hand. Ciel: A universal execution engine for distributed dataflow computing. In *NSDI'11*, 2011.

16. Daniel Peng and Frank Dabe. Large-scale incremental processing using distributed transactions and notifications. In *Proceedings of the 9th Conference on Symposium on Opearting Systems Design and Implementation (OSDI'10)*, pages 1–15, 2010.

17. Russell Power and Jinyang Li. Piccolo: Building fast, distributed programs with partitioned tables. In *Proceedings of the 9th USENIX Symposium on Operating Systems Design and Implementation (OSDI'10)*, OSDI'10, pages 1–14, 2010.

18. Matei Zaharia, Mosharaf Chowdhury, Tathagata Das, Ankur Dave, Justin Ma, Murphy McCauley, Michael J. Franklin, Scott Shenker, and Ion Stoica. Resilient distributed data sets: A fault-tolerant abstraction for in-memory cluster computing. In *Proceedings of USEINX Symposium Networked Systems Design and Implementation (NSDI'12)*, 2012.

19. Matei Zaharia, Andy Konwinski, Anthony D. Joseph, Randy Katz, and Ion Stoica. Improving MapReduce performance in heterogeneous environments. In *Proceedings of the 8th USENIX Symposium on Operating Systems Design and Implementation (OSDI'08)*, pages 29–42, 2008.

20. Yanfeng Zhang, Qinxin Gao, Lixin Gao, and Cuirong Wang. iMapReduce: A distributed computing framework for iterative computation. In *Proceedings of the 1st International Workshop on Data Intensive Computing in the Clouds (DataCloud'11)*, pages 1112–1121, 2011.

21. Yanfeng Zhang, Qinxin Gao, Lixin Gao, and Cuirong Wang. iMapReduce: A distributed computing framework for iterative computation. *Journal of Grid Computing*, 10:47–68, March 2012.

22. Yanfeng Zhang, Qixin Gao, Lixin Gao, and Cuirong Wang. Priter: A distributed framework for prioritized iterative computations. In *Proceedings of the 2nd ACM Symposium on Cloud Computing (SOCC'11)*, pages 13:1–13:14, 2011.

4 Incremental MapReduce Computations

Pramod Bhatotia, Alexander Wieder, Umut A. Acar, and Rodrigo Rodrigues

CONTENTS

4.1 INTRODUCTION

Distributed processing of large data sets has become an important task in the life of various companies and organizations, for whom data analysis is an important vehicle to improve the way they operate. This area has attracted a lot of attention from both researchers and practitioners over the last few years, particularly after the introduction of the MapReduce paradigm for large-scale parallel data processing [19].

A usual characteristic of the data sets that are provided as inputs to large-scale data-processing jobs is that they do not vary dramatically over time. Instead, the same job is often invoked consecutively with small changes in this input from one run to the next. For instance, researchers have reported that the ratio between old and new data when processing consecutive web crawls may range from 10 to 1000× [28].

Motivated by this observation, there have been several proposals for large-scale *incremental* data-processing systems, such as Percolator [33] or CBP [28], to name a few early and prominent examples. In these systems, the programmer is able to devise an incremental update handler, which can store state across successive runs, and contains the logic to update the output as the program is notified about input changes. While this approach allows for significant improvements when compared with the "single-shot" approach, that is, re-processing all the data each time that part of the input changes or that inputs are added and deleted, it also has the downside of requiring programmers to adopt a new programming model and API. This has two negative implications. First, there is the programming effort to port a large set of existing applications to the new programming model. Second, it is often difficult to devise the logic for incrementally updating the output as the input changes: research in the area of dynamic algorithms (i.e., algorithms to solve problems that are formulated in terms of deltas to their input) shows that such algorithms can be very complex, even in cases where the normal, non-incremental algorithm was easy to devise [16,20].

In this chapter, we present an overview of our prior work on designing and building a system called Incoop for large-scale incremental computations [11]. Incoop extends the Hadoop open-source implementation of the MapReduce paradigm to run unmodified MapReduce programs in an incremental way. The design and implementation of Incoop is inspired by recent advances on self-adjusting computation [3,5,6,15,24], which offers a solution to the problem of automatic incrementalization of programs, and draws on techniques developed in that line of work. The idea behind Incoop is to enable the programmer to incrementalize automatically existing MapReduce programs without the need to make any modifications to the code. To this end, Incoop records information about previously executed MapReduce tasks so that it can be reused in future MapReduce computations when possible.

The basic approach taken by Incoop consists of (1) splitting the computation into subcomputations, where the natural candidate for a subcomputation is a MapReduce task; (2) memoizing the inputs and outputs of each subcomputation; and (3) in an incremental run, checking the inputs to a subcomputation and using the memoized output without rerunning the task when the input remains unchanged. Despite being a good starting point, this basic approach has several shortcomings that motivated us to introduce several technical innovations in Incoop, namely:

- **Incremental HDFS.** We introduce a file system called Inc-HDFS that provides a scalable way of identifying the deltas in the inputs of two consecutive job runs. This reuses an idea from the LBFS local file system [31], which is to avoid splitting the input into fixed-size chunks, and instead split it based on the contents such that small changes to the input keep most chunk boundaries. The new file system is able to achieve a large reuse of input chunks while maintaining compatibility with HDFS, which is the most common interface to provide the input to a job in Hadoop.
- **Contraction phase.** To avoid rerunning a large reduce task when only a small subset of its input changes, we introduce a new phase in the MapReduce

framework called the contraction phase. This consists of breaking up the Reduce task into smaller subcomputations that form an inverted tree, such that, when a small portion of the input changes, only the path from the corresponding leaf to the root needs to be recomputed.

- **Memoization-aware scheduler.** We modify the scheduler of Hadoop to take advantage of the locality of memoized results. The new scheduler uses a work stealing strategy to decrease the amount of data movement across machines when reusing memoized outputs, while still allowing tasks to execute on machines that are available.

We present an overview of the design and implementation of Incoop, and we report experimental results using five MapReduce applications. The results from this evaluation show that we achieve significant performance gains, while paying a modest cost during the initial run or during runs that cannot take advantage of previously computed results.

The rest of this chapter is organized as follows. We first present an overview of Incoop in Section 4.2. The system design is detailed in Sections 4.3, 4.4, and 4.5. We present the experimental evaluation in Section 4.6. Related work and conclusions are discussed in Sections 4.7 and 4.8, respectively.

4.2 SYSTEM OVERVIEW

We present first a basic design that we use as a starting point, highlight the limitations of this basic design, the challenges in overcoming them, and briefly overview the main ideas behind Incoop, which addresses the limitations of the basic design. Our basic strategy is to adapt the principles of self-adjusting computation to the MapReduce paradigm, and in particular to Hadoop. We start with some background on self-adjusting computation.

4.2.1 SELF-ADJUSTING COMPUTATION

Self-adjusting computation [3,5,6,15,24] offers a solution to the incremental-computation problem by enabling any computation to respond to changes in its data by efficiently recomputing only the subcomputations that are affected by the changes. To this end, a self-adjusting computation tracks dependencies between the inputs and the outputs of subcomputations, and in incremental runs, only rebuilds subcomputations affected (transitively) by modified inputs. To identify the affected subcomputations, the approach represents a computation as a dependency graph of subcomputations, where two subcomputations are data-dependent if one of them uses the output of the other as input and control-dependent if one takes place within the dynamic scope of another. Subcomputations are also memoized based on their inputs to enable reuse even if they are control-dependent on some affected subcomputation. Given the "delta," the modifications to the input, a *change-propagation algorithm* pushes the modifications through the dependency graph, rebuilding affected subcomputations, which it identifies based on both data and control dependencies. Before rebuilding a subcomputation, change propagation recovers subcomputations that can be reused, even partially, by using a computation memoization technique that remembers (and re-uses) not just input–output relationships but also the dependency graphs of memoized subcomputations [5].

The efficiency of a self-adjusting computation in responding to an input modification is determined by the stability of the computation. Informally speaking, we call a computation stable when the set of subcomputations performed on similar input data sets themselves are similar, that is, many of the subcomputations are in fact the same and thus can be reused. For a more precise definition of stability, we refer the interested reader to the previous work [3,27]. One way to ensure stability is to make sure that (1) the computation is divided into small subcomputations and (2) no long chain of dependencies exists between computations. Since MapReduce framework is naturally parallel, it naturally has short dependency chains at the granularity of tasks. As we will see, however, it can yield unstable computations, because a small change to the input can cause the input for many MapReduce tasks to change, and because reduce tasks can be large.

For the sake of simplicity in design and implementation, Incoop, does not construct the dependency graph of subcomputations explicitly, and thus does not perform change propagation on the dependency graph. Instead, the graph is recorded implicitly by memoizing subcomputations—MapReduce tasks—and change propagation is performed by revisiting all subcomputations and reusing those that can be reused via memoization. While this approach simplifies the design and the implementation, it can yield asymptotically suboptimal performance, because it requires touching all subcomputations (for the purposes of memoization and reuse) even if they may not be affected by the input modifications. Since, however, subcomputations (tasks) are relatively large, the cost of reusing an unaffected subcomputation is small compared with rebuilding it. The approach therefore can perform well in practice (Section 4.6).

4.2.2 BASIC DESIGN

Our goal is to design a system for large-scale incremental data processing that is able to leverage the performance benefits of incremental computation, while also being transparent, meaning that it does not require changes to existing programs. In particular, we consider MapReduce programs for distributed large-scale data processing. We assume the reader is familiar with the MapReduce paradigm, and refer to prior publications on the subject for more information [19].

To achieve this goal, we apply the principles of self-adjusting computation to the MapReduce paradigm. To this end, we first need to decide what forms a subcomputation. The natural candidate in our system is to use MapReduce tasks as subcomputations; this makes it possible to view the data-flow graph of the MapReduce job as a subgraph of the dependency graph, which in addition has control dependencies. Since MapReduce frameworks implicitly keep track of this graph when implementing the data movement and synchronization between the various tasks, building the dependency graph becomes easy and natural.

This decision leads to our basic design, which is shown in Figure 4.1. In this design, the MapReduce scheduler orchestrates the execution of every MapReduce job normally, by spawning and synchronizing tasks and performing data movement as in a

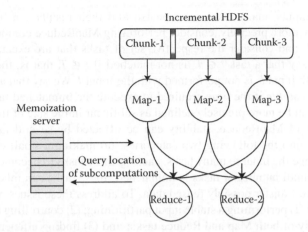

FIGURE 4.1   Basic design of Incoop.

normal MapReduce execution. To record and update the dependency graph implicitly, our design includes a *memoization server* that stores a mapping from the input of a previously run task to the location of the corresponding memoized output. When a task completes, its output is memoized persistently, and a mapping from the input to the location of the output is stored in the memoization server. Then, during an incremental run, when a task is instantiated, the memoization server is queried to check if the inputs to the task match those of a previous run. If so, the system reuses the outputs from the previous run. Otherwise, the task runs normally and the mapping from its input to the location of the newly produced output is stored in the memoization server.

This basic design raises a series of challenges, which we describe next. In subsequent sections, we describe our key technical contributions that we propose to address these challenges.

4.2.3   CHALLENGE: TRANSPARENCY

Self-adjusting computation requires knowing the modifications to the input to update the output. To this end, it requires a new interface for making changes to the input, so that the edits, which are clearly identified by the interface, can be used to trigger an incremental update. We wish to achieve the efficiency benefits of self-adjusting computation *transparently* without requiring the programmer to change the way they run MapReduce computations. This goal seems to conflict with the fact that HDFS (the system employed to store inputs to MapReduce computations in Hadoop) is an append-only file system, making it impossible to convey input deltas. To overcome this challenge, we store the inputs and outputs of consecutive runs in separate HDFS files and compute a delta between two HDFS files in a way that is scalable and performs well.

4.2.4   CHALLENGE: EFFICIENCY

To achieve efficient incremental updates, we must ensure that MapReduce computations remain stable under small changes to their input, meaning that, when executed with similar inputs, many tasks are repeated and their results can be reused. To define stability more precisely, consider performing MapReduce computations with inputs I and I' and consider the respective set of tasks that are executed, denoted T and T'. We say that a task $t \in T'$ is not matched if $t \notin T$, that is, the task that is performed with input I' is not performed with the input I. We say that a MapReduce computation is *stable* if the time required to execute the unmatched tasks is small, where small can be more precisely defined as sublinear in the size of the input.

In the case of MapReduce, stability can be affected by several factors, which we can group into the following two categories: (a) making a small change to the input can change the input to many tasks, causing these tasks to become unmatched; (b) even if a small number of tasks is unmatched, these tasks can take a long time to execute or to transfer possibly reused data. To address these issues, we introduce techniques for (1) performing a stable input partitioning; (2) controlling the granularity and stability of both Map and Reduce tasks; and (3) finding efficient scheduling mechanisms to avoid unnecessary movement of memoized data.

Stable input partitioning. To see why using HDFS as an input to MapReduce jobs leads to unstable computations, consider inserting a single data item in the middle of an input file. Since HDFS files are partitioned into fixed-sized chunks, this small change will shift each partition point following the input change by a fixed amount. If this amount is not a multiple of the chunk size, all subsequent map tasks will be unmatched. (On average, a single insert will affect half of all map tasks.) The problem gets even more challenging when we consider more complex changes, like the order of records being permuted; such changes can be common, for instance, if a crawler uses a depth-first strategy to crawl the web, and a single link change can move the position of an entire subtree in the input file. In this case, using standard algorithms to compute the differences between the two input files is not viable, since this would require running a polynomial-time algorithm (e.g., an edit-distance algorithm). We explain how our new file system called Inc-HDFS leads to stable input partitioning without compromising efficiency in Section 4.3.

Granularity control. A stable partitioning leads directly to the stability of map tasks. The input to the reduce tasks, however, is determined only by the outputs of the map tasks, since each reduce task processes all values produced in the map phase and associated with a given key. Consider, for instance, the case when a single key-value pair is added to a reduce task that processes a large number of values (e.g., linear in the size of the input). This is problematic since it causes the entire task to be recomputed. Furthermore, even if we found a way of dividing large reduce tasks into multiple smaller tasks, this per se would not solve the problem, since we still need to aggregate the results of the smaller tasks in a way that avoids a large recomputation. Thus, we need a way to (i) split the reduce task into smaller tasks and (ii) eliminate potentially long (namely linear-size) dependencies between these smaller tasks. We solve this problem with a new contraction phase, where reduce tasks are broken into subtasks organized in a tree. This breaks up the reduce task while ensuring that long dependencies between tasks are not formed, since all paths in the tree will be of logarithmic length. Section 4.4 describes our proposed approach.

Scheduling. To avoid a large movement of memoized data, it is important to schedule a task on the machine that stores the memoized results that are being reused. To ensure this, we introduce a modification to the scheduler used by Hadoop, to incorporate a notion of *affinity*. The new scheduler takes into account affinities between machines and tasks by keeping a record of which nodes have executed which tasks. This allows for scheduling tasks in a way that decreases the movement of memoized intermediate results, but at the cost of a potential degradation of job performance due to stragglers [38]. This is because a strict affinity of tasks results in deterministic scheduling, which prevents a lightly loaded node from performing work when the predetermined node is heavily loaded. Our scheduler therefore needs to strike a balance between work stealing and affinity of memoized results. Section 4.5 describes our modified scheduler.

4.3   INCREMENTAL HDFS

In this section, we present tncremental HDFS (Inc-HDFS), a distributed file system that enables stable incremental computations in Incoop, while keeping the interface provided by HDFS. Inc-HDFS builds on HDFS, but modifies the way that files are partitioned into chunks to use content-based chunking, a technique that was introduced in LBFS [31] for data deduplication. At a high-level, content-based chunking defines chunk boundaries based on finding certain patterns in the input, instead of using fixed-size chunks. As such, insertions and deletions cause small changes to the set of chunks. In the context of MapReduce, this ensures that the input to map tasks remains mostly unchanged, which translates into a stable recomputation. Figure 4.2 illustrates the differences in the strategies for determining chunk boundaries in HDFS and Inc-HDFS. To perform content-based chunking, we scan the entire file, examining the contents of a fixed-width window whose initial position is incremented one byte at a time. For each window, we compute its Rabin fingerprint, and if the fingerprint matches a certain pattern (called a *marker*) we place a chunk boundary at that position. In addition, this approach can be extended to avoid creating chunks that are too small or too large, which could affect the overheads and load balancing properties of MapReduce. (Note that all the system designer can tune is the likelihood of finding a marker, but the actual spacing depends on the input.) This is achieved by setting minimum and maximum chunk sizes: after we find a marker m_i at position p_i, we skip a fixed *offset* O and continue to scan the input after position $p_i + O$. In addition, we bound the chunk length by setting a marker after M content bytes even if no marker is found. Despite the possibility of affecting stability in rare cases, for example, when skipping the offset leads to skipping disjoint sets of markers in two consecutive runs, we found this to be a very limited problem in practice.

An important design decision is whether to perform chunking during the creation of the input or when the input is read by the map task. We chose the former because the cost of chunking can be amortized when chunking and producing the input data are done in parallel. This is relevant in cases where the generation of input data is not limited by the storage throughput.

To parallelize the chunking process on multicore machines, our implementation uses multiple threads, each of which starts the search for the marker at a different position. The markers that each thread finds cannot be used immediately to define the chunk boundaries, since some of them might have to be skipped due to the minimum

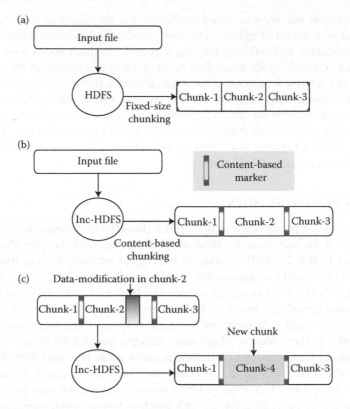

FIGURE 4.2 Chunking strategies in HDFS and Inc-HDFS. (a) Fixed-size chunking in HDFS. (b) Content-based chunking in Inc-HDFS. (c) Example of stable partitioning.

chunk size. Therefore, we collect the markers in a centralized list, and scan the list to determine which markers are skipped; the remaining ones form the chunk boundaries. Our experimental evaluation (Section 4.6.4) highlights the performance gains of this optimization, showing that it is instrumental in keeping the performance of Inc-HDFS close to that of HDFS.

4.4   INCREMENTAL MapReduce

This section presents our design for incremental MapReduce computations. We split the presentation by describing the map and reduce phases separately.

Incremental map. For the map phase, the main challenges have already been addressed by Inc-HDFS, which partitions data in such a way that the input to map tasks ensures stability and also allows for controlling the average granularity of the input that is provided to these tasks. In particular, this granularity can be adjusted by changing how likely it is to find a marker, and it should be set in a way that strikes a good balance between the following two characteristics: incurring the overhead associated with scheduling many map tasks when the average chunk size is low, and having to recompute a large map task if a small subset of its input changes when the average chunk size is large.

Therefore, the main job of map tasks in Incoop is to implement task-level memoiza-tion. To do this, after a map task runs, we store its results persistently (instead of discarding them after the job execution) and insert a corresponding reference to the result in the memoization server.

During incremental runs, map tasks query the memoization server to determine if their output has already been computed. If so, they output the location of the memoized result, and conclude. Figure 4.3 illustrates this process: part (a) describes the initial run and part (b) describes the incremental run where chunk 2 is modi-fied (and replaced by chunk 4) and the map tasks for chunks 1 and 3 can reuse the memoized results.

Incremental reduce. The reduce task processes the output of the map phase: each reduce task has an associated key k, collects all the key-value pairs generated by all map tasks for k, and applies the reduce function. For efficiency, we apply two levels of memoization in this case. First, we memoize the inputs and outputs of the entire reduce task to try to reuse these results in a single step. Second, we break down the reduce phase into a contraction phase followed by a smaller invocation of the reduce function to address the stability issues we discussed.

The first level of memoization is very similar to that of map tasks: the memoiza-tion server maintains a mapping from a hash of the input to the location of the result of the reduce task. A minor difference is that a reduce task receives input from several map tasks, and as such the key of that mapping is the concatenation of the collision-resistant hashes from all these outputs. For the reduce task to compute this key, instead of immediately copying the output from all map tasks, it fetches the hashes only to determine if the reduce task can be skipped entirely. Only if this is not the case the data is transferred from map to reduce tasks.

As we mentioned, this first level has the limitation that small changes in the input cause the entire reduce task to be re-executed, which can result in work that is linear

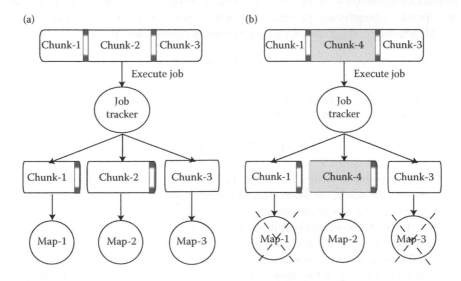

FIGURE 4.3   Incremental map tasks. (a) Initial run. (b) Incremental run.

in the size of the original input, even if the delta in the input is small. In fact it may be argued that the larger the reduce task the more likely it is that a part of its input may change. To prevent this stability problem, we need to find a way to control the granularity of the subcomputations in the reduce phase, and organize these subcomputations in way that avoids creating a long dependence chain between subcomputations, otherwise, a single newly computed subcomputation could also trigger a large amount of recomputation.

To reduce the granularity of reduce tasks, we propose a new *contraction phase*, which is run by reduce tasks. This new phase takes advantage of *combiners*, a feature of the MapReduce framework [18], also implemented by Hadoop, which originally aims at saving bandwidth by offloading part of the computation performed by the reduce task to the map task. To this end, the programmer specifies a combiner function, which is invoked by the map task, and pre-processes a part of the map output, that is, a set of ⟨key,value⟩ pairs, merging them into a smaller number of pairs. The signature of the combiner function uses the same input and output type to be interposed between the map and reduce phase. Its inputs and output arguments are a sequence of ⟨key,value⟩ pairs. In all the MapReduce applications we analyzed so far, the combiners and the reduce functions perform similar work.

The contraction phase uses combiners to break up reduce tasks into several applications of the combine function. In particular, we start by splitting the reduce input into chunks, and apply the combine function to each chunk. Then we recursively form chunks from the aggregate result of all the combine invocations and apply the combine function to these new chunks. The data size gets smaller in each level, and in the last level, we apply the reduce function to the output of all the combiners from the second to last level.

Given the signature of combiner functions we described before, it is syntactically correct to interpose any number of combiner invocations between the map and Reduce functions. However, semantically, combiners are invoked by the MapReduce or Hadoop frameworks at most once per key/value pair that is output by a map task, and therefore MapReduce programs are only required to ensure the correctness of the MapReduce computation for a single combiner invocation, that is,

$$R \circ C \circ M = R \circ M$$

where R, C, and M represent the reduce, combiner, and map function, respectively. Our new use of combiner functions introduces a different requirement, namely,

$$R \circ C^n \circ M = R \circ M, \forall n > 0$$

It is conceivable to write a combiner that meets the original requirement but not the new one. However, we found that, in practice, all of the combiner functions we have seen obey the new requirement.

Stability of the contraction phase. When deciding how to partition the input to the contraction phase, the same issue that was faced by the map phase arises: if a part of the input to the contraction phase is removed or a new part is added, then a fixed-size partitioning of the input would not ensure the stability of the dependence graph. This problem is illustrated in Figure 4.4, which shows two consecutive runs of

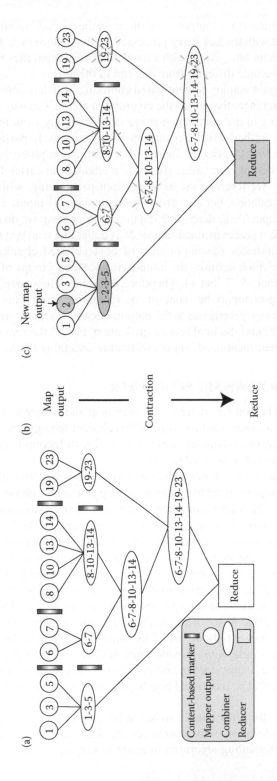

FIGURE 4.4 Stability of the contraction phase. (a) First run. (b) Legend for (a) and (c). (c) Incremental run.

a reduce task, where a map task (output 2) produces in the second but not in the first run a value associated with the key being processed by this reduce task. In this case, a partitioning of the input into groups with a fixed number of input files would cause all groups of files to become different from one run to the next.

To solve this, we again employ content-based chunking, which is applied to every level of the tree of combiners that forms the contraction phase. The way we perform content-based chunking in the contraction phase differs slightly from the approach we took in Inc-HDFS, for both efficiency and simplicity reasons. In particular, given that the Hadoop framework splits the input to the contraction phase into multiple files coming from different map tasks, we require chunk boundaries to be at file boundaries. This way we leverage the existing input partitioning, which not only simplifies the implementation, but also avoids reprocessing this input, since we can use the hash of each input file to determine if a marker is present: we do this by testing if the hash modulo a predetermined integer M is equal to a constant $k < M$.

Figure 4.4 also illustrates the importance of content-based chunking. In this example, the marker, which delimits the boundaries between groups of input files, is present only in outputs 5, 7, and 14. Therefore, inserting a new map output will change the first group of inputs but none of the remaining ones. This figure also illustrates how this change propagates to the output: it leads to a new combiner invocation (labeled 1-2-3-5) and the final reduce invocation. For all the remaining combiners we can reuse their memoized outputs without re-executing them.

4.5   MEMOIZATION-AWARE SCHEDULER

The main job of the Hadoop scheduler is to assign map and reduce tasks to cluster machines, taking into account machine availability, cluster topology, and the locality of input data. However, this scheduler does not fit well with Incoop because it does not consider the location of memoized results.

The memoization-aware scheduler addresses this shortcoming. To understand the goals that guide its design we need to consider the map and reduce phases separately.

For the map phase, the location of memoized results is irrelevant, since, in case the map task is able to reuse these results, it can just communicate the location of the results to the scheduler, who then points the reduce tasks to this location. Therefore, the memoization-aware scheduler works like the Hadoop scheduler in the map phase.

For scheduling reduce tasks, which now perform the contraction phase as well as the final reduce invocation, the memoization-aware scheduler must try to schedule them in nodes where the memoized results they may use are stored. This is important because the contraction phase often uses a combination of newly computed and memoized results, whenever only a part of its inputs has changed. In addition to this design goal, the scheduler must provide some flexibility by allowing tasks to be scheduled on nodes that do not store memoized results, otherwise it can lead to the presence of stragglers, that is, individual poorly performing nodes that can delay the job completion [38].

The new scheduler for reduce tasks strikes a balance between these two goals by being aware of the location of memoized results, while at the same time implementing a simple work-stealing algorithm to adapt to varying resource availability.

The scheduler maintains a separate queue of pending reduce tasks for each node in the cluster (instead of a single queue for all nodes). Each queue is populated with the tasks that should run on that node to exploit the location of memoized results. Whenever a node requests more work, the scheduler dequeues the first task from the corresponding queue and assigns the task to the node for execution. In case the queue for the requesting node is empty, the scheduler attempts to steal work from other task queues, by choosing a pending task from the task queue with maximum length. Our experimental evaluation (Section 4.6.6) shows the effectiveness of the new scheduler.

4.6 IMPLEMENTATION AND EVALUATION

This section describes the implementation and experimental evaluation of Incoop.

4.6.1 IMPLEMENTATION

We built a prototype of Incoop based on Hadoop-0.20.2. The implementation of Inc-HDFS extends HDFS with stable input partitioning, and incremental MapReduce extends Hadoop with support for memoization, the contraction phase, and the memoization-aware scheduler.

The Inc-HDFS file system keeps exactly the same interface and semantics for all existing HDFS calls, and implements the parallel scanning scheme to find markers that we described in Section 4.3. For our experiments, we set the minimum chunk size (i.e., the number of Bytes skipped after finding a marker) to 40 MB, unless otherwise noted. In HDFS, we use a chunk size of 64 MB.

The memoization server is built as a wrapper around the in-memory key/value store memcached v1.4.5 system. The memcached server is colocated with the name node, which is the directory server from Hadoop. All the memoized results are stored on Inc-HDFS with a replication factor of one. This implies that in case of a data node crash these results need to be recomputed. We implemented a simple garbage collection scheme to discard old memoized results, which only retains the results from the most recent run of a given MapReduce job, and discards all results from previous runs.

Finally, the contraction phase is implemented by aggregating all keys that are processed by each node, instead of building one contraction tree for each key processed by that node, since this is closer to the original Hadoop implementation.

4.6.2 APPLICATIONS

We evaluated Incoop using a set of MapReduce applications from the open-source Apache Mahout project summarized in Table 4.1. These applications cover a wide range of domains such as machine learning, natural language processing, pattern recognition, and document analysis. Furthermore, this set includes both data-intensive (WordCount, CoMatrix, BiCount), and CPU-intensive (KNN and K-Means) computations, corresponding to different ratios of I/O to CPU load. We did not have to modify any of these applications to work with Incoop.

The three data-intensive applications use documents written in a natural language as input. In our benchmarks, we used as input the contents of Wikipedia

TABLE 4.1
Applications Used in the Performance Evaluation

Application	Description
K-Means	K-Means clustering is a method of cluster analysis for partitioning n data points into k clusters, in which each observation belongs to the cluster with the nearest mean.
WordCount	Word count determines the frequency of words in a document.
KNN	K-nearest neighbors classifies objects based on the closest training examples in a feature space.
CoMatrix	Co-occurrence matrix generates an $N \times N$ matrix, where N is the number of unique words in the corpus. A cell m_{ij} contains the number of times word w_i co-occurs with word w_j.
BiCount	Bigram count measures the prevalence of each subsequence of two items within a given sequence.

from a public data set.* The two CPU-intensive applications use a set of points in a d-dimensional space as input. In this case we used a set of randomly generated points in a 50-dimensional unit cube. To obtain reasonable running times, we chose all the input sizes in a way that the running time of each job would be approximately 1 hour.

4.6.3 OVERVIEW OF THE EXPERIMENTS

Our evaluation tries to answer the following questions:

- What are the overheads introduced by Inc-HDFS compared with HDFS? (Section 4.6.4)
- What are the performance gains of using Incoop when compared with recomputing from scratch? (Section 4.6.5)
- How important are each of the design features we introduce? (Section 4.6.6)
- What are the overheads introduced by Incoop when a job is executed for the first time? (Section 4.6.7)

To answer these questions, we ran experiments using the following setting and measured the following data.

Experimental setup. We ran experiments on a cluster of 20 machines, running the Linux kernel 2.6.32 in 64-bit mode, connected by a gigabit ethernet. The name node and the job tracker of Hadoop ran on a master machine, which had a 12-core Intel Xeon processor and 12 GB of RAM. When we run an Inc-HDFS client on this machine, the parallel chunking code in Inc-HDFS is parameterized to spawn 12 threads, that is, one thread per core. The data nodes and task trackers of Hadoop ran on the remaining 19 machines, which had AMD Opteron-252 processors and 4 GB

---

* Wikipedia data set: http://wiki.dbpedia.org/.

of RAM. The task trackers were parameterized to use two map and two reduce slots per worker machine.

Work and time. We separately measure work and time to compare the performance across runs. *Work* is the sum of all the computation time performed by all the tasks, which eliminates the effects of having some machines idling waiting to synchronize with other machines. *(Parallel) time* refers to the total running time for the job. The two metrics are related through the work-time principle, which states that a computation with W work can be executed on P machines (or processors) in $\frac{w}{p}$ time if there are no scheduling overheads. Note that the work measurements include the additional computational work performed by tasks that are speculatively executed by the Hadoop framework (e.g., Hadoop can run the same task on two different machines to improve performance if there is spare capacity on the cluster). Therefore, a difference in the number of speculative tasks that are launched will be reflected in the comparison of work.

Initial and incremental runs. When evaluating Incoop, we need to consider two types of runs. The *initial run* operates on data that was never seen before, and therefore can start with an empty memoization server, which is then populated by the initial run. The *incremental run* corresponds to a subsequent run where the input is modified by a certain fraction, and the system tries to reuse subcomputations to the extent possible.

Speedup. We present the results comparing the performance of Incoop and Hadoop by plotting the speedup, that is, the ratio of the work or parallel time required by Hadoop to the work or time required by Incoop. In most cases we plot how this speedup varies as we change the fraction of the input that differs from the initial to the incremental run. To run an experiment where $x\%$ of the input data differs between the two runs, we randomly chose $x\%$ of the chunks in the input and replaced them with new equally sized chunks with new content.

4.6.4 Incremental HDFS

We compare the throughput during an upload of a data set of 3 GB in HDFS and Inc-HDFS, for a varying number of skipped bytes in Inc-HDFS. The client machine that is writing to the file system runs on the same machine as the name node of Hadoop. The results of this experiment are summarized in Table 4.2. Overall, Inc-HDFS adds only a small throughput overhead compared with HDFS, which can be attributed to the fingerprint computation.

TABLE 4.2
Throughput of HDFS and Inc-HDFS

Version	Skip Offset (MB)	Throughput (MB/s)
HDFS	–	34.41
Incremental HDFS	20	32.67
	40	34.19
	60	32.04

This overhead becomes more visible for the smallest skip offset of 20 MB. This was expected since the Rabin fingerprint needs to be computed for a larger fraction of the data. Somewhat more surprising was the reduction in throughput for the largest skip offset of 60 MB. This is due to the fact that increasing the skip offset leads to an increase in the average chunk size, which in turn leads to decreasing the amount of parallelism toward the end of the data upload. We therefore found 40 MB to be a reasonable compromise between these two negative factors.

4.6.5   WORK AND TIME SPEEDUP

We report the speedup of Incoop relative to Hadoop in terms of work and time in Figure 4.5a and b, respectively. The results show that incremental computations Incoop are significantly faster than recomputing the data from scratch using Hadoop,

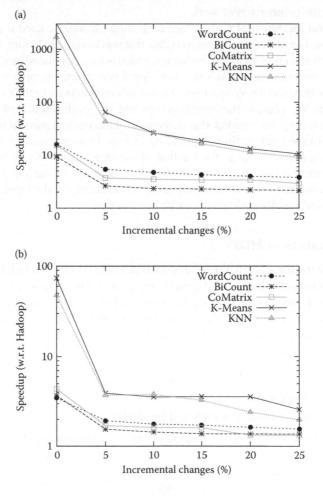

FIGURE 4.5   Performance gains for Incoop in comparison to Hadoop. (a) Work speedups vs. change size. (b) Time speedups vs. change size.

with work and time speedups ranging from 3 to 1000× for incremental modifications
of up to 25%. The results also point out that CPU-intensive applications can obtain
larger speedups than data-intensive ones, most likely because some data movement
is unavoidable in the incremental run (e.g., to read the new input or to write the new
output). Finally, we note that the speedups decrease with the fraction of changed
data, as expected. However, with very small changes, speedups in work are not translated into speedups in time, because of the effect of there being less parallelism
available when only a few tasks need to be rerun.

4.6.6 INDIVIDUAL DESIGN FEATURES

Next we evaluate the some of the design features individually, namely the contraction phase and the new scheduler.

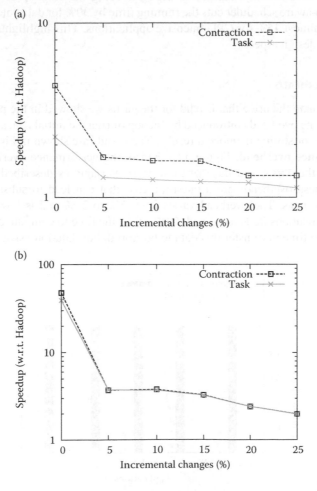

FIGURE 4.6 Performance gains comparison between `Contraction` and `Task` variants.
(a) Co-occurrence matrix. (b) k-NN classifier.

Contraction phase. To evaluate the contraction phase, we run two versions of Incoop, a version that only memoizes the output of an entire reduce task, and the full design that includes the contraction phase. We identify these two versions as `Task` and `Contraction`. Figure 4.6 compares the work and time speedup of the two versions using an application of each class (`CoMatrix` is data-intensive and KNN is CPU-intensive). The contraction phase does not change the performance of KNN but significantly improves the performance of `CoMatrix`. This is related to the fact that the reduce phase in KNN performs a simple computation and thus has little to gain from the contraction phase. Given this fact, it is noteworthy that the contraction phase did not add significant overhead.

Scheduler modification. We now evaluate the effectiveness of the memoization-aware scheduler. In Figure 4.7, we compare the time to run the various applications in Incoop using the new and the original Hadoop scheduler. The Y-axis presents the total running time normalized to the time using the Hadoop scheduler. The memoization-aware scheduler cuts the running time by 30% for data-intensive applications and almost 15% for CPU-intensive applications. This highlights the importance of this design aspect.

4.6.7 Overheads

Next we evaluate the price that is paid for the gains we showed in the previous section, namely the overheads introduced by Incoop during the initial run, and the space requirements for storing memoized results. The results are shown in Figure 4.8.

Performance overhead. Figure 4.8a depicts the performance overhead for the first run for the `Task` and the `Contraction` variants as described before. We stress that these overheads are a one-time cost that can lead to substantial gains in subsequent runs. The overhead varies from 5% to 22% and is lower for CPU-intensive applications (`K-Means` and KNN), since the time to compute over the data dominates the time to transfer this data to be stored. For data-intensive applications

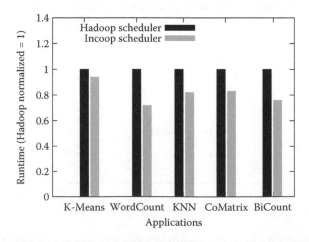

FIGURE 4.7 Effectiveness of scheduler optimizations.

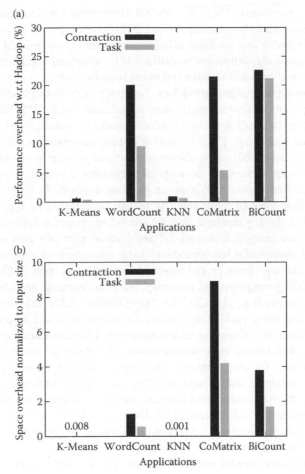

FIGURE 4.8 Overheads imposed by Incoop in comparison to Hadoop. (a) Performance overhead for the first job run. (b) Space overhead.

(`WordCount`, `CoMatrix`, and `BiCount`), the overheads using the `Contraction` approach are higher, due to the overheads for processing all levels of the tree of the contraction phase.

Space overhead. Figure 4.8b shows the space overhead for storing memoized results as a fraction of the input size. The results show that the contraction approach requires more space to store the results for all the levels of the tree, as expected. Overall, space overheads can reach up to 9× (`CoMatrix`), highlighting the trade-off between space in time that is enabled by this approach.

4.7 RELATED WORK

Several fields and research communities have looked into related problems. In this section, we present an overview of this body of related work.

Dynamic algorithms. There are several algorithms for a variety of problems that are designed for a dynamic input [3,16,20,21,35]. This body of work shows that dynamic algorithms can be more efficient than their conventional counterparts. However, dynamic algorithms can be difficult to develop and implement: some problems took years of research to solve and many remain open.

Programming language approaches. This body of work proposes programming language support to achieve automatic incrementalization (e.g., [35]). Recent advances on self-adjusting computation propose general-purpose techniques that can achieve optimal update times (e.g., [5,6,24]). Self-adjusting computation offers abstractions for automatic incrementalization, allowing programs written in a conventional style to be compiled to programs that can respond to changes in their data inputs automatically. While earlier proposals [4] required program annotations for efficiency, recent results show that some of these annotations can be inferred by type systems [15]. Stability, one of the key concepts that we use in this paper was developed initially as an algorithmic analysis technique [3] and later as part of a cost semantics [27]. Self-adjusting computation has been shown to be effective for a wide variety of problems and has led to progress on and sometimes solutions to open problems in several domains including computational geometry, machine learning, and checking of data structural invariants (e.g., [5,8,9,36,37]). Some earlier [7,23] and more recent work [13] realized that many parallel algorithms are amenable to self-adjusting computation and developed techniques for taking advantage of both simultaneously.

Incremental database view maintenance. The database community proposed several techniques for incrementally updating a database view (a predetermined query) as the database state is updated. This can be implemented either directly by modifying the database engine internals or using database triggers that update the view whenever the data changes [14]. Even though we share the same goals as incremental view maintenance, the techniques used by this class of systems are very specific to database semantics.

Large-scale incremental processing. We split the prior work on incremental parallel computations for large data sets into two categories: nontransparent and transparent proposals.

Nontransparent approaches are exemplified by Google's Percolator [33], which provides the programmer with the ability to write a handler (called an observer) that is triggered upon data changes. Observers in turn can modify other data forming a dependence chain that implements the incremental data processing. Similarly, continuous bulk processing (CBP) [28] offers a new programming model with primitives to store and reuse prior state for incremental processing upon the arrival of new data. Naiad [30] is another proposal for incremental processing that offers differential data flow. These proposals have two drawbacks, which are addressed by Incoop. The first is that they depart from existing models and therefore do not allow for reusing the large existing base of MapReduce programs. The second is that the programmer must devise a dynamic algorithm, which, as mentioned, can be difficult to design with efficiency for many problems.

Examples of transparent approaches include DryadInc [34], which like Incoop, caches task results, and Nectar [22], which caches prior results of entire LINQ subexpressions. Also, although not fully transparent, Haloop [12] provides task-level memoization techniques for iterative computations. Incoop improves on these proposals using a set of principles from related work to identify and overcome the situations where task-level memoization is inefficient, such as the stable input partitioning or the contraction phase.

Our own short position paper [10] makes the case for applying techniques inspired by self-adjusting computation to large-scale data processing in general and uses MapReduce as an example. This position paper, however, models MapReduce in a sequential, single-machine implementation of self-adjusting computation called CEAL [24] and does not offer a full-scale distributed design and implementation such as the system we presented.

Finally, the idea of breaking up the work of a reduce task using combiner functions was also adopted for the purpose of minimizing network bandwidth overheads [17,29].

Stream processing systems. Comet [25] proposed the Batched Stream Processing (BSP) model, where queries are triggered upon appending a chunk of data to an input stream. In contrast to Comet, we are compatible with the MapReduce model and focus on several issues like controlling task granularity or input partitioning that do not arise in Comet's model.

NOVA [32] allow for the incremental execution of Pig programs as new data continuously arrives. Much like the work on incremental view maintenance, NOVA introduces a workflow manager that rewrites the computation to identify the parts of the computation affected by incremental changes and produce the necessary update function, which in turn runs on top of the existing Pig/Hadoop framework. However, as noted by the authors of NOVA, an alternative, more efficient design would be to modify the underlying Hadoop system to support this functionality. This is precisely that path we took in Incoop. Furthermore, our work is more general since it can be applied to any MapReduce program and not only the programs produced by the Pig framework.

Other systems such as Storm [2] or S4 [1] work at a finer granularity by triggering a processing routine each time a (possibly small) input arrives. Deduce [26] presents a hybrid solution for real-time data analytics using a combination of techniques from batch processing in MapReduce and streaming processing in IBM's System S. In contrast to these proposals, the focus of Incoop is to provide incremental processing in batch processing workloads.

4.8 CONCLUSION

This chapter presents a set of principles and techniques for performing incremental MapReduce computations. We build on prior work from several fields, most notably contributions from the programming languages community on self-adjusting computation, a technique for incremental computations, which we extend to large-scale parallel computations. The resulting system combines the efficiency of recomputing a small subset of subcomputations affected by each input change with the ability to transparently execute existing MapReduce computations. This work thus has the potential to bring substantial performance improvements to MapReduce computations when these computations are repeated on evolving data.

We achieve the efficiency improvements by reorganizing MapReduce computations to be executed slightly differently in a way that is consistent with the principles of self-adjusting computation so that the benefits of incremental computation can be delivered transparently. Specifically, Incoop organizes a MapReduce computation such that it remains stable even as the input data set changes—that is, computations performed on similar data sets themselves remain similar. To ensure the stability of the map phase, Incoop incorporates content-based chunking to the file system to detect incremental changes in the input file and to partition the data; this maximizes reuse of the results of the map phase. To ensure the stability of the reduce phase, Incoop performs an additional contraction phase, where results from smaller reductions are combined to form larger reductions in a balanced-tree fashion; this enables the reuse of results from the intermediate states of an otherwise large reduction. Incoop proposes a memoization-aware scheduler that improves efficiency by taking the location of previously computed results into account.

We view this work as a first step in taking advantage of the benefits of transparent incremental computation in parallel and distributed systems. We envision that the work will open many avenues of research for applying similar incrementalization techniques to other distributed systems.

ACKNOWLEDGMENTS

This experimental evaluation is supported by AWS in Education Grant award. The research of R. Rodrigues has received funding from the European Research Council under an ERC starting grant.

REFERENCES

1. Apache s4 (http://incubator.apache.org/s4/). May 2013.
2. Storm (http://storm-project.net/). May 2013.
3. U. A. Acar. *Self-Adjusting Computation*. PhD thesis, Department of Computer Science, Carnegie Mellon University, May 2005.
4. U. A. Acar, G. E. Blelloch, M. Blume, R. Harper, and K. Tangwongsan. A library for self-adjusting computation. *Electronic Notes in Theoretical Computer Science*, 148(2), 2006.
5. U. A. Acar, G. E. Blelloch, M. Blume, R. Harper, and K. Tangwongsan. An experimental analysis of self-adjusting computation. *ACM Trans. Programming Languages and Systems*, 32(1):1–53, 2009.
6. U. A. Acar, G. E. Blelloch, and R. Harper. Adaptive functional programming. *ACM Trans. Programming Languages and Systems*, 28(6):990–1034, 2006.
7. U. A. Acar, G. E. Blelloch, R. Harper, J. L. Vittes, and M. Woo. Dynamizing static algorithms with applications to dynamic trees and history independence. In *ACM-SIAM Symposium on Discrete Algorithms*, pp. 531–540, 2004.
8. U. A. Acar, G. E. Blelloch, K. Tangwongsan, and D. Türkoğlu. Robust kinetic convex hulls in 3D. In *Proceedings of the 16th Annual European Symposium on Algorithms*, September 2008.
9. U. A. Acar, A. Cotter, B. Hudson, and D. Türkoğlu. Dynamic well-spaced point sets. In *Proceedings of the 26th Symposium on Computational Geometry (SCG'10)*, 2010.

10. P. Bhatotia, A. Wieder, I. E. Akkus, R. Rodrigues, and U. A. Acar. Large-scale incremental data processing with change propagation. In *USENIX Workshop on Hot Topics in Cloud Computing (HotCloud'11)*.

11. P. Bhatotia, A. Wieder, R. Rodrigues, U. A. Acar, and R. Pasquini. Incoop: MapReduce for incremental computations. In *SoCC*.

12. Y. Bu, B. Howe, M. Balazinska, and M. D. Ernst. HaLoop: Efficient iterative data processing on large clusters. In *36th International Conference on Very Large Data Bases*, Singapore, September 14–16, 2010.

13. S. Burckhardt, D. Leijen, C. Sadowski, J. Yi, and T. Ball. Two for the price of one: A model for parallel and incremental computation. In *ACM SIGPLAN Conference on Object-Oriented Programming, Systems, Languages, and Applications*, 2011.

14. S. Ceri and J. Widom. Deriving production rules for incremental view maintenance. In *Proceedings of the 17th International Conference on Very Large Data Bases*, pp. 577–589, 1991.

15. Y. Chen, J. Dunfield, and U. A. Acar. Type-directed automatic incrementalization. In *ACM SIGPLAN Conference on Programming Language Design and Implementation (PLDI)*, June 2012.

16. Y.-J. Chiang and R. Tamassia. Dynamic algorithms in computational geometry. *Proceedings of the IEEE*, 80(9):1412–1434, 1992.

17. P. Costa, A. Donnelly, A. Rowstron, and G. O'Shea. Camdoop: Exploiting in-network aggregation for Big Data applications. In *NSDI*, 2012.

18. J. Dean and S. Ghemawat. MapReduce: Simplified data processing on large clusters. In *Proceedings of the 6th Symposium on Operating Systems Design and Implementation (OSDI'04)*.

19. J. Dean and S. Ghemawat. MapReduce: Simplified data processing on large clusters. *Communications of the ACM*, 51(1):107–113, 2008.

20. C. Demetrescu, I. Finocchi, and G. Italiano. *Handbook on Data Structures and Applications*, Chapter 36: Dynamic Graphs. CRC, 2005.

21. C. Demetrescu, I. Finocchi, and G. Italiano. *Handbook on Data Structures and Applications*, Chapter 35: Dynamic Trees. Dinesh Mehta and Sartaj Sahni (eds.), CRC Press Series, in *Computer and Information Science*, 2005.

22. P. K. Gunda, L. Ravindranath, C. A. Thekkath, Y. Yu, and L. Zhuang. Nectar: Automatic management of data and computation in data centers. In *Proceedings of the 9th Symposium on Operating Systems Design and Implementation (OSDI'10)*.

23. M. Hammer, U. A. Acar, M. Rajagopalan, and A. Ghuloum. A proposal for parallel self-adjusting computation. In *DAMP'07: Proceedings of the First Workshop on Declarative Aspects of Multicore Programming*, 2007.

24. M. A. Hammer, U. A. Acar, and Y. Chen. CEAL: A C-based language for self-adjusting computation. In *Proceedings of the 2009 ACM SIGPLAN Conference on Programming Language Design and Implementation*, June 2009.

25. B. He, M. Yang, Z. Guo, R. Chen, B. Su, W. Lin, and L. Zhou. Comet: Batched stream processing for data intensive distributed computing. In *Proceedings of the 1st Symposium on Cloud Computing (SoCC'10)*.

26. V. Kumar, H. Andrade, B. Gedik, and K.-L. Wu. Deduce: At the intersection of mapreduce and stream processing. In *EDBT*, 2010.

27. R. Ley-Wild, U. A. Acar, and M. Fluet. A cost semantics for self-adjusting computation. In *Proceedings of the 26th Annual ACM Symposium on Principles of Programming Languages*, 2009.

28. D. Logothetis, C. Olston, B. Reed, K. C. Webb, and K. Yocum. Stateful bulk processing for incremental analytics. In *1st Symposium on Cloud Computing (SoCC'10)*.

29. D. Logothetis, C. Trezzo, K. C. Webb, and K. Yocum. In-situ MapReduce for log processing. In *USENIX ATC*, 2011.

30. F. McSherry, R. I. Isaacs, M. Isard, and D. G. Murray. Composable incremental and iterative data-parallel computation with naiad. *MSR-TR-2012-105*, 2012.
31. A. Muthitacharoen, B. Chen, and D. Mazières. A low-bandwidth network file system. In *Proceedings of the 18th Symposium on Operating Systems Principles (SOSP'01)*.
32. C. Olston et al. Nova: Continuous pig/hadoop workflows. In *Proceedings of the 2011 International Conference on Management of Data*, SIGMOD, 2011.
33. D. Peng and F. Dabek. Large-scale incremental processing using distributed transactions and notifications. In *Proceedings of the 9th Symposium on Operating Systems Design and Implementation (OSDI'10)*.
34. L. Popa, M. Budiu, Y. Yu, and M. Isard. DryadInc: Reusing work in large-scale computations. In *Workshop on Hot Topics in Cloud Computing (HotCloud'09)*.
35. G. Ramalingam and T. Reps. A categorized bibliography on incremental computation. In *Proceedings of the 20th Symposium Principles of Programming Languages (POPL'93)*.
36. A. Shankar and R. Bodik. DITTO: Automatic incrementalization of data structure invariant checks (in Java). In *Proceedings of the ACM SIGPLAN 2007 Conference on Programming Language Design and Implementation*, 2007.
37. O. Sümer, U. A. Acar, A. Ihler, and R. Mettu. Adaptive exact inference in graphical models. *Journal of Machine Learning*, 8:180–186, 2011.
38. M. Zaharia, A. Konwinski, A. D. Joseph, R. Katz, and I. Stoica. Improving mapreduce performance in heterogeneous environments. In *Proceedings of the 8th USENIX Conference on Operating Systems Design and Implementation, OSDI'08*, 2008.

5 Large-Scale RDF Processing with MapReduce

Alexander Schätzle, Martin Przyjaciel-Zablocki,
Thomas Hornung, and Georg Lausen

CONTENTS

5.1 INTRODUCTION

Most of the information in the classical "Web of Documents" is designed for human readers, whereas the idea behind the semantic web is to build a "web of data" that enables computers to understand and use the information in the web. The advent of this web of data gives rise to new challenges with regard to query evaluation on the semantic web. The core technologies of the semantic web are the Resource Description Framework (RDF) [1] for representing data in a machine-readable format and SPARQL [2] for querying RDF data. However, querying RDF data sets at web scale is challenging, especially because the computation of SPARQL queries usually requires several joins between subsets of the data. On the other side, classical single-place machine approaches have reached a point where they cannot scale with respect to the ever increasing amount of available RDF data (cf. [3]).

The advent of Google's *MapReduce* programming model [4] in 2004 opened up new ways for parallel processing of very large data sets distributed over a computer cluster. Hadoop [5] is the most popular open-source implementation of MapReduce. In the last few years many companies have built-up their own Hadoop infrastructure, but there are also ready-to-use cloud services like Amazon's Elastic Compute Cloud (EC2), offering the Hadoop platform as a service (PaaS). Thus, in contrast to specialized distributed RDF systems like YARS2 [6] or 4store [7], the use of existing Hadoop MapReduce infrastructures enables scalable, distributed and fault-tolerant SPARQL processing out-of-the-box without any additional installation or management overhead. However, developing on the MapReduce level is still technically challenging as it requires profound knowledge about how to program and optimize Hadoop in an appropriate way. Therefore, Yahoo! developed Pig Latin [8] a language for the analysis of large data sets based on Hadoop that gives the user a simple level of abstraction by providing high-level primitives like *Filters* and *Joins*.

In the first part of this chapter we describe PigSPARQL [9], a translation framework from full SPARQL 1.0 to Pig Latin, which allows a scalable processing of SPARQL queries on a MapReduce cluster without any additional programming efforts. It can be downloaded* and executed on each Hadoop cluster with Apache Pig installed and benefits from further developments of Apache Pig without changing a single line of code. The second part of the chapter focuses on an optimized join technique for selective queries. We present the *Map-Side Index Nested Loop Join* (MAPSIN join), which combines the scalable indexing capabilities of the NoSQL data store HBase with MapReduce for efficient large-scale join processing.

This chapter is structured as follows: Section 5.2 gives an introduction to RDF and SPARQL, and also provides an overview of distributed processing with MapReduce (with a special focus on join computation) and PigLatin. Section 5.3 describes the translation process from SPARQL queries to PigLatin programs. Section 5.5 discusses experimental results of the PigSPARQL implementation for the SP^{2}Bench SPARQL benchmark [10]. Section 5.6 presents the RDF storage organization for HBase. Section 5.7 takes another look at join processing with MapReduce and suggests the MAPSIN join technique as a flexible alternative to the commonly used reduce-side join. Section 5.8 demonstrates the effectiveness of this approach for selective queries by a comparison of the MAPSIN join with PigSPARQL native joins for a selection of LUBM [11] benchmark queries. Finally, Section 5.8 gives an overview of related work, and Section 5.9 concludes this chapter with a short summary.

---

* http://dbis.informatik.uni-freiburg.de/PigSPARQL.

5.2 FOUNDATIONS

5.2.1 RDF AND SPARQL

RDF [1] is the W3C recommended standard model for representing knowledge about arbitrary resources, for example, articles, authors. An RDF data set consists of a set of RDF triples in the form (*subject, predicate, object*) that can be interpreted as "*subject* has property *predicate* with value *object*." URIs (Uniform Resource Identifier) are globally unique identifiers used to represent resources in RDF (e.g., URLs are a subset of URIs). For clarity of presentation, we use a simplified RDF notation without URI prefixes in the following. It is possible to visualize an RDF data set as directed, labeled graph where every triple corresponds to an edge (predicate) from subject to object. Figure 5.1 shows an RDF graph with information about users and their friendship relationships.

SPARQL is the W3C recommended declarative query language for RDF. A SPARQL query defines a graph pattern *P* that is matched against an RDF graph *G*. This is done by replacing the variables in *P* with elements of *G* such that the resulting graph is contained in *G* (pattern matching). The most basic constructs in a SPARQL query are *Triple Patterns*, that is, RDF triples where subject, predicate, and object can be variables (?*v*), for example, (?*s*, p, ?*o*). A set of triple patterns concatenated by AND (.) is called a *Basic Graph Pattern* (BGP). In general, a SPARQL 1.0 graph pattern can be defined recursively as follows:

- A BGP is a graph pattern.
- If *P*, *P'* are graph patterns, then
  {*P*}.{*P'*}, {*P*} UNION {*P'*} and {*P*} OPTIONAL {*P'*} are also graph patterns.
- If *P* is a graph pattern and *R* is a filter condition, then
  P FILTER (*R*) is also a graph pattern.
- If *P* is a graph pattern, *u* an URI and ?*v* a variable, then

GRAPH *u* {*P*} and GRAPH ?*v* {*P*} are also graph patterns.

FILTER can be used to restrict the values of variables and OPTIONAL allows to add additional information to the result of a query. If the desired information does not exist, the optional variables remain *unbound* in the query result. UNION can be used to define two alternative graph patterns where the query results must match at least one of the patterns. A SPARQL query can also address several RDF graphs

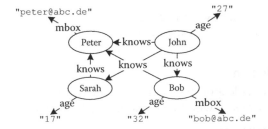

```
Example SPARQL Query
SELECT *
WHERE {
    { ?person knows Peter
      ?person age    ?age }
    OPTIONAL { ?person mbox ?mb }
    FILTER (?age >= 18)
}
```

FIGURE 5.1 RDF graph and SPARQL query.

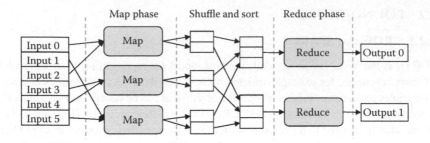

FIGURE 5.2   MapReduce data flow.

using the GRAPH operator. For a detailed definition of the SPARQL syntax we refer
the interested reader to the official W3C Recommendation [2]. A formal definition of
the SPARQL semantics can also be found in [12]. The SPARQL query in Figure 5.1
returns all persons who know "Peter" and are at least 18 years old together with their
mailboxes, if they exist. Executed on the corresponding RDF graph there are two
results for "John" and "Bob" where only "Bob" has a known email address.

5.2.2 MAPREDUCE

The MapReduce programming model [4] enables scalable, fault tolerant, and massively
parallel computations using a computer cluster. The basis of Google's MapReduce is the
distributed file system GFS [13] where large files are split into equal sized blocks, spread
across the cluster and fault tolerance is achieved by replication. We use *Apache Hadoop**
as it is the most popular open-source implementation of Google's GFS and MapReduce
framework that is used by many companies like Yahoo!, IBM, or Facebook.†

The workflow of a MapReduce program is a sequence of MapReduce iterations
each consisting of a *map* and a *reduce* phase separated by a so-called *Shuffle* and *Sort*
phase (see Figure 5.2). A user has to implement *map* and *reduce* functions, which
are automatically executed in parallel on a subset of the data. The map function gets
invoked for every input record represented as a key-value pair. It outputs a list of new
intermediate key-value pairs that are then sorted and grouped by their key. The reduce
function gets invoked for every distinct intermediate key together with the list of all
according values and outputs a list of values that can be used as input for the next
MapReduce iteration. The signatures of the map and reduce functions are therefore
as follows:

```
map: (inKey, inValue) -> list(outKey, tmpValue)
reduce: (outKey, list(tmpValue)) -> list(outValue)
```

5.2.2.1 Map-Side vs. Reduce-Side Join

Processing joins with MapReduce is a challenging task as data sets are typically very
large [14,15]. If we want to join two data sets with MapReduce, $L \bowtie R$, we have to

---

* http://hadoop.apache.org/.
† http://wiki.apache.org/hadoop/PoweredBy.

ensure that the subsets of *L* and *R* with the same join key values can be processed on the same machine. Hence, for joining arbitrary data sets on arbitrary keys we generally have to shuffle data over the network or choose appropriate prepartitioning and replication strategies.

The most prominent and flexible join technique in MapReduce is called *reduce-side join* [14,15]. Some literature also refer to it as *repartition join* [14] as the idea is based on reading both data sets (map phase) and repartition them according to the join key (shuffle phase). The actual join computation is done in the reduce phase. The main drawback of this approach is that both data sets are completely transferred over the network regardless of the join output. This is especially inefficient for selective joins and consumes a lot of network bandwidth. Another group of joins is based on getting rid of the shuffle and reduce phase to avoid transferring both data sets over the network. This kind of join technique is called *map-side join* since the actual join processing is done in the map phase. The most common one is the *map-side merge join* [15]. However, this join cannot be applied on arbitrary data sets since a preprocessing step is necessary to fulfill several requirements: data sets have to be sorted and equally partitioned according to the join key. If the preconditions are fulfilled, the map phase can process an efficient parallel merge join between presorted partitions and data shuffling is not necessary. In a sequence of such joins, the shuffle and reduce phases are indeed needed to fulfill the preconditions for the next join iteration. Therefore, map-side joins are generally hard to cascade and the advantage of avoiding a shuffle and reduce phase is lost. In Section 5.6, we present our MAPSIN join approach that is designed to overcome this drawback by using the distributed index of the NoSQL data store HBase.

5.2.3 PIG LATIN

Pig Latin [8] is a language for the analysis of very large data sets based on Apache Hadoop developed by Yahoo! Research. The implementation of Pig Latin for Hadoop, *Pig*, is an Apache top-level project that automatically translates a Pig Latin program into a series of MapReduce jobs.

Data Model: Pig Latin has a fully nested data model that allows more flexibility than at tables required by the first normal form in relational databases. The data model of Pig Latin provides four different types:

- **Atom**: Contains a simple atomic value like a string or number, for example, `'Sarah'` or `24`.
- **Tuple**: Sequence of fields of any type. Every field can have a name (alias) that can be used to reference the field, for example, `('John', 'Doe')` with alias (*firstname, lastname*).
- **Bag**: Collection of tuples with possible duplicates. The schemas of the tuples do not have to match, that is, the number and types of fields can differ.

$$\left\{ \begin{array}{c} (\text{'Bob','Sarah'}) \\ (\text{'Peter',('likes','football')}) \end{array} \right\}$$

- **Map**: Collection of data items where each item can be looked up by an associated key.

$$
\left[\begin{array}{l} \text{'name'} \rightarrow \text{'John'} \\ \text{'knows'} \left\{ \begin{array}{l} (\text{'Sarah'}) \\ (\text{'Bob'}) \end{array} \right\} \end{array} \right]
$$

Operators: A Pig Latin program consists of a sequence of instructions where each instruction performs a single data transformation. We shortly introduce those Pig Latin operators that we used for our translation. The interested reader can find a more detailed description of Pig Latin in [16].

- **LOAD** deserializes the input data and maps it to the data model of Pig Latin. The user can implement a *User Defined Function* (UDF) that defines how to map an input tuple to a Pig Latin tuple as shown in the following example. The result of LOAD is a bag of tuples.

```
people = LOAD 'input' USING myLoad() AS (name, age);
```

- **FOREACH** can be used to apply some processing on every tuple of a bag. It can also be used for projection or adding new fields to a tuple.

```
A = FOREACH people GENERATE name, age >= 18? 'adult' :
'minor' AS type;
```

- **FILTER** allows to remove unwanted tuples of a bag.

```
B = FILTER people BY age >= 18;
```

- **[OUTER] JOIN** performs an equi or outer join between bags. It can also be applied to more than two bags at once (multijoin).

```
C = JOIN A BY name [LEFT OUTER], B BY name;
```

- **UNION** can be used to combine two or more bags. Unlike relational databases, the schemas of the tuples do not have to match although this is not recommended in general since the schema information, especially the alias names of the fields, is lost in such cases.

```
D = UNION B, C;
```

- **SPLIT** partitions a bag into two or more bags that do not have to be distinct or complete, that is, tuples can end up in more than one partition or no partition at all.

```
SPLIT people INTO E IF age < 18, F IF age >= 21;
```

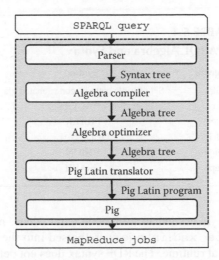

FIGURE 5.3 Modular translation process.

5.3 SPARQL TRANSLATION

A translation of SPARQL to Pig Latin enables SPARQL query processing on a MapReduce cluster, with the great advantage that it benefits from further developments of Apache Pig without any additional programming effort. This includes both, performance enhancements and the support for newer versions of Hadoop like the upcoming YARN* (MRv2) framework. For translating SPARQL to Pig Latin we follow a standard approach that centers on an algebraic representation of SPARQL expressions (cf. Figure 5.3). First, a SPARQL query is parsed to generate an abstract syntax tree that is then translated into a SPARQL algebra tree as described by the W3C documentation [2]. For the syntax and algebra tree generation we used the well-known ARQ† engine of the Jena framework. Before translating the resulting algebra expressions into Pig Latin, certain optimizations are applied that will be explained later.

The semantics of a SPARQL query is defined on the algebra level and an expression of the SPARQL algebra can be represented as a tree that is evaluated *bottom-up*. Table 5.1 shows the operators of the SPARQL algebra and the corresponding syntax expressions.

5.3.1 RDF DATA MAPPING

To process RDF data sets with Pig Latin, we first have to define how to represent an RDF triple in Pig Latin. An RDF triple is a tuple with three fields that can consist of *URIs* (Uniform Resource Identifier), RDF *literals* or *blank nodes*. Since URIs are strings in a special format, we represent them as atoms in angle brackets (`<URI>`). Simple and typed RDF literals can also be represented as atoms using a compound value for literals with a language or data type tag (`"literal"@lang`,

---

* http://hadoop.apache.org/docs/current/hadoop-yarn/hadoop-yarn-site/YARN.html.
† http://jena.sourceforge.net/ARQ.

TABLE 5.1

SPARQL Algebra and Syntax

Algebra	Syntax
BGP	Set of triple patterns concatenated via.
Join	Concatenation of two groups {…} . {…}
Filter	FILTER
LeftJoin	OPTIONAL
Union	UNION
Graph	GRAPH

`"literal"^^type`). If needed in arithmetic expressions, numeric literals (e.g., `literals of type xsd:integer`) are parsed into the appropriate numeric data type of Pig Latin at runtime. The RDF syntax does not define an internal structure of blank nodes, they just have to be distinguishable from URIs and literals. Thus, we can also represent them as atoms with a leading underscore (`_:nodeID`). Hence, an RDF triple can be represented as a tuple with three fields of atomic type (`chararray`) with schema (`s:chararray, p:chararray, o:chararray`).

5.3.2 ALGEBRA TRANSLATION

For each operator of the SPARQL algebra we give a translation into a sequence of Pig Latin commands illustrated by a representative example (P1–P6). First, we introduce the needed terminology analogous to [12]: Let V be the infinite set of query variables and T be the set of valid RDF terms (URIs, RDF literals, blank nodes).

Definition 5.1

A *(solution) mapping* μ is a partial function $\mu : V \rightarrow T$. We call $\mu(?v)$ the variable binding of μ for $?v$. Abusing notation, for a triple pattern p we call $\mu(p)$ the triple pattern that is obtained by substituting the variables in p according to μ. The domain of μ, $dom(\mu)$, is the subset of V where μ is defined and the domain of p, $dom(p)$, is the subset of V used in p. The result of a SPARQL query is a multiset of solution mappings Ω. ∎

Definition 5.2

Two mappings μ_1, μ_2 are compatible iff, for every variable $?v \in dom(\mu_1) \cap dom(\mu_2)$, it holds that $\mu_1(?v) = \mu_2(?v)$. It follows that mappings with disjoint domains are always compatible and the set-union (merge) of μ_1 and μ_2, $\mu_1 \cup \mu_2$, is also a mapping. ∎

Basic Graph Pattern (BGP). BGPs are the basis of all SPARQL queries as it is the only operator that is evaluated directly on the underlying RDF data. The result of a BGP is a multiset of solution mappings that serves as input for other operators. Solution mappings can be represented in Pig Latin as a (flat) bag where each tuple is a single solution mapping and the fields of a tuple correspond to the variable bindings of that tuple. This bag can be seen as a table where the rows are the solution mappings and the columns are the corresponding variable bindings. The corresponding Pig Latin program for P1 consists of a LOAD (1), followed by several FILTER/ FOREACH (2) and several JOIN/FOREACH (3) statements.

P1. Persons Who Know "Bob" with Age and Mailbox

```
SP     BGP(?a knows Bob . ?a age ?b . ?a mbox ?c)
PL     A = LOAD 'RDFGraph' USING RDFLoader() AS (s,p,o);  (1)
       t1 = FILTER A BY p=='knows' AND o=='Bob';       (2)
       t1 = FOREACH t1 GENERATE s AS a;
       t2 = FILTER A BY p=='age';
       t2 = FOREACH t2 GENERATE s AS a, o AS b;
       t3 = FILTER A BY p=='mbox';
       t3 = FOREACH t3 GENERATE s AS a, o AS c;
       j1 = JOIN t1 BY a, t2 BY a;        (3)
       j1 = FOREACH j1 GENERATE t1::a AS a, b;
       j2 = JOIN j1 BY a, t3 BY a;
       P1 = FOREACH j2 GENERATE j1::a AS a, b, c;
```

1. We implemented a loader UDF for RDF data that maps RDF triples to the data model of Pig Latin as described in Section 5.31.
2. For every triple pattern, we need a FILTER to select those RDF triples of the input that match the pattern. FOREACH is used to remove unnecessary columns (columns that do not correspond to a variable binding) and update the schema information with the names of the variables.
3. The results of the Triple Patterns are successively joined to compute the final result. If a BGP consists of n Triple Patterns we need $n - 1$ JOINs in general. The predicate of the join is given by the shared variables of both sides, that is, the join combines the compatible solution mappings. If there are no shared variables we have to compute the cross product.

Filter. A Filter removes those solution mappings from a multiset of solution mappings that do not satisfy the filter expression. A Filter can be directly expressed as FILTER in Pig Latin (cf. P2). To support the SPARQL built-in functions one could implement them as UDFs in Pig Latin. We did not do this, as this is not interesting from a research point of view.

P2. Filter P1 for Persons with Ages between 30 and 40 Years

```
SP     Filter(?b >= 30 && ?b <= 40, P1)
PL     P2 = FILTER P1 BY (b >= 30 AND b <= 40);
```

Join. The Join merges the compatible mappings of two multisets of solution mappings. A Join can be expressed as a JOIN in Pig Latin on the shared variables (cf. P3, assuming the results of the BGPs are stored in `BGP1` and `BGP2`). Again, FOREACH is used to remove unnecessary columns and update the schema information as illustrated in the following.

P3. Persons Who Know Somebody with the Same Age

```
SP      Join(BGP(?a knows ?b),
            BGP(?a age ?c . ?b age ?c))
PL      j1 = JOIN BGP1 BY (a,b), BGP2 BY (a,b);
        P3 = FOREACH j1 GENERATE
            BGP1::a AS a, BGP1::b AS b, c;
```

LeftJoin. The LeftJoin operator adds additional information to the result, if it exists. This additional information can be restricted by a filter expression. In Pig Latin, we can first use a FILTER to restrict the values of the additional information before performing an OUTER JOIN on the shared variables as illustrated in the following.

P4. Persons with Mailbox and Optional Age

```
SP      LeftJoin(BGP(?a mbox ?b),
            BGP(?a age ?c), ?c >= 18)
PL      f1= FILTER BGP2 BY c >= 18;
        lj= JOIN BGP1 BY a LEFT OUTER, BGP2 BY a;
        P4= FOREACH lj GENERATE BGP1::a AS a, b, c;
```

Union. The Union operator combines two multisets of solution mappings (Ω_1, Ω_2) to a single multiset without any further changes, that is, it unifies the results of two graph patterns. The problem of Union is that for two mappings $\mu_1 \in \Omega_1$ and $\mu_2 \in \Omega_2$ it can be that $dom(\mu_1) \neq dom(\mu_2)$ as it is the case for P5 where ?b is not defined in the second BGP. To have a common schema in Pig Latin we add a new column to the result of the second BGP and use null values to indicate that the variable binding for ?b is not defined.

P5. Persons Who Know "Bob" and Have a Mailbox or Persons Who Know "John"

```
SP      Union(BGP(?a knows Bob . ?a mbox ?b),
            BGP(?a knows John))
PL      BGP2 = FOREACH BGP2 GENERATE a, null as b;
        P5 = UNION BGP1, BGP2;
```

Graph. A SPARQL query data set is a collection of RDF graphs with one *default graph* and zero or more additional *named graphs*. In general, a graph pattern is applied to the default graph. The graph operator can be used to apply a pattern to one or all of the named graphs. A named graph is referenced by an unique URI, and for each graph that is used in the query, we need a pair *(URI, graph)* that specifies where to find the corresponding RDF graph. If a variable is used in the Graph operator instead of a specific graph URI, the pattern must be applied to all named graphs.

As we want to execute SPARQL queries on large RDF graphs in a MapReduce cluster, all graphs must be stored in the distributed file system. Applying a pattern to one of the named graphs with Pig Latin simply means loading the corresponding data.

P6. Persons in Graph graphURI Who Know Somebody

```
SP      Graph(graphURI, BGP(?a knows ?b))
PL      graph1 = LOAD 'pathToGraphURI'
                 USING RDFLOader() AS (s,p,o);
        t1 = FILTER graph1 BY p == 'knows';
        P6 = FOREACH t1 GENERATE s AS a, o AS b;
```

Joins and Null values. As we use at bags to represent solution mappings in Pig Latin and all tuples of a bag have the same schema we use null values to indicate that a variable is unbound in a solution mapping. This typically occurs when using OPTIONAL to add additional information to a solution mapping. The result of OPTIONAL is a set of solution mappings (i.e., a bag in Pig Latin) where the optional variables can be unbound for some solution mappings (i.e., some tuples of the bag contain null values). However, this is problematic if the further processing of the query requires a join over these possibly unbound variables. In SPARQL an unbound variable is compatible to any other binding of that variable but since Pig Latin follows the relational algebra, a JOIN in Pig Latin is null rejecting. Assume we have two bags of solution mappings R, S with schemas (A,B) and (B,C) where R can contain null values for variable B as illustrated in the following example.

R			S			A	B	C
A	B		B	C		a_1	b_1	c_1
a_1	b_1	$\bowtie$ *SPARQL*	b_1	c_1	$=$	a_2	b_1	c_1
a_2	*null*		b_2	c_2		a_2	b_2	c_2

The second tuple of R is compatible to any tuple of S since variable B is unbound. In Pig Latin, we would only get one tuple as join result since the second tuple of R will not match with any tuple of S. To get the same result in Pig Latin we split R into two bags (with and without `null` values) and process them separately, that is, we perform an equi join for all tuples without `null` values and a crossproduct for the tuples with `null` values.

```
PL      SPLIT R INTO R1 IF B is not null,
                       R2 IF B is null;
        j1 = JOIN R1 BY B, S BY B;
        j1 = FOREACH j1 GENERATE A, R1::B AS B, C;
        j2 = CROSS R2, S;
        j2 = FOREACH j2 GENERATE A, S::B AS B, C;
        J  = UNION j1, j2;
```

The complexity increases with the number of join variables that can be unbound, for example, for two possibly unbound join variables we already have to split the bag into four distinct paritions (one for every possible combination). Our translator recognizes if a join contains possibly unbound variables and performs the necessary changes to the translation automatically. Fortunately, this situation does not occur in most SPARQL queries. In fact, if a SPARQL query is *well designed* according to [12], there are no joins over unbound variables at all.

5.3.3 OPTIMIZATIONS

The optimization of SPARQL queries is a subject of current research [17–19]. As we will demonstrate in the evaluation, optimizing the SPARQL query execution based on Pig Latin means reducing I/O required to transfer data between the map and the reduce phase as well as the data that is read or stored in the distributed file system.

1. **SPARQL algebra.** We investigated some well-known optimization strategies for the SPARQL algebra to reduce the amount of intemediate results, especially the early execution of filters and the reordering of triple patterns by selectivity [19]. We used a fixed scheme without statistical information on the RDFdata set (called *variable counting*) where triple patterns with one variable are considered to be more selective than triple patterns with two variables and bounded subjects are considered to be more selective than bounded predicates or objects.
2. **Translation.** The early projection of redundant data ("*project early and often,*" e.g., duplicate columns after joins or bounded values that should not occur in the result) as well as the application of multijoins to reduce the number of joins in Pig Latin has proven to be very effective. We can use a multijoin if several consecutive joins refer to the same svariables. Assume we have three bags (A,B,C) to join by the common variable ?v. Instead of using two joins, we can use a single multijoin as shown in the following example.

   ```
   JOIN A BY v, B BY v, C BY v;
   ```

3. **Data model.** In a typical SPARQL query the predicate of a triple pattern is mostly bounded, that is, variables are typically used in the subject and object position. Therefore, *a vertical partitioning* [20] of the RDF data by predicates reduces the amount of RDF triples that must be loaded for query

execution. This vertical partitioning can be done once in advance using a single MapReduce job and does not cost more disk space. All RDF triples with the same predicate are stored in the same partition and every predicate has its own partition. For queries with unbounded predicate all partitions have to be processed again, which corresponds to processing the unpartitioned RDF data.

5.3.4 EXAMPLE

Figure 5.4 shows the algebra tree after optimization (pushing Filter execution before LeftJoin) for the SPARQL query of Section 5.21 (Figure 5.1). The tree is traversed bottom-up and translated into the following sequence of Pig Latin commands, assuming a vertical partitioning of the RDF data.

```
PL      -- Left BGP                                              (1)
        knows = LOAD 'rdf/knows' USING RDFLoader() AS (s,o);
        age   = LOAD 'rdf/age' USING RDFLoader() AS (s,o);
        f1 = FILTER knows BY o == 'Peter';
        t1 = FOREACH f1 GENERATE s AS person;
        t2 = FOREACH age GENERATE s AS person, o AS age;
        j1 = JOIN t1 BY person, t2 BY person;
        BGP1 = FOREACH j1 GENERATE
                t1::person AS person, t2::age AS age;
        -- FILTER                                                (2)
        F = FILTER BGP1 BY age >= 18;
        -- Right BGP                                             (3)
        mbox = LOAD 'rdf/mbox' USING RDFLoader() AS (s,o);
        BGP2 = FOREACH mbox GENERATE s AS person,o AS mb;
        -- LEFTJOIN                                              (4)
        lj = JOIN F BY person LEFT OUTER, BGP2 BY person;
        LJ = FOREACH lj GENERATE F::person AS person,
                F::age AS age, BGP2::mb AS mb;
        STORE LJ INTO 'output' USING resultWriter();
```

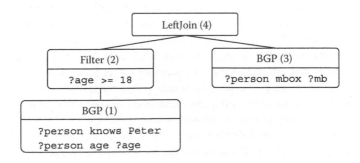

FIGURE 5.4 SPARQL algebra tree.

5.4 PIGSPARQL EVALUATION

We evaluated our implementation on 10 Dell PowerEdge R200 servers connected via a gigabit network. Each server was equipped with a Dual Core 3.16-GHz processor, 4-GB RAM, 1-TB hard disk, and Hadoop 0.20.2 as well as Pig 0.5.0 installed. Due to the replication of the distributed file system (HDFS), the actual available payload was 2.5 TB.

We investigated the execution times, the amount of data read from HDFS (*HDFS Bytes Read*), the amount of data written to HDFS (*HDFS Bytes Written*), and the amount of data that was transferred during the shuffle phase (*Reduce Shuffle Bytes*). We used the SP²Bench [10], a SPARQL specific performance benchmark that covers a wide range of SPARQL features. The SP²Bench data generator was used to produce RDF data sets of up to 1.6 billion triples based on the DBLP library [21]. In the following, we present the evaluation of three representative and rather complex SP²Bench queries, that cover interesting aspects like queries that involve many joins or an OPTIONAL with a FILTER for unbounded values.

Q2. Extract All Inproceedings with the Given Properties and Optional Abstract, Sorted by the Year of Publication

```
SELECT *
WHERE {
       ?inproc rdf:type bench:Inproceedings.
       ?inproc dc:creator ?author.
       ?inproc bench:booktitle ?booktitle.
       ?inproc dc:title ?title.
       ?inproc dcterms:partOf ?proc.
       ?inproc rdfs:seeAlso ?ee.
       ?inproc swrc:pages ?page.
       ?inproc foaf:homepage ?url.
       ?inproc dcterms:issued ?yr
       OPTIONAL { ?inproc bench:abstract ?abstract }
} ORDER BY ?yr
```

Q2. The left side of the OPTIONAL contains a BGP with nine triple patterns that requires (without any optimization) eight joins. In addition, the results should be emitted in a sorted order. Since all eight joins apply to the same variable ?inproc they can be implemented by a single multijoin (Q2 opt). As a result, the number of MapReduce jobs that are necessary for executing Q2 is reduced from 12 to 5. The query also benefits from the vertical partitioning (Q2 opt+part) as all predicates are bounded, which leads to an overall query execution time reduction of nearly 90% (a).

Q6. This query implements a (closed world) negation by the combination of OPTIONAL and a FILTER for unbounded values. None of the considered optimizations on the algebra level is possible for this query. As a consequence, the computation of the OPTIONAL produces many intermediate results. In fact, 75% of the aggregated I/O values (diagram d of Figure 5.5) arise in a single MapReduce job (computation of

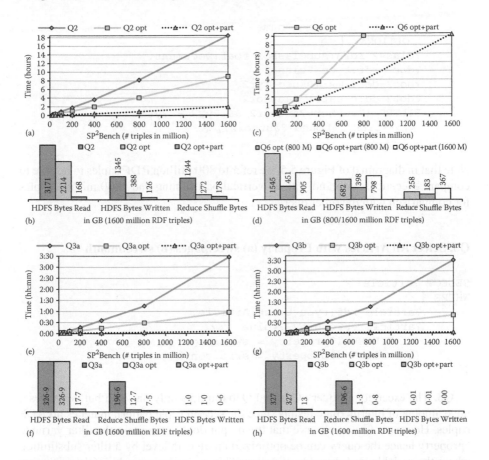

FIGURE 5.5 Runtimes and IO costs for SP²Bench queries Q2 (a+b), Q6 (c+d), Q3a (e+f), and Q3b (g+h).

OPTIONAL), making the query especially challenging. Only when using a vertical partitioned data set, the capacity of our cluster was sufficient for executing Q6 with 1600 million triples. Without vertical partitioning, there was not enough local and distributed disk space. To overcome such situation we could make use of the horizontal scalability of MapReduce and simply add more machines to the cluster.

Q6. Return, for each Year, All Publications of Persons That Have Not Published in Years Before

```
SELECT ?yr ?name ?doc
WHERE {
        ?class rdfs:subClassOf foaf:Document.
        ?doc rdf:type ?class.
        ?doc dcterms:issued ?yr.
        ?doc dc:creator ?author.
```

```
?author foaf:name ?name
  OPTIONAL {
?class2 rdfs:subClassOf foaf:Document.
?doc2 rdf:type ?class2.
?doc2 dcterms:issued ?yr2.
?doc2 dc:creator ?author2
FILTER (?author=?author2 && ?yr2 < ?yr)
  } FILTER (!bound(?author2))
}
```

Note that in diagram d of Figure 5.5, we refer to 800 million RDF triples to be able to compare executions with and without vertical partitioning and 1600 million triples for comparison with the other queries.

Q3. Select All Articles with Property (a) swrc:pages (b) swrc:month

```
SELECT ?article
WHERE {
        ?article rdf:type bench:Article.
        ?article ?property ?value
        (a) FILTER (?property = swrc:pages)
        (b) FILTER (?property = swrc:month)
}
```

Q3. The execution of query Q3a and Q3b requires only one join but generates a huge amount of intermediate results since the second triple pattern matches all RDF triples. However, we can observe that the output does not contain the filter variable ?property hence the query can be optimized on algebra level by a filter substitution where the variable is replaced by its value. This optimization reduces the execution time of this query by 70% (e)+(g) due to a significant reduction of the reduce shuffle bytes (f)+(h). A positive side effect of this optimization is the elimination of the unbounded predicate in the second triple pattern. Thus, using a vertical partitioned data set, only two predicates must be considered, which results in a significant reduction of data read from HDFS (opt+part). The filter optimization and the vertical partitioning reduces the execution time of this query by 97%.

The difference between Q3a and Q3b is the selectivity of the property used in the filter expression. While the property swrc:pages is rather unselective as it retains 92.61% of all articles, the property swrc:month retains only 0.62% of all articles [10]. But as we compare the query execution times in (e) and (g), there is not much difference since the query processing does not really exploit this fact as dangling articles are discarded in the reduce phase where the join between the two triple patterns is actually computed. For these kind of very selective patterns, it would be way more efficient to discard the dangling mappings already in the map phase before they are transferred over the network. We will discuss this in more detail in the following sections.

As an immediate observation our experiments confirm a linear scalability of the query processing time with respect to the size of the data, a well-known feature of the MapReduce paradigm. This underlines that PigSPARQL indeed is an effective application of the MapReduce paradigm for SPARQL. Our evaluations demonstrate how dramatically PigSPARQL's optimization reduces the amount of data to be handled and the corresponding query processing time. Along other optimizations, especially the vertical partitioning [20], which has a wide influence on the overall performance, but comes at the cost of a preprocessing step, that has to be done once in advance. However, we would like to stress that we could observe linear scalability also for query Q6, which might be highly problematic when not executed in a distributed environment. This claim is justified by the observation that in Q6 we first have to compute all publications with respect to all authors before we can find out those authors who have not published in the years before; hence, the query produces a large amount of intermediate results. One further important advantage of PigSPARQL is its simplicity in the sense of usability. Other research approaches in this area often do not provide their implementations at all or they cannot be used out of the box, as they are either not maintained anymore or just nonstable proof-of-concept implementations. In contrast, PigSPARQL is ready to download and can be executed on every Hadoop cluster with Apache Pig installed. There is neither an installation nor a configuration required, as even the data loading and partitioning is done using an included Pig Latin script. Moreover, as PigSPARQL translates SPARQL into Pig Latin, it benefits from further developments of Apache Pig and stays compatible with newer versions of Hadoop. Updating Apache Pig from version 0.5.0 to 0.10.0 improved our execution times in a range of 20% to 40% without changing a single line of code.

However, while the performance and scaling properties of PigSPARQL for complex analytical queries are competitive, the performance for selective queries is not satisfying. The reduce-side-based query execution requires to transfer the whole data that is going to be joined together through the network as join computation is done in the reduce phase. In particular rather selective queries suffer from this fact, since a large amount of unneeded data is processed, which could be avoided using more sophisticated join techniques based on index structures. In the following sections we describe an alternative join approach optimized for selective patterns where join computation is done in the map phase by utilizing the NoSQL data store HBase as a distributed index structure. While this approach retains the flexibility of commonly used reduce-side joins, it leverages the effectiveness of map-side joins without any changes to the underlying MapReduce framework. As we show in a further evaluation in Section 5.7, MAPSIN can improve query performance for selective queries by an order of magnitude compared with a classical reduce-side join execution, as used for PigSPARQL.

5.5 RDF STORAGE SCHEMA FOR HBase

Before introducing MAPSIN, we first have to discuss our RDF storage schema, that enables the storage of arbitrary RDF graphs in HBase as there is no straightforward mapping from the RDF data model to the HBase data model. Therefore, we will start the second part of this chapter with a short outline of HBase followed by a presentation of our RDF storage schema for HBase, that provides the required preconditions for processing MAPSIN joins without the usage of a reduce phase. HBase is a distributed, scalable, and strictly consistent column-oriented NoSQL data store, inspired by Google's Bigtable [22] and well integrated into Hadoop. Hadoop's distributed file system, HDFS, is designed for sequential reads and writes of very large files in a batch processing manner but lacks the ability to access data randomly in close to real time. HBase can be seen as an additional storage layer on top of HDFS that supports efficient random access. The data model of HBase corresponds to a sparse multidimensional sorted map with the following access pattern:

$$(Table,\ RowKey,\ Family,\ Column,\ Timestamp) \rightarrow Value$$

The rows of a table are sorted and indexed according to their *row key* and every row can have an arbitrary number of *columns*. Columns are grouped into *column families* and column values (denoted as cell) are timestamped and thus support multiple versions. HBase tables are dynamically split into *regions* of contiguous row ranges with a configured maximum size. When a region becomes too large, it is automatically split into two regions at the middle key (auto-sharding). However, HBase has neither a declarative query language nor built-in support for native join processing, leaving higher-level data transformations to the overlying application layer. In our approach we propose a map-side join strategy that leverages the implicit index capabilities of HBase to overcome the usual restrictions of map-side joins as outlined in Section 5.2.2.

In [23], the authors adopted the idea of Hexastore [24] to index all possible orderings of an RDF triple for storing RDF data in HBase. This results in six tables in HBase allowing to retrieve results for any possible SPARQL triple pattern with a single lookup on one of the tables (except for a triple pattern with three variables). However, as HDFS has a default replication factor of three and data in HBase is stored in files on HDFS, an RDF data set is actually stored 18 times using this schema. But it's not only about storage space, also loading a web-scale RDF data set into HBase becomes very costly and consumes many resources. Our storage schema for RDF data in HBase is inspired by [25] and uses only two tables, T_{s_po} and T_{o_ps}. We extend the schema with a triple pattern mapping that leverages the power of predicate push-down filters in HBase to overcome possible performance shortcomings of a two table schema. Furthermore, we improve the scalibility of the schema by introducing a modified row key design for class assignments in RDF, which would otherwise lead to overloaded regions constraining both scalability and performance.

In a T_{s_po} table, an RDF triple is stored using the subject as row key, the predicate as column name and the object as column value. If a subject has more than one object for a given predicate (e.g., an article having more than one author), these objects are stored as different versions in the same column. The notation T_{s_po} indicates that the table is indexed by subject. Table T_{o_ps} follows the same design. In both tables there is only one single column family that contains all columns. Tables 5.2 and 5.3 illustrate the corresponding tables for the RDF graph in Figure 5.6.

At first glance, this storage schema seems to have performance drawbacks when compared with the six table schema in [23] since there are only indexes for subjects and objects. However, we can use the HBase Filter API to specify additional column filters for table index lookups. These filters are applied directly on server

TABLE 5.2

T_{s_po} **Table for RDF Graph in Figure 5.6**

Rowkey	Family:Column→Value
Article1	p:title→{"PigSPARQL"},
	p:year→{"2011"},
	p:author→{Alex, Martin}
Article2	p:title→{"RDFPath"},
	p:year→{"2011"},
	p:author→{Martin, Alex},
	p:cite→{Article1}

TABLE 5.3

T_{o_ps} **Table for RDF Graph in Figure 5.6**

Rowkey	Family:Column→Value
"2011"	p:year→{Article1, Article2}
"PigSPARQL"	p:title→{Article1}
"RDFPath"	p:title→{Article2}
Alex	p:author→{Article1, Article2}
Article1	p:cite→{Article2}
Martin	p:author→{Article2, Article1}

FIGURE 5.6 RDF graph and SPARQL query.

side such that no unnecessary data must be transferred over the network (*predicate push-down*). As already mentioned in [25], a table with predicates as row keys causes scalability problems since the number of predicates in an ontology is usually fixed and relatively small, which results in a table with just a few very fat rows. Considering that all data in a row is stored on the same machine, the resources of a single machine in the cluster become a bottleneck. Indeed, if only the predicate in a triple pattern is given, we can use the HBase Filter API to answer this request with a table scan on T_{s_po} or T_{o_ps} using the predicate as column filter. Table 5.4 shows the mapping of every possible triple pattern to the corresponding HBase table. Overall, experiments on our cluster showed that the two-table schema with server side filters

TABLE 5.4

SPARQL Triple Pattern Mapping Using HBase Predicate Push-Down Filters

Pattern	Table	Filter
(s, p, o)	T_{s_po} or T_{o_ps}	Column and value
(?s, p, o)	T_{o_ps}	Column
(s, ?p, o)	T_{s_po} or T_{o_ps}	Value
(s, p, ?o)	T_{s_po}	Column
(?s, ?p, o)	T_{o_ps}	
(?s, p, ?o)	T_{s_po} or T_{o_ps} (table scan)	Column
(s, ?p, ?o)	T_{s_po}	
(?s, ?p, ?o)	T_{s_po} or T_{o_ps} (table scan)	

has similar performance characteristics compared to the six-table schema but uses only one third of storage space.

Our experiments also revealed some fundamental scaling limitations of the storage schema caused by T_{o_ps}. In general, an RDF data set uses a relatively small number of classes but contains many triples that link resources to classes, for example, (Alex, type, Person). Thus, using the object of a triple as row key means that all resources of the same class will be stored in the same row. With increasing data set size these rows become very large and exceed the configured maximum region size resulting in overloaded regions that contain only a single row. Since HBase cannot split these regions, the resources of a single machine become a bottleneck for scalability. To circumvent this problem we use a modified T_{o_ps} row key design for triples with predicate type. Instead of using the object as row key we use a compound row key of object and subject, for example, (PersonjAlex). As a result, we cannot access all resources of a class with a single table lookup, but as the corresponding rows will be consecutive in T_{o_ps}, we can use an efficient range scan starting at the first entry of the class.

5.6 MAPSIN JOIN

The indexing capabilities of HBase lay the foundation for our Map-Side Index Nested Loop Join (MAPSIN) that improves the query performance of selective queries. This allows us to retain the flexibility of reduce-side joins while utilizing the effectiveness of a map-side join without any changes to the underlying frameworks. We start the discussion by introducing the base case of our join technique followed by our strategy for cascading a sequence of joins. To the end, we will propose optimizations for multiway joins and one-pattern queries.

5.6.1 BASE CASE

To compute the join between two triple patterns, $p_1 \bowtie p_2$, we have to merge the compatible mappings for p_1 and p_2. Therefore, it is necessary that subsets of both multisets of mappings are brought together such that all compatible mappings can be processed on the same machine. Our MAPSIN join technique computes the join between p_1 and p_2 in a single map phase. At the beginning, the map phase is initialized with a parallel distributed HBase table scan for the first triple pattern p_1 where each machine retrieves only those mappings that are locally available. This is achieved by utilizing a mechanism for allocating local records to map functions, which is supported by the MapReduce input format for HBase. The map function is invoked for each retrieved mapping μ_1 for p_1. To compute the partial join between p_1 and p_2 for the given mapping μ_1, the map function needs to retrieve those mappings for p_2 that are compatible to μ_1 based on the shared variables between p_1 and p_2. At this point, the map function utilizes the input mapping μ_1 to substitute the shared variables in p_2, that is, the join variables. The substituted triple pattern, $p_2^{sub} = \mu_1(p_2)$, is then used to retrieve the compatible mappings with a table lookup in HBase following the triple pattern mapping outlined in Table 5.4. Since there is no guarantee that the corresponding HBase entries reside on the same machine, the results of the request have to be transferred over the network in general. However, in contrast to a reduce-side join approach where a lot of data is transferred over the network, we only transfer the data that is really needed. Finally, the computed multiset of mappings is stored in HDFS.

Figure 5.7 is an example for the base case that illustrates the join between the first two triple patterns of the SPARQL query in Figure 5.6. While the mappings for the first triple pattern (*?article*, title, *?title*) are retrieved locally using a distributed table scan (step 1+2), the compatible mappings for (*?article*, author, *?author*) are requested within the map function (step 3) and the resulting set of mappings is stored in HDFS (step 4).

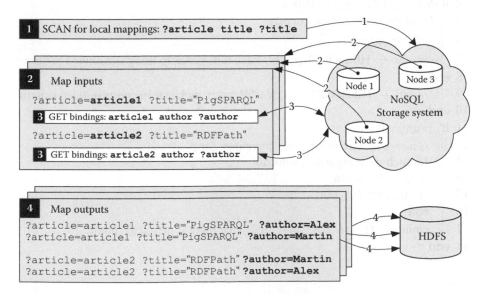

FIGURE 5.7 MAPSIN join base case for the first two triple patterns of query in Figure 5.6.

5.6.2 CASCADING JOINS

Chains of concatenated triple patterns require some slight modifications to the previously described base case. To compute a query of at least three triple patterns we have to process several joins successively, for example, $p_1 \bowtie p_2 \bowtie p_3$. The processing of the first two patterns $p_1 \bowtie p_2$ correspond to the base case and the results are stored in HDFS. The additional triple pattern p_3 is then joined with the mappings for $p_1 \bowtie p_2$. To this end, an additional map-phase (without any intermediate shuffle or reduce phase) is initialized with the previously computed mappings as input. Since these mappings reside in HDFS, they are retrieved locally in parallel such that the map function gets invoked for each mapping μ_2 for $p_1 \bowtie p_2$. The compatible mappings for p_3 are retrieved using the same strategy as for the base case, that is, μ_2 is used to substitute the shared variables in p_3, $p_3^{sub} = \mu_2(p_3)$, and compatible mappings are retrieved following the triple pattern mapping outlined in Table 5.4. Algorithm 5.1 outlines one iteration of the MAPSIN join. The input for the map function contains either a mapping for the first triple pattern (via distributed table scan) or a mapping for previously joined triple patterns (loaded from HDFS).

Algorithm 5.1: MAPSIN Join: map(inKey, inValue)

> **input** : *inKey, inValue:* value contains input mapping, key can be ignored
> **output**: multiset of mappings
> 1 $p_{n+1} \leftarrow$ Config.getNextPattern()
> 2 $\mu_n \leftarrow inValue$.getInputMapping()
> 3 $\Omega_{n+1} \leftarrow \emptyset$
> 4   **if** $dom(\mu_n) \cap dom(p_{n+1}) = \emptyset$ **then**
> 5   // substitute shared vars in p_{n+1}
> 6 $p_{n+1}^{sub} \leftarrow \mu_n(p_{n+1})$
> 7   *results* $\leftarrow$ HBase.GET(p_{n+1}^{sub}) // table index lookup using substituted pattern
> 8   **else**
> 9   *results* $\leftarrow$ HBase.GET(p_{n+1}) // table index lookup using unsubstituted pattern
> 10   **end**
> 11   **if** results $\neq \emptyset$ **then**
> 12   // merge μ_n with compatible mappings for p_{n+1}
> 13   **foreach** *mapping μ in results* **do**
> 14 $\mu_{n+1} \leftarrow \mu_n \cup \mu$
> 15 $\Omega_{n+1} \leftarrow \Omega_{n+1} \cup \mu_{n+1}$
> 16   **end**
> 17   emit(*null*, Ω_{n+1}) // key is not used since there is no reduce phase
> 18   **end**

5.6.3 MULTIWAY JOIN OPTIMIZATION

Instead of processing concatenated triple patterns successively as a sequence of two-way joins, some basic graph patterns allow to apply a multiway join approach to process joins between several concatenated triple patterns at once in a single map phase. This is typically the case for star pattern queries where triple patterns share the same join variable. The SPARQL query introduced in Section 5.5 is an example for such a query as all triple patterns share the same join variable ?*article*. This query can be processed by a three-way join in a single map-phase instead of two consecutive two-way joins.

We extended our approach to support this multiway join optimization. Again, the first triple pattern p_1 is processed using a distributed table scan as input for the map phase. But instead of using a sequence of n map phases to compute $p_1 \bowtie p_2 \bowtie \ldots \bowtie p_{n+1}$ we use a single map phase thus saving $n - 1$ MapReduce iterations. Hence, the map function needs to retrieve all mappings for $p_2, p_3, \ldots, p_{n+1}$ that are compatible to the input mapping μ_1 for p_1. Therefore, the join variable $?v_s$ in $p_2, p_3, \ldots, p_{n+1}$ (e.g., ?*article*) is substituted with the corresponding variable binding $\mu_1(?v_s)$. The substituted triple patterns $p_2^{sub}, p_3^{sub}, \ldots, p_{n+1}^{sub}$ with $p_i^{sub} = \mu_1(p_i)$ are then used to retrieve the compatible mappings using HBase table lookups. This general case of the MAPSIN multiway join is outlined in Algorithm 5.2.

Algorithm 5.2: MAPSIN multiway join: map(inKey, inValue)

    input : *inKey, inValue:* value contains input mapping, key can be ignored
    output: multiset of mappings
1 $p_{n+i} \leftarrow$ Config.getNextPattern()
2 $\mu_n \leftarrow inValue$.getInputMapping()
3 $\Omega_n \leftarrow \{\mu_n\}$
4 // iterate over all subsequent multiway patterns
5 **for** $i \leftarrow 1$ **to** #p **do**
6     $\Omega_{n+i} \leftarrow \emptyset, p_{n+i} \leftarrow$ Config.getNextPattern()
7     $p_{n+i}^{sub} \leftarrow \mu_n(p_{n+i})$// substitute shared vars in p_{n+i}
8   *results* $\leftarrow$ HBase.GET(p_{n+i}^{sub}) // table index lookup using substituted pattern
9   **if** *results* $\neq \emptyset$ **then**
10   // merge previous mappings with compatible mappings for p_{n+i}
11   **foreach** *mapping μ in results* **do**
12   **foreach** *mapping μ' in Ω_{n+i-1}*
13           $\Omega_{n+i} \leftarrow \Omega_{n+i} \cup (\mu \cup \mu')$
14   **end**
15   **end**
16   **else**
17   // no compatible mappings for p_{n+i} hence join result for μ_n is empty
18   return
19   **end**
20 **end**
21 emit(*null*, $\Omega_{n+\#p}$) // key is not used since there is no reduce phase

The performance of MAPSIN joins strongly correlates with the number of index lookups in HBase. Hence, minimizing the number of lookups is a crucial point for optimization. In many situations, it is possible to reduce the number of requests by leveraging the RDF schema design for HBase outlined in Section 5.5. If the join variable for all triple patterns is always on subject or always on object position, then all mappings for $p_2, p_3, \ldots, p_{n+1}$ that are compatible to the input mapping μ_1 for p_1 are stored in the same HBase table row of T_{s_po} or T_{o_ps}, respectively, making it possible to use a single instead of n subsequent table lookups. Hence, all compatible mappings can be retrieved at once thus saving $n - 1$ lookups for each invocation of the map function. Algorithm 5.3 outlines this optimized case.

Algorithm 5.3: MAPSIN Optimized Multiway Join: map(inKey, inValue)

    input : *inKey, inValue:* input mapping
    output: multiset of solution mappings
1 #p   Config.getNumberOfMultiwayPatterns()
2 $\mu_n \leftarrow inValue$.getInputMapping()
3 $\Omega_{n+\#p} \leftarrow \emptyset$
4 // iterate over all subsequent multiway patterns
5 **for** $i \leftarrow 1$ **to** #p **do**
6     $p_{n+i} \leftarrow$ Config.getNextPattern()
7     $p_{n+i}^{sub} \leftarrow \mu_n(p_{n+i})$// substitute shared vars in p_{n+i}
8 **end**
9 *results* $\leftarrow$ HBase.GET($p_{n+i}^{sub}, \ldots, p_{n+\#p}^{sub}$) // table index lookup with substituted pattern
10 **if** *results* $\neq \emptyset$ **then**
11   // merge μ_n with compatible mappings for $p_{n+i}, \ldots, p_{n+\#p}$
12   **foreach** *mapping μ in results* **do**
13         $\mu_{n+\#p} \leftarrow \mu_n \cup \mu'$
14         $\Omega_{n+\#p} \leftarrow \Omega_{n+\#p} \cup \mu_{n+\#p}$
15   **end**
16   emit(*null*, $\Omega_{n+\#p}$)
17 **end**

5.6.4 ONE-PATTERN QUERIES

Queries with only one single triple pattern, that return only a small number of solution mappings, can be executed locally on one machine. In general however, the number of solution mappings can exceed the capabilities of a single machine for large data sets. Thus, concerning scalability, it is advantageous to use a distributed execution with MapReduce even if we do not need to perform a join. The map phase is initialized with a distributed table scan for the single triple pattern p_1. Hence, map functions get only those mappings as input, which are locally available. The map function itself has only to emit the mappings to HDFS without any further requests to HBase. If the query result is small, nondistributed query execution can reduce query execution time significantly as MapReduce initialization takes up to 30 seconds in our cluster, which clearly dominates the execution time.

5.7 MAPSIN EVALUATION

The evaluation was performed on the same cluster used for the evaluation in Section 5.4, but we increased the RAM configuration of every server to 8 GB since HBase consumes a lot of RAM. We used HBase in the version 0.90.4.

We used the well-known Lehigh University Benchmark (LUBM) [11] as the queries can easily be formulated as SPARQL basic graph patterns. The generated data sets ranged from 1000 up to 3000 universities using the WebPIE inference engine for Hadoop [26] to precompute the transitive closure. The loading times for both tables T_{s_po} and T_{o_ps} as well as all data sets are listed in Table 5.5. We illustrate the performance comparison of PigSPARQL and MAPSIN for some selected LUBM queries that represent the different query types in Figure 5.8. Our proof-of-concept implementation is currently limited to a maximum number of two join variables as the goal was to demonstrate the feasibility of the approach for selective queries rather than supporting all possible BGP constellations. For detailed comparison, the runtimes of all executed queries are listed in Table 5.6.

LUBM queries Q1, Q3, Q5, Q11, Q13 demonstrate the base case with a single join between two triple patterns (cf. Figure 5.8a). MAPSIN joins performed 8 to 13 times faster compared to the reduce-side joins of PigSPARQL. Furthermore, the performance gain increases with the size of the data set.

LUBM queries Q4 (5 triple patterns), Q7 (4 triple patterns), Q8 (5 triple patterns) demonstrate the more general case with a sequence of cascaded joins (cf. Figure 5.8b). In these cases, MAPSIN joins perform up to 28 times faster than PigSPARQL. Of particular interest is query Q4 of LUBM, since it supports the multiway join optimization outlined in Section 5.6.3, as all triple patterns share the same join variable. This kind of optimization is also supported by PigSPARQL such that both approaches can compute the query results with a single multiway join (cf. Figure 5.8c). The MAPSIN multiway join optimization improves the basic MAPSIN join execution time by a factor of 3.3 (LUBM Q4), independently of the data size. Moreover, the MAPSIN multiway join optimization performs 19 to 28 times faster than the reduce-side based multiway join implementation of PigSPARQL.

The remaining queries (LUBM Q6, Q14) consist of only one single triple pattern. Consequently, they do not contain a join processing step and illustrate primarily the advantages of the distributed HBase table scan compared with the HDFS storage

---

TABLE 5.5

LUBM Loading Times for Tables T_{s_po} and T_{o_ps} (hh:mm:ss)

LUBM	1000	1500	2000	2500	3000
# RDF triples	~210 million	~315 million	~420 million	~525 million	~630 million
T_{s_po}	00:28:50	00:42:10	00:52:03	00:56:00	01:05:25
T_{o_ps}	00:48:57	01:14:59	01:21:53	01:38:52	01:34:22
Total	01:17:47	01:57:09	02:13:56	02:34:52	02:39:47

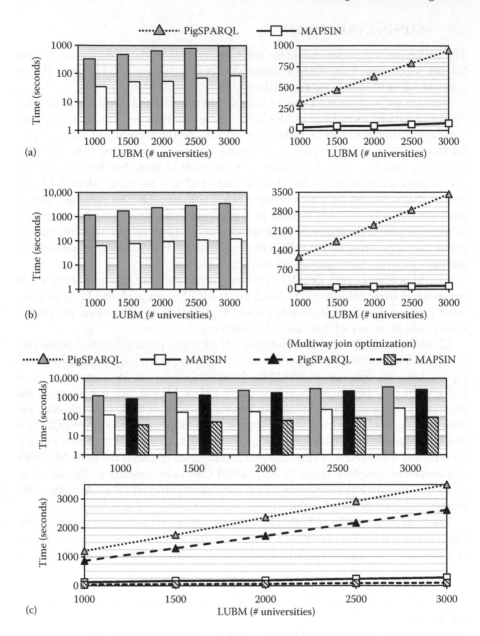

FIGURE 5.8 Performance comparison for LUBM Q1 (a), Q8 (b), and Q4 (c).

access of PigSPARQL. Improvements are still present but less significant, resulting in an up to five times faster query execution.

An open issue of the evaluation remains the actual data flow between HBase and MapReduce, as HBase is like a black box where data distribution and partitioning is handled by the system automatically. Since data locality is an important

TABLE 5.6
Query Execution Times for PigSPARQL (P) and MAPSIN (M) (in seconds)

	1000		1500		2000		2500		3000	
LUBM	P	M	P	M	P	M	P	M	P	M
Q1	324	34	475	51	634	53	790	70	944	84
Q3	324	33	480	42	642	49	805	59	961	72
Q4	1202	121	1758	167	2368	182	2919	235	3496	279
Q4 MJ	861	37	1297	53	1728	62	2173	81	2613	92
Q5	329	33	484	44	640	53	800	66	955	80
Q6	149	48	214	60	284	69	355	84	424	104
Q7	1013	62	1480	68	1985	93	2472	114	2928	123
Q8	1172	64	1731	77	2318	33	2870	108	3431	121
Q11	319	33	469	46	620	53	780	69	931	79
Q13	325	44	482	72	645	84	800	108	957	128
Q14	149	43	214	70	288	79	364	89	434	107

aspect of distributed systems, it is crucial to examine additional measures for future optimizations.

Overall, the MAPSIN join approach clearly outperforms the reduce-side join based query execution for selective queries. Both approaches reveal a linear scaling behavior with the input size but the slope of the MAPSIN join is much smaller. Especially for LUBM queries, MAPSIN joins outperform reduce-side joins by an order of magnitude, as these queries are generally rather selective. Moreover, the application of the multiway join optimization results in a further significant improvement of the total query execution times.

5.8 RELATED WORK

Single machine RDF systems like *Sesame* [27] and *Jena* [28] are widely used since they are user-friendly and perform well for small- and medium-sized RDF data sets. *RDF-3X* [29] is considered one of the fastest single machine RDF systems in terms of query performance that vastly outperforms previous single machine systems but performance degrades for queries with unbound objects and low selectivity factor [30]. Furthermore, as the amount of RDF data continues to grow, it will become more and more difficult to store entire data sets on a single machine due to the limited scaling capabilities [3].

In [31], a translation from SPARQL to Pig Latin has already been mentioned. However, the authors provide no further information or technical details about it. To the best of our knowledge, we present the first detailed and comprehensive translation from SPARQL to Pig Latin that also considers efficient optimizations on different levels and is evaluated with a SPARQL performance benchmark that also contains queries with the SPARQL-specific OPTIONAL operator.

The authors in [32] also consider the execution of SPARQL queries based on Hadoop. In contrast to our approach a query is directly mapped into a sequence of MapReduce jobs. They also provide evaluation results for the SP^{2}Bench queries Q1, Q2, and Q3a on a Hadoop cluster of ten nodes similar to our cluster. A comparison of the results confirms that both approaches have a similar performance whereby our implementation is more than 40% faster for Q3a. This demonstrates that our approach based on mapping SPARQL to Pig Latin achieves an execution of SPARQL queries that keeps up with a direct mapping to MapReduce with respect to efficiency if not being more efficient. Another direct mapping approach is also proposed in [33]. In contrast to these approaches, our translation supports all SPARQL 1.0 operators and also benefits from further developments of Pig [34]. As we map to Pig Latin, we can expect a greater independence from possible changes inside the underlying MapReduce layer in comparison to a direct mapping.

There is also a large body of work dealing with join processing in MapReduce considering various aspects and application fields [14,15,35–39]. In Section 5.2.2, we briefly outlined the advantages and drawbacks of the general-purpose reduce-side and map-side (merge) join approaches in MapReduce. Though map-side joins are generally more efficient, they are hard to cascade due to the strict preconditions. Our MAPSIN approach leverages HBase to overcome the shortcomings of common map-side joins without the use of auxiliary shuffle and reduce phases, making MAPSIN joins easily cascadable. In addition to these general-purpose approaches there are several proposals focusing on certain join types or optimizations of existing join techniques for particular application fields. In [37], the authors discussed how to process arbitrary joins (theta joins) using MapReduce, whereas [35] focuses on optimizing multiway joins. However, in contrast to our MAPSIN join, both approaches process the join in the reduce phase including a costly data shuffle phase.

Map–reduce–merge [39] describes a modified MapReduce workflow by adding a merge phase after the reduce phase, whereas *map–join–reduce* [36] proposes a join phase in between the map and reduce phases. Both techniques attempt to improve the support for joins in MapReduce but require profound modifications to the MapReduce framework. In [40], the authors present a noninvasive index and join techniques for SQL processing in MapReduce that also reduce the amount of shuffled data at the cost of an additional co-partitioning and indexing phase at load time. However, the schema and workload are assumed to be known in advance, which is typically feasible for relational data but does not hold for RDF in general.

HadoopDB [41] is a hybrid of MapReduce and DBMS where MapReduce is the communication layer above multiple single-node DBMS. The authors in [3] adopt this hybrid approach for the semantic web using RDF-3X. However, the initial graph partitioning is done on a single machine and has to be repeated if the data set is updated or the number of machines in the cluster change. As we use HBase as an underlying storage layer, additional machines can be plugged in seamlessly and updates are possible without having to reload the entire data set. *HadoopRDF* [30] is a MapReduce-based RDF system that stores data directly in HDFS and does also not require any changes to the Hadoop framework. It is able to rebalance automatically when cluster size changes but join processing is also done in the reduce phase. Our MAPSIN join does not use any shuffle or reduce phase at all, even in consecutive iterations.

Instead of a general MapReduce cluster, some RDF stores are built on top of a specialized computer cluster. Virtuoso Cluster Edition [42] is a cluster extension of the well-known Virtuoso RDF store. 4store [7] is a ready-to-use RDF store that divides the cluster in storage and processing nodes. Nevertheless, the usage of a specialized cluster has the disadvantage that it requires a dedicated infrastructure and pose additional installation and management overhead whereas our approach builds upon the idea to use existing infrastructures that are well known and widely used. As we do not require any changes to Hadoop or HBase at all, it is possible to use any existing Hadoop cluster or cloud service (e.g., Amazon EC2) out of the box.

5.9 CONCLUSION

In this chapter, we presented PigSPARQL, a new approach for the scalable execution of SPARQL queries on very large RDF data sets. For this purpose, we designed and implemented a translation from SPARQL to Pig Latin. The resulting Pig Latin program is translated into a sequence of MapReduce jobs and executed in parallel on a Hadoop cluster. Following such an approach, we benefit from further developments of Apache Pig without any additional programming effort. This includes performance enhancements as well as major changes of Hadoop like the upcoming YARN (MRv2) framework. PigSPARQL is available for download and can be used out of the box on every Hadoop cluster with Apache Pig installed, since there is neither an installation nor a configuration process required. Our evaluation with a SPARQL specific benchmark confirmed that PigSPARQL is well suited for the scalable execution of SPARQL queries on large RDF data sets with Hadoop. This is also demonstrated by the used data set size of up to 1.6 billion RDF triples that already exceeds the capabilities of many single machine systems [10].

Although PigSPARQL offers an easy and efficient way to take advantage of the performance and scalability of Hadoop for the distributed and parallelized execution of SPARQL queries, the performance of selective queries was not satisfying. This is attributed to principle of a reduce-side join, where dangling tuples are thrown out in the reduce phase, which causes a large amount of probably unneeded data that has to be shuffled through the network in general. To overcome this issue, we introduced the Map-Side Index Nested Loop Join (MAPSIN join), which combines the advantages of the NoSQL data store HBase with the well known and approved distributed processing facilities of MapReduce. In general, map-side joins are more efficient than reduce-side joins in MapReduce as there is no expensive data shuffle phase involved. However, current map-side join approaches suffer from strict preconditions what makes them hard to apply in general, especially in a sequence of joins. The combination of HBase and MapReduce allows us to cascade a sequence of MAPSIN joins without having to sort and repartition the intermediate output for the next iteration. Furthermore, with the multiway join optimization, we can reduce the number of MapReduce iterations and HBase requests. Using an index to selectively request only those data that is really needed also saves network bandwidth, making parallel query execution more efficient. The evaluation with the LUBM benchmark demonstrated the advantages of our approach compared with the commonly used reduce-side join approach. For selective queries, the MAPSIN join based SPARQL query execution outperformed the reduce-side join based execution in PigSPARQL by an order of magnitude while scaling very smoothly with the input size. Lastly, our approach did not require any changes to Hadoop and HBase at all. Consequently, MAPSIN joins could be run on any existing Hadoop infrastructure and also on an instance of Amazon's Elastic Compute Cloud (EC2) without additional installation or management overhead.

REFERENCES

1. Manola, F., Miller, E., McBride, B.: RDF Primer. W3C Recom. Available at http://www.w3.org/TR/rdf-primer/ (2004).
2. Prud'hommeaux, E., Seaborne, A.: SPARQL Query Language for RDF. W3C Recom. Available at http://www.w3.org/TR/rdf-sparql-query/ (2008).
3. Huang, J., Abadi, D.J., Ren, K.: Scalable SPARQL Querying of Large RDF Graphs. *PVLDB* 4(11), 1123–1134 (2011).
4. Dean, J., Ghemawat, S.: MapReduce: Simplified Data Processing on Large Clusters. *Commun. ACM* 51(1), 107–113 (2008).
5. White, T.: *Hadoop—The Definitive Guide: Storage and Analysis at Internet Scale* (2nd ed.). O'Reilly (2011) Sebastopol (CA, USA).
6. Harth, A., Umbrich, J., Hogan, A., Decker, S.: YARS2: A Federated Repository for Querying Graph Structured Data from the Web. *Semantic Web* 4825, 211–224 (2007).
7. Harris, S., Lamb, N., Shadbolt, N.: 4store: The Design and Implementation of a Clustered RDF Store. In: *SSWS*, pp. 94–109 (2009).
8. Olston, C., Reed, B., Srivastava, U., Kumar, R., Tomkins, A.: Pig Latin: A Not-So-Foreign Language for Data Processing. In: *Proc. SIGMOD*, pp. 1099–1110. ACM (2008).
9. Schätzle, A., Przyjaciel-Zablocki, M., Lausen, G.: PigSPARQL: Mapping SPARQL to Pig Latin. In: *Proceedings of the International Workshop on Semantic Web Information Management (SWIM)*, pp. 4:1–4:8 (2011).
10. Schmidt, M., Hornung, T., Lausen, G., Pinkel, C.: SP2Bench: A SPARQL Performance Benchmark. In: *Proc. ICDE*, pp. 222–233 (2009).
11. Guo, Y., Pan, Z., Heflin, J.: LUBM: A Benchmark for OWL Knowledge Base Systems. *Web Semantics* 3(2), 158–162 (2005).
12. Pérez, J., Arenas, M., Gutierrez, C.: Semantics and Complexity of SPARQL. *ACM Trans. Database Syst. (TODS)* 34(3), 16 (2009).
13. Ghemawat, S., Gobioff, H., Leung, S.T.: The Google File System. In: *Proc. SOSP*, pp. 29–43 (2003).
14. Blanas, S., Patel, J.M., Ercegovac, V., Rao, J., Shekita, E.J., Tian, Y.: A Comparison of Join Algorithms for Log Processing in MapReduce. In: *SIGMOD* (2010).
15. Lee, K.H., Lee, Y.J., Choi, H., Chung, Y.D., Moon, B.: Parallel Data Processing with MapReduce: A Survey. *SIGMOD Rec.* 40(4), 11–20 (2011).
16. Apache: Pig Latin Reference Manual 1 and 2. Available at http://pig.apache.org/docs/ (2010).
17. Hartig, O., Heese, R.: The SPARQL Query Graph Model for Query Optimization. In: *The Semantic Web: Research and Applications*, pp. 564–578 (2007).
18. Schmidt, M., Meier, M., Lausen, G.: Foundations of SPARQL Query Optimization. In: *Proc. ICDT*, pp. 4–33 (2010).
19. Stocker, M., Seaborne, A., Bernstein, A., Kiefer, C., Reynolds, D.: SPARQL Basic Graph Pattern Optimization Using Selectivity Estimation. In: *Proc. WWW*, pp. 595–604 (2008).
20. Abadi, D.J., Marcus, A., Madden, S., Hollenbach, K.J.: Scalable Semantic Web Data Management Using Vertical Partitioning. In: *Proc. VLDB*, pp. 411–422 (2007).
21. Ley, M.: DBLP Bibliography. Available at http://www.informatik.uni-trier.de/ley/db/ (2010).

22. Chang, F., Dean, J., Ghemawat, S., Hsieh, W., Wallach, D., Burrows, M., Chandra, T., Fikes, A., Gruber, R.: Bigtable: A Distributed Storage System for Structured Data. *ACM Trans. Comput. Syst. (TOCS)* 26(2), 4 (2008).

23. Sun, J., Jin, Q.: Scalable RDF Store Based on HBase and MapReduce. In: *ICACTE*, vol. 1, pp. 633–636 (2010).

24. Weiss, C., Karras, P., Bernstein, A.: Hexastore: Sextuple Indexing for Semantic Web Data Management. *PVLDB* 1(1), 1008–1019 (2008).

25. Franke, C., Morin, S., Chebotko, A., Abraham, J., Brazier, P.: Distributed Semantic Web Data Management in HBase and MySQL Cluster. In: *IEEE International Conference on Cloud Computing (CLOUD)*, pp. 105–112 (2011).

26. Urbani, J., Kotoulas, S., Maassen, J., van Harmelen, F., Bal, H.: OWL Reasoning with WebPIE: Calculating the Closure of 100 Billion Triples. In: *ESWC*, pp. 213–227 (2010).

27. Broekstra, J., Kampman, A., van Harmelen, F.: Sesame: A Generic Architecture for Storing and Querying RDF and RDF Schema. In: *Proc. ISWC* (2002).

28. Wilkinson, K., Sayers, C., Kuno, H.A., Reynolds, D.: Efficient RDF Storage and Retrieval in Jena2. In: *SWDB*, pp. 131–150 (2003).

29. Neumann, T., Weikum, G.: RDF-3X: A RISC-Style Engine for RDF. *PVLDB* 1(1), 647–659 (2008).

30. Husain, M.F., McGlothlin, J.P., Masud, M.M., Khan, L.R., Thuraisingham, B.M.: Heuristics-Based Query Processing for Large RDF Graphs Using Cloud Computing. *IEEE TKDE* 23(9), 1312–1327 (2011).

31. Mika, P., Tummarello, G.: Web Semantics in the Clouds. *IEEE Intell. Syst.* 23(5), 82–87 (2008).

32. Husain, M., Khan, L., Kantarcioglu, M., Thuraisingham, B.: Data Intensive Query Processing for Large RDF Graphs Using Cloud Computing Tools. In: *Proc. CLOUD*, pp. 1–10. IEEE (2010).

33. Myung, J., Yeon, J., Lee, S.: SPARQL Basic Graph Pattern Processing With Iterative MapReduce. In: *Proc. MDAC*, pp. 1–6. ACM (2010).

34. Gates, A.F., Natkovich, O., Chopra, S., Kamath, P., Narayanamurthy, S.M., Olston, C., Reed, B., Srinivasan, S., Srivastava, U.: Building a High-Level Dataflow System on Top of Map-Reduce: The Pig Experience. *PVLDB* 2(2), 1414–1425 (2009).

35. Afrati, F.N., Ullman, J.D.: Optimizing Multiway Joins in a Map-Reduce Environment. *IEEE TKDE* 23(9), 1282–1298 (2011).

36. Jiang, D., Tung, A.K.H., Chen, G.: Map-Join-Reduce: Toward Scalable and Efficient Data Analysis on Large Clusters. *IEEE TKDE* 23(9), 1299–1311 (2011).

37. Okcan, A., Riedewald, M.: Processing Theta-Joins Using MapReduce. In: *SIGMOD Conference*, pp. 949–960 (2011).

38. Przyjaciel-Zablocki, M., Schätzle, A., Hornung, T., Lausen, G.: RDFPath: Path Query Processing on Large RDF Graphs with MapReduce. In: *ESWC Workshops*, pp. 50–64 (2011).

39. Yang, H.-C., Dasdan, A., Hsiao, R.-L., Parker, S.: Map-Reduce-Merge: Simplified Relational Data Processing on Large Clusters. In: *SIGMOD* (2007).

40. Dittrich, J., Quiané-Ruiz, J.A., Jindal, A., Kargin, Y., Setty, V., Schad, J.: Hadoop++: Making a Yellow Elephant Run Like a Cheetah (Without It Even Noticing). *PVLDB* 3(1), 518–529 (2010).

41. Abouzeid, A., Bajda-Pawlikowski, K., Abadi, D.J., Rasin, A., Silberschatz, A.: HadoopDB: An Architectural Hybrid of MapReduce and DBMS Technologies for Analytical Workloads. *PVLDB* 2(1), 922–933 (2009).

42. Erling, O., Mikhailov, I.: Towards Web Scale RDF. In: *Proc. SSWS* (2008).

6 Algebraic Optimization of RDF Graph Pattern Queries on MapReduce

Kemafor Anyanwu, Padmashree Ravindra, and HyeongSik Kim

CONTENTS

6.1   INTRODUCTION

The growing success of the Semantic Web and Web of data initiatives has ushered in the era of "Big Semantic Web Data." Data sets such as the Billion Triple Challenge [2] are in the order of billions of triples and scientific data collections like the Open Science Data cloud [3] are approaching petabyte scale. A crucial question now is how to meet the scalability challenges of processing such data collections. Further, emerging applications are introducing nontraditional scalability requirements where scalability needs are elastic, varying significantly at different periods. For example, a biologist may want to analyze their protein data by linking to other publicly available related data. This data maybe from their domain, or other domains, for example, data about chemical compounds for helping interdisciplinary research is increasingly demanding such holistic perspectives on data.

A biologist may not have the resources for locally storing and managing the large amounts of biological data available on the Web (data sets like Uniprot are updated monthly), nor may they be interested in managing data from other disciplines, for example, chemistry, locally. To satisfy the needs of these applications, cloud data services are increasing in popularity, and while most are still in their nascent phases, significant activity is on to increase usability and performance of these systems. Many cloud data services are based on the MapReduce programming model [12] or other similar models, made popular by Google's expository [12] on their data-processing stack. Its attractiveness is the simplicity of its programming model which helps usability, its ability to support clusters made from commodity-grade machines, making it inexpensive. An open-source implementation of MapReduce called *Hadoop* [9] is now available. Hadoop-based extensions such as Apache Pig [32] and

Hive [44] provide high-level data flow or query languages and automatic optimization techniques a la relational database systems, and are gaining popularity.

In the context of scalable processing of Semantic Web data, query processing techniques have to address the unique challenges posed by semantic graph data models such as W3C's *Resource Description Framework* (RDF). In RDF, data is modeled at a fine-grained level in the form of what are called *statements* or *triples*. A *triple* (*Subject*, *Property*, *Object*) asserts that a resource (the *Subject*) has a *Property* whose value (the *Object*) is another resource or a literal. Figure 6.1a shows a subset of triples describing vendor-product offerings in the commerce context. The example triple (*&Off*1, *product*, *&Pr*1) states that an offer *&Off*1 is for a product *&Pr*1. Further, nodes and edges may be linked to an ontological layer that defines types of nodes and edges and relationships between node types and edge types. Therefore, an RDF model may entail additional statements beyond what is explicitly asserted, and entailed statements can be derived using inferencing techniques. An RDF database is a collection of triples but can also be viewed as a directed labeled graph with nodes representing *subjects* and *objects*, and labeled edges denoting *property* types.

The foundational construct for querying an RDF graph is a *triple pattern*, which is a triple with a variable (denoted by leading '?') in any of the Subject, Property, or Object positions, for example, (*?o vendor ?v*). A triple t in the database is considered a valid "match" for a triple pattern tp if some substitution of the variables in tp with RDF terms (resources or literals), yields t. For example, triple $t =$ (*&Off*1, *vendor*, *&V*1) is a match for triple pattern (*?o vendor ?v*) because the substitutions *?o/&Off*1 and *?v/&V*1 produce a valid triple t in the database. Multiple triple patterns can be combined using combination operators to form *Graph Patterns*. A *Basic Graph Pattern* is a conjunction of two or more triple patterns and shared variables across triple patterns implicitly represent equi-joins. The example query Q1 in Figure 6.1b is a graph pattern with 10 triple patterns with 9 implicit joins (3 with *?v*, 3 with *?o*, 2 with *?r*, 1 with *?prod*). The answer to a graph pattern is the list of substitutions for each variable that agree across triple patterns (i.e., meet join conditions).

An important consequence of RDF's fine-grained data model is that query workloads contain much larger number of joins than relational workloads. In fact, up to 100 join operations have been reported in queries for some real applications [43]. This number can be further increased if a complete result, including entailed triples, is desired and inferencing is done as query expansion during processing. The first challenge in this context is that relational query plan generation strategies will be confounded by the large search space generated by such numbers of joins. Further, the heuristics that are used to prune search space such as restricting to only left-linear plans, are not ideal for RDF queries. In fact, bushy plans are often preferred since many of the joins are m-way star joins and can be evaluated as merge joins if suitable sorted indexes exist. Consequently, such queries have a much larger query plan search space than existing strategies are suited for. A second subtle but critical point is that cost-based query optimization techniques used for ordering join operations assume conditions that do not carry over to RDF models. For example, the *containment of value sets* assumption that underlies join cardinality estimation exploits the referential integrity constraint in relational models that allows this assumption to hold in many relational join scenarios (e.g., join between foreign and primary key fields). However,

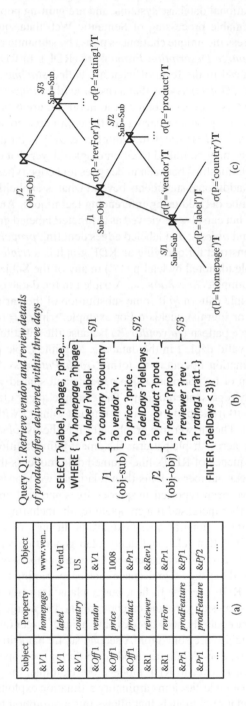

(a)

Query Q1: *Retrieve vendor and review details*
of product offers delivered within three days

SELECT ?vlabel, ?hpage, ?price,....
WHERE { ?v homepage ?hpage.
         ?v label ?vlabel.
    J1 ⎡ ?v country ?vcountry.
(obj-sub) ⎣ ?o vendor ?v .
         ?o price ?price .
         ?o delDays ?delDays .
    J2 ⎡ ?o product ?prod .
(obj-obj) ⎣ ?r revFor ?prod .
         ?r reviewer ?rev.
         ?r rating1 ?rat1 .}
    FILTER (?delDays < 3)}

(b)

(c)

FIGURE 6.1 (a) Example RDF triple relation T, (b) example SPARQL query Q1, and (c) corresponding relational algebra plan.

these constraints are not present in RDF models. The consequence of this mismatch in assumptions may not be easily observable when dealing with very small data sets or data sets generated using synthetic benchmarks like LUBM and BSBM that generate data fairly systematically, causing such assumptions to hold artificially. However, when processing large real data sets, this issue becomes very apparent.

Distributed and Parallel Graph Pattern Query Evaluation. Systems such as Virtuoso [14] use distributed and parallel processing schemes for scalable RDF query processing on cluster-based architectures. Other systems use a hybrid of MapReduce for distributed processing and traditional RDF database systems for processing within a partition [21]. Some others use only MapReduce processing [22,36,41]. Overall, in most of these existing systems, data partitioning is done using some sort of key range partitioning [17,18,22,43]. However, [21] uses a structure-based partitioning scheme that clusters related nodes and edges at a coarser level of granularity—connected subgraphs. The nature of data partitioning impacts the kind of parallelism that can be enabled for processing. For example, key range partitioning on a column of a triple relation will allow join operations on that column to be executed using *partitioned parallelism*, where same operator is executed across partitions. If there are multiple such joins, that is, a star join, then potentially, *pipelined parallelism* of the join operations that constitute a star join, could be supported within each partition. For most existing systems, this is the extent of parallelism that is supported. The implication is that from a global perspective, the context of every execution is either a single join or a single star join. This means that when there are multiple star joins there are multiple partition phases with potential costs of materializing intermediate results and transporting them across the network. In MapReduce platforms, the cost of each execution phase is more significant than traditional processing models, so that it is more critical to focus on having plans with as few phases as possible, that is, shorter execution workflows. One may consider using structure-based partitioning schemes such as in [21] to achieve a coarser-grained partitioning, so that complete matches for large subqueries or even entire queries may be found within individual partitions, thus minimizing the number of phases needed. However, the need for such specialized partitioning only adds to the already significant preprocessing time required by existing systems for constructing a large number of indexes and statistical profiles (HadoopRDF [22] reported up to 56 hrs for 3.3 billion triples in systems like RDF-3X [30]). Significant preprocessing requirements may not be ideal in elastic, on-demand, leased cloud-usage scenarios because there are financial implications for such times that may not be recouped in the short terms that services are rented. Further, it delays time-to-first-result, which is critical in exploratory phases where users want to get a quick sense before determining exactly what they want to do with the data. In addition, the goal of keeping execution workflow shorter may conflict with optimization goals of non-MapReduce cost-based techniques based on just statistics. For example, using relational join cardinality estimation techniques, the optimal query plan selected may be a more linear query plan with a longer MapReduce execution workflow than if using number of MapReduce cycles as a primary optimization goal. This has been echoed in [6,22], and we present an empirical validation in the next section.

To enable fewer MapReduce cycles it will be useful to investigate other kinds of inter-operator parallelism. HadoopRDF [22] explored this idea by making some modifications to Hadoop. Another approach to achieve this is to use algebraic optimization—rewriting queries using a new set of operators that can achieve the same goal. In [36], such an approach has been presented. However, this approach has additional advantages over the approach in HadoopRDF in terms of management of intermediate results because it uses a nested data model as opposed to the classical relational model. Also, HadoopRDF, like most systems, requires a preprocessing phase.

This book chapter will discuss state-of-art techniques that have been proposed for RDF data processing, particularly graph pattern matching queries, on MapReduce. It will also cover related techniques that have not yet been applied to RDF query processing but are applicable. The chapter will cover algorithms for MapReduce-based physical operators, Hadoop-only and hybrid computational architectures, query compilation, cost models, and heuristics for cost-based optimization techniques, data model and algebras for algebraic optimization, and dynamic and adaptive optimization techniques. We will end the chapter with a short discussion on the feasibility of current approaches with more complex SPARQL graph pattern fragments, for example, queries with unbound predicates, optional clauses, or queries with grouping and aggregation.

6.2   DATA PROCESSING USING MapReduce—AN OVERVIEW

Encoding tasks using the MapReduce programming model is done in terms of two functions:

$$map(K1, V1) \rightarrow list(K2, V2)$$

$$\texttt{reduce}(K2, list(V2)) \rightarrow (K2, V3)$$

where map() processes input key-value pairs $(K1, V1)$ and produces intermediate key-value pairs $(K2, V2)$. The reduce() aggregates the group of values associated with an intermediate key such as $K2$ in this example, to produce an output key-value pair for each group. MapReduce execution platforms like Hadoop use a master–slave architecture where a master node (*JobTracker*) splits the input file into "chunks" and schedules m instances of slave nodes called *mappers* such that each is assigned some chunk to process, that is, execute the map() function on its input, partition the map output based on the key and write results to their local disks. Subsequently, the *JobTracker* schedules r instances of *reducers* to *reduce* some assigned partition of mapper output values in a process that consists of three phases: *copy*—copying the sorted map output from mappers' disks to reducer nodes; *merge*—merging the sorted output lists from the different mappers based on the intermediate key, and *reduce*—reduce() is invoked once for each intermediate key, and applied to the associated group of values. The output of the reduce phase is saved to the *Hadoop Distributed File System* (HDFS).

Remark 6.1

The dominant cost components in a MapReduce cycle include, M_{Read}—the cost of mappers reading input; data-shuffling costs that involve M_{Write}—local disk writes at the mappers, MR_{Sort}—sort–merge costs, as well as MR_{TR}—network transfer costs, and finally R_{Write}—the cost of writing the reduce output to the HDFS, that is, cost of a MapReduce cycle MR_i can be summarized as

$$M_{Read} + (M_{Write} + MR_{Sort} + MR_{TR}) + R_{Write}$$

■

6.2.1   RDF DATA PROCESSING ON MAPREDUCE

Most nontrivial data-processing tasks will require multiple MapReduce cycles that are chained together into sequential, but data dependency-preserving, execution workflows. There are often multiple possible decompositions of a task into cycles or subtasks. Therefore, given a data-processing task, a key question is to find a decomposition that produces a low overall workflow cost. Since, as mentioned earlier, each MapReduce cycle incurs a significant amount of overhead, decompositions that result in shorter workflows have a better chance of fulfilling that requirement. In the context of RDF data processing, the decomposition problem is the distribution of SELECT, PROJECT, and particularly JOIN operations, into subtasks where each subtask is supported by a MapReduce cycle. The decomposition issue is related to the ordering of operations because only neighboring operations in a query plan can be effectively grouped into the same subtask. In the MapReduce context, it is helpful to guide the ordering of operations based on key partitioning requirements so that neighboring operations do not have conflicting partitioning requirements. This would force a repartitioning step between such operations, delineating them into different cycles. For example, the two JOIN operations that join the first three triple patterns in our example query Q1 (refer Figure 6.1b) can be computed as a multiway join on the Subject column (*star-join*), and hence can be grouped and executed in the same MapReduce (MR) cycle. Figure 6.1c shows the relational algebra plan after decomposing query Q1 based on star joins, which required a total of 5 MR cycles—one for each of the three star joins (*SJ1*, *SJ2*, *SJ3*), and two MR cycles to compute the joins between the stars (*J1* and *J2*). To understand the impact of length of workflow on performance, we present a case study that empirically evaluates query execution strategies on MapReduce.

6.2.2   CASE STUDY: DIFFERENT GROUPINGS OF STAR-JOINS

Figure 6.2 shows a case study with 6 test queries (each with two star subpatterns) using the BSBM synthetic benchmark data set (43 GB) on a 10-node Hadoop cluster. The test queries have varying join structures with object–subject join (Q1a, Q1b, Q2a, Q2b) and object–object join (Q3a, Q3b) between star patterns. Queries Q1b, Q2b, Q3b are variations of Q1a, Q2a, Q3a, respectively, where one of the two star joins is highly selective due to an additional filter on the object column. We evaluated three approaches that execute, (i) a star join per cycle approach (*SJ-per-cycle*), (ii) most selective grouping of joins first but preserving star structure as much as possible to minimize MR cycles (*Sel-SJ-first*), and (iii) grouping-based approach that concurrently computes all star joins in a single cycle (*NTGA*). *SJ-per-cycle* approach requires three MR cycles for all queries (two of three cycles require full scan of

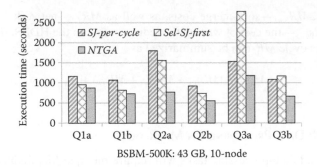

BSBM-500K: 43 GB, 10-node

FIGURE 6.2   A comparative evaluation of different groupings of star-joins.

triple relation). For object–subject joins, *Sel-SJ-first* approach can group joins into just two MR cycles (both cycles scan entire triple relation). For the object–object join (Q3a, Q3b), *Sel-SJ-first* still requires three MR cycles, but more importantly has very high HDFS reads due to full scan of triple relation in all three cycles. In contrast, the *NTGA* approach is able to minimize the number of MR cycles (two cycles for all queries), as well as minimize the required number of full scans of the triple relation, thus outperforming the other two approaches for all the test queries.

   Besides the issue of workflow execution length, the sizes of intermediate outputs and inputs, have an impact on performance. This is because M_{Read}, M_{Write}, MR_{Sort}, MR_{TR}, and R_{Write}, are all functions of the size of data. In addition to the impact of the intermediate data size on disk I/Os and network traffic, which affect query latency, size of intermediate results also impact the disk space requirements for a MapReduce workflow. This is because systems such as Hadoop provide fault-tolerance by storing intermediate results, until the workflow completes. Therefore, to successfully complete the execution of a workflow with k MR cycles MR_1 to MR_k, the amount of available disk space should be at least equal to

$$\left(|Inp| + \left|Out_{MR_1}\right| + \left|Out_{MR_2}\right| + ... + \left|Out_{MR_k}\right| \right) \times Rep_{DFS}$$

where Inp is the initial input, Out_{MR_i} is reduce output for the ith MR cycle, and Rep_{DFS} is the configured replication factor of the distributed file system.

Remark 6.2

The above discussion highlights that two key objectives for optimizing evaluation of queries on MapReduce platforms are minimizing length of execution workflow and minimizing the footprint of intermediate results.   ∎

6.3   RELATED WORK

Over the last decade, there has been significant research in developing efficient and scalable RDF processing systems. State-of-the-art single-node systems [10,30,46] have integrated various optimization techniques for efficient query processing, for example, histograms, summary statistics, dictionary mapping, and sideway information passing with comprehensive indexes. Furthermore, bushy execution plans and compressed bitmap data structures have been adopted [8,16,45]. However, as shown in [22], most single-node systems require huge main memory and a significant loading/preprocessing time.

6.3.1 DISTRIBUTED RDF QUERY PROCESSING SYSTEMS

Distributed RDF databases [14,17,18,43] have been studied to improve the scalability and fault-tolerance of RDF query processing systems. Generally, they are also equipped with exhaustive indexes, which are distributed based on key ranges (e.g., S in SPO index) or a global hash/randomized function for load balancing. However, such systems have typically been tested with a relatively small number of nodes and limited size of data sets, for example, 16 nodes and approximately 600 GB data sets in YARS2 [18]. As an alternative, graph-oriented approaches [42,47] have been explored to manipulate RDF data sets based on graph-based approaches in a distributed environment. However, the performance of such systems still relies on large memory with expensive network devices, for example, 96 GB RAM and InfiniBand network in Trinity [47]. Recently, extensive efforts have been made to leverage commodity-grade machines on generic cloud platforms to process massive amounts of RDF data sets. In particular, the MapReduce framework has been popularly used to build scalable RDF processing systems. The main difference across such systems is the translation strategy from relational plans to MapReduce plans. In this section, we mainly discuss existing RDF query processing systems and optimization techniques that have been developed for vanilla Hadoop as well as Hadoop-based extended platforms.

6.3.2 QUERY PROCESSING SYSTEMS ON VANILLA HADOOP PLATFORM

A common strategy for evaluating RDF graph pattern queries on MapReduce is translating queries to corresponding relational-style plans, for example, SHARD [38], PigSPARQL [41], HadoopRDF [22]. SHARD employs a MapReduce execution plan in which the first MapReduce job preprocesses the data (groups related triples), while the subsequent MapReduce jobs implement a *clause–iteration evaluation technique* that executes each join with a triple pattern in a separate MapReduce job. A final MapReduce job then projects the specified columns, leading to a total of $(n + 1)$ cycles for a query with n triple patterns that is, $(n - 1$ joins). SHARD has a fairly limited support of the SPARQL language—as of time of this writing, does not support FILTER operations. Some research efforts have developed optimization techniques that attempt to reduce cost by minimizing the number of MapReduce jobs required to process queries [22]. HadoopRDF preprocesses data into a storage model consisting of files of predicate–object splits of data. This allows for selective retrieval of splits based on predicates and objects in a query. While queries are interpreted using the traditional relational-like algebra, it employs a greedy strategy to find an optimal grouping of "non-conflicting" join operators in the same cycle. This approach results in a shorter MapReduce workflow length than the traditional approach.

6.3.3 QUERY PROCESSING SYSTEMS ON EXTENDED HADOOP PLATFORMS

A variety of Hadoop-based platforms support extensions to the data flow specification layer, the data-processing layer, as well as the underlying storage models as shown in Figure 6.3. Systems such as Apache Hive and Pig allow users to express data-processing tasks using high-level query primitives that are automatically compiled into low-level map and reduce functions. Works such as PigSPARQL translate a SPARQL query into Pig's high-level data flow language called as Pig Latin, incorporating basic optimizations such as early filter/projection and the rearrangement of triple patterns based on variable counting. Similar to SHARD, this translation produces one JOIN command in Pig for each join in query. A detailed description of the query compilation process in Pig will be discussed in the next section. Extended platforms with indexed access methods have also been proposed to support efficient random access, which is expensive over HDFS. Hybrid database-Hadoop architectures such as HadoopDB [5] take advantage of the available indexes as well as the traditional database optimization techniques. HadoopDB employs data partitioning schemes that allow part of the query evaluation to be pushed into the database, thus reducing the required number of MapReduce cycles. HadoopDB's storage and processing layer has also been extended [21] to include RDF-3X [30], an RDF storage and retrieval system for SPARQL query support. RDF data is partitioned into multiple nodes with some overlaps, and most query processing is pushed into each single-node equipped with RDF-3X instead of RDBMS. Some other works [15,33,40] have proposed RDF storage models and SPARQL query translation algorithms that exploit distributed databases such as HBase [1]. The MAPSIN [40] join algorithm uses HBase to selectively retrieve mapping values for variables in a graph pattern and avoids the need for an expensive reduce phase for join execution. H2RDF [33] indexes data into HBase with a statistical profile on data sets, and the query engine adaptively selects the most feasible join algorithm based on query selectivity and the inherent characteristics of MapReduce and HBase systems. EAGRE [48] introduces an RDF data representation and layout schemes to efficiently locate RDF triples that match a graph pattern. Additionally, adaptive scheduling strategies and a consulting protocol are used to evaluate queries in a way that minimizes disk and network I/O costs, as well as the total execution time.

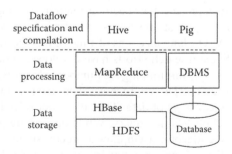

FIGURE 6.3 Hadoop-based data processing platforms.

6.3.4 COMPLEMENTARY OPTIMIZATION TECHNIQUES ON MAPREDUCE

There have been other compile-time and run-time techniques to optimize join processing on MapReduce. Though some of this work is pursued outside the context of RDF and SPARQL, they are very relevant to this discussion. Compile-time optimizations include techniques that share scans or results of subexpressions within [28] or across queries [13,31,35]. A multiway join algorithm [6] has also been proposed that efficiently partitions and replicates tuples across reducers in a way that minimizes the communication cost as well as the required number of MapReduce cycles. Run-time optimization techniques such as side-way information passing [19,20] have also been adapted for Hadoop platforms. These techniques exploit join information from subqueries to prune out input that is irrelevant to subsequent join operations, thus reducing the materialization and network transfer costs. Other run-time techniques [25,26] address data skew problems that result in overloaded reducers impacting the overall performance. Rather than the timeout approach used in traditional Hadoop, SkewTune [26] proactively detects skewed jobs and repartitions remaining unprocessed data into other available nodes. The problem of skew is expected to be common when processing web-scale RDF data sets since some subsets of subject/property values occur in very high frequencies than others, for example, the resources related with RDF schema. A skew-resistant join algorithm [25] that uses bifocal samplings and replicated join techniques has been proposed for Pig. A comprehensive survey on other available optimization techniques for MapReduce framework can be found here [27,39].

6.4 SPARQL QUERY COMPILATION ON HADOOP-BASED PLATFORMS—A CASE STUDY ON APACHE PIG

Hadoop-based extended platforms such as Hive and Pig allow users to express data-processing tasks using high-level query primitives. For example, Pig provides a high level data flow language called *Pig Latin* with which users specify their tasks as a sequence of data transformation commands, for example, LOAD, SPLIT, JOIN, etc. A high-level data flow script is automatically translated into logical/physical plan and a MapReduce (MR) execution plan.

Example 6.1: SPARQL Query in Pig Latin

Suppose we have a query with the two star patterns (*S/*1 and *S/*2) each with two triple patterns whose properties are *p*1, *p*2, and *p*3, *p*4, respectively. A group of Pig Latin commands can be used for this purpose, for example, Pig's SPLIT operator for vertical partitioning of the input relation based on properties, and the JOIN operator for processing joins in a query, and a Pig Latin version of the query can be expressed as Program 6.1.

6.4.1 LOGICAL PLAN TRANSLATION

The data flow compilation translates Pig Latin program into a Pig logical plan. LOLoad, is used to load the triple relation from HDFS. The next pair of operators LOSplit and `LOSplitOutput` are responsible for splitting the triple relation into vertical partitions based on the properties in a graph pattern, that is, four `LOSplitOutput` operators are linked with a `LOSplit` indicating that the input relation T will be split into four subrelations whose properties are $p1$, $p2$, and $p3$, $p4$, respectively. Two `LOJoin` operators follow for each star join $SJ1$ and $SJ2$. Then, another operator `LOJoin` is used to join the two star subpatterns, and finally, an operator `LOStore` stores the output of `LOJoin` to disk. The complete logical plan is illustrated in Figure 6.4a.

Program 6.1: A Pig Latin Program for the Example Query

```
T = Load 'input.nt' using PigStorage(' ') as (S,P,O) ;
SPLIT T into P1 if P eq 'P1', P2 if P eq 'P2', P3 if P eq 'P3', P4 if P eq 'P4' ;
SJ1 = JOIN P1 by S, P2 by S ;
SJ2 = JOIN P3 by S, P4 by S ;
J1 = JOIN SJ1 by $0, SJ2 by $2 ;
STORE J1; ;
```

6.4.2 PHYSICAL PLAN TRANSLATION

The logical plan is translated to a physical plan as shown in Figure 6.4b. The logical operator `LOLoad` is mapped to a physical operator `POLoad` (Pig uses LO and PO prefixes for logical and physical operators, respectively). The operators `LOSplit` and `LOSplitOutput` are then transformed into a physical operator `POFilter` with subexpression operators to select only the triples matching each triple pattern, that is, a `POFilter` denotes a selection operation on T based on some conditions that are described with expression operators, for example, `POProject` for σ and P, `POConstant` for $p1$, and `EqualTo` for = in $\sigma_{(P = 'p1')}(T)$. Pig then maps the logical operator `LOJoin` into a set of physical operators: `POLocalRearrange`—for annotating triples from `POFilter` with their *subjects*; `POUnion`—for unioning annotated triples in the operator `POUnion`, and `POJoinPackage`—for packaging (joining) triples joined by *Subject* into n-tuples. Each gray-dotted box in Figure 6.4b and c denotes a set of operators that annotate triples that match a triple pattern with its *Subject*, for example, the `POFilter` and `POLocalRearrange` in the first box annotating the triples matching the triple pattern with the property $p1$ (the operators for other properties ($p2$, $p3$, and $p4$) are omitted). As a final step, the logical operator `LOStore` is mapped into a physical operator `POStore`. The mappings between logical/physical operators are denoted by black-dotted boxes in Figure 6.4a and b.

6.4.3 MAPREDUCE PLAN TRANSLATION

In the final phase of data flow compilation, a physical plan is decomposed into MR jobs with job dependencies recorded. This is shown in Figure 6.4c. Besides deciding which MR job an operator should be assigned to, the compiler must also determine whether the operator executes in the Map or Reduce phase. For example, while most

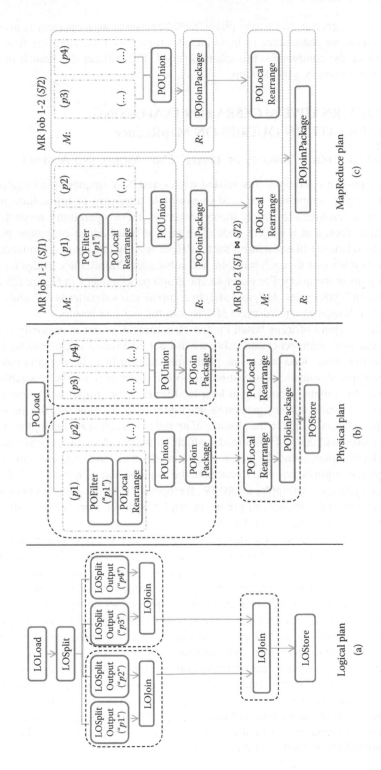

FIGURE 6.4 (a–c) Translation from logical-to-physical-to-MapReduce plan in Pig.

operators are assigned to some map phase, a `POJoinPackage` operator is always assigned to a reduce phase since its input includes tuples with the same key from all mappers. Once the compilation process is finished, Pig initiates the launch of the first MR job for execution on Hadoop.

6.5   AN ALTERNATIVE ALGEBRA FOR EVALUATING GRAPH PATTERN QUERIES ON MapReduce

6.5.1   THE CASE FOR A "GROUPS OF TRIPLES" DATA MODEL AND ALGEBRA

Relational equi-join operations link related triples and very frequently a large proportion of the join operations are used to assemble attributes or immediate relationships of a resource. In graph theoretic terms, these operations reconstruct star-subgraphs rooted at a subject node. The typical MapReduce execution plans generated by relational-like platforms such as Hive and Pig consist of a sequence of MapReduce cycles, one for each star-join, and subsequent MapReduce cycles for the remaining joins in the query. For example, the graph pattern query in Figure 6.5 can be evaluated in 3 MR cycles: MR_1 and MR_2 to compute star subpatterns $SJ1$ and $SJ2$, respectively, followed by a third-cycle MR_3 to join the star-join results.

However, grouping of joins based on star structures does not necessarily result in the typical join order generated using traditional cost-based optimization. One challenge is that most cloud processing platforms are used in an on-demand model, where precomputed statistics for cost-based optimization may not be available or take too long to compute, resulting in long lead times. More importantly, ordering joins in terms of their costs may generate some linear subplans requiring one input as the full triple relation, which in the absence of an index is a full scan. Such plans may incur larger overhead due to HDFS reads, which outweighs the savings achieved by pushing selective joins ahead. However, if we consider a different representation for related triples, it might be possible to compute the required star subgraphs with fewer MapReduce cycles. For example, a `GROUP BY` operation on the subject column of the triple relation will produce all groups of triples with the same subject, that is, equivalent to star-subgraphs in a relation.

As an illustration, consider the star subqueries $SJ1$ and $SJ2$ in the query and the result of the `GROUP BY` operation on input relation T as shown in Figure 6.5. The groups of triples or *triplegroups* tg_1, tg_2, and tg_3 can be seen as potential matches to the star subpatterns $SJ1$ and $SJ2$, respectively. They contain the same content or are *"content-equivalent"* to n-tuples resulting from the corresponding relational-style join operations. In other words, given a query with n star subpatterns, the grouping-based approach results in an MR execution plan with n MR cycles, as opposed to $(2n - 1)$ cycles using the relational-style approach.

The triplegroup model has another important property in that it represents multi-valued relationships implicitly. Join operations involving multivalued relationships result in redundant information due to the repetition of associated attributes with each distinct value of the multivalued relationship. However, the triplegroup model eliminates such redundancy by implicitly representing subgraphs that contain multi-valued relationships. We will revisit this issue in a later section.

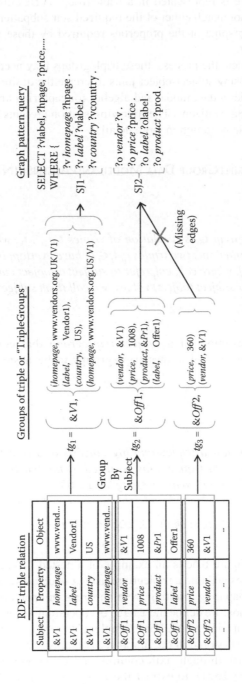

FIGURE 6.5   Group By on the Subject column of a triple relation yields groups of triples that are potential matches to the star subpatterns in the query.

The idea of triplegroup "matching" a star subpattern in a query has to ensure that the underlying structure is represented in a triplegroup. For example, triplegroup tg_3 in Figure 6.5 does not match either of the required star subpatterns since it does not contain triples with some of the properties required by those subpatterns, for example, *label, product.*

In addition, to complete the process, these triplegroups may need to be "joined" together, for example, using subject-object joins to create the desired subgraph. All of this essentially implies a data model and algebra for capturing and manipulating "triplegroups" as first-class citizens. The following section presents this data model and algebra and its implementation in more detail.

6.5.2 The Nested TripleGroup Data Model and Algebra (NTGA)

Definition 6.1

(TripleGroup) A triplegroup tg is a relation of triples $t_1, t_2, \ldots t_k$, whose schema is defined as (S, P, O). Further, any two triples $t_i, t_j \in tg$ have overlapping components, that is, $t_i [col_i] = t_j [col_j]$, where col_i, col_j refer to subject or object component. When all triples agree on their subject (object) values, we call them subject (object) triplegroups, respectively. ∎

Figure 6.6a is an example of a *subject triplegroup* that corresponds to a star subgraph. Our data model allows triplegroups to be nested at the object component.

Definition 6.2

(Nested TripleGroup) A nested triplegroup ntg consists of a root triplegroup ntg. root *and one or more child triplegroups returned by the function ntg.*child() *such that: For each child triplegroup ctg ∈ ntg.*child()*,*

- $\exists\ t_1 \in ntg.$root, $t_2 \in ctg$ *such that* $t_1.$Object $= t_2$. ∎

Triplegroup *ntg* in Figure 6.6c is an example of a nested triplegroup. A nested triplegroup can be "unnested" into a triplegroup using the unnest operator. Figure 6.6d shows the triplegroup *untg* resulting from an unnest operation on the nested triplegroup *ntg*. In addition, we define the flatten operation to generate an "equivalent" n-tuple for a given triplegroup. For example, if $tg = t_1, t_2, \ldots$, then the n-tuple *tu* has triple $t_1 = (s1, p1, o1)$ stored in the first three columns of *tu*, triple $t_2 = (s2, p2, o2)$ is stored in the fourth through sixth column, and so on. For convenience, we define the function triples() to extract the triples in a triplegroup. For triplegroup *tg* in Figure 6.6a, the flatten is computed as *tg*.triples(*label*) ⋈ *tg*.triples(*country*) ⋈ *tg*.triples(*homepage*), resulting in an n-tuple *nt*

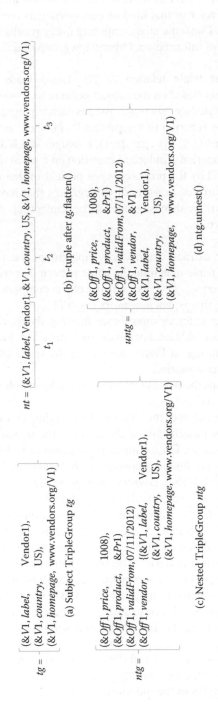

FIGURE 6.6 Examples of (a) Subject TripleGroup *tg*, (b) corresponding flattened n-tuple, (c) Nested TripleGroup *ntg*, and (d) corresponding unnested TripleGroup.

as shown in Figure 6.6b. It is easy to observe that the information content in both formats is equivalent. We refer to this kind of equivalence as *content equivalence*, which we will denote as $\cong$. Consequently, computing query results in terms of triplegroups is lossless in terms of information. Other triplegroup functions are defined as shown in Figure 6.7b.

Given a query Q over triple relation T, TG_Load loads the triples, and TG_GroupBy groups them based on the subject column to produce a set of triplegroups TG. The *structure-labeling function* λ assigns each triplegroup tg, with a label that is constructed as some function of tg.props(). Further, for two triplegroups tg_1, tg_2 such that tg_1.props() $\subseteq$ tg_2.props(), λ assigns labels such that tg_1.λ() $\subseteq$ tg_2.λ(). The labeling function λ induces a partition on a set of triplegroups based on the structure represented by the property types present in that triplegroup. Each equivalence class in the partition consists of triplegroups that have the exact same set of property types. Next, we discuss some of the triplegroup operators that are formally defined in Figure 6.7c.

- **TG_Proj** operator extracts from each triplegroup, the required triple component from the triple matching the triple pattern. For triplegroup tg in Figure 6.6a, TG_Proj$_{?hpage}(TG)$ extracts the object component of the triple with property *hpage*, that is, *www.vendors.org/V1*}.
- **TG_Filter** operator enforces *value-based filtering*, that is, checks if triplegroups satisfy the filter condition. For our example data, TG_Filter$_{price<500}(TG)$ eliminates triplegroup *ntg* in Figure 6.6c since the triple (&*Offer*1, *price*, 1008) violates the filter condition.
- **TG_GroupBy** groups the triples t_i based on the subject column to produce a set of triplegroups TG.
- **TG_GroupFilter** enforces the structural constraints in a star subpattern such that triplegroups missing any of the edges in the structure are pruned (*structure-based filtering*). For example, triplegroup tg in Figure 6.6a is a valid match for the set of bound properties {*label, country, homepage*} but violates the structure in {*label, country, homepage, mbox*}.
- **TG_Join** operator is semantically equivalent to the relational join operator but is defined on triplegroups. The join expression TG_Join $\left(?v_{tp_x}:TG_x,?v_{tp_y}:TG_y\right)$ computes the join between a triplegroup tg_x in equivalence class TG_x with a triplegroup tg_y in equivalence class TG_y based on the given triple patterns. The triple patterns tp_x and tp_y share a common variable $?v$ at O or S component. The result of an object–subject (O–S) join is a nested triplegroup in which tg_y is nested at the O component of the join triple in tg_x. For example, Figure 6.6c shows the nested triplegroup resulting from the TG_Join operation between equivalence classes $TG_{\{price,product,validFrom,vendor\}}$ and $TG_{\{label,country,homepage\}}$ that join based on triple patterns {?o *vendor* ?v} and {?v *country* ?vcountry}, respectively. For object–object (O–O) joins, the TG_Join operator computes a triplegroup by union of triples in the individual triplegroups.

(a)

Symbol	Description
tg	TripleGroup
TG	Set of TripleGroups
tp	Triple pattern
ntg.root	Root of the nested TripleGroup
ntg.child()	Children of the nested TripleGroup
$?v_{tp}$	A variable in the triple pattern tp

(b)

Function	Returns
tg.props()	Set union of property types in tg
tg.triples()	Set union of triples in tg
tg.triples(p_i)	Triples in tg with property type p_i
$tg.\lambda()$	Structure label for tg based on tg.props()
$\delta(tp)$	A triple matching the triple pattern tp
$\delta(?v_{tp})$	A variable substitution in the triple matching tp

(c)

Operator	Definition
TG_Load($\{t_i\}$)	$\{tg_i \mid tg_i.\text{triples}() = t_i,$ and t_i is an input triple$\}$
TG_Proj$_{?v_{tp}}(TG)$	$\{\delta_i(?v_{tp}) \mid \delta_i(tp) \in tg_i, tg_i \in TG$ and $tp.\lambda() \subseteq tg_i.\lambda()\}$
TG_Filter$_{\Theta(?v_{tp})}(TG)$	$\{tg_i \mid tg_i \in TG$ and $\exists\, \delta_i(tp) \in tg_i$ such that $\delta_i(?v_{tp})$ satisfies the filter condition $\Theta(?v_{tp})\}$
TG_GroupFilter(TG, P)	$\{tg_i \mid tg_i \in TG$ and $tg_i.\text{props}() = P\}$
TG_Join($?v_{tp_x}; TG_x, ?v_{tp_j}; TG_y$)	Assume $tg_x \in TG_x, tg_y \in TG_y, \exists\, \delta_1(tg_x) \in tg_x, \delta_2(tg_y) \in tg_y,$ and $\delta_1(?v_{tp_x}) = \delta_2(?v_{tp_y})$ if O-S join, then $\{ntg_i \mid ntg_i.\text{root} = tg_x, \delta_1(tp_x).\text{Object} = tg_y\}$ else $\{tg_x \cup tg_y\}$
tg.flatten()	$\{tg.\text{triples}(p_1) \bowtie tg.\text{triples}(p_2)... \bowtie tg.\text{triples}(p_n)$ where $p_i \in tg.\text{root}\}$
ntg.unnest()	$\{t_i \mid t_i$ is a non-nested triple in $tg.\text{root}\}$ $\cup \{(s, p, s') \mid t' = (s, p, (s', p', o'))$ is a nested triple in $tg.\text{root}\}$ $\cup \{ctg_i.\text{unnest}() \mid ctg_i \in tg.\text{child}()\}$

FIGURE 6.7 NTGA quick reference: (a) symbols, (b) functions, and (c) operators.

6.5.2.1 Content Equivalence

Triplegroups produced by the grouping-based star-join computation are considered to be "content-equivalent" (represented as $\cong$) to the set of n-tuples computed using a set of relational star joins. Let Stp be a star subpattern comprising of the set of bound properties $\{P_1, P_2, ..., P_k\}$ and Tup_{Stp} be the join result of vertically partitioned subset relations $T_{P_1}, T_{P_2}, ..., T_{P_k}$. Let Tup_{Stp_s} represent the subset of Tup_{Stp} with subject Sub = s.

$$Tup_{Stp_s} = \sigma_{Sub=s}(T_{P_1} \bowtie T_{P_2} \bowtie ... \bowtie T_{P_k})$$

Each tuple in Tup_{Stp_s} is of 3k arity (each property in Stp is associated with three columns). Let π_{P_i} denote the projection of the (Sub, Prop, Obj) columns corresponding to the parent relation T_{P_i} with bound property P_i. Let tg_s represent the set union of triples formed by the three columns, that is,

$$tg_s = \pi_{P_1}\left(Tup_{Stp_s}\right) \cup \pi_{P_2}\left(Tup_{Stp_s}\right) \cup ... \cup \pi_{P_k}\left(Tup_{Stp_s}\right)$$

Remark 6.3

In summary, the tuples in Tup_{Stp_s} can be vertically partitioned into "triples" whose union is equivalent to a subject triplegroup tg_s in the NTGA data model. For our example data in Figure 6.5, we have

$$tg_1 \cong \sigma_{Sub = \&V1}(T_{homepage} \bowtie T_{label} \bowtie T_{country})$$

$$tg_2 \cong \sigma_{Sub = \&Off1}(T_{vendor} \bowtie T_{price} \bowtie T_{product} \bowtie T_{label})$$

Note that the two n-tuples corresponding to $SJ1$ containing a multivalued property *home-page* are implicitly represented using a single triplegroup tg_1 as shown in Figure 6.5. ∎

6.6 RAPID+—AN IMPLEMENTATION OF NTGA

6.6.1 SYSTEM ARCHITECTURE

In this section, we discuss our implementation strategy for NTGA in a system called RAPID+ [23], which is an extension of Apache Pig. Figure 6.8 shows the overall system architecture of RAPID+. (The gray boxes denote new or extended components.) The user interface layer introduces support for expression of graph pattern matching queries via either an integrated SPARQL query interface that integrates Jena's ARQ [29] or NTGA-related high level commands that have been added to the Pig Latin language. A SPARQL query is parsed and compiled into an ARQ-compliant SPARQL S-expression tree [4]. The *query analyzer* and the *Pig Latin/NTGA plan generator* are added as new components in the logical plan layer. Based on the given query execution

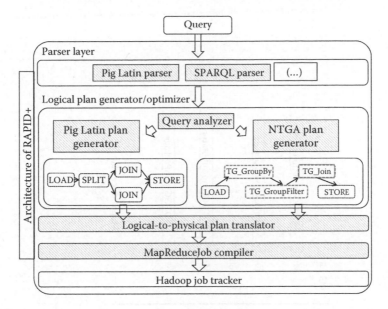

FIGURE 6.8   Overall data flow and architecture of RAPID+.

parameters, the query analyzer routes the execution flow either into the Pig Latin/NTGA logical plan generator. These generators compile the given SSE tree into the logical plan with Pig Latin/NTGA operators. The Logical-to-Physical plan translator and Job Compiler are also extended to recognize NTGA operators and compile the NTGA-based plan into the corresponding physical/MapReduce Plan. (Details can be found in [7]).

6.6.2   SPARQL QUERY COMPILATION IN RAPID+

RAPID+ follows similar query compile process to the one used in Pig.

Example 6.2: Query Compilation Process with NTGA Operators

Here, we specifically describe the case that executes a SPARQL query with NTGA operators. We use the same example query with the two star patterns (*SJ*1 and *SJ*2) shown in Section 6.3. Figure 6.9a–c show the translations from the logical plan to the MapReduce one. Once the query is parsed into the SSE tree by the SPARQL parser, the NTGA plan generator traverses the tree and generates corresponding logical plan. The plan starts with the operator LOTGLoadFilter corresponding to TG_LoadFilter in NTGA. The operator LOTGGroupBy and LOTGGroupFilter are then connected, which correspond to TG_GroupBy and TG_GroupFilter, respectively. To join the two stars (*SJ*1 and *SJ*2), the logical operator LOTGJoin is connected, which implements the operator TG_Join. As a next step, the logical plan is compiled into the physical one. In this process, a common theme is to *coalesce* operators

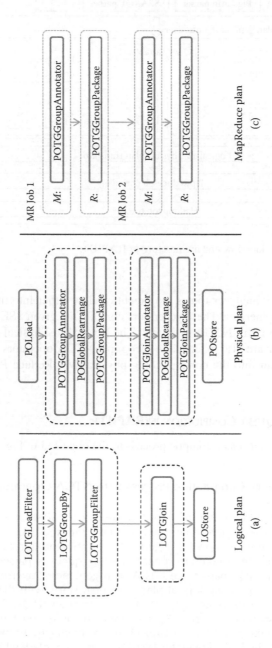

FIGURE 6.9 (a–c) Translation from logical-to-physical-to-MapReduce plan in RAPID+.

where possible to minimize the costs of parameter passing, context switching between methods, and the number of MR jobs required. For example, the traditional execution plan would execute the grouping step in the reduce phase of a MapReduce cycle, then the groupfiltering phase in a map cycle of the subsequent MapReduce cycle, thus requiring at least 2 MapReduce cycles. In RAPID+, both operations are merged into a single MapReduce cycle by the introduction of a new operator called `POTGPackage`, which coalesces the `TG_GroupFilter` operator into the reduce-side of Pig's relational `GROUP BY` operator (`POPackage`). Other logical operators are mapped into the physical ones similar to the Pig's case; for example, the `LOTGJoin` is mapped into multiple physical operators (e.g., `POTGJoinAnnotator` and `POTGJoinPackage`). Finally, the physical plan is divided into multiple MR jobs shown in Figure 6.9c. Note that the relational-style plan shown in Section 6.3 needs three MR jobs while the NTGA-based plan only requires two MR jobs, saving one MR cycle.

Remark 6.4

Generally, the relational-style approach using Pig Latin operators requires the $(2n - 1)$ MR jobs to process the query with n star subpatterns. In the NTGA-based MR workflow, the number of MR jobs for producing stars is always one because grouping operation essentially produces all the stars in the first MR job. Therefore, NTGA-based plan processes the same query using only n MR jobs.   ∎

6.6.3 IMPLEMENTATION OF NTGA OPERATORS

6.6.3.1 Data Model Representation—RDFMap

The Pig Latin data model supports a collection data type called a *bag* that can be used to capture a group of tuples or in the NTGA context, a triplegroup. A bag is implemented as an array list of tuples and provides an iterator to process them. Consequently, implementing NTGA operators such as `TG_Filter`, `TG_GroupFilter`, `TG_Join`, etc., using this data structure requires an iteration through the data bag, which is expensive. For example, given a graph pattern with a set of triple patterns *TP* and a data graph represented as a set of triplegroups *TG*, the `TG_GroupFilter` operator requires matching each triple pattern in *TP* with each tuple *t* for each triplegroup $tg \in TG$. In addition, representing triples as 3-tuple (*s*, *p*, *o*) results in redundant *s*(*o*) components for subject (object) triplegroups. RAPID+ uses an extended map structure called *RDFMap* that captures, (i) the subject *Sub* associated with the triples in a triplegroup, (ii) a hashmap *propMap* that records the mappings from property types to object values, and (iii) a structure-label *EC* that encodes property types in the triplegroup. This enables efficient look-up of triples matching a given triple pattern and a compact representation of intermediate results. Since subject of triples in a triplegroup are often repeated, RDFMap avoids this redundancy using a single-field *Sub* to represent the subject component. Using this representation model, a nested triplegroup can be supported using a nested *propMap*, which contains another RDFMap as a value. The *prop-Map* provides a property-based indexed structure that eliminates the need to iterate through the tuples in each bag.

6.6.3.2   Implementation of TG_GroupBy

In the physical layer, TG_GroupBy in NTGA is mapped into the physical operators POTGGroupAnnotator and POTGGroupPackage. As a reminder, physical operators in MapReduce-based systems are executed in *map*() and *reduce*() functions. In the *map* phase, the TripleLoader loads triples from HDFS and filters them out if their properties do not match with any properties in a graph pattern. This filtering process offers some cost savings by avoiding future processing and materialization for irrelevant triples to a given query. The operator POTGGroupAnnotator comes next to annotate the triples based on the *S* component, for example, tag *t* in triples *T* as (*t.S, t*). In the *reduce* function, the operator POTGGroupPackage is executed, which packages the same *S* component into an *RDFMap* that corresponds to a subject triplegroup (line 5–7 of Algorithm 6.1).

Algorithm 6.1: POTGGroupPackage

> **Reduce** (*key:Subject Sub,val:List of tuples T*) ;
> //locBitSet—record property types in T
> //ECList—list of global BitSets for all ECs
> **1 for each** *tup(s, p, o)* ∈ *T* **do**
> **2**   set *p* in *locBitset* ;
> **3**   add *(p,o)* to *tempMap* ;
> **4** *matchedECList* ← *match(locBitSet, ECList)* ;
> **5 foreach** *EC* ∈ *matchedECList* **do**
> **6**   *propMap* ← extract subset of *tempMap* based on
>   properties in *EC* ;
> **7**   emit ⟨*RDFMap(Sub, EC, propMap)*⟩ ;

6.6.3.3   Implementation of TG_GroupFilter

TG_GroupFilter is also mapped into the POTGGroupPackage, that is, the structure-based filter in TG_GroupFilter is integrated into the POTGGroupPackage to filter irrelevant triplegroups based on the query substructures before generating actual *RDFMap* instances. Algorithm 6.1 describes the algorithm of this operator using the two types of bit patterns: *global* and *local* bit patterns. The global ones represent the property types in the query substructures.

Example 6.3: Structure-Based Filtering

Figure 6.10b shows that properties in the two star patterns (*SJ*1 and *SJ*2 in Figure 6.10a) are encoded into two 6-bit bitmaps. The local ones keep track of the property types processed as the triples are packaged into a triplegroup (lines 1–3),

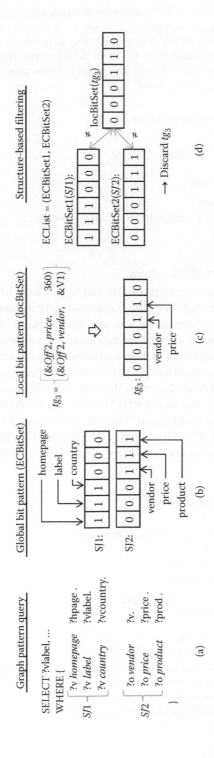

FIGURE 6.10 (a) Example SPARQL query, (b) corresponding global bit patterns, (c) local bit patterns for triplegroup tg_3, and (d) structure-based filtering process.

for example, marking the bits corresponding to the property *vendor* and *price* in Figure 6.10c. After processing all triples in a group, if the local BitSet (`locBitSet`) does not match the global BitSet (`ECBitSet`), the structure is incomplete and the group of triples is eliminated (line 4). Figure 6.10d shows that `locBitSet` of triplegroup tg_3 is not matched with any global bit patterns representing the two star patterns; therefore, tg_3 is discarded.

Algorithm 6.2: POTGJoinAnnotator

> **Map** (*key:null, val: RDFMap rMap*) ;
> 1 **if** *join on Sub* **then**
> 2 $\quad\lfloor\quad joinKey \leftarrow rMap.Sub$;
>
> $\quad$ **else if** *join on Obj* **then**
> 3 $\quad\lfloor\quad joinKey \leftarrow$ extract joinKey from $rMap.propMap$;
> 4 emit $\langle joinKey, rMap \rangle$;

6.6.3.4 Implementation of TG_Join

The physical operators `POTGJoinAnnotator` and `POTGJoinPackage` are mapped into the operator `TG_Join` in NTGA. Both operators take as input a single relation containing RDFMaps, and computes the join operation between star patterns. In the *map* phase, the physical operator `POTGJoinAnnotator` annotates the RDFMaps based on the join key corresponding to their equivalence class (lines 1–4 of Algorithm 6.2). In the *reduce* phase, the physical operator `POTGJoinPackage` is executed. The operator separates the RDFMaps based on their equivalence class *EC* (lines 1–4 of Algorithm 6.3) and packages the joined RDFMaps into a new RDFMap (lines 5–11), which corresponds to a nested triplegroup. The equivalence class *EC* of the new joined RDFMap is a function of the *EC* of the individual RDFMaps (line 8). In our implementation, the *Sub* field is a concatenation of the *Sub* fields of the joining RDFMaps.

Algorithm 6.3: POTGJoinPackage

> **Reduce** (*key:joinKey, val:List of RDFMaps R*) ;
> 1 **foreach** *rMap* ∈ *R* **do**
> 2 $\quad$ **if** *rMap.EC* == *EC1* **then**
> 3 $\quad\quad\lfloor$ add *rMap* to *leftList* ;
>
> $\quad\quad$ **else if** *rMap.EC* == *EC2* **then**
> 4 $\quad\quad\lfloor$ add *rMap* to *rightList* ;
>
> 5 **foreach** *left* ∈ *leftList* **do**
> 6 $\quad$ **foreach** *right* ∈ *rightList* **do**
> 7 $\quad\quad$ $propMap' \leftarrow$ joinProp(*left.propMap, right.propMap*) ;
> 8 $\quad\quad$ $EC' \leftarrow$ joinEC(*left.EC, right.EC*) ;
> 9 $\quad\quad$ $Sub' \leftarrow$ joinSub(*left.Sub, right.Sub*) ;
> 10 $\quad\quad$ $rMap' \leftarrow$ RDFMap(*Sub', EC', propMap*) ;
> 11 $\quad\quad$ emit $\langle rMap' \rangle$;

6.7   CASE STUDY: EVALUATION OF NTGA EXECUTION PLANS

In this section, we present results comparing the performance of evaluating graph pattern queries using NTGA execution plans against relational-style execution plans in Apache Pig. We evaluated scalability in terms of number of join operations and the size of the cluster.

6.7.1   SETUP AND TESTBED

Experiments were conducted on 5- to 30-node Hadoop clusters. Two synthetic data sets were used—data set $D1$ with size 51 GB (approximately 200 million n-triples) generated using the BSBM benchmark generator and $D2$—modified version of the analysis benchmark data set used in [34] with size 43 GB (approximately 1 billion 3-ary triples).

6.7.2   SCALABILITY WITH INCREASING JOINS

Figure 6.11a shows the results of queries—Q1, Q2, Q3, Q4 with 3, 5, 9, and 11 joins, respectively. The number of star subpatterns varies from one in Q1 to four in Q4,

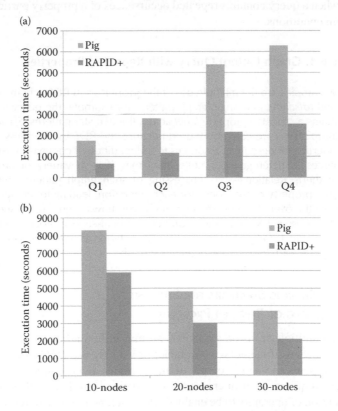

FIGURE 6.11   Scalability study with (a) increasing joins using the 51 GB data set on a 10-node cluster and (b) increasing cluster size using the 43 GB data set.

respectively. The experiments were conducted on a 10-node cluster with D1 data set (51 GB). The results show that RAPID+ shows a performance gain of 60% over the default Pig implementation. This is due to the reduced MapReduce execution workflow length, for example, 4 MR cycles for Q4 vs. 7 MR cycles for Pig.

6.7.3 SCALABILITY WITH INCREASING CLUSTER SIZE

Figure 6.11b demonstrates the scalability of NTGA-based approach in RAPID+, against relational-style approach in Pig with varying size of clusters. Evaluation was done using query Q5 with 7 triple patterns evaluated on D2 data set (43 GB). RAPID+ shows a performance gain of 31% over Pig approach with the 10-node cluster, which increases to 41% as we increase the cluster size to 30-nodes. The increase in cluster size enables more parallelization of the grouping based star-join computation in RAPID+, further reducing the overall execution time.

6.8 INTRAQUERY SCAN SHARING FOR NTGA EXECUTION PLANS

In this section, we consider the problem of sharing scans within a query. This problem arises when a query contains repeated occurrences of a property participating in different join operations.

Example 6.4: Graph Pattern Query with Repeated Properties

Common examples are the multiple use of the properties in RDF schema such as *rdf:type* and *rdfs:label* in a single graph pattern, for example, the query in Figure 6.12a contains a repeated property *label* across the two star patterns, *SJ*1 and *SJ*2. Such graph patterns are commonly used because the RDF model allows liberal use of properties for describing resources to reflect different contexts of resources and resources in heterogeneous collections may have a variety of properties describing them. Relational-style processing of such graph patterns, results in scanning the property relation once for each operation, leading to multiple scans that increase the overall I/O overhead of such workflows. Figure 6.12c shows the MR workflows using 3 MR jobs based on the relational-style approach. In this MR workflow, the job 1 and 2 scan the input relation twice to select the same triples whose properties are (*type, label, date*) in each job.

6.8.1 SCAN-SHARING STRATEGIES FOR EFFICIENT
PROCESSING OF REPEATED PROPERTIES

To avoid such multiple scans on a relation, we may either buffer the relation for the duration it is needed (if memory is available) or we may use DAG (directed acyclic graph)-shaped plans so that the output of an operator can be sent to more than one operator. This requires either interoperator or pipelined parallelism that allows concurrent execution of operators to be enabled. However, neither one of these scenarios is possible in the MapReduce model. Hence, there is a need for approaches that

SELECT * WHERE{
?producer **type** Producer .
?producer **label** ?prcLabel .
?producer **date** ?prcdate .
?producer hpage ?hpage .

?product pub ?producer .
?product **type** Product .
?product **label** ?prodLabel .
?product **date** ?prodDate .
}

(a)

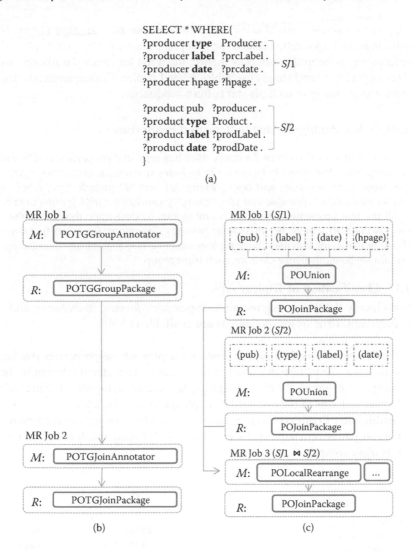

(b)   (c)

FIGURE 6.12   (a) Example SPARQL query, (b) MR execution workflow for the example query using NTGA operators, and (c) corresponding workflow using Pig Latin operators.

enable scan sharing while processing graph pattern queries with repeated properties. In NTGA, the scan sharings are naturally made while processing such graph
patterns because all star subpatterns are executed as a grouping operation, requiring
only one scan of the entire input set. Therefore, the triples for a particular property
are scanned only once regardless of how many times that property is used in a query.
Figure 6.12b shows the NTGA-based **MR** workflows, which scans the input data set
only once. However, this scan sharing in the presence of repeated properties can lead
to ambiguities in the semantics of triplegroups because triplegroups are assumed to

be mapped to a single equivalence class in the current `TG_GroupFilter`. This assumption is no longer valid because the grouping operation (`TG_GroupBy`) does not enforce any structural constraints (hence, the need for structural filtering using `TG_GroupFilter`) and simply assembles related triples. Consequently, the triples in a triplegroup may span multiple star pattern subqueries.

Example 6.5: Ambiguity due to Repeated Properties

This ambiguity can also occur if a query itself has repeated properties in different star subqueries. The query in Figure 6.12a includes five unique properties (*hpage, type, label, date,* and *pub*) and both patterns *SJ*1 and *SJ*2 include *type, label,* or *date.* In addition, it is possible that `TG_GroupBy` produces a triplegroup containing all the five properties. Hence, it is ambiguous to determine the equivalence class partition to which the triplegroup belongs. Therefore, we need to extend NTGA for managing and identifying triplegroups in a way that relaxes the assumption of a single equivalence class for each triplegroup.

6.8.1.1   Classification of Triplegroups

We first classify the triplegroup into three types: *well-formed, ambiguous,* and *perfect* triplegroups. (The formal definitions are available in [24]).

- **Well-Formed Triplegroup:** It contains triples whose properties overlap with some star pattern in a query; thus, it can be considered relevant to the query. For example, the triplegroups tg_0, tg_1, and tg_2 in Figure 6.13b are well formed in terms of the extended example query in Figure 6.13a.
- **Ambiguous Triplegroup:** It is a triplegroup whose properties span multiple star patterns in a query, for example, tg_0 in Figure 6.13b is an ambiguous triplegroup.

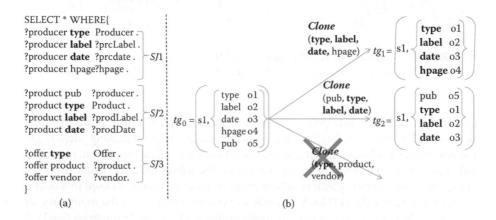

FIGURE 6.13   (a) Extended query and (b) cloning in the context of ambiguous triplegroups.

- **Perfect Triplegroup:** It is an unambiguous triplegroup, which contains no properties except those in specific star patterns. Therefore, it can be considered as a valid answer for a query. The triplegroups tg_1 and tg_2 in Figure 6.13b are examples of perfect triplegroups.

Since the current `TG_GroupFilter` semantics assume perfect triplegroups as input, we need to extend its definition to deal with ambiguous triplegroups. Specifically, the `TG_GroupFilter` needs to split any ambiguous triplegroup *ta* into a set of subgroups (not necessarily disjoint) representing all perfect triplegroups that are derivable *ta* with respect to the query. However, care must be taken not to introduce redundant or invalid triplegroups, which could result in spurious results. This is handled by a concept we call *cloning*, generating perfect triplegroups from an ambiguous triplegroup.

Example 6.6: Clone Operation

Figure 6.13b shows how perfect triplegroups tg_1 and tg_2 are cloned from the ambiguous triplegroup tg_0 (note that tg_0 does not contain triples matching SJ3 and hence no triplegroup TG_{type, product, vendor} is generated ["_" means the subscript notation]). (The detail on the concept of the clone operation and the proof on losslessness are available in [24].)

6.8.1.2   Implementation of Clone Operation

Algorithm 6.4 shows the algorithm of the extended operator `POTGGroupPackage`, which supports handling of ambiguous triplegroups. In the `reduce` phase, all tuples corresponding to the same subject component are processed in the same reduce function. A bitmap (locBitset) is used to keep track of the property types processed (line 3) and the (Property, Object) pairs are stored in a temporary map (tempMap in line 4). After processing all tuples in the group, the locBitSet is matched with all the equivalence classes (star subpatterns) in the query (ECList in line 5). A match with a single equivalence class represents a perfect triplegroup (line 10). A match with more than one equivalence class indicates an ambiguous triplegroup and the temporary map is cloned to retrieve the relevant (Property, Object) pairs corresponding to the matched star subpatterns (lines 7–8). The cloned maps are then used to create perfect triplegroups (line 9) corresponding to the star subpatterns required in the query. A mismatch with ALL star subpatterns results in filtering out of the group of tuples.

6.8.2   CASE STUDY: IMPACT OF SCAN-SHARING FOR GRAPH PATTERN QUERIES WITH REPEATED PROPERTIES

To compare the performance of the relational-style and NTGA-based approaches and their ability to share scans while processing query patterns involving repeated properties (*DupPs*), we present a case study evaluating three approaches, (i) 1-join-per-cycle (SHARD), (ii) 1-star-join-per-cycle (VP approach), and (iii) all-star-joins-1-cycle (NTGA).

Algorithm 6.4: The Extended `POTGGroupPackage`

    Reduce (*key:Sub, val: List of tuples T*) ;
1 **foreach** *tup(s, p, o)* ∈ *T* **do**
2   set *p* in *locBitstet* ;
3   add (*p,o*) to *tempMap* ;
4 *matchedList = match(locBitSet, ECList)* ;
5 **if** (|*matchedList*| > 1) **then**
       //Ambiguous TripleGroup
6   **foreach** *EC* ∈ *matchedList* **do**
7   *propMap* ← *cloneMap(tempMap, EC.propList)* ;
8   emit ⟨RDFMap(*Sub, EC, propMap*)⟩ ;

  else
       //Perfect TripleGroup
9   emit ⟨*RDFMap(Sub, matchedList*[0], *tempMap*)⟩ ;

6.8.2.1 Setup and Testbed

The evaluation was conducted on a 10-node Hadoop cluster with BSBM-250k data set (approximately 86M triples with 250k Products {22 GB}). Four queries (*dq*0 to *dq*4) containing two star patterns are considered, with varying numbers of repeated properties (from 0 to 4, respectively) in the second star subpattern. Figure 6.14 shows the graph representation of queries *dq*0 and *dq*4 (black and gray edges denote an arbitrary unique property and a repeated property, respectively). The queries include the following DupPs: *dq*0 (none), *dq*1 (*publisher*), *dq*2 (*publisher, type*), *dq*3 (*publisher, type, label*), and *dq*4 (*publisher, type, label, date*). To evaluate scalability with increasing size of data, four BSBM data sets were used—BSBM-{250k, 500k, 750k, 1000k}, with data size ranging from BSBM-250k to BSBM-1000k (22 to 86 GB).

6.8.2.2 Varying Number of Repeated Properties across a Query

Figure 6.15a shows the execution time and the number of bytes read from HDFS using the three approaches. In general, SHARD results in highest execution time and

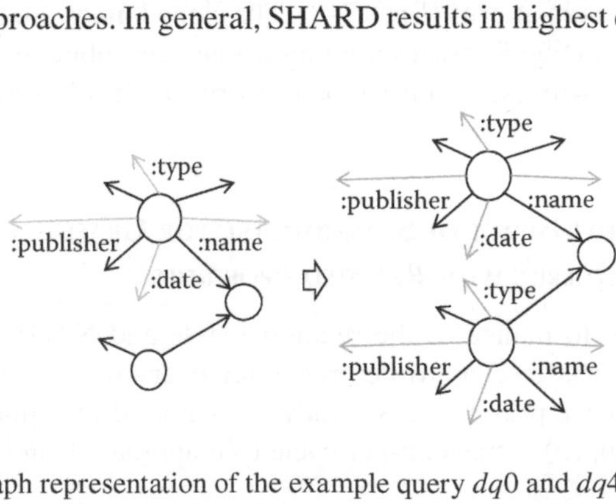

FIGURE 6.14 Graph representation of the example query *dq*0 and *dq*4.

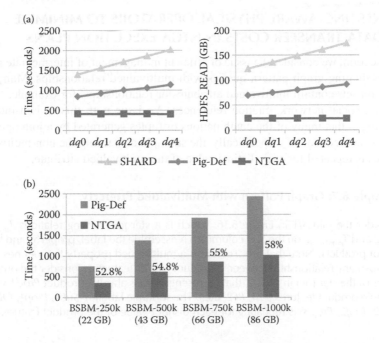

FIGURE 6.15 (a) A comparative evaluation of the three approaches (SHARD, Pig-Def, NTGA) for the queries with repeated properties. (b) Scalability study of scan-sharing approach for query $dq4$ with increasing sizes of RDF graphs.

I/O compared with other two approaches. Further, the execution time in SHARD increases as the number of triple patterns increases from 8 to 12 in $dq0$ to $dq4$, respectively. Pig-Def shows relatively better performance compared with SHARD because the number of MR jobs for star join is mainly affected by the number of star patterns in the queries. However, the amount of HDFS reads for all queries in Pig-Def is still larger than the one in NTGA because the DupPs are scanned and processed in BOTH the star-join cycles (MR1 and MR2 among 3 MR jobs) in Pig-Def, which results in an increasing amount of HDFS bytes read as the number of DupPs increase. In NTGA, it is observed that the execution time and the amount of HDFS reads do not change much with varying numbers of DupPs because the grouping-based star-join computation approach in NTGA enables a scan sharing for DupPs while processing star subpatterns containing DupPs.

6.8.2.3 Varying Size of RDF Graphs

Figure 6.15b shows a comparative evaluation of the two approaches (Pig-Def and NTGA) with increasing number of RDF triples. The NTGA approach scales well with a performance gain of 52% to 58% ranging over BSBM-250k to BSBM-1000k data sizes, respectively. The gain varies because the number of triples containing repeated properties is not linearly increased when increasing the size of the data sets.

6.9 NESTING-AWARE PHYSICAL OPERATORS TO MINIMIZE DATA TRANSFER COSTS IN NTGA EXECUTION PLANS

In this section, we consider the issue of efficient management of intermediate results while evaluating graph pattern queries with multivalued relationships. Many real-world data sets contain multivalued attributes or relationships, for example, friend-ships in a social network, citation references. An issue with this in join-intensive processing is that many of the combinations of tuples generated by a join operation contain some redundancy. Specifically, the subtuple containing the non-multivalued attributes is repeated for each distinct value of the multivalued attribute.

Example 6.7: Graph Pattern with Multivalued Property

Consider the join $SJ1$ in Figure 6.16, which is a star join among relations T_{pLabel}, T_{pProp}, and $T_{prodFeature}$ on the Sub column, to reassemble the label, property, and fea-ture of products. Note that $prodFeature$ is a multivalued property that defines the one-to-many relationship between a product and its features. Consider the output tuples of the star join in Out_{MR1} that represents details about a product $Prod1$ with multiple product features ($PF1$, $PF2$, etc.). The subtuple labeled ($Sub1$, $Prop1$, $Obj1$, $Prop2$, $Obj2$, $Prop3$) is repeating for each distinct value of the product feature.

Remark 6.5

We define *redundancy factor* of an output as the portion of redundant data in the output, that is written onto the HDFS at the end of a MapReduce cycle. Typically, the redundancy factor is proportional to the multiplicity of the multivalued attribute. Multivalued properties with high multiplicity such as Facebook friends of highly social persons, result in a high redundancy factor in intermediate results when part of graph pattern queries. ■

Impact of Redundancy on Processing Costs. The redundancy factor is likely to compound across subsequent join operations, that is, the portion of redundant data in Out_{MR1} increases further after join $J1'$ (refer to Out_{MR3} in Figure 6.16). This ripple effect of redundancy in intermediate results has a negative impact on the HDFS writes of the current cycle, as well as the HDFS reads and data-shuffling costs of subsequent cycles. The impact on HDFS writes is significant while using flat data models. Additionally, the bloated intermediate results also impact the total disk space requirements in systems such as Hadoop, that store intermediate results till the completion of the entire execution workflow. Hence, efficient management of redundancy while processing join-intensive data-processing workloads is important to keep MR workflows nimble and cost-effective.

Remark 6.6

NTGA's nested data model already enables concise representation of intermediate results. For example, m star subgraphs containing redundant information due to the

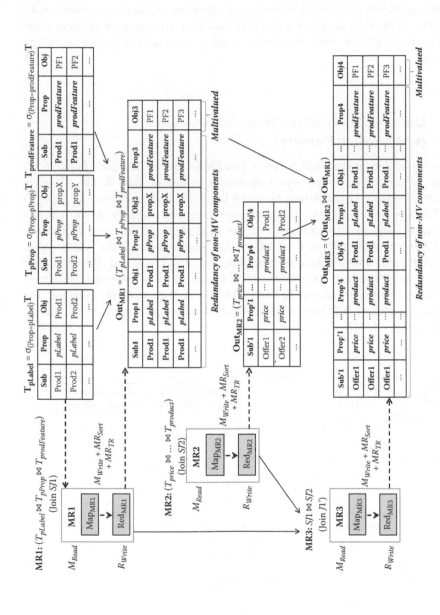

FIGURE 6.16 Star-join results Out_{MR1} containing a multivalued attribute prodFeature and repeated values for the non-multivalued attributes, and a ripple effect of the redundancy factor in the subsequent join result Out_{MR3}.

presence of a multivalued property with multiplicity *m* can be implicitly represented as a single triplegroup in NTGA. However, similar to systems such as Pig that support nested data models but do not support nesting-aware operators, the earlier generation NTGA operators require *unnesting* of such implicit representations prior to any subsequent join operation. This unnesting introduces redundancy in intermediate results. In the next section, we describe unnesting strategies for efficient management of redundancy while processing graph pattern queries with multivalued properties.   ■

6.9.1 Unnesting Strategies for Efficient Management of Multivalued Properties

Given a nested data model, there are three possible unnesting strategies (Figure 6.17) that can be considered to deal with redundancy in intermediate results, (i) *early complete unnesting* in the reduce phase of the cycle that generates the input to the *MVJoin* operation, (ii) *lazy complete unnesting*, and (iii) *lazy partial unnesting*. Both (ii) and (iii) are processed in the map phase of the cycle processing the *MVJoin* operation. Figure 6.17 denotes the stages at which the intermediate results containing a multivalued property are nested and unnested (flattened). For the rest of this discussion, we use *Star-MVP* to denote a star subgraph containing a multivalued property (such as *SJ*1 in Figure 6.16). We use *RedF$_i$* to denote the redundancy factor of *MR$_i$*, that is, the amount of redundant content in the reduce output of MR cycle *MR$_i$*.

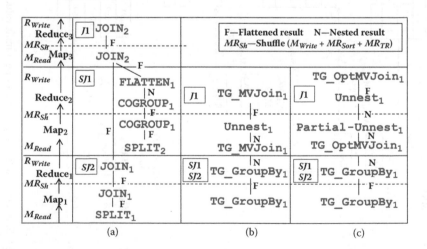

(a)   (b)   (c)

FIGURE 6.17 Unnesting strategies for a *MVJoin* J1 between two star subpatterns *SJ*1 and *SJ*2 (a) early complete unnesting in reduce of *MR$_{SJ1}$*, (b) lazy complete unnesting, and (c) lazy partial unnesting in map of *MR$_{J1}$*.

COGROUP *pLabel* by Sub, *pProp* by Sub...*prodFeature* by Sub;

$$\left[\textbf{Prod1,} \left\{ (\text{Prod1}, pLabel, \text{Prod1}) \right\}, \left\{ (...,pProp,...) \right\},...., \left\{ \begin{array}{l} (\text{Prod1}, prodFeature, \text{PF1}) \\ (\text{Prod1}, prodFeature, \text{PF2}) \\ (\text{Prod1}, prodFeature, \text{PF3}) \\ (\text{Prod1}, prodFeature, \text{PF4}) \end{array} \right\} \right]$$

FIGURE 6.18   Nested tuple resulting from a COGROUP on vertically partitioned relations.

Early Complete Unnesting: Reduce-Side Full Replication. Apache Pig's nested data model can be exploited to eliminate data redundancy while representing star-join results corresponding to Star-MVP. This can be achieved by processing star joins as a COGROUP operation that is used to group multiple relations on the same column, such as the Subject column in this case. A COGROUP on N relations, results in a nested tuple with N columns, where each column is a bag containing corresponding tuples from the participating relations as represented in Figure 6.18. The COGROUP-based star-join computation of Star-MVPs minimizes the redundancy factor for MR_{SJ1} ($RedF_{SJ1} = 0$), and reduces the amount of disk writes (R_{Write}) in MR_{SJ1}. However, each "column" in the result of a COGROUP is a bag of tuples, and Pig's JOIN operator is not defined on nested columns. Hence, processing any subsequent join operation requires unnesting (or flattening in Pig Latin parlance) of the join column.

Remark 6.7

In the case of a join operation on any of the single-valued columns such as object of *pLabel*, we may *partially* unnest the nested tuple based on the required column, which does not affect redundancy. However, a join on the multivalued column requires complete unnesting of the tuples resulting in redundant information about the single-valued columns. Both partial and complete unnesting can be achieved using the FLATTEN operator at the end of the reduce phase that generates the input to the *MVJoin* operation (MR_{SJ1} as shown in Figure 6.17a). Complete unnesting of the nested tuple results in full replication of the Star-MVP, and the replication factor *Rep* is a function of the multiplicity of the multivalued property.   ∎

Lazy Complete Unnesting: Map-Side Full Replication. NTGA operators are nesting-aware and do not require unnesting before operations such as join. This allows the unnesting of Star-MVPs to be delayed to the map phase of the *MVJoin* operation (MR_{J1} in Figure 6.17b) as opposed to the reduce phase of a previous cycle (MR_{SJ1} in Figure 6.17a). To support multivalued properties, RDFMap is extended to support (*Property*, List⟨*Object*⟩) pairs such as (*prodFeature*, {*PF*1, *PF*2, *PF*3, *PF*4, *PF*5}) as shown in Figure 6.19. For the rest of this discussion, we use the notation *Pr*1_*rMap* – *PF*1, ..., *PFn* to refer to a triplegroup corresponding to Product *Pr*1 and containing an MV property *prodFeature* with n object values *PF*1, ..., *PFn*.

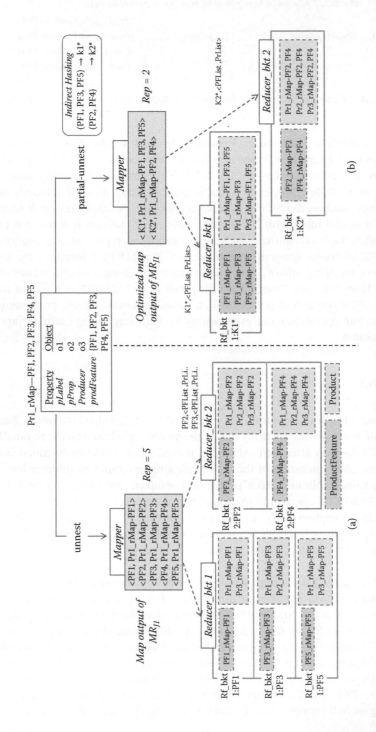

FIGURE 6.19 Lazy map-side unnest strategies: (a) complete unnesting (*Rep* = 5) and (b) partial unnesting (*Rep* = 2).

Example 6.8: Lazy Unnesting

The lazy unnesting approach delays the unnesting of $Pr1\_rMap$ till the map phase of the $MVJoin$, thus minimizing the redundancy factor in the output of MR_{SJ1}. This translates to savings in disk writes (R_{Write}) in the star-join phase as well as reduced amount of reads (M_{Read}) in the subsequent $MVJoin$ phase. NTGA's TG_MVJoin operator implements the map-side unnest operation, which completely unnests a Star-MVP and generates a map output tuple for each attened copy of the Star-MVP. For example, $Pr1\_rMap$ is unnested into five triplegroups, one for each of the distinct product features. Hence, the replication factor Rep is a function of the multiplicity of the multivalued property.

Lazy Partial Unnesting: Map-Side Partial Replication. If the multiplicity of a multivalued property is greater than the number of partitions in the reducer space, it is likely that multiple copies of the Star-MVP are assigned to the same partition. Consider Figure 6.19 with 2 reducers ($r = 2$), where 3 copies of the map output value $Pr1\_rMap$ corresponding to the join keys $PF1$, $PF3$, $PF5$, respectively, are mapped to the same $Reducer\_bkt$ 1. The map-side sorting costs (MR_{Sort}), local writes (M_{Write}), and network communication costs (MR_{TR}) can be reduced if the references to $Pr1\_rMap$ can be shared across the reduce function space (rf_bkt or a group of tuples processed by the same reduce function), that is, if the replication factor Rep can be reduced. This can be achieved using an extended partitioning scheme that allows sharing data references in the map output to avoid full replication.

Example 6.9: Lazy Partial Unnesting

For our map input $Pr1\_rMap$ shown in Figure 6.19, an example partition scheme $func^*$ could map the keys {$PF1$, $PF3$, $PF5$} to the same group key $k1^*$ as shown in Figure 6.19b. Consequently, only 1 copy of $Pr1\_rMap$ is transferred to $Reducer\_bkt$ 1, reducing the shuffle costs. The partial unnest operation partially unnests triplegroups based on the grouping function $func^*$ and is integrated into the map phase of an optimized join operator, TG_OptMVJoin.

Implementation of TG_OptMVJoin. The optimized NTGA operator TG_OptMVJoin, implements the lazy partial unnesting strategy for joins involving multivalued property. Algorithm 6.5 shows the extensions to POTGJoinAnnotator to enable partial unnesting. In the map phase, RDFMaps that join on subject Sub are annotated using its group key k^* computed by $k^* = func^*(Sub)$ (lines 1–2). For joins on object, RDFMap is partially unnested using the partial-unnest operation (lines 7–11). The partial-unnest operator splits the object list of the multivalued property based on the Object's group key $k^* = func^*(Obj)$, resulting in a list of partially unnested RDFMaps ($pList$ in line 3). A map output tuple is generated for each partially unnested RDFMap, annotated by its group key (lines 4–6). The replication factor Rep is now a function of $func^*$.

Algorithm 6.5: Extended POTGJoinAnnotator (TG_OptMVJoin)

    Map (*key:null, val: RDFMap rMap*) ;
1 **if** *join* on *Sub* **then**
2   ⌊ emit ⟨ func*(*rMap.Sub*), *rMap*⟩ ;

    else if *join* on *Obj* **then**
      //Partially unnest MVP's ObjList in *rMap* based on
      $k* = func* (Obj)$
3   *pList* ← **partial-unnest** (*rMap, func**) ;
4   **foreach** *partialMap* ∈ *pList* **do**
5   ⌊ *key* ← extract $k*$ for *partialMap* ;
6   ⌊ emit ⟨*key, partialMap*⟩ ;

    partial-unnest (*RDFMap rMap, func**) ;
    //RDFMap(*Sub, EC, propMap*)
7 *objList* ← extract MV prop's list of objects from *propMap* ;
8 **foreach** obj ∈ *objList* **do**
9   *groupKey* ←func* (*obj*);
10 ⌊ add (*prop, obj*) to *partialList* [*groupKey*] ;

11 emit *partialList* ;

Algorithm 6.6 shows the extensions to POTGJoinPackage operator, where all RDFMaps corresponding to the same group key $k*$ but different join keys are processed in the same reduce(). For example, RDFMaps in *Reducer_bkt*1 correspond to group key $k1*$ but different original keys *PF*1, *PF*3, and *PF*5. This requires selectively joining RDFMaps based on the original join key. RDFMaps corresponding to the left relation (*leftEC*) are extracted into a list (line 1). RDFMaps from the right relation (*rightEC*) are unnested and hashed based on the join key (line 2). The algorithm iterates through each RDFMap in the left relation (line 3), and probes the hashed relation for each distinct object value (join key) for each property (lines 4–6). When a match is found the RDFMaps are joined (line 7) as per the definition of TG_Join. Additional details about the partitioning scheme and a discussion on the implementation issues can be found here [37].

Algorithm 6.6: Extended POTGJoinPackage (TG_OptMVJoin)

    Reduce (*key:k**, *val:List of RDFMaps R*) ;
1 *leftList* ← extract leftEC RDFMaps from *R* //MV
2 *rightHash* ← extract rightEC RDFMaps from *R* //non-MV
3 **foreach** *leftR* ∈ *leftList* **do**
    //Handle multivalued property
4   *MVList* ← extract *prop's objList* from *leftR* ;
5   **foreach** *joinKey* ∈ *MVList* **do**
6   ⌊ *rightR* ← *rightHash*.get(*joinKey*) ;
7   ⌊ emit ⟨ joinRDFMaps(*leftR, rightR*)⟩ ;

6.9.2   CASE STUDY: IMPACT OF NESTING AND LAZY UNNESTING STRATEGIES FOR GRAPH PATTERN QUERIES WITH MULTIVALUED PROPERTIES

This section presents a study on the impact of the proposed nesting and unnesting strategies on minimizing the redundancy factor in intermediate results while processing graph pattern queries. The comparative evaluation included two popular relational-style systems, Apache Pig (*Pig-Opt* with COGROUP-based star-join computation) and Hive (*Hive*), both of which support tuple-based algebra. *NTGA-Opt* denotes NTGA with lazy partial unnesting strategy.

Setup and Testbed. Experiments were conducted on a 10-node Hadoop cluster with Pig release 0.10.0, Hive 0.8.1, and Hadoop 0.20.2. The BSBM [11] synthetic benchmark data set was used for evaluation, which consists of two multivalued properties *productFeature* with approximate multiplicity 19 and product *type* with multiplicity 6. The results presented in this section are for *BSBM-500K* data set with 500,000 products (43 GB in size). Two categories of queries that involve multivalued properties were considered, (i) *non-MV join*—the join variable is single-valued, and (ii) *MVJoin*—the join variable is the object of a multivalued property.

Impact of the Nesting Strategy. Figure 6.20a shows the performance evaluation of the approaches for queries containing one multivalued property with low (product type with 6) and high (product feature with 19) multiplicity, respectively. Figure 6.20b denotes the redundancy factor in intermediate results while evaluating the queries using at tuple-based algebra in Hive. Queries *low-1Star* and *high-1Star* (both with one star subpattern) can be computed in a single MR cycle (MR_{S1}) and their reduce output contains a redundancy factor of 0.72 and 0.82, respectively, when evaluated using Pig/Hive. The two star subpattern queries (*low-2Star* and *high-2Star*) demonstrate how the redundancy factor compounds across the subsequent join cycle. While the redundancy factor of *low-2Star* increases from 0.72 (in MR_{S1}) to 0.78 after the subsequent join in $MR_{S1 \bowtie S2}$, for *high-2Star* it increases from 0.82 (in MR_{S1}) to 0.89 (in $MR_{S1 \bowtie S2}$).

The impact of the redundancy factor on HDFS writes can be seen in Figure 6.20a. Both *Hive/Pig-Opt* approaches failed to complete execution for *high-2Star* on a 10-node cluster due to insufficient disk space (denoted as a missing bar for Hive). This failure can be attributed to the blow-up of the intermediate results. *Hive* approach occupied 52% more disk space after the star-join phase when compared with the nested approaches. On the contrary, the nested approaches (*Pig-Opt* and *NTGA*) required 71.5% / 86.6% less disk space overall, when compared with Hive for queries *low-1Star/high-2Star*, respectively.

Impact of the Lazy Unnesting Strategy. This evaluation included four MVJoin queries with varying density of star subpattern containing the multivalued property— *MV-2p* to *MV-5p* whose *Star-MVP* consists of 2 to 5 triple patterns, respectively. Denser star-join structures result in larger size of non-MV components and hence a higher redundancy factor. The lazy unnesting strategies in *NTGA* outperform both *Hive* and the early complete unnesting in *Pig-Opt* for all queries. As the size of the redundant component increases, *NTGA* shows an increasing performance gain over *Pig-Opt* from 61% in *MV-2p* to 68% in *MV-5p*.

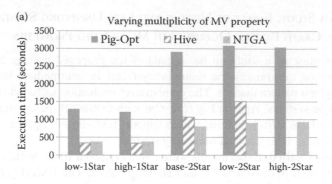

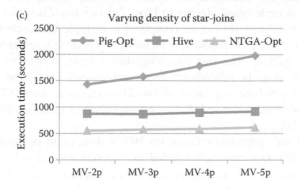

(b)

Redundancy factor across the MapReduce workflow			
Query	MR_{S1}	MR_{S2}	$MR_{S1 \bowtie S2}$
Low-1Star	0.72 (1.5 GB)	–	–
High-1Star	0.82 (5.2 GB)	–	–
Base-2Star	0 (0.2 GB)	0 (7.7 GB)	0 (12.7 GB)
Low-2Star	0.72 (1.6 GB)	0 (7.7 GB)	0.78 (75.8 GB)
High-2Star	0.82 (5.4 GB)	0 (7.7 GB)	0.89 (250 GB)

FIGURE 6.20 (a) Comparative evaluation using one and two star subpattern queries containing low and high multiplicity MV property, (b) redundancy factor in reduce output while evaluating test queries using flat algebra, (c) impact of lazy unnesting strategy with increasing cardinality of star-joins (BSBM-500k, 10-node).

6.10 CONCLUDING REMARKS

This chapter discusses the challenges and strategies for RDF query processing on MapReduce platforms. The impetus for this research direction is the range of emerging applications that rely on increasing amounts of publicly available Semantic Web data as background knowledge for analysis. In many scenarios, the computational needs required to incorporate such large amounts of Semantic Web data in processing are episodic and elastic so that the trend is to leverage resources from the cloud when possible. A number of cloud data-processing platforms have emerged in recent times to support such applications, with many of them based on query processing infrastructure similar to relational query engines. However, relational model and algebra have some limitations with respect to the requirements of Semantic Web processing—large number of joins, irregular structure, inferencing with querying, and these limitations have an appreciable negative impact in MapReduce context.

This chapter reviews query evaluation techniques for graph pattern queries on MapReduce platforms in terms of two query algebras: derivatives of relational algebra and an alternative algebra called the *Nested TripleGroup Data Model and Algebra (NTGA)*. It discusses the advantage of NTGA over relational-style query plans and data representation, due to concurrent execution of "star joins," which reduces workflow length and enables shared table scans while keeping the footprint of intermediate results minimized. The chapter presents some evaluation results that show up to 60% performance advantage for relatively basic queries involving 2 to 3 star patterns. This advantage is expected to be even larger in more complex queries with more star patterns because of the concurrent star-join execution enabled by NTGA plans.

Ongoing and future work in NTGA optimization is focused on including necessary extensions (logical and physical operators and query rewriting rules) to enable translation of more complex graph pattern queries like graph patterns with unbound properties, with optional fragments, ontological queries, and analytical queries to NTGA. Some preliminary results for some of these more complex classes, specifically ontological queries, have shown up to orders of magnitude in performance advantage and are thus very promising.

REFERENCES

1. Apache HBase. http://hbase.apache.org/.
2. Billion Triple Challenge. http://challenge.semanticweb.org/.
3. Open Science Data Cloud. https://www.opensciencedatacloud.org/.
4. SPARQL S-Expressions. http://jena.apache.org/documentation/notes/sse.html.
5. Azza Abouzeid, Kamil Bajda-Pawlikowski, Daniel Abadi, Avi Silberschatz, and Alexander Rasin. HadoopDB: An Architectural Hybrid of MapReduce and DBMS Technologies for Analytical Workloads. *Proc. VLDB*, 2:922–933, 2009.
6. Foto N. Afrati and Jeffrey D. Ullman. Optimizing Multiway Joins in a Map-Reduce Environment. *Proc. TKDE*, 23(9):1282–1298, 2011.
7. Kemafor Anyanwu, HyeongSik Kim, and Padmashree Ravindra. Algebraic Optimization for Processing Graph Pattern Queries in the Cloud. *IEEE Internet Comput.*, 17(2):52–61, 2013.
8. Medha Atre, Vineet Chaoji, Mohammed J. Zaki, and James A. Hendler. Matrix Bit Loaded: A Scalable Lightweight Join Query Processor for RDF data. In *Proc. Int. Conf. World Wide Web*, pp. 41–50, 2010.
9. Andrzej Bialecki, Michael Cafarella, Doug Cutting, and Owen O'Malley. *Hadoop: A Framework for Running Applications on Large Clusters Built of Commodity Hardware.*
10. Barry Bishop, Atanas Kiryakov, Damyan Ognyanoff, Ivan Peikov, Zdravko Tashev, and Ruslan Velkov. OWLIM: A Family of Scalable Semantic Repositories. *Semantic Web*, 2(1):33–42, 2011.

11. Christian Bizer and Andreas Schultz. The Berlin SPARQL Benchmark. *International Journal on Semantic Web and Information Systems*, 5(2):1–24, 2009.
12. Jeffrey Dean and Sanjay Ghemawat. MapReduce: Simplified Data Processing on Large Clusters. In *Proc. OSDI*, pp. 10–10, 2004.
13. Iman Elghandour and Ashraf Aboulnaga. ReStore: Reusing Results of MapReduce jobs. *Proc. VLDB*, 5(6):586–597, February 2012.
14. Orri Erling and Ivan Mikhailov. Virtuoso: RDF Support in a Native RDBMS. In *Semantic Web Inform. Manag.*, pp. 501–519, 2010.
15. Craig Franke, Samuel Morin, Artem Chebotko, John Abraham, and Pearl Brazier. Distributed Semantic Web Data Management in HBase and MySQL Cluster. In *Proc. CLOUD*, pp. 105–112, 2011.
16. Olaf Gorlitz and Steffen Staab. SPLENDID: SPARQL Endpoint Federation Exploiting VOID Descriptions. In *Proc. COLD*, 2011.
17. Steve Harris, Nick Lamb, and Nigel Shadbolt. 4store: The Design and Implementation of a Clustered RDF store. In *Proc. SSWS*, pp. 94–109, 2009.
18. Andreas Harth, Jurgen Umbrich, Aidan Hogan, and Stefan Decker. YARS2: A Federated Repository for Querying Graph Structured Data from the Web. In *Proc. ISWC*, pp. 211–224, 2007.
19. Seokyong Hong and Kemafor Anyanwu. HIP: Information Passing for Optimizing Join-Intensive Data Processing Workloads on Hadoop. In *Proc. DEXA*, pp. 384–391, 2012.
20. Seokyong Hong, Padmashree Ravindra, and Kemafor Anyanwu. Adaptive Information Passing for Early State Pruning in MapReduce Data Processing Workflows. In *Proc. ICAC*, pp. 133–143, 2013.
21. Jiewen Huang, Daniel J. Abadi, and Kun Ren. Scalable SPARQL Querying of Large RDF Graphs. *Proc. VLDB*, 4(11), 2011.
22. Mohammad Farhan Husain, James McGlothlin, Mohammad Mehedy Masud, Latifur R. Khan, and Bhavani Thuraisingham. Heuristics-Based Query Processing for Large RDF Graphs Using Cloud Computing. *TKDE*, 23:1312–1327, 2011.
23. HyeongSik Kim, Padmashree Ravindra, and Kemafor Anyanwu. From SPARQL to MapReduce: The Journey Using a Nested TripleGroup Algebra. *Proc. VLDB*, 4(12), 2011.
24. HyeongSik Kim, Padmashree Ravindra, and Kemafor Anyanwu. Scan-Sharing for Optimizing RDF Graph Pattern Matching on MapReduce. In *Proc. CLOUD*, pp. 139–146, 2012.
25. Spyros Kotoulas, Jacopo Urbani, Peter Boncz, and Peter Mika. Robust Runtime Optimization and Skew-Resistant Execution of Analytical SPARQL Queries on Pig. In *Proc. ISWC*, pp. 247–262, 2012.
26. YongChul Kwon, Magdalena Balazinska, Bill Howe, and Jerome Rolia. SkewTune: Mitigating Skew in Mapreduce Applications. In *Proc. SIGMOD*, pp. 25–36, 2012.
27. Kyong-Ha Lee, Yoon-Joon Lee, Hyunsik Choi, Yon Dohn Chung, and Bongki Moon. Parallel Data Processing with MapReduce: A Survey. *SIGMOD Rec.*, 40(4):11–20, January 2012.
28. Rubao Lee, Tian Luo, Yin Huai, Fusheng Wang, Yongqiang He, and Xiaodong Zhang. YSmart: Yet Another SQL-to-MapReduce Translator. In *Proc. ICDCS*, pp. 25–36, 2011.
29 Brian McBride. Jena: A Semantic Web Toolkit. *Internet Computing, IEEE*, 6(6):55–59, 2002.
30. Thomas Neumann and Gerhard Weikum. The RDF-3X Engine for Scalable Management of RDF Data. *VLDB J.*, 19:91–113, 2010.
31. Tomasz Nykiel, Michalis Potamias, Chaitanya Mishra, George Kollios, and Nick Koudas. MRShare: Sharing across Multiple Queries in MapReduce. *Proc. VLDB*, 3:494–505, 2010.
32. Christopher Olston, Benjamin Reed, Utkarsh Srivastava, Ravi Kumar, and Andrew Tomkins. Pig Latin: A Not-So-Foreign Language for Data Processing. In *Proc. SIGMOD*, 2008.

33. Nikolaos Papailiou, Ioannis Konstantinou, Dimitrios Tsoumakos, and Nectarios Koziris. H2RDF: Adaptive Query Processing on RDF Data in the Cloud. In *Proc. WWW*, pp. 397–400, 2012.

34. Andrew Pavlo, Erik Paulson, Alexander Rasin, Daniel J. Abadi, David J. DeWitt, Samuel Madden, and Michael Stonebraker. A Comparison of Approaches to Large-Scale Data Analysis. In *Proc. SIGMOD*, pp. 165–178, 2009.

35. Sriram Rao, Raghu Ramakrishnan, Adam Silberstein, Mike Ovsiannikov, and Damian Reeves. Sailfish: A Framework for Large Scale Data Processing. In *Proc. SoCC*, pp. 4:1–4:14, 2012.

36. Padmashree Ravindra, HyeongSik Kim, and Kemafor Anyanwu. An Intermediate Algebra for Optimizing RDF Graph Pattern Matching on MapReduce. In *Proc. ESWC*, volume 6644, pp. 46–61, 2011.

37. Padmashree Ravindra, HyeongSik Kim, and Kemafor Anyanwu. To Nest or Not to Nest, When and How Much: Representing Intermediate Results of Graph Pattern Queries in MapReduce Based Processing. In *Proc. 4th International Workshop on Semantic Web Information Management*, SWIM'12, 2012.

38. Kurt Rohloff and Richard E. Schantz. High-Performance, Massively Scalable Distributed Systems Using the MapReduce Software Framework: The SHARD Triple-Store. In *Proc. PSI EtA*, pp. 4:1–4:5, 2010.

39. Sherif Sakr, Anna Liu, and Ayman G. Fayoumi. The Family of MapReduce and Large Scale Data Processing Systems. *CoRR*, abs/1302.2966, 2013.

40. Alexander Schatzle, Martin Przyjaciel-Zablocki, Christopher Dorner, Thomas Hornung, and Georg Lausen. Cascading Map-Side Joins over HBase for Scalable Join Processing. In *Proc. SSWS+HPCSW*, pp. 59–74, 2012.

41. Alexander Schatzle, Martin Przyjaciel-Zablocki, and Georg Lausen. PigSPARQL: Mapping SPARQL to Pig Latin. In *Proc. SWIM*, pp. 4:1–4:8, 2011.

42. Philip Stutz, Abraham Bernstein, and William Cohen. Signal/Collect: Graph Algorithms for the (Semantic) Web. In *Proc. ISWC*, pp. 764–780, 2010.

43. Bryan Thompson and Mike Personick. BigData: The Semantic Web on an Open Source Cloud. In *Proc. ISWC*, 2009.

44. Ashish Thusoo, Joydeep Sen Sarma, Namit Jain, Zheng Shao, Prasad Chakka, Suresh Anthony, Hao Liu, Pete Wyckoff, and Raghotham Murthy. Hive: A Warehousing Solution over a MapReduce Framework. *Proc. VLDB*, 2:1626–1629, 2009.

45. Maria-Esther Vidal, Edna Ruckhaus, Tomas Lampo, Amadis Martinez, Javier Sierra, and Axel Polleres. Efficiently Joining Group Patterns in SPARQL Queries. In *Proc. ESWC*, pp. 228–242, 2010.

46. Cathrin Weiss, Panagiotis Karras, and Abraham Bernstein. Hexastore: Sextuple Indexing for Semantic Web Data Management. *Proc. VLDB*, 1:1008–1019, 2008.

47. Kai Zeng, Jiacheng Yang, Haixun Wang, Bin Shao, and Zhongyuan Wang. A Distributed Graph Engine for Web Scale RDF Data. In *Proc. VLDB*, pp. 265–276, 2013.

48. Xiaofei Zhang, Lei Chen, Yongxin Tong, and Min Wang. EAGRE: Towards Scalable I/O Efficient SPARQL Query Evaluation on the Cloud. In *Proc. ICDE*, pp. 565–576, 2013.

7 Network Performance Aware Graph Partitioning for Large Graph Processing Systems in the Cloud

Rishan Chen, Xuetian Weng, Bingsheng He,
Byron Choi, and Mao Yang

CONTENTS

7.1 INTRODUCTION

A wide variety of recent applications model their data in graphs/networks such as social networks, web graphs, and protein–protein interaction networks. Efficient processing for large graph data poses new challenges for almost all components of state-of-the-art data management systems. To list a few examples: (i) graph data are complex structures and cannot be efficiently stored as relational tables; (ii) the access patterns of large graph processing are complex, which results in inefficient disk accesses or network communications; and (iii) last but not least, to tackle scalability issues, graph processing must be efficiently distributed in a networked environment.

Researchers have been actively proposing many innovative solutions to address the new challenges of large graph processing. In particular, a notable number of techniques have recently been proposed to utilize the cloud. The objectives of this chapter are (i) to introduce typical examples of large graph processing, (ii) to give an overview of existing cloud-based graph processing platforms, and more importantly, (iii) to emphasize a network performance aware data partitioning approach, which bridges large graph processing and cloud-based platforms. In particular, the network bandwidth may not be uniform across the large network in a cloud; a network with higher bandwidth between its machines can support more intermachine computation.

The chapter is structured as follows. We survey some typical examples of large graph processing in Section 7.2. In Section 7.3, we list some representative cloud-based graph processing platforms. Section 7.4 presents the network unevenness in cloud-based systems and Section 7.5 introduces network performance aware graph partitioning. For the completeness of discussions, Section 7.7 gives an introduction to existing graph partitioning approaches, although they may not be related to the cloud technologies. A discussion of open problems is provided in Section 7.8. We summarize the chapter in Section 7.9.

7.2 APPLICATIONS OF LARGE GRAPHS

Large graphs have arisen in a wide range of data-intensive applications. To begin our discussions, we first describe a small and non-exhaustive set of typical examples of large graphs and their applications.

7.2.1 SOCIAL NETWORKS

In social networks, nodes often represent users and edges may often represent relationships between users (friendships). Today, there are plenty of large social networks. For example, the social network of Facebook consisted of 1 billion nodes and more than 100 billion edges in 2012 [70]. The largest publicly available social network (contributed by Yahoo!*) consists of more than 1 billion nodes. The social network of LinkedIn contained almost 218 million nodes in the first quarter of 2013 [54]. The project FlockDB manages social graphs with more than 13 billion edges [40]. Moreover, social networks are evolving at an unprecedented rate. For example, it has been reported that, between 2004 and 2012, the Facebook network increased from roughly 1 million to 1 billion users [70].

Analysis on social networks has become a hot research topic. Work has been conducted identifying and searching user communities from the networks, and studies have been carried out to estimate the diameter and the radius of a network (e.g., [42]). These studies show how users are connected and indicate which users are outliers of the network. It is reported that the small-world phenomenon has been found in social networks [42]. In practice, despite the large number of users on social networks, it is often a user's close friends who often have the most influence on him/her. It is desirable to determine two- or three-hop friend lists for a social network user. Another application of the networks is to help organizing activities. An organizer can find not only a group of his/her close friends, but also groups that contain people who are close friends of each other.

7.2.2 WEB GRAPHS

Another example of large graphs is the WWW graph. The nodes represent web pages and edges represent hyperlinks. Google estimates that there are over 1 trillion web pages. The indexed web contained at least 4.6 billion web pages as of June 2013.† Today, the WWW graphs for experimentation contain more than 20 billion web pages and 160 billion hyperlinks. The web page hyperlink connectivity graph of Yahoo! AltaVista of 2002 is publicly available.‡ The well-known application of

---

* Webscope from Yahoo! Labs. Graph, and Social Data. http://webscope.sandbox.yahoo.com/catalog.php?datatype=g.
† WorldWideWebSize.com: http://www.worldwidewebsize.com/.
‡ Webscope from Yahoo! Labs. Graph and Social Data. http://webscope.sandbox.yahoo.com/catalog.php?datatype=g.

the WWW graph is the computation of web pages' PageRank [63] for web searches. Let the engineering details such as damping factor alone, the PageRank algorithm iteratively computes the PageRank of each page from the PageRanks of the pages that link to it. The algorithm terminates when the PageRanks of the pages converge. The PageRank algorithm is often used as an example to illustrate performance characteristics of cloud-based platforms.

7.2.3 INFORMATION NETWORKS

Resource Description Framework (RDF) has been an official W3C recommendation for the semantic web. The triplets of RDF naturally form a graph. Among others, RDF has been applied to knowledge bases, such as DBpedia [6]. The ontology of DBpedia derived from Wikipedia contains 3.7 millions of "things" and 400 millions of facts.* Such data are particularly useful for users to formulate complex queries about the information represented in the RDF. Applications of the semantic web continue to emerge each year [1].

Search engine providers are actively engaged in introducing semantics for next generation search engines (e.g., Probase [78]).† A recent report of the graph-based knowledge base Satori [13] from Microsoft, which enhances the search capabilities of Bing, consists of more than 300 million nodes and 800 million edges. Google's knowledge graph has 570 million objects and 18 billion facts about the relationships between different objects. The knowledge graphs are expected to enhance the ranking mechanisms of search results.

7.2.4 MISCELLANEOUS

Other examples of large graphs are the citation relationship of research articles, relationships between US patents,‡ Wordnet,§ communication networks, transportation or road networks, and many others. Some of these graphs can be found in the a nice collection of graphs of the Stanford Network Analysis Project (SNAP) [53].

7.3 CLOUD-BASED GRAPH PROCESSING PLATFORMS

As described in the previous section, graph data are ubiquitous and their volume is ever increasing. New computationally and data-intensive analysis tasks on graphs are continuously being reported. The deployments of applications on such data have been moving from a small number of high-performance servers or super computers [31,46] toward a *cloud* with a large number of commodity servers [43,58].

A number of general-purpose development platforms such as MapReduce [23], its open-source variant, Hadoop [33], and Dryad [37] have been proposed to help users to develop custom applications on the cloud, without worrying about the complexity beneath the cloud. For instance, data may be stored in distributed and replicated file

---

* DBpedia SPARQL Benchmark: http://aksw.org/Projects/DBPSB.html.
† Probase: http://research.microsoft.com/probase/.
‡ US Patent: http://vlado.fmf.uni-lj.si/pub/networks/data/patents/Patents.htm.
§ Wordnet: http://vlado.fmf.uni-lj.si/pub/networks/data/dic/Wordnet/Wordnet.zip.

systems such as GFS [30] or BigTable [17]. Such systems are suitable for processing flat data structures, not just graph structured data. In particular, it is known that much graph analysis inherently involves random access and direct adoption of the technologies for flat files or relations may lead to high (network) communication costs in the cloud. It is desirable to have a graph-processing platform that automatically handles optimization details for users.

Graph processing platforms for the cloud have recently been proposed. Most of these platforms (e.g., [42,43,81]) are built on top of MapReduce [23]. In this section, we give a brief survey of some representative solutions.

7.3.1 SURVEY OF EXISTING SYSTEMS

7.3.1.1 Pregel

Pregel [58] is a vertex-oriented graph processing engine that implements a Bulk Synchronous Parallel (BSP) model. Pregel passes computational results between workers. It provides a user-defined API *Compute()* executed on vertices. In one iteration of BSP (i.e., *superstep* in Pregel's terminology), Pregel executes *Compute()* on all the vertices in parallel. Messages are passed over the network. Vertices vote to halt if they have no work to do.

7.3.1.2 PEGASUS

PEGASUS [43] is an open-source Hadoop-based library that supports typical graph mining operations including PageRank, spectral clustering, diameter and radius estimations, and connected components. An important observation is that many such mining operations can be readily expressed as an iterative matrix-vector multiplication. PEGASUS therefore proposes a scalable, highly optimized primitive called generalized iterated matrix–vector multiplication that includes block multiplication, clustered edges, and diagonal block iteration.

7.3.1.3 HADI

HADI [42] is a graph mining implementation (developed on Hadoop) that estimates the radii and diameter of a large graph. To tackle the scale of large graphs, HADI proposes an approximation algorithm implemented and optimized for the cloud framework Hadoop/MapReduce.

7.3.1.4 Surfer

Surfer [18] is a large graph processing engine that provides two primitives for developing applications on the cloud: MapReduce and propagation. MapReduce is useful for applications processing flat data structures. In comparison, the second primitive propagation operation is designed for developing edge-oriented tasks on large graphs. A prototype [19] is developed on top of Pregel extended with a network performance-aware partitioning framework.

7.3.1.5 Trinity

Trinity [67] is a distributed memory-based general purpose graph engine. An observation is that MapReduce implementation of graph processing can lead to huge I/O and communication overhead. Trinity exploits the memory of the machines in the cloud forming a "memory cloud," which enables fast random data access, which is particularly useful for computation on graphs. In addition, Trinity consists of a native graph storage engine. These techniques significantly speed up large graph processing. Trinity supports both transactional and batched graph processing.

7.3.1.6 GraphLab

GraphLab [56] is specially designed for machine learning and data mining algorithms, which are not naturally supported by MapReduce. The GraphLab abstraction enables developers to specify asynchronous, dynamic, graph-parallel computation while ensuring data consistency and achieving a high degree of parallel performance in the shared-memory setting. GraphLab uses an asynchronous parallel model different from the BSP model used by Pregel. Additionally, The GraphLab framework has been extended to the distributed setting while preserving strong data consistency guarantees [55].

Other cloud-based solutions for graph processing include the following. DisG [81] is an ongoing project for web graph reconstruction using Hadoop. Pujol et al. [65] studied different replication methods to scale social network analysis. Hama [5] and Giraph [4] are two open-source projects targeting large graph processing. They adopt Pregel's programming model and their storage is built on top of the Hadoop Distributed File System. While the solutions mentioned above focus on batch processing, there are transactional graph processing databases such as Neo4j and InfiniteGraph. Finally, recently, a number of cloud-based data management systems have been developed for other important workloads such as data warehousing [2,35,77] and on-line transaction processing [22], which are beyond the scope of this chapter.

7.3.2 COMPARISON OF EXISTING SYSTEMS

Table 7.1 provides a brief comparison of a number of representative graph processing systems with respect to their properties of graph storage, support of online processing, main-memory processing and distributed processing. Neo4j and HyperGraphDB

TABLE 7.1
Comparison of Representative Systems (An Extended Version Based on Table 2 in Previous [68])

	Native Graphs	Online Query Processing	Memory-Based Exploration	Distributed Parallel Processing
Neo4j	Yes	Yes	No	No
HyperGraphDB	No	Yes	No	No
InfiniteGraph	Yes	Yes	No	Yes
MapReduce	No	No	No	Yes
PEGASUS	No	No	No	Yes
Surfer	Yes	No	Yes	Yes
Googles Pregel	No	No	No	Yes
Microsofts Trinity	Yes	Yes	Yes	Yes

are two centralized graph processing engines that do not partition data graphs to multiple machines. Both can support online query processing. However, their scalability is limited, because they cannot handle very large graphs efficiently, due to the costly disk accesses. For distributed graph processing systems, many engines are disk-based, mainly for reliability, and scalability. In-memory graph explorations resolve the random I/O bottleneck of Trinity and Surfer. As for graph partitioning, most graph engines (except Surfer) use random hash partitioning by default. Surfer adopts the network performance aware graph partitioning, specifically designed for cloud environments.

To illustrate the differences between these systems with an example, we briefly compare their reported performances of the PageRank computation, which is a typical algorithm for benchmarking graph processing.

Neo4j and HyperGraphDB are centralized graph processing engines, and hence, the graphs that they can process are obviously limited by the centralized server. As graph processing often involves random data accesses, graphs that cannot fit into main memory may incur numerous disk accesses that significantly affects performance.

Pegasus supports iterative matrix–vector multiplications and implemented the matrix approach for computing PageRank and its optimizations. Their experiments confirmed that performance improves as the number of machines increases and performance scales linearly as graph size increases beyond 1 billion nodes. Pegasus finished one PageRank iteration in around 100 seconds on YahooWeb (1.4 billion nodes) under the default setting of 9 supercomputers.

Pregel implemented a vertex-oriented PageRank algorithm under the message passing paradigm. To handle large graph data, its original implementation uses a default random hash function to partition graph data to worker processes. Giraph [4] is a publicly available implementation for Pregel. Its performance of PageRank has been reported in comparison with Trinity [67]. Trinity also implemented a vertex-oriented PageRank algorithm and ran it on eight commodity machines. Trinity keeps graphs in the main memory, which leads to superior efficiency. In particular, Trinity completes one PageRank iteration on a 1 billion node graph in less than 1 minute. In comparison, Giraph is at least two orders of magnitude slower and runs out of memory processing some large graphs.

Surfer tested the Network Rank algorithm* on a social network that consists of more than half a billion nodes and about 30 billion edges. The main focus of Surfer is to show the improvement in performance due to its network performance aware graph partitioning. The speedup of the response time observed from the MapReduce engine built on top of a MapReduce platform ranges from 1.7 to 5.8 times faster than the original response times, under different network topology settings.

7.3.3   OTHER GRAPH PROCESSING PLATFORMS/SYSTEMS

We have recently seen that cloud computing platforms have been equipped with emerging hardware such as multicore CPUs and GPUs (Graphics Processing Units).

---

* Network ranking is the generation of a ranking on the vertices in the graph using PageRank or its variants.

Beyond machine-level parallelism, it is desirable to exploit intra-machine parallelism. On multicore CPUs, parallel libraries like MTGL [12] have been developed for parallel graph algorithms. MTGL offers a set of data structures and APIs for building graph algorithms. The MTGL API is modeled after the Boost Graph Library [69] and optimized to leverage shared memory multithreaded machines. The SNAP framework [7] provides a set of algorithms and building blocks for graph analysis, especially for small-world graphs. On the GPU, a general-purpose programming framework called Medusa [80] has been developed. The goal is to hide the details of graph programming and GPU runtime from users. In contrast to Pregel, Medusa adopts very fine-grained processing on vertices/edges/messages to exploit the massive parallelism of the GPU. Additionally, there are specific parallel graph algorithms on the GPU [34,36,48,75].

7.4 UNEVEN BANDWIDTH BETWEEN THE MACHINES OF THE CLOUD

The cloud-based solutions discussed in the previous section provide a user-friendly platform for users to develop their custom logic without worrying how the underlying interconnected machines operates. However, the unique network environment that consists such number of servers does further add fuel to the challenges of large graph processing. In this section, we discuss the factors on the cloud (such as hardware and software) that reveal the major factors of network bandwidth unevenness in the cloud.

7.4.1 FACTOR 1: NETWORK ENVIRONMENT

Due to the significant scale, the cloud network environment is significantly different from those in previous distributed environment [44,46,52], for example, Cray supercomputers or a small-scale cluster. In a small-scale cluster, the network bandwidth is often roughly the same for every machine pair. However, the network bandwidth of the cloud environment is uneven among different machine pairs.

Current cloud infrastructures often use a switch-based tree structure to interconnect the servers [10,32,41]. Machines are first grouped into *pods*, and then pods are connected to higher-level switches. A natural consequence of such a topology is that the network bandwidth of any machine pair is not uniform that is influenced by the switches that connect the two machines [37]. The intra-pod bandwidth is much higher than the cross-pod bandwidth.

The knowledge of network topology (such as multilevel data reduction along the tree topology [23] and partition-based locality optimizations [64]) and scheduling techniques [38] are crucial for advanced optimization in the cloud. However, it should also be remarked that the topology information in the cloud is usually not available to cloud users due to the virtualization and system management issues.

Finally, a simple reason for network unevenness can be that the commodity computers in the cloud may not have a uniform network configuration (e.g., network adaptors). As the cloud evolves, its computers may become heterogeneous from generations to generations [79]. For example, current mainstream network adaptors provide 1 Gb/sec, and the adaptors with 10 Gb/sec has been gradually employed. These hardware factors result in the unevenness of the network bandwidth among machines in the cloud.

7.4.1.1   Case Study

As discussed, the network bandwidth among different machine pairs can vary significantly. Such network bandwidth unevenness has been observed by cloud providers [10,41]. He et al. [19] have also observed significant network bandwidth unevenness in Amazon EC2. Figure 7.1 shows the network bandwidth of every machine pair among 64 and 128 small instances (i.e., virtual machine) on Amazon EC2. The network bandwidth varies significantly. The mean (MB/sec) and standard deviation are (112.8, 37.5) and (115.0, 40.2) for 64 and 128 small instances, respectively. It is observed that some pairwise bandwidth are very high (e.g., more than 500 MB/sec). The possible reason is that those small instances can be allocated to the same physical machine.

He et al. [19] also note that the network bandwidth between two instances in the public cloud is temporarily stable, with similar results observed in the another study [76]. This allows to develop network performance aware optimizations based on the network bandwidths measured at a particular recent time point.

7.4.2   FACTOR 2: VIRTUALIZATION

In addition to hardware factors, software techniques in the cloud can result in network bandwidth unevenness. In particular, virtualization has been a crucial facility of the cloud. It hides the network topology or the real configurations of the machines underneath a cloud system from users. In fact, in cloud environments, users do not have administrator privileges on the hardware under the virtualization layer. A popular optimization in virtualization is virtual machine consolidation, for better resource utilization of virtualization. However, the consolidation process may induce concurrent tasks to compete for the network bandwidth on the same physical machine. Different degrees of consolidation cause the network bandwidth unevenness among physical machines.

7.5   NETWORK BANDWIDTH AWARE GRAPH PARTITIONING TECHNIQUE FOR THE CLOUD

Due to the massive volume of graph data, even a baseline graph processing engine should store a large graph into partitions, as opposed to a single flat storage. However, graph partitioning itself should be effectively integrated into the large processing in the cloud environment. There are a number of challenging issues in such an integration. First, graph partitioning itself is a very costly task, which in particular generates much network traffic. Second, the network bandwidth unevenness described in Section 1.3 affects the way of graph partitioning and graph partition storage on the machines. Since the number of graph partitions and the number of machines for graph processing can be very large, the possible solution space of storing graph partitions to the machines is huge. Consider P partitions to be stored on P machines. The space includes $P!$ possible solutions. Another problem is how to make both the graph

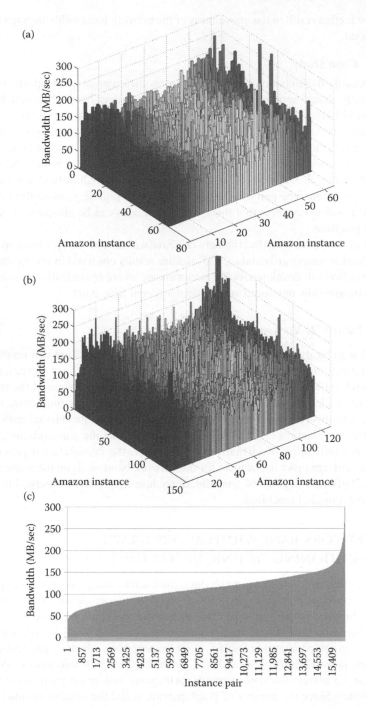

FIGURE 7.1 Network bandwidth unevenness in Amazon EC2: (a, b) pairwise network bandwidth varying the number of small instances, (c) the distribution of pairwise network bandwidth. The y-axis of all figures is capped at 300 for clarity.

partitioning and graph processing algorithm aware of the bandwidth unevenness for networking efficiency.

Foremost, graph partitioning has been a classical combinatorial optimization problem, with an input objective function. The input objective function is to minimize the number of cross-partition edges with the constraint of all partitions with similar number of edges. This is because the total number of cross-partition edges is often a good indicator of the amount of communication between partitions in distributed computation. It is an NP-complete problem [50].

The network performance aware graph partitioning framework discussed in this section improves the network performance of graph partitioning process itself. Moreover, the partitions generated from the framework improve the network performance of graph processing tasks. The basic idea of the framework is to partition, store, and process the graph partitions according to their numbers of cross-partition edges such that the partitions with a large number of cross-partition edges are stored in the machines with high network bandwidth between them, as the network traffic requirement for those graph partitions is high. To achieve this, the framework partitions both the data graph and a "machine graph" (defined next) simultaneously.

7.5.1 MACHINE GRAPH

To capture the network bandwidth unevenness, a complete weighted undirected graph (namely *machine graph*) models the machines chosen for graph partitioning. Each machine is modeled as a vertex; an edge represents the connectivity between the two machines, and the bandwidth between any two machines is represented as the weight of an edge. For simplicity, assume that each machine has the same configuration in terms of computation power and main memory. In practice, users usually acquire the virtual machines of the same type for one application, because of convenience and management. In addition, an undirected graph is used in the model, as the bandwidth can often be similar in both directions.

Machine Graph Building. The machine graph can be built without the knowledge or control of the network physical topology, as follows.

Given a set of machines for partitioning, the machine graph can be constructed by calibrating the network bandwidth between any two machines in the set. The network bandwidth can be measured by sending a data chunk of 8 MB and using the average of twenty measurements as the estimated bandwidth. For N virtual machines, only N iterations of calibrations are needed to measure all pairwise performance. In each iteration, $\frac{N}{2}$ machine pairs are calibrated. The maintenance is based on the classic exponential average by getting the bandwidth of data transfer in the graph processing.

Example

The left part of Figure 7.2a illustrates the machine graph for four machines in a cluster with tree topology. The edge thickness represents the weight: a thicker edge means a link with higher bandwidth. The example cluster consists of two

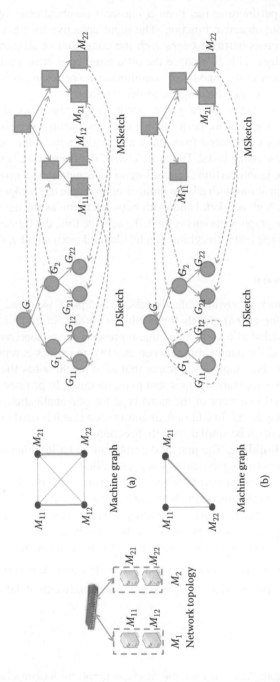

FIGURE 7.2 Mapping on the partition sketches between the machine graph and the data graph. (a) Four machines are chosen. (b) Three machines are chosen.

pods, and each pod consists of two machines. Assuming that the intra-pod network bandwidth is higher than the inter-pod one, and the intra-pod bandwidth is the same across pods, the machine graph consists of four vertices and six edges. The intra-pod connections are represented as thicker edges, indicating that they have a higher interconnected bandwidth.

7.5.2 PARTITION SKETCH

The *process* of a multilevel graph partitioning algorithm is modeled as a tree structure (namely *partition sketch*). Each node in the partition sketch represents the graph acting as the input for the partition operation at a level of the entire graph partitioning process: the root node representing the input graph; nonleaf nodes at level $(i + 1)$ representing the partitions of the ith iteration; the leaf nodes representing the graph partitions generated by the multilevel graph partitioning algorithm. The partition sketch is a k-ary tree for k-section-based graph partitioning algorithm. In practice, graph partitioning is often done using bisections iteratively, and hence, the partition sketch is represented as a binary tree. If the number of graph partitions is P, the number of levels of the partition sketch is ($\lceil \log_2 P \rceil + 1$).

Example

Figure 7.3 illustrates the correspondence between partition sketch and the bisections in the entire graph partitioning process. In the figure, the graph is divided into four partitions, and the partition sketch has three levels.

7.5.2.1 Design Principles of Ideal Partition Sketch

Among various partition sketches, an *ideal partition sketch* describes the partitioning process that strikes a balance between partitioning time and partition quality.

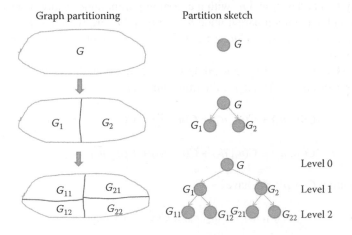

FIGURE 7.3 Correspondence between bisections and the partition sketch for the process of partitioning the graph into four partitions.

The ideal partition sketch represents the iterative partition process with the optimal bisection on each partition. In each bisection, the optimal bisection minimizes the number of cross-partition edges between the two generated partitions. This is the best case that existing bisection-based algorithms [44,46,47] can achieve. Partitioning with optimal bisections does not necessarily result in partitions with the globally minimum number of cross-partition edges. However, existing studies [44,46] have demonstrated that they can achieve relatively good partitioning quality, approaching the global optimum. Furthermore, the ideal partition sketch exhibits a few interesting properties:

7.5.2.1.1 Local Optimality

Denote $C(n_1, n_2)$ as the number of cross-partition edges between two nodes n_1 and n_2 in the partition sketch. Given any two nodes n_1 and n_2 with a common parent node p in the ideal partition sketch, we have $C(n_1, n_2)$ is the minimum among all the possible bisections on p.

By definition of the ideal partition sketch, the local optimality is achieved on each bisection.

7.5.2.1.2 Monotonicity

Suppose the total number of cross-partition edges among any partitions at the same level l in the partition sketch to be T_l. The monotonicity of the ideal partition sketch is that $T_i \leq T_j$, if $i \leq j$.

Proof (sketch). According to multilevel graph partitioning, a cross-partition edge in level i is still a cross-partition edge in level $i + 1$. Additionally, more cross-partition edges are created during the bi-section at level i. Thus, the set of cross-partition edge in level i is a subset of that in level $i + 1$. Thus, $T_i \leq T_{i+1}$. Therefore, $T_i \leq T_j$, if $i \leq j$. $\square$

The monotonicity reflects the increase in the number of cross-partition edges in the recursive partitioning process.

7.5.2.1.3 Proximity

Given any two nodes n_1 and n_2 with a common parent node p, any other two nodes n_3 and n_4 with a common parent node p', and p and p' are with the same parent, we have $C(n_1, n_2) + C(n_3, n_4) \geq C(n_{\pi(1)}, n_{\pi(2)}) + C(n_{\pi(3)}, n_{\pi(4)})$ where π is any permutation on (1, 2, 3, 4).

Proof (sketch). According to local optimality, we know that $C(p, p') = C(n_1, n_3) + C(n_1, n_4) + C(n_2, n_3) + C(n_2, n_4)$ is the minimum. Thus, we have

$$C(n_1, n_2) + C(n_1, n_4) + C(n_3, n_2) + C(n_3, n_4) \geq C(p, p') \tag{7.1}$$

$$C(n_1, n_2) + C(n_1, n_3) + C(n_4, n_2) + C(n_4, n_3) \geq C(p, p') \tag{7.2}$$

Substituting $C(p, p')$, we have

$$C(n_1, n_3) + C(n_2, n_4) \leq C(n_1, n_2) + C(n_3, n_4) \tag{7.3}$$

$$C(n_2, n_3) + C(n_1, n_4) \leq C(n_1, n_2) + C(n_3, n_4) \tag{7.4}$$

That means, we have $C(n_1, n_2) + C(n_3, n_4) \geq C(n_{\pi(1)}, n_{\pi(2)}) + C(n_{\pi(3)}, n_{\pi(4)})$ where π is any permutation on (1, 2, 3, 4). $\square$

The intuition of the proximity is, at a certain level of the ideal partition sketch, the partitions with a low common ancestor have a larger number of cross-partition edges than those with a high common ancestor.

These properties of the partitioning sketch indicate the following design principles for graph partitioning and processing, to match the network bandwidth with the number of cross-partition edges.

P_1. Graph partitioning and processing should gracefully adapt to the bandwidth unevenness in the cloud network. The number of cross-partition edges is a good indicator on bandwidth requirements. According to the local optimality, the two partitions generated in a bisection on a graph should be stored on two machine sets such that the total bandwidth between the two machine sets is the lowest.

P_2. The partition size should be carefully chosen for the efficiency of processing. The number of partitions should be no smaller than the number of machines available for parallelism. According to the monotonicity, a small partition size increases the number of levels of the partition sketch, resulting in a large number of cross-partition edges. On the other hand, a large partition may not fit into main memory of a machine, which results in random disk I/O in accessing the graph data.

P_3. According to proximity, the nodes with a low common ancestor should be stored together in the machine sets with high interconnected bandwidth to reduce the performance impact of the large number of cross-partition edges.

7.5.3 Bandwidth Aware Graph Partitioning

The network bandwidth aware framework for graph partitioning and processing in the cloud exploits the ideal partition sketch and the machine graph discussed in Sections 7.5.1 and 7.5.2, which enhances a popular *multilevel graph partitioning algorithm* with the *network performance awareness*. This subsection presents some design issues and an overview of such a framework.

7.5.3.1 Background on the Bisection in the Multilevel Graph Partitioning

Since graph bisection has been a key operation in multilevel graph partitioning [44,46], we briefly introduce the process of bisection. There are three phases in a graph bisection, namely *coarsening*, *partitioning*, and *uncoarsening*, as illustrated in Figure 7.4. The coarsening phase consists of multiple iterations. In each iteration, multiple adjacent vertices in the graph are coarsened into one according to some heuristics, and the graph is condensed into a smaller graph. The coarsening phase ends when the graph is small enough, in the scale of thousands of vertices. The partitioning phase divides the coarsened graph into two partitions

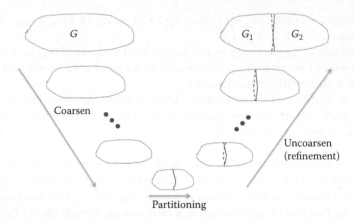

Coarsen

Uncoarsen
(refinement)

Partitioning

FIGURE 7.4 The three phases in graph bisection: *coarsening, partitioning,* and *uncoarsening.*

using a sequential and high-quality partitioning algorithm such as GGGP (Greedy Graph Growing Partitioning) [45]. In the uncoarsening phase, the partitions are then iteratively projected back toward the original graph, with a local refinement on each iteration.

The iterations are highly parallelizable, and their efficiency and scalability has been evaluated on shared-memory architectures (such as Cray supercomputers) [44,46]. However, in the coarsening and uncoarsening phases, all the edges may be accessed, generating a lot of network traffic if the input graph is stored in distributed machines.

7.5.3.2 Network Transfer due to Cross Edges

Given a set of machines to partition the graph, the graph is initially stored in those machines (usually according to the simple hash function). At each bisection, all edges and vertices are accessed multiple times for coarsening and uncoarsening. It generates a lot of network traffic. Thus, bisection should be designed to be aware of the network bandwidth unevenness.

Assume that the amount of network traffic sent along each cross-partition edge is the same (denoted as b). Denote the number of cross-partition edges from partition G_i to G_j to be $C(G_i, G_j)$, and the network bandwidth between the machines stored G_i and G_j to be $B_{i,j}$. Since network bandwidth is a scarce resource in the cloud environment [23,37], the bandwidth can be considered as the main indicator for network performance, and it approximates the network data transfer time from G_i to G_j to be $\dfrac{c(G_i, G_j) \times b}{B_{i,j}}$. This approximation is sufficient for large graph processing in both private and public cloud environments. Assuming P graph partitions are stored on P different machines, the total network data transfer time incurred in all partition pairs is $\displaystyle\sum_{i=0}^{P-1} \sum_{j=0}^{P-1} \dfrac{C(G_i, G_j) \times b}{B_{i,j}}$.

Clearly, if the network bandwidth among different machine pairs $(B_{i,j}, \forall i, j < P)$ is constant, minimizing the total number of cross-partition edges also minimizes the total network data transfer time.

7.5.3.3 Partitioning the Machine Graph

An observation on multilevel graph partitioning algorithms is that *due to the divide-and-conquer nature, there is no data exchange between the two bisection subpartitions generated from the same bisection.* Suppose a distinct subset of machines is responsible for each of the two subpartitions. The network connections between the two subsets of machines are no longer involved in the deeper levels of the bisection. That means, the partitioning algorithm should pick the high bandwidth connections remaining in the subset of machines, and leave the low bandwidth connections as those between the two subsets of machines. This is analogous to performing graph partitioning on the machine graph with respect to minimizing the total bandwidth between two subsets of machines. That results in the correspondence between partitioning the data graph and partitioning the machine graph, and the algorithm gradually assigns the subset of machines that are suitable to handle graph partitioning at a certain level.

7.5.3.4 Network Performance Aware Partitioning

Putting these together, the algorithm traverses the partition sketches of the machine graph and the data graph and builds a mapping between the machines and the partitions. At each level of graph partitioning, the framework partitions the data graph and machine graph *simultaneously* and matches the network bandwidth in the cloud to the number of cross-partition edges according to the partition sketch and the machine graph. The mapping guides the machines where the graph partition is further partitioned, and where the graph partition is stored. At the leaf level, graph partitions are stored in the machine in the corresponding node in the machine graph. Finally, the partition sketches for both machine graph and data graph are generated.

Example

Figure 7.2 illustrates the mapping between two machine graphs and a data graph for the partitioning framework. Take case (a) where four machines are selected as an example. The bisection on the entire graph G is done on all the four machines. At the next level, the bisections on G_1 and G_2 are performed on pods M_1 and M_2, respectively. Finally, the partitions are stored in the machines according to the mapping.

Regarding the local graph partitioning algorithm, any classical graph partitioning algorithms such as Metis [47] can be used. For example, Metis can be used to partition the machine graph, since the machine graph can often fit into the main memory of a single machine. On the bisection of the machine graph, the objective function is to minimize the weight of the cross-partition edges with the constraint of two partitions having around the same number of machines. This objective function matches the bandwidth unevenness of the selected machines. The goal of minimizing the weight of cross-partition edges in the machine graph corresponds to minimizing the number of cross-partition edges in the data graph. This is a graceful adaptation on assigning the network bandwidth to partitions with different number of cross-partition edges.

7.5.3.5 Partition Numbers

A minor detail is that it is preferable to make partitions with the roughly same number of machines is for load-balancing purpose, since partitions in the data graph also have similar sizes. On the other hand, the number of partitions returned by the algorithm may also be specified by the user. A reasonable choice is to determine P so that each graph partition can fit into the main memory of a machine. This is to avoid the significant performance degradation due to the random disk I/O in graph processing.

Finally, the partitioning algorithm discussed in this section satisfies the three design principles: (1) the number of cross-partition edges is gradually adapted to the network bandwidth. In each bisection of the recursion, the cut with the minimum number of cross-partition edges in the data graph coincides that with minimum aggregated bandwidth in the machine graph. (2) The partition size is tuned according to the amount of main memory available to reduce the random disk accesses. (3) In the iteration, the proximity among partitions in the machine graph matches that in the data graph.

7.6   HIERARCHICAL COMBINATION OF EXECUTION

With partitioned graph, the graph execution model may exploit data locality to reduce network traffic in data-intensive computing systems [23,37]. The basic idea is to apply a *Combine*() function (i.e., *Combiner* in Pregel), and perform partial merging of the intermediate data before they are sent over the network. Combination is applicable when the combination function is annotated as an associative and commutative function.

A basic approach is *local combination*. Current cloud-based graph engines like Pregel and Trinity support this basic approach. For all the graph partitions on a machine, one may apply the local combination on the boundary vertices belonging to the same remote partition and send the combined intermediate results back to the local partition for further processing.

Local combination is not aware of the network bandwidth unevenness in the cloud network environment. This motivates the approach of *hierarchical combination*. In local combination, it requires network data transfer for the boundary vertices of the graph partition. Due to the irregular graph structures, the source vertices are likely to be scattered on many different machines. Thus, many data transfers are performed on the relatively low-bandwidth machine pairs caused by the network bandwidth unevenness. Therefore, instead of direct data transfers after local combination, one may exploit the machine graphs for local combination as follows.

The data of the source vertices can be combined among the machines with high bandwidth before sending them to the target machine via the connections with low bandwidth. Hierarchical combination applies this idea in multiple levels according to

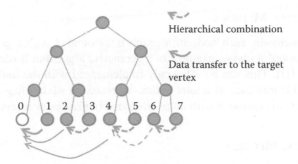

FIGURE 7.5 Hierarchical combination according to the partition sketch of the machine graph of eight machines.

the partition sketch of the machine graph. With the hierarchical combination optimization, the data transfer on the low-bandwidth connection is reduced.

Example

Figure 7.5 illustrates one example of performing hierarchical combination on eight machines. Suppose each machine holds one graph partition and machine 0 needs to read data from other machines. Note that the partition sketch of the machine graph has captured the network bandwidth unevenness. After local combination on each machine, the first-level combination between two machines (for example, between machines 6 and 7) are performed, and the result is stored on a *representative* machine. Let us assume machines 2, 4, and 6 are the representative machines at the first-level combination. Further combination is performed on the representative machines. Finally, all the partial results are sent to machine 0. On the low-bandwidth connections between machine 0 and machine i ($4 \leq i \leq 7$), hierarchical combination has only one data transfer for the partial results, compared with four in the baseline implementation with local combination.

7.7 RELATED WORK ON GRAPH PARTITIONING

In addition to the recent work on network performance aware partitioning, a large number of graph partitioning techniques have been proposed. In this section, we provide a review of general graph partitioning algorithms and then highlight some existing distributed graph partitioning algorithms.

Graph partitioning is important not only in emerging applications like Web and social graphs, as discussed in previous sections, but also traditional applications such as circuit placement and matrix factorization. The problem is NP-hard for general graphs [15,29]. There have been many studies on graph partitioning problems, which we can divide into five major categories: geometric methods [11,26,60], spectral methods [25,71], multilevel methods [44,46], metaheuristic-based approaches [51], and streaming graph partitioning [3,72,74]. We also refer the readers to two comprehensive surveys [28,51] for more related work on graph partitioning.

7.7.1 GEOMETRIC METHODS

In geometric methods, each node of a graph is associated with a geometric location (or coordinate). A classic example of a geometric algorithm is recursive coordinate bisection [11]. This can be efficiently implemented with the multidimensional
binary tree or kD tree data structure. Follow-up research studies (e.g., [26,60]) have
improved the classic methods with more advanced heuristics or bisection methods.

7.7.2 SPECTRAL METHODS

Spectral graph theory studies the relationships of fundamental properties of graphs
(e.g., algebraic connectivity) and the eigenvectors and eigenvalues of the Laplacian
matrix associated with the graphs [14,20]. In particular, the eigenvector associated
with algebraic connectivity (also known as the Fiedler vector) can be used to partition
graphs. There have many proposals on spectral partitioning and spectral bisection.
With spectral bisections, one can incorporate them into multilevel graph partitioning. It should be remarked that most of the results from spectral graph theory are
specific to undirected graphs.

An advantage of the spectral techniques is that they are supported by industrial-
strength softwares, not to mention the availability of advanced optimizations.

7.7.3 METAHEURISTIC-BASED APPROACHES

In general, it is difficult to produce high-quality solutions with approximation
algorithms of theoretical bounds. The metaheuristic approaches have mostly con-
centrated on finding high-quality solutions without performance guarantee in a
reasonable amount of time. Representatives of metaheuristic approaches include
simulated annealing [39], tabu search [66], ant colony optimization [16], and
genetic algorithms [57]. More details of these algorithms can be found in the
survey [51].

7.7.4 STREAMING GRAPH PARTITIONING

Instead of optimizing the graph partitioning quality, streaming graph partitioning emphasizes the graph partitioning performance while achieving a much better
graph partitioning quality than random hashing. It usually requires a simple pass (or
scan) of the graph, and generates the graph partitioning during the scan. Due to the
streaming nature, this category of graph partitioning algorithm can also be applicable to streaming graphs. For online streaming graphs, Aggarwal et al. [3] proposed
an algorithm for clustering graph streams. They used a hash-based compression of
the edges to create microclusters onto a smaller domain space. They showed that
their method provides bounded accuracy in terms of distance computations. Stanton
et al. [72] developed simple heuristics for streaming graph and demonstrated their
effectiveness against simple hashing and Metis schemes. Fennel [74] is a general
framework for streaming graph partitioning. All these studies have demonstrated
significant gains in terms of the communication cost and runtime.

7.7.5 Distributed Graph Partitioning Algorithms

Prior to the network bandwidth aware framework described in the previous sections, distributed graph partitioning [24,47,52] was the traditional way of reducing data shuffling in distributed graph processing. The commonly used distributed graph processing algorithms are multilevel algorithms [44,46,73], which are also used in the partitioning algorithm described in this chapter. They have been proved efficient in many applications.

7.7.6 The Metis Framework

A highly popular tool Metis [47] is a multilevel graph partitioning framework whose implementation is fast, robust, and easy to use. The multilevel graph partitioning framework contains three phases: (1) "coarsening by maximal match until the graph is small enough"; (2) partitioning the coarsest graph by any reasonable partition algorithm; and (3) refining the partitions by vertex swapping algorithm. ParMetis [44,46] is a parallel multilevel graph partitioning algorithm, with a minimum bisection on each level. It has been demonstrated to perform very well on shared-memory architectures [46]. Additionally, various different heuristics have been proposed for the quality of coarsening and refinement (e.g., [9,59]).

7.8 OPEN PROBLEMS

Despite recent efforts in large-graph processing in the cloud, many open problems remain to be explored in future [68]. As suggested by Shao et al., these open problems include architectural design, application needs, computation model, and ownership. We briefly elaborate on the problems as follows.

7.8.1 Architectural Design

Currently, in-memory processing is the key technique for resolving the random I/O in graph processing (besides algorithmic design). However, as the increasing popularity of graph-centric applications (such as the fast growing social graphs and web graph), it is yet to confirm whether the in-memory solution is the most favorable system design in terms of performance, energy consumption, and total ownership cost, among other things. Thus, in addition to main-memory based solutions, one may investigate other emerging storages such as solid state drives (SSD), which also exhibits much faster random I/O speed than hard disks. A hybrid storage system of SSD and main memory may also be possible for increasingly large graphs. More research work is required on efficient data structures and algorithms for graphs on such a hybrid system.

7.8.2 Application Needs

Web and social networks have been the two main driving applications for graph processing. Their application needs evolve from offline to online processing. Many application needs, such as data consistency and transaction management, have received relatively little research attention. These needs are already difficult problems in the context of flat data-like distributed relational databases [8,21], and they will be more challenging for graph systems.

7.8.3 COMPUTATION MODEL

"One size does not fit all." Application needs drive the computation model. Current systems are mainly based on MapReduce and the vertex oriented execution model. However, it is an open problem to extend these models with indexes and different application needs such as consistency and transaction management.

7.8.4 COST OF OWNERSHIP

Ideally, users want to minimize the cost of ownership while satisfying the performance requirement and other quality of service attributes. However, the design space is huge for various different hardware and software components. As specific to the cloud, different cloud providers offer very different price structures. Even for the same cloud provider, the capabilities of virtual machines can be quite different [27]. More research has to be conducted on automatic and customizable design for the cost of ownership.

7.9   SUMMARY

In this chapter, we have surveyed a number of applications of large graphs and existing representative cloud-based large graph processing systems. One of the classic techniques for handling large graphs is graph partitioning. The chapter reviewed the network unevenness of the cloud, which poses new challenges to graph partitioning techniques. In particular, networks with high bandwidth between machines can process more tasks on cross-partition edges. This chapter then focused on network performance aware graph partitioning. The techniques include modeling machines and the network bandwidth between them as a machine graph, and partitioning the graph corresponding to the machine graph. These techniques minimize network traffic in both partitioning and processing. The processing on partition graphs may further exploit the locality of the partitions to reduce communications. There are many open problems that require more research efforts in this field.

REFERENCES

1. A new application award: Semantic web challenge. http://challenge.semanticweb.org/, 2013.
2. A. Abouzeid, K. Bajda-Pawlikowski, D. Abadi, A. Silberschatz, and A. Rasin. Hadoopdb: An architectural hybrid of MapReduce and DBMS technologies for analytical workloads. *Proc. VLDB Endow.*, 2009.
3. C. C. Aggarwal, Y. Zhao, and P. S. Yu. A framework for clustering massive graph streams: Submission to best of SDM 2010 issue. *Stat. Anal. Data Min.*, 3(6):399–416, December 2010.
4. Apache Giraph. http://giraph.apache.org/.

5. Apache Hama. http://hama.apache.org/.

6. S. Auer, C. Bizer, G. Kobilarov, J. Lehmann, and Z. Ives. Dbpedia: A nucleus for a web of open data. In *6th International Semantic Web Conference*, pages 11–15, 2007.

7. D. Bader and K. Madduri. SNAP, small-world network analysis and partitioning: An open-source parallel graph framework for the exploration of large-scale networks. In *IPDPS*, pages 1–12, 2008.

8. P. Bailis, A. Fekete, A. Ghodsi, J. M. Hellerstein, and I. Stoica. Hat, not cap: Highly available transactions. *CoRR*, abs/1302.0309, 2013.

9. U. Benlic and J.-K. Hao. An effective multilevel memetic algorithm for balanced graph partitioning. In *ICTAI* (1), pages 121–128, 2010.

10. T. Benson, A. Akella, and D. A. Maltz. Network traffic characteristics of data centers in the wild. In *IMC*, 2010.

11. M. J. Berger and S. H. Bokhari. A partitioning strategy for nonuniform problems on multi-processors. *IEEE Trans. Comput.*, 36(5):570–580, May 1987.

12. J. W. Berry, B. Hendrickson, S. Kahan, and P. Konecny. Software and algorithms for graph queries on multithreaded architectures. In *IPDPS*, pages 1–14, March 2007. IEEE.

13. Bing Index Team. Understand your world with Bing. http://hk.bing.com/blogs/site blogs/b/search/archive/2013/03/21/satorii.aspx, 2013.

14. A. E. Brouwer and W. H. Haemers. *Spectra of Graphs*. Springer, 2012.

15. T. N. Bui and C. Jones. Finding good approximate vertex and edge partitions is np-hard. *Inf. Process. Lett.*, 42(3):153–159, May 1992.

16. T. N. Bui and L. C. Strite. An ant system algorithm for graph bisection. In *GECCO*, pages 43–51, 2002.

17. F. Chang, J. Dean, S. Ghemawat, W. C. Hsieh, D. A. Wallach, M. Burrows, T. Chandra, A. Fikes, and R. E. Gruber. Bigtable: A distributed storage system for structured data. In *OSDI*, pages 205–218, 2006.

18. R. Chen, X. Weng, B. He, and M. Yang. Large graph processing in the cloud. In *Proceedings of the 2010 ACM SIGMOD International Conference on Management of data, SIGMOD'10*, pages 1123–1126, New York, 2010. ACM.

19. R. Chen, M. Yang, X. Weng, B. Choi, B. He, and X. Li. Improving large graph processing on partitioned graphs in the cloud. In *SoCC*, pages 3:1–3:13, 2012.

20. F. Chung. Spectral Graph Theory. Conference Board of the Mathematical Sciences, 1997.

21. J. C. Corbett, J. Dean, M. Epstein, A. Fikes, C. Frost, J. J. Furman, S. Ghemawat et al. Spanner: Google's globally-distributed database. In *Proceedings of the 10th USENIX Conference on Operating Systems Design and Implementation, OSDI'12*, pages 251–264, Berkeley, CA, USA, 2012. USENIX Association.

22. S. Das, D. Agrawal, and A. El Abbadi. G-store: A scalable data store for transactional multi key access in the cloud. In *SoCC: ACM Symposium on Cloud Computing*, 2010.

23. J. Dean and S. Ghemawat. MapReduce: Simplified data processing on large clusters. *Commun. ACM*, 51(1):107–113, January 2008.

24. B. Derbel, M. Mosbah, and A. Zemmari. Fast distributed graph partition and application. In *IPDPS*, 2006.

25. W. E. Donath and A. J. Hoffman. Lower bounds for the partitioning of graphs. *IBM J. Res. Dev.*, 17(5):420–425, September 1973.

26. C. Farhat and M. Lesoinne. Automatic partitioning of unstructured meshes for the parallel solution of problems in computational mechanics. *Int. J. Numer. Methods Eng.*, 36(5):745–764, 1993.

27. B. Farley, A. Juels, V. Varadarajan, T. Ristenpart, K. D. Bowers, and M. M. Swift. More for your money: Exploiting performance heterogeneity in public clouds. In *Proceedings of the Third ACM Symposium on Cloud Computing, SoCC'12*, pages 20:1–20:14, New York, 2012. ACM.

28. P.-O. Fjallstrom. Algorithms for graph partitioning: A survey. *Linkoping Electronic Articles in Computer and Information Science*, 1998.
29. M. R. Garey, D. S. Johnson, and L. Stockmeyer. Some simplified np-complete problems. In *Proceedings of the Sixth Annual ACM Symposium on Theory of Computing, STOC'74*, pages 47–63, New York, 1974. ACM.
30. S. Ghemawat, H. Gobioff, and S.-T. Leung. The Google file system. *SIGOPS Oper. Syst. Rev.*, 37(5):29–43, 2003.
31. D. Gregor and A. Lumsdaine. The parallel BGL: A generic library for distributed graph computations. In *Parallel Object-Oriented Scientific Computing (POOSC)*, 2005.
32. C. Guo, H. Wu, K. Tan, L. Shi, Y. Zhang, and S. Lu. Dcell: A scalable and fault-tolerant network structure for data centers. *SIGCOMM*, 38(4):75–86, 2008.
33. Hadoop. http://hadoop.apache.org/.
34. P. Harish and P. J. Narayanan. Accelerating large graph algorithms on the GPU using CUDA. In *Proceedings of the 14th International Conference on High Performance Computing, HiPC'07*, pages 197–208, 2007. Springer-Verlag.
35. B. He, M. Yang, Z. Guo, R. Chen, B. Su, W. Lin, and L. Zhou. Comet: Batched stream processing for data intensive distributed computing. In *Proceedings of the 1st ACM Symposium on Cloud Computing, SoCC'10*, pages 63–74, New York, 2010. ACM.
36. G. He, H. Feng, C. Li, and H. Chen. Parallel SimRank computation on large graphs with iterative aggregation. In *SIGKDD*, 2010.
37. M. Isard, M. Budiu, Y. Yu, A. Birrell, and D. Fetterly. Dryad: Distributed data-parallel programs from sequential building blocks. *SIGOPS Oper. Syst. Rev.*, 41(3):59–72, 2007.
38. M. Isard, V. Prabhakaran, J. Currey, U. Wieder, K. Talwar, and A. Goldberg. Quincy: Fair scheduling for distributed computing clusters. In *SOSP*, 2009.
39. D. S. Johnson, C. R. Aragon, L. A. McGeoch, and C. Schevon. Optimization by simulated annealing: An experimental evaluation. Part I, graph partitioning. *Oper. Res.*, 37(6):865–892, October 1989.
40. N. Kallen, R. Pointer, J. Kalucki, and E. Ceaser. Github. https://github.com/twitter/flockdb, 2013.
41. S. Kandula, S. Sengupta, A. Greenberg, P. Patel, and R. Chaiken. The nature of data center traffic: Measurements and analysis. In *IMC*, 2009.
42. U. Kang, C. Tsourakakis, A. P. Appel, C. Faloutsos, and J. Leskovec. HADI: Fast diameter estimation and mining in massive graphs with Hadoop. Technical Report CMU-ML-08-117, CMU, 2008.
43. U. Kang, C. E. Tsourakakis, and C. Faloutsos. PEGASUS: A peta-scale graph mining system–implementation and observations. In *Proceedings of the 2009 Ninth IEEE International Conference on Data Mining, ICDM'09*, pages 229–238, 2009.
44. G. Karypis and V. Kumar. Parallel multilevel k-way partitioning scheme for irregular graphs. In *Proceedings of the 1996 ACM/IEEE Conference on Supercomputing, Supercomputing'96*, 1996. IEEE Computer Society Press.
45. G. Karypis and V. Kumar. A fast and high quality multilevel scheme for partitioning irregular graphs. *SIAM J. Sci. Comput.*, 20(1):359–392, 1998.
46. G. Karypis and V. Kumar. A parallel algorithm for multilevel graph partitioning and sparse matrix ordering. *J. Parallel Distrib. Comput.*, 48(1):71–95, 1998.
47. Karypis Lab. *Family of Graph and Hypergraph Partitioning Software*, 2013.
48. G. J. Katz and J. T. Kider, Jr. All-pairs shortest-paths for large graphs on the GPU. In *Graphics Hardware*, pages 47–55, 2008.
49. KEGG Laboratories. KEGG: Kyoto encyclopedia of genes and genomes. http://www.genome.jp/kegg/kegg1.html, 2013.
50. B. W. Kernighan and S. Lin. An efficient heuristic procedure for partitioning graphs. *Bell System Technical Journal*, 49(1):291–307, 1970.

51. J. Kim, I. Hwang, Y.-H. Kim, and B.-R. Moon. Genetic approaches for graph partitioning: A survey. In *Proceedings of the 13th Annual Conference on Genetic and Evolutionary Computation, GECCO'11*, pages 473–480, New York, 2011. ACM.

52. S. Koranne. A distributed algorithm for k-way graph partitioning. In *EUROMICRO*, 1999.

53. J. Leskovec. Stanford network analysis project. http://snap.stanford.edu/, 2013.

54. LinkedIn. Numbers of LinkedIn members as of 1st quarter 2013. http://www.statista.com/statistics/198224/quarterly-member-numbers-of-linkedin/, 2013.

55. Y. Low, D. Bickson, J. Gonzalez, C. Guestrin, A. Kyrola, and J. M. Hellerstein. Distributed graphlab: A framework for machine learning and data mining in the cloud. *Proc. VLDB Endow.*, 5(8):716–727, April 2012.

56. Y. Low, J. Gonzalez, A. Kyrola, D. Bickson, C. Guestrin, and J. Hellerstein. Graphlab: A new framework for parallel machine learning. In *UAI*, 2010.

57. H. Maini, K. Mehrotra, C. Mohan, and S. Ranka. Genetic algorithms for graph partitioning and incremental graph partitioning. In *Proceedings of the 1994 ACM/IEEE Conference on Supercomputing, Supercomputing'94*, pages 449–457, Los Alamitos, CA, 1994. IEEE Computer Society Press.

58. G. Malewicz, M. H. Austern, A. J. C. Bik, J. C. Dehnert, I. Horn, N. Leiser, and G. Czajkowski. Pregel: A system for large-scale graph processing. In *Proceedings of the 2010 ACM SIGMOD International Conference on Management of Data. SIGMOD'10*, pages 135–146, 2010.

59. J. Maue and P. Sanders. Engineering algorithms for approximate weighted matching. In *Proceedings of the 6th International Conference on Experimental Algorithms, WEA'07*, pages 242–255, Berlin, Heidelberg, 2007. Springer-Verlag.

60. G. L. Miller, S. Teng, W. Thurston, and S. A. Vavasis. Automatic mesh partitioning. Technical Report, Ithaca, NY, 1992.

61. NCBI. PubChem. http://pubchem.ncbi.nlm.nih.gov, 2013.

62. NCBI. Submit data to NCBI. http://pubchem.ncbi.nlm.nih.gov/search/#, 2013.

63. L. Page, S. Brin, R. Motwani, and T. Winograd. The PageRank citation ranking: Bringing order to the web. Technical Report 1999-66, 1999.

64. R. Power and J. Li. Piccolo: Building fast, distributed programs with partitioned tables. In *Proceedings of the 9th USENIX Conference on Operating Systems Design and Implementation, OSDI'10*, pages 1–14, 2010.

65. J. M. Pujol, V. Erramilli, G. Siganos, X. Yang, N. Laoutaris, P. Chhabra, and P. Rodriguez. The little engine(s) that could: Scaling online social networks. In *Proceedings of the ACM SIGCOMM 2010 Conference, SIGCOMM'10*, pages 375–386, 2010.

66. E. Rolland, H. Pirkul, and F. Glover. Tabu search for graph partitioning. Annals of Operations Research, 1996.

67. B. Shao, H. Wang, and Y. Li. The trinity graph engine. Technical report, Microsoft Research, 2012.

68. B. Shao, H. Wang, and Y. Xiao. Managing and mining large graphs: Systems and implementations. In *Proceedings of the 2012 ACM SIGMOD International Conference on Management of Data, SIGMOD'12*, pages 589–592, New York, 2012. ACM.

69. J. Siek, L.-Q. Lee, and A. Lumsdaine. The Boost Graph Library: User Guide and Reference Manual. Addison-Wesley, 2002.

70. Socialbakers. Facebook pages statistics. http://www.socialbakers.com/facebook-pages/, 2011.

71. D. Spielman. Spectral graph theory and its applications. In *48th Annual IEEE Symposium on Foundations of Computer Science, 2007. FOCS'07*, pages 29–38, 2007.

72. I. Stanton and G. Kliot. Streaming graph partitioning for large distributed graphs. In *Proceedings of the 18th ACM SIGKDD International Conference on Knowledge Discovery and Data Mining, KDD'12*, pages 1222–1230, New York, 2012. ACM.

73. A. Trifunović and W. J. Knottenbelt. Parallel multilevel algorithms for hypergraph partitioning. *J. Parallel Distrib. Comput.*, 68, May 2008.
74. C. E. Tsourakakis, C. Gkantsidis, B. Radunovic, and M. Vojnovic. Fennel: Streaming graph partitioning for massive scale graphs. Technical Report MSR-TR-2012-113, Microsoft Research, 2012.
75. V. Vineet and P. J. Narayanan. CUDA cuts: Fast graph cuts on the GPU. In *2012 IEEE Computer Society Conference on Computer Vision and Pattern Recognition Workshops*, pages 1–8, 2008.
76. G. Wang and T. S. E. Ng. The impact of virtualization on network performance of Amazon EC2 data center. In *Proceedings of the 29th Conference on Information Communications, INFOCOM'10*, pages 1163–1171, 2010.
77. J. Wang, S. Wu, H. Gao, J. Li, and B. C. Ooi. Indexing multi-dimensional data in a cloud system. In *Proceedings of the 2010 ACM SIGMOD International Conference on Management of Data, SIGMOD'10*, pages 591–602, 2010.
78. W. Wu, H. Li, H. Wang, and K. Q. Zhu. Probase: A probabilistic taxonomy for text understanding. In *SIGMOD*, pages 481–492, 2012.
79. M. Zaharia, A. Konwinski, A. D. Joseph, R. Katz, and I. Stoica. Improving MapReduce performance in heterogeneous environments. In *OSDI*, pages 321–330, 2008.
80. J. Zhong and B. He. Medusa: Simplified graph processing on GPUS. *IEEE TPDS*, 2013.
81. A. Zhou, W. Qian, D. Tao, and Q. Ma. DisG: A distributed graph repository for web infrastructure (invited paper). In *International Symposium on Universal Communication*, 0:141–145, 2008.

8 PEGASUS
A System for Large-Scale Graph Processing

Charalampos E. Tsourakakis

CONTENTS

8.1 INTRODUCTION

The scale of graph data that is nowadays collected and required to be processed is massive. For example, in the context of online services, the web graph amounts to at least 1 trillion of links [1]. Facebook recently reported more than 1 billion of users and 140 billion of friend connections [2], and Twitter reported in 2009 more than 40 million of users and about 1.5 billion of social relations [30]. The unprecedented proliferation of data provides us with new opportunities and benefits but also poses hard computational challenges. Frequent graph computations such as community detection [25], finding connected components [29], iterative computations using graph input data such as computing PageRank and its variations [41], and shortest path and radius computations [17,28] become challenging computational tasks in the realm of big graph data.

In this chapter, we describe PEGASUS, an open-source Peta Graph Mining library, which performs typical graph mining tasks such as computing the diameter of a graph, computing the radius of each node, finding the connected components, and computing the importance score of nodes. The main idea behind PEGASUS is to capitalize on matrix–vector multiplication as a main primitive for the software engineer. Inspired by the work of [47], which showed that triangles can be estimated by few matrix–vector multiplications, PEGASUS introduces a set of different operators that solve a variety of graph mining tasks together with an optimized implementation of matrix–vector multiplications in MapReduce. PEGASUS is a solid engineering effort that allows us to manipulate large-scale graphs. Since the introduction of PEGASUS, other large-scale graph processing systems have been introduced, among them Google's Pregel [36], LinkedIn's Giraph [3], and GraphLab [34]. It is worth mentioning that Giraph uses several algorithms and ideas from PEGASUS, including the connected components algorithm. Also, PEGASUS has been included in Hadoop for Windows Azure [4]. PEGASUS provides us with the ability to investigate the structure of large-scale graphs. This allows us to detect outliers and obtain significant structural patterns.

This chapter is organized as follows: Section 8.2 presents related work. Section 8.3 presents the proposed method. Section 8.4 presents Hadoop implementations and Section 8.5 timings. Section 8.6 shows findings of PEGASUS in several real-world networks.

8.2 RELATED WORK

In Section 8.2.1, we discuss two established patterns, the bow-tie structure of the web and the six degrees of separation theory. In Section 8.2.2, we provide basic graph theoretic definitions for our work. In Section 8.2.3, we discuss work related to computing the diameter and radii of a graph. Finally, in Section 8.2.4, we present briefly, work related to space efficient algorithms for finding the number of distinct elements in a multiset. Throughout the chapter, we use *n, m* for the number of vertices and edges of the graph *G*.

8.2.1 STRUCTURE OF REAL-WORLD NETWORKS

8.2.1.1 Bow-Tie Structure of the Web Graph

In 1999, Andrei Broder et al. [16], performed an influential study of the web graph using strongly connected components (SCCs) as their building blocks. Specifically, they proposed the bow-tie model for the structure of the web graph based on their findings on the index of pages and links of the AltaVista search engine. According to the bow-tie structure of the web, there exists a single giant SCC. Broder et al. [16] positioned the remaining SCCs with respect to the giant SCC as follows:

- IN: vertices that can reach the giant SCC but cannot be reached from it.
- OUT: vertices that can be reached from the giant SCC but cannot be reached from it.
- Tendrils: These are vertices that either are reachable from IN but cannot reach the giant SCC or the vertices that can reach OUT but cannot be reached from the giant SCC.
- Disconnected: vertices that belong to none of the above categories. These are the vertices that even if we ignore the direction of the edges have no path connecting them to the giant SCC.

A schematic picture of the bow-tie structure of the web is shown in Figure 8.1. This structure has been verified in other studies as well [12,20].

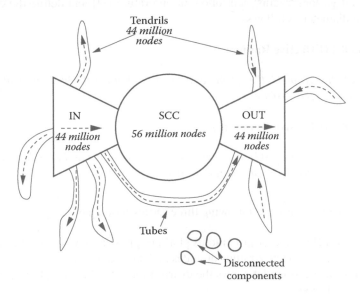

FIGURE 8.1 Bow-tie structure of the web graph. (Image from A. Broder et al., *Comput. Networks*, 33(1), 309–320, 2000.)

8.2.1.2 Six Degrees of Separation

Six degrees of separation is the theory that anyone in the world is no more than six relationships away from any other person. In the early twentieth century, Nobel Peace Prize winner Guglielmo Marconi, the father of modern radio, suggested that it would take only six relay stations to cover and connect the earth by radio [37]. It is likely that this idea was the seed for the six degrees of separation theory, which was further supported by Frigyes Karinthy in a short story called *Chains*. Since then, many scientists, including Michael Gurevich, Ithiel De Sola Pool have worked on this theory. In a famous experiment, Stanley Milgram asked people to route a postcard to a fixed recipient by passing them to direct acquaintances [39]. Milgram observed that depending on the sample of people chosen the average number of intermediaries was between 4.4 and 5.7.

Nowadays, the World Wide Web and online social networks provide us with data that reach the planetary scale. Recently, Backstrom, Boldi, Rosa, Ugander, and Vigna show that the world is even smaller than what the six degrees of separation theory predicts [7]. Specifically, they perform the first world-scale social-network graph-distance computation, using the entire Facebook network of active users (at that time 721 million users, 69 billion friendship links) and observe an average distance of 4.74.

8.2.2 GRAPH THEORETIC DEFINITIONS

First, we review basic graph theoretic definitions [14] and then introduce the notions of effective radius and diameter. Let $G(V, E)$ be a directed graph. The radius/eccentricity of a vertex v is the greatest shortest-path distance between v and any other vertex. The radius $r(G)$ is the minimum radius of any vertex. The diameter $d(G)$ is the maximum radius of any vertex. Since the radius and the diameter are susceptible to outliers (e.g., long chains), we follow the literature [31] and define the effective radius and diameter as follows.

Definition 8.1 (Effective Radius)

For a node v in a graph G, the effective radius $r_{\text{eff}}(v)$ of v is the 90th percentile of all the shortest distances from v.   ∎

Definition 8.2 (Effective Diameter)

The effective diameter $d_{\text{eff}}(G)$ of a graph G is the minimum number of hops in which 90% of all connected pairs of nodes can reach each other.   ∎

In Section 8.6, we use the following three radius-based plots:

1. **Static Radius Plot** (or just "radius plot") of graph G shows the distribution (count) of the effective radius of nodes at a specific time.
2. **Temporal Radius Plot** shows the distributions of effective radius of nodes at several times.
3. **Radius–Degree Plot** shows the scatter-plot of the effective radius $r_{\text{eff}}(v)$ vs. the degree d_v for each node v.

8.2.3 Computing Radius and Diameter

Typical algorithms to compute the radius and the diameter of a graph include Breadth First Search (BFS) and Floyd's algorithm [19] when no negative cycles are present. Both approaches are prohibitively slow for large-scale graphs, requiring $O(n^2 + nm)$ and $O(n^3)$ time, respectively. For the same reason, related BFS or all-pair shortest-path based algorithms like [8,22,35,46] cannot handle large-scale graphs.

A sampling approach starts BFS from a subset of nodes, typically chosen at random as in [16]. Despite its practicality, this approach has no obvious solution for choosing the representative sample for BFS. An interesting approach has been proposed by Cohen [18], but according to practitioner's experience [13] it appears not to be as scalable as the ANF algorithm [42]. The latter is closely related to our work since it is a sequential algorithm based on Flajolet–Martin sketches [23]. We review its key idea in the next section.

8.2.4 Distinct Elements in Multisets

Let $A = \{a_1,..., a_m\}$ be a multiset where $a_i \in [n]$ for all $i = 1,...,$ m. Let $m_i = |\{j : a_j = i\}|$. For each $k \geq 0$ define $F_k = \sum_{i=1}^{n} m_i^k$. The numbers F_k are called frequency moments of the multiset, and provide useful statistics. We notice that F_0 is the number of distinct elements in A, $F_1 = m$. Historically, Morris was the first to show that F_1 can be approximated with $O(\log \log m) = O(\log \log n)$ [40]. Flajolet and Martin designed an algorithm that needs $O(\log n)$ bits of memory to approximate F_0 [23]. Since PEGASUS implements Flajolet-Martin sketches, we briefly describe the main idea of their algorithm. Let $h : M \to \{0, 1,..., 2^L - 1\}$ be a hash function that hashes the elements of the multiset uniformly over the allowed range of values. Here, L has to satisfy $2^L \geq n$. The algorithm maintains a bitmask, which is initially set to zero and its ith bit is set to one if there exists an element $a_j \in A$ whose hash value $h(a_j)$ ends in i consecutive zeros. Notice that the pattern 0^i of i trailing zeros occurs with probability 2^{-i} under the assumption of uniform hashing. Therefore, when i is significantly larger than $\log_2 (n)$ we expect to observe zeros but when $i \approx \log_2 (n)$ we expect to observe both. Flajolet and Martin showed that the expected value of the leftmost zero position R in the bitmask is $E(R) = \log_2 (\phi n)$ where $\phi = 0.77351$ and that the variance is 1.12. To reduce the variance, typically, we use several hash functions and use the average. For further improvements on this problem, the interested reader may read [6,9–11,18,21,24,26,48]. Recently, Kane, Nelson, and Woodruff provided an optimal algorithm for estimating F_0 [27].

Before we delve into the details of the proposed algorithm, we outline the high-level goal of PEGASUS. A large number of important computational tasks can be solved by iterating matrix–vector multiplication. For instance, computing the diameter, radius distributions, PageRank scores, spectral clustering and connected components fall into this class of computational problems. PEGASUS implements optimized programming primitives to handle this class of problems.

Consider the following assignment $v' \leftarrow M \times v$ where $M \in \mathbb{R}^{m \times n}$; $v \in \mathbb{R}^n$. The ith coordinate of v' is $v_i' = \sum_{j=1}^{n} m_{i,j} v_j$, $i = 1, ..., m$. Typically, in our applications, M is the adjacency matrix representation of a graph, and therefore we are going to assume in the following that $m = n$, unless otherwise noticed.

There are three types of operations in the previous formula:

1. combine2: multiply $m_{i,j}$ and v_j.
2. combineAll: sum n multiplication results for node i.
3. assign: overwrite the previous value of v_i with the new result to make v_i'.

We introduce an abstraction of the basic matrix–vector multiplication, called generalized iterative matrix–vector multiplication. The corresponding programming primitive is the GIM-V primitive on which PEGASUS is based. The "Iterative" in GIM-V denotes that we apply the $\times_G$ operation until a convergence criterion is met. Specifically, let us define the operator $\times_G$ as follows:

$$v' = M \times_G v$$

where $v_i' = \text{assign}(v_i, \text{combineAll}_i(\{x_j \mid j = 1..n, \text{ and } x_j = \text{combine2}(m_{i,j}, v_j)\}))$.

The functions combine2(), combineAll(), and assign() have the following interpretation, generalizing the product, sum, and assignment of the traditional matrix–vector multiplication:

1. combine2$(m_{i,j}, v_j)$: combine $m_{i,j}$ and v_j.
2. combineAll$_i(x_1,..., x_n)$: combine all the results from combine2() for node i.
3. assign(v_i, v_{new}) : decide how to update v_i with v_{new}.

In the following sections we show how different choices of combine2(), combineAll$_i$(), and assign() allow us to solve several important graph mining tasks. Before that, we want to highlight the strong connection of GIM-V with SQL. When combineAll$_i$() and assign() can be implemented by user defined functions, the operator $\times_G$ can be expressed concisely in terms of SQL. This viewpoint is important when we implement GIM-V in large-scale parallel processing platforms, including Hadoop, if they can be customized to support several SQL primitives including JOIN and GROUP BY. Suppose we have an edge table E(sid, did, val) and a vector table V(id, val), corresponding to a matrix and a vector, respectively. Then, $\times_G$ corresponds to the SQL statement in Table 8.1. We assume that we have (built-in or user-defined) functions, combineAll$_i$() and combine2(), and we also assume that the resulting table/vector will be fed into the assign() function (omitted, for clarity).

TABLE 8.1

GIM-V in Terms of SQL

SELECT E.sid, combineAll$_{E.sid}$(combine2(E.val,V.val))
  FROM E, V
   WHERE E.did=V.id
   GROUP BY E.sid

In the following sections, we show how we can customize GIM-V to handle important graph mining operations including PageRank, Random Walk with Restart, diameter estimation, and connected components.

8.3   PROPOSED METHOD

8.3.1   GIM-V AND PAGERANK

Our first warm-up application of GIM-V is PageRank, a famous algorithm that was used by Google to calculate relative importance of web pages [15]. The PageRank vector p of n web pages satisfies the following eigenvector equation:

$$p = (cE^T + (1 - c)U)p$$

where c is a damping factor (usually set to 0.85), E is the row-normalized adjacency matrix (source, destination), and U is a matrix with all elements set to $1/n$.

To calculate the eigenvector p we can use the power method, which multiplies an initial vector with the matrix, several times. We initialize the current PageRank vector p^{cur} and set all its elements to $1/n$. Then the next PageRank p^{next} is calculated by $p^{next} = (cE^T + (1 - c)U)p^{cur}$. We continue to perform the multiplication until p converges.

PageRank is a direct application of GIM-V, that is, $p^{next} = M \times_G p^{cur}$. Matrix M is E^T, that is, the column-normalized version of the adjacency matrix. The three operations are defined as follows:

1. $\mathtt{combine2}(m_{i,j}, v_j) = c \times m_{i,j} \times v_j$
2. $\mathtt{combineAll}_i(x_1, \ldots, x_n) = \dfrac{(1-c)}{n} + \sum_{j=1}^{n} x_j$
3. $\mathtt{assign}(v_i, v_{new}) = v_{new}$

8.3.2   GIM-V AND RANDOM WALK WITH RESTART

Random Walk with Restart (RWR) is closely related to Personalized PageRank [43], a popular algorithm to measure the relative proximity of vertices with respect to a given vertex. In RWR, the proximity vector r_k of vertex k satisfies the equation:

$$r_k = cMr_k + (1 - c)e_k$$

where e_k is the kth unit vector in $\mathbb{R}^n$, c is a restart probability parameter, which is typically set to 0.85 [43], and M is as in Section 8.3.1. In GIM-V, RWR is formulated by $r_k^{next} = M \times_G r_k^{cur}$ where the three operations are defined as follows:

1. $\mathtt{combine2}(m_{i,j}, v_j) = c \times m_{i,j} \times v_j$
2. $\mathtt{combineAll}_i(x_1, \ldots, x) = (1-c)\delta_{ik} + \sum_{j=1}^{n} x_j$, where δ_{ik} is the *Kronecker delta*, equal to 1 if $i = k$ and 0 otherwise
3. $\mathtt{assign}(v_i, v_{new}) = v_{new}$

8.3.3 GIM-V AND DIAMETER ESTIMATION

Estimating the diameter and radius distribution falls within the framework of iterative matrix–vector computations. In [28], we presented the Hadi algorithm that estimates the diameter and radius distribution of a large-scale graph. Hadi can be presented within the framework of PEGASUS, since the number of neighbors reachable from vertex i within h hops is encoded in a probabilistic bitstring b_i^h, which is updated as follows [23]:

$$b_i^{h+1} = b_i^h \text{BITWISE-OR}\left\{b_k^h \mid (i,k) \in E\right\}$$

In GIM-V, the bitstring update of Hadi is represented by

$$b^{h+1} = M \times_G b^h$$

where M is the adjacency matrix, b^{h+1} is a vector of length n, which is updated by $b_i^{h+1} = \text{assign}\big(b_i^h, \text{combineAll}, (\{x_j \mid j = 1...n, \text{ and } x_j = \text{combine2}(m_{i,j}, b_j^h)\})\big)$, and the three PEGASUS operations are defined as follows:

1. $\text{combine2}(m_{i,j}, v_j) = m_{i,j} \times v_j$.
2. $\text{combineAll}_i(x_1,..., x_n) = \text{BITWISE-OR}\{x_j \mid j = 1...n\}$
3. $\text{assign}(v_i, v_{new}) = \text{BITWISE-OR}(v_i, v_{new})$.

The $\times_G$ operation is run iteratively until the bitstring of each vertex remains the same.

8.3.4 GIM-V AND CONNECTED COMPONENTS

We propose Hcc, a new algorithm for finding connected components in large graphs. The main idea is as follows: for each vertex i in the graph, we maintain a component identification number (id) c_i^h, which is the minimum vertex id within h hops from i.

Initially, c_i^h of vertex i is set to i, that is, $c_i^0 = i$. In each iteration, each vertex sends its current c_i^h to its neighbors. Then c_i^{h+1} is set to the minimum value among its current component id and the received component ids from its neighbors. The crucial observation is that this communication between neighbors can be formulated in GIM-V as follows:

$$c^{h+1} = M \times_G c^h$$

where M is the adjacency matrix, c^{h+1} is a vector of length n, which is updated by $c_i^{h+1} = \text{assign}\big(c_i^h, \text{combineAll}_i(\{x_j \mid j = 1...n, \text{ and } x_j = \text{combine2}(m_{i,j}, c_j^h)\})\big)$, and the three PEGASUS operations are defined as follows:

1. $\mathtt{combine2}(m_{i,j}, v_j) = m_{i,j} \times v_j$.
2. $\mathtt{combineAll}_i(x_1, \ldots, x_n) = \min\{x_j \mid j = 1..n\}$.
3. $\mathtt{assign}(v_i, v_{new}) = \min(v_i, v_{new})$.

By repeating this process, component ids of nodes in a component are set to the minimum node id of the component. We iteratively do the multiplication until component ids converge. The upper bound of the number of iterations in Hcc is d, where d is the diameter of the graph. We notice that because of the small-world phenomenon, see Section 8.2, the diameter of real graphs is small, and therefore, in practice, Hcc completes after a small number of iterations. For a recent work with better practical performance, see [45].

8.4   HADOOP IMPLEMENTATION

Given the main goal of the PEGASUS project is to provide an efficient system to the user, we discuss different Hadoop implementation approaches, starting out with a naive implementation and progressing to faster methods for GIM-V. The proposed versions are evaluated in Section 8.5.

8.4.1   GIM-V BASE: NAIVE MULTIPLICATION

GIM-V BASE is a two-stage algorithm whose pseudocode is in Algorithms 8.1 and 8.2. The inputs are an edge file and a vector file. Each line of the edge file has the form $(id_{src}, id_{dst}, mval)$, which corresponds to a nonzero entry in the adjacency matrix. Similarly, each line of the vector file has the form $(id, vval)$, which corresponds to an element in vector v. Stage1 performs the combine2 operation by combining columns of matrix (id_{dst} of M) with rows of the vector (id of V). The output of Stage1 are (key, value) pairs where the key is the source vertex id of the matrix (id_{src} of M), and the value is the partially combined result (combine2($mval$, $vval$)). This output of Stage1 becomes the input of Stage2. Stage2 combines all partial results from Stage1 and updates the vector. The combineAll$_i$() and assign() operations are done in line 15 of Stage2, where the "self" and "others" tags in lines 15 and 21 of Stage1 are needed by Stage2 to distinguish cases appropriately. We note that in Algorithm 8.4 and 8.5, Output(k, v) means to output data with the key k and the value.

8.4.2   GIM-V BL: BLOCK MULTIPLICATION

GIM-V BL is a fast algorithm for GIM-V, which is based on block multiplication. The main idea is to group elements of the input matrix into blocks/submatrices of size b by b. Also, we group elements of input vectors into blocks of length b. In practice, grouping means we place all elements of a group into one line of input file. Each block contains only nonzero elements of the matrix/vector. The format of a matrix block with k nonzero elements

Algorithm 8.1 GIM-V BASE Stage 1.

Input: Matrix $M = \{(id_{src}, (id_{dsrt}, mval))\}$, Vector $V = \{(id, vval)\}$
Output: Partial vector $V' = \{id_{src}, \text{combine2}(mval, vval)\}$
1: Stage1-Map(Key k, Value v):
2: **if** (k, v) is of type V **then**
3:     Output (k, v);   // (k: id, v: $vval$)
4: **else if** (k, v) is of type M **then**
5:     $(id_{dst}, mval) \leftarrow v$;
6:     Output($id_{dst}, (k, mval)$);   // (k: id_{src})
7: **end if**
8:
9: Stage1-Reduce(Key k, Value $v[1..m]$):
10: $saved\_kv \leftarrow [\ ]$;
11: $saved\_v \leftarrow [\ ]$;
12: **for** $v \in v[1..m]$ **do**
13:   **if** (k, v) is of type V **then**
14:     $saved\_v \leftarrow v$;
15:     Output $(k, (\text{“self”}; saved\_v))$;
16:   **else if** (k, v) is of type M **then**
17:     Add v to $saved\_kv$;   // (v: $(id_{src}, mval)$)
18:   **end if**
19: **end for**
20: **for** $(id'_{src}, mval') \in saved\_kv$ **do**
21:   Output($id'_{src}, (\text{“others”}, \text{combine2}(mval', saved\_v))$));
22: **end for**

Algorithm 8.2 GIM-V BASE Stage 2.

Input: Partial vector $V' = \{(id_{src}, vval')\}$
Output: Result vector $V = \{(id_{src}, vval)\}$
1: Stage2-Map(Key k, Value v):
2: Output(k, v);
3:
4: Stage2-Reduce(Key k, Value $v[1..m]$):
5: $others\_v \leftarrow [\ ]$;
6: $self\_v \leftarrow [\ ]$;
7: **for** $v \in v[1..m]$ **do**
8:   $(tag, v') \leftarrow v$;
9:   **if** $tag = \text{“same”}$ **then**
10:     $self\_v \leftarrow v'$;
11:   **else if** $tag = \text{“others”}$ **then**
12:     Add v' to $others\_v$;
13:   **end if**
14: **end for**
15: Output(k, assign($self\_v$, combineAll$_k$($others\_v$)));

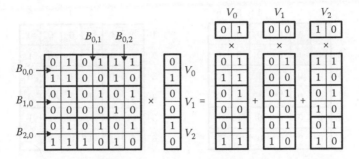

FIGURE 8.2 GIM-V BL using 2×2 blocks. $B_{i,j}$ represents a matrix block and v_i represents a vector block. The matrix and vector are joined block-wise, not element-wise.

is $\left(row_{block}, col_{block}, row_{elem_1}, col_{elem_1}, mval_{elem_1}, \ldots, row_{elem_k}, col_{elem_k}, mval_{elem_k} \right)$. Similarly, the format of a vector block with k nonzero elements is $\left(id_{block}, id_{elem_1}, vval_{elem_1}, \ldots, id_{elem_k}, vval_{elem_k} \right)$. Only blocks with at least one nonzero elements are saved to disk. This block encoding forces nearby edges in the adjacency matrix to be closely located; it is different from Hadoop's default behavior, which does not guarantee co-locating them. After grouping, GIM-V is performed on blocks, not on individual elements. GIM-V BL is illustrated in Figure 8.2.

In Section 8.5, we observe that GIM-V BL is at least 5 times faster than GIM-V BASE. There are two main reasons for this speedup.

- **Sorting Time**: Block encoding decreases the number of items to be sorted in the shuffling stage of Hadoop. We observe that one of the main efficiency bottlenecks in Hadoop is its shuffling stage where network transfer, sorting, and disk I/O take place.
- **Compression**: The size of the data decreases significantly by converting edges and vectors to block format. The reason is that in GIM-V BASE, we need $2 \times 4 =$ 8 bytes to save each (srcid, dstid) pair. However in GIM-V BL we can specify each *block* using a block row id and a block column id with two 4-byte integers and refer to elements inside the block using $2 \times \log b$ bits. This is possible because we can use $\log b$ bits to refer to a row or column inside a block. By this block method, we decrease the edge file size. For instance, using block encoding, we are able to decrease the size of the Yahooweb graph more than 50%.

8.4.3 GIM-V CL: CLUSTERED EDGES

We use co-clustering heuristics, see [44] as a preprocessing step to obtain a better clustering of the edge set. Figure 8.3 illustrates the concept. The preprocessing step needs to be performed only once. If the number of iterations required for the execution of an algorithm is large, then it is beneficial to perform this preprocessing step. Notice that we have two variants of GIM-V: GIM-V CL and GIM-V BL-CL, which are GIM-V BASE and GIM-V BL with clustered edges, respectively.

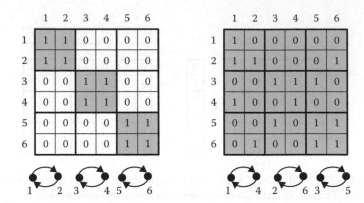

FIGURE 8.3 Clustered vs. nonclustered adjacency matrices for two isomorphic graphs. The edges are grouped into 2 × 2 blocks. The left graph uses only 3 blocks, whereas the right graph uses 9 blocks.

8.4.4 GIM-V DI: DIAGONAL BLOCK ITERATION

Reducing the number of iterations required for executing an algorithm in MapReduce mitigates the computational cost a lot, since the main bottleneck of GIM-V is its shuffling and disk I/O steps. In Hcc, it is possible to decrease the number of iterations when the graph has long chains. The main idea is to multiply diagonal matrix blocks and corresponding vector blocks as much as possible in one iteration. This is illustrated in Figure 8.4.

Algorithm 8.3 Renumbering the minimum node

Input: Edge $E = \{(id_{src}, id_{dst})\}$,
      current minimum vertex id $minid_{cur}$,
      new minimum vertex id $minid_{new}$
Output: Renumbered Edge $V = \left\{ \left(id'_{src}, id'_{dst} \right) \right\}$
  1: Renumber–Map(key k, value v):
  2: $src \leftarrow k$;
  3: $dst \leftarrow v$;
  4: **if** $src = minid_{cur}$ **then**
  5:    $src \leftarrow minid_{new}$;
  6: **else if** $src = minid_{new}$ **then**
  7:    $src \leftarrow minid_{cur}$;
  8: **end if**
  9: **if** $dst = minid_{cur}$ **then**
 10:    $dst \leftarrow minid_{new}$;
 11: **else if** $dst = minid_{new}$ **then**
 12:    $dst \leftarrow minid_{cur}$;
 13: **end if**
 14: Output(src, dst);

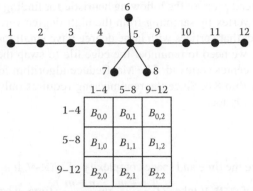

(a) Example of graph and block adjacency matrix

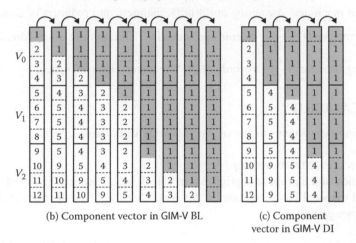

(b) Component vector in GIM-V BL   (c) Component
                                                    vector in GIM-V DI

FIGURE 8.4 Propagation of component id(=1) when block width is 4. Each element in the adjacency matrix of (a) represents a 4 × 4 block; each column in (b) and (c) represents the vector after each iteration. GIM-V DL finishes in 4 iterations while GIM-V BL requires 8 iterations.

8.4.5 GIM-V NR: NODE RENUMBERING

In HCC, the minimum vertex id is propagated to the other parts of the graph within at most d steps, where d is the diameter of the graph. If the vertex with the minimum id (which we call "minimum node") is located at the center of the graph, then the number of iterations is small, close to $d/2$. However, if it is located at the boundary of the network, then the number of iterations can be close to d. Therefore, if we preprocess the edges so that the minimum vertex id is swapped to the center vertex id, the number of iterations and the total running time of HCC would decrease.

Finding the center vertex with the minimum radius could be done with the Hadi algorithm. However, the algorithm is expensive for the preprocessing step of HCC.

Therefore, we instead propose the following heuristic for finding the center node: we choose the center vertex by sampling from the high-degree vertices. This heuristic is based on the fact that vertices with large degree have small radii [28]. After finding a center node, we need to renumber the edge file to swap the current minimum vertex id with the center vertex id. The MapReduce algorithm for this renumbering is shown in Algorithm 8.6. Since the renumbering requires only filtering, it can be done with a map-only job.

8.4.6 ANALYSIS

Finally, we analyze the time and space complexity of GIM-V. It is not hard to observe that one iteration of GIM-V takes $O\left(\dfrac{n+m}{M}\log\dfrac{n+m}{M}\right)$ time, where M stands for the number of machines. Assuming uniformity, mappers and reducers of Stage1 and Stage2 receive $O\left(\dfrac{n+m}{M}\right)$ records per machine. The running time is dominated by the sorting time for $\dfrac{n+m}{M}$ records. GIM-V requires $O(n + m)$ space.

8.5 SCALABILITY

We perform experiments to answer the following questions:

- How does GIM-V scale up?
- Which of the proposed optimizations (block multiplication, clustered edges, and diagonal block iteration, vertex renumbering) gives the highest performance gains?

The graphs we use in our experiments are shown in Table 8.2. We run PEGASUS in M45 Hadoop cluster by Yahoo! and our own cluster composed of 9 machines. M45 is one of the top 50 supercomputers in the world with the total 1.5-PB storage and 3.5-TB memory. For the performance and scalability experiments, we used synthetic Kronecker graphs [31] since we can generate them with any size, and they are one of the most realistic graphs among synthetic graphs.

8.5.1 RESULTS

We first show how the performance of our method changes as we add more machines. Figure 8.5 shows the running time and performance of GIM-V for PageRank with Kronecker graph of 282 million edges and size 32 blocks if necessary.

In Figure 8.5a, for all of the methods the running time decreases as we add more machines. Note that clustered edges (GIM-V CL) did not help performance unless it is combined with block encoding. When it is combined, however, it showed the best performance (GIM-V BL-CL).

In Figure 8.5b, we see that the relative performance of each method compared with GIM-V BASE method decreases as number of machines increases. With three

TABLE 8.2

Order and Size of Networks

Name	Vertices	Edges	Description
YahooWeb	1413 million	6636 million	WWW pages in 2002
LinkedIn	7.5 million	58 million	Person–person in 2006
	4.4 million	27 million	Person–person in 2005
	1.6 million	6.8 million	Person–person in 2004
	85 thousand	230 thousand	Person–person in 2003
Wikipedia	3.5 million	42 million	Doc–doc in 2007/02
	3 million	35 million	Doc–doc in 2006/09
	1.6 million	18.5 million	Doc–doc in 2005/11
Kronecker	177 thousand	1977 million	Synthetic
	120 thousand	1145 million	Synthetic
	59 thousand	282 million	Synthetic
	19 thousand	40 million	Synthetic
WWW-Barabasi	325 thousand	1497 thousand	WWW pages in nd.edu
DBLP	471 thousand	112 thousand	Document–document
Flickr	404 thousand	2.1 million	Person–person
Epinions	75 thousand	508 thousand	Who trusts whom

machines (minimum number of machines, which Hadoop "distributed mode" supports), the fastest method (GIM-V BL-CL) ran 5.27 times faster than GIM-V BASE. With 90 machines, GIM-V BL-CL ran 2.93 times faster than GIM-V BASE. This is expected since there are fixed component (JVM load time, disk I/O, network communication), which cannot be optimized even if we add more machines.

Next, we show how the performance of our methods changes as the input size grows. Figure 8.5c shows the running time of GIM-V with different number of edges under 10 machines. As we can see, all of the methods scale linearly with the number of edges.

Next, we compare the performance of GIM-V DI and GIM-V BL-CL for Hcc in graphs with long chains. For this experiment, we made a new graph whose diameter is 17, by adding a length 15 chain to the 282 million Kronecker graph, which has diameter 2. As we see in Figure 8.6, GIM-V DI finished in 6 iterations, whereas GIM-V BL-CL finished in 18 iterations. The running time of both methods for the first 6 iterations are nearly same. Therefore, the diagonal block iteration method decreases the number of iterations while not affecting the running time of each iteration much.

Finally, we compare the number of iterations with/without renumbering. Figure 8.7 shows the degree distribution of LinkedIn. Without renumbering, the minimum vertex has degree 1, which is not surprising since about 46% of the vertices have degree 1 due to the power law behavior of the degree distribution. We show the number of iterations after changing the minimum vertex to each of the top 5 highest degree vertices in Figure 8.8. We see that the renumbering

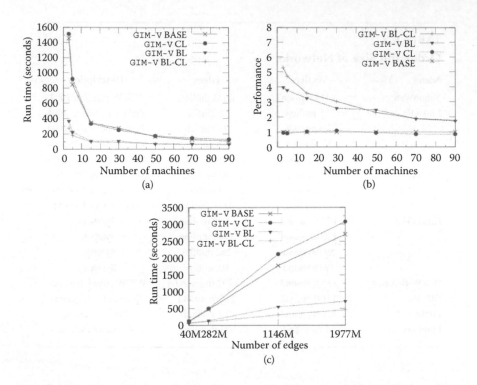

FIGURE 8.5 Scalability and performance of GIM-V. (a) Running time decreases quickly as more machines are added. (b) The performance (=1/*running time*) of "BL-CL" wins more than 5× (for n=3 machines) over the "BASE." (c) Every version of GIM-V shows linear scalability.

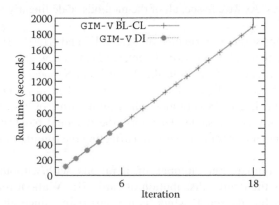

FIGURE 8.6 Comparison of GIM-V DI and GIM-V BL-CL for Hcc. GIM-V DI finishes in 6 iterations, whereas GIM-V BL-CL finishes in 18 iterations due to long chains.

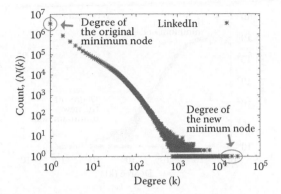

FIGURE 8.7 Degree distribution of LinkedIn. Notice that the original minimum vertex has degree 1, which is highly probable given the power law behavior of the degree distribution. After the renumbering, the minimum vertex is replaced with a highest-degree node.

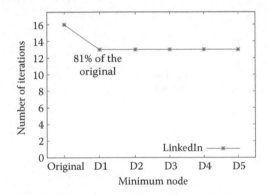

FIGURE 8.8 Number of iterations vs. the minimum vertex of LinkedIn, for connected components. Di represents the vertex with ith largest degree. Notice that the number of iterations decreased by 19% after renumbering.

decreased the number of iterations to 81% of the original. Similar results are observed for the Wikipedia graph in Figures 8.9 and 8.10. The original minimum vertex has degree 1, and the number of iterations decreased to 83% of the original after renumbering.

8.6 PEGASUS AT WORK

In this section, we evaluate PEGASUS on real-world networks. Specifically, Section 8.6.1 presents our findings with respect to connected components of real-world networks. Section 8.6.2 presents our findings on the PageRank scores and Section 8.6.3 presents our findings on the diameter and radii distribution of real-world networks.

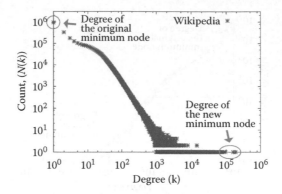

FIGURE 8.9 Degree distribution of Wikipedia. Notice that the original minimum vertex has degree 1, as in LinkedIn. After the renumbering, the minimum vertex is replaced with a highest-degree node.

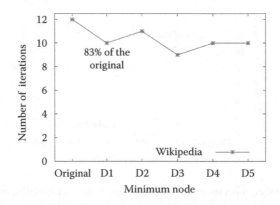

FIGURE 8.10 Number of iterations vs. the minimum vertex of Wikipedia, for connected components. D*i* represents the vertex with *i*th largest degree. Notice that the number of iterations decreased by 17% after renumbering.

8.6.1 Connected Components of Real-World Networks

Figure 8.11 shows the evolution of connected components of LinkedIn and Wikipedia graphs. Figure 8.12 shows the distribution of connected components in the YahooWeb graph. We make the following set of observations.

8.6.1.1 Power Laws in Connected Components Distributions

We observe a power law relation between the count and size of small connected components in Figures 8.11a, b and 8.12. This reflects that the connected components in real networks are formed by preferential attachment processes.

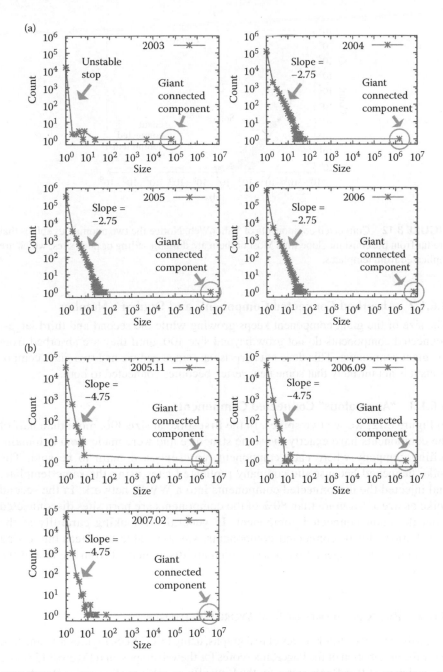

FIGURE 8.11 The evolution of connected components of (a) LinkedIn and (b) Wikipedia graphs. The giant connected component grows each year. The second largest connected components do not grow above Dunbar's number (≈150) and the slope of the size distribution remains constant after the gelling point at year 2003. As in LinkedIn, notice the growth of giant connected component and the constant slope of the size distribution.

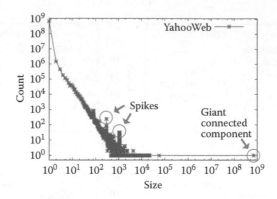

FIGURE 8.12 Connected components of YahooWeb. Notice the two anomalous spikes that are far from the constant-slope line. Most of them are domain selling or porn sites, which are replicated from templates.

8.6.1.2 Absorbed Connected Components and Dunbar's Number

The size of the giant component keeps growing while the second and third largest connected components do not grow beyond size 100, until they are absorbed from the giant component. This does not surprise us, since had we had two giant components it is not unlikely that some new vertex becomes connected to both.

8.6.1.3 "Anomalous" Connected Components

In Figure 8.12, we see two spikes. In the first spike at size 300, more than half of the components have exactly the same structure and were made from a domain-selling company where each component represents a domain to be sold. The spike happened because the company replicated sites using the same template, and injected the disconnected components into a WWW network. In the second spike at size 1101, more than 80% of the components are porn sites disconnected from the giant connected component. In general, by looking carefully at the distribution plot of connected components, we were able to detect interesting communities with special purposes, which are disconnected from the rest of the Internet.

8.6.2 PAGERANK SCORES OF REAL-WORLD NETWORKS

We analyze the PageRank scores of real graphs, using PEGASUS. Figures 8.13 and 8.14 show the distribution of the PageRank scores for theweb graphs, and Figure 8.15 shows the evolution of PageRank scores for the LinkedIn and Wikipedia graphs. We observe power-law relations between the PageRank score and the number of vertices with such PageRank. The top 3 highest PageRank sites for the year 2002 are `www.career bank.com`, `access.adobe.com`, and `top100.rambler.ru`. As expected, they have huge in-degrees (from ≈70K to ≈70M).

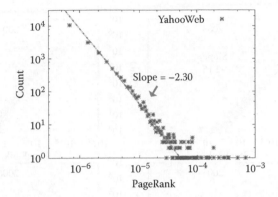

FIGURE 8.13 PageRank distribution of YahooWeb. The distribution follows a power law with an exponent 2.30.

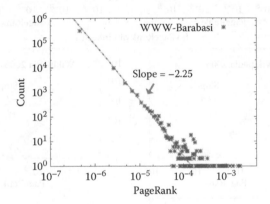

FIGURE 8.14 PageRank distribution of WWW-Barabasi. The distribution follows a power law with an exponent 2.25.

8.6.3 DIAMETER OF REAL-WORLD NETWORKS

PEGASUS reveals new patterns in massive graphs, which we present in this section. We distinguish these new patterns into *static* (Section 8.6.4) and *temporal* (Section 8.6.5).

8.6.4 STATIC PATTERNS

8.6.4.1 Diameter

What is the diameter of the web? Albert et al. [5] computed the diameter on a directed web graph with approximately 0.3 million vertices and conjectured that it should be

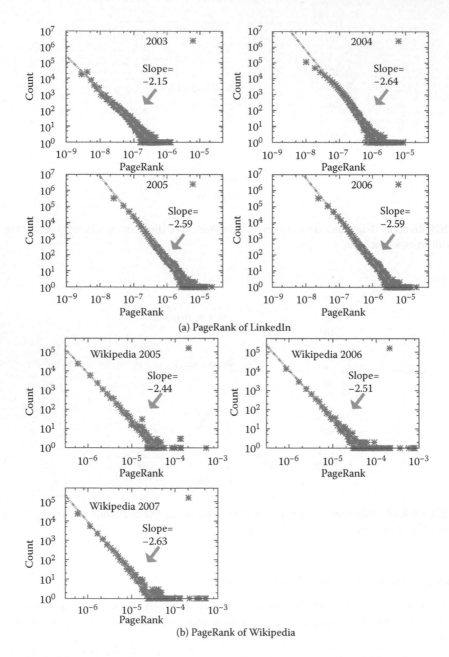

FIGURE 8.15 The evolution of PageRank. (a) The distributions of PageRank follows a power law. However, the exponent at year 2003, which is around the gelling point, is much different from year 2004, which are after the gelling point. The exponent increases after the gelling point and becomes stable. Also, notice the maximum PageRank after the gelling point is about 10 times larger than that before the gelling point due to the emergence of the giant connected component. (b) Again, the distributions of PageRank follows a power law. Since the gelling point is before year 2005, the three plots show similar characteristics: the maximum PageRank and the slopes are similar.

around 19 for a 1.4 billion-vertex web graph as shown in the upper line of Figure 8.17. Broder et al. [16] used their sampling approach from approximately 200 million vertices and reported 16.15 and 6.83 as the diameter for the directed and the undirected cases, respectively. What should the effective diameter be, for a significantly larger crawl of the web, with billions of vertices? Figure 8.16 gives the surprising answer:

Observation 1 (Small Web) *The effective diameter of the* YahooWeb *graph (year: 2002) is surprisingly small, between 7 and 8.*

The previous results from Albert et al. [5] and Broder et al. [16] also consider the undirected version of the web graph. We compute the average diameter and show the comparison of diameters of different graphs in Figure 8.17. We first observe that the average diameters of all graphs are relatively small (<20) for both the directed and the undirected cases. We also observe that the Albert et al.'s conjecture for the diameter of the directed graph is overpessimistic: both the sampling approach and Hadi output smaller values for the diameter of the directed graph.

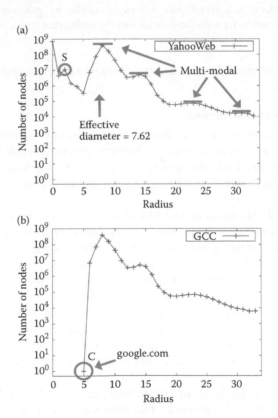

FIGURE 8.16   (a) Radius plot (count vs. radius) of the YahooWeb graph. Notice the effective diameter is surprisingly small. Also notice the peak (marked "S") at radius 2, due to star-structured disconnected components. (b) Radius plot of GCC (giant connected component) of YahooWeb graph. The *only* vertex with radius 5 (marked "C") is google.com.

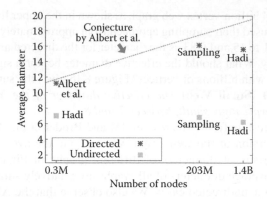

FIGURE 8.17   Average diameter vs. number of vertices in lin–log scale for the three different web graphs, where M and B stand for millions and billions, respectively. (0.3M): web pages inside nd.edu at 1999, from Albert et al.'s work. (203M): web pages crawled by Altavista at 1999, from Broder et al.'s work (1.4B): web pages crawled by Yahoo at 2002. Notice the relatively small diameters for both the directed and the undirected cases.

For the diameter of the undirected graph, we observe the constant/shrinking diameter pattern [32].

8.6.4.2   Shape of Distribution

Figure 8.16 shows that the radii distribution in the web graph is multimodal. In other relatively smaller networks, we observe a bimodal structure. As shown in the radius plot of U.S. Patent and LinkedIn network in Figure 8.18, they have a peak at zero, a dip at a small radius value (9 and 4, respectively) and another peak very close to the dip.

Observation 2 (Multimodal and Bimodal) *The radius distribution of the web graph has a multimodal structure. Smaller networks have a bimodal structure.*

A natural question to ask with respect to the bimodal structure is what are the common properties of the vertices that belong to the first peak; similarly, for the vertices in the first dip, and the same for the vertices of the second peak. After investigation, the former are vertices that belong to disconnected components (DCs); vertices in the dip are usually core vertices in the giant connected component (GCC), and the vertices at the second peak are the vast majority of well-connected vertices in the GCC. Figure 8.19 exactly shows the radii distribution for the vertices of the GCC (in blue), and the vertices of the few largest remaining components.

In Figure 8.19, we clearly see that the second peak of the bimodal structure came from the giant connected component. However, where does the first peak around radius 0 come from? We can get the answer from the distribution of connected component of the same graph in Figure 8.20. Since the ranges of radius are limited by the size of connected components, we see the first peak of radius plot came from the disconnected components whose size follows a power law.

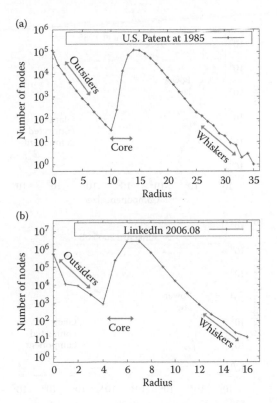

FIGURE 8.18 Static radius plot (count vs. radius) of (a) U.S. Patent and (b) LinkedIn graphs. Notice the bimodal structure with "outsiders" (vertices in the DCs), "core" (central vertices in the GCC), and "whiskers" (vertices connected to the GCC with long paths).

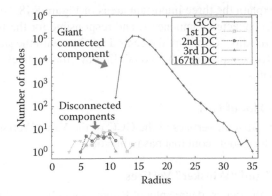

FIGURE 8.19 Radius plot (count vs. radius) for the giant connected components and other smaller connected components of the U.S. Patent data in 1985.

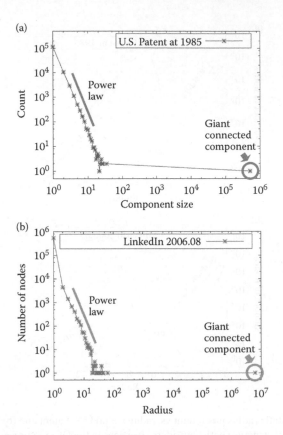

FIGURE 8.20 Size distribution of connected components of (a) U.S. Patent and (b) LinkedIn graphs. Notice the size of the disconnected components (DCs) follows a power law, which explains the first peak around radius 0 of the radius plots in Figure 8.18.

Now we can explain the three important areas of Figure 8.18: "*outsiders*" are the vertices in the disconnected components, and responsible for the first peak and the negative slope to the dip. "*Core*" are the central vertices with the smallest radii from the giant connected component. "*Whiskers*" [33] are the vertices connected to the GCC with long paths.

8.6.4.3 Radius Plot of GCC

Figure 8.16b shows that all vertices of the GCC of the YahooWeb graph have radius 6 or more except for google.com that has radius one.

8.6.4.4 "Core" and "Whisker" Vertices

Figure 8.21 shows the radius–degree plot of Patent, YahooWeb, and LinkedIn graphs. The radius–degree plot is a scatterplot with one dot for every vertex plotting the degree of the vertex vs. its radius. The points corresponding to vertices in the GCC are colored with blue, while the rest is in magenta. We observe that the highest

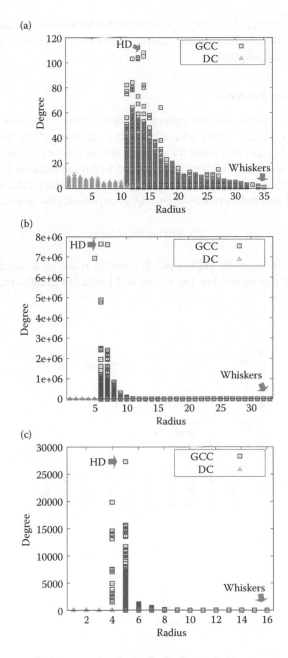

FIGURE 8.21 Radius–degree plots of (a) Patent, (b) YahooWeb and (c) LinkedIn graphs. HD represents the vertex with the highest degree. Notice that HD belongs to core vertices inside the GCC, and whiskers have small degree.

degree vertices belong to the set of core vertices inside the GCC but are not necessarily the ones with the smallest radius. Finally, the whisker vertices have small degree and belong to chain subgraphs.

8.6.5 TEMPORAL PATTERNS

Here we study the radius distribution as a function of time. We know that the diameter of a graph typically grows with time, spikes at the "gelling point," and then shrinks [32,38]. Indeed, this holds for our data sets as shown in Figure 8.22.

Figure 8.23 shows our findings. The radius distribution expands to the right until it reaches the gelling point. Then, it contracts to the left. Finally, the decreasing segments of several real radius plots seem to decay exponentially, that is,

$$count(r) \propto \exp(-cr) \tag{8.1}$$

for every time tick *after* the gelling point. $count(r)$ is the number of vertices with radius r and c is a constant. For the Patent and LinkedIn graphs, the absolute correlation coefficient.

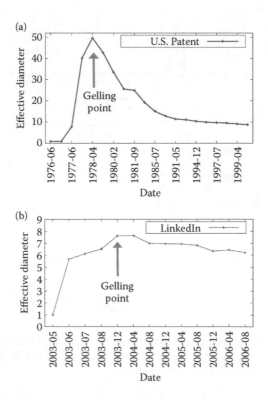

FIGURE 8.22 Evolution of the effective diameter of (a) U.S. Patent and (b) LinkedIn graphs. The diameter increases until a "gelling" point and starts to decrease after that point.

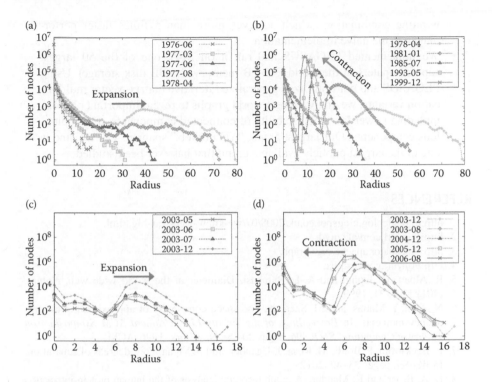

FIGURE 8.23 Radius distribution over time for (a), (b) U.S. Patent and (c), (d) LinkedIn graphs. "Expansion": the radius distribution moves to the right until the gelling point. "Contraction": the radius distribution moves to the left after the gelling point.

8.7 CONCLUSION

In this chapter, we presented PEGASUS [29], a graph mining package for very large graphs using the Hadoop architecture. Since the introduction of PEGASUS, many other graph-processing systems have been proposed [3,34,36]. The PEGASUS source code can be downloaded from http://www.cs.cmu.edu/~pegasus/. We illustrated case studies where PEGASUS allows us to obtain insights from large-scale graphs, such as the important case of the web graph. Finding other novel applications of the tools developed is left as an interesting direction to the interested practitioners. We summarize the contributions of PEGASUS:

- We identified the common, underlying primitive of several graph mining operations, and we showed that it is a generalized form of a matrix–vector multiplication. We call this operation generalized iterative matrix–vector multiplication and showed that it includes the diameter estimation, the PageRank estimation, RWR calculation, and finding connected components, as special cases.
- Given its importance, we proposed several optimizations (block multiplication, diagonal block iteration, node renumbering, etc.) and reported the

winning combination, which achieves more than 5 times faster performance to the naive implementation.

- We implemented PEGASUS and ran it on M45, one of the 50 largest supercomputers in the world (3.5 TB memory, 1.5 PB disk storage). Using PEGASUS and our optimized generalized iterative matrix–vector multiplication variants, we analyzed real-world graphs to reveal important patterns including power law tails, stability of connected components, and anomalous components. Our largest graph, "YahooWeb," spanned 120 Gb, and is one of the largest publicly available graph that has ever been studied.

REFERENCES

1. http://googleblog.blogspot.co.uk/2008/07/we-knew-web-was-big.html.
2. http://tinyurl.com/afzzuvd.
3. http://incubator.apache.org/giraph/.
4. http://tinyurl.com/csqljsr.
5. R. Albert, H. Jeong, and A.-L. Barabasi. Diameter of the world wide web. *Nature*, (401):130–131, 1999.
6. N. Alon, Y. Matias, and M. Szegedy. The space complexity of approximating the frequency moments. In *Proceedings of the Twenty-Eighth Annual ACM Symposium on Theory of Computing, STOC'96*, pages 20–29, New York, 1996. ACM.
7. L. Backstrom, P. Boldi, M. Rosa, J. Ugander, and S. Vigna. Four degrees of separation. In *WebSci*, pages 33–42, 2012.
8. D. A. Bader and K. Madduri. A graph-theoretic analysis of the human protein-interaction network using multicore parallel algorithms. *Parallel Computing*, 34(11):627–639, 2008.
9. Z. Bar-Yossef, T. S. Jayram, R. Kumar, D. Sivakumar, and L. Trevisan. Counting distinct elements in a data stream. In *Proceedings of the 6th International Workshop on Randomization and Approximation Techniques, RANDOM'02*, pages 1–10. Springer-Verlag, 2002.
10. Z. Bar-Yossef, R. Kumar, and D. Sivakumar. Reductions in streaming algorithms, with an application to counting triangles in graphs. In *Proceedings of the Thirteenth Annual ACM-SIAM Symposium on Discrete Algorithms, SODA'02*, pages 623–632, Philadelphia, PA, USA, 2002. Society for Industrial and Applied Mathematics.
11. K. Beyer, P. J. Haas, B. Reinwald, Y. Sismanis, and R. Gemulla. On synopses for distinct-value estimation under multiset operations. In *Proceedings of the 2007 ACM SIGMOD International Conference on Management of data, SIGMOD'07*, pages 199–210, New York, 2007. ACM.
12. K. Bharat, B.-W. Chang, M. R. Henzinger, and M. Ruhl. Who links to whom: Mining linkage between web sites. In *Proceedings of the 2001 IEEE International Conference on Data Mining, ICDM'01*, pages 51–58, Washington, DC, USA, 2001. IEEE Computer Society.
13. P. Boldi, M. Rosa, and S. Vigna. Hyperanf: Approximating the neighbourhood function of very large graphs on a budget. In *Proceedings of the 20th International Conference on World Wide Web, WWW'11*, pages 625–634, New York, 2011. ACM.
14. J. A. Bondy and U. S. Ramachandra Murty. *Graph Theory with Applications*, volume 290. MacMillan, London, 1976.
15. S. Brin and L. Page. The anatomy of a large-scale hypertextual (web) search engine. In *Proceedings of the 7th International World Wide Web Conference (WWW7)/Computer Networks*, pages 107–117, 1998. Published as Proc. 7th International World Wide Web Conference (WWW7)/Computer Networks, volume 30, number 1–7.

16. A. Broder, R. Kumar, F. Maghoul, P. Raghavan, S. Rajagopalan, R. Stata, A. Tomkins, and J. Wiener. Graph structure in the web. *Comput. Networks*, 33(1):309–320, 2000.

17. B. V. Cherkassky, A. V. Goldberg, and T. Radzik. Shortest paths algorithms: Theory and experimental evaluation. In *SODA'94*, pages 516–525, Philadelphia, PA, USA, 1994. Society for Industrial and Applied Mathematics.

18. E. Cohen. Size-estimation framework with applications to transitive closure and reachability. *J. Comput. Syst. Sci.*, 55(3):441–453, 1997.

19. T. Cormen, C. Leiserson, and R. Rivest. *Introduction to Algorithms*. The MIT Press, 1990.

20. D. Donato, L. Laura, S. Leonardi, and S. Millozzi. The web as a graph: How far we are. *ACM Trans. Internet Technol.*, 7(1), 2007.

21. M. Durand and P. Flajolet. Loglog counting of large cardinalities (extended abstract). In *ESA*, pages 605–617, 2003.

22. J.-A. Ferrez, K. Fukuda, and T. M. Liebling. Parallel computation of the diameter of a graph. In *High Performance Computing Systems and Applications*, pages 283–296, 1998. Springer.

23. P. Flajolet and G. Nigel Martin. Probabilistic counting algorithms for data base applications. *J. Comput. Syst. Sci.*, 1985.

24. P. Flajolet, Eric Fusy, O. Gandouet et al. Hyperloglog: The analysis of a near-optimal cardinality estimation algorithm. In *AOFA'07: Proceedings of the 2007 International Conference on Analysis of Algorithms*, 2007.

25. S. Fortunato. Community detection in graphs. CoRR, abs/0906.0612, 2009.

26. P. Indyk and D. Woodruff. Tight lower bounds for the distinct elements problem. In *Proceedings of the 44th Annual IEEE Symposium on Foundations of Computer Science*, pages 283–288, 2003. IEEE.

27. D. M. Kane, J. Nelson, and D. P. Woodruff. An optimal algorithm for the distinct elements problem. In *Proceedings of the Twenty-Ninth ACM SIGMOD-SIGACT-SIGART Symposium on Principles of Database Systems, PODS'10*, pages 41–52, New York, 2010. ACM.

28. U. Kang, C. E. Tsourakakis, A. P. Appel, C. Faloutsos, and J. Leskovec. Hadi: Mining radii of large graphs. *ACM Trans. Knowl. Discov. Data*, 5(2):8:1–8:24, 2011.

29. U. Kang, C. Tsourakakis, and C. Faloutsos. Pegasus: A peta-scale graph mining system implementation and observations. In *Ninth IEEE International Conference on Data Mining, ICDM'09*, pages 229–238, 2009. IEEE.

30. H. Kwak, C. Lee, H. Park, and S. Moon. What is twitter, a social network or a news media? In *Proceedings of the 19th International Conference on World Wide Web, WWW'10*, pages 591–600, 2010. ACM.

31. J. Leskovec, D. Chakrabarti, J. M. Kleinberg, and C. Faloutsos. Realistic, mathematically tractable graph generation and evolution, using kronecker multiplication. In *PKDD*, pages 133–145, 2005.

32. J. Leskovec, J. Kleinberg, and C. Faloutsos. Graph evolution: Densification and shrinking diameters. *ACM Trans. Knowl. Discov. Data*, 1(1):2, 2007.

33. J. Leskovec, K. J. Lang, A. Dasgupta, and M. W. Mahoney. Statistical properties of community structure in large social and information networks. In *Proceedings of the 17th International Conference on World Wide Web*, pages 695–704, 2008. ACM.

34. Y. Low, D. Bickson, J. Gonzalez, C. Guestrin, A. Kyrola, and J. M. Hellerstein. Distributed graphlab: A framework for machine learning and data mining in the cloud. *Proc. VLDB Endow.*, 5(8):716–727, 2012.

35. J. Ma and S. Ma. Efficient parallel algorithms for some graph theory problems. *J. Comput. Sci. Technol.*, 8(4):362–366, 1993.

36. G. Malewicz, M. H. Austern, A. J. C. Bik, J. C. Dehnert, I. Horn, N. Leiser, and G. Czajkowski. Pregel: A system for large-scale graph processing. In *Proceedings of the 2010 ACM SIGMOD International Conference on Management of Data*, pages 135–146, 2010. ACM.

37. G. Marconi. Wireless telegraphic communication. *Nobel Price Lecture*, 1909.
38. M. McGlohon, L. Akoglu, and C. Faloutsos. Weighted graphs and disconnected components: Patterns and a generator. In *Proceedings of the 14th ACM SIGKDD International Conference on Knowledge Discovery and Data Mining*, pages 524–532, 2008. ACM.
39. S. Milgram. The small world problem. *Psychology*, 2(1):60–67, 1967.
40. R. Morris. Counting large numbers of events in small registers. *Communications of the ACM*, 21(10):840–842, 1978.
41. L. Page, S. Brin, R. Motwani, and T. Winograd. The PageRank citation ranking: Bringing order to the web. Technical report, Stanford InfoLab, 1999.
42. C. R. Palmer, P. B. Gibbons, and C. Faloutsos. Anf: A fast and scalable tool for data mining in massive graphs. In *Proceedings of the Eighth ACM SIGKDD International Conference on Knowledge Discovery and Data Mining*, pages 81–90, 2002. ACM.
43. J.-Y. Pan, H.-J. Yang, C. Faloutsos, and P. Duygulu. Automatic multimedia cross-modal correlation discovery. In *Proceedings of the Tenth ACM SIGKDD International Conference on Knowledge Discovery and Data Mining*, pages 653–658, 2004. ACM.
44. S. Papadimitriou and J. Sun. Disco: Distributed co-clustering with map–reduce: A case study towards petabyte-scale end-to-end mining. In *Eighth IEEE International Conference on Data Mining, ICDM'08*, pages 512–521, 2008. IEEE.
45. T. Seidl, B. Boden, and S. Fries. CC-MR-finding connected components in huge graphs with mapreduce. *Machine Learn. Knowledge Discov. Databases*, pages 458–473, 2012.
46. B. P. Sinha, B. B. Bhattacharya, S. Ghose, and P. K. Srimani. A parallel algorithm to compute the shortest paths and diameter of a graph and its vlsi implementation. *IEEE Trans. Comput.*, 35(11):1000–1004, 1986.
47. C. E. Tsourakakis. Fast counting of triangles in large real networks without counting: Algorithms and laws. In *Proceedings of the 2008 Eighth IEEE International Conference on Data Mining, ICDM'08*, pages 608–617, Washington, DC, USA, 2008. IEEE Computer Society.
48. D. Woodruff. Optimal space lower bounds for all frequency moments. In *Proceedings of the Fifteenth Annual ACM-SIAM Symposium on Discrete Algorithms, SODA'04*, pages 167–175, Philadelphia, PA, USA, 2004. Society for Industrial and Applied Mathematics.

9 An Overview of the NoSQL World

Liang Zhao, Sherif Sakr, and Anna Liu

CONTENTS

Over the past decade, rapidly growing Internet-based services such as e-mail, blogging, social networking, search, and e-commerce have substantially redefined the way consumers communicate, access contents, share information and purchase products. Relational database management systems (RDBMS) have been considered as the *one-size-fits-all* solution for data persistence and retrieval for decades. However, the ever-increasing need for scalability and new application requirements have created new challenges for traditional RDBMS. Recently, a new generation of low-cost, high-performance database software, aptly named as *NoSQL* (Not Only SQL), has emerged to challenge the dominance of RDBMS. The main features of these systems include ability to horizontally scale, supporting weaker consistency models, using flexible schemas and data models and supporting simple low-level query interfaces. In this chapter, we explore the recent advancements and the new approaches of web-scale data management. We discuss the advantages and disadvantages of several recently introduced approaches and its suitability to support certain class of applications and end users. Finally, we present and discuss some of the current challenges and open research problems to be tackled to improve the current state-of-the-art.

9.1 INTRODUCTION

Over the past decade, rapidly growing Internet-based services such as e-mail, blogging, social networking, search, and e-commerce have substantially redefined the way consumers communicate, access contents, share information, and purchase products. In particular, the recent advances in the web technology have made it easy for any user to provide and consume content of any form. For example, building a personal web page (e.g., Google Sites*), starting a blog (e.g., WordPress,[†] Blogger,[‡] LiveJournal[§]), and making both searchable for the public have become a commodity that is available for users all over the world. Arguably, the main goal of the next wave is to facilitate the job of implementing every application as a distributed, scalable, and widely accessible service on the web. Services such as Facebook,[¶] Flickr,** YouTube,[††] Zoho,[‡‡] and LinkedIn[§§] are currently leading this approach. Such applications are both *data-intensive* and very *interactive*. For example, the Facebook social network has announced that it has more than 800 millions of monthly active users.[¶¶] Each user has an average of 130 friendship relations. Moreover, there are about 900 million objects that registered users interact with, such as pages, groups, events, and community pages. Other smaller scale social networks such as LinkedIn, which is mainly used for professionals, has more than 120 million registered users. Twitter has also claimed to have over 100 million active monthly users. Therefore, it becomes an ultimate goal to make it easy for every application to achieve such high scalability and availability goals with minimum efforts.

In general, relational database management systems (e.g., MySQL, PostgreSQL, SQL Server, Oracle) have been considered as the *one-size-fits-all* solution for data persistence and retrieval for decades. They have matured after extensive research and development efforts and very successfully created a large market and solutions in different business domains. However, the ever-increasing need for scalability and new application requirements have created new challenges for traditional RDBMS. Therefore, recently, there has been some dissatisfaction with this *one-size-fits-all* approach in some web-scale applications [58]. Nowadays, the most common architecture to build enterprise web applications is based on a three-tier approach: the web server layer, the application server layer, and the data layer. In practice, data partitioning [50] and data replication [40] are two well-known strategies to achieve the availability, scalability, and performance improvement goals in the distributed

---

* http://sites.google.com/.
[†] http://wordpress.org/.
[‡] http://www.blogger.com/.
[§] http://www.livejournal.com/.
[¶] http://www.facebook.com/.
** http://www.flickr.com/.
[††] http://www.youtube.com/.
[‡‡] http://www.zoho.com/.
[§§] http://www.linkedin.com/.
[¶¶] http://www.facebook.com/press/info.php?statistics.

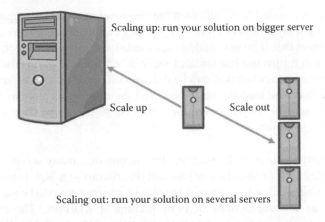

Scaling up: run your solution on bigger server

Scale up   Scale out

Scaling out: run your solution on several servers

FIGURE 9.1   Database scalability options.

data management world. In particular, when the application load increases, there are two main options for achieving scalability at the database tier that enables the applications to cope with more client requests (Figure 9.1) as follows:

1. *Scaling up*: aims at allocating a bigger machine to act as database servers.
2. *Scaling out*: aims at *replicating* and *partitioning* data across more machines.

In fact, the scaling up option has the main drawback that large machines are often very expensive and eventually a physical limit is reached where a more powerful machine cannot be purchased at any cost. Alternatively, it is both extensible and economical–especially in a dynamic workload environment–to scale out by adding storage space or buying another commodity server, which fits well with the new *pay-as-you-go* philosophy of cloud computing.

Recently, a new generation of low-cost, high-performance database software has emerged to challenge the dominance of relational database management systems. A big reason for this movement, named as *NoSQL* (Not Only SQL), is that different implementations of web, enterprise, and cloud computing applications have different database requirements (e.g., not every application requires rigid data consistency). For example, for high-volume web sites (e.g., eBay, Amazon, Twitter, Facebook), scalability and high availability are essential requirements that cannot be compromised. For these applications, even the slightest outage can have significant financial consequences and impacts customers' trust.

In general, the *CAP* theorem [15,34] and the *PACELC* model [1] describe the existence of direct tradeoffs between consistency and availability as well as consistency and latency. For example, the *CAP* theorem shows that a distributed database system can only choose at most two out of three properties: <u>C</u>onsistency, <u>A</u>vailability, and *tolerance to <u>P</u>artitions*. Therefore, there is a plethora of alternative consistency models, which have been introduced for offering different performance tradeoffs such as *session guarantees, causal consistency* [7], *causal+ consistency* [48], and *parallel snapshot isolation* [57]. In practice, the new wave of

NoSQL systems decided to compromise on the strict consistency requirement. In particular, they apply a relaxed consistency policy called *eventual consistency* [63], which guarantees that if no new updates are made to a replicated object, eventually all accesses will return the last updated value. If no failures occur, the maximum size of the inconsistency window can be determined based on factors such as communication delays, the load on the system, and the number of replicas involved in the replication scheme. In particular, these new NoSQL systems have a number of design features in common:

- The ability to horizontally scale out throughput over many servers.
- A simple call level interface or protocol (in contrast to a SQL binding).
- Supporting weaker consistency models in contrast to ACID guaranteed properties for transactions in most traditional RDBMS. These models are usually referred to as *BASE* models (*B*asically *A*vailable, *S*oft state, *E*ventually consistent) [53].
- Efficient use of distributed indexes and RAM for data storage.
- The ability to dynamically define new attributes or data schema.

These design features are made to achieve the following system goals:

- *Availability*: They must always be accessible even during network failure or a whole datacenter going offline.
- *Scalability*: They must be able to support very large databases with very high request rates at very low latency.
- *Elasticity*: They must be able to satisfy changing application requirements in both directions (scaling up or scaling down). Moreover, the system must be able to gracefully respond to these changing requirements and quickly recover its steady state.
- *Load balancing*: They must be able to automatically move load between servers so that most of the hardware resources are effectively utilized and to avoid any resource overloading situations.
- *Fault tolerance*: They must be able to deal with the situation that the rarest hardware problems go from being freak events to eventualities. While hardware failure is still a serious concern, this concern needs to be addressed at the architectural level of the database, rather than requiring developers, administrators, and operations staff to build their own redundant solutions.
- *Ability to run in a heterogeneous environment*: On scaling out environment, there is a strong trend toward increasing the number of nodes that participate in query execution. It is nearly impossible to get homogeneous performance across hundreds or thousands of compute nodes. Part failures that do not cause complete node failure, but result in degraded hardware performance become more common at scale. Hence, the system should be designed to run in a heterogeneous environment and must take appropriate measures to prevent performance degradation that are due to parallel processing on distributed nodes.

This chapter explores the recent advancements and the new approaches of the web-scale data management. We discuss the advantages and the disadvantages of each approach and its suitability to support certain class of applications and end users. Section 9.2 describes the NoSQL systems that are introduced and used internally in the key players: Google, Yahoo, and Amazon, respectively. Section 9.3 provides an overview of a set of open-source projects, which have been designed following the main principles of the NoSQL systems. Section 9.4 discusses the notion of providing database management as a service and gives an overview of the main representative systems and their challenges. The web-scale data management tradeoffs and open research challenges are discussed in Section 9.5 before we conclude the chapter in Section 9.7.

9.2 NoSQL KEY SYSTEMS

This section provides an overview of the main NoSQL systems which has been introduced and used internally by three of the key players in the web-scale data management domain: Google, Yahoo, and Amazon.

9.2.1 GOOGLE: BIGTABLE

Bigtable is a distributed storage system for managing structured data that is designed to scale to a very large size (petabytes of data) across thousands of commodity servers [21]. It has been used by more than 60 Google products and projects such as Google search engine,* Google Finance,† Orkut,‡ Google Docs,§ and Google Earth.¶ These products use Bigtable for a variety of demanding workloads, which range from throughput-oriented batch-processing jobs to latency-sensitive serving of data to end users. The Bigtable clusters used by these products span a wide range of configurations, from a handful to thousands of servers, and store up to several hundred terabytes of data.

Bigtable does not support a full relational data model. However, it provides clients with a simple data model that supports dynamic control over data layout and format. In particular, a Bigtable is a sparse, distributed, persistent multidimensional sorted map. The map is indexed by a row key, column key, and a timestamp. Each value in the map is an uninterpreted array of bytes. Thus, clients usually need to serialize various forms of structured and semistructured data into these strings. A concrete example that reflects some of the main design decisions of Bigtable is the scenario of storing a copy of a large collection of web pages into a single table. Figure 9.2 illustrates an example of this table where *URLs* are used as row keys and various aspects of web pages as column names. The contents of the web pages are stored in a single column that stores multiple versions of the page under the timestamps when they were fetched.

The row keys in a table are arbitrary strings where every read or write of data under a single row key is atomic. Bigtable maintains the data in lexicographic order

---

* http://www.google.com/.
† http://www.google.com/finance.
‡ http://www.orkut.com/.
§ http://docs.google.com/.
¶ http://earth.google.com/.

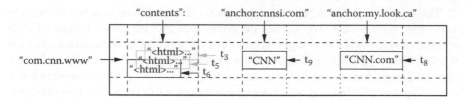

FIGURE 9.2   Sample Bigtable structure. (From F. Chang et al., *ACM Trans. Comput. Syst.*, 26, 2008.)

by row key where the row range for a table is dynamically partitioned. Each row range is called a *tablet*, which represents the unit of distribution and load balancing. Thus, reads of short row ranges are efficient and typically require communication with only a small number of machines. Bigtables can have an unbounded number of columns that are grouped into sets called *column families*. These column families represent the basic unit of access control. Each cell in a Bigtable can contain multiple versions of the same data that are indexed by their timestamps. Each client can flexibly decide the number of n versions of a cell that need to be kept. These versions are stored in decreasing timestamp order so that the most recent versions can be always read first.

The Bigtable API provides functions for creating and deleting tables and column families. It also provides functions for changing cluster, table, and column family metadata, such as access control rights. Client applications can write or delete values in Bigtable, look up values from individual rows, or iterate over a subset of the data in a table. At the transaction level, Bigtable supports only *single-row* transactions, which can be used to perform atomic read–modify–write sequences on data stored under a single row key (i.e., no general transactions across row keys).

At the physical level, Bigtable uses the distributed Google File System (GFS) [33] to store log, and data files. The Google *SSTable* file format is used internally to store Bigtable data. An SSTable provides a persistent, ordered immutable map from keys to values, where both keys and values are arbitrary byte strings. Bigtable relies on a distributed lock service called *Chubby* [17], which consists of five active replicas, one of which is elected to be the *master* and actively serves requests. The service is live when a majority of the replicas are running and can communicate with each other. Bigtable uses Chubby for a variety of tasks such as (1) ensuring that there is at most one active master at any time, (2) storing the bootstrap location of Bigtable data, (3) storing Bigtable schema information and to the access control lists. The main limitation of this design is that if Chubby becomes unavailable for an extended period of time, the whole Bigtable becomes unavailable. At the runtime, each Bigtable is allocated to one master server and many tablet servers, which can be dynamically added (or removed) from a cluster based on the changes in workloads. The master server is responsible for assigning tablets to tablet servers, balancing tablet-server load, and garbage collection of files in GFS. In addition, it handles schema changes such as table and column family creations. Each tablet server manages a set of tablets. The tablet server handles read and write requests to the tablets that it has loaded, and also splits tablets that have grown too large.

9.2.2 YAHOO: PNUTS

The *PNUTS* system (renamed later to Sherpa) is a massive-scale hosted database system that is designed to support Yahoo!s web applications [25,56]. The main focus of the system is on data serving for web applications, rather than complex queries. It relies on a simple relational model where data is organized into tables of records with attributes. In addition to typical data types, *blob* is a main valid data type, which allows arbitrary structures to be stored inside a record, but not necessarily large binary objects like images or audio. The PNUTS system does not enforce constraints such as referential integrity on the underlying data. Therefore, the schema of these tables are flexible where new attributes can be added at any time without halting any query or update activity. In addition, it is not required that each record have values for all attributes.

Figure 9.3 illustrates the system architecture of PNUTS. The system is divided into regions where each region contains a full complement of system components and a complete copy of each table. Regions are typically, but not necessarily, geographically distributed. Therefore, at the physical level, data tables are horizontally partitioned into groups of records called *tablets*. These tablets are scattered across many servers where each server might have hundreds or thousands of tablets. The assignment of tablets to servers is flexible in a way that allows balancing the workloads by moving a few tablets from an overloaded server to an underloaded server.

The query language of PNUTS supports selection and projection from a single table. Operations for updating or deleting existing records must specify the primary key. The system is designed primarily for online serving workloads that consist mostly of queries that read and write single records or small groups of records. Thus, it provides a *multiget* operation that supports retrieving multiple records in parallel by specifying a set of primary keys and an optional predicate. The *router* component (Figure 9.3) is responsible of determining which storage unit needs to be accessed for a given record to be read or written by the client. Therefore, the primary-key space of a table is divided into intervals where each interval corresponds to one tablet. The router stores an interval mapping that defines the boundaries of each tablet and maps each tablet to a storage unit. The query model of PNUTS does not support join operations that are too expensive in such massive scale systems.

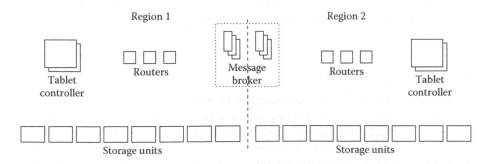

FIGURE 9.3 PNUTS system architecture. (From B. F. Cooper et al., *PVLDB*, 1, 1277–1288, 2008.)

The PNUTS system does not have a traditional database log or archive data. However, it relies on a pub/submechanism that act as a redo log for replaying updates that are lost before being applied to disk due to failure. In particular, PNUTS provides a consistency model that is between the two extremes of general serializability and eventual consistency [63]. The design of this model is derived from the observation that web applications typically manipulate one record at a time while different records may have activity with different geographic locality. Thus, it provides *per-record timeline* consistency where all replicas of a given record apply all updates to the record in the same order. In particular, for each record, one of the replicas (independently) is designated as the master where all updates to that record are forwarded to the master. The master replica for a record is adaptively changed to suit the workload where the replica receiving the majority of write requests for a particular record is selected to be the master for that record. Relying on the per-record timeline consistency model, the PNUTS system supports the following range of API calls with varying levels of consistency guarantees

- *Read-any*: This call has a lower latency as it returns a possibly stale version of the record.
- *Read-critical (required version)*: This call returns a version of the record that is strictly newer than or the same as the *required version*.
- *Read-latest*: This call returns the latest copy of the record that reflects all writes that have succeeded. It is expected that the *read-critical* and *read-latest* can have a higher latency than *read-any* if the local copy is too stale and the system needs to locate a newer version at a remote replica.
- *Write*: This call gives the same ACID guarantees as a transaction with a single write operation in it (e.g., blind writes).
- *Test-and-set-write (required version)*: This call performs the requested write to the record if and only if the present version of the record is the same as the required version. This call can be used to implement transactions that first read a record, and then do a write to the record based on the read, e.g., incrementing the value of a counter.

Since the system is designed to scale to cover several worldwide replicas, automated failover, and load balancing is the only way to manage the operations load. Therefore, for any failed server, the system automatically recovers by copying data from a replica to other live servers.

9.2.3 AMAZON: DYNAMO

Amazon runs a worldwide e-commerce platform that serves tens of millions customers at peak times using tens of thousands of servers located in many data centers around the world. In this environment, there are strict operational requirements on Amazon's platform in terms of performance, reliability, and efficiency, and to support Amazon's continuous growth the platform needs to be highly scalable. Reliability is one of the most important requirements because even the slightest outage has significant financial consequences and impacts customer trust.

The Dynamo system [30] is a highly available and scalable distributed key/value-based datastore built for supporting *internal* Amazon's applications. Dynamo is used to manage the state of services that have very high reliability requirements and need tight control over the tradeoffs among availability, consistency, cost-effectiveness, and performance. There are many services on Amazons platform that only need primary-key access to a data store. The common pattern of using a relational database would lead to inefficiencies and limit the ability to scale and provide high availability. Thus, Dynamo provides a simple primary-key-only interface to meet the requirements of these applications. The query model of the Dynamo system relies on simple read and write operations to a data item that is uniquely identified by a key. State is stored as binary objects (blobs) identified by unique keys. No operations span multiple data items.

Dynamo's partitioning scheme relies on a variant of consistent hashing mechanisms [39] to distribute the load across multiple storage hosts. In this mechanism, the output range of a hash function is treated as a fixed circular space or ring (i.e., the largest hash value wraps around to the smallest hash value). Each node in the system is assigned a random value within this space, which represents its position on the ring. Each data item identified by a key is assigned to a node by hashing the data item's key to yield its position on the ring, and then walking the ring clockwise to find the first node with a position larger than the item's position. Thus, each node becomes responsible for the region in the ring between it and its predecessor node on the ring. The principle advantage of consistent hashing is that departure or arrival of a node only affects its immediate neighbors and other nodes remain unaffected.

In the Dynamo system, each data item is replicated at N hosts where N is a parameter configured per-instance. Each key k is assigned to a coordinator node. The coordinator is in charge of the replication of the data items that fall within its range. In addition to locally storing each key within its range, the coordinator replicates these keys at the $(N - 1)$ clockwise successor nodes in the ring. This results in a system where each node is responsible for the region of the ring between it and its Nth predecessor. As illustrated in Figure 9.4, node B replicates the key k at nodes C and D

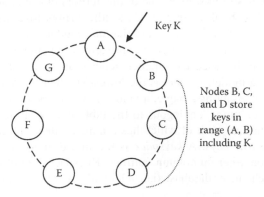

FIGURE 9.4 Partitioning and replication of keys in the Dynamo ring. (From G. DeCandia et al., Dynamo: Amazon's highly available key-value store, in *SOSP*, pp. 205–220, 2007.)

in addition to storing it locally. Node *D* will store the keys that fall in the ranges (*A*, *B*), (*B*, *C*), and (*C*, *D*). The list of nodes that is responsible for storing a particular key is called the preference list. The system is designed so that every node in the system can determine which nodes should be in this list for any particular key.

9.3 NoSQL OPEN SOURCE PROJECTS

In practice, most NoSQL data management systems that are introduced by the key players (e.g., Bigtable, Dynamo, PNUTS) are meant for their internal use only and are thus, not available for public users. Therefore, many open-source projects have been built to implement the concepts of these systems and make it available for public users [18,54]. Due to the ease in which they can be downloaded and installed, these systems have attracted a lot of interest from the research community. There are not many details that have been published about the implementation of most of these systems. In general, the NoSQL open-source projects can be broadly classified into the following categories:

- *Key-value stores*: These systems use the simplest data model, which is a collection of objects where each object has a unique key and a set of attribute/value pairs.
- *Document stores*: These systems have the data models that consists of objects with a variable number of attributes with a possibility of having nested objects.
- *Extensible record stores*: They provide variable-width tables (Column Families) that can be partitioned vertically and horizontally across multiple nodes.

Here, we give a brief introduction about some of these projects. For the full list, we refer the reader to the NoSQL database website.*

Cassandra† is presented as a highly scalable, eventually consistent, distributed, structured key-value store [44,45]. It was open-sourced by Facebook in 2008. It is designed by Avinash Lakshman (one of the authors of Amazon's Dynamo) and Prashant Malik (Facebook engineer). Cassandra brings together the distributed systems technologies from Dynamo and the data model from Google's Bigtable. Like Dynamo, Cassandra is eventually consistent. Like Bigtable, Cassandra provides a column family-based data model richer than typical key/value systems. In Cassandra's data model, *column* is the lowest/smallest increment of data. It is a tuple (triplet) that contains a name, a value, and a timestamp. A *column family* is a container for columns, analogous to the table in a relational system. It contains multiple columns, each of which has a name, value, and a timestamp, and are referenced by row keys. A *keyspace* is the first dimension of the Cassandra hash, and is the container for column families. Keyspaces are of roughly the same granularity as a schema or database (i.e., a logical collection of tables) in RDBMS.

---

* http://NoSQL-database.org/.
† http://cassandra.apache.org/.

They can be seen as a namespace for ColumnFamilies and is typically allocated as one per application. *SuperColumns* represent columns that themselves have subcolumns (e.g., Maps). Like Dynamo, Cassandra provides a tunable consistency model that allows the ability to choose the consistency level that is suitable for a specific application. For example, it allows to choose how many acknowledgments are required to be received from different replicas before considering a *WRITE* operation to be successful. Similarly, the application can choose how many successful responses need to be received in the case of *READ* before returning the result to the client. In particular, every *write* operation can choose one of the following consistency levels:

a. *ZERO*: It ensures nothing. The write operation will be executed asynchronously in the system background.
b. *ANY*: It ensures that the write operation has been executed in at least one node.
c. *ONE*: It ensures that the write operation has been committed to at least 1 replica before responding to the client.
d. *QUORUM*: It ensures that the write has been executed on ($N/2 + 1$) replicas before responding to the client where N is the total number of system replicas.
e. *ALL*: It ensures that the write operation has been committed to all N replicas before responding to the client.

On the other hand, every *read* operation can choose one of the following available consistency levels:

a. *ONE*: It will return the record of the first responding replica.
b. *QUORUM*: It will query all replicas and return the record with the most recent timestamp once it has at least a majority of replicas ($N/2 + 1$) reported.
c. *ALL*: It will query all replicas and return the record with the most recent timestamp once all replicas have replied.

Therefore, any unresponsive replicas will fail the read operation. For read operations, in the *ONE* and *QUORUM* consistency levels, a consistency check is always done with the remaining replicas in the system background to fix any consistency issues.

HBase* is another project is based on the ideas of Bigtable system. It uses the Hadoop distributed filesystem (HDFS)† as its data storage engine. The advantage of this approach is that HBase does not need to worry about data replication, data consistency, and resiliency because HDFS already considers and deals with them. However, the downside is that it becomes constrained by the characteristics of HDFS, which is that it is not optimized for random read access. In the HBase architecture, data is stored in a farm of Region Servers. A *key-to-server* mapping is used to locate

---

* http://hbase.apache.org/.
† http://hadoop.apache.org/hdfs/.

the corresponding server. The in-memory data storage is implemented using a distributed memory object caching system called *Memcache*,* while the on-disk data storage is implemented as a HDFS file residing in the Hadoop data node server.

The HyperTable[†] project is designed to achieve a high performance, scalable, distributed storage, and processing system for structured and unstructured data. It is designed to manage the storage and processing of information on a large cluster of commodity servers, providing resilience to machine and component failures. Like HBase, Hypertable also runs over HDFS to leverage the automatic data replication, and fault tolerance that it provides. In HyperTable, data is represented in the system as a multidimensional table of information. The HyperTable systems provides a low-level API and Hypertable Query Language (HQL) that provides the ability to create, modify, and query the underlying tables. The data in a table can be transformed and organized at high speed by performing computations in parallel, pushing them to where the data is physically stored.

CouchDB[‡] is a document-oriented database that is written in Erlang and can be queried and indexed in a MapReduce fashion using JavaScript. In CouchDB, documents are the primary unit of data. A CouchDB document is an object that consists of named fields. Field values may be strings, numbers, dates, or even ordered lists and associative maps. Hence, a CouchDB database is a flat collection of documents where each document is identified by a unique ID. CouchDB provides a RESTful HTTP API for reading and updating (add, edit, delete) database documents. The CouchDB document update model is lockless and optimistic. Document edits are made by client applications. If another client was editing the same document at the same time, the client gets an edit conflict error on save. To resolve the update conflict, the latest document version can be opened, the edits reapplied, and the update retried again. Document updates are all or nothing, either succeeding entirely or failing completely. The database never contains partially saved or edited documents.

MongoDB[§] is another example of distributed schema-free document-oriented database, which is created at *10gen*.[¶] It is implemented in C++ but provides drivers for a number of programming languages including C, C++, Erlang. Haskell, Java, JavaScript, Perl, PHP, Python, Ruby, and Scala. It also provides a JavaScript command-line interface. MongoDB stores documents as *BSON* (Binary JSON), which are binary encoded JSON like objects. BSON supports nested object structures with embedded objects and arrays. At the heart of MongoDB is the concept of a *document* that is represented as an ordered set of keys with associated values. A *collection* is a group of documents. If a document is the MongoDB analog of a row in a relational database, then a collection can be thought of as the analog to a table. Collections are schema-free. This means that the documents within a single collection can have any number of different shapes. MongoDB groups collections into *databases*. A single instance of MongoDB can host several databases, each of which can be thought of as completely independent. It provides eventual consistency

---

* http://memcached.org/.
† http://hypertable.org/.
‡ http://couchdb.apache.org/.
§ http://www.mongodb.org/.
¶ http://www.10gen.com/.

guarantees in a way that a process could read an old version of a document even if another process has already performed an update operation on it. In addition, it provides no transaction management so that if a process reads a document and writes a modified version back to the database, there is a possibility that another process may write a new version of the same document between the read and the write operation of the first process. MongoDB supports indexing the documents on multiple fields. In addition, it provides a very rich API interface that supports different batch operations and aggregate functions.

Many other variant projects have followed the NoSQL movement and support different types of data stores such as key-value stores (e.g., Voldemort,* Dynomite†), document stores (e.g., Riak‡), and graph stores (e.g., Neo4j,§ DEX¶).

9.4 DATABASE-AS-A-SERVICE

Multitenancy, a technique which is pioneered by *salesforce.com*,** is an optimization mechanism for hosted services in which multiple customers are consolidated onto the same operational system and thus the economy of scale principles help to effectively drive down the cost of computing infrastructure. In particular, multitenancy allows pooling of resources that improves utilization by eliminating the need to provision each tenant for their maximum load. Therefore, multitenancy is an attractive mechanism for both of the service providers who are able to serve more customers with a smaller set of machines, and also to customers of these services who do not need to pay the price of renting the full capacity of a server. Database-as-a-service (DaaS) is a new paradigm for data management in which a third–party service provider hosts a database as a service [3,37]. The service provides data management for its customers and thus alleviates the need for the service user to purchase expensive hardware and software, deal with software upgrades, and hire professionals for administrative and maintenance tasks. Since using an external database service promises reliable data storage at a low cost, it represents a very attractive solution for companies especially that of startups. In this section, we give an overview of the state-of-the-art of different options of DaaS from the key players Google, Amazon, and Microsoft.

9.4.1 GOOGLE DATASTORE

Google has released the Google AppEngine datastore,†† which provides a scalable schemaless object data storage for web application. It performs queries over data objects, known as *entities*. An entity has one or more *properties* where one property can be a reference to another entity. Datastore entities are schemaless where two entities of the same kind are not obligated to have the same properties, or use the same value types

---

* http://project-voldemort.com/.
† http://wiki.github.com/cliffmoon/dynomite/dynomite-framework.
‡ http://wiki.basho.com/display/RIAK/Riak.
§ http://neo4j.org/.
¶ http://www.dama.upc.edu/technology-transfer/dex.
** http://www.salesforce.com/.
†† http://code.google.com/appengine/docs/python/datastore/.

```
SELECT [* | __key__ ] FROM <kind>
[WHERE <condition> [AND <condition> ...]]
[ORDERBY <property> [ASC | DESC] [, <property> [ASC | DESC] ...]]
[LIMIT [<offset>,] <count>]
[OFFSET <offset>]

<condition> : = <property> {< | <= | > | >= | = | != } <value>
<condition> : = <property> IN <list>
<condition> : = ANCESTOR IS <entity or key>
```

FIGURE 9.5   Basic GQL syntax.

for the same properties. Each entity also has a key that uniquely identifies the entity. The simplest key has a kind and a unique numeric ID provided by the datastore. An application can fetch an entity from the datastore using its key or by performing a query that matches the entity's properties. A query can return zero or more entities and can return the results sorted by property values. A query does not allow the number of results returned by the datastore to be very large to conserve memory and run time.

With the AppEngine datastore, every attempt to create, update, or delete an entity happens in a transaction. A transaction ensures that every change made to the entity is saved to the datastore. However, in the case of failure, none of the changes are made. This ensures consistency of data within an entity. The datastore uses optimistic concurrency to manage transactions. The datastore replicates all data to multiple storage locations, so if one storage location fails, the datastore can switch to another and still access the data. To ensure that the view of the data stays consistent as it is being updated, an application uses one location as its primary location and changes to the data on the primary are replicated to the other locations in parallel. An application switches to an alternate location only for large failures. For small failures in primary storage, such as a single machine becoming unavailable temporarily, the datastore waits for primary storage to become available again to complete an interrupted operation. This is necessary to give the application a reasonably consistent view of the data, since alternate locations may not yet have all of the changes made to the primary. In general, an application can choose between two read policies: (1) a read policy of *strong consistency*, which always reads from the primary storage location, and (2) a policy of *eventual consistency* [63], which will read from an alternate location when the primary location is unavailable.

The AppEngine datastore provides a Python* interface, which includes a rich data modeling API and a SQL-like query language called *GQL*.[†] Figure 9.5 depicts the basic syntax of GQL. A GQL query returns zero or more entities or keys of the requested kind. In principle, a GQL query cannot perform a SQL-like "join" query. Every GQL query always begins with either *SELECT* * *FROM* or *SELECT (key) FROM* followed by the name of the kind. The optional *WHERE* clause filters the result set to those entities that meet one or more conditions. Each condition compares a property of the entity with a value using a comparison operator. GQL does

---

* http://www.python.org/.
† http://code.google.com/appengine/docs/python/datastore/gqlreference.html.

not have an *OR* operator. However, it does have an IN operator that provides a limited form of *OR*. The optional *ORDER BY* clause indicates that results should be returned are sorted by the given properties in either ascending (ASC) or descending (DESC) order. An optional *LIMIT* clause causes the query to stop returning results after the first count entities. The *LIMIT* can also include an offset to skip the specified number of results to find the first result to be returned. An optional *OFFSET* clause can specify an offset if the no *LIMIT* clause is present. Chohan et al. [23] have presented *AppScale* as an open-source extension to the Google AppEngine that facilitates distributed execution of its applications over virtualized cluster resources, including Infrastructure-as-a-Service (IaaS) cloud systems such as Amazon EC2 and Eucalyptus.* They have used AppScale to empirically evaluate and compare how well different NoSQL systems (e.g., Cassandra, HBase, Hypertable, MemcacheDB, MongoDB, Voldemort) map to the GAE Datastore API [16].

Google Cloud SQL† is another Google service that provide the capabilities and functionality of MySQL database servers, which are hosted in Google's cloud. Although there is tight integration of the services with the *Google App Engine*, it allows the software applications to easily move their data in and out of Google's cloud without any obstacles.

9.4.2 AMAZON: S3/SIMPLEDB/AMAZON RDS

Amazon Simple Storage Service (S3) is an online public storage web service offered by Amazon Web Services. Conceptually, S3 is an infinite store for objects of variable sizes. An object is simply a byte container, which is identified by a URI. Clients can read and update S3 objects remotely using a simple web services (SOAP or REST-based) interface. For example, *get(uri)* returns an object and *put(uri, bytestream)* writes a new version of the object. In principle, S3 can be considered as an online backup solution or for archiving large objects, which are not frequently updated.

Amazon has not published details on the implementation of S3. However, Brantner et al. [14] have presented initial efforts of building web-based database applications on top of S3. They described various protocols for storing, reading, and updating objects and indexes using S3. For example, the *record manager* component is designed to manage records where each record is composed of a key and payload data. Both key and payload are bytestreams of arbitrary length where the only constraint is that the size of the whole record must be smaller than the page size. Physically, each record is stored in exactly one page, which in turn is stored as a single object in S3. Logically, each record is part of a *collection* (e.g., a table). The record manager provides functions to create new objects, read objects, update objects, and scan collections. The *page manager* component implements a buffer pool for S3 pages. It supports reading pages from S3, pinning the pages in the buffer pool, updating the pages in the buffer pool, and marking the pages as updated. All these functionalities are implemented in a straightforward way just as in any standard database system. Furthermore, the page manager implements the commit

---

* http://www.eucalyptus.com/.
† https://developers.google.com/cloud-sql/.

and abort methods where it is assumed that the write set of a transaction (i.e., the set of updated and newly created pages) fits into the clients main memory or secondary storage (flash or disk). If an application commits, all the updates are propagated to S3 and all the affected pages are marked as unmodified in the clients buffer pool. Moreover, they implemented standard B-tree indexes on top of the page manager and basic redo log records. On the other hand, there are many database-specific issues that have not yet been addressed by this work. For example, DB-style strict consistency and transactions mechanisms are not provided. Furthermore, query processing techniques (e.g., join algorithms and query optimization techniques) and traditional database functionalities such as bulkload a database, create indexes, and drop a whole collection, still need to be devised.

SimpleDB is another Amazon service that is designed for providing structured data storage in the cloud and backed by clusters of Amazon-managed database servers. It is a highly available and flexible nonrelational data store that offloads the work of database administration. Storing data in SimpleDB does not require any predefined schema information. Developers simply store and query data items via web services requests and Amazon SimpleDB does the rest. There is no rule that forces every data item (data record) to have the same fields. However, the lack of schema also means that there are no data types, as all data values are treated as variable length character data. Hence, the drawbacks of a schema-less data storage also include the lack of automatic integrity checking in the database (no foreign keys) and an increased burden on the application to handle formatting and type conversions. Following the AWS' pay-as-you-go pricing philosophy, SimpleDB has a pricing structure that includes charges for data storage, data transfer, and processor usage. There are no base fees and there are no minimums. Similar to most AWS services, SimpleDB provides a simple API interface, which follows the rules and the principles for both of REST and SOAP protocols where the user sends a message with a request to carry out a specific operation. The SimpleDB server completes the operations, unless there is an error, and responds with a success code and response data. The response data is an HTTP response packet, which has headers, storing metadata, and some payload, which is in XML format.

The top level abstract element of data storage in SimpleDB is the *domain*. A domain is roughly analogous to a database table where the user can create and delete domains as needed. There are no design or configuration options to create a domain. The only parameter you can set is the domain name. All the data stored in a SimpleDB domain takes the form of key-value attribute pairs. Each attribute pair is associated with an item that plays the role of a table row. The attribute name is similar to a database column name. However different items (rows) can contain different attribute names, which give you the freedom to store different attributes in some items without changing the layout of other items that do not have the same attributes. This flexibility allows the painless addition of new data fields in the most common situations of schema changing or schema evolution. In addition, it is possible for each attribute to have not just one value (multivalued attributes) but an array of values. In this case, all the user needs to do is add another attribute to an item and use the same attribute name but with a different value. Each value is automatically indexed as it is added. However, there are no explicit indexes to maintain. Therefore, the user has no index maintenance work of any kind to do. On the other side, the user does not have any direct control over the created indices. SimpleDB provides a small group of API calls that enables the core functionality for building client applications such as *CreateDomain*, *DeleteDomain*, *PutAttributes*, *DeleteAttributes*, and *GetAttributes*. The SimpleDB API also provides a query language that is similar to the SQL *Select* statement. Hence, this query language makes SimpleDB Selects very familiar to the typical database user that ensures a gentle learning curve. However, it should be noted that the language supports issuing queries only over the scope of a single domain (no joins, multidomain, or subselect queries).

SimpleDB is implemented with complex replication and failover mechanisms behind the scenes. Therefore, it can provide a high availability guarantee with the stored data replicated to different locations automatically. Hence, a user does not need to make any extra effort or become an expert on high availability or the details of replication techniques to achieve the high availability goal. SimpleDB supports two options for each user read request: eventual consistency or strong consistency. In general, using the option of a consistent read eliminates the consistency window for the request. The results of a consistent read are guaranteed to return the most up-to-date values. In most cases, a consistent read is no slower than an eventually consistent read. However, it is possible for consistent read requests to show higher latency and lower bandwidth on some occasions (e.g., high workloads). SimpleDB does not offer any guarantees about the eventual consistency window but it is frequently less than one second. There are quite a few limitations that a user needs to consider while using the simpleDB service such as the maximum storage size per domain is 10 GB, the maximum attribute values per domain is 1 billion, the maximum attribute values per item is 256, the maximum length of item name, attribute name, or value is 1024 bytes, the maximum query execution time is 5 seconds, the max query result is 2500, and the maximum query response size is 1 MB.

Amazon Relational Database Service (RDS) is another Amazon service that gives access to the full capabilities of the familiar MySQL, Oracle, and SQL Server relational database systems. Hence, the code, applications, and tools that are already designed on existing databases of these system can work seamlessly with Amazon RDS. Once the database instance is running, Amazon RDS can automate common administrative tasks, such as performing backups or patching the database software. Amazon RDS can also provide data replication synchronization and automatic failover management services.

9.4.3 MICROSOFT SQL AZURE

Microsoft has recently released the Microsoft SQL Azure Database system,* which has been announced as a cloud-based relational database service that has been built on Microsoft SQL Server technologies [12]. It provides a highly available, scalable, multi-tenant database service hosted by Microsoft in the cloud. So, applications can create, access, and manipulate tables, views, indexes, referential constraints, roles, stored procedures, triggers, and functions. It can execute complex queries, joins

---

* http://www.microsoft.com/windowsazure/sqlazure/.

across multiple tables, and supports aggregation and full-text queries. It also supports Transact-SQL (T-SQL), native ODBC, and ADO.NET data access.* In particular, the SQL Azure service can be seen as running an instance of SQL server in a cloud hosted server, which is automatically managed by Microsoft instead of running on-premise managed server.

In SQL Azure, a logical database is called a *table group*, which can be keyless or keyed. A keyless table group is an ordinary SQL server database where there are no restrictions on the choices of keys for the tables. On the other hand, if a table group is keyed, then all of its tables must have a common column called the *partitioning key*, which does not need not to be a unique key for each relation. A *row group* is a set of all rows in a table group that have the same partition key value. SQL Azure requires that each transaction executes on one table group. If the table group is keyed, then the transaction can read and write rows of only one row group. Based on these principles, there are two options for building transaction application that can scale out using SQL Azure. The first option is to store the data in multiple groups where each table group can fit comfortably on a single machine. In this scenario, the application takes the responsibility for scaling out by partitioning the data into separate table groups. The second option is to design the database as keyed table group so that the SQL Azure can perform the scale out process automatically.

In SQL Azure, the *consistency unit* of an object is the set of data that can be read and written by an ACID transaction. Therefore, the consistency unit of a keyed table group is the row group while the consistency unit of a keyless table group is the whole table group. Each replica of a consistency unit is always fully contained in a single instance of SQL server running one machine. Hence, using the two-phase commit protocol is never required. A query can execute on multiple partitions of a keyed table group with an isolation level of read-committed. Thus, data that the query read from different partitions may reflect the execution of different transactions. Transactionally consistent reads beyond a consistency unit are not supported.

At the physical level, a keyed table group is split into partitions based on ranges of its partitioning key. The ranges must cover all values of the partitioning key and must not overlap. This ensures that each row group resides in exactly one partition and hence that each row of a table has a well-defined home partition. Partitions are replicated for high availability. Therefore, a partition is considered to be the failover unit. Each replica is stored on one server. Each row group is wholly contained in one replica of each partition that is scattered across servers such that no two copies reside in the same *failure domain*. The transaction commitment protocol requires that only a quorum of the replicas be up. A Paxos-like consensus algorithm is used to maintain a set of replicas to deal with replica failures and recoveries. Dynamic quorums are used to improve availability in the face of multiple failures. In particular, for each partition, at each point in time one replica is designated to be the primary. A transaction executes using the primary replica of the partition that contains its row group and thus is nondistributed. The primary replica processes all queries, updates, and data definition language operations. The primary replica is also

---

* http://msdn.microsoft.com/en-us/library/h43ks021(VS.71).aspx.

responsible for shipping the updates and data definition language operations to the secondary replicas.

Since some partitions may experience higher load than others, the simple technique of balancing the number of primary and secondary partitions per node might not balance the loads. The system can rebalance dynamically using the failover mechanism to tell a secondary on a lightly loaded server to become the primary, by either demoting the former primary to secondary, or moving the former primary to another server. A keyed table group can be partitioned dynamically. If a partition exceeds the maximum allowable partition size (either in bytes or the amount of operational load it receives), it is split into two partitions. In general, the size of each hosted SQL Azure database cannot exceed the limit of 50 GB.

9.5 WEB SCALE DATA MANAGEMENT: TRADEOFFS

An important issue in designing large-scale data management applications is to avoid the mistake of trying to be *"everything for everyone."* As with many types of computer systems, no one system can be best for all workloads and different systems make different tradeoffs to optimize for different applications. Therefore, the most challenging aspects in these application is to identify the most important features of the target application domain and to decide about the various design tradeoffs, which immediately lead to performance tradeoffs. To tackle this problem, Jim Gray came up with the heuristic rule of *"20 queries"* [38]. The main idea of this heuristic is that on each project, we need to identify the 20 most important questions the user wanted the data system to answer. He argued that five questions are not enough to see a broader pattern, and a hundred questions would result in a shortage of focus.

In general, it is hard to maintain ACID guarantees in the face of data replication over large geographic distances. The CAP theorem [15,34] shows that a shared-data system can only choose at most two out of three properties: *Consistency* (all records are the same in all replicas), *Availability* (a replica failure does not prevent the system from continuing to operate), and *tolerance to Partitions* (the system still functions when distributed replicas cannot talk to each other). When data is replicated over a wide area, this essentially leaves just consistency and availability for a system to choose between. Thus, the C (consistency) part of ACID is typically compromised to yield reasonable system availability [2]. Therefore, most of the cloud data management overcomes the difficulties of distributed replication by relaxing the ACID guarantees of the system. In particular, they implement various forms of weaker consistency models (e.g., eventual consistency, timeline consistency, session consistency [60]) so that all replicas do not have to agree on the same value of a data item at every moment of time. Hence, NoSQL systems can be classified based on their support of the properties of the CAP theorem into three categories:

- *CA systems*: Consistent and highly available, but not partition-tolerant
- *CP systems*: Consistent and partition-tolerant, but not highly available
- *AP systems*: Highly available and partition-tolerant, but not consistent

In principle, choosing the adequate NoSQL system (from the very wide available spectrum of choices) with design decisions that best fit with the requirements of a software application is not a trivial task and requires careful consideration. Table 9.1 provides an overview of different design decision for sample NoSQL systems.

In practice, transactional data management applications (e.g., banking, stock trading, supply chain management) that rely on the ACID guarantees that databases provide, tend to be fairly write-intensive or require microsecond precision and are less obvious candidates for the cloud environment until the cost and latency of wide-area data transfer decreases. Cooper et al. [26] discussed the tradeoffs facing cloud data management systems as follows:

- *Read performance vs. write performance*: Log-structured systems that only store update deltas can be very inefficient for reads if the data is modified over time. On the other hand, writing the complete record to the log on each update avoids the cost of reconstruction at read time but there is a correspondingly higher cost on update. Unless all data fits in memory, random I/O to the disk is needed to serve reads (e.g., as opposed to scans). However, for write operations, much higher throughput can be achieved by appending all updates to a sequential disk-based log.
- *Latency vs. durability*: Writes may be synched to disk before the system returns success to the user or they may be stored in memory at write time and synched later. The advantages of the latter approach are that avoiding disk access greatly improves write latency, and potentially improves

TABLE 9.1
Design Decisions of Various Web-Scale Data Management Systems

System	Data Model	Query Interface	Consistency	CAP Options	License
Bigtable	Column Families	Low-Level API	Strict	CP	Internal at Google
Google AppEng	Column Families	Python API-GQL	Strict	CP	Commercial
PNUTS	Key-Value Store	Low-Level API	Multiple	AP	Internal at Yahoo
Dynamo	Key-Value Store	Low-Level API	Eventual	AP	Internal at Amazon
S3	Large Objects Store	Low-Level API	Eventual	AP	Commercial
SimpleDB	Key-Value Store	Low-Level API	Multiple	AP	Commercial
RDS	Relational Store	SQL	Strict	CA	Commercial
SQL Azure	Relational Store	SQL	Strict	CA	Commercial
Cassandra	Column Families	Low-Level API	Tunable	AP	Open source—Apache
Hypertable	Multidimensional Table	Low-Level API, HQL	Eventual	AP	Open source—GNU
CouchDB	Document-Oriented Store	Low-Level API	Eventual	AP	Open source—Apache

throughput The disadvantage is the greater risk of data loss if a server crashes and loses unsynched updates.

- *Synchronous vs. asynchronous replication*: Synchronous replication ensures all copies are up-to-date but potentially incurs high latency on updates. Furthermore, availability may be impacted if synchronously replicated updates cannot complete while some replicas are offline. Asynchronous replication avoids high write latency but allows replicas to be stale. Furthermore, data loss may occur if an update is lost due to failure before it can be replicated.
- *Data partitioning*: Systems may be strictly row-based or allow for column storage. Row-based storage supports efficient access to an entire record and is ideal if we typically access a few records in their entirety. Column-based storage is more efficient for accessing a subset of the columns, particularly when multiple records are accessed.

Florescu and Kossmann [32] argued that in a cloud environment, the main metric that needs to be optimized is the cost as measured in dollars. Therefore, the big challenge of data management applications is no longer on how fast a database workload can be executed or whether a particular throughput can be achieved; instead, the challenge is how many machines are necessary to meet the performance requirements of a particular workload. This argument fits well with a rule-of-thumb calculation that has been proposed by Jim Gray regarding the opportunity costs of distributed computing on the Internet as opposed to local computations [35]. Gray reasons that except for highly processing-intensive applications outsourcing computing tasks into a distributed environment does not pay off because network traffic fees outnumber savings in processing power. In principle, calculating the tradeoff between basic computing services can be useful to get a general idea of the economies involved. This method can easily be applied to the pricing schemes of cloud computing providers (e.g., Amazon, Google). Florescu and Kossmann [32] have also argued in the new large-scale web applications, the requirement to provide 100% read and write availability for all users has over-shadowed the importance of the ACID paradigm as the gold standard for data consistency. In these applications, no user is ever allowed to be blocked. Hence, consistency has turned to be an optimization goal in modern data management systems to minimize the cost of resolving inconsistencies and not a constraint as in traditional database systems. Therefore, it is better to design a system that it deals with resolving inconsistencies rather than having a system that prevents inconsistencies under all circumstances.

Kossmann et al. [41] conducted an end-to-end experimental evaluation for the performance and cost of running enterprise web applications with OLTP workloads on alternative cloud services (e.g., RDS, SimpleDB, S3, Google AppEngine, Azure). The results of the experiments showed that the alternative services varied greatly both in cost and performance. Most services had significant scalability issues. They confirmed the observation that public clouds lack of support for uploading large data volumes. It was difficult for them to upload 1 TB or more of raw data through the APIs provided by the providers. With regard to cost, they concluded that Google seems to be more interested in small applications with light workloads whereas Azure is currently the most affordable service for medium to large services.

With the goal of facilitating performance comparisons of the tradeoffs cloud data management systems, the Yahoo! Cloud Serving Benchmarks, YCSB* [26] and YCSB++[52], have been presented as frameworks and core set of benchmarks for NoSQL systems. The benchmarking tools have been made available via open-source to allow extensible development of additional cloud benchmark suites that represent different classes of applications and to facilitate the evaluation of different cloud data management systems.

9.6 CHALLENGES OF THE NEW WAVE OF NoSQL SYSTEMS

In this section, we shed the lights on a set of novel research challenges, that have been introduced by the new wave of NoSQL systems that need to be addressed to ensure that the vision of designing and implementing successful scalable data management solutions can be achieved.

9.6.1 TRUE ELASTICITY

A common characteristic of internet-scale applications and services is that they can be used by large numbers of end users and highly variable load spikes in the demand for services that can occur depending on the day and the time of year and the popularity of the application. In addition, the workload characteristic could vary significantly from one application type to another where possible fluctuations on the workload characteristics that could be of several orders of magnitude on the same business day may also occur [13]. In principle, elasticity and horizontal scalability are considered to be of the most important features that are provided by NoSQL systems [59]. In practice, both of the commercial NoSQL offerings (e.g., Amazon SimpleDB) and commercial DaaS offerings (e.g., Amazon RDS, Microsoft SQL Azure) do not provide their users with any flexibility to dynamically increase or decrease the allocated computing resources of their applications. While NoSQL offerings claim to provide elastic services of their tenants, they do not provide any guarantee that their provider-side elasticity management will provide scalable performance with increasing workloads [10]. Moreover, commercial DaaS pricing models require their users to predetermine the computing capacity that will be allocated to their database instance as they provide standard packages of computing resources (e.g., *Micro, Small, Large*, and *Extra Large* DB Instances). In practice, predicting the workload behavior (e.g., arrival pattern, I/O behavior, service time distribution) and consequently accurate planning of the computing resource requirements with consideration of their monetary costs are very challenging tasks. Therefore, the user might still tend to overprovide the allocated computing resources for the database tier of their application to ensure satisfactory performance for their workloads. As a

---

result of this, the software application is unable to fully utilize the elastic feature of the cloud environment.

Xiong et al. [66] have presented a provider-centric approach for intelligently managing the computing resources in a shared multi-tenant database system at the virtual machine level. The proposed approach consists of two main components:

1. The system modeling module that uses machine learning techniques to learn a model that describes the potential profit margins for each tenant under different resource allocations. The learned model considers many factors of the environment such as SLA cost, client workload, infrastructure cost, and action cost.
2. The resource allocation decision module dynamically adjusts the resource allocations, based on the information of the learned model, of the different tenants to achieve the optimum profits.

Tatemura et al. [61] proposed a declarative approach for achieving elastic OLTP workloads. The approach is based on defining the following two main components:

1. The transaction classes required for the application.
2. The actual workload with references to the transaction classes.

Using this information, a formal model can be defined to analyze elasticity of the workload with transaction classes specified. In general, we believe that there is a lack of flexible and powerful consumer-centric elasticity mechanisms that enable software application to have more control on allocating the computing resources for the database tier of their applications over the application running time and make the best use of the elasticity feature of the cloud computing environments. More attention from the research community is required to address these issues in future work.

9.6.2 Data Replication and Consistency Management

In general, stateless services are easy to scale since any new *replicas* of these services can operate completely independently of other instances. In contrast, scaling stateful services, such as a *database system*, needs to guarantee a consistent view of the system for users of the service. However, the cost of maintaining several database replicas that are always strongly consistent is very high. As we have previously described, according to the *CAP* theorem, most of the NoSQL systems overcome the difficulties of distributed replication by relaxing the consistency guarantees of the system and supporting various forms of weaker consistency models (e.g., eventual consistency [63]). In practice, a common feature of the *NoSQL* and *DaaS* cloud offerings is the creation and management of multiple replicas (usually 3) of the stored data while a replication architecture is running behind-the-scenes to enable automatic failover management and ensure high availability of the service. In general, replicating for performance differs significantly from replicating for availability or fault tolerance. The distinction between the two situations is mainly reflected by the higher degree of replication, and as a consequence the need for supporting weak consistency when scalability is the motivating factor for replication [19].

Several studies have been presented as an attempt to quantify the consistency guarantees of cloud storage services. Wada et al. [64] presented an approach for measuring time-based staleness by writing timestamps to a key from one client, reading the same key, and computing the difference between the reader's local time and the timestamp read. Bermbach and Tai [11] have tried to address a side of these limitations by extending original the experiments of [64] using a number of readers that are geographically distributed. They measure the consistency window by calculating the difference between the latest read timestamp of version n and the write timestamp of version $n+1$. Their experiments with Amazon S3 showed that the system frequently violates monotonic read consistency. Anderson et al. [4] presented an offline algorithm that analyzes the trace of interactions between the client machines and the underlying key-value store and reports how many violations for consistent reads are there in the trace. This approach is useful for checking the safety of running operations and detecting any violation on the semantics of the executed operations. However, it is not useful for any system that requires online monitoring for their data staleness or consistency grantees. Zellag and Kemme [67] have proposed an approach for real-time detection of consistency anomalies for arbitrary cloud applications accessing various types of cloud datastores in transactional or nontransactional contexts. In particular, the approach builds the dependency graph during the execution of a cloud application and detect cycles in the graph at the application layer and independently of the underlying datastore. Bailis et al. [8] presented an approach that provides expected bounds on staleness by predicting the behavior of eventually consistent quorum-replicated data stores using Monte Carlo simulations and an abstract model of the storage system including details such as the distribution of latencies for network links.

Kraska et al. [42] have argued that finding the right balance among cost, consistency, and availability is not a trivial task. High consistency implies high cost per transaction and, in some situations, reduced availability but avoids penalty costs. Low consistency leads to lower costs per operation but might result in higher penalty costs. Hence, they presented a mechanism that not only allows designers to define the consistency guarantees on the data instead at the transaction level, but also allows them to automatically switch consistency guarantees at runtime. They described a dynamic consistency strategy, called *Consistency Rationing*, to reduce the consistency requirements when possible (i.e., the penalty cost is low) and raise them when it matters (i.e., the penalty costs would be too high). The adaptation is driven by a cost model and different strategies that dictate how the system should behave. In particular, they divide the data items into three categories (A, B, C) and treat each category differently depending on the consistency level provided. The A category represents data items for which we need to ensure strong consistency guarantees as any consistency violation would result in large penalty costs, the C category represents data items that can be treated using session consistency as temporary inconsistency is acceptable, while the B category comprises all the data items where the consistency requirements vary over time depending on the actual availability of an item. Therefore, the data of this category is handled with either strong or session consistency depending on a statistical-based policy for decision making. Keeton et al. [24] have proposed a similar approach in a system called *LazyBase* that allows users to trade off query performance and result freshness. LazyBase breaks up metadata processing into a pipeline of ingestion, transformation, and query stages that can be parallelized to improve performance and efficiency. By breaking up the processing, LazyBase can independently determine how to schedule each stage for a given set of metadata, thus providing more flexibility than existing monolithic solutions. LazyBase uses models of transformation and query performance to determine how to schedule transformation operations to meet users' freshness and performance goals and to utilize resources efficiently.

In general, the simplicity of key-value stores comes at a price when higher levels of consistency are required. In these cases, application programmers need to spend extra time and exert extra effort to handle the requirements of their applications with no guarantee that all corner cases are handled, which consequently might result in an error-prone application. In practice, data replication across different data centers is expensive. Inter-datacenter communication is prone to variation in round-trip times (RTTs) and loss of packets. For example, RTTs are in the order of hundreds of milliseconds. Such large RTTs cause the communication overhead that dominates the commit latencies observed by users. Therefore, systems often sacrifice strong consistency guarantees to maintain acceptable response times. Hence, many solutions rely on asynchronous replication mechanism and weaker consistency guarantees. Some systems have been recently proposed to tackle these challenges. For example, *Google Megastore* [9] has been presented as a scalable and highly available datastore that is designed to meet the storage requirements of large-scale interactive Internet services. It relies on the *Paxos* protocol [20], a proven optimal fault-tolerant consensus algorithm with no requirement for a distinguished master, for achieving synchronous wide area replication. Megastore's replication mechanism provides a single, consistent view of the data stored in its underlying database replicas. Megastore replication semantics is done on *entity group* basis, a priori grouping of data for fast operations, basis by synchronously replicating the group's transaction log to a quorum of replicas. In particular, it uses a write-ahead log replication mechanism over a group of symmetric peers where any node can initiate reads and writes. Each log append blocks on acknowledgments from a majority of replicas and replicas in the minority catch up as they are able. Kraska et al. [43] have proposed the *MDCC* (*M*ulti-*D*ata *C*enter *C*onsistency) commit protocol for providing strongly consistent guarantees at a cost that is comparable to eventually consistent protocols. In particular, in contrast to transactional consistency two-phase commit protocol (2PC), MDCC is designed to commit transactions in a single round-trip across data centers in the normal operational case. It also does not require a master node so that apply reads or updates from any node in any data center by ensuring that every commit has been received by a quorum of replicas. It does not also impose any database partitioning requirements. The MDCC commit protocol can be combined with different read guarantees where the default configuration is to guarantee read committed consistency without any lost updates. In principle, we believe that the problem of data replication and consistency management across different data centers in the cloud environment has, thus far, not attracted sufficient attention from the research community, and it represents a rich direction of future research and investigation. Nawab et al. [49] presented *Message Futures*, a distributed multi-datacenter transaction management system that provides strong consistency guarantees while maintaining low commit latency. It achieves an average commit latency of around one RTT. In this approach, a transaction is committed when a commit condition on mutual information is met. The commit condition is designed to be true, at any point in time, for any single object in at least one datacenter. The protocol utilizes a replicated log (RLog) [65] to continuously share transactions and state information among datacenters, which allows a datacenter to commit transactions without initiating a new wide-area message exchange with other datacenters and improves the protocol's resilience to node and communication failures.

The *COPS* system (Clusters of Order-Preserving Servers) [48] has been designed to provide geo-replicated and distributed data stores that support complex online applications, such as social networks, which must provide an *always on* facility where operations always complete with low latency. In particular, it provides causal+ consistency where it executes all *put* and *get* operations in the local datacenter in a linearizable fashion, and it then replicates data across datacenters in a causal+ consistent order in the background. COPS achieves the causal+ consistency by tracking and explicitly checking that causal dependencies are satisfied before exposing writes in each cluster.

9.6.3 SLA MANAGEMENT

An SLA is a contract between a service provider and its customers. *Service level agreements* (SLAs) capture the agreed upon guarantees between a service provider and its customer. They define the characteristics of the provided service including service level objectives (SLOs) (e.g., maximum response times) and define penalties if these objectives are not met by the service provider. In practice, flexible and reliable management of SLA agreements is of paramount importance for both cloud service providers and consumers. For example, Amazon found that every 100 ms of latency costs them 1% in sales and Google found that an extra 500 ms in search page generation time dropped traffic by 20%. In addition, large enterprise web applications (e.g., eBay and Facebook) need to provide high assurances in terms of SLA metrics such as response times and service availability to their users. Without such assurances, service providers of these applications stand to lose their user base, and hence their revenues.

In general, SLA management is a common general problem for the different types of software systems that are hosted in cloud environments for different reasons such as the unpredictable and bursty workloads from various users in addition to the performance variability in the underlying cloud resources [26,55]. In practice, resource management and SLA guarantee falls into two layers: the *cloud service providers* and the *cloud consumers* (users of cloud services). In particular, the cloud service provider is responsible for the efficient utilization of the physical resources and guarantee their availability for their customers (cloud consumers). The cloud consumers are responsible for the efficient utilization of their allocated resources to satisfy the SLA of their customers (application end users) and achieve their business goals. The state-of-the-art cloud databases do not allow the specification of SLA metrics at the application nor at the end-user level. In practice, cloud service providers guarantee only the availability (uptime guarantees), but not the performance, of their services [6,10,31]. In addition, sometimes the granularity of the uptime guarantees is also weak. For example, the uptime guarantees of Amazon EC2 is on a per data center basis where a data center is considered to be unavailable if a customer cannot access any of its instances or cannot launch replacement instances for a contiguous interval of five minutes. In practice, traditional cloud monitoring technologies (e.g., *Amazon CloudWatch*) focus on low-level computing resources (e.g., *CPU speed, CPU utilization, I/O disk speed*). In general, translating the SLO of software application to the thresholds of utilization for low-level computing resources is a very challenging task and is usually done in an ad hoc manner due to the complexity and dynamism inherent in the interaction between the different tiers and components of the system. Furthermore, cloud service providers do not automatically detect SLA violation and leave the burden of providing the violation proof on the customer [10].

In the multi-tenancy environment of DaaS, it is an important goal for DaaS providers to promise high performance to their tenants. However, this goal normally conflicts with another goal of minimizing the overall running servers and thus operating costs by tenant consolidation. In general, increasing the *degree* of multi-tenancy (number of tenants per server) is normally expected to decrease per-tenant-allocated resources and thus performance, but on the other hand, it also reduces the overall operating cost for the DaaS provider and vice versa. Therefore, it is necessary, but challenging for the DaaS providers to balance between the performance that they can deliver to their tenants and the data center's operating costs. Several provider-centric approaches have been proposed to tackle this challenge. Chi et al. [22] have proposed a cost-aware query scheduling algorithm, called *iCBS*, that takes the query costs derived from the SLAs between the service provider and its customers (in terms of response time) into account to make cost-aware scheduling decisions that aims to minimize the total expected cost. *SLA-tree* is another approach that have been proposed to efficiently support profit-oriented decision making of query scheduling. SLA-tree uses the information about the buffered queries that are waiting to be executed in addition to the SLA for each query that indicates the different profits for the query for varying query response times and provides support for the answering of certain profit-oriented *what if* type of questions. Lang et al. [46] presented a framework that takes as input the tenant workloads, their performance SLA, and the server hardware that is available to the DaaS provider, and produces server characterizing models that can be used to provide constraints into an optimization module. By solving this optimization problem, the framework provides a cost-effective hardware provisioning policy and a tenant scheduling policy on each hardware resource. The main limitation of this approach is that the input information of the tenant workloads is not always easy to specify and model accurately. *PIQL* (*Performance Insightful Query Language*) [5] is a declarative language that has been proposed with a SLA compliance prediction model. The PIQL query compiler uses static analysis to select only query plans where it can calculate the number of operations to be performed at every step in their execution. In particular, PIQL extends

SQL to allow developers to provide extra bounding information to the compiler. In contrast to traditional query optimizers, the objective of the query compiler is not to find the fastest plan but to avoid performance degradation. Thus, the compiler choose a potentially slower bounded plan over an unbounded plan that happens to be faster given the current database statistics. If the PIQL compiler cannot create a bounded plan for a query, it warns the developer and suggests possible ways to bound the computation.

In general, adequate SLA monitoring strategies and timely detection of SLA violations represent challenging research issues in the cloud computing environments. Salman [10] has suggested that it may be necessary, in the future, for cloud providers to offer performance-based SLAs for their services with a tiered pricing model, and charge a premium for guaranteed performance. While this could be one of the directions to solve this problem, we believe that it is a very challenging goal to delegate the management of the fine-granular SLA requirements of the consumer applications to the side of the cloud service provider due to the wide heterogeneity in the workload characteristics, details, and granularity of SLA requirements, and cost management objectives of the very large number of consumer applications (tenants) that can be running simultaneously in a cloud environment. Therefore, it becomes a significant issue for the cloud consumers to be able to monitor and adjust the deployment of their systems if they intend to offer viable SLAs to their customers (end users). It is an important requirement for cloud service providers to enable the cloud consumers with a set of facilities, tools and framework that ease their job of achieving this goal effectively.

9.6.4 TRANSACTION SUPPORT

A transaction is a core concept in the data management world that represents a set of operations that are required to be executed *atomically* on a single consistent view of a database [36]. In general, the expertise gained from building distributed database systems by researchers and practitioners have shown that supporting distributed transactions hinder the ability of building scalable and available systems [51]. Therefore, to satisfy the scalability requirements of large-scale internet services, many systems have sacrificed the ability to support distributed transactions. For example, most of the NoSQL systems (e.g., Bigtable, Dynamo, SimpleDB) supports atomic access only at the granularity of single keys. This design choice allows these systems to horizontally partition the tables, without worrying about the need for distributed synchronization and transaction support. While many web applications can live with single key access patterns [21,30], many other applications (e.g., payment, auction services, online gaming, social networks, collaborative editing) would require atomicity guarantee on multikey accesses patterns. In practice, leaving the burden of ensuring transaction support to the application programmer normally leads to increased code complexity, slower application development, and low-performance client-side transaction management. Therefore, one of the main challenges of cloud-hosted database systems that has been considered is to support transactional guarantees for their applications without compromising the scalability property as one of the main advantages of the cloud environments.

The *G-Store* system [29] has been presented as a scalable data store that provides transactional multikey access guarantees over non-overlapping groups of keys using a key-value store. The main idea of GStore is the *Key Group* abstraction that defines a relationship between a group of keys and represents the granule for on-demand transactional access. This abstraction allows the Key Grouping protocol to collocate control for the keys in the group to allow efficient access to the group of keys. In particular, the Key Grouping protocol enables the transfer of ownership for all keys in a group to a single-node that then efficiently executes the operations on the Key Group. At any instance of time, each key can only belong to a single group and the Key Group abstraction does not define a relationship between two groups. Thus, groups are guaranteed to be independent of each other and the transactions on a group guarantee consistency only within the confines of a group. The Key Grouping protocol ensures that the ownership of the members of a group reside with a single node. Thus, the implementation of the transaction manager component does not require any distributed synchronization and is similar to the transaction manager of any single-node relational database management systems. The key difference is that in G-Store, transactions are limited to smaller logical entities (key groups). A similar approach has been followed by the *Google Megastore system* [9]. It implements a transactional record manager on top of the Bigtable data store [21] and provides transaction support across multiple data items where programmers have to manually link data items into hierarchical groups and each transaction can only access a single group. Megastore partitions the data into a collection of *entity groups*, a priori user-defined grouping of data for fast operations, where each group is independently and synchronously replicated over a wide area. In particular, Megastore tables are either entity group root tables or child tables. Each child table must declare a single distinguished foreign key referencing a root table. Thus, each child entity references a particular entity in its root table (called the root entity). An entity group consists of a root entity along with all entities in child tables that reference it. Entities within an entity group are mutated with single-phase ACID transactions (for which the commit record is replicated via Paxos). Operations across entity groups could rely on expensive two-phase commit operations but they could leverage the built-in Megastore's efficient asynchronous messaging to achieve these operations. Google's *Spanner* [27] has been presented as a scalable and globally distributed database that shards data across many sets of Paxos state machines in datacenters that are spread all over the world. Spanner automatically reshards data across machines as the amount of data or the number of servers changes, and it automatically migrates data across machines (even across datacenters) to balance load and in response to failures. It supports general-purpose transactions, and provides a SQL-based query language.

Deuteronomy [47] have presented a radically different approach toward scaling databases and supporting transactions in the cloud by *unbundling* the database into two components: (1) The *transactional component* (TC) that manages transactions and their concurrency control and undo/redo recovery but knows nothing about physical data location. (2) The *data component* (DC) that maintains a data cache and uses access methods to support a record-oriented interface with atomic operations but knows nothing about transactions. Applications submit requests to the TC, which uses a lock manager and a log manager to logically enforce transactional concurrency control and recovery. The TC passes requests to the appropriate data component (DC). The DC, guaranteed by the TC to never receive conflicting concurrent operations, needs to only support atomic record operations, without concern for transaction properties that are already guaranteed by the TC. In this architecture, data can be stored anywhere (e.g., local disk, in the cloud) as the TC functionality in no way depends on where the data is located. The TC and DC can be deployed in a number of ways. Both can be located within the client, and that is helpful in providing fast transactional access to closely held data. The TC could be located with the client while the DC could be in the cloud, which is helpful in case a user would like to use its own subscription at a TC service or wants to perform transactions that involve manipulating data in multiple locations. Both TC and DC can be in the cloud, which is helpful if a cloud data storage provider would like to localize transaction services for some of its data to a TC component. There can be multiple DCs serviced by one TC, where transactions spanning multiple DCs are naturally supported because a TC does not depend on where data items are stored. Also, there can be multiple TCs, yet, a transaction is serviced by one specific TC.

The *Calvin system* [62] has been designed to run alongside a nontransactional storage system with the aim of transforming it into a shared-nothing (near-)linearly scalable database system that provides high availability and full ACID transactions. These transactions can potentially span multiple partitions spread across the shared-nothing cluster. Calvin accomplishes this goal by providing a layer above the storage system that handles the scheduling of distributed transactions, as well as replication and network communication in the system. The key technical feature of Calvin is that it relies on a deterministic locking mechanism that enables the elimination of distributed commit protocols. In particular, the essence of Calvin lies in separating the system into three separate layers of processing:

- *The sequencing layer* intercepts transactional inputs and places them into a global transactional input sequence, which represents the order of transactions to which all replicas will ensure serial equivalence during their execution.
- *The scheduling layer* orchestrates transaction execution using a deterministic locking scheme to guarantee equivalence to the serial order specified by the sequencing layer while allowing transactions to be executed concurrently by a pool of transaction execution threads.
- *The storage layer* handles all physical data layout. Calvin transactions access data using a simple CRUD interface. Therefore, any storage engine supporting a similar interface can be directly plugged into Calvin.

Each node in a Calvin deployment typically runs one partition of each layer. It supports horizontal scalability of the database and unconstrained ACID-compliant distributed transactions by supporting both asynchronous and Paxos-based synchronous replication, both within a single data center and across geographically separated data centers.

9.7 DISCUSSION AND CONCLUSIONS

For more than a quarter of a century, the relational database management systems (RDBMS) have been the dominant model for database management. They provide an extremely attractive interface for managing and accessing data and have proven to be wildly successful in many financial, business, and Internet applications. However, with the new trends of web-scale data management, they started to suffer from some serious limitations [28]:

* *Database systems are difficult to scale.* Most database systems have hard limits beyond which they do not easily scale. Once users reach these scalability limits, time consuming and expensive manual partitioning, data migration, and load balancing are the only recourse.
* *Database systems are difficult to configure and maintain.* Administrative costs can easily account for a significant fraction of the total cost of ownership of a database system. Furthermore, it is extremely difficult for untrained professionals to get good performance out of most commercial systems.
* *Diversification in available systems complicates its selection.* The rise of specialized database systems for specific markets (e.g., main memory systems for OLTP or column stores for OLAP) complicates system selection, especially for customers whose workloads do not neatly fall into one category.
* *Peak provisioning leads to unnecessary costs.* Web-scale workloads are often bursty in nature, and thus, provisioning for the peak often results in excess of resources during off-peak phases, and thus unnecessary costs.

Recently, the new wave of NoSQL systems have started to gain some mindshares as an alternative model for database management. In principle, some of the main advantages of NoSQL systems can be summarized as follows:

* *Elastic scaling*: For years, database administrators have relied on the *scale up* approach rather than the *scale out* approach. However, with the current increase in the transaction rates and high availability requirements, the economic advantages of the scaling out approach on commodity hardware has become very attractive. RDBMS might not scale out easily on commodity clusters but NoSQL systems are initially designed with the ability to expand transparently to take advantage of the addition of any new nodes.
* *Less administration*: Despite the many manageability improvements introduced by RDBMS vendors over the years, high-end RDBMS systems cannot be maintained without the assistance of expensive, highly trained DBAs. DBAs are intimately involved in the design, installation, and ongoing tuning of high-end RDBMS systems. On the contrary, NoSQL databases are generally designed from the ground up to require less management. For example, automatic repair and the simpler data model features should lead to lower administration and tuning requirements.

- *Better economics*: While RDBMS tends to rely on expensive proprietary servers and storage systems, NoSQL databases typically use clusters of cheap commodity servers to manage the exploding data and transaction volumes. Therefore, the cost per gigabyte or transactions per second for NoSQL can be many times less than the cost for RDBMS, which allows a NoSQL setup to store and process more data at a much lower price. Moreover, when an application uses data that is distributed across hundreds or even thousands of servers, simple economics points to the benefit of using no-cost server software as opposed to that of paying per-processor license fees. Once freed from license fees, an application can safely scale horizontally with complete avoidance of the capital expenses.
- *Flexible data models*: Even minor changes to the data model of a large production RDBMS have to be carefully managed and may necessitate downtime or reduced service levels. NoSQL databases have more relaxed (if any) data model restrictions. Therefore, application changes and database schema changes can be changed more softly.

These advantages have given NoSQL systems a lot of attractions. However, there are many obstacles that still need to be overcome before theses systems can appeal to mainstream enterprises such as:*

- *Programming model*: NoSQL databases offer few facilities for ad hoc query and analysis. Even a simple query requires significant programming expertise. Missing the support of declaratively expressing the important join operation has been always considered one of the main limitations of these systems.
- *Transaction support*: Transaction management is one of the powerful features of RDBMS. The current limited support (if any) of the transaction notion from NoSQL database systems is considered as a big obstacle toward their acceptance in implementing mission critical systems.
- *Maturity*: RDBMS systems are well known with their high stability and rich functionalities. In comparison, most NoSQL alternatives are in preproduction versions with many key features either being not stable enough or yet to be implemented. Therefore, enterprises are still approaching this new wave with extreme caution.
- *Support*: Enterprises look for the assurance that if a the system fails, they will be able to get timely and competent support. All RDBMS vendors go to great lengths to provide a high level of enterprise support. In contrast, most NoSQL systems are open-source projects. Although there are few firms offering support for each NoSQL database, these companies often are small start-ups without the global reach, support resources, or credibility of the key market players such as Oracle, Microsoft, or IBM.

---

* http://blogs.techrepublic.com.com/10things/?p=1772.

- *Expertise*: There are millions of developers throughout the world, and in every business segment, who are familiar with RDBMS concepts and programming. In contrast, almost every NoSQL developer is in a learning mode. This situation will be addressed naturally over time. However, currently, it is far easier to find experienced RDBMS programmers or administrators than a NoSQL expert.

Currently, there is a big debate between the NoSQL and RDBMS campuses that is centered on the right choice for implementing online transaction processing systems. RDBMS proponents think that the NoSQL camp has not spent sufficient time to understand the theoretical foundation of the transaction processing model. For example, the eventual consistency model is still not well defined, and different implementations may differ significantly with each other. This means figuring out all these inconsistent behaviors lands on the application developer's responsibilities and makes their life very much harder. On the other side, the NoSQL camp argues that this is actually a benefit because it gives the domain-specific optimization opportunities back to the application developers who are now no longer constrained by a one-size-fits-all model. However, they admit that making such optimization decisions requires a lot of experience and can be very error-prone and dangerous if the decisions are not made by experts.

In principle, we believe that it is not expected that the new wave of NoSQL data management systems will provide a complete replacement of the relational data management systems. Moreover, there will not be a single winner (one-size-fits-all) solution. However, it is more expected that different data management solutions will coexist at the same time for a single application (Figure 9.6). For example, we can imagine an application that uses different datastores for different purposes as follows:

- MySQL for low-volume, high-value data-like user profiles and billing information.
- A key value store (e.g., Hbase) for high-volume, low-value data-like hit counts and logs.

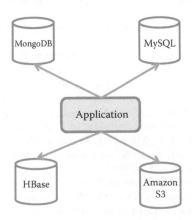

FIGURE 9.6 Coexistence of multiple data management solution in one application.

- Amazon S3 for user-uploaded assets like photos, sound files, and big binary files.
- MongoDB for storing the application documents (e.g., bills).

Finally, we believe that there is still a huge amount of required research and development efforts for improving the current state-of-the-art in tackling the current limitations in both of all campuses: NoSQL database systems, data management service providers, and traditional relational database management systems.

REFERENCES

1. Daniel Abadi. Consistency tradeoffs in modern distributed database system design: CAP is only part of the story. *IEEE Computer*, 45(2), 2012.
2. Daniel J. Abadi. Data Management in the cloud: Limitations and opportunities. *IEEE Data Eng. Bull.*, 32(1):3–12, 2009.
3. Divyakant Agrawal, Amr El Abbadi, Fatih Emekçi, and Ahmed Metwally. Database management as a service: Challenges and opportunities. In *ICDE*, pages 1709–1716, 2009.
4. Eric Anderson, Xiaozhou Li, Mehul A. Shah, Joseph Tucek, and Jay J. Wylie. What consistency does your key-value store actually provide? In *HotDep*, 2010.
5. Michael Armbrust, Kristal Curtis, Tim Kraska, Armando Fox, Michael J. Franklin, and David A. Patterson. PIQL: Success-tolerant query processing in the cloud. *PVLDB*, 5(3):181–192, 2011.
6. Michael Armbrust, Armando Fox, Rean Griffith, Anthony D. Joseph, Randy H. Katz, Andrew Konwinski, Gunho Lee, et al. Above the clouds: A berkeley view of cloud computing, 2009.
7. Peter Bailis, Alan Fekete, Ali Ghodsi, Joseph M. Hellerstein, and Ion Stoica. The Potential Dangers of Causal Consistency and an Explicit Solution. In *SoCC*, 2012.
8. Peter Bailis, Shivaram Venkataraman, Michael J. Franklin, Joseph M. Hellerstein, and Ion Stoica. Probabilistically bounded staleness for practical partial quorums. *PVLDB*, 5(8), 2012.
9. Jason Baker, Chris Bond, James Corbett, J. J. Furman, Andrey Khorlin, James Larson, Jean-Michel Leon, Yawei Li, Alexander Lloyd, and Vadim Yushprakh. Megastore: Providing scalable, highly available storage for interactive services. In *CIDR*, pages 223–234, 2011.
10. Salman Abdul Baset. Cloud SLAs: Present and future. *Operating Systems Review*, 46(2):57–66, 2012.
11. David Bermbach and Stefan Tai. Eventual consistency: How soon is eventual? An evaluation of Amazon S3's consistency behavior. In *Proceedings of the 6th Workshop on Middleware for Service Oriented Computing*, 2011.
12. Philip A. Bernstein, Istvan Cseri, Nishant Dani, Nigel Ellis, Ajay Kalhan, Gopal Kaki-vaya, David B. Lomet, Ramesh Manne, Lev Novik, and Tomas Talius. Adapting Microsoft SQL server for cloud computing. In *ICDE*, pages 1255–1263, 2011.
13. Peter Bodík, Armando Fox, Michael J. Franklin, Michael I. Jordan, and David A. Patterson. Characterizing, modeling, and generating workload spikes for stateful services. In *SoCC*, pages 241–252, 2010.
14. Matthias Brantner, Daniela Florescu, David A. Graf, Donald Kossmann, and Tim Kraska. Building a database on S3. In *SIGMOD Conference*, pages 251–264, 2008.
15. Eric A. Brewer. Towards robust distributed systems (abstract). In *PODC*, page 7, 2000.

16. Chris Bunch, Navraj Chohan, Chandra Krintz, Jovan Chohan, Jonathan Kupferman, Puneet Lakhina, Yiming Li, and Yoshihide Nomura. An evaluation of distributed data-stores using the AppScale Cloud Platform. In *IEEE CLOUD*, pages 305–312, 2010.

17. Michael Burrows. The Chubby Lock service for loosely-coupled distributed systems. In *OSDI*, pages 335–350, 2006.

18. Rick Cattell. Scalable SQL and NoSQL data stores. *SIGMOD Record*, 39(4):12–27, 2010.

19. Emmanuel Cecchet, George Candea, and Anastasia Ailamaki. Middleware-based data-base replication: The gaps between theory and practice. In *SIGMOD Conference*, pages 739–752, 2008.

20. Tushar Deepak Chandra, Robert Griesemer, and Joshua Redstone. Paxos made live: An engineering perspective. In *PODC*, pages 398–407, 2007.

21. Fay Chang, Jeffrey Dean, Sanjay Ghemawat, Wilson C. Hsieh, Deborah A. Wallach, Michael Burrows, Tushar Chandra, Andrew Fikes, and Robert E. Gruber. Bigtable: A distributed storage system for structured data. *ACM Trans. Comput. Syst.*, 26(2), 2008.

22. Yun Chi, Hyun Jin Moon, and Hakan Hacigümüs. iCBS: Incremental Costbased Scheduling under piecewise linear SLAs. *PVLDB*, 4(9):563–574, 2011.

23. Navraj Chohan, Chris Bunch, Sydney Pang, Chandra Krintz, Nagy Mostafa, Sunil Soman, and Richard Wolski. AppScale: Scalable and Open AppEngine Application Development and Deployment. In *CloudComp*, pages 57–70, 2009.

24. James Cipar, Gregory R. Ganger, Kimberly Keeton, Charles B. Morrey, Craig A. N. Soules, and Alistair C. Veitch. LazyBase: Trading freshness for performance in a scalable database. In *EuroSys*, pages 169–182, 2012.

25. Brian F. Cooper, Raghu Ramakrishnan, Utkarsh Srivastava, Adam Silberstein, Philip Bohannon, Hans-Arno Jacobsen, Nick Puz, Daniel Weaver, and Ramana Yerneni. PNUTS: Yahoo!'s hosted data serving platform. *PVLDB*, 1(2):1277–1288, 2008.

26. Brian F. Cooper, Adam Silberstein, Erwin Tam, Raghu Ramakrishnan, and Russell Sears. Benchmarking cloud serving systems with YCSB. In *ACM SoCC*, pages 143–154, 2010.

27. James C. Corbett, Jeffrey Dean, Michael Epstein, Andrew Fikes, Christopher Frost, JJ Furman, Sanjay Ghemawat, et al. Spanner: Google's globally-distributed database. In *OSDI*, 2012.

28. Carlo Curino, Evan Jones, Yang Zhang, Eugene Wu, and Sam Madde. Relational cloud: The case for a database service. In *CIDR*, 2011.

29. Sudipto Das, Divyakant Agrawal, and Amr El Abbadi. G-Store: A scalable data store for transactional multi key access in the cloud. In *SoCC*, pages 163–174, 2010.

30. Giuseppe DeCandia, Deniz Hastorun, Madan Jampani, Gunavardhan Kakulapati, Avinash Lakshman, Alex Pilchin, Swaminathan Sivasubramanian, Peter Vosshall, and Werner Vogels. Dynamo: Amazon's highly available key-value store. In *SOSP*, pages 205–220, 2007.

31. Dave Durkee. Why cloud computing will never be free. *Commun. ACM*, 53(5), 2010.

32. Daniela Florescu and Donald Kossmann. Rethinking cost and performance of database systems. *SIGMOD Record*, 38(1):43–48, 2009.

33. Sanjay Ghemawat, Howard Gobioff, and Shun-Tak Leung. The Google file system. In *SOSP*, pages 29–43, 2003.

34. Seth Gilbert and Nancy A. Lynch. Brewer's conjecture and the feasibility of consistent, available, partition-tolerant web services. *SIGACT News*, 33(2):51–59, 2002.

35. Jim Gray. Distributed computing economics. Microsoft Research Technical Report MSRTR-2003-24, Microsoft Research, 2003.

36. Jim Gray and Andreas Reuter. *Transaction Processing: Concepts and Techniques*. The Morgan Kaufmann Series in Data Management Systems, 1992.

37. Hakan Hacigümüs, Sharad Mehrotra, and Balakrishna R. Iyer. Providing database as a service. In *ICDE*, 2002.

38. Tony Hey, Stewart Tansley, and Kristin Tolle, editors. *The fourth paradigm: Data-intensive scientific discovery*. Microsoft Research, 2009.

39. David R. Karger, Eric Lehman, Frank Thomson Leighton, Rina Panigrahy, Matthew S. Levine, and Daniel Lewin. Consistent hashing and random trees: Distributed caching protocols for relieving hot spots on the World Wide Web. In *STOC*, pages 654–663, 1997.

40. Bettina Kemme, Ricardo Jiménez-Peris, and Marta Patiño-Martínez. *Database Replication*. Synthesis Lectures on Data Management. Morgan & Claypool Publishers, 2010.

41. Donald Kossmann, Tim Kraska, and Simon Loesing. An evaluation of alternative architectures for transaction processing in the cloud. In *SIGMOD Conference*, pages 579–590, 2010.

42. Tim Kraska, Martin Hentschel, Gustavo Alonso, and Donald Kossmann. Consistency Rationing in the cloud: Pay only when it matters. *PVLDB*, 2(1):253–264, 2009.

43. Tim Kraska, Gene Pang, Michael J. Franklin, and Samuel Madden. MDCC: Multi-data center consistency. *CoRR*, abs/1203.6049, 2012.

44. Avinash Lakshman and Prashant Malik. Cassandra: Structured storage system on a p2p network. In *PODC*, page 5, 2009.

45. Avinash Lakshman and Prashant Malik. Cassandra: A decentralized structured storage system. *Operating Systems Review*, 44(2):35–40, 2010.

46. Willis Lang, Srinath Shankar, Jignesh M. Patel, and Ajay Kalhan. Towards multi-tenant performance SLOs. In *ICDE*, pages 702–713, 2012.

47. Justin J. Levandoski, David B. Lomet, Mohamed F. Mokbel, and Kevin Zhao. Deuteronomy: Transaction support for cloud data. In *CIDR*, pages 123–133, 2011.

48. Wyatt Lloyd, Michael J. Freedman, Michael Kaminsky, and David G. Andersen. Don't settle for eventual: Scalable causal consistency for wide-area storage with COPS. In *SOSP*, 2011.

49. Faisal Nawab, Divyakant Agrawal, and Amr El Abbadi. Message futures: Fast commitment of transactions in multi-datacenter environments. In *CIDR*, 2013.

50. M. Tamer Özsu and Patrick Valduriez. *Principles of distributed database systems, second edition*. Prentice-Hall, 1999.

51. M. Tamer Ozsu and Patrick Valduriez. *Principles of Distributed Database Systems*. Springer, 3rd edition, 2011.

52. Swapnil Patil, Milo Polte, Kai Ren, Wittawat Tantisiriroj, Lin Xiao, Julio López, Garth Gibson, Adam Fuchs, and Billie Rinaldi. YCSB++: Benchmarking and performance debugging advanced features in scalable table stores. In *SOCC*, 2011.

53. Dan Pritchett. BASE: An Acid Alternative. *ACM Queue*, 6(3):48–55, 2008.

54. Sherif Sakr, Anna Liu, Daniel M. Batista, and Mohammad Alomari. A survey of large scale data management approaches in cloud environments. *IEEE Communications Surveys and Tutorials*, 13(3):311–336, 2011.

55. Jörg Schad, Jens Dittrich, and Jorge-Arnulfo Quiané-Ruiz. Runtime measurements in the cloud: Observing, analyzing, and reducing variance. *PVLDB*, 3(1), 2010.

56. Adam Silberstein, Jianjun Chen, David Lomax, B. McMillan, M. Mortazavi, P. P. S. Narayan, Raghu Ramakrishnan, and Russell Sears. PNUTS in flight: Web-scale data serving at Yahoo. *IEEE Internet Computing*, 16(1):13–23, 2012.

57. Yair Sovran, Russell Power, Marcos K. Aguilera, and Jinyang Li. Transactional storage for geo-replicated systems. In *SOSP*, 2011.

58. Michael Stonebraker. One size fits all: An idea whose time has come and gone. *Commun. ACM*, 51(12):76, 2008.

59. Basem Suleiman, Sherif Sakr, Ross Jeffrey, and Anna Liu. On understanding the economics and elasticity challenges of deploying business applications on public cloud infrastructure. *Internet Services and Applications*, 3(2):173–193, 2012.

60. Andrew S. Tanenbaum and Maarten van Steen, editors. *Distributed systems: Principles and paradigms*. Prentice Hall, 2002.

61. Jun'ichi Tatemura, Oliver Po, and Hakan Hacigümüs. Microsharding: A declarative approach to support elastic OLTP workloads. *Operating Systems Review*, 46(1):4–11, 2012.

62. Alexander Thomson, Thaddeus Diamond, Shu-Chun Weng, Kun Ren, Philip Shao, and Daniel J. Abadi. Calvin: Fast distributed transactions for partitioned database systems. In *SIGMOD Conference*, pages 1–12, 2012.

63. Werner Vogels. Eventually consistent. *Commun. ACM*, 52(1):40–44, 2009.

64. Hiroshi Wada, Alan Fekete, Liang Zhao, Kevin Lee, and Anna Liu. Data consistency properties and the trade-offs in commercial cloud storage: The consumers' perspective. In *CIDR*, 2011.

65. Gene T. J. Wuu and Arthur J. Bernstein. Efficient Solutions to the Replicated Log and Dictionary Problems. *Operating Systems Review*, 20(1):57–66, 1986.

66. PengCheng Xiong, Yun Chi, Shenghuo Zhu, Hyun Jin Moon, Calton Pu, and Hakan Hacigümüs. Intelligent management of virtualized resources for database systems in cloud environment. In *ICDE*, pages 87–98, 2011.

67. Kamal Zellag and Bettina Kemme. How consistent is your cloud application? In *SoCC*, 2012.

10 Consistency Management in Cloud Storage Systems

Houssem-Eddine Chihoub, Shadi Ibrahim,
Gabriel Antoniu, and Maria S. Perez

CONTENTS

10.1 INTRODUCTION

Cloud computing has recently emerged as a popular paradigm for harnessing a large number of commodity machines. In this paradigm, users acquire computational and storage resources based on a pricing scheme similar to the economic exchanges in the utility market place: users can lease the resources they need in a *pay-as-you-go* manner [1]. For example, the *Amazon Simple Storage Service* (S3) is using a pricing scheme based on data size/transfer per Gigabyte (e.g., $0.095 per GB for the first terabyte and $0.020 per GB inter-region transfer [2]) and the *Amazon Elastic Compute Cloud* (EC2) service is using a pricing scheme based on virtual machine (VM) hours (e.g., $0.065 per small instance hour [3]).

Meanwhile, we have entered the era of Big Data, where the size of data generated by digital media, social networks, and scientific instruments is increasing at an extreme rate. With data growing rapidly and applications becoming more data-intensive, many organizations have moved their data to the cloud, aiming to provide cost-efficient, scalable, reliable, and highly available services (Animoto*, a start-up for video generating and sharing, had successfully used Amazon Web Services to cope with the huge increase of users from 5000 a day to 250,000 a day without investing any money in building new servers [4], and since then they have shifted their service completely to Amazon). Cloud providers allow service providers to deploy and customize their environment in multiple physically separate datacenters to meet the ever-growing user needs. Services therefore can replicate their state across geographically diverse sites and direct users to the closest or least loaded site. Replication has become an essential feature in storage systems and is extensively leveraged in cloud environments [5–7]. It is the main reason behind several features such as fast accesses, enhanced performance, and high availability.

- For **fast access**, user requests can be directed to the closest datacenter to avoid communications' delays and thus insure fast response time and low latency.

---

* http://www.animoto.com.

- For **enhanced performance**, user requests can be redirected to other replicas within the same datacenter (but different racks) to avoid overloading one single copy of the data and thus improve the performance under heavy load.
- For **high availability**, failure and network partitions are common in large-scale distributed systems; by replicating, we can avoid single points of failure.

A particularly challenging issue that arises in the context of storage systems with geographically distributed data replication is how to ensure a consistent state of all the replicas. Insuring strong consistency by means of synchronous replication introduces an important performance overhead due to the high latencies of networks across datacenters (the average round trip latency in *Amazon* sites varies from 0.3 ms in the same site to 380 ms in different sites [8]). Consequently, several weaker consistency models have been implemented (e.g., casual consistency, eventual consistency, timeline consistency). Such relaxed consistency models allow the system to return some stale data at some points in time.

Many cloud storage services opt for weaker consistency models to achieve better availability and performance (i.e., such consistency models allow cloud storage systems to replicate their data and scale out their infrastructure on multiple geographically distributed datacenters—to cope with the ever-growing size of Big Data and the increasing number of users (worldwide) – while simultaneously aid in retaining performance requirements of users, and availability guarantees of data). For example, Facebook uses the eventually consistent storage system Cassandra to scale up to host data for more than 800 million active users [9]. This comes at the cost of a high probability of stale data being read (i.e., the replicas involved in the reads may not always have the most recent write). As shown in [10], under heavy reads and writes some of these systems may return up to 66.61% stale reads, although this may be tolerable for users in the case of social network. With the ever-growing diversity in the access patterns of cloud applications along with the unpredictable diurnal/monthly changes in services loads and the variation in network latency (intra- and inter-sites), static and traditional consistency solutions are not adequate for the cloud. With this in mind, several adaptive consistency solutions, among which, our automated and self-adaptive approach (i.e., Harmony [11]) has been introduced to adaptively tune the consistency level at run-time to improve the performance/availability of cloud storage systems while simultaneously maintaining a low fraction of stale reads. Harmony, to be application-adaptive, takes into account the application needs expressed by the stale reads rate that can be tolerated. At run-time, Harmony collects relevant information about the storage system (i.e., the network latency, which directly affects updates propagation to replicas) and the application demands (i.e., the frequency of access patterns during reads, writes, and updates) to estimate the stale reads rate and make a decision accordingly (i.e., change the number of replicas involved in the read operation).

In summary, it is useful to take a step back, consider the variety of consistency solutions offered by different cloud storage systems, and describe them in an unified way, putting the different uses and types of consistency in perspective; this is the main purpose of this book chapter. The rest of this chapter is organized as follows: in Section 10.2, we briefly introduce the *CAP* theorem and its implications in cloud systems. Then, we present the different types of consistency in Section 10.3. After that, we briefly introduce the four main cloud storage systems used by big cloud vendors in Section 10.4. To complete our survey, we present different adaptive consistency approaches in Section 10.5 and detail our approach Harmony in Section 10.6. A conclusion is provided in Section 10.7.

10.2 THE *CAP* THEOREM AND BEYOND

10.2.1 THE *CAP* THEOREM

In his keynote speech [12], Brewer introduced what is known as the *CAP* theorem. This theorem states that at most only two out of the three following properties can be achieved simultaneously within a distributed system: Consistency, Availability, and Partition Tolerance. The theorem was later proven by Gilbert and Lynch [13]. The three properties are important for most distributed applications such as web applications. However, within the *CAP* theorem, one property needs to be forfeited, thus introducing several tradeoffs. To better understand these tradeoffs, we will first highlight the three properties and their importance in distributed systems.

10.2.1.1 Consistency

The consistency property guarantees that an operation or a transaction is performed atomically and leaves the systems in a consistent state, or fails instead. This is equivalent to the atomicity and consistency properties (*AC*) of the *ACID* (atomicity, consistency, isolation, and Durability) semantics in relational database management systems (*RDBMs*), where a common way to guarantee a strong level of consistency is applying one-copy serializability.

10.2.1.2 Availability

In their *CAP* theorem proof [13], the authors define a distributed storage system as continuously available if every request received by a nonfailing node must result in a response. On the other hand, when introducing the original *CAP* theorem, *Brewer* qualified a system to be available if *almost* all requests receive a response.

10.2.1.3 Partition Tolerance

In a system that is partition tolerant, the network is allowed to loose messages between nodes from different components (datacenters for instance). When a network partition appears, the network communication between two components (racks, datacenters, etc.) is off and all the messages are lost. Since replicas may be spread over different partitions in such a case, this property has a direct impact on both consistency and availability.

The implications of the *CAP* theorem introduced challenging and fundamental tradeoffs for distributed systems and service designers. Systems that are designed to be deployed on single entities, such as an RDBM, aim to provide both availability and consistency properties since partitions are not an issue. However, for distributed systems that rely on networking, such as georeplicated systems, partition tolerance is a must for a big majority of them. This in turn introduces, among other tradeoffs derived from the *CAP* theorem, the *Consistency vs. Availability* as a major tradeoff. As shown in Figure 10.1, user requests can be served from different replicas in

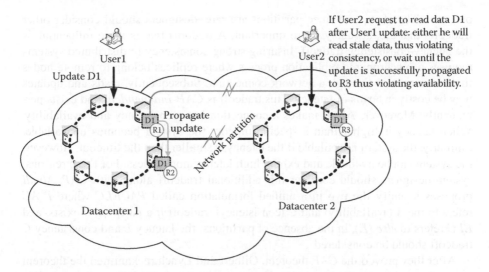

If User2 request to read data D1 after User1 update: either he will read stale data, thus violating consistency, or wait until the update is successfully propagated to R3 thus violating availability.

FIGURE 10.1   Consistency vs. availability in geo-replicated systems.

the system. If partitions occur, an update on one replica cannot be propagated to other replicas on different partitions. Therefore, these replicas could be made either *available* to the clients, thus violating consistency, or otherwise, made *unavailable* until they converge to a *consistent* state, which can happen after recovering from the network partition.

10.2.2   BEYOND THE *CAP* THEOREM

The proposal of the *CAP* theorem a few years ago had a huge impact on the design of distributed systems and services. Moreover, the ever-growing volume of data along with the huge expansion of distributed systems scales makes the implications of the *CAP* theorem of even higher importance. Twelve years after the introduction of his *CAP* theorem, *Brewer* still ponders its implications [14]. He estimates that the theorem achieved its purpose in the past in the way it brought the community's attention to the related design challenges. On the other hand, he judges some interpretations of the implications as misleading, in particular, the two out of three tradeoff properties. The general belief is that the partition tolerance property *P* is insurmountable for wide-area systems. This often leads designers to completely forfeit consistency *C* or availability *A* for each other. Given that partitions are rare. *Brewer* states that the modern goal of the *CAP* theorem should be to maximize combinations of *C* and *A*. In addition, system designers should develop mechanisms that detect the start of partitions, enter an explicit partition mode with potential limitations of some operations, and finally initiate partition recovery when communication is restored.

Abadi [15] states as well that the *CAP* theorem was misunderstood. *CAP* trade-offs should be considered under network failures. In particular, the consistency–availability tradeoff in *CAP* is for when partitions appear. The theorem property *P* implies that a system is partition-tolerant and more importantly, is enduring a partition. Therefore, and since partitions are rare, designers should consider other tradeoffs that are, arguably, more important. A tradeoff that is more influential, is the latency-consistency tradeoff. Insuring strong consistency in distributed systems requires a synchronized replication process where replicas belong to remote nodes that communicate through a network connection. Subsequently, reads and updates may be costly in terms of latency. This tradeoff is *CAP-Independent* and exists permanently. Moreover, Abadi makes a connection between latency and availability. When latency is higher than a specific timeout the system becomes unavailable. Similarly, the system is available if the latency is smaller than the timeout. However, the system can be available and exhibit high latency nonetheless. For these reasons, system designers should consider this additional tradeoff along with *CAP*. *Abadi* proposes to unify the two in a unified formulation called *PACELC* where *P AC* refers to the *A* (availability) and *C* (consistency) tradeoff *if* a partition *P* exists, and *ELC* refers to *else* (*E*), in the absence of partitions, the latency *L* and consistency *C* tradeoff should be considered.

After they proved the *CAP* theorem, Gilbert and Lynch reexamined the theorem properties and its implications [16]. The tradeoff within *CAP* is another example of the more general tradeoff between *safety* and *liveness* in unreliable systems. Consistency can be seen as a *safety* property for which every response to client requests is correct. In contrast, availability is a *liveness* property that implies that every client request would eventually receive a response. Hence, viewing *CAP* in the broader context of safety–liveness tradeoffs provides insight into the feasible design space for distributed systems [16]. Therefore, they reformulate the *CAP* theorem as follows: "CAP states that any protocol implementing an atomic read/write register cannot guarantee both safety and liveness in a system prone to partitions." As a result, the practical implications dictate that designers opt for best-effort availability, thus guaranteeing consistency, and best-effort consistency for systems that must guarantee availability. A pragmatic way to handle the tradeoff is by balancing the consistency–availability tradeoff in an adaptive manner. We will further explore this idea in Section 10.5.

10.3   CONSISTENCY MODELS

In this section, we present multiple consistency models. For every model, we show its specified guarantees to provide consistency at the system side. Eventually, and considering the strength level of these guarantees, we discuss the potential solutions to manage updates conflict situations. The consistency models are then summarized in Table 10.1.

10.3.1   STRONG CONSISTENCY

In traditional distributed storage and database systems, the instinctive and correct way to handle replicas consistency was to insure a strong consistency state of all replicas in the system at all time. For example, the RDBMs were based on ACID semantics. These semantics are well defined and insure a strong consistency behavior of the RDBM based on the atomicity and consistency properties. Similarly, the

TABLE 10.1
Consistency Models

Consistency Model		Guarantees
Strong consistency	Serializability	Serial order of concurrent executions of a set of serialization units (set of operations).
	Linearizability	Global total order of operations (single operations), every operation is perceived instantaneously.
Weak consistency	Read-your-writes	A process always sees its last update with read operations.
	Session consistency	Read-your-writes consistency is guaranteed only within a session.
	Monotonic reads	Successive reads must always return the same or more recent value than a previous read.
	Monotonic writes	A write operation must always complete before any successive writes.
Causal consistency		Total ordering between operations that have causal relation.
Eventual consistency		In the absence of updates, all replicas will gradually and eventually become consistent.
Timeline consistency		All replicas perform operations on one record in the same "correct order."

POSIX standard for file systems implies that data replicated in the system should always be consistent. Strong consistency guarantees that all replicas are in a consistent state immediately after an update, before it returns a success. In a perfect world, such semantics and a strong consistency model are the properties that every storage system should adopt. However, insuring strong consistency requires mechanisms that are very costly in terms of performance and availability and limit the system scalability. This was not an issue in the early years of distributed storage systems as the scale and the performance needed at the time were not as important. However, in the era of Big Data and cloud computing, this consistency model can be penalizing, in particular if such a strong consistency is actually not required by the applications.

10.3.1.1 System-Side Guarantees

Several models and correctness conditions to insure strong data consistency have been proposed over the years. Two of the most common models are *serializability* [17] and *linearizability* [18].

10.3.1.1.1 Serializability

The execution of a set of concurrent actions on a set of objects is serializable if it is equivalent to a serial execution. Every action is considered as a serialization unit and consists of one or more operations. Each operation may be performed concurrently with other operations from different serialization units. Serialization units are equivalent to transactions in RDBMs and a single file system call in the case of file systems.

A concurrent execution on a set of replicated objects is *one-copy equivalent* if it is equal to an execution on the same set of objects without replication. As a result, the execution of concurrent actions is said to be one-copy serializable if it is serializable and one-copy equivalent. Moreover, a one-copy serializable execution is considered global one-copy serializable if the partial orderings of serialization units, which are perceived by each process, are preserved.

10.3.1.1.2 Linearizability

The linearizability or the atomicity of a set of operations on a shared data object is considered as a correctness condition for concurrent shared data objects [18]. Linearizibility is achieved if every operation performed by a concurrent process appears instantaneously to the other concurrent processes at some moment between its invocation and response. Linearizability can be viewed as a special case of global one-copy serializability where a serialization unit (a transaction) is restricted to consist of a single operation [18]. Subsequently, linearizability provides locality property. A system is linearizable if every individual object is linearizable [18]. This enhances concurrency and modularity. Moreover, linearizability is a nonblocking property in the sense that processes invoking totally defined operations are never forced to wait [18].

Given these models strength, no further guarantees are required at the client side. All situations that lead to updates conflict or inconsistency are efficiently handled at the system-side (with eventually performance overhead).

10.3.2 WEAK CONSISTENCY

The implementation of strong consistency models imposes, in many cases, limitations in both system's design choices and application's performance. Moreover, insuring strong global total ordering has a heavy performance overhead. As to overcome these limitations, Dubois et al. [19] first introduced the weak ordering model that relax the strong ordering guarantees for enhanced performance.

10.3.2.1 System-Side Guarantees

Data accesses (read and write operations) are considered as weakly ordered if they satisfy the following three conditions:

- All accesses to a shared synchronization variables are strongly (sequentially) ordered. All processes perceive the same order of operations.
- Data accesses to a synchronization variable are not issued by processors before all previous global accesses have been globally performed.
- A global data access is not allowed by processors until a previous access to synchronization variable is globally performed.

From these three conditions, the order of read and write operations, outside critical sections (synchronization variables), can be seen in different orders by different processes as long as they do not violate the aforementioned conditions. However, in [20,21], it has been argued that not all the three conditions are necessary to reach the intuitive goals of weak ordering. Numerous variation models have been proposed since. Bisiani et al. [22] proposed an implementation of weak consistency on distributed memory systems. Timestamps are used to achieve a weak ordering of the operations. A synchronization operation is completed only after all previous operations in the systems reach a completion state. Various weaker consistency models derived from the weak ordering. The following client-side models are weak consistency models, but provide further guarantees to the client.

10.3.2.2 Client-Side Guarantees

10.3.2.2.1 Read-Your-Writes

This model guarantees that a process that commits an update will always be able to see its updated value with the read operation and not an older one. This might be an important consistency property to provide with weakly ordered systems for a large class of applications. As will be seen further in this section, this is a special case of causal consistency.

10.3.2.2.2 Session Consistency

Read-your-writes consistency is guaranteed in the context of a *session* (which is a sequence of accesses to data, usually with an explicit beginning and ending). As long as the users access data during the same session, they are guaranteed to access their latest updates. However, the read-your-writes property is not guaranteed to be spanned over different sessions.

10.3.2.2.3 Monotonic Reads

A process should never read a data item value older than what it has read before. This consistency guarantees that a process's successive read returns always the same value or a more recent one than the previous read.

10.3.2.2.4 Monotonic Writes

This property guarantees the serialization of the writes by one process. A write operation on a data object or item must be completed before any successive writes by the same process. Systems that do not guarantee this property are notoriously hard to program [23].

10.3.3 EVENTUAL CONSISTENCY

In a replicated storage system, the consistency level defines the behavior of divergence of replicas of logical objects in the presence of updates [24]. Eventual consistency [23–25], is the weakest consistency level that guarantees convergence. In the absence of updates, data in all replicas will gradually and *eventually* become consistent.

10.3.3.1 System-Side Guarantees

Eventual consistency ensures the convergence of all replicas in systems that implement lazy, update-anywhere, or optimistic replication strategies [26]. For such systems, updates can be performed on any replica hosted on different nodes. The update propagation is done in a lazy fashion. Moreover, this update propagation process may encounter even more delays considering cases where network latency is of a high order such as for georeplication. Eventual consistency is ensured through mechanisms that will guarantee the propagation process will successfully terminate at a future (maybe unknown) time. Furthermore, Vogels [23] judges that, if no failures occur, the size of the inconsistency window can be determined based on factors such as communication delays, the load on the system, and the number of replicas in the system.

Eventual consistency by the mean of lazy asynchronous replication may allow better performance and faster accesses to data. Every client can read data from local replicas located in a geographically close datacenter. However, if an update is performed on one of the replicas and is yet to be propagated to others because of the asynchronous replication mechanism, a client reading from a distant replica may read stale data.

10.3.3.2 Updates Conflict Handling

Eventual consistency is most suitable for a given class of applications. Therefore, its updates conflict management may present serious problems for other types of applications. In [25], two examples that illustrate the typical use case and show the potential gains with this consistency model were presented. The worldwide domain name system (DNS) is a perfect example of a system for which eventual consistency is the best fit. The DNS namespace is partitioned into domains where each domain is assigned to a naming authority. This is an entity that will be responsible for this domain and is the only one that can update it. This scheme eliminates the update–update conflict. Therefore, only the read–update conflict needs to be handled. As updates are less frequent, to maintain system availability and fast accesses for users read operations, lazy replication is the best fit solution. Another example is the World Wide Web. In general, each web page is updated by a single authority, the webmaster. This also avoids any update–update conflict. However, to improve performance and lower read access latency, browsers, and web proxies are often configured to keep a fetched page in a local cache for future requests. As a result, a stale out-of-date page may be read. However, many users find this inconsistency acceptable (to a certain degree) [25].

Within many applications, many updates conflicts may not need a strict ordering between them but can be handled based on the application semantics instead. A famous example of this case is the Amazon user *shop cart* application where updates can be easily merged no matter their order of occurrence. In this context, eventually consistent systems provide, generally, mechanisms to handle updates conflicts.

10.3.4 CAUSAL CONSISTENCY

Causal consistency is another model that relax strong consistency ordering as to reduce the performance overhead. It utilizes the causal relation between operations to provide minimum causality guarantees.

10.3.4.1 System-Side Guarantees

Causal consistency is a consistency model where a sequential ordering is always preserved only between operations that have causal relation. Operations that execute concurrently do not share a causality relation. Therefore, causal consistency does not order concurrent operations. In [27,28], two operations, a and b, have a potential causality if one of the two following conditions are met: a and b are executed in a single thread and one operation execution precedes the other in time, or if b reads a value that is written by a. Moreover, a causality relation is transitive. If a and b have a causal relation, b and c have a causal relation as well, then a and c have a causal relation.

10.3.4.2 Updates Conflict Handling

In [28], a model that combines causal consistency and convergent conflict handling is presented and called causal+. Since concurrent operations are not ordered by causal consistency, two writes to the same key or data object would lead to concurrent updates conflict where different data changes are performed at the level of at least two different replicas. The main challenge for such situations is to ensure replicas convergence to the same state. In contrast to eventual consistency, the updates conflict is a direct result of performing updates concurrently. With eventual consistency, however, a conflict may occur with two updates to the same data but not at the same time. The convergent conflict handling aims at handling all the replicas in the same manner using a handler function to ensure that all replicas will be in the same state at a latter time. To reach handling convergence, all conflicting replicas should consent to an agreement. Various conflict handling methods were proposed such as last-writer-wins rule [29], through user intervention, or using versioning mechanisms that allow merging of different versions in one as in Amazon's eventually consistent Dynamo storage system. In this context, it has been shown that implementing causal consistency with last-writer-wins rule to handle updates conflicts at wide scales provides performance comparable to that of eventually consistent systems [30].

10.3.5 Timeline Consistency

The timeline consistency model was proposed specifically for the design of Yahoo! PNUTS [31], the storage system designed for Yahoo! web applications. This consistency model was proposed to overcome the inefficiency of serializability of transactions at massive scales and georeplication. Moreover, it aims to limit the weakness of eventual consistency.

10.3.5.1 System-Side Guarantees

Transaction serializability was avoided as a design choice within Yahoo! PNUTS. This was mainly due to the observation that web applications typically manipulate one record at a time. Therefore, a per-record timeline consistency was introduced. Unlike eventual consistency, where operations order can vary from one replica to another, all replicas of a record perform the operations in the same "correct" order. For instance, if two concurrent updates are performed, all replicas will execute them in the same order and thereby avoid inconsistencies. Nevertheless, data propagation to replicas is done lazily, which makes the convergence of all replicas eventual. This allows clients to read data from local replicas that may be in a stale version. To preserve the order of operations for a given record, one replica is designated dynamically as a master replica for the record that handles all the updates.

This model avoids major problems related to updates conflict, which eventually consistent systems might suffer from, since update operations are all executed at the same order everywhere. Moreover, the model still provides some flexibility to allow read update conflicts and therefore reducing performance overhead caused by synchronization. However, eventual consistency still, conceptually, outperforms timeline consistency.

10.3.6 DISCUSSION

Table 10.1 summarizes the presented consistency models. These models provide different levels of guarantees and are designed for different classes of applications and use cases. Strong models such as linearizability and serializability provide the strongest forms of consistency that eliminates operations conflict situations. However, this comes at the cost of performance overhead due to the application of expensive necessary mechanisms to deliver such guarantees. In this context, the weak consistency models were introduced to relax the strong guarantees for applications that do not require the strongest forms of consistency. As a result, the performance overhead is significantly reduced. To deal with weak guarantees, additional operation ordering requirements can be imposed on the client level as to cope with the consistency needs. In the context of relaxing the strong consistency guarantees, three models have become very popular in recent years. They differ mainly in the way they handle conflicts. Eventual consistency is the weakest consistency model that guarantees the convergence of replicas. In this model, updates conflict resolution is postponed to a future time favoring availability of data. Causal consistency, however, does not allow the violation of causal relations between updates. Therefore, only concurrent simultaneous updates can lead to the conflict situations. As opposed to these two models, timeline consistency orders updates deterministically and does not allow updates conflicts. Data propagation is, however, eventual and thus, read–update conflicts may occur.

10.4 CLOUD STORAGE SYSTEMS

In this section, we describe some state-of-the-art cloud storage systems, which are adopted by the big cloud vendors, such as Amazon Dynamo, Apache Cassandra, Yahoo! PNUTS, and Google Spanner. Every system is presented by introducing its targeted applications and use cases, its data model, its design principles and adopted consistency, and its API. We then give an overview of their real-life applications and use cases in Table 10.2.

10.4.1 AMAZON DYNAMO

Amazon Dynamo [32], is a storage system designed by Amazon engineers to fit the requirements of their web services. Dynamo provides the storage backend for the highly available worldwide Amazon.com e-commerce platform and overcomes the

TABLE 10.2

Cloud Storage Systems

Storage System	Consistency Model	Data Model	Cloud Applications/Services	API
Amazon Dynamo	Eventual consistency	Key/value	Amazon.com e-commerce platform, Few AWS (Amazon Web Services) (e.g., DynamoDB)	Multiple consistency levels
Cassandra	Eventual consistency	Column families	Facebook inbox search, Twitter, Netflix, eBay, SOUNDCLOUD, RackSpace Cloud	Multiple consistency levels
Riak [38]	Eventual consistency	Key/value	Yammer private social network, Clipboard, GitHub, enStratus Cloud	Multiple consistency levels
Voldemort [39]	Eventual consistency	Key/value	LinkedIn, eHarmony, GiltGroup, Nokia	Multiple consistency levels
CouchDB [40]	Eventual consistency	Document-oriented	Ubuntu One cloud, BBC (Dynamic Content Platform), Credit Suisse (Market Place Framework)	RESTful API
MongoDB [41]	Eventual consistency	Document-oriented	SAP AG Software Entreprise, MTV, and Sourceforge	CRUD API
Yahoo PNUTS!	Timeline consistency	Relational-like	Yahoo web applications	Multiple consistency guarantees
Google BigTable [6]	Strong consistency	Column families	Google analytics, Google earth, Google personalized search	NoSQL API
Google Megastore [42]	Strong consistency	Semi-relational	Google applications: Gmail, Picasa, Google Calendar, Android Market, and AppEngine	SQL-like
Google Spanner	Strong consistency	Semi-relational	Google F1	SQL-like
Redis [43]	Strong consistency	Key/value	Instagram, Flickr, The guardian news paper	NoSQL API
Microsoft Azure Storage [44]	Strong consistency	Blob tables	Microsoft internal applications: networking search, serving video, music, and game content, Blob storage cloud service	RESTful API
Apache HBase [45]	Strong consistency	Column families	Facebook messaging system, traditionally used with Hadoop for large set of applications	NoSQL API

inefficiency of RDBMs for this type of applications. Reliability and scaling requirements within this platform services are high. Moreover, availability is very important, as the increase of latencies by only minimal fractions can cause financial losses. Dynamo provides a flexible design where services may control availability, consistency, cost-effectiveness and performance tradeoffs. Dynamo's data model rely on a simple key/value scheme. Since the targeted applications and services within Amazon do not require complex querying models, a record- or key-based queries are considered both enough in term of requirements and efficient in terms of performance scaling.

Dynamo's design relies on a consistent hashing-based partitioning scheme [33]. In the implemented scheme, the resulting range or space of a hash function is considered as a ring. Every member of the ring is a virtual node (host) where a physical node may be responsible for one or more virtual nodes. The introduction of virtual nodes, instead of using fixed physical nodes on the ring, is a choice that provides better availability and load balancing under failures. Each data item can be assigned to a node on the ring based on its key. The hashed value of the key determines its position on the ring. Data then, is assigned to the closest node on the ring clockwise. Moreover, data is replicated on the successive $(K - 1)$ nodes for a given replication factor K, avoiding virtual nodes that belong to the same physical nodes. All the nodes on Dynamo are considered equals and are able to compute the *reference list* for any given key. The *reference list* is the list of nodes that store a copy of data referenced by the key.

Dynamo is an eventually consistent system. Updates are asynchronously propagated to replicas. As data is usually available while updates are being propagated, clients may perform updates on older versions of data for which the last updates have not yet been committed. As a result, the system may suffer from updates conflicts. To deal with these situations, Dynamo relies on data versioning. Every updated replica is assigned a new immutable version. The conflicting versions of data resulting from concurrent updates may be solved at a latter time. This allows the system to be always available and fast to respond to client requests. Versions that share a causal relation are easy to solve by the system based on syntactic reconciliation. However, a difficulty arises with versions branching. This often happens in the presence of failures combined with concurrent updates and results in conflicting versions of data. The reconciliation in this case is left to the client rather than the system because the latter lacks the semantic context. The reconciliation is performed by collapsing the multiple data versions into one (semantic reconciliation). A simple example is the case of the *shopping cart* application. This application chooses to merge the diverging versions as a reconciliation strategy. To detect inconsistencies between replicas and repair them in the event of failures and other threats to data durability, Dynamo implements an anti-entropy replicas synchronization protocol.

Clients can interact with dynamo through a flexible API that provides various consistency configurations. Replica consistency is handled by a quorum-like system. In a system that maintains N replicas, R is the minimum number of nodes (replicas) that must participate in the read operation, and W is the minimum number of nodes that must participate in the write operation, which are configured on a per operation basis and are of high importance. By setting these two parameters, one can define the tradeoff between consistency and latency. A configuration that provides $R + W > N$

is a quorum-like setting. This configuration insures that the last up-to-date replica is included in the quorum and thus the response. However, the operation latencies are as small as the longest replica response time. In a configuration where $R + W < N$, clients may be exposed to stale versions of data.

10.4.2 CASSANDRA

Many web services and social networks are data-intensive and deal with the problem of data deluge. The Facebook social networking platform is the largest networking platform serving hundred millions of users at peak times and having no less than 900 million active users [9]. Therefore, and in order to keep users satisfied within such services, an efficient Big Data management that guarantees high availability, performance, and reliability is required. Moreover, a storage system that fulfills these needs must be able to elastically scale out to meet the continuous growth of the data-intensive platform. Cassandra [34] is a highly available, highly scalable, distributed storage system that was first built within Facebook. It was designed for managing large objects of structured data spread over a large amount of commodity hardware located in different datacenters worldwide.

The design of Cassandra was highly inspired by that of two other distributed storage systems. Implementation choices and consistency management are very similar to the ones of Amazon Dynamo (except for in-memory management) while its data model is derived from the Google BigTable [6] model. Therefore, the model adopted is column family based. Data are stored in tables and indexed by row keys. For each table, column families are defined and column keys within a column family can be created dynamically. Every operation on a single row key is atomic per a replica without the consideration of which columns are accessed. Such a data model provides great abilities for structured large data, as it offers a more flexible yet efficient data access. Moreover, it enables a better dynamic memory management. Like BigTable, Cassandra keeps data in-memory in small tables called *memtables*. When a memtable size grows over a given threshold, it is considered as full and data is flushed into an *sstable* that will be dumped to the disk.

The Cassandra partitioning scheme is based on consistent hashing. Unlike Dynamo, which uses virtual nodes to overcome the non-uniformity of load distribution, every node on the ring is a physical host. Therefore, and to guarantee uniform load distribution, Cassandra uses the same technique as in [35], where lightly loaded nodes move on the ring. Replication in Cassandra is performed in the same manner as in Dynamo. Moreover, Cassandra implements few replication strategies that consider the system topology. Therefore, strategies that are *Rack UnAware*, *Rack Aware*, and *Datacenter Aware* are provided. For the two latter strategies, Cassandra implements algorithms in Zookeeper [36] to compute *the reference list* for a given key. This list is cached locally at the level of every node as to preserve the zero-hop property of the system.

Similar to Amazon Dynamo, Cassandra storage system provides a flexible API to clients. In this context, various consistency levels [37] are proposed per operation. A write of consistency level *One* implies that data has to be written to the commit log and memory table of at least one replica before returning a success. Moreover, as shown in Figure 10.2, a read operation with consistency level *All* (strong consistency)

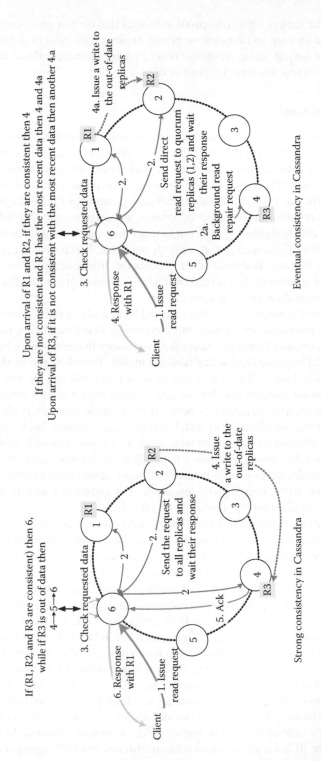

FIGURE 10.2 Synchronous replication vs. Quorum replication in Cassandra [11].

implies that the read operation must wait for all the replicas to reply and insures that all replicas are consistent to return the data to the client. In contrast, in a read consistency of level of *Quorum* (Quorum is computed as $\left\lfloor \dfrac{replication\ factor}{2} + 1 \right\rfloor$), two out of the three (the replication factor is set to three) replicas are contacted to fulfill the read request and the replica with the most recent version would return the requested data. In the background, a read repair will be issued to the third replica and will check for consistency with the first two. If inconsistency occurs, an asynchronous process will be launched to repair the stale nodes at a later time.

10.4.3   YAHOO! PNUTS

Yahoo!'s requirements for a data management platform that provides scalability, fast response, reliability, and high availability in different geographical areas, led them to the design and implementation of PNUTS [31]. PNUTS is a massively parallel geographically distributed storage system. Its main purpose is to host and serve data for Yahoo! web applications. PNUTS relies on a novel relaxed consistency model to cope with availability and fault-tolerance requirements at large scale. PNUTS provides the user with a simplified relational model. Data is stored in a set of tables of records with multiple attributes. An additional data type provided to the users is the "blob" type. A blob encapsulates arbitrary data structures (not necessarily large objects) inside records.

PNUTS divides the system into a set of regions. Regions are typically, but not necessarily, geographically distributed. Every region consists of a set of *storage units*, a *tablet controller*, and a set of *routers*. Data tables are decomposed horizontally into smaller data structures called *tablets* that are stored across storage units (servers) within multiple regions. On the other hand, the routers functionality is to locate data within tablets and storage units based on a *mapping* computed and provided by the tablet controller. PNUTS introduces the novel consistency model of *per record timeline consistency* described in Section 10.3. Therefore, it uses an asynchronous replication scheme. To provide reliability and replication, PNUTS relies on a pub/submechanism, called *Yahoo! Message Broker* (YMB). With YMB, PNUTS avoids other asynchronous replication protocols such as Gossip, and optimizes geographical replication. Moreover, a replica does not need to acquire the location of other replicas. Instead, it needs to just subscribe to the data updates within YMB.

For applications and users to deal with timeline consistency, API calls, which provide varying consistency guarantees, were proposed. The *read-any* call may return stale data to the users favoring performance and fast response to consistency. In common cases, a class of applications require the read data to be more recent than a given version. The API call *read-critical (required_version)* is proposed to deal with these requirements. In contrast, the *read-latest* call always returns the most recent version of data. This call, however, may be costly in terms of latency. Moreover, the API provides two calls for writing data. The *write* call gives ACID guarantees for the write (a write is a transaction with a single operation). In contrast, *test-and-set-write(required_version)* checks the version of the actual data in the system. If, and only if, the version matches *required_version*, the write is performed. This flexible API calls give a degree of freedom to applications and users to choose their consistency guarantees and control their availability, consistency, and performance tradeoffs.

10.4.4 GOOGLE SPANNER

Spanner [46] is a scalable, globally distributed database that provides synchronous replication and ensures strong consistency. While many applications within Google require georeplication for global availability and geographical locality reasons, a large class of these applications still needs a strong consistency and an SQL-like query model. Google BigTable [6] still serves and manages data efficiently for many applications, but it only guarantees eventual consistency at global scale and provides a NoSQL API. Therefore, Spanner is designed to overcome BigTable insufficiencies for the aforementioned class of applications and provides global scale external consistency (linearizability) and SQL-like query language similar to that of Google Megastore [42]. Data is stored into semi-relational tables to support an SQL-like query language and general-purpose transactions.

The Spanner architecture consists of a *universe* that may contain several *zones* where zones are the unit of administrative deployment. A zone additionally presents a location where data may be replicated. Each zone encapsulates a set of *spanservers* that host data tables that are split into data structures called *tablets*. Spanner timestamps data to provide multi-versioning features. A *zonemaster* is responsible for assigning data to spanservers whereas, the *location proxies* components provide clients with information to locate the spanserver responsible for its data. Moreover, Spanner introduces an additional data abstraction called *directories*, which are kinds of buckets to gather data that have the same access properties. The directory abstraction is the unit used to perform and optimize data movement and location. Replication is supported by implementing a Paxos protocol. Each spanserver associates a Paxos state machine with a tablet. The set of replicas for a given tablet is called a *Paxos group*. For each tablet and its replicas, a long-lived Paxos leader is designated with a time-based leader lease. The Paxos state machines are used to keep a consistent state of replicas. Therefore, writes must all initiate the Paxos protocol at the level of the Paxos leader while reads can access Paxos states at any replica that is sufficiently up-to-date. At the level of the leader replica, a lock table is used to manage concurrency control based on a two-phase locking (2PL) protocol. Consequently, all operations that require synchronization should acquire locks at the lock table.

To manage the global ordering and external consistency, Spanner relies on a time API called *TrueTime*. This API exposes clock uncertainty and allows Spanner to assign globally meaningful commit timestamps. The clock uncertainty is kept small within the TrueTime API relying on atomic clocks and GPS-based clocks at the level of every datacenter. Moreover, when uncertainty grows to a large value, Spanner slows down to wait out that uncertainty. The TrueTime API is then used to guarantee spanner desired correctness properties for concurrent executions, therefore, providing external consistency (linearizability) while enabling lock-free read-only transactions and nonblocking reads in the past.

Spanner presents a novel globally distributed architecture that implements the first globally ordered system with external consistency guarantees. While such guarantees were estimated to be fundamental for many applications within Google, it is unclear how such an implementation affects latency, performance, and availability. In particular, the write throughput might suffer from the two-phase locking mechanism, which is known to be very expensive at wide scale. Moreover, it is not obvious how Spanner deals with availability during network failures.

10.4.5 DISCUSSION

As cloud computing technology emerges, more and more cloud storage systems have been developed. Table 10.2 gives an overview of the four aforementioned cloud storage systems along with several other storage system examples. Many systems implement eventual consistency. These systems are usually destined to serve social networks, web shop applications, document-based applications, and cloud services. Commonly, they adopt one of the following data models: key/value, column families, and document-oriented. Moreover, many of these systems provide the user with a flexible API that offers various consistency levels. On the opposite side, systems that implement strong consistency serve many applications including services such as mail service, advertisement, image hosting platforms, data analytics applications, and a few cloud services as well. These applications, in general, require strong consistency while their availability and performance requirements are not as high as web shop services for instance. These systems implement, generally, a semi-relational data model, column families, and rarely, a key/value model. Moreover, they usually provide users with SQL-like API.

10.5 ADAPTIVE CONSISTENCY

A wide range of applications either require a strictly strong form of consistency or settle for only static eventual consistency. However, for another class of applications, consistency requirements are not obvious as they depend on data access behavior dynamicity, clients needs, and the consequences (or the cost) of reading inconsistent data. Typical applications that fall in this class include auction systems and web shop applications. For these types of applications, availability and fast accesses are vital. Therefore, strong consistency mechanisms may be too costly. While high levels of consistency are strongly desired for these particular applications, it is not always required. In the start of an auction or in the not so busy periods for a web shop, a weaker form of consistency is sufficient and does not cause anomalies that the storage system cannot handle. However, strong consistency is required toward the end of the auction as well as in the busy holiday periods, as heavy accesses are expected and data inconsistency might be of disastrous consequences. As with this type of situations, static eventual or strong forms of consistency lead both to undesirable consequences.

To cope with the dynamicity of accesses behavior at the massive cloud scale, various adaptive and dynamic consistency approaches were introduced. Their goal is to use strong consistency only when it is necessary. These approaches differ in the target consistency tradeoffs (e.g., consistency-cost in [47,48] and consistency performance in [8,11,49]) and in the way they define the consistency requirements. Hereafter, we present two adaptive consistency models (next section will be devoted to our adaptive consistency solution Harmony). For both models, we start by presenting the motivation and the use case, then we present the adaptive approach, and finally we describe the model implementation on the targeted infrastructure.

10.5.1 REDBLUE CONSISTENCY

Due to the high network latencies, strong consistency guarantees are too expensive when storage systems are geographically distributed. Therefore, weaker consistency semantics such as eventual consistency is the most popular choice for applications that require high availability and performance. However, weaker consistency models are not suitable for all applications classes, even if most operations within one application require only eventual consistency. For instance, in the case of a social network, a transaction that might combine privacy-related updates among other social activity operations might need more than eventual consistency. Privacy-related operations require strong ordering at all geographical sites in order not to violate the privacy setting of the user. On the other hand, social activity operations might only require eventual convergence of replicas no matter the ordering of the operations.

RedBlue consistency [8] is introduced to provide as fast responses as possible and consistency when necessary. It provides two types of operations: Red and Blue. Blue operations are executed locally and replicated lazily. Therefore, their ordering can vary from site to site. In contrast, Red operations require a stronger consistency. They must satisfy serializable ordering with each other and as a result generate communication across sites for coordination. Subsequently, the RedBlue order is defined as a partial ordering for which all Red operations are totally ordered. Moreover, every site has a local causal serialization that provides a total ordering of operations that are applied locally. This definition of the RedBlue consistency does not guarantee the replicas state convergence. Convergence is reached if all causal serializations of operations at the level of each site reach the same state. However, with the RedBlue consistency, blue operations might have different orders in different sites. Therefore, noncommutative operations executed in a different order would not allow replicas convergence. As a result, noncommutative operations should not be tagged as blue if the convergence is to be insured. An extension of the RedBlue consistency consists in splitting original application operations into two components. A *generator operation* that has no side-effect and is executed only at the primary site and *shadow operation*, which is executed at every site. *Shadow operations* that are noncommutative or violate the application variant (e.g., negative values for a positive variable) are labeled Red while all other *shadow operations* are labeled blue.

The RedBlue consistency is implemented in a system called *Gemini* storage system. Gemini uses MySQL as its storage backend. Its deployment consists of several sites where each site is composed of four components: a *storage engine*, a *proxy server*, *concurrency coordinator*, and *data writer*. The proxy server is the component that processes client requests for data hosted on the storage engine (a relational database). *Generator operations* are performed on a temporary private scratchpad, resulting in a virtual private copy of the service state. Upon the completion of a *generator operation*, the proxy server sends the *shadow operation* to the concurrency coordinator. The latter notifies the proxy server whether the operation is accepted or rejected according to the RedBlue consistency. If accepted, the operation is then delegated to the local data writer to be executed in the storage engine.

10.5.2 CONSISTENCY RATIONING

Data created and processed by the same application might be different, and so might the consistency requirements on them. For instance, data processed by a web shop service can be of different kinds. Data kinds may include customers profiles and credit card information, product sold data, user preferences, etc. Not all these data kinds have the same requirements in terms of consistency and availability. Moreover, within the same category, data might exhibit dynamic and changing consistency requirements. As an example, an auction system data might require lower levels of consistency at the start of the auction than towards the end of it.

The *consistency rationing* model [47] allows designers to define consistency requirements on data instead of transactions. It divides data into three categories: *A*, *B*, and *C*. Category *A* data requires strong consistency guarantees. Therefore, all transactions on this data are serializable. However, serializability requires protocols and implementation techniques as well as coordination, which are expensive in terms of monetary cost and performance. Data within *C* category is data for which temporary inconsistency is acceptable. Subsequently, only weaker consistency guarantees, in the form of session consistency, are implemented for this category. This comes at a cheaper cost per transaction and allows better availability. The *B* category on the other hand presents data for which consistency requirements change in time as in the case for many applications. These data endure adaptive consistency that switch between serializability and session consistency at runtime whenever necessary. The goal of the adaptive consistency strategies is to minimize the overall cost of the provided service in the cloud. The general policy is an adaptive consistency model that relies on updates conflict probability. It observes the data access frequency to data items to compute the probability of access conflicts. When this probability grows over an adaptive threshold, serializability is selected. The computation of the adaptive threshold is based on the monetary cost of weak and strong consistency and the expected cost of violating consistency.

Consistency rationing is implemented in a system that provides storage on top of *Amazon Simple Storage Service* (S3) [2], which provides only eventual consistency. Clients Requests are directed to application servers. These servers are hosts on *Amazon EC2* [3]. Therefore, application servers interact with the persistent storage on *Amazon S3*. To provide consistency guarantees, the update requests are buffered in queues called pending updates queues that are implemented on the *Amazon Simple Queue Service* (SQS) [50]. Session consistency is provided by always routing requests from the same client to the same server within a session. In contrast, and to provide serializability, a two-phase locking protocol is used.

10.6 HARMONY: AUTOMATED SELF-ADAPTIVE CONSISTENCY

Most of the existing adaptive consistency approaches require a global knowledge of the application access pattern (e.g., consistency rationing requires the data to be categorized in advance). However, with the tremendous increase in data size along with the significant variation in the service's load, this task is hard to accomplish and will add an extra overhead to the system. Moreover, these approaches cover a small set of applications where operation orderings are strictly required. In this context, we introduce our approach Harmony [11], an *automated self-adaptive* approach that considers applications tolerance rate for stale reads (i.e., Harmony complements other adaptive approaches as it targets applications with stale reads consideration rather than operation orderings, see Table 10.3).

Rather than relying on a standard model based only on the access pattern to define the consistency requirement of an application—which is the case for most existing work—Harmony, instead, uses the *stale read rate* of the application to precisely define such requirement: by doing so, Harmony retains the same rate of stale reads regardless the variation in the access loads and patterns of an application or the changes on the network latency of the system. Consequently, Harmony embraces an intelligent estimation model to automatically identify the key parameters affecting the stale reads such as the system states (network latency) and application's requirements (current access pattern). Harmony, therefore, elastically scales up/down the number of replicas involved in read operations to maintain a low (possibly zero) tolerable fraction of stale reads, hence, improving the performance of the applications while meeting the desired consistency level.

In the rest of this section, we will first present design trend in Harmony of using stale reads rate to define the consistency requirement of an application. Then, we discuss how to estimate the amount of stale reads in the system. We then describe the Harmony implementation, and integration into Cassandra cloud storage system [34] and present detailed results of experimental evaluations on Amazon EC2 [3].

TABLE 10.3
Adaptive Consistency Approaches

	Consistency Specification Level	Cloud Storage System: Implemented Within	Testbed for Evaluating the Solution	Automated Consistency	Tradeoff
RedBlue Consistency [8]	Operations	Gemini	Amazon EC2 in different availability zones	No	Consistency–performance
Consistency Rationing [47]	Data	Amazon S3	Amazon S3	Yes	Consistency–cost
Harmony [11]	Operations	Apache Cassandra	Grid'5000 and Amazon EC2	Yes	Consistency–performance

10.6.1 WHY USE THE STALE READS RATE TO DEFINE THE CONSISTENCY REQUIREMENTS OF AN APPLICATION?

We consider two applications that may at some point have the same access pattern. One is a web-shop application that can have heavy reads and writes during the busy holiday periods, and a social network application that can also have heavy access during important events or in the evening of a working day. These two applications may have the same behavior at some point and are the same from the point of view of the system when monitoring data accesses and network state, thus they may be given the same consistency level. However, the cost for stale reads is not the same for both applications. A social network application can tolerate a higher number of stale reads than a web-shop application: a stale read has no effects on the former, whereas it could result in anomalies for the latter. Consequently, defining the consistency level in accordance to the stale reads rate can precisely reflect the application requirements. Furthermore, this allow Harmony to always retain the same consistency guarantees (i.e., predefined stale reads rate) while offering the best-effort performance (i.e., finding the minimum number of replicas that satisfy the predefined consistency). For example, Harmony can offer strong consistency guarantees to the same application (by setting the stale reads rate to low value or "zero"), but with adaptive number of involved replicas (e.g., less replicas will be involved when the service load or the network latency are low).

10.6.2 STALE READS PROBABILISTIC ESTIMATION

The estimation model requires basic knowledge of the application access pattern and of the storage system network latency. Network latency in this case is of high importance, since it is the determinant of the updates propagation time to other replicas. The access pattern, which includes read rates and write rates is a key factor to determine consistency requirements in the storage system. For instance, it is obvious that a heavy read–write access pattern would produce higher stale reads when adopting eventual consistency.

We define the situation that leads to a stale read in Figure 10.3. The read may be stale if its starting time X_r is in the time interval between the starting time of the last write and the end of the propagation time of data to the other replicas. This situation is repeatable for any of the writes that may occur in the system. T_p in Figure 10.3 is the time necessary for the propagation of a write or an update to all the replicas. It is computed based on the network latency L_n and the average write size avg_w and should be represented as $T_p(L_n, avg_w)$, but to simplify the representation, it will be denoted as T_p in the rest of the chapter.

Transactions arrivals are generally considered as a Poisson process as it is the common way to model them in literature [10,51]. We assume that the writes and the reads arrivals follow the Poisson distribution of parameter λ_w^{-1} (we chose λ_w^{-1} instead of λ_w to simplify subsequent formulas where the parameter will be inverted) and λ_r, respectively. These parameters values change dynamically at run time following the read and write requests arrivals monitored in the storage system. Since the distribution of waiting time between two Poisson arrivals is an exponential process, the

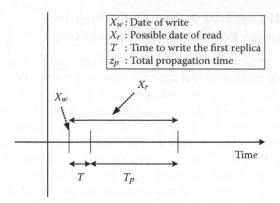

FIGURE 10.3 Situation that leads to a stale read.

stochastic variables X_w and X_r of a write time and read time follow an exponential distribution of parameters λ_w^{-1} and λ_r, respectively. The probability of the next read being stale corresponding to the aforementioned situation is given by Equation 10.1, with N being the replication factor in the system and X being the number of replicas involved in the read operation, and T_p is the average time to propagate an update to other replicas. Here $X_n = 1$ for the basic eventual consistency.

$$Pr(stale\_read) = \sum_{i=0}^{\infty} \left(\frac{N-(X_n=1)}{N} Pr\left(X_w^i < X_r < X_w^i + T + T_p \right) + \frac{X_n=1}{N} Pr\left(X_w^i < X_r < X_w^i + T \right) \right)$$

(10.1)

After simplifying (more details can be found in [11]), the final value of the probability of next read to be stale, is given by

$$Pr(stale\_read) = \frac{(N-1)(1-e^{-\lambda_r T_p})(1+\lambda_r\lambda_w)}{N\lambda_r\lambda_w}$$

(10.2)

10.6.3 HARMONY IMPLEMENTATION

Harmony can be applied to different cloud storage systems that are featured with flexible consistency rules. The current implementation of Harmony operates on top of *Apache Cassandra* storage [52] and consists of two modules. The monitoring module collects relevant metrics about data access in the storage system: read rates and write rates, as well as network latencies. These data are further fed to the adaptive consistency module. This module is the heart of the Harmony implementation where the estimation and the resulting consistency level computations are performed: the Harmony estimation model, which is based on probabilistic computations, predicts the stale read rate in accordance to the statics fed by the monitoring module. Accordingly, as shown in Algorithm 10.1, Harmony chooses whether to select the basic consistency level ONE (involving only one replica) or else, computes the number of involved replicas necessary to maintain an acceptable stale reads rate while allowing a better performance.

Algorithm 1: Harmony: Consistency Tuning Algorithm

Input: *app_stale_rate* is the predefined consistency requirement.
Description: θ_{stale} is estimated stale reads rate.
Output: X_n is the number of replicas that retain the same consistency requirements.
if *app_stale_rate* $\geq \theta_{stale}$ then
  | Choose eventual consistency (Consistency Level = One)
else
  | Compute X_n the number of always consistent replicas necessary to have
  | *app_stale_rate* $\geq \theta_{stale}$
  | Choose consistency level based on X_n
end

As shown in Algorithm 10.1, the default consistency level is the basic eventual consistency that allows reading from only one replica. When such a level may not satisfy the consistency requirements of an application due to the growing number of stale reads, the number of replicas X_n that should be involved in the reading requests is computed as given in formula (10.3). All the following read requests will be performed with consistency level X_n.

$$X_n = \left\lfloor \frac{N((1-e^{-\lambda_r T_P})(1+\lambda_r\lambda_w) - app\_stale\_rate\lambda_r\lambda_w)}{(1-e^{-\lambda_r T_P})(1+\lambda_r\lambda_w)} \right\rfloor \qquad (10.3)$$

10.6.4 Harmony Evaluation

To validate Harmony, a set of experimental evaluations was conducted on Amazon Elastic Cloud Compute (EC2) [3]. For all experiments we ran Apache Cassandra-1.0.2 as an underlying storage system, and used the Yahoo Cloud Serving Benchmark! (YCSB) [53]. We deployed Cassandra on 20 VMs on Amazon EC2. The goal of these experiments is to evaluate system performance and measure the staleness rate. We used Workload-A: a heavy read–update workload from YCSB! with two data sets with the size of 23.85 GB for EC2 and a total of 5 million operations.

10.6.4.1 Throughput and Latency

We compare Harmony with two settings (two different tolerable stale read rates of an application) with strong and eventual consistency (i.e., the ONE level). The first tolerable stale read rate is 60% for Amazon EC2 (this rate tolerates more staleness in the system implying lower consistency levels and thus less waiting time) and the second tolerable stale read rate is 40% for Amazon EC2 (this rate is more restrictive than the first one, meaning that the number of read operations performed with a higher level of consistency is larger). Network latency is high and varies in time in Amazon EC2 (we observe it is 5 times higher than in a local cluster). We run workload-A while varying the number of client threads.

Figure 10.4a presents the 99th percentile latency of read operations when the number of client threads increases on EC2. The strong consistency approach provides the highest latency having all reads to wait for responses from all replicas that are spread over different racks and clusters. Eventual consistency is the approach that provides the smallest latencies since all read operations are performed on one local replica (possibly at the cost of consistency violation). We can clearly see that Harmony with both settings provides almost the same latency as a basic static eventual consistency. Moreover, the latency increases by decreasing the tolerable stale reads rate of an application as the probability of stale read can easily get higher than these rates, which requires higher consistency levels and, as a result, a higher latency.

In Figure 10.4b, we show the overall throughput for read and write operations with different numbers of client threads. The throughput increases as the number of threads increases. However, the throughput decreases with more than 90 threads. This is because the number of client threads is higher than the number of storage hosts and threads are served concurrently. We can observe that the throughput is smaller with strong consistency. This is because of the extra network traffic generated by the synchronization process as well as the high operation latencies. We can notice that our approach with a stale reads rate of 60%, provides very good throughput that can be compared with the one of static eventual consistency approach. While exhibiting high throughput, our adaptive policies provide fewer stale reads as higher consistency levels are chosen only when it matters.

10.6.4.2   Staleness

In Figure 10.4c, we show that Harmony, with both policies with different application tolerated stale reads rates, provides less stale reads than the eventual consistency approach. Moreover, we can see that, with a more restrictive tolerated stale reads rate, we get a smaller number of stale reads. We observe that with rates of 40%, the number of stale reads decreases when the number of threads grows over 40 threads. This is explained by the fact that with more than 40 threads the estimated rate grows higher than 40%, for most of the run time due to concurrent accesses, and higher consistency levels are chosen, thus decreasing the number of stale reads. It is important to note that that this number of stale reads is not the actual number of stale reads in the system in the normal run, but it is representative.

In fact, to measure the number of stale reads, we perform two read operations for every read operation in the workload. The first read is performed with the relevant consistency level chosen by our approach, and the second read is performed with the strongest consistency level. Then, we compare the returned timestamps from both reads, and if they do not match, it means that the read is stale.

To see the impact of network latency on the stale reads estimation we ran workload-A—varying the number of threads starting with 90 threads, then, 70, 40, 15, and finally, one thread–on Amazon EC2 and measure the network latency during the runtime. Figure 10.4d shows that high network latency causes higher stale reads

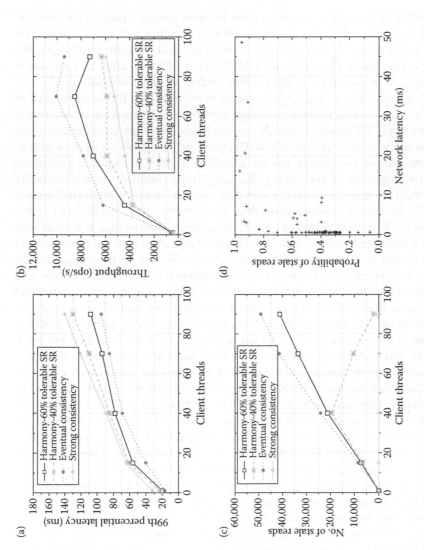

FIGURE 10.4   Harmony with $S\%$ tolerable stale reads (Harmony-$S\%$ Tolerable SR) against strong and eventual consistency on Amazon EC2. (a) Shows the 99th percentile latency of read operations, (b) shows the overall throughput for read and write operations, (c) shows the number of stale reads, and (d) shows the impact of network latency on the stale reads estimation employed by Harmony.

regardless of the number of the threads (higher latency dominates the probability of stale reads), while when the latency is small, the access pattern has more influence on the probability.

10.7 CONCLUSION

This chapter addresses a major open issue in cloud storage systems: the management of consistency for replicated data. Despite a plethora of cloud storage systems available today, data consistency schemes are still far from satisfactory. We take this opportunity to ponder the *CAP* theorem 13 years after its formulation and discuss its implications in the modern context of cloud computing. The tension among consistency, availability, and partition tolerance has been handled in various ways in existing distributed storage systems (e.g., by relaxing consistency at wide-area level). We therefore provide an overview of the major consistency models and approaches used for providing scalable, yet highly available services on clouds. We categorize the consistency models according to their consistency guarantees into: (1) strong form of consistency including linearizability and serializability and (2) weaker form of consistency including eventual causal and timeline consistency. For the weaker consistency models, we elaborate on what additional operation ordering is applied to handle conflict situations. Cloud storage is foundational to cloud computing because it provides a backend for hosting not only user data but also the system-level data needed by cloud services. We survey the state-of-the-art cloud storage systems used by the main cloud vendors (i.e., in Amazon, Google, and Facebook). In addition to a general presentation of these systems architectures and use cases, we discuss the employed consistency model by each cloud storage system. The survey helps to understand the mapping between the applied consistency technique and target requirements of the applications using these cloud solutions. Moreover, and to handle the tremendous size of Big Data, the scale of cloud systems is extremely increasing and the cloud applications are significantly diversifying (e.g., access pattern and diurnal/monthly loads). We advocate self-adaptivity as a key means to approach the tradeoffs that must be handled by the user applications. We review several approaches of adaptive consistency that provide flexible consistency management for users to reduce performance overhead and monetary cost when data are distributed across geographically distributed sites. Then, we discuss in detail our adaptive consistency solution Harmony: a novel approach that handles data consistency in cloud storage adaptively by choosing the most appropriate consistency level dynamically at run time. In Harmony, we collect relevant information about the storage system to estimate the stale read rate when consistency is eventual, and make a decision accordingly. To be application-adaptive, Harmony takes into account the application's needs expressed by the stale read rate that can be tolerated. Harmony is evaluated with the Cassandra cloud storage on Amazon EC2. The chapter helps to fill the gap between the conceptual overview of consistency models and how they are used in practise in real cloud systems. Also, this chapter emphasizes on the importance of the adaptive consistency approaches to cope with the cloud/data scale and applications diversity and offer insights into designing new consistency approaches for Big Data storage systems.

REFERENCES

1. H. Jin, S. Ibrahim, T. Bell, L. Qi, H. Cao, S. Wu, and X. Shi, "Tools and technologies for building the clouds," *Cloud Computing: Principles Systems and Applications*, pp. 3–20, 2010.
2. "Amazon Simple Storage Service (Amazon S3)," February 2013. [Online]. Available: http://aws.amazon.com/s3/.
3. "Amazon Elastic Compute Cloud (Amazon EC2)," February 2013. [Online]. Available: http://aws.amazon.com/ec2/.
4. "Amazon Case Studies," February 2013. [Online]. Available: http://aws.amazon.com/solutions/case-studies/.
5. S. Ghemawat, H. Gobioff, and S.-T. Leung, "The Google file system," *SIGOPS—Oper. Syst. Rev.*, vol. 37, no. 5, pp. 29–43, 2003.
6. F. Chang, J. Dean, S. Ghemawat, W. C. Hsieh, D. A. Wallach, M. Burrows, T. Chandra, A. Fikes, and R. E. Gruber, "Bigtable: A distributed storage system for structured data," in *Proceedings of the 7th Conference on USENIX Symposium on Operating Systems Design and Implementation*, pp. 205–218, 2006.
7. S. Ibrahim, H. Jin, L. Lu, B. He, G. Antoniu, and S. Wu, "Maestro: Replica-aware map scheduling for mapreduce," in *Proceedings of the 12th IEEE/ACM International Symposium on Cluster, Cloud and Grid Computing (CCGrid 2012)*, Ottawa, Canada, pp. 59–72, 2012.
8. C. Li, D. Porto, A. Clement, J. Gehrke, N. Preguiça, and R. Rodrigues, "Making geo-replicated systems fast as possible, consistent when necessary," in *Proceedings of the 10th USENIX Conference on Operating Systems Design and Implementation*, ser. OSDI'12, Berkeley, CA, USA: USENIX Association, pp. 265–278, 2012.
9. "Facebook Statistcs," February 2013. [Online]. Available: http://newsroom.fb.com/content/default.aspx?NewsAreaId=22.
10. H. Wada, A. Fekete, L. Zhao, K. Lee, and A. Liu, "Data consistency properties and the trade-offs in commercial cloud storage: The consumers' perspective," in *CIDR 2011, Fifth Biennial Conference on Innovative Data Systems Research, Online Proceedings*, Asilomar, CA, USA, pp. 134–143, January 9–12, 2011.
11. H.-E. Chihoub, S. Ibrahim, G. Antoniu, and M. S. Pérez-Hernández, "Harmony: Towards automated self-adaptive consistency in cloud storage," in *2012 IEEE International Conference on Cluster Computing (CLUSTER'12)*, Beijing, China, pp. 293–301, 2012.
12. E. A. Brewer, "Towards robust distributed systems (abstract)," in *Proceedings of the Nineteenth Annual ACM Symposium on Principles of Distributed Computing*, ser. PODC'00, New York, USA: ACM, p. 7, 2000.
13. S. Gilbert, and N. Lynch, "Brewer's conjecture and the feasibility of consistent available partition-tolerant web services," in *ACM SIGACT News*, 2002, p. 2002.
14. E. Brewer, "Cap twelve years later: How the 'rules' have changed," *Computer*, vol. 45, no. 2, pp. 23–29, 2012.
15. D. J. Abadi, "Consistency tradeoffs in modern distributed database system design: Cap is only part of the story," *Computer*, vol. 45, pp. 37–42, 2012.
16. S. Gilbert, and N. Lynch, "Perspectives on the cap theorem," *Computer*, vol. 45, no. 2, pp. 30–36, 2012.
17. P. A. Bernstein, V. Hadzilacos, and N. Goodman, *Concurrency Control and Recovery in Database Systems*. Boston, USA: Addison-Wesley Longman Publishing Co., Inc., 1987.
18. M. P. Herlihy, and J. M. Wing, "Linearizability: A correctness condition for concurrent objects," *ACM Trans. Program. Lang. Syst.*, vol. 12, no. 3, pp. 463–492, 1990.
19. M. Dubois, C. Scheurich, and F. Briggs, "Memory access buffering in multiprocessors," in *25 Years of the International Symposia on Computer Architecture (Selected Papers)*, ser. ISCA'98, New York, USA: ACM, pp. 320–328, 1998.

20. C. Scheurich, and M. Dubois, "Concurrent miss resolution in multiprocessor caches," in *ICPP (1)*, pp. 118–125, 1988.
21. S. V. Adve, and M. D. Hill, "Weak ordering—A new definition," *SIGARCH Comput. Archit. News*, vol. 18, no. 3a, pp. 2–14, 1990.
22. R. Bisiani, A. Nowatzyk, and M. Ravishankar, "Coherent shared memory on a distributed memory machine," in *ICPP (1)*, pp. 133–141, 1989.
23. W. Vogels, "Eventually consistent," *Commun. ACM*, vol. 52, no. 1, pp. 40–44, 2009.
24. M. Shapiro, and B. Kemme, "Eventual Consistency," in Encyclopedia of Database Systems (online and print), M. T. Ozsu and L. Liu, Eds. Springer US, 2009.
25. A. S. Tanenbaum, and M. V. Steen, *Distributed Systems: Principles and Paradigms*, (2nd Edition). Upper Saddle River, NJ, USA: Prentice-Hall, Inc., 2006.
26. Y. Saito, and M. Shapiro, "Optimistic replication," *ACM Comput. Surv.*, vol. 37, no. 1, pp. 42–81, 2005.
27. M. Ahamad, G. Neiger, J. E. Burns, P. Kohli, and P. W. Hutto, "Causal memory: Definitions, implementation, and programming," *Distrib. Comput.*, vol. 9, no. 1, pp. 37–49, 1995.
28. W. Lloyd, M. J. Freedman, M. Kaminsky, and D. G. Andersen, "Don't settle for eventual: Scalable causal consistency for wide-area storage with cops," in *Proceedings of the Twenty-Third ACM Symposium on Operating Systems Principles*, ser. SOSP'11, New York, USA: ACM, pp. 401–416, 2011.
29. R. H. Thomas, "A majority consensus approach to concurrency control for multiple copy databases," *ACM Trans. Database Syst.*, vol. 4, no. 2, pp. 180–209, June 1979.
30. W. Lloyd, M. J. Freedman, M. Kaminsky, and D. G. Andersen, "Stronger semantics for low-latency geo-replicated storage," in *Proceedings of the 10th USENIX Conference on Networked Systems Design and Implementation*, ser. nsdi'13, Berkeley, CA, USA: USENIX Association, pp. 313–328, 2013.
31. B. F. Cooper, R. Ramakrishnan, U. Srivastava, A. Silberstein, P. Bohannon, H.-A. Jacobsen, N. Puz, D. Weaver, and R. Yerneni, "Pnuts: Yahoo!'s hosted data serving platform," *Proc. VLDB Endow.*, vol. 1, no. 2, pp. 1277–1288, 2008.
32. G. DeCandia, D. Hastorun, M. Jampani, G. Kakulapati, A. Lakshman, A. Pilchin, S. Sivasubramanian, P. Vosshall, and W. Vogels, "Dynamo: Amazon's highly available key-value store," in *Proceedings of Twenty-First ACM SIGOPS Symposium on Operating Systems Principles*, ser. SOSP'07, New York, USA: ACM, pp. 205–220, 2007.
33. D. Karger, E. Lehman, T. Leighton, R. Panigrahy, M. Levine, and D. Lewin, "Consistent hashing and random trees: Distributed caching protocols for relieving hot spots on the world wide web," in *Proceedings of the Twenty-Ninth Annual ACM Symposium on Theory of Computing*, ser. STOC'97, New York, USA: ACM, pp. 654–663, 1997.
34. A. Lakshman, and P. Malik, "Cassandra: A decentralized structured storage system," *SIGOPS Oper. Syst. Rev.*, vol. 44, pp. 35–40, 2010.
35. I. Stoica, R. Morris, D. Karger, M. F. Kaashoek, and H. Balakrishnan, "Chord: A scalable peer-to-peer lookup service for internet applications," in *Proceedings of the 2001 Conference on Applications, Technologies, Architectures, and Protocols for Computer Communications*, ser. SIGCOMM'01, New York, USA: ACM, 2001, pp. 149–160.
36. P. Hunt, M. Konar, F. P. Junqueira, and B. Reed, "Zookeeper: Wait-free coordination for internet-scale systems," in *Proceedings of the 2010 USENIX Conference on USENIX Annual Technical Conference*, ser. USENIXATC'10, Berkeley, CA, USA: USENIX Association, pp. 11–11, 2010.
37. "About Data Consistency in Cassandra," February 2012. [Online]. Available: http://www.datastax.com/docs/1.0/dml/data_consistency.
38. "Riak," February 2013. [Online]. Available: http://basho.com/riak/.
39. "Voldemort," February 2013. [Online]. Available: http://www.project-voldemort.com/voldemort/.

40. "Apache CouchDB," February 2013. [Online]. Available: http://couchdb.apache.org/.
41. "MongoDB," February 2013. [Online]. Available: http://www.mongodb.org/.
42. J. Baker, C. Bond, J. C. Corbett, J. Furman, A. Khorlin, J. Larson, J.-M. Leon, Y. Li, A. Lloyd, and V. Yushprakh, "Megastore: Providing scalable, highly available storage for interactive services," in *Proceedings of the Conference on Innovative Data system Research (CIDR)*, pp. 223–234, 2011.
43. "Redis," February 2013. [Online]. Available: http://redis.io/.
44. B. Calder, J. Wang, A. Ogus, N. Nilakantan, A. Skjolsvold, S. McKelvie, Y. Xu et al. "Windows azure storage: A highly available cloud storage service with strong consistency," in *Proceedings of the Twenty-Third ACM Symposium on Operating Systems Principles*, ser. SOSP'11, New York, USA: ACM, pp. 143–157, 2011.
45. "Apache HBase," February 2013. [Online]. Available: http://hbase.apache.org/.
46. J. C. Corbett, J. Dean, M. Epstein, A. Fikes, C. Frost, J. J. Furman, S. Ghemawat et al. Spanner: Google's globally-distributed database," in *Proceedings of the 10th USENIX Conference on Operating Systems Design and Implementation*, ser. OSDI'12, Berkeley, CA, USA: USENIX Association, pp. 251–264, 2012.
47. T. Kraska, M. Hentschel, G. Alonso, and D. Kossmann, "Consistency rationing in the cloud: Pay only when it matters," *Proc. VLDB Endow.*, vol. 2, pp. 253–264, 2009.
48. H.-E. Chihoub, S. Ibrahim, G. Antoniu, and M. S. Pérez-Hernández, "Consistency in the cloud: when money does matter!" in *13th IEEE/ACM International Symposium on Cluster, Cloud and Grid Computing (CCGrid 2013)*, Delft, the Netherlands, 2013.
49. R. Liu, A. Aboulnaga, and K. Salem, "Dax: A widely distributed multitenant storage service for dbms hosting," in *Proceedings of the 39th International Conference on Very Large Data Bases*, ser. PVLDB'13, VLDB Endowment, pp. 253–264, 2013.
50. "Amazon Simple Queue Service (Amazon SQS)," February 2013. [Online]. Available: http://aws.amazon.com/sqs/.
51. A. T. Tai, and J. F. Meyer, "Performability management in distributed database systems: An adaptive concurrency control protocol," in *Proceedings of the 4th International Workshop on Modeling, Analysis, and Simulation of Computer and Telecommunications Systems*, ser. MASCOTS'96, Washington, DC, USA: IEEE Computer Society, 1996.
52. "Apache Cassandra," February 2012. [Online]. Available: http://cassandra.apache.org/.
53. B. F. Cooper, A. Silberstein, E. Tam, R. Ramakrishnan, and R. Sears, "Benchmarking cloud serving systems with ycsb," in *Proceedings of the 1st ACM Symposium on Cloud Computing*, ser. SoCC'10, New York, USA: ACM, pp. 143–154, 2010.

11 CloudDB AutoAdmin
A Consumer-Centric Framework for SLA Management of Virtualized Database Servers

Sherif Sakr, Liang Zhao, and Anna Liu

CONTENTS

One of the main advantages of the cloud computing paradigm is that it simplifies the time-consuming processes of hardware provisioning, hardware procurement and software deployment. Currently, we are witnessing a proliferation in the number of cloud-hosted applications with a tremendous increase in the scale of the data generated as well as being consumed by such applications. Cloud-hosted database systems powering these applications form a critical component in the software stack of these applications. *Service Level Agreements* (SLA) represent the contract, which captures the agreed upon guarantees between a service provider and its customers. The specifications of existing service level agreements (SLA) for cloud services are not designed to flexibly handle even relatively straightforward performance and technical requirements of consumer applications. In this chapter, we present an approach for SLA-based management of cloud-hosted databases from the *consumer perspective*. We present, cloudDB AutoAdmin, an end-to-end framework for *consumer-centric* SLA management of cloud-hosted databases. The framework facilitates adaptive and dynamic provisioning of the database tier of the software applications based on application defined policies for satisfying their own SLA performance requirements, avoiding the cost of any SLA violation and controlling the monetary cost of the allocated computing resources. In this framework, the SLA of the consumer applications are declaratively defined in terms of *goals* that are subjected to a number of constraints that are specific to the application requirements. The framework continuously monitors the application-defined SLA and automatically triggers the execution of necessary corrective actions (scaling out/in the database tier) when required. The framework is database platform-agnostic, uses virtualization-based database replication mechanisms and requires zero source code changes of the cloud-hosted software applications. The experimental results demonstrate the effectiveness of our SLA-based framework in providing the consumer applications with the required flexibility for achieving their SLA requirements.

11.1 INTRODUCTION

Cloud computing technology represents a new paradigm for the provisioning of computing infrastructure. This paradigm shifts the location of this infrastructure to the network to reduce the costs associated with the management of hardware and software resources. Hence, businesses and users become able to access application services from anywhere in the world on demand. Therefore, it represents the long-held dream of envisioning computing as a utility [2] where the economy of scale principles help to effectively drive down the cost of computing infrastructure. Cloud computing simplifies the time-consuming processes of hardware provisioning, hardware procurement, and software deployment. Therefore, it promises a number of advantages for the deployment of data-intensive applications such as elasticity of resources, pay-per-use cost model, low time to market, and the perception of (virtually) unlimited resources and infinite scalability. Hence, it becomes possible, at least theoretically, to achieve unlimited throughput by continuously adding computing resources (e.g., database servers) if the workload increases.

In practice, the advantages of the cloud computing paradigm opens up new avenues for deploying novel applications that were not economically feasible in a traditional enterprise infrastructure setting. Therefore, the cloud has become an increasingly popular platform for hosting software applications in a variety of domains such as e-retail, finance, news, and social networking. Thus, we are witnessing a proliferation in the number of applications with a tremendous increase in the scale of the data generated as well as being consumed by such applications. *Cloud-hosted database systems powering these applications form a critical component in the software stack of these applications.*

Cloud computing is by its nature a fast changing environment that is designed to provide services to unpredictably diverse sets of clients and heterogeneous workloads. Several studies have also reported that the variation of the performance of cloud computing resources is high [6,18]. These characteristics raise serious concerns from the cloud consumers' perspective regarding the manner in which the SLA of their application can be managed. According to a Gartner market report released in November 2010, SaaS is forecast to have a 15.8% growth rate through 2014, which makes SaaS and cloud very interesting to the services industry, but the viability of the business models depends on the practicality and the success of the terms and conditions (SLAs) being offered by the service provider(s) in addition to their satisfaction to the service consumers. Therefore, successful SLA management is a critical factor to be considered by both providers and consumers alike. Existing service level agreements (SLAs) of cloud providers are not designed for supporting the straightforward requirements and restrictions under which SLA of consumers' applications need to be handled. Particularly, most providers guarantee only the availability (but not the performance) of their services [21]. Therefore, consumer concerns on SLA handling for their cloud-hosted databases along with the limitations of existing SLA frameworks to express and enforce SLA requirements in an automated manner creates the need for SLA-based management techniques for cloud-hosted databases. In this chapter, we present a novel approach for SLA-based management of cloud-hosted databases from the *consumer* perspective. In particular, we summarize the main contributions of this chapter as follows:

- We present the design and implementation details of an end-to-end framework that enables the cloud consumer applications to *declaratively* define and manage their SLA for the cloud-hosted database tiers in terms of goals that are subjected to a number of constraints that are specific to their application requirements. The presented framework is database platform-agnostic and relies on virtualization-based database replication mechanism.
- We present consumer-centric dynamic provisioning mechanisms for cloud-hosted databases based on adaptive application requirements for two of the most important SLA metrics, namely, data freshness and transactions response times.
- We conduct an extensive set of experiments that demonstrate the effectiveness of our framework in providing the cloud consumer applications with the required flexibility for achieving their SLA requirements of the cloud-hosted databases.

The remainder of this chapter is structured as follows. Section 11.2 provides a brief overview of the virtualized database servers techniques for hosting database tiers of software applications in cloud environments. Section 11.3 discusses the main challenges of SLA Management for cloud-hosted databases. Section 11.4 presents an overview of our framework architecture for consumer-centric SLA management. An experimental evaluation for the performance characteristics of database replication in virtualized cloud environments is presented in Section 11.5. Our mechanism for provisioning the database tier based on the consumer-centric SLA metric of data freshness is presented in Section 11.6 and for the SLA metric of the response times of application transactions is presented in Section 11.7. Section 11.8 summarizes the related work before we conclude the chapter in Section 11.9.

11.2 VIRTUALIZED DATABASE SERVER

Virtualization is a key technology of the cloud computing paradigm. Virtual machine technologies are increasingly being used to improve the manageability of software systems and lower their total cost of ownership. They allow resources to be allocated to different applications on demand and hide the complexity of resource sharing from cloud users by providing a powerful abstraction for application and resource provisioning. In particular, resource virtualization technologies add a flexible and programmable layer of software between applications and the resources used by these applications. The virtualized database server approach takes an existing application that has been designed to be used in a conventional data center, and then port it to virtual machines in the public cloud. Such migration process usually requires minimal changes in the architecture or the code of the deployed application. In this approach, database servers, like any other software components, are migrated to run in virtual machines. *Our framework presented in this chapter belongs to this approach.*

In principle, one of the major advantages of the *virtualized database server* approach is that the application can have full control in dynamically allocating and configuring the physical resources of the database tier (database servers) as needed [5,17,20]. Hence, software applications can fully utilize the elasticity feature of the cloud environment to achieve their defined and customized scalability or cost reduction goals. However, achieving these goals requires the existence of an admission control component, which is responsible for monitoring the system state and taking the corresponding actions (e.g., allocating more/less computing resources) according to the defined application requirements and strategies. Several approaches have been proposed for building admission control components that are based on the *efficiency of utilization* of the allocated resources [5,20]. In our approach, we focus on building an SLA-based admission control component as a more practical and *consumer-centric* view for achieving the requirements of their applications.

11.3 CHALLENGES OF SLA MANAGEMENT FOR VIRTUALIZED DATABASE SERVERS

An SLA is a contract between a service provider and its customers. *Service level agreements* (SLAs) capture the agreed upon guarantees between a service provider and its customer. They define the characteristics of the provided service including service level objectives (SLOs) (e.g., maximum response times, minimum throughput rates, data freshness) and define penalties if these objectives are not met by the service provider. In general, SLA management is a common general problem for the different types of software systems, which are hosted in cloud environments for different reasons such as the unpredictable and bursty workloads from various users in addition to the performance variability in the underlying cloud resources. In particular, there are three typical parties in the cloud. To keep a consistent terminology throughout the rest of the chapter, these parties are defined as follows:

- *Cloud Service Providers (CSP)*: They offer client-provisioned and metered computing resources (e.g., CPU, storage, memory, network) that can be rented for flexible time durations. In particular, they include Infrastructure-as-a-Service providers (IaaS), Platform-as-a-Service providers (PaaS), and Database-as-a-Service (DaaS). Examples include Amazon, Microsoft, and Google.
- *Cloud Consumers*: They represent the cloud-hosted software applications that utilize the services of CSP and are financially responsible for their resource consumptions.
- *End Users*: They represent the legitimate users for the services (applications) that are offered by cloud consumers.

While cloud service providers charge cloud consumers for renting computing resources to deploy their applications, cloud consumers may charge their end users for processing their workloads (e.g., SaaS) or may process the user requests for free (cloud-hosted business application). In both cases, the cloud consumers need to guarantee their users' SLA. Penalties are applied in the case of SaaS and reputation loss is incurred in the case of cloud-hosted business applications. For example, Amazon found that every 100 ms of latency costs them 1% in sales and Google found that an extra 500 ms in search page generation time dropped traffic by 20%.* In addition, large enterprise web applications (e.g., eBay, Facebook) need to provide high assurances in terms of SLA metrics such as response times and service availability to their users. Without such assurances, service providers of these applications stand to lose their user base, and hence their revenues.

In practice, resource management and SLA guarantee falls into two layers: the cloud service providers and the cloud consumers. In particular, the cloud service provider is responsible for the efficient utilization of the physical resources and guarantee their availability for their customers (cloud consumers). The cloud consumers are responsible for the efficient utilization of their allocated resources to satisfy the SLA of their customers (end users) and achieve their business goals. Therefore, we distinguish between two types of service level agreements (SLAs):

1. *Cloud Infrastructure SLA (I-SLA)*: These SLAs are offered by cloud providers to cloud consumers to assure the quality levels of their cloud computing resources (e.g., server performance, network speed, resources availability, storage capacity).
2. *Cloud-hosted Application SLA (A-SLA)*: These guarantees relate to the levels of quality for the software applications, which are deployed on a cloud infrastructure. In particular, cloud consumers often offer such guarantees to their application's end users to assure the quality of services that are offered such as the application's response time and data freshness.

---

* http://glinden.blogspot.com/2006/11/marissa-mayer-at-web-20.html.

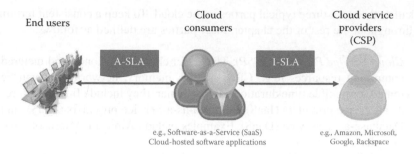

End users   Cloud   Cloud service
                             consumers   providers
                                                          (CSP)

A-SLA   I-SLA

e.g., Software-as-a-Service (SaaS)   e.g., Amazon, Microsoft,
Cloud-hosted software applications   Google, Rackspace

FIGURE 11.1   SLA parties in cloud environments.

Figure 11.1 illustrates the relationship between I-SLA and A-SLA in the software stack of cloud-hosted applications. In practice, traditional cloud monitoring technologies (e.g., Amazon CloudWatch*) focus on low-level computing resources (e.g., CPU speed, CPU utilization, disk speed). In principle, translating the SLAs of applications' transactions to the thresholds of utilization for low-level computing resources is a very challenging task and is usually done in an ad hoc manner due to the complexity and dynamism inherent in the interaction between the different tiers and components of the system. In particular, meeting SLAs that are agreed with end users by consumer applications of cloud resources using the traditional techniques for resource provisioning is a very challenging task due to many reasons such as the following:

- *Highly dynamic workload*: An application service can be used by large numbers of end users and highly variable load spikes in demand can occur depending on the day and the time of year, and the popularity of the application. In addition, the characteristic of workload could vary significantly from one application type to another and possible fluctuations on the workload characteristics that could be of several orders of magnitude on the same business day may occur [3]. Therefore, predicting the workload behavior (e.g., arrival pattern, I/O behavior, service time distribution) and consequently accurate planning of the computing resource requirements are very challenging tasks.
- *Performance variability of cloud resources*: Several studies have reported that the variation of the performance of cloud computing resources is high [6,18]. As a result, currently, cloud service providers do not provide adequate SLAs for their service offerings. Particularly, most providers guarantee only the availability (but not the performance) of their services [2,8].
- *Uncertain behavior*: One complexity that arises with the virtualization technology is that it becomes harder to provide performance guarantees

* http://aws.amazon.com/cloudwatch/.

and to reason about a particular application's performance because the performance of an application hosted on a virtual machine becomes a function of applications running in other virtual machines hosted on the same physical machine. In addition, it may be challenging to harness the full performance of the underlying hardware, given the additional layers of indirection in virtualized resource management [14].

In practice, it is a very challenging goal to delegate the management of the SLA requirements of the consumer applications to the side of the *cloud service provider* due to the wide heterogeneity in the workload characteristics, details, and granularity of SLA requirements, and cost management objectives of the very large number of consumer applications (tenants) that can be simultaneously running in a cloud environment. Therefore, it becomes a significant issue for the cloud consumers to be able to monitor and adjust the deployment of their systems if they intend to offer viable service level agreements (SLAs) to their customers (end users) [17]. Failing to achieve these goals will jeopardize the sustainable growth of cloud computing in the future and may result in valuable applications being moved away from the cloud. In the following sections, we present our *consumer-centric* approach for managing the SLA requirements of cloud-hosted databases.

11.4   FRAMEWORK ARCHITECTURE

In this section, we present an overview of our consumer-centric framework that enables the cloud consumer applications to *declaratively* define and manage their SLA for the cloudhosted database tiers in terms of goals that are subjected to a number of constraints that are specific to their application requirements. The framework also enables the consumer applications to declaratively define a set of application-specific rules (*action rules*) where the admission control component of the database tier needs to take corresponding actions to meet the expected system performance or to reduce the cost of the allocated cloud resources when they are not efficiently utilized. The framework continuously monitors the database workload, tracks the satisfaction of the application-defined SLA, evaluates the condition of the action rules, and takes the necessary actions when required. The design principles of our framework architecture are to be *application-independent* and to require *no code modification* on the consumer software applications that the framework will support. In addition, the framework is database *platform-agnostic* and relies on *virtualization-based database replication* mechanism. To achieve these goals, we rely on a database proxying mechanism that provides the ability to forward database requests to the underlying databases using an intermediate piece of software, the proxy, and to return the results from those request transparently to the client program without the need of having any database drivers installed. In particular, a database proxy software is a simple program that sits between the client application and the database server that can monitor, analyze, or transform their communications. Such flexibility allows for a wide variety of uses such as load balancing, query analysis, and query filtering.

In general, there exists many forms of SLAs with different metrics. In this chapter, we focus on the following two main consumer-centric SLA metrics:

- *Data freshness*, which represents the tolerated window of data staleness for each database replica. In other words, it represents the time between a committed update operation on the master database and the time when the operation is propagated and committed to the database replica (Section 11.6).
- *Transaction response time*, which represents the time between a transaction is presented to the database system and the time when the transaction execution is completed (Section 11.7).

Figure 11.2 shows an overview of our framework architecture, which consists of three main modules: the *monitor module,* the *control module*, and the *action module*. In this architecture, the consumer application is only responsible for configuring the control module of the framework by declaratively defining (using an XML dialect) the specifications of the SLA metrics of their application. In addition, the consumer application declaratively defines (using another XML dialect) a set of rules that specify the actions that should be taken (when a set of conditions are satisfied) to meet the expected system performance or to reduce the cost of the allocated cloud resources when they are not efficiently utilized. More details and examples about the declarative definitions of the application-specific SLA metrics and action rules will be presented in Sections 11.6 and 11.7. The control module also maintains the information about the configurations of the load balancer (e.g., proxy address, proxy script), the access information of each database replica (e.g., host address, port number), and the location information of each database replica (e.g., us-east, us-west,

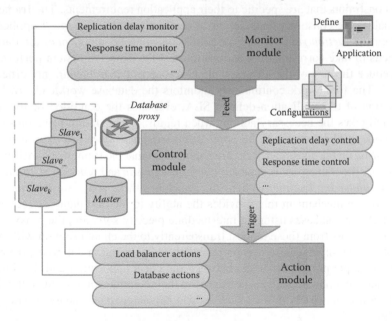

FIGURE 11.2 Framework architecture.

eu-west). On the runtime, the monitor module is responsible of continuously tracking the application-defined SLAs and feeding the control module with the collected information. The control module is responsible for continuously checking the monitored SLA values against their associated application-defined SLAs and triggers the action module to scale out/in the database according to the application-defined action rules.

In general, dynamic provisioning at the database-tier involves increasing or decreasing the number of database servers allocated to an application in response to workload changes. *Data replication* is a well-known strategy to achieve the availability, scalability, and performance improvement goals in the data management world. In particular, when the application load increases and the database tier becomes the *bottleneck* in the stack of the software application, there are two main options for achieving scalability at the database tier to enable the application to cope with more client requests:

1. *Scaling up (vertical scalability)*, which aims at allocating a bigger machine with more horsepower (e.g., more processors, memory, bandwidth) to act as a database server.
2. *Scaling out (horizontal scalability)*, which aims at replicating the data across more machines.

In practice, the scaling up option has the main drawback that large machines are often very expensive and eventually a physical limit is reached where a more powerful machine cannot be purchased at any cost. Alternatively, it is both extensible and economical, especially in a dynamic workload environment, to scale out by adding another commodity server that fits well with the pay-as-you-go pricing philosophy of cloud computing. In addition, the scale out mechanism is more adequate for achieving the elasticity benefit of cloud platforms by facilitating the process of horizontally adding or removing (in case of scaling in), as necessary, computing resources according to the application workload and requirements.

In database replication, there are two main replication strategies: *master–slave* and *multimaster*. In master–slave, updates are sent to a single master node and lazily replicated to slave nodes. Data on slave nodes might be stale, and it is the responsibility of the application to check for data freshness when accessing a slave node. Multimaster replication enforces a serializable execution order of transactions between all replicas so that each of them applies update transactions in the same order. This way, any replica can serve any read or write request. Our framework mainly considers the master–slave architecture as it is the most common architecture employed by most web applications in the cloud environment. For the sake of simplicity of achieving the consistency goal among the database replicas and reducing the effect of network communication latency, we employ the ROWA (read-once write-all) protocol on the Master copy [13]. However, our framework can be easily extended to support the multimaster replication strategy as well.

In general, provisioning of a new database replica involves extracting database content from an existing replica and copying that content to a new replica. In practice, the time taken to execute these operations mainly depends on the database size. To provision database replicas in a timely fashion, it is necessary to periodically snapshot the database state to minimize the database extraction and copying time to that of only the snapshot synchronization time. Clearly, there is a tradeoff between the time to snapshot the database, the size of the transactional log and the amount of update transactions in the workload. In our framework this trade-off can be controlled by application-defined parameters. This tradeoff can be further optimized by applying recently proposed live database migration techniques [9,24].

11.5 PERFORMANCE EVALUATION OF DATABASE REPLICATION ON VIRTUALIZED CLOUD ENVIRONMENTS

The CAP theorem [4] shows that a shared-data system can only choose at most two out of three properties: Consistency (all records are the same in all replicas), Availability (all replicas can accept updates or inserts), and tolerance to Partitions (the system still functions when distributed replicas cannot talk to each other). In practice, it is highly important for cloud-based applications to be always available and accept update requests of data and at the same time cannot block the updates even while they read the same data for scalability reasons. Therefore, when data is replicated over a wide area, this essentially leaves just consistency and availability for a system to choose between. Thus, the C (consistency) part of **CAP** is typically compromised to yield reasonable system availability [1]. Hence, most of the cloud data management overcome the difficulties of distributed replication by relaxing the consistency guarantees of the system. In particular, they implement various forms of weaker consistency models (e.g., eventual consistency [22]) so that all replicas do not have to agree on the same value of a data item at every moment of time. In particular, the eventual consistency policy guarantees that if no new updates are made to the object, eventually all accesses will return the last updated value. If no failures occur, the maximum size of the *inconsistency window* can be determined based on factors such as communication delays, the load on the system and the number of replicas involved in the replication scheme.

In this section, we present an experimental evaluation for the performance characteristics of the master–slave database replication strategy on virtualized database server in cloud environments [25]. In particular, the main goals of the experiments of this section are the following:

- To investigate the scalability characteristics of the master–slave replication strategy with an increasing workload and an increasing number of database replicas in a virtualized cloud environment. In particular, we try to identify what factors act as limits on achievable scale in such deployments.
- To measure the average replication delay (window of data staleness) that could exist with an increasing number of database replicas and different configurations to the geographical locations of the slave databases.

11.5.1 EXPERIMENT DESIGN

The Cloudstone benchmark* has been designed as a performance measurement tool for Web 2.0 applications. The benchmark mimics a Web 2.0 social events calendar

---

* http://radlab.cs.berkeley.edu/wiki/Projects/cloudstone.

that allows users to perform individual operations (e.g., browsing, searching, creating events) as well as social operations (e.g., joining, tagging events) [19]. Unlike Web 1.0 applications, the more interactive nature of Web 2.0 applications places many different demands on the database tier of software applications. One of the differences is on the write pattern, as contents of Web 2.0 applications depend on user contributions via blogs, photos, videos, and tags. Therefore, more write transactions are expected to be processed. Another difference is on the tolerance with regards to data consistency. In general, Web 2.0 applications are more acceptable to data staleness. For example, it might not be a mission-critical goal for a social network application (e.g., Facebook) to *immediately* have a user's new status available to his friends. However, a *consistency window* of some seconds (or even some minutes) would still be acceptable. Therefore, we believe that the design and workload characteristics of the Cloudstone benchmark is more suitable for the purpose of our study rather than other benchmarks such as TPC-W* or RUBiS,[†] which are more representative of Web 1.0-like applications.

The original software stack of Cloudstone consists of 3 components: web application, database, and load generator. Throughout the benchmark, the load generator generates the load against the web application, which in turn makes use of the database. The benchmark designs well for benchmarking performance of each tier for Web 2.0 applications. However, the original design of the benchmark makes it hard to push the database performance to its performance limits, which limits its suitability for our experiments of focusing mainly on the database tier of the software stack. In general, a user's operation, which is sent by a load generator has to be interpreted as database transactions in the web tier based on a predefined business logic before passing the request to the database tier. Thus, the saturation on the web tier usually happens earlier than the saturation on the database tier. Therefore, we modified the design of the original software stack by removing the web server tier. In particular, we reimplemented the business logic of the application in a way that a user's operation can be processed directly at the database tier without any intermediate interpretation at the web server tier. Meanwhile, on top of our Cloudstone implementation, we also implemented a connection pool (i.e., DBCP[‡]) and a proxy (i.e., MySQL Connector/J[§]) components.

The pool component enables the application users to reuse the connections that have been released by other users who have completed their operations to save the overhead of creating a new connection for each operation. The proxy component works as a load balancer among the available database replicas where all write operations are sent to the master while all read operations are distributed among slaves.

The database tier is composed of multiple MySQL replicas. For the purpose of monitoring replication delay in MySQL, we have created a *Heartbeats* database and a time/date function for each replica. The *Heartbeats* database, synchronized in the format of SQL statement across replicas, maintains a *"heartbeat"* table, which

---

* http://www.tpc.org/tpcw/.
† http://rubis.ow2.org/.
‡ http://commons.apache.org/dbcp/.
§ http://www.mysql.com/products/connector/.

records an id and a timestamp in each row. A heartbeat plug-in for Cloudstone is implemented to insert a new row with a global id and a local timestamp to the master periodically during the experiment. Once the insert query is replicated to slaves, every slave re-executes the query by committing the global id and its own local timestamp. The replication delay from the master to slaves is then calculated as the difference of two timestamps between the master and each slave. In practice, there are two challenges with respect to achieving a fine-grained measurement of replication delay: the resolution of the time/date function and the clock synchronization between the master and slaves. The time/date function offered by MySQL has a resolution of a second that represents an unacceptable solution because accurate measuring of the replication delay requires a higher precision. We, therefore, implemented a user defined time/date function with a microsecond resolution that is based on a proposed solution to MySQL Bug #8523.* The clock synchronizations between the master and slaves are maintained by NTP[†] (Network Time Protocol) on Amazon EC2. We set the NTP protocol to synchronize with multiple time servers every second to have a better resolution.

With the customized Cloudstone[‡] and the heartbeat plug-in, we are able to achieve our goal of measuring the end-to-end database throughput and the replication delay. In particular, we defined two configurations with read/write ratios of 50/50 and 80/20. We also defined three configurations of the geographical locations based on availability zones (they are distinct locations within a region) and regions (they are separated into geographic areas or countries) as follows: *same zone* where all slaves are deployed in the same Availability Zone of a Region of the master database; *different zones* where the slaves are in the same Region as the master database, but in different availability zones; *different regions* where all slaves are geographically distributed in a different region from where the master database is located. The workload and the number of database replicas start with a small number and gradually increase at a fixed step. Both numbers stop increasing if there are no throughputs gained.

11.5.2 Experiment Setup

We conducted our replication experiments in Amazon EC2 service with a three-layer implementation (Figure 11.3). The first layer is the Cloudstone benchmark that controls the read/write ratio and the workload by separately adjusting the number of read and write operations, and the number of concurrent users. As a large number of concurrent users emulated by the benchmark could be very resource-consuming, the benchmark is deployed in a large instance to avoid any overload on the application tier. The second layer includes the master database that receives the write operations from the benchmark and is responsible for propagating the write sets to the slaves. The master database runs in a small instance so that saturation can be expected to be observed

* http://bugs.mysql.com/bug.php?id=8523.
† http://www.ntp.org/.
‡ The source code of our Cloudstone customized implementation is available on http://code.google.com/p/clouddbreplication/.

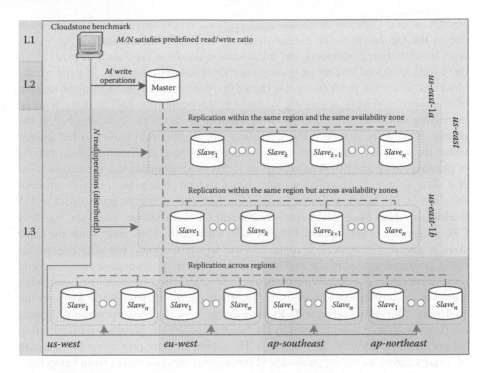

FIGURE 11.3 Database replication on virtualized cloud servers.

early. Both the master database server and the application benchmark are deployed in *us-east-1a* location. The third layer is a group of slaves that arc responsible for processing read operations and updating write sets. The number of slaves in a group varies from one to the number where throughput limitation is achieved. Several options for the deployment locations of the slaves have been used, namely, the same zone as the master in *us-east-1a*, a different zone in *us-east-1b*, and four possible different regions, ranging among *us-west*, *eu-west*, *ap-southeast*, and *ap-northeast*. All slaves run in small instances for the same reason of provisioning the master instance.

Several sets of experiments have been implemented to investigate the end-to-end throughput and the replication delay. Each of these sets is designed to target a specific configuration regarding the geographical locations of the slave databases and the read/write ratio. Multiple runs are conducted by compounding different workloads and numbers of slaves. The benchmark is able to push the database system to a limit where no more throughput can be obtained by increasing the workload and the number of database replicas. Every run lasts 35 minutes, including 10-minute ramp-up, 20-minute steady stage, and 5-minute ramp down. Moreover, for each run, both the master and slaves should start with a preloaded, fully synchronized database.

11.5.3 END-TO-END THROUGHPUT EXPERIMENTS

Figures 11.4 and 11.5 show the throughput trends for up to 4 and 11 slaves with mixed configurations of three locations and two read/write ratios. Both results indicate that

MySQL with asynchronous master–slave replication is limited in its ability to scale due to the saturation to the master database. In particular, the throughput trends react to saturation movements and transitions in database replicas in regards to an increasing workload and an increasing number of database replicas. In general, the observed saturation point (the point right after the observed maximum throughput of a number of slaves), appearing in slaves at the beginning, moves along with an increasing workload when an increasing number of slaves are synchronized to the master. Eventually, however, the saturation will transit from slaves to the master where the scalability limit is achieved. Taking throughput trends with configurations of the same zone and 50/50 ratio (Figure 11.5a) as an example, the saturation point of 1 slave is initially observed at under 100 workloads due to the full utilization of the slave's CPU. When a second slave is attached, the saturation point shifts to 175 workloads where both slaves reach maximum CPU utilization while the master's CPU usage rate is also approaching its utilization limit. Thus, ever since the third slave is added, 175 workloads remain as the saturation point, but with the master being saturated instead of slaves. Once the master is in the saturation status, adding more slaves does not help with improving the scalability, because the overloaded master fails to offer extra capacity for improving write throughput to keep up the read/write ratio that corresponds to the increment of the read throughput. Hence, the read throughput is suppressed by the benchmark, for the purpose of maintaining the predefined read/write ratio at 50/50. The slaves are over provisioned in the case of 3 and 4 slaves, as the suppressed read throughput prevents slaves from being fully utilized. The similar saturation transition also happens to 3 slaves at 50/50 ratio in the other two locations (Figure 11.4b and 11.4c) and 10 slaves at 20/80 ratio in the same zone (Figure 11.5a) and different zone (Figure 11.5b) and also 9 slaves at 20/80 ratio in different regions (Figure 11.5c).

The configuration of the geographic locations is a factor that affects the end-to-end throughput, in the context of locations of users. In the case of our experiments, since all users emulated by Cloudstone send read operations from *us-east-1a*, distances between the users and the slaves increase, following the order of same zone, different zone, and different region. Normally, a long distance incurs a slow round-trip time, which results in a smaller throughput for the same workload. Therefore, it can be expected that a decrease in maximum throughput would be observed when configurations of locations follow the order of same zone, different zone, and different region. Moreover, the throughput degradation is also related to read percentages where higher read percentages would result in larger degradations. It explains why degradation of maximum throughput is more significant with configuration of 80/20 read/write ratio (Figure 11.5). Hence, it is a good strategy to distribute replicated slaves to places that are close to users to improve end-to-end throughput.

The performance variation of instances is another factor that needs to be considered when deploying databases in the cloud. For throughput trends of 1 slave at 50/50 read/write ratio with configurations of different zone and different region, respectively, if the configuration of locations is the only factor, the maximum throughput in the different zone (Figure 11.4b) should be larger than the one in the different region (Figure 11.4c). However, the main reason of throughput difference here is

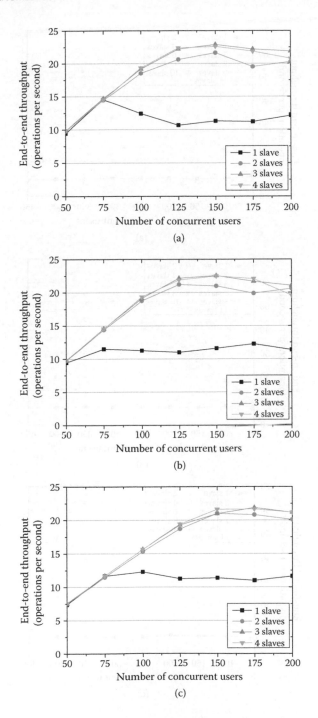

FIGURE 11.4 End-to-end throughput of the workload with the read/write ratio 50/50.
(a) Same zone (*us-west-1a*). (b) Different zone (*us-west-1b*). (c) Different region (*eu-west-1a*).

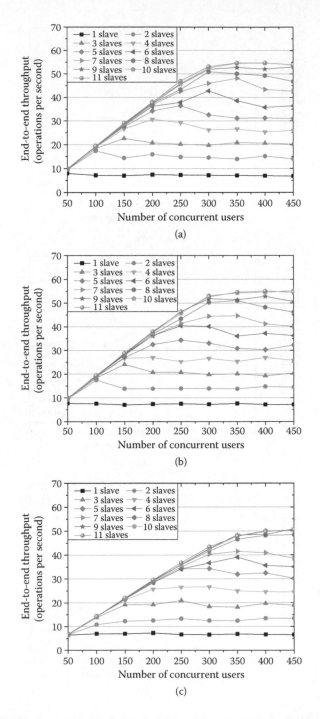

FIGURE 11.5 End-to-end throughput of the workload with the read/write ratio 80/20. (a) Same zone (*us-west-1a*). (b) Different zone (*us-west-1b*). (c) Different region (*eu-west-1a*).

caused by the performance variation of instances rather than the configuration of locations. The first slave from the same zone runs on top of a physical machine with an Intel Xeon CPU E5430 2.66GHz, while another first slave from the different zone is deployed in a physical machine powered by an Intel Xeon CPU E5507 2.27GHz. Because of the performance differences between physical CPUs, the slave from same zone performs better than the one from different zone. Previous research indicated that the coefficient of variation of CPU of small instances is 21% [18]. Therefore, it is a good strategy to validate instance performance before deploying applications into the cloud, as poor-performing instances are launched randomly and can largely affect application performance.

11.5.4 REPLICATION DELAY EXPERIMENTS

Figures 11.6 and 11.7 show the trends of the average relative replication delay for up to 4 and 11 slaves with mixed configurations of three locations and two read/write ratios. The results of both figures imply that the configurations of the geographical locations have a lower impact on the replication delay than that of the workload characteristics. The trends of the average relative replication delay respond to an increasing workload and an increasing number of database replicas. For most cases, with the number of database replicas being kept constant, the average relative replication delay surges along with an increasing workload, which leads to more read and write operations sent to the slaves and the master database, respectively. It turns out that the increasing number of read operations result in a higher resource demand on every slave while the increasing write operations on the master database leads to, indirectly, increasing resource demand on slaves as more writesets are propagated to be committed on slaves. The two increasing demands push resource contention higher, resulting in the delay of committing writesets, which subsequently results in higher replication delay. Similarly, the average relative replication delay decreases along with an increasing number of database replicas as the addition of a new slave leads to a reduction in the resource contention and subsequent decrease in replication delay.

As previously mentioned, the configuration of the geographic location of the slaves play a less significant role in affecting replication delay, in comparison to the changes of the workload characteristics. We measured the half round-trip time between the master in *us-west-1a* and the slave that uses different configurations of geographic locations by running the ping command every second for a 20-minute period. The results suggest an average of 16, 21, and 173 milliseconds half round-trip time for the same zone (Figures 11.6a and 11.7a), different zones (Figures 11.6b and 11.7b), and different regions (Figures 11.6c and 11.7c), respectively. However, the trends of the average relative replication delay can usually go up from two to four orders of magnitude (Figure 11.6), or one to three orders of magnitude (Figure 11.7). Therefore, it could be suggested that geographic replication would be applicable in the cloud as long as workload characteristics can be well managed (e.g., having a smart load balancer that is able to balance the operations based on estimated processing time).

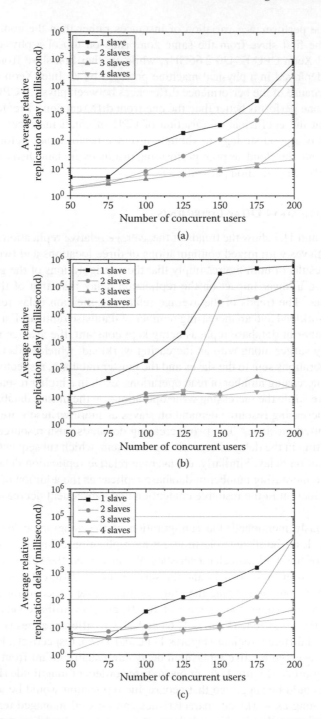

FIGURE 11.6 Average relative replication delay of the workload with the read/write ratio is 50/50. (a) Same zone (*us-west-1a*). (b) Different zone (*us-west-1b*). (c) Different region (*eu-west-1a*).

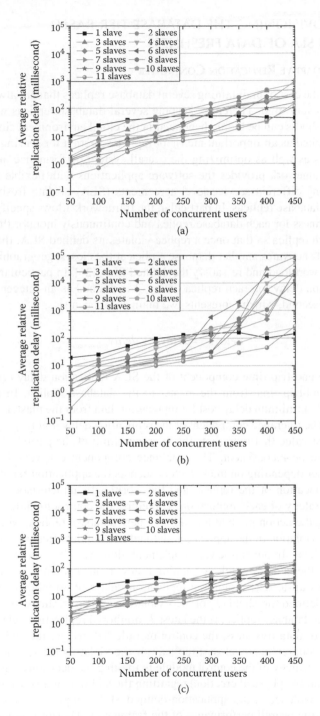

FIGURE 11.7 Average relative replication delay of the workload with the read/write ratio is 80/20. (a) Same zone (*us-west-1a*). (b) Different zone (*us-west-1b*). (c) Different region (*eu-west-1a*).

11.6   PROVISIONING THE DATABASE TIER BASED ON SLA OF DATA FRESHNESS

11.6.1   ADAPTIVE REPLICATION CONTROLLER

In practice, the cost of maintaining several database replicas that are always strongly consistent is very high. Therefore, keeping several database replicas with different levels of freshness can be highly beneficial in the cloud environment since freshness can be exploited as an important metric of replica selection for serving the application requests as well as optimizing the overall system performance and monetary cost. Our framework provides the software applications with flexible mechanisms for specifying different service level agreements (SLA) of data freshness for the underlying database replicas. In particular, the framework allows specifying an SLA of data freshness for each database replica and continuously monitor the replication delay of each replica so that once a replica violates its defined SLA, the framework automatically activates another database replica at the closest geographic location to balance the workload and re-satisfy the defined SLA [26]. In particular, the SLA of the replication delay for each replica ($delay_{sla}$) is defined as an integer value in the unit of millisecond, which represents two main components:

$$delay_{sla} = delay_{rtt} + delay_{tolerance}$$

where the round-trip time component of the SLA replication delay ($delay_{rtt}$) is the average round-trip time from the master to the database replica. In particular, it represents the minimum delay cost for replicating data from the master to the associated slave. The tolerance component of the replication delay ($delay_{tolerance}$) is defined by a constant value that represents the tolerance limit of the period of the time for the replica to be inconsistent. This tolerance component can vary from one replica to another depending on many factors such as the application requirements, the geographic location of the replica, and the workload characteristics and the load balancing strategy of each application. Therefore, the control module is responsible of triggering the action module for adding a new database replica, when necessary, to avoid any violation in the application-defined SLA of data freshness for the active database replicas. In our framework implementation, we follow an intuitive strategy that triggers the action module for adding a new replica when it detects a number of continuous up-to-date monitored replication delays of a replica that exceeds its application defined threshold (T) of SLA violation of data freshness. In other words, for a running database replica, if the latest T monitored replication delays are violating its SLA of data freshness, the control module will trigger the action module to activate the geographically closest replica (for the violating replica). It is worthy to note that the strategy of the control module in making the decisions (e.g., the timing, the placement, the physical creation) regarding the addition of a new replica in order to avoid any violence of the application-defined SLA can play an important role in determining the overall performance of the framework. However, it is not the main focus of this chapter to investigate different strategies for making these decisions. We leave this aspect for future work.

11.6.2 EXPERIMENTAL EVALUATION

We implemented two sets of experiments to evaluate the effectiveness of our adaptive replication controller in terms of its effect on the end-to-end system throughput and the replication delay for the underlying database replicas. Figure 11.8 illustrates the setup of our experiments using Amazon EC2 platform. In the first set of experiments, we fix the value of the tolerance component ($delay_{tolerance}$) of the SLA replication delay to 1000 milliseconds and vary the monitor interval ($intvl_{mon}$) among the following set of values: 60, 120, 240, and 480 seconds. In the second set of experiments, we fix the monitor interval ($intvl_{mon}$) to 120 seconds and adjust the SLA of replication delay ($delay_{sla}$) by varying the tolerance component of the replication delay ($delay_{tolerance}$) among the following set of values: 500, 1000, 2000, and 4000 milliseconds. We have been evaluating the round-trip component ($delay_{rtt}$) of the replication delays SLA ($delay_{sla}$) for the database replicas in the three geographical regions of our deployment by running ping command every second for a 10-minute period. The resulting average three round-trip times ($delay_{rtt}$) are 30, 130, and 200 milliseconds for the master to slaves in *us-west*, *us-east*, and *eu-west*, respectively. Every experiment is executed for a period of 3000 seconds with a starting workload of 220 concurrent users and database requests with a read/write ratio of 80/20. The

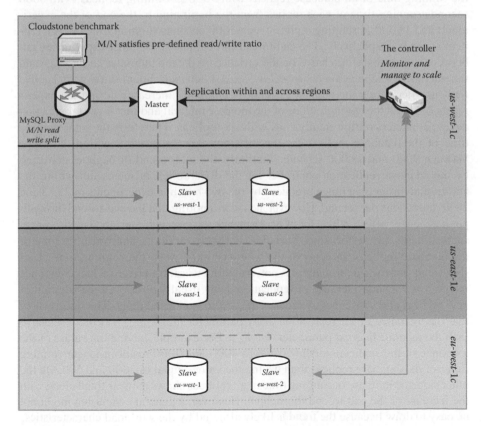

FIGURE 11.8 Adaptive replication controller.

workload gradually increases in steps of 20 concurrent users every 600 seconds so that each experiment ends with a workload of 300 concurrent users. Each experiment deploys 6 replicas in 3 regions where each region hosts two replicas: the first replica is an active replica that is used from the start of the experiment for serving the database requests of the application, while the second replica is a hot backup that is not used for serving the application requests at the beginning of the experiment but can be added by the action module, as necessary, when triggered by the control module. Finally, in addition to the two sets of experiments, we conducted two experiments without our adaptive replication controller to measure the end-to-end throughputs and replication delays of 3 (the minimum number of running replicas) and 6 (the maximum number of running replicas) slaves in order to measure the baselines of our comparison.

11.6.2.1 End-to-End Throughput

Table 11.1 presents the end-to-end throughput results for our set of experiments with different configuration parameters. The baseline experiments represent the *minimum* and *maximum* end-to-end throughput results with 22.33 and 38.96 operations per second, respectively. They also represent the minimum and maximum baseline for the running time of all database replicas with 9000 (3 running replicas, with 3000 seconds running time of each replica from the beginning to the end of the experiment) and 18,000 (6 running replicas, with 3000 seconds running time of each replica) seconds, respectively. The end-to-end throughput of the other experiments fall between the two baselines based on the variance on the monitor interval ($intvl_{mon}$) and the tolerance of replication delay ($delay_{tolerance}$). Each experiment starts with 3 active replicas after which the number of replicas gradually increases during the experiments based on the configurations of the monitor interval and the SLA of replication delay parameters until it finally ends with six replicas. Therefore, the total running time of the database replicas for the different experiments fall within the range between 9000 and 18,000 seconds. Similarly, the end-to-end throughput delivered by the adaptive replication controller for the different experiments fall within the end-to-end throughput range produced by the two baseline experiments of 22.33 and 38.96 operations per second. However, it is worth noting that the end-to-end throughput can be still affected by a lot of performance variations in the cloud environment such as hardware performance variation, network variation, and warm up time of the database replicas. In general, the relationship between the running time of all slaves and end-to-end throughput is not straightforward. Intuitively, a longer monitor interval or a longer tolerance of replication delay usually postpones the addition of new replicas and consequently reduces the end-to-end throughput. The results show that the tolerance of the replication delay parameter ($delay_{tolerance}$) is more sensitive than the monitor interval parameter ($intvl_{mon}$). For example, having the values of the tolerance of the replication delay equal to 4000 and 1000 result in longer running times of the database replicas than having the values equal to 2000 and 500. On the other side, the increase of running time of all replicas shows a linear trend along with the increase of the end-to-end throughput. However, a general conclusion might not be easy to draw because the trend is likely affected by the workload characteristics.

TABLE 11.1
Effect of the Adaptive Replication Controller on the End-to-End System Throughput

Experiment Parameters	Monitor Interval ($intvl_{mon}$) (seconds)	Tolerance of Replication Delay ($delay_{tolerance}$) (msec)	Number of Running Replicas	Running Time of All Replicas (seconds)	End-to-End Throughput (operations per seconds)	Replication Delay
Baselines with fixed number of replicas	N/A	N/A	3	9000	22.33	Figure 11.9a
	N/A	N/A	6	18000	38.96	Figure 11.9b
Varying the monitor interval ($intvl_{mon}$)	60	1000	3 → 6	15837	38.43	Figure 11.10a
	120	1000	3 → 6	15498	36.45	Figure 11.9c
	240	1000	3 → 6	13935	34.12	Figure 11.10b
	480	1000	3 → 6	12294	31.40	Figure 11.10c
Varying the tolerance of replication delay ($delay_{tolerance}$)	120	500	3 → 6	15253	37.44	Figure 11.10d
	120	1000	3 → 6	15498	36.45	Figure 11.9c
	120	2000	3 → 6	13928	36.33	Figure 11.10e
	120	4000	3 → 6	14437	34.68	Figure 11.10f

11.6.2.2   Replication Delay

Figure 11.10 illustrates the effect of the adaptive replication controller on the performance of the replication delay for the cloud-hosted database replicas. Figure 11.9a and b shows the replication delay of the two baseline cases for our comparison. They represent the experiments of running with a fixed number of replicas (3 and 6, respectively) from the starting times of the experiments to their end times. Figure 11.9a shows that the replication delay tends to follow different patterns for the different replicas. The two trends of *us-west*-1 and *eu-west*-1 surge significantly at 260 and 280 users, respectively. At the same time, the trend of *us-east*-1 tends to be stable throughout the entire running time of the experiment. The main reason behind this is the performance variation between the hosting EC2 instances for the database replicas.* Due to the performance differences between the physical CPUs specifications, *us-east*-1 is able to handle the amount of operations that saturate *us-west*-1 and *eu-west*-1. Moreover, with an identical CPU for *us-west*-1 and *eu-west*-1, the former seems to surge at an earlier point than the latter. This is basically because of the difference in the geographical location of the two instances. As illustrated in Figure 11.8, the MySQL Proxy location is closer to *us-west*-1 than *eu-west*-1. Therefore, the forwarded database operations by the MySQL Proxy take less time to arrived at *us-west*-1 than *eu-west*-1, which leads to more congestion on the *us-west*-1 side. Similarly, in Figure 11.9b, the replication delay tends to surge in both *us-west*-1 and *us-west*-2 for the same reason of the difference in the geographic location of the underlying database replica.

Figures 11.9c and 11.10d–f show the results of the replication delay for our experiments using different values for the monitor interval ($intvl_{mon}$) and the tolerance of replication delay ($delay_{tolerance}$) parameters. For example, Figure 11.9c shows that the *us-west*-2, *us-east*-2, and *eu-west*-2 replicas are added in sequence at the 255th, 407th, and 1843th seconds, where the drop lines are emphasized. The addition of the three replicas are caused by the SLA-violation of the *us-west*-1 replicas at different periods. In particular, there are four SLA-violation periods for *us-west*-1 where the period must exceed the monitor interval, and all calculated replication delays in the period must exceed the SLA of replication delay. These four periods are: (1) 67:415 (total of 349 seconds). (2) 670:841 (total of 172 seconds). (3) 1373:1579 (total of 207 seconds). (4) 1615:3000 (total of 1386 seconds). The addition of new replicas is only triggered on the first and the fourth periods based on the time point analysis. The second and the third periods do not trigger the addition of new replica as the number of detected SLA violations does not exceed the defined threshold (T).

Figures 11.9c and 11.10a–c show the effect of varying the monitor interval ($intvl_{mon}$) on the replication delay of the different replicas. The results show that *us-west*-2 is always the first location that adds a new replica because it is the closest location to *us-west*-1, which hosts the replica that first violates its defined SLA data freshness. The results also show that as the monitor interval increases, the triggering points for adding new replicas are usually delayed. On the contrary, the results of Figures 11.9c and 11.10d–f show that increasing the value of the tolerance of the replication delay parameter ($delay_{tolerance}$) does not necessarily cause a delay in the triggering point for adding new replicas.

---

* Both *us-west*-1 and *eu-west*-1 are powered by Intel® Xeon® CPU E5507 at 2.27GHz, whereas *us-east*-1 is deployed with a better CPU, Intel® Xeon® CPU E5645 @ 2.40GHz.

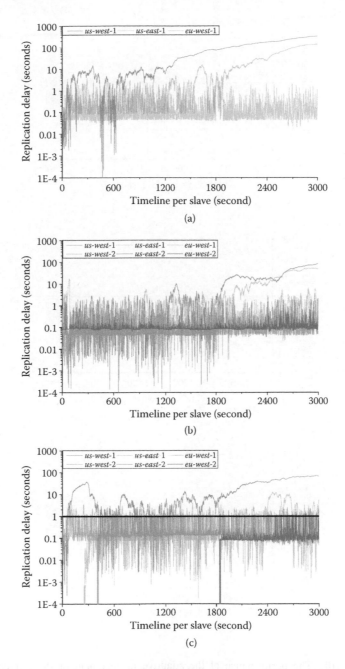

FIGURE 11.9 The performance of the adaptive management of the replication delay for the cloud-hosted database replicas. (a) Fixed 3 running replicas. (b) Fixed 6 running replicas. (c) $delay_{tolerance} = 1000$ ms and $intvl_{mon} = 120$ sec.

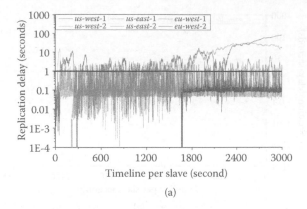

(a)

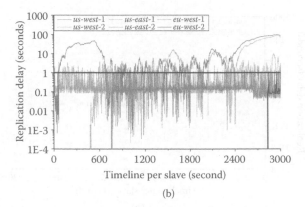

(b)

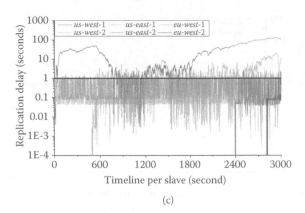

(c)

FIGURE 11.10 The performance of the adaptive management of the replication delay for the cloud-hosted database replicas. (a) $intvl_{mon}$ = 60 seconds. (b) $intvl_{mon}$ = 120 seconds. (c) $intvl_{mon}$ = 480 seconds. (d) $delay_{tolerance}$ = 480 milliseconds. (e) $delay_{tolerance}$ = 2000 milliseconds. (f) $delay_{tolerance}$ = 4000 milliseconds.

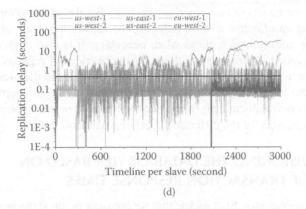

(d)

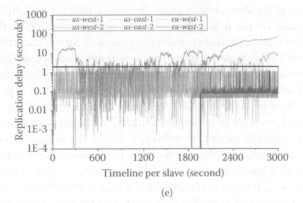

(e)

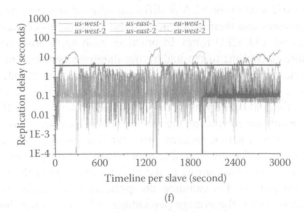

(f)

FIGURE 11.10 (Continued) The performance of the adaptive management of the replication delay for the cloud-hosted database replicas. (a) $intvl_{mon}$ = 60 seconds. (b) $intvl_{mon}$ = 120 seconds. (c) $intvl_{mon}$ = 480 seconds. (d) $delay_{tolerance}$ = 480 milliseconds. (e) $delay_{tolerance}$ = 2000 milliseconds. (f) $delay_{tolerance}$ = 4000 milliseconds.

In general, the results of our experiments show that the adaptive replication controller can play an effective role on reducing the replication delay of the underlying replicas by adding new replicas when necessary. It is also observed that with more replicas added, the replication delay for the overloaded replicas can dramatically drop. Moreover, it is more cost-effective in comparison to the overprovisioning approach for the number of database replicas that can ensure low replication delay because it adds new replicas only when necessary based on the application-defined SLA of data freshness for the different underlying database replicas.

11.7 PROVISIONING THE DATABASE TIER BASED ON SLA OF TRANSACTION RESPONSE TIMES

Another consumer-centric SLA metric that we consider in our framework is the total execution times of database transactions (response time). In practice, this metric has a great impact on the user experience and thus satisfaction of the underlying services. In other words, individual users are generally more concerned about when their transaction will complete rather than how many transactions the system will be able to execute in a second (system throughput) [11]. To illustrate, assuming a transaction (T) with an associated SLA for its execution time (S) is presented to the system at time 0, if the system is able to finish the execution of the transaction at time $(t \leq S)$ then the service provider has achieved his target otherwise if $(t > S)$, then the transaction response cannot be delivered within the defined SLA, and hence, a penalty p is incurred. In practice, the SLA requirements can vary between the different types of application transactions (for example, a login application request may have an SLA of 100 ms execution time, a search request may have an SLA of 600 ms while a request of submitting an order information would have 1500 ms). Obviously, the variations in the SLA of different applications transactions is due to their different natures and their differences in the consumption behavior of system resources (e.g., disk I/O, CPU time). In practice, each application transaction can send one or more operations to the underlying database system. Therefore, in our framework, consumer applications can define each transaction as pattern(s) of SQL commands where the transaction execution time is computed as the total execution time of these individual operations in the described pattern. Thus, the monitoring module is responsible for correlating the received database operations based on their sender to detect the transaction patterns [16]. Our framework also enables the consumer application to declaratively define application-specific action rules to adaptively scale out or scale in according to the monitored status of the response times of application transactions. For example, an application can define to scale out the underlying database tier if the average percentage of SLA violation for transactions T_1 and T_2 exceeds 10% (of the total number of T_1 and T_2 transactions) for a continuous period of more than 8 minutes. Similarly, the application can define to scale in the database tier if the average percentage of SLA violation for transactions T_1 and T_2 is less than 2% for a continuous period that is more than 8 minutes and the average number of concurrent users per database replica is less than 25.

We conducted our experiments with 4 different rules for achieving elasticity and dynamic provisioning for the database tier in the cloud. Two rules are defined based

on the average CPU utilization of allocated virtual machines for the database server
as follows: scale out the database tier (add one more replica) when the average CPU
utilization of the virtual machines exceeds of 75% for (**R1**) and 85% for (**R2**) over a
continuous period of 5 minutes. Two other rules are defined based on the percentage
of the SLA satisfaction of the workload transactions (the SLA values of the different transactions are defined as specified in the Cloudstone benchmark) as follows:
scale out the database tier when the percentage of SLA satisfaction is less than 97%
for (**R3**) and 90% for (**R4**) over a continuous period of 5 minutes. Our evaluation
metrics are the overall percentage of SLA satisfaction and the number of provisioned
database replicas during the experimental time.

Figure 11.11 illustrates the results of running our experiments over a period of one
hour for the 80/20 workload (Figure 11.11a) and the 50/50 workload (Figure 11.11b).

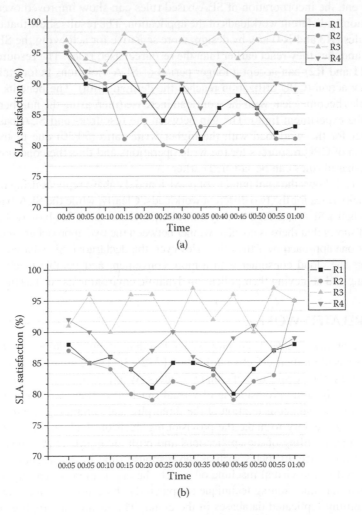

FIGURE 11.11 Comparison of SLA-based vs. resource-based database provisioning rules.
(a) Workload: 80/20 (r/w). (b) Workload: 50/50 (r/w).

TABLE 11.2
Number of Provisioned Database Replicas

Workload/Rule	R1	R2	R3	R4
80/20	4	3	5	5
50/50	5	4	7	6

In these figures, the *X-axis* represents the elapsed time of the experiment while the *Y-axis* represents the SLA satisfaction of the application workload according to the different elasticity rules. In general, we see that, even for this relatively small deployment, the incorporation of SLA-based rules can show improved overall SLA satisfaction of different workloads of the application. The results show that the SLA-based rules (**R3** and **R4**) are, by design, more sensitive for achieving the SLA satisfaction, and thus they react earlier than the resourcebased rules. The resource-based rules (**R1** and **R2**) can accept a longer period of SLA violations before taking any necessary action (CPU utilization reaches the defined limit). The benefits of SLA-based rules become clear with the workload increase (increasing the number of users during the experiment time). The gap between the resource- and SLA-based rules is smaller for the workload with the higher write ratio (50/50) due to the higher contention of CPU resources for the write operations and thus the conditions of the resource-based rules can be satisfied earlier.

Table 11.2 shows the total number of provisioned database replicas using the different elasticity rules for the two different workloads. Clearly, while the SLA-based rules achieves better SLA satisfaction, they may also provision more database replicas. This trade-off shows that there is no clear winner between the two approaches, and we cannot favor one approach over the other. However, the declarative SLA-based approach empowers the cloud consumer with a more convenient and flexible mechanism for controlling and achieving their policies in dynamic environments such as the cloud.

11.8   RELATED WORK

Several approaches have been proposed for dynamic provisioning of computing resources based on their effective utilization [7,12,23]. These approaches are mainly geared toward the perspective of cloud providers. Wood et al. [23] have presented an approach for dynamic provisioning of virtual machines. They define a unique metric based on the data consumption of the three physical computing resources: CPU, network, and memory to make the provisioning decision. Padala et al. [12] carried out black box profiling of the applications and built an approximated model, which relates performance attributes such as the response time to the fraction of processor allocated to the virtual machine on which the application is running. Dolly [5] is a virtual machine cloning technique to spawn database replicas and provisioning shared-nothing replicated databases in the cloud. The technique proposes database provisioning cost models to adapt the provisioning policy to the low-level cloud resources according to the application requirements. Rogers et al. [15] proposed two approaches for managing the resource provisioning challenge for cloud databases. The black-box provisioning uses end-to-end performance results of sample query executions, whereas white-box provisioning uses a finer grained approach that relies on the DBMS optimizer to predict the physical resource (e.g., I/O, memory, CPU) consumption for each query. Floratou et al. [10] have studied the performance and cost in the relational database as a service environments. The results show that given a range of pricing models and the flexibility of the allocation of resources in cloud-based environments, it is hard for a user to figure out their actual monthly cost upfront. Soror et al. [20] introduced a virtualization design advisor that uses information about the database workloads to provide offline recommendations of workload-specific virtual machines configurations. To the best of our knowledge, our approach is the first to tackle the problem of dynamic provisioning the cloud resources of the database tier based on consumer-centric and application-defined SLA metrics.

11.9 CONCLUSIONS

In this chapter, we presented the design and implementation details* of an end-to-end framework that facilitates adaptive and dynamic provisioning of the database tier of the software applications based on consumer-centric policies for satisfying their own SLA performance requirements, avoiding the cost of any SLA violation and controlling the monetary cost of the allocated computing resources. The framework provides the consumer applications with declarative and flexible mechanisms for defining their specific requirements for fine-grained SLA metrics at the application level. The framework is database platform-agnostic, uses virtualization-based database replication mechanisms and requires zero source code changes of the cloud-hosted software applications.

REFERENCES

1. Daniel J. Abadi. Data management in the cloud: Limitations and opportunities. *IEEE Data Eng. Bull.*, 32(1), 2009.
2. Michael Armbrust, Armando Fox, Rean Griffith, Anthony D. Joseph, Randy H. Katz, Andrew Konwinski, Gunho Lee et al. Above the clouds: A berkeley view of cloud computing. Technical Report UCB/EECS-2009-28, 2009.
3. Peter Bodík, Armando Fox, Michael J. Franklin, Michael I. Jordan, and David A. Patterson. Characterizing, modeling, and generating workload spikes for stateful services. In *SoCC*, pages 241–252, 2010.
4. Eric Brewer. Towards robust distributed systems. In *PODC*, 2000.
5. Emmanuel Cecchet, Rahul Singh, Upendra Sharma, and Prashant J. Shenoy. Dolly: Virtualization-driven database provisioning for the cloud. In *VEE*, 2011.
6. Brian F. Cooper, Adam Silberstein, Erwin Tam, Raghu Ramakrishnan, and Russell Sears. Benchmarking cloud serving systems with YCSB. In *SoCC*, 2010.
7. Italo S. Cunha, Jussara M. Almeida, Virgilio Almeida, and Marcos Santos. Self-adaptive capacity management for multi-tier virtualized environments. In *Integrated Network Management*, 2007.
8. Dave Durkee. Why cloud computing will never be free. *Commun. ACM*, 53(5), 2010.

---

* http://cdbslaautoadmin.sourceforge.net/.

9. Aaron J. Elmore, Sudipto Das, Divyakant Agrawal, and Amr El Abbadi. Zephyr: Live migration in shared nothing databases for elastic cloud platforms. In *SIGMOD*, 2011.

10. Avrilia Floratou, Jignesh M. Patel, Willis Lang, and Alan Halverson. When free is not really free: What does it cost to run a database workload in the cloud? In *TPCTC*, pages 163–179, 2011.

11. Daniela Florescu and Donald Kossmann. Rethinking cost and performance of database systems. *SIGMOD Record*, 38(1), 2009.

12. Pradeep Padala, Kang G. Shin, Xiaoyun Zhu, Mustafa Uysal, Zhikui Wang, Sharad Singhal, Arif Merchant, and Kenneth Salem. Adaptive control of virtualized resources in utility computing environments. In *EuroSys*, 2007.

13. Christian Plattner and Gustavo Alonso. Ganymed: Scalable replication for transactional web applications. In *Middleware*, 2004.

14. Thomas Ristenpart, Eran Tromer, Hovav Shacham, and Stefan Savage. Hey, you, get off of my cloud: Exploring information leakage in third-party compute clouds. In *ACM CCS*, 2009.

15. Jennie Rogers, Olga Papaemmanouil, and Ugur Çetintemel. A generic auto-provisioning framework for cloud databases. In *ICDE Workshops*, 2010.

16. Sherif Sakr and Anna Liu. SLA-based and consumer-centric dynamic provisioning for cloud databases. In *IEEE Cloud*, 2012.

17. Sherif Sakr, Liang Zhao, Hiroshi Wada, and Anna Liu. CloudDB AutoAdmin: Towards a truly elastic cloud-based data store. In *ICWS*, 2011.

18. Jörg Schad, Jens Dittrich, and Jorge-Arnulfo Quiané-Ruiz. Runtime measurements in the cloud: Observing, analyzing, and reducing variance. *PVLDB*, 3(1), 2010.

19. Will Sobel, Shanti Subramanyam, Akara Sucharitakul, Jimmy Nguyen, Hubert Wong, Arthur Klepchukov, Sheetal Patil, Armando Fox, and David Patterson. Cloudstone: Multi-platform, multi-language benchmark and measurement tools for web 2.0. In *Proceedings of Cloud Computing and Its Applications (CCA)*, 2008.

20. Ahmed A. Soror, Umar Farooq Minhas, Ashraf Aboulnaga, Kenneth Salem, Peter Kokosielis, and Sunil Kamath. Automatic virtual machine configuration for database workloads. *ACM Trans. Database Syst.*, 35(1), 2010.

21. Basem Suleiman, Sherif Sakr, Ross Jeffrey, and Anna Liu. On understanding the economics and elasticity challenges of deploying business applications on public cloud infrastructure. *Internet Services and Applications*, 3(2), 2012.

22. Werner Vogels. Eventually consistent. *Queue*, 6:14–19, 2008.

23. Timothy Wood, Prashant J. Shenoy, Arun Venkataramani, and Mazin S. Yousif. Blackbox and gray-box strategies for virtual machine migration. In *NSDI*, 2007.

24. Yangyang Wu and Ming Zhao. Performance modeling of virtual machine live migration. In *IEEE CLOUD*, 2011.

25. Liang Zhao, Sherif Sakr, Alan Fekete, Hiroshi Wada, and Anna Liu. Application managed database replication on virtualized cloud environments. In *ICDE Workshops*, 2012.

26. Liang Zhao, Sherif Sakr, and Anna Liu. Application-managed replication controller for cloud-hosted databases. In *IEEE Cloud*, 2012.

12 An Overview of Large-Scale Stream Processing Engines

Radwa Elshawi and Sherif Sakr

CONTENTS

12.1 INTRODUCTION

Today's era of Big Data is witnessing a continuous increase of user and machine connectivity that produces an overwhelming flow of data that demands a paradigm shift in the computing architecture requirements and large-scale data-processing mechanisms. Therefore, concurrent computations have been receiving increased attention due to the widespread adoption of multicore processors and the emerging advancements of cloud computing technology. For example, the MapReduce framework has been introduced as a scalable and fault-tolerant data-processing framework that enables the processing of a massive volume of data in parallel on clusters of horizontally scalable commodity machines. By virtue of its simplicity, scalability, and fault-tolerance, MapReduce is becoming ubiquitous and gaining significant momentum within both industry and academia. However, the MapReduce framework, open-sourced by the Hadoop* Implementation, and its related large-scale data-processing technologies (e.g., Pig,† Hive‡) have been mainly designed for supporting batch processing tasks, but they are not adequate for supporting real-time stream processing

---

* http://hadoop.apache.org/.
† http://pig.apache.org/.
‡ http://hive.apache.org/.

tasks [19]. The ubiquity of mobile devices, location services, sensor pervasiveness and real-time network monitoring have created the crucial need for building scalable and parallel architectures to process vast amounts of streamed data.

In general, stream processing systems support a large class of applications in which data are generated from multiple sources and are pushed asynchronously to servers that are responsible for processing. Therefore, stream processing applications are usually deployed as continuous jobs that run from the time of their submission until their cancellation. Many applications in several domains such as telecommunications, network security, and large-scale sensor networks require online processing of continuous data flows. They produce very high loads that require aggregating the processing capacity of many nodes. Rather than processing stored data like in traditional database systems, stream processing engines process tuples on-the-fly. This is due to the amount of input that discourages persistent storage and the requirement of providing prompt results. Queries of streaming application are generally continuous and stateful. Once a query is registered, it starts processing events and only stops when the system terminates or the query is deregistered from the system. Queries typically maintain state such as aggregates of windows or local variables. Query state is kept on the same node that executes the query.

In the last decade, there have been substantial advancements in the field of data stream processing. From centralized stream processing systems, the state-of-the-art has advanced to stream processing engines with the ability to distribute different queries among a cluster of nodes [10,11,18]. This chapter provides an overview of a set of the main systems that have been presented for achieving scalable processing of streaming data.

12.2   AURORA

The *Aurora* [2,7] is a centralized stream processor that is fundamentally presented as a data-flow system and uses the popular boxes and arrows paradigm. In aurora, a stream is modeled as an append-only sequence of tuples with uniform type (schema). In addition to application-specific data fields $A_1,..., A_n$, each tuple in a stream has a timestamp (ts) that specifies its time of origin within the Aurora network. The Aurora data model supports out-of-order data arrival. Tuples flow through a loop-free, directed graph of processing operators (i.e., boxes). Ultimately, output streams are presented to applications, which must be constructed to handle the asynchronously arriving tuples in an output stream. Each operator accepts input streams, transforms them in some way, and produces one or more output streams. By default, queries are continuous in that they can potentially run forever over push-based inputs. Figure 12.1 illustrates an overview of the Aurora system.

The Aurora *Stream Query Algebra* (SQuAl) supports seven operators that are used to construct Aurora networks queries. The operators are analogous to operators in the relational algebra. However, they differ in fundamental ways in the way they address the special requirements of stream processing. They can be divided into two main sections: (1) order-agnostic operators (filter, map, and union) and (2) order-sensitive operators (BSort, Aggregate, Join, and Resample). The behavior of these operators are described as follows:

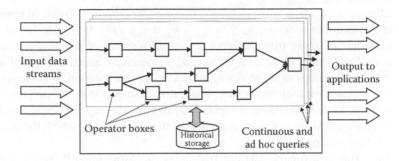

FIGURE 12.1 The system of Aurora.

- *Filter*: This operator is used to route input tuples to alternative streams. It takes the form $Filter(P_1,..., P_m)(S)$ such that $P_1,..., P_m$ are predicates over tuples on the input stream, S. Its output consists of $m + 1$ streams $(S_1,..., S_{m+1})$ such that the tuples on the input stream that satisfy predicate P_1 are the output on the first output stream, tuples on the input stream that satisfy predicate P_2 (but not P_1) are output on the second output stream, and so on. The $(m + 1)$ stream contains all tuples satisfying none of the predicates. The output tuples of the *Filter* operator have the same schema and values as input tuples.
- *Map*: This is a generalized projection operator that takes the form $Map(B_1 = F_1,..., B_m = F_m)(S)$ such that $B_1,..., B_m$ are names of attributes and $F_1,..., F_m$ are functions over tuples on the input stream, S. *Map* outputs a stream consisting of tuples of the form $(TS = t.TS, B_1 = F_1(t),..., B_m = Fm(t))$ for each input tuple, t. The resulting stream of this operator can have a different schema than the input stream, but the timestamps of input tuples are preserved in corresponding output tuples.
- *Union*: This operator is used to merge two or more streams into a single output stream and takes the form $Union(S_1,..., S_n)$ such that $S_1,..., S_n$ are streams with a common schema. *Union* can output tuples in any order, though one obvious processing strategy is to emit tuples in the order in which they arrive regardless of which input stream they arrive on.
- *BSort*: This is an approximate sort operator that takes the form $BSort$ $(Assuming\ O)\ (S) such that O = Order\ (On\ A,\ Slack\ n,\ GroupBy\ B_1,..., B_m)$, which is a specification of the assumed ordering over the output stream. While a complete sort is not possible over an infinite stream with finite time or space, *BSort* performs a buffer-based approximate sort equivalent to n passes of a bubble sort where $slack = n$. This is achieved by maintaining a buffer of $n + 1$ tuples while processing the input stream. Every time the buffer is filled, a tuple in the buffer with minimal value for A is evicted from the buffer and emitted as output.
- *Aggregate*: This operator applies *"window functions"* to sliding windows over its input stream. It has the form $Aggregate\ (F, Assuming\ O, Size\ s, Advance\ i)\ (S)$ such that F is a window function, $O = Order\ (On\ A,\ Slack\ n, GroupBy\ B_1,..., B_m)$ is an order specification over input stream S, s is the size of the window, and i is an integer or predicate that specifies how to

advance the window when it slides. This operator outputs a stream of tuples of the form $(TS = ts, A = a, B_1 = u_1,..., B_m = u_m)$ ++$(F(W))$ such that W is a window of tuples from the input stream with values of A between a and $a+s - 1$ and values for $B_1,..., B_m$ of $u_1,..., u_m$, respectively, and ts is the smallest of the timestamps associated with tuples in W. The notation "++" denotes the concatenation of two tuples. Thus, it is assumed that the function F returns a tuple of aggregate computations and that this tuple is concatenated to a tuple consisting of fields that identify the window over which the computation took place ($B_1,..., B_m$, and A).

- *Join*: This is a binary operator that takes the form *Join (P, Size s, Left Assuming O_1, Right Assuming O_2) (S_i, S_2)* such that P is a predicate over pairs of tuples from input streams S_1 and S_2, s is an integer, and O_1 and O_2 are specifications of assumed orderings of S_1 and S_2, respectively. For every in-order tuple t in S_1 and u in S_2, the concatenation of t and u (t ++u) is output if $|t.A - u.B| \le s$ and P holds of t and u. The *Join* operator does need not sort its inputs to process disordered streams but can instead delay pruning tuples to account for slack. The *Join* operator also permits one or both of its inputs to be static tables. A static table is a special case of a window on a stream that is infinite in size.

- *Resample*: It is an asymmetric, semi-join-like synchronization operator that can be used to align pairs of streams. This operator takes the form *Resample(F, Size s, Left Assuming O_1, Right Assuming O_2) (S_1, S_2)* such that F is a window functionover S_1, s is an integer, A is an attribute over S_1, and O_1 and O_2 are specifications of orderings assumed of S_1 and S_2, respectively. F or every tuple, t, from S_1, tuple ($B_1 : u.B_1,..., B_m : u.B_m, A : t.A$) ++ $F(W(t))$ is output such that $W(t) = u \in S_2 - u$ in order wrt O_2 in $S_2 \wedge - t.A - u.B - \le s$. Thus, for every tuple in S_1, an interpolated value is generated from S_2 using the interpolation function, F, over a window of tuples of size 2s.

Figure 12.2 illustrates the runtime architecture of Aurora. The basic purpose of an Aurora run-time network is to process data flows through a potentially large workflow diagram where inputs from data sources and outputs from boxes are fed to the router, which forwards them either to external applications or to the storage manager to be placed on the proper queue. The storage manager is responsible for maintaining the box queues and managing the buffer.

Conceptually, the scheduler picks a box for execution, ascertains what processing is required, and passes a pointer to the box description to the multithreaded box processor. The box processor executes the appropriate operation and then forwards the output tuples to the router. The scheduler then ascertains the next processing step and the cycle is repeated. The QoS monitor continually monitors system performance and activates the load shedder when it detects an overload situation and poor system performance. The load shedder then sheds load until the performance of the system reaches an acceptable level. The catalog contains information regarding the network topology, inputs, outputs, QoS information, and relevant statistics (e.g., selectivity, average box processing costs), which are essentially used by all components.

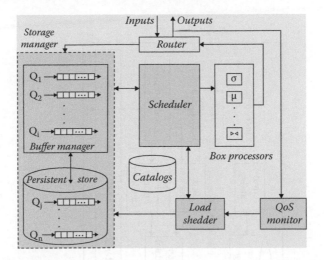

FIGURE 12.2   The runtime architecture of Aurora.

12.3 BOREALIS

Borealis [1,6,12] is one of the early presented distributed stream processing engines. In Borealis, the collection of continuous queries submitted to the system can be seen as one giant network of operator query diagram whose processing is distributed to multiple sites. Each site runs a Borealis server where the *Query Processor* (QP) is a single-site processor. Figure 12.3 illustrates the system architecture of Borealis where input streams are fed into the QP an results are pulled through *I/O Queues*, which route tuples to and from remote Borealis nodes and clients. The QP is controlled by the *Admin* module that sets up locally running queries and takes care of moving query diagram fragments to and from remote Borealis nodes, when instructed to do so by another module. System control messages issued by the Admin are fed into the *Local Optimizer*. Local Optimizer further communicates with major run-time components of the QP to supply them with performance improving directions. These components are

- *Priority scheduler*, which determines the order of box execution based on tuple priorities.
- *Box processors*, with one for each different type of box, which can change behavior on the fly based on control messages from the local optimizer.
- *Load shedder*, which discards low-priority tuples when the node is overloaded.

The QP also contains the *storage manager*, which is responsible for the storage and retrieval of data that flows through the arcs of the local query diagram. The *local catalog* stores query diagram descriptions and metadata, which are accessible by all the components.

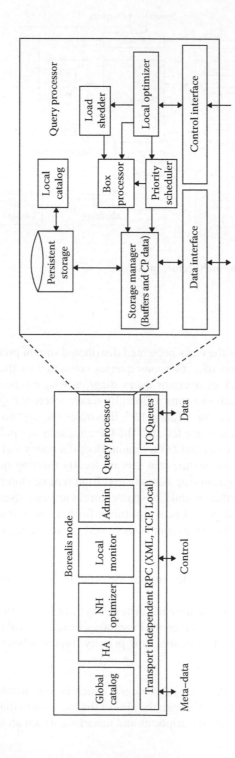

FIGURE 12.3 The architecture of Borealis.

Borealis uses an extended Aurora data model where streams are modeled as append-only sequences of tuples of the form $(k_1,..., k_n, a_1,..., a_m)$, where $k_1,..., k_n$ comprise a key for the stream, and $a_1,..., a_m$ provide attribute values. In particular, Borealis generalizes this model to support three kinds of stream messages (i.e., tuples):

- *Insertion messages* (+, *t*), where *t* is a new tuple to be inserted with a new key value.
- *Deletion messages* (–, *t*), where *t* consists of the key attributes for some previously processed message.
- *Replacement messages* (#, *t*), where *t* consists of key attributes for some previously processed message, and nonkey attributes with revised values for that message.

Borealis inherits the boxes-and-arrows model from Aurora for specifying continuous queries where boxes represent query operators and arrows represent the data flow between boxes. Queries are composed of extended versions of Aurora operators that support revision messages where each operator processes revision messages based on its available message history and emits other revision messages as output. Aurora's connection points (CPs) buffer stream messages that compose the message history required by operators. An important addition to the Aurora query model is the ability to change box semantics on the fly. Borealis boxes are provided with special control lines in addition to their standard data input lines. These lines carry control messages that include revised box parameters and functions to change box behavior.

As in Aurora, a quality of service model forms the basis of resource management decisions in Borealis. Unlike Aurora, where each query output is provided with QoS functions, Borealis allows QoS predictions to operated at any point in a data flow. For this purpose, messages are supplied with a *vector of metrics* (VM). These metrics include content-related properties (e.g., message importance) or performance-related properties (e.g., message arrival time, total resources consumed for processing the message up to the current point in the query diagram, number of dropped messages preceding this message). The attributes of the VM are predefined and identical on all streams. As a message flows through a box, some fields of the VM can be updated by the box code. A diagram administrator (DA) can also place special map boxes into the query diagram to change the VM. Furthermore, there is a universal, parameterizable Score Function for an instantiation of the Borealis System that takes in VM and returns a value in [0, 1], that shows the current predicted impact of a message on QoS. This function is known to all run-time components (such as the scheduler) and shapes their processing strategies. The overall goal is to deliver maximum average QoS at system outputs.

A Borealis application, which is a single connected diagram of processing boxes, is deployed on a network of *N* sites. Borealis optimization consists of multiple collaborating monitoring and optimization components. These components continuously optimize the allocation of query network fragments to processing sites. Monitors, in particular, have two types:

1. *Local monitor* (LM) runs at each site and produces a collection of local statistics, which it forwards periodically to the end-point monitor (EM). LM maintains various box- and site-level statistics regarding utilization and queuing delays for various resources including CPU, disk, bandwidth, and power (only relevant to sensor proxies).
2. *Endpoint monitor* (EM) runs at every site that produces Borealis outputs. EM evaluates QoS for every output message and keeps statistics on QoS for all outputs for the site.

In addition, there are three levels of collaborating optimizers:

1. *Local optimizer* runs at every site and is responsible for scheduling messages to be processed as well as deciding where in the locally running diagram to shed load, if required.
2. *Neighborhood optimizer* runs at every site and is primarily responsible for load balancing the resources at a site with those of its immediate neighbors.
3. *Global optimizer* is responsible for accepting information from the endpoint monitors and making global optimization decisions.

Monitoring components run continuously and trigger optimizer(s) when they detect problems (e.g., resource overload) or optimization opportunities (e.g., neighbor with significantly lower load). The local monitor triggers the local optimizer or neighborhood optimizer while the end-point the monitors will trigger the global optimizer. Each optimizer tries to resolve the situation itself. If it cannot achieve this within a predefined period, monitors trigger the optimizer at the higher level. This approach strives to handle problems locally when possible because in general, local decisions are cheaper to make and realize with the added benefit of being less disruptive. Another implication is that transient problems are dealt with locally, whereas more persistent problems potentially require global intervention.

12.4 IBM SYSTEM S AND IBM SPADE

The IBM System S [3,4,20] is a large-scale, distributed data stream processing middleware that supports structured as well as unstructured data stream processing and can be scaled to a large number of compute nodes. The System S runtime can execute a large number of long-running queries that take the form of data-flow graphs. A data-flow graph consists of a set of *processing elements* (PEs) connected by streams, where each stream carries a series of tuples. The PEs implement data stream analytics and are basic execution containers that are distributed over the compute nodes. The compute nodes are organized as a shared-nothing *cluster of workstations* (COW). The PEs communicate with each other via their input and output ports, connected by streams. The PE ports as well as the streams connecting them are typed. PEs can be explicitly connected using hard-coded links or through implicit links that rely on type compatibility. System S also provides several other services, such as fault tolerance, scheduling, and placement optimization, distributed job management, storage services, and security.

The *Spade* system (Stream Processing Application Declarative Engine) [10] is the declarative stream processing engine of System S. It provides a rapid application development front end for System S using the following features:

- An intermediate language for flexible composition of parallel and distributed data-flow graphs. This language sits in between higher-level programming tools and languages such as the System S IDE or Stream QL, and the lower-level System S programming APIs.
- A toolkit of type generic built-in stream processing operators. Spade supports all basic stream-relational operators with rich windowing and punctuation semantics. It also seamlessly integrates built-in operators with user-defined ones.
- A broad range of stream adapters. These adapters are used to ingest data from outside sources and publish data to outside destinations, such as network sockets, relational and XML databases and file systems.

The Spade language provides a stream-centric, operator-level programming model. The stream-centric design implies building a programming language where the basic building block is a stream. The operators can be used to implement any relational query with windowing extensions used in streaming applications. Examples of these operators are

- **Source**, used for creating a stream from data flowing from an external source. This operator is capable of performing parsing and tuple creation and can interact with a diverse set of external devices.
- **Sink**, used for converting a stream into a flow of tuples that can be used by components that are not part of System S. Its main task consists of converting tuples into objects accessible externally through devices such as the file system or the network.
- **Functor**, used for performing tuple-level manipulations such as filtering, projection, mapping, attribute creation, and transformation. In these manipulations, the Functor operator can access tuples that have appeared earlier in the input stream.
- **Aggregate**, used for grouping and summarization of incoming tuples. This operator supports a large number of grouping mechanisms and summarization functions.
- **Join**, used for correlating and pairing two streams.
- **Sort**, used for imposing an order on incoming tuples in a stream.
- **Barrier**, used as a synchronization point that consumes tuples from multiple streams, outputting a tuple only when a tuple from each of the input streams has arrived.
- **Punctor**, used for performing tuple-level manipulations where conditions on the current tuple as well as on past tuples are evaluated for generating punctuations in the output stream.
- **Split**, used for routing incoming tuples to different output streams based on a user-supplied routing condition.
- **Delay**, used for delaying a stream based on a user-supplied time interval.

The Spade language also provides the capability for extending the basic building block operators by supporting user-defined operators. These operators can make use of external libraries and implement operations that are customized to a particular application domain. Spade uses code generation to fuse operators into PEs. The PE code generator produces code that

- Fetches tuples from the PE input buffers and relays them to the operators within.
- Receives tuples from operators within and inserts them into the PE output buffers.
- For all the intra-PE connections between the operators, it fuses the outputs of operators with the inputs of downstream ones using function calls.

This fusion of operators with function calls results in a depth-first traversal of the operator subgraph that corresponds to the partition associated with the PE, with no queuing involved in between. This code generation approach is extremely powerful because through simple recompilation one can go from a fully fused application to a fully distributed one, adapting to different ratios of processing to I/O provided by different computational architectures. The fusion of operators is controlled through compiler directives and primitives in the Spade code.

SPL [13] is a stream processing language that allows the composition of streaming applications by assembling operators and expressing their stream interconnections. In SPL, operators can implement any logic (e.g., filtering, aggregation, image processing) and be arbitrarily interconnected. The language allows developers to define composite operators that represent a logically related subgraph that can be reused to assemble more complex graphs. These composite operators are important for application modularization. To execute an application, the SPL compiler places operators into processing elements (PEs), which are runtime containers for one or more operators. During execution, each PE maps to an operating system process, which can execute in any host available to the stream processing infrastructure. The compiler partitions operators into PEs based on performance measurements and following partition constraints informed by the developers. During runtime, PEs are distributed over hosts according to host placement constraints informed by developers as well as the resource availability of hosts and load balance. The SPL compiler can also group operators that belong to different composites into the same PE. This means that the physical streaming graph layout does not reflect the fact that some operators are logically grouped.

When the SPL compiler builds an application, it generates C++ code for each used operator and a file with the application description called ADL. The ADL is an XML description that includes the name of each operator in the graph, their interconnections, their composite containment relationship, their PE partitioning, and the PE's host placement constraints. Both the System S runtime and its visualization tools use the ADL for tasks such as starting the application and reporting runtime information to the users.

12.5 DEDUCE

In general, while MapReduce offers the capability to analyze several terabytes of stored data, stream processing solutions offer the ability to process, possibly, a few million updates every second. However, there is an increasing number of data-processing applications, which need a solution that effectively and efficiently combines the benefits of MapReduce and stream processing to address their data-processing needs. *DEDUCE* [16] is a middleware that has been designed to offer a unified abstraction and runtime for addressing the needs of modern data-processing applications. It attempts to combine real-time stream processing with the capabilities of a massive data analysis framework like MapReduce by providing the following features:

- *Language Constructs*: DEDUCE extends SPADE'S data-flow composition language to enable the specification and use of MapReduce jobs as data-flow elements.
- *Reusable Modules*: DEDUCE provides the capability to describe reusable modules for implementing offline MapReduce tasks aimed at calibrated analytic models.
- *Runtime Support*: DEDUCE augments the System S runtime infrastructure to support the execution and optimized deployment of map and reduce tasks.
- *Control Parameters*: DEDUCE provides configuration parameters (e.g., update frequency, resource utilization hints, etc.) associated with the MapReduce jobs that can be tweaked to perform end-to-end system optimizations and shared resource management.

The DEDUCE-specific language extensions to the SPADE language has been designed to achieve the following goals:

1. To be able to easily specify the MapReduce jobs
2. To support MapReduce jobs as composable data-flow elements
3. To provide the capability for creating domain-specific collection of map and reduce modules

In particular, the DEDUCE language extensions consists of two important components: the DEDUCE Operator Toolkit and the module specification framework. DEDUCE Operator Toolkit contains the following operators:

- *MapReduce Operator*: DEDUCE models the MapReduce job as a SPADE operator. This approach simplifies the design of applications that combine the data at rest with the data in motion. While the input data set for a MapReduce job can either be specified as a parameter to the operator or as a punctuated input stream containing the location of directories or files to be processed, the output of the MapReduce job is written to a prespecified location on the distributed file system and the location of this output data is optionally available as a punctuated output stream from the MapReduce operator.

- *Data Input and Output Operators*: DEDUCE provides an implementation of operators that can read and write data to the underlying distributed file system, while conforming to a certain data format. These operators, besides being used by the users, are also used by the map and the reduce tasks to access data that is assumed to be formatted in conformance to the input-Format and the outputFormat parameters that are specified as part of the MapReduce operator. These operators also hide the underlying distributed file system using a common interface to access the file system.

DEDUCE also supports the creation of domain-specific MapReduce toolkits. A toolkit is a collection of domain-specific UBOPs (possibly implemented by a domain expert) and prewritten modules that may use the UBOPs specified in the toolkit. The UBOPs contained in the toolkit typically implement functional units that, for example, perform fast Fourier transforms on streamed digital signals. In other words, operators are the building blocks employed for specifying a map/reduce module. Prewritten modules can be directly used by DEDUCE developers to rapidly prototype and deploy domain-specific MapReduce jobs.

12.6   STREAMCLOUD

The *StreamCloud* (SC) system [11] has been presented as a scalable and elastic distributed stream processing engine that builds on top of *Borealis* to provide transparent query parallelization. In particular, the SC compiler takes the abstract query and generates its parallel version that is deployed on a cluster that can consists of a large set of shared-nothing nodes. In this approach, logical data streams are split into multiple physical data substreams that flow in parallel, thus avoiding single-node bottlenecks. Communication across different nodes is minimized and only performed to guarantee semantic transparency. SC performs content-aware stream splitting and encapsulates the parallelization logic within smart operators that make sure that the outcome of the parallel execution matches the output of the centralized execution. SC monitors its activity and dynamically reacts to workload variations by reorganizing the load among its nodes as well as provisioning or decommissioning nodes. Elastic resource management is performed on-the-fly with very low intrusiveness, thus making provisioning and decommissioning cost-effective.

In SC, the main two main factors for the estimating the parallelization cost are the number of hops performed by each tuple and the communication fan-out of each node with the others. It strikes the best balance between communication and fan-out overhead where queries are split into subqueries and each *subquery* is allocated to a set of SC instances grouped in a *subcluster*. Data flows from one subcluster to the next one, until the output of the system. All instances of a subcluster run the same subquery, called *local subquery*, for a fraction of the input data stream, and produce a fraction of the output data stream. Communication between subclusters guarantees semantic transparency. Input queries are written in the Borealis query language and automatically parallelized by SC through its query compiler. The latter allows easy deployment of arbitrary complex queries over large clusters with just a few steps. The user is only required to input a query written in the Borealis query language and the elasticity rules.

Figure 12.4 illustrates the elastic management architecture of StreamCloud where each SC instance runs a *local manager* (LM) that monitors resource utilization and incoming load, and is able to reconfigure the local *load balancer* (LB). Each LM periodically reports monitoring information to the *elastic manager* (EM) that aggregates it on a per subcluster basis. Based on the collected data, the EM may decide to reconfigure the system either to balance the load, to provision, or decommission instances. Reconfiguration decisions are taken and executed independently for each subcluster. If instances must be provisioned or decommissioned, the EM interacts with the *resource manager* (RM), which keeps a pool of instances where SC software is running but no query is deployed. Once the EM receives a new instance, the subquery is deployed and the instance is added to the subcluster that was about to saturate.

SC complements elastic resource management with dynamic load balancing to guarantee that new instances are only provisioned when a subcluster is not able to cope with the incoming load. Both techniques facilitate the ability to reconfigure the system in an online and nonintrusive manner. Reconfiguring a subcluster requires transferring the ownership of one or more buckets from one instance (old owner) to another (new owner) in the same subcluster. For instance, bucket ownership of an overloaded instance may be transferred to a less loaded instance or to a new one.

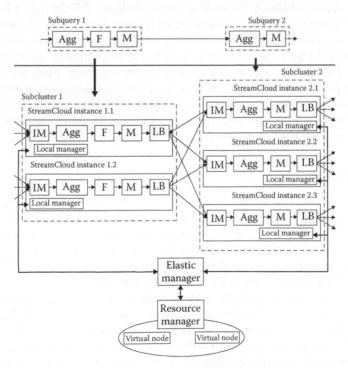

FIGURE 12.4 The elastic management architecture of StreamCloud. (From V. Gulisano et al., *IEEE Trans. Parallel Distrib. Syst.*, 23, 2351–2365, 2012.)

The basic idea is to define a point in time p so that tuples of bucket b earlier than p are processed by the old owner and tuples later than p are processed by the new one. This is straightforward for stateless operators. However, it is more challenging when reconfiguring stateful operators. Due to the sliding window semantics used in stateful operators, a tuple might contribute to several windows. Thus, there will be tuples that need to be processed by both the old and new owners. SC reconfigures a subcluster by triggering one or more reconfiguration actions. Each action changes the ownership of a bucket from the old owner to the new one within the same subcluster. Reconfiguration actions only affect the instances of the subcluster being reconfigured and the upstream LBs.

Elasticity rules are specified as thresholds that set the conditions that trigger provisioning, decommissioning or load balancing. Provisioning and decommissioning are triggered if the average CPU utilization is above the *upper-utilization-threshold* (UUT) or below the *lower-utilization-threshold* (LUT). Reconfiguration actions aim to achieve an average CPU utilization figure that is as close as possible to the *target-utilization-threshold* (TUT). Load balancing is triggered when the standard deviation of the CPU utilization is above the *upper-imbalance-threshold* (UIT). A *minimum-improvement-threshold* (MIT) specifies the minimum performance improvement to endorse a new configuration. That is, the new configuration is applied only if the imbalance reduction is above the MIT. The goal is to keep the average CPU utilization within upper and lower utilization thresholds and the standard deviation below the upper imbalance threshold in each subcluster. SC features a load-aware provisioning strategy. When provisioning instances, a naive strategy would be to provision one instance at a time (individual provisioning). However, individual provisioning might lead to cascaded provisioning, that is, continuous allocation of new instances. This might happen with steadily increasing loads when the additional computing power provided by the new instance does not decrease the average CPU utilization below UUT. To overcome this problem, SC load-aware provisioning takes into account the current subcluster size and load to decide how many new instances to provide in order to reach for TUT.

12.7 STORMY

The *Stormy* system [18] has been presented as a distributed stream processing service for continuous data processing that relies on techniques from existing cloud storage systems that are adapted to efficiently execute streaming workloads. It uses a synthesis of well-known techniques from cloud storage systems [9,15,17] to achieve the scalability and availability goals. It uses distributed hash tables (DHT) [5] to distribute queries across all nodes, and route events from query to query according to the query graph. To achieve high availability, Stormy uses a replication mechanism where queries are replicated on several nodes, and events are concurrently executed on all replicas. As Stormy's architecture is by design decentralized, there is no single point-of-failure. However, Stormy uses the assumption that a query can be completely executed on one node. Thus, there is an upper limit on the number of incoming events of a stream. The API of Stormy consists of only four functions:

- **registerStream(description) –> SID**: Registers an external data stream and returns the generated internal SID for this stream.
- **registerQuery(name, query, input SIDs) –> SID**: Adds a query with the parameters name, query, and a set of one or more input SIDs. It returns the SID of the query output stream.
- **registerOutput(SID, target)**: Registers an output destination that receives the data from the given SID. The target parameter contains the host address and port of the output location.
- **pushEvents(SID, events)**: Pushes a set of one or more events with the given input stream SID to the system.

Figure 12.5 illustrates the distributed stream processing in Stormy. Multiple clients can register streams, queries, and output destinations; either independently of each other, or they may even share queries or output destinations. Stormy uses a consistent hashing mechanism [14] to distribute queries among the available nodes where the output range of a hash function can be treated as a fixed circular space, or "ring." Each node in the system gets assigned a random value that defines its position on this ring. If a new item is inserted into the system, the hash value of its key is calculated and the item is assigned to the first node reached by following the ring clockwise starting at the location of the item's hash value. In other words, every node becomes responsible for the key space between its own position and the position of its predecessor. The mapping of ranges to nodes is maintained using a DHT where every node knows the mapping of keys to nodes and can therefore forward an incoming request to the responsible node. If the DHT changes, the new version of the mapping is propagated through the system using a gossip protocol. A gossip protocol distributes new information to all nodes in the system, typically with some time delay. Therefore, it might happen that a node with outdated mapping information forwards the request to the wrong node. However, the request will eventually arrive at the correct node as the new mapping information is gossiped through the system.

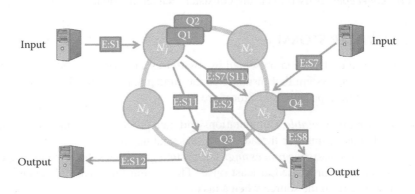

FIGURE 12.5 Execution of distributed stream processing in Stormy. (From S. Loesing et al., Stormy: An elastic and highly available streaming service in the cloud, in *EDBT/ICDT Workshops*, pages 55–60, 2012.)

To achieve high availability, Stormy uses a successor list replication mechanism, as proposed in Chord [21], where every query is replicated on several nodes, and a replication protocol takes care that every incoming event is executed by every replica. To cope with overload situations, Stormy uses two main techniques:

1. *Load balancing*: The decision to balance load is made locally by a node, based on its current utilization. Each node continuously measures its resource utilization of CPU, memory, network consumption, and disk space. These parameters form a utilization factor, which is disseminated via the gossip protocol to all other nodes in the system. In regular intervals, a node compares its utilization factor to those of its immediate neighbors. If the load difference is above a specified threshold, the node initiates a load-balancing step; that is, the node transfers part of its data range to its less loaded neighbor. As every node makes the decision to balance load locally, several load-balancing steps can happen in parallel, which allows the whole system to react efficiently to load variations.
2. *Cloud bursting*: If the overall load of the system is getting too high, a new node has to be added to the system. The decision to cloud-burst is made by only one node in the system, the elected cloud bursting leader. This leader initiates the cloud bursting procedure, which brings up and adds a new node to the system. This new node takes a random position on the ring, takes over parts of the data range from its neighbors, and finally updates the DHT. If the overall load of the system is too low, the cloud bursting leader decides to drop a node from the system. Similar to adding a new node, we first move the queries and their state to the node that takes over the range, update the DHT, and terminate the old node.

Stormy has been implemented on top of the *Cloudy* [15] system that offers a DHT to distribute and replicate events across the nodes of the system and therefore already provides scalability and elasticity. On top of Cloudy, *MXQuery* stream processing engine* is used to execute any XQuery query with additional streaming constructs. *Apache Zookeeper*[†] is used to ensure consistent leader election.

12.8   TWITTER STORM

The *Storm* system[‡] has been presented by Twitter as a distributed and fault-tolerant stream processing system that instantiates the fundamental principles of Actor theory. The key design principles of Storm are

- *Horizontally scalable*: Computations and data processing are performed in parallel using multiple threads, processes, and machines.
- *Guaranteed message processing*: The system guarantees that each message will be fully processed at least once. The system takes care of replaying messages from the source when a task fails.

---

* http://mxquery.org/.
† http://zookeeper.apache.org/.
‡ http://github.com/nathanmarz/storm.

- *Fault-tolerant*: If there are faults during execution of the computation, the system will reassign tasks as necessary.
- *Programming language agnostic*: Storm tasks and processing components can be defined in any language, making Storm accessible to nearly anyone. Clojure, Java, Ruby, and Python are supported by default. Support for other languages can be added by implementing a simple Storm communication protocol.

The core abstraction in Storm is the *stream*. A stream is an unbounded sequence of *tuples*. Storm provides the primitives for transforming a stream into a new stream in a distributed and reliable way. The basic primitives Storm provides for performing stream transformations are *spouts* and *bolts*. A *spout* is a source of streams. A *bolt* consumes any number of input streams, carries out some processing, and possibly emits new streams. Complex stream transformations, such as the computation of a stream of trending topics from a stream of tweets, require multiple steps and thus multiple bolts. A *topology* is a graph of stream transformations where each node is a spout or bolt. Edges in the graph indicate which bolts are subscribing to which streams. When a spout or bolt emits a tuple to a stream, it sends the tuple to every bolt that subscribed to that stream. Links between nodes in a topology indicate how tuples should be passed around. Each node in a Storm topology executes in parallel. In any topology, we can specify how much parallelism is required for each node, and then Storm will spawn that number of *threads* across the cluster to perform the execution.

Figure 12.6 depicts a sample Storm topology.

The Storm system relies on the notion of *stream grouping* to specify how tuples are sent between processing components. In other words, it defines how that stream should be partitioned among the bolt's tasks. In particular, Storm supports different types of stream groupings such as

1. *Shuffle grouping*, where stream tuples are randomly distributed such that each bolt is guaranteed to get an equal number of tuples
2. *Fields grouping*, where the tuples are partitioned by the fields specified in the grouping
3. *All grouping*, where the stream tuples are replicated across all the bolts
4. *Global grouping*, where the entire stream goes to a single bolt

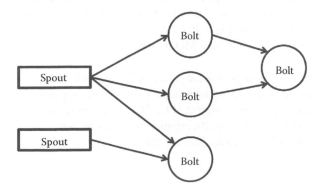

FIGURE 12.6 Sample Storm topology.

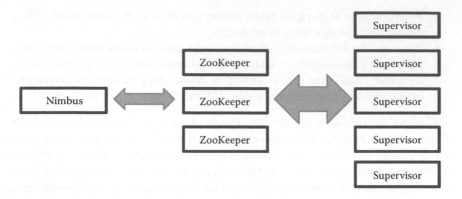

FIGURE 12.7   Storm cluster.

In addition to the supported built-in stream grouping mechanisms, the Storm system allows its users to define their own custom grouping mechanisms.

In general, a Storm cluster is superficially similar to a Hadoop cluster. One key difference is that a MapReduce job eventually finishes while a Storm job processes messages forever (or until the user kills it). In principle, there are two kinds of nodes on a Storm cluster:

- *The Master node* runs a daemon called *Nimbus* (similar to Hadoop's JobTracker), which is responsible for distributing code around the cluster, assigning tasks to machines, and handling failures.
- The *Worker nodes* run a daemon called the *Supervisor*. The supervisor listens for work assigned to its machine and starts or stops worker processes as necessary based on what Nimbus has assigned to it.

Figure 12.7 illustrates the architecture of a Storm cluster. In a Storm cluster all the interactions between Nimbus and the Supervisors are done through a *ZooKeeper* cluster, an open-source configuration and synchronization service for large distributed systems. Both the Nimbus daemon and Supervisor daemons are fail-fast and stateless, where all state is kept in ZooKeeper or on local disk. Communication between workers living on the same host or on different machines is based on *ZeroMQ* sockets* over which serialized java objects (representing tuples) are being passed. Some of the feature of ZeroMQ include

- Socket library that acts as a concurrency framework
- Faster than TCP, for clustered products and supercomputing
- Carries messages across inproc, IPC, TCP, and multicast
- Asynch I/O for scalable multicore message-passing apps
- Connect N-to-N via fanout, pubsub, pipeline, request-reply

---

* http://www.zeromq.org/.

12.9 CONCLUSION

In this chapter, we presented an overview of a set of approaches and systems that have presented for developing scalable stream data-processing systems and solutions. Although we have been focusing on the main research and open-source projects in this domain, we also acknowledge the existence of other commercial systems and technologies such as Microsoft StreamInsight* and StreamBase.† In general, we notice that although the domain of designing distributed stream processing engine has attracted the attention of the research community in the last few years, we are convinced that there is still room for further optimization and advancement in different directions. For example, defining the right and most convenient programming abstractions and standard declarative interfaces of these systems is an important research direction that will need to be tackled. Designing innovative frameworks and mechanisms that can combine the capabilities of large-scale distributed batch processing systems (e.g., MapReduce) with the strengths of distributed stream processing engine represents a clear gap in the area of advanced data-processing techniques of Big Data that has yet to attract sufficient attention from the research community.

REFERENCES

1. Daniel J. Abadi, Yanif Ahmad, Magdalena Balazinska, Ugur Çetintemel, Mitch Cherniack, Jeong-Hyon Hwang, Wolfgang Lindner, et al. Design of the Borealis Stream Processing Engine. In *CIDR*, pages 277–289, 2005.
2. Daniel J. Abadi, Donald Carney, Ugur Çetintemel, Mitch Cherniack, Christian Convey, Sangdon Lee, Michael Stonebraker, Nesime Tatbul, and Stanley B. Zdonik. Aurora: A new model and architecture for data stream management. *VLDB J.*, 12(2):120–139, 2003.
3. Henrique Andrade, Bugra Gedik, Kun-Lung Wu, and Philip S. Yu. Scale-Up Strategies for Processing High-Rate Data Streams in System S. In *ICDE*, pages 1375–1378, 2009.
4. Henrique Andrade, Bugra Gedik, Kun-Lung Wu, and Philip S. Yu. Processing high data rate streams in System S. *J. Parallel Distrib. Comput.*, 71(2):145–156, 2011.
5. Hari Balakrishnan, M. Frans Kaashoek, David R. Karger, Robert Morris, and Ion Stoica. Looking up data in p2p systems. *Commun. ACM*, 46(2):43–48, 2003.
6. Magdalena Balazinska, Hari Balakrishnan, Samuel Madden, and Michael Stonebraker. Fault-tolerance in the borealis distributed stream processing system. *ACM Trans. Database Syst.*, 33(1), 2008.
7. Mitch Cherniack, Hari Balakrishnan, Magdalena Balazinska, Donald Carney, Ugur Çetintemel, Ying Xing, and Stanley B. Zdonik. Scalable Distributed Stream Processing. In *CIDR*, 2003.
8. Jeffrey Dean and Sanjay Ghemawat. MapReduce: Simplified data processing on large clusters. In *OSDI*, pages 137–150, 2004.
9. Giuseppe DeCandia, Deniz Hastorun, Madan Jampani, Gunavardhan Kakulapati, Avinash Lakshman, Alex Pilchin, Swaminathan Sivasubramanian, Peter Vosshall, and Werner Vogels. Dynamo: Amazon's highly available key-value store. In SOSP, pages 205–220, 2007.

---

* http://msdn.microsoft.com/en-us/sqlserver/ee476990.aspx.
† http://www.streambase.com/.

10. Bugra Gedik, Henrique Andrade, Kun-Lung Wu, Philip S. Yu, and Myungcheol Doo. SPADE: The system s declarative stream processing engine. In SIGMOD Conference, pages 1123–1134, 2008.
11. Vincenzo Gulisano, Ricardo Jiménez-Peris, Marta Patiño-Martínez, Claudio Soriente, and Patrick Valduriez. StreamCloud: An Elastic and Scalable Data Streaming System. *IEEE Trans. Parallel Distrib. Syst.*, 23(12):2351–2365, 2012.
12. Jeong-Hyon Hwang, Sanghoon Cha, Ugur Çetintemel, and Stanley B. Zdonik. Borealis-R: A replication-transparent stream processing system for wide-area monitoring applications. In *SIGMOD Conference*, pages 1303–1306, 2008.
13. Gabriela Jacques-Silva, Bugra Gedik, Rohit Wagle, Kun-Lung Wu, and Vibhore Kumar. Building User-defined Runtime Adaptation Routines for Stream Processing Applications. *PVLDB*, 5(12):1826–1837, 2012.
14. David R. Karger, Eric Lehman, Frank Thomson Leighton, Rina Panigrahy, Matthew S. Levine, and Daniel Lewin. Consistent hashing and random trees: Distributed caching protocols for relieving hot spots on the world wide web. In *STOC*, pages 654–663, 1997.
15. Donald Kossmann, Tim Kraska, Simon Loesing, Stephan Merkli, Raman Mittal, and Flavio Pfaffhauser. Cloudy: A modular cloud storage system. *PVLDB*, 3(2):1533–1536, 2010.
16. Vibhore Kumar, Henrique Andrade, Bugra Gedik, and Kun-Lung Wu. DEDUCE: At the intersection of MapReduce and stream processing. In *EDBT*, pages 657–662, 2010.
17. Avinash Lakshman and Prashant Malik. Cassandra: A decentralized structured storage system. *Operating Systems Review*, 44(2):35–40, 2010.
18. Simon Loesing, Martin Hentschel, Tim Kraska, and Donald Kossmann. Stormy: An elastic and highly available streaming service in the cloud. In *EDBT/ICDT Workshops*, pages 55–60, 2012.
19. Sherif Sakr, Anna Liu, Daniel M. Batista, and Mohammad Alomari. A survey of large scale data management approaches in cloud environments. *IEEE Communications Surveys and Tutorials*, 13(3):311–336, 2011.
20. Scott Schneider, Henrique Andrade, Bugra Gedik, Alain Biem, and Kun-Lung Wu. Elastic scaling of data parallel operators in stream processing. In *IPDPS*, pages 1–12, 2009.
21. Ion Stoica, Robert Morris, David R. Karger, M. Frans Kaashoek, and Hari Balakrishnan. Chord: A scalable peer-to-peer lookup service for internet applications. In *SIGCOMM*, pages 149–160, 2001.

13 Advanced Algorithms for Efficient Approximate Duplicate Detection in Data Streams Using Bloom Filters

Sourav Dutta and Ankur Narang

CONTENTS

13.1   INTRODUCTION AND MOTIVATION

Unprecedented technological advancements in diverse fields have led to an explosion of the amount of data stored worldwide. With the volume of information breaking the barrier of petabytes, efficient management, indexing, retrieval, and processing has occupied a central research focus in most data-intensive applications. Myriad sources such as telecommunication call data records, telescopic imagery, online transactions, web pages, stock markets, climate warning systems, medical records, etc., demand resource and compute efficiency for such massively exponential data. Removal of redundancy from such multibillion record data sets constitutes an important area of study.

"Intelligent Compression" or data de-duplication in streaming scenarios, for computational efficiency in downstream processing, calls for precise identification and elimination of duplicates on-the-fly from such unbounded data streams. The real-time nature of such applications requiring processing capacity of greater than 1 GB/s constitutes an even greater challenge in this domain. This chapter highlights the problems of detecting and eliminating redundant records arriving in large streaming data sets and provides to the readers a detailed description of the state-of-art solutions to tackle this ever-growing problem.

Consider a national telecommunication network that generates call data records (*CDR*) and stores important information such as the callee number, caller number, duration, etc., for further analytics. However, redundant or duplicate records may be generated due to errors in the procedure. Storing of such billions of CDRs in real time in the central data repository calls for duplicate detection and removal to enhance performance. Typical approaches involving the use of database queries or Bloom filter [20] methods are prohibitively slow due to disk access, defeating the real-time criteria of most applications, or are extremely resource intensive requiring around 20 GB for storing the entire data (~6 billion CDRs) for exact match. Even disk-based algorithms [20] have a heavy performance impact. Hence, there is a paramount need for de-duplication algorithms involving in-memory operations, real-time performance along with tolerable false-positive (FP) and false-negative (FN) rates.

The growth of search engines is another area where de-duplication algorithms are important. The search engines need to regularly crawl the web to extract new URLs and update their corpus. Given a list of extracted URLs, the search engines need to perform a probe of its corpus to identify if the current URL is already present in its corpus [24]. This calls for efficient duplicate detection, wherein a small performance hit can be tolerated. A high FN rate (FNR) triggering recrawling of URLs will lead to a severe performance degradation of the search engine, and a high FP rate (FPR) leading to new URLs being ignored will produce a stale corpus. Hence, a balance in both FPR and FNR needs to be targeted.

Another interesting application for approximate duplicate detection in streaming environment is the detection of fraudulent advertiser clicks [30]. In the web advertising domain, for the sake of profit it is possible that the publisher fakes a certain amount of the clicks (using scripts). Thus, there is a strong need to detect such malpractices. Detection of same user ID or click generation IP in these cases can help in minimizing frauds. Solutions involving database access or probing of the archives are prohibitively compute expensive and time consuming. Naïve string matching algorithms also do not provide a feasible solution to the demand of in-memory real-time algorithms for the *data redundancy removal* (DRR) problem.

Most duplicate detection approaches use the Bloom filter structure [8,9]. The literature hosts a large number of Bloom filter variations such as the counting [16], compressed [31], space-code, and spectral Bloom filters to name a few. Even sliding window models [30], and Bloom filter arrays have been proposed. Further, memory-efficient de-duplication algorithms and their parallel versions have also been proposed in [20]. The inherent limitations of the existing procedures while considering 100s of petabytes of data and also in the streaming scenarios have been studied. This has led to the development of new innovative approaches for the massive or streaming de-duplication problem.

This chapter delves into solutions pertaining to approximate duplicate detection, wherein the application can tolerate a small fraction of *false-positive* and *false-negative* results. The event of *false positive* (FP) occurs when a distinct element is wrongly reported as duplicate. The opposite scenario of *false negative* (FN) occurs when a duplicate entity is falsely reported as nonduplicate. Since the in-memory storage of all elements from a possibly unbounded stream is infeasible, de-duplication algorithms tend to minimize the FP and FN rates.

This chapter introduces in details the working principle of the different variants of de-duplication techniques, their merits, and disadvantages. Most approaches suffer from high FP and FN rates or are ill-suited for the applications at hand. However, two recent Bloom filter–based algorithms, *stable Bloom filter* (SBF) [12], and *reservoir sampling–based stable Bloom filter* (RSBF) [15] guaranteeing a novel characteristic, *stability*, providing high-performance throughput have been discussed in this chapter. The SBF and RSBF currently offers the best performance guarantees for duplicate detection. Coupled with the *stability* property, they far outperform other existing methods in this domain. These structures and algorithms demonstrate that their FP and FN rates become constant as the stream length increases, thereby making them extremely attractive for de-duplication applications. Hence, detailed insights into the working principles of these state-of-art algorithms are presented to the reader. A complete theoretical analysis of FPR, FNR, and stability of these two approaches along with their experimental comparison for different data have also been discussed here.

This chapter aims to establish an exhaustive and detailed reference to the current scenarios in the de-duplication problem, and highlight future roadmaps, and challenges in the de-duplication problem for petabytes of data. In particular, this chapter presents to the readers *RSBF* as the state-of-art data structure for approximate duplicate detection combining attractive features such as low error rates, theoretical guarantees, stability, and low memory requirement. It is in this context that SBF has been selected for direct comparison.

The next section describes the various existing de-duplication methods and data structures. Section 13.3 introduces the working concepts of the *stable Bloom filter*, theoretical properties and its stability property. Section 13.4 then briefly discusses the method of *reservoir sampling*. Section 13.5 provides the detailed algorithmic overview and theoretical bounds for the *reservoir sampling–based stable Bloom filter*, offering the best error rates. Empirical results comparing the performance of the two techniques (SBF and RSBF) over varied data sets along with the setting of parameters are depicted in Section 13.6. Finally, Section 13.7 concludes the chapter summarizing the findings and also citing possible future work directions.

13.2 DUPLICATE DETECTION APPROACHES AND DATA STRUCTURES

Duplicate detection provides a classical problem within the ambit of data storage and databases giving rise to numerous buffering solutions. With the advent of online arrival of data and transactions, detection of duplicates in such streaming environment using buffering and caching mechanisms [19] corresponds to a naïve solution. The inability to store all the data arriving on the stream led to the design of approximate de-duplication methods.

Management of large data streams for computing approximate frequency moments [4], element classification [23], correlated aggregate queries [21], and others with limited memory and acceptable error rates have become a spotlight among the research community. *Bit Shaving*, the problem of fraudulent advertisers not paying commission for a certain amount of the traffic or hits have also been studied in this context [34]. This prompted the growth of approximate duplicate detection techniques in the area of both databases and web applications. Redundancy removal algorithms for search engines were first studied in [10,11,28].

Formally, the *duplicate detection* problem is defined as: *Given a data stream, S, and fixed memory space, M, we need to report if an element e_i in S has already occurred previously among e_1, e_2,..., e_{i-1} or not*. As the storage of the entire stream, which can possibly be unbounded, is infeasible, an approximate estimate minimizing the error rates is required.

13.2.1 DATABASE QUERY AND BUFFERING TECHNIQUES

Straightforward approaches using traditional database queries or pairwise string matching algorithms become prohibitively slow involving disk accesses, defeating the real-time demands of the streaming applications. Naïve caching and buffering methods [19] involve populating a fixed-sized buffer memory with elements arriving on the stream. The membership query of an element is then performed by checking if the element is present in the buffer or not. However, once the buffer becomes completely filled, the storage of a new element involves the eviction of an element present in the buffer. Several such eviction or *replacement policies* have been studied in [19]. Nevertheless, the performance of these methods depends heavily on the choice of the replacement policy adopted.

To study the performance of approximate duplicate detection mechanisms, fuzzy algorithms were also proposed in [7,39]. *Bit shaving* in the context of fraudulent advertiser traffic was studied in [34], and duplicate detection for web applications was presented in [10,11,28]. File-level hashing was used in storage systems for de-duplication [1,14,37], but they provided a low compression ratio. Even secure hashes were proposed for fixed-sized data blocks [33].

13.2.2 BLOOM FILTERS

Bloom filters [8,9] are space-efficient probabilistic bit-vector data structures providing fast membership queries on sets [8]. A Bloom filter consists of a bit vector and k hash functions. An element is hashed onto k bit positions of the Bloom filter using the hash functions. Typical Bloom filter approaches involve k comparisons for each record for checking the corresponding bit positions of the Bloom filter array. However, the efficiency of Bloom filters come at the cost of a small false-positive rate, wherein the Bloom filter falsely reports the presence of the query element. This occurs due to hash collision of multiple elements onto a single bit position of the Bloom filter. Interestingly false negatives are never encountered. The probability of a false positive for a standard Bloom filter is given by [9]: $FPR \approx (1 - e^{-kn/m})^k$, where m is the number of elements in the stream and n is the number of distinct elements observed. Given n and m, the optimal number of hash functions $k = \ln 2(m/n)$. Bloom filters were first used by TAPER system [26] depicting ease of implementation and fast performance.

13.2.3 COUNTING AND WINDOW BLOOM FILTERS

Counting Bloom filters [16] were introduced to support the scenario where the contents of a set change over time due to insertions and deletions. In this approach the bits were replaced by small counters that stored the number of elements hashed onto the particular bit position, and were updated with insertion and deletion of elements. However, the support for deletion operations from the structure now gives rise to false negatives. To meet the needs of varied application scenarios, a large number of Bloom filter variants were proposed such as the compressed Bloom filter [31], space-code Bloom filter [27], and spectral Bloom filter [35] to name but a few. Even window model of Bloom filters were proposed [30] such as landmark window, jumping window, sliding window [36], etc. These models operate on a definite amount of history of objects observed in the stream to draw conclusions for processing of future elements.

Bloom filters have even been applied to network related applications such as finding heavy flows for stochastically fair blue queue management [17], packet classification [6], per-flow state management, and longest prefix matching [13]. Multiple Bloom filters in conjunction with hash tables have been studied to represent items with multiple attributes accurately and efficiently with low false-positive rates [25]. *Bloomjoin* used for distributed joins have also been extended to minimize network usage for query execution based on database statistics. Bloom filters have also been used for speeding up name-to-location resolution processes [29].

13.2.4 PARALLEL BLOOM FILTERS

To cater to enormous data in the order of petabytes and multiple input stream scenarios, parallel variants of Bloom filters have been explored [20]. Adhering to the real-time needs of de-duplication applications, even disk based Bloom filters exist in the literature. The advent of *MapReduce* and other techniques for parallelization tools catering to massive data analytics, paved the path for efficient implementation of parallel Bloom filters and their variants. For a single data element, all the bit positions of the Bloom filters could be accessed simultaneously, giving enormous performance gains. The two approaches discussed in this chapter can trivially be implemented in a parallel system.

13.3   STABLE BLOOM FILTER (SBF)

In data stream applications, as more and more elements arrive, the fraction of zeros in the Bloom filter decreases continuously and the false-positive rate increases finally reaching 1. Usual solutions employ random eviction policies for bits from the Bloom filters to accommodate the new elements and keep the FPR at bay. An interesting Bloom filter structure proposed recently is the *stable Bloom filter*, SBF [12]. It provides a stable performance guarantee on a very large stream. This constant performance is of huge importance for de-duplication applications. SBF works by continuously evicting stale information from the Bloom filters. Although it achieves a tight upper bound on FPR, the stability of the algorithm is reached theoretically at infinite stream length.

The regular bits of a Bloom filters are changed to a collection of bits in the Stable Bloom filter. New elements arriving on the stream are mapped into k positions of the Bloom filter by k uniform and independent hash functions. The membership query for the new element proceeds as in regular Bloom filters, wherein the selected locations are probed.

Algorithm 13.1: *SBF (S)*

Require: Stream (S) and Number of bits at each Bloom filter position (d)
Ensure: Detecting *duplicate* and *distinct* elements in S

```
 1:  SBF is initialized to 0
 2:  for each e_i ∈ S do
 3      Select k cells of SBF
 4:      if none of the above cells is 0 then
 5:         Result ← DUPLICATE
 6:      else
 7:         Result ← DISTINCT
 8:      end if
 9:      Select p cells of SBF uniformly randomly
10:      for each cells selected above do
11:         if cell, C_i has value ≥ 1 then
12:             C_i ← C_i − 1
13:         end if
14:      end for
15:      for each of the k cells previously selected do
16:         Set cell value to Max = 2^d − 1
```

17:   **end for**
18:   Output *Result*
19:   **end for**

SBF is then updated by again randomly uniformly selecting p bits locations, at which the count is decremented by 1, thereby making room for new elements of the stream. The k positions previously selected are now set to $Max = 2^d - 1$, where d is the number of bits at each position of the Bloom filter. The setting of Max value at the SBF locations enable it to delete older data to incorporate the new arriving elements. The pseudo-code of SBF is presented in Algorithm 13.1. The details of the working of SBF can be found in [12].

13.3.1 STABILITY PROPERTY

The *stable Bloom filter* introduces a unique property called "stability." The *stability* guarantees that the number of zeroes in SBF become constant after a number of elements arrive on the data stream. Since the false-positive rate depends on the number of zeroes in the Bloom filters, SBF demonstrates constant FPR once the stability point is achieved. Ref. [12] proves that at stability, the FPR and FNR of SBF are *constant*. At this stage, the expected number of zeros in SBF are shown to be constant for a sufficiently large stream. Interesting, the expected fractions of 0s in SBF is monotonically nonincreasing and the FPR at stability is bounded by

$$FPR = \left(1 - \left(\cfrac{1}{1 + \cfrac{1}{p(1/k - 1/m)}} \right)^{Max} \right)^k,$$

where m is the number of elements already occurred on the stream S. The above equation shows a strong correlation between the FPR an the values of k and p. Similarly, the FNR can be computed and was seen to also exhibit similar properties. The convergence of SBF to stability was shown to be at an exponential rate on expectation. For detailed proofs and properties, the readers are referred to [12]. The stability property provides an excellent domain for de-duplication applications to limit the FP and FN rates to the desired acceptable tolerance level independent of the stream length. Ref. [12] considered the underlying data distribution of the input stream to be constant.

The working of SBF also depends on the appropriate setting of its parameters. In [12], the parameters have been set so as to minimize the average FN rate, while bounding the FP rate within acceptable thresholds following the theoretical bounds obtained. *Max* can be empirically set to enhance the performance of SBF.

SBF mainly suffers from the limitation that the stability is theoretically reached at infinite stream length. Also the underlying distribution of the input data is assumed to be constant in SBF. SBF performs substantially better than most of the other Bloom filter approaches for duplicate detection, exhibiting low FPR and considerable stability of FP and FN rates at large stream lengths. However, the FNR attained, although constant, is extremely high.

13.4   RESERVOIR SAMPLING MECHANISM

Finding the number of distinct elements in a stream was explored in [18]. The problem of synopsis maintenance [5,22] has been studied in great detail for its extensive application in query estimation [32]. Many synopsis methods such as sampling, wavelets, histograms, and sketches have been designed for approximate query answering. A comprehensive survey of stream synopsis methods can be found in [2]. An important class of synopsis construction methods is the *reservoir sampling* [38]. This sampling method has great appeal as it generates a sample of original multi-dimensional data for various data mining applications.

In reservoir sampling, one maintains a reservoir of size n from the data stream. After the first n points have been added to the reservoir, subsequent elements are inserted into the reservoir with an *insertion probability* given by n/t for the tth element of the stream. An interesting characteristic of this algorithm is that it is extremely easy to implement and that all subsets of data are equi-probable to be present in the reservoir. Each data point is also associated with a bias function representing its probability to be inserted into the reservoir. Hence, the biasing function captures the changing behavior of the stream.

Property

After t points in the data stream have been processed, the probability of any point in the stream belonging to the sample of size n is equal to n/t.   ■

One interesting characteristic of this maintenance algorithm is that it is extremely efficient to implement in practice. When new points in the stream arrive, it needs to be decided whether or not to insert into the current sample array that represents the reservoir. The sample array can then be overwritten at a random position. The bias function [3] associated with the rth data point at the time of arrival of the tth point $(r \leq t)$ is given by $f(r, t)$ and is related to the probability $p(r, t)$ of the rth point belonging to the reservoir at the time of arrival of the tth point. Specifically, $p(r, t)$ is proportional to $f(r, t)$. The function $f(r, t)$ is monotonically decreasing with t (for fixed r) and monotonically increasing with r (for fixed t). Therefore, the use of a bias function ensures that recent points have higher probability of being represented in the sample reservoir. Hence, defining the concept of a bias-sensitive sample $S(t)$, which in turn is defined by the bias function $f(r, t)$ as

Definition Let $f(r, t)$ be the bias function for the rth point at the arrival of the tth point. A biased sample $S(t)$ at the time of arrival of the tth point in the stream is defined as a sample such that the relative probability $p(r, t)$ of the rth point belonging to the sample $S(t)$ (of size n) is proportional to $f(r, t)$.   ■

A memory-less temporal bias functions for streams for evolving streams have been proposed in [3]. Apart from $O(1)$ processing time per stream element, incorporating the bias results in upper bounds of reservoir sizes limiting the maximum space requirement to nearly constant in most cases even for an infinitely long data stream. The next section presents biased reservoir sampling techniques on the Bloom filters for the de-duplication problem.

13.5   RESERVOIR SAMPLING–BASED BLOOM FILTER (RSBF) APPROACH

This section discusses the design and working model of the *reservoir sampling–based stable Bloom filter* (RSBF) for de-duplication in large data streams. *RSBF* intelligently combines the concepts of reservoir sampling techniques [15] and that of Bloom filter approach. *RSBF* provides the first of such an integration to exhibit enhanced performance for de-duplication.

RSBF comprises k Bloom filters, each of size s bits and are initially set to 0. On arrival of a new element, e it is hashed to one of the s bits in each of the k Bloom filters with the help of k different uniform random hash functions. The existence of the element is verified by checking whether these k bit positions are set. If all the k bit positions are set to 1, then RSBF reports the element to be duplicate, else to be distinct. RSBF directly inserts the initial s elements of the stream into the structure by setting the corresponding k bit positions in the Bloom filter. Each element e_i, for $i > s$, is then first probed against the Bloom filter structure to determine the duplicate or distinct status. If e_i is reported as distinct, it is inserted in the structure with probability $p_i = s/i$ (insert probability), where i is the current length of the stream and s is the size of each of the Bloom filter.

However, with the increase in the number of bits set in the Bloom filters, RSBF would suffer from a high rate of *false positives* wherein a distinct element is falsely reported as duplicate. As the length of the stream increases, it can be observed that the probability of an element being a duplicate increases (since the elements are drawn from a finite universe). The reservoir sampling method implicitly helps to prevent such a scenario by increasingly rejecting elements from being inserted into the structure (as the *insert probability* decreases). Insertion of elements from a possibly infinite stream would inevitable lead to the setting of nearly all the bits of RSBF to 1, thereby incurring a high false-positive rate (FPR). To alleviate this problem, whenever an element is inserted into RSBF, the algorithm also deletes k randomly uniformly chosen bit (one from each Bloom filter) by setting it to 0. It should be observed that such deletion operation invariably leads to the presence of *false negatives*.

Applications involving duplicate detection demand low tolerance for both false positive as well as false-negative rates (FNR). The use of reservoir sampling helps to keep the false-positive rate significantly lower. However, the repeated rejection of elements (possibly distinct) with increase in the stream length may result in an increase of the FNR, thereby degrading the performance of RSBF. To address this problem, RSBF uses a weak form of biasing on the reservoir sampling operation performed on the stream elements. When the insert probability of an element decreases beyond a specified threshold, p^*, and is reported as distinct by probing its bits, the

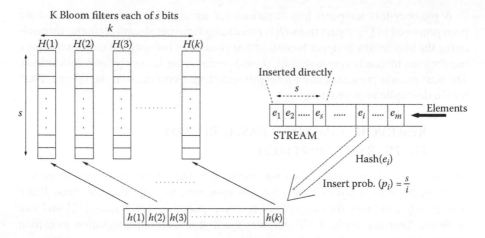

FIGURE 13.1 The working model of RSBF.

element is inserted. This novel combination of reservoir sampling with thresholding thus helps to reduce FNR to acceptable limits. This procedure also helps RSBF to dynamically adapt itself to an evolving stream.

It must be emphasized that along with observing a low FPR and FNR, RSBF also exhibits faster convergence to stability, as compared with that of SBF, as the setting and deletion of k bits lead to a near constant number of 1s and 0s in the structure. The pseudo-code of RSBF is given in Algorithm 13.2 and its structure is diagrammatically represented by Figure 13.1.

13.5.1 THEORETICAL FRAMEWORK

This section provides a snapshot of the theoretical bounds and analysis of FPR, FNR, and convergence rate of the RSBF structure. The readers are referred to [15] for extensive proof statements. Table 13.1 describes the symbols used for the theoretical outline presented here.

TABLE 13.1
Symbol List

Symbols	Meanings
M	Available memory (in bits)
k	Number of bloom filters
s	Size of each bloom filter (in bits)
p_i	Prob. of insertion by reservoir sampling
p^*	Insertion threshold prob. for distinct elements
h_i	Hash position within the ith bloom filter
S	Stream of input elements

13.5.1.1 False-Positive Rate

A false positive, FP, occurs when a distinct element of the stream is reported as a duplicate. Consider the FP of e_{m+1}, the $(m + 1)$th element of the stream. The elements of the stream are assumed to be uniformly drawn at random from a finite universe Γ, with $|\Gamma| = U$.

Let P_{unique} be the probability that e_{m+1} has not occurred in the first m elements of the stream, and let e_{m+1} hash to $H = \{h_1, h_2,..., h_k\}$ positions, where $h_i \in [1, s]$ for the ith Bloom filter. e_{m+1} will be reported as a duplicate when all the bit positions in H are set to 1 after the first m stream elements. Since all the Bloom filters are identical and are independently processed, the argument for one of them can be extended for the others.

Assume element e_l hashes to position h_1 in the first Bloom filter. Initially, all the bits of the Bloom filters are set to 0. Let the latest transition of h_1, from 0 to 1, occur at the lth iteration, and thereafter h_1 is never reset, that is, set to 0. In RSBF a bit will not be reset to 0 in an iteration if the stream element for the iteration is not selected for insertion or a different bit of the Bloom filter is chosen for deletion when the element is to be inserted. The probability of such a transition of h_1 is represented by P_{trans}. Therefore,

$$P_{trans} = P(e_l \text{ is inserted}) \, P(e_l \text{ selects } h_1) \, P(h_1 \text{ is not reset})$$

$$= p_l \frac{1}{s} \prod_{i=l+1}^{m}\left[(1 - p_i) + p_i \frac{s-1}{s}\right] = \frac{s}{l}\frac{1}{s}\prod_{i=l+1}^{m}\left(1 - \frac{1}{i}\right) = \frac{1}{m}$$

Algorithm 13.2: *RSBF(S)*

Require: Threshold FPR *(FPR₁)*, Memory in bits *(M)*, and Stream *(S)*
Ensure: Detecting *duplicate* and *distinct* elements in *S*

```
 1: Compute the value of k from FPRₜ.
 2: Construct k Bloom filters each having M/k bits of memory.
 3: iter ← 1
 4: for each element e of S do
 5:    Hash e into k bit positions, H = h₁, ⋯, hₖ.
 6:    if all bit positions in H are set then
 7:        Result ← DUPLICATE
 8:    else
 9:        Result ← DISTINCT
10:    end if
11:    if iter ≤ s then
12:        Set all the bit positions in H.
13:    else
14:        if (s/iter) ≤ p* then
15:            for all positions hᵢ in H do
```

16:        **if** $h_i = 0$ **then**
17:            Find a bit in ith bloom filter which is set to 1, and reset to 0.
18:            Set the bit at h_i position to 1
19:        **end if**
20:        **end for**
21:    **else**
22:        With probability (s/$iter$) insert e by setting all the bit positions in H.
23:        If e was decided to be inserted then randomly reset one bit positions
           from each of the k Bloom filters.
24:    **end if**
25:    **end if**
26:    $iter \leftarrow iter + 1$
27: **end for**

This transition (Event 1) may happen during any of the iterations from ($s + 1$) to m. Hence, $l \in [s + 1, m]$. Since the different Bloom filters are independent, the final decision (*distinct or duplicate*) regarding e_{m+1} is taken after probing all the bit positions of H, and hence,

$$P_H = \left(1 - \frac{s}{m}\right)^k \approx 1 - \frac{ks}{m} \tag{13.1}$$

It can be observed that the transition of the bit may also be possible during the first s elements of the stream (Event 2). Since the first s elements of the stream are always inserted, all the bit positions in H should be set at least once during this period for an element to be reported as duplicate. Therefore, using similar computations as above, the probability that all the bits for e_{m+1} in H is set in the initial s iterations is given by

$$P_{H_s} = \left(\left[1 - \frac{1}{e}\right]\frac{s}{m}\right)^k \tag{13.2}$$

Either of the above two events will contribute to the FPR, hence the probability of e_{m+1} being reported as an FP can be obtained using Equations 13.1 and 13.2, which is given by

$$P_{FPR} = \left(\frac{U-1}{U}\right)^m \left[1 - \frac{ks}{m} + \left(\left[1 - \frac{1}{e}\right]\frac{s}{m}\right)^k\right] \tag{13.3}$$

The detailed proof can be found in [15]. Analyzing Equation 13.3, it can be seen that as the stream length m tends to infinity, the right multiplicative factor tends to 1. However, as $U - 1 < U$ the left multiplicative term tends to 0. Hence as the stream length increases, the observed FPR decreases and nearly becomes constant. This leads to a stable performance of RSBF similar to that of SBF. However, RSBF achieved this convergence much faster as opposed to SBF as discussed in [15].

13.5.1.2   False-Negative Rate

A false-negative error occurs in the stream when a duplicate element is recognized as distinct. This section focuses on determining the probability of occurrence of an FN. As per the working of RSBF (Algorithm 13.2), an element e will be an FN if it has occurred in the stream earlier and one of the following two cases hold:

1. At least one of the k bits of the hash positions of e (set during the previous occurrence of e) has been reset during the insertion of another stream element into the reservoir.
2. When e occurred earlier in the stream it was not inserted due to low insertion probability of the stream then (by reservoir sampling). However, according to the threshold p^* in Algorithm 13.2, every distinct element in the stream is inserted if the current insertion probability, $p_i \leq p^*$. Therefore, if previous appearances of e had occurred before p_i was less than p^* and were not inserted, then it is likely to be detected as an FN when e repeats for the first time after the insertion probability of the reservoir falls below p^*.

Consider the probability of occurrence of an FN for an element e_{m+1}, at the $(m + 1)$th iteration. Let the previous occurrence of element e_{m+1} be at position x, where it was inserted into the reservoir. Therefore, $\Pr(e_{m+1}$ occurs at x *and* is inserted$) = P_x = p_x/U$. Now, for all iterations from $(x + 1)$ to m, either e_{m+1} has not occurred in the stream or was not inserted. Thus, $\Pr(e_{m+1}$ has not occurred OR e_{m+1} has not been inserted after $x)$ is given by

$$P_{x'} = \prod_{i=x+1}^{m} \left[\frac{U-1}{U} + \frac{1-p_i}{U} \right] \leq \left[1 - \frac{s}{Um} \right]^{m-x} \leq e^{\frac{-s(m-x)}{Um}} \left[\therefore p_i = s/i \text{ and } \frac{s}{Um} \text{ is small} \right]$$

Now, $\Pr(e_{m+1}$ was last inserted at position $x)$ is given by

$$P_l = P_x P_{x'} \leq \frac{s}{Ux} e^{\frac{-s(m-x)}{Um}} \tag{13.4}$$

Since e_{m+1} was last inserted at position x, the k bits corresponding to e_{m+1} were all set to 1. Therefore, e_{m+1} will be a FN if at least one of those k bits is reset to 0. Due to the deletion operation in case of insertion of an element into the reservoir, some of those k bits can be reset again. Let y be the last iteration where there is a transition from 0 to 1 for any of the k n = bits corresponding to e_{m+1}, after which it is not reset again until the mth iteration, and hence $x \leq y \leq m$. Therefore, $\Pr(a$ bit is set at $y) = P_y = p_y/s = 1/y$. Also, $\Pr(that$ bit is not reset after $y)$ is given as

$$P_{y'} = \prod_{i=y+1}^{m} = \left[p_i \left(1 - \frac{1}{s} \right) + (1 - p_i) \right] = \frac{y}{m} \tag{13.5}$$

Hence, Pr(the last transition of the bit from 0 to 1 in a buffer at y) can be expressed as a product of P_y and $P_{y'}$, which is equal to $1/m$.

As y can vary from x to m, Pr (the bit remains set at m) $= \sum_{y=x}^{m} \frac{1}{m} = \frac{m-x+1}{m}$. So, Pr (at least one of those k bits is reset at m) $= P_r = 1 - \text{Pr(the bit remains set at } m)^k = 1 - \left(\frac{m-x+1}{m} \right)^k$. Now, $\Pr(e_{m+1}$ is last inserted at x AND at least one of those k bits is reset at m) is given by

$$P_{lr} = P_l P_r \le \frac{s}{Ux} e^{\frac{-s(m-x)}{Um}} \left[1 - \left(\frac{m-x+1}{m} \right)^k \right] \le \frac{1}{Ux} \left[1 - \left(\frac{m-x+1}{m} \right)^k \right] \quad (13.6)$$

However, the value of x can vary within the range $[(s+1), m]$. Hence, the probability of e_{m+1} being reported as a FN becomes

$$P_{FNR} \le \frac{k(m-s)}{Um} \quad (13.7)$$

Similarly, if e_{m+1} had occurred in the first s iterations, then it had definitely been inserted, and e_{m+1} will be a FN if at least one of the bits is 0 at the $(m+1)$th iteration. The probability that the last insertion of e_{m+1} occurs in the first s iterations is

$$P_{in\,s} = \left[1 - \left(\frac{U-1}{U} \right)^s \right] \prod_{i=s+1}^{m} \left[\frac{1}{U}(1 - p_i) + \frac{U-1}{U} \right]$$

$$\le \left[1 - \left(\frac{U-1}{U} \right)^s \right] \prod_{i=s+1}^{m} \left[1 - \frac{s}{mU} \right] = \frac{s}{U} e^{-\frac{s}{Um}(m-s)} \le \frac{1}{U} \quad (13.8)$$

Similar to the previous arguments, probability of transition of a bit from 0 to 1 is $1/m$. As the position y can vary within $[s+1, m]$, the probability that the bit is set after $(m+1)$th iteration is $\left(\frac{m-s}{m} \right)$. Hence for all the Bloom filters, the probability of at least one bit being zero is given by

$$P_{set} = 1 - \left[1 - \frac{s}{m} \right]^k \approx \frac{sk}{m} \quad (13.9)$$

From Equations 13.8 and 13.9, the FNR in this context is given by $\frac{sk}{Um}$. Using Equation 13.7 and the above result (both can produce an FNR), the probability of e_{m+1} being reported as a FN can be bounded by

$$P_{FNR} \approx O\left(\frac{k}{U} \right) \quad (13.10)$$

Hence, RSBF tends to observe a constant *FNR* much lower than that of SBF as the stream length increases. Readers can find the detailed proof in [15].

13.5.1.3 Stability Factor

SBF introduced the concept of *stability* of a Bloom filter, whereby the number of 1s or 0s in the structure become constant after a time period. It should be noted that as the FPR and FNR is dependent on the 1s and 0s present in the Bloom filter, respectively, stability of their counts nearly guarantees constant performance of the data structure. In the following analysis, RSBF structure is shown to attain stability much earlier compared with SBF. The complete proof was presented in [15].

The following theorem bounds the expected fraction of 1s in the RSBF. The fraction of 1s (or 0s) is important because the false-positive rate (or FNR) is dependent on the fraction of 1s (or 0s). The faster stability is attained, the better will be the overall performance of the structure. Let $E(X)$ be the expected count of 1s in one of the k Bloom filters of RSBF; then the expected fraction of 1s in RSBF, (ζ) can be approximated by $\dfrac{E(X)}{s}$, where s is the size of each Bloom filter (in bits).

Theorem 1.5.1

Given an RSBF with ks bits, at any iteration i, the expected fraction of 1s (ζ) is a constant, $\forall i > s$.   ∎

Proof

Let λ denote the count of 1s in a Bloom filter after iteration $(i - 1)$. The analysis is performed on a single Bloom filter as other Bloom filters (and the operations on them) are identical. According to Algorithm 13.2, the count of 1s can either increase or decrease by one only or remain the same in iteration i. Therefore, the expected count of 1s can be expressed as

$$E(X) = (\lambda - 1)\,\Pr(\lambda - 1) + \lambda\,\Pr(\lambda) + (\lambda + 1)\,\Pr(\lambda + 1) \tag{13.11}$$

since $\Pr(\lambda \pm j) = 0$, where $j \geq 2$.

The count of 1s in a Bloom filter can decrease by one when an element is inserted and the bit selected to be set was already set to 1, and during deletion, 1 of the set bits is reset to 0. The probability is given by

$$\Pr(\lambda - 1) = p_i \left[\frac{\lambda\,(\lambda - 1)}{s^2} \right] \tag{13.12}$$

The count of 1s can remain the same when the ith element e_i in the stream is not inserted. Further, if the element is inserted, the count of 1s can still remain the same if a 0 bit is selected to be set to 1 and a 1 bit is reset to 0 during deletion. Also, if the bit to be set to 1 is already set and that to be reset is already 0, the count of 1s remain constant. Hence,

$$\Pr(\lambda) = (1 - p_i) + p_i \left[\frac{\lambda (s - \lambda + 1)}{s^2} + \frac{\lambda (s - \lambda)}{s^2} \right] \tag{13.13}$$

Similarly, the count increases by one if a 0 bit is set to 1 and during deletion a 0 bit is selected.

$$\Pr(\lambda + 1) = p_i \left(\frac{s - \lambda}{s} \right)^2 \tag{13.14}$$

Substituting Equations 13.12, 13.13, and 13.14 in Equation 13.11,

$$E(X) = p_i \left[\lambda \left(\frac{1 - s}{s} \right)^2 + 1 \right] + \lambda (1 - p_i) = \lambda + p_i \in \tag{13.15}$$

For any value that λ can assume, $0 \leq |\in| \leq 1$ and therefore the fraction of 1s, $E(X)/s$ in a buffer is a constant. Moreover, the fraction $|p_i.\in|$ is monotonically decreasing with increasing values of i, which is the stream length. Hence for large i, $\in$ is practically 0. This analysis holds identically for all the remaining $(k - 1)$ buffers. Therefore ζ is a constant for RSBF. ∎

By algebraic manipulations, the variance of the count of 1s in RSBF, $Var[X]$ is

$$Var[X] = p_i (\beta^2 + (\beta - 1)^2) - p_i^2, \text{ where } 0 \leq \beta \leq 1 \tag{13.16}$$

Equation 13.16 implies that the variance of the count of 1s in the Bloom filters for RSBF is significantly low. For instance, when $\beta = 0.5$, the variance is only $(p_i/2 - p_i^2)$. Further, as the length of the stream increases, the variance of the number of ones decreases. This analysis implies a faster convergence to stability for RSBF with respect to SBF.

13.6 EXPERIMENTS AND RESULTS

13.6.1 SETTING OF PARAMETERS

This section discusses the procedure of setting the parameters for the proposed algorithm to optimize its performance. Given a fixed amount of memory space, M in bits, the best setting for the number of Bloom filters, k and the size of each Bloom filter, s such that $sk = M$, is to be found.

SBF in this case establishes a constraint on p depending on a threshold FPR given as input by the application, and then computes the optimal value of k by varying the values of *Max*. Also, the nature of the stream and the expected number of FNs are used to compute the best value of *Max*. In case, no such prior data is available, *Max* is set to 1.

RSBF, on the other hand, accepts the threshold FPR, FPR_t as input, and computes the optimal value of k and s for overall low *FPR* and *FNR*. Assume that the algorithm conforms to the threshold FPR, FPR_t after the initial s elements of the stream has been processed. An FPR will occur for an element e_{s+1} if all the corresponding bits in the Bloom filter for e_{s+1} are set. Considering a single Bloom filter, the particular bit into which e_{s+1} hashes to will be set if at least one of the s elements maps into it. Hence, by similar computations

$$\left(1 - \frac{1}{e}\right)^k = FPR_t$$

$$\therefore k = \frac{\ln(FPR_t)}{\ln\left(1 - \frac{1}{e}\right)}, \text{ and } s = \frac{M}{k} \tag{13.17}$$

FPR is found to decrease with increase in the value of k, while *FNR* is the lowest when $k = 1$. Hence, to optimize this trade-offs, the value of k is set as the *arithmetic mean* of 1 and that obtained in Equation 13.17. Given the value of k, s is thus appropriately set accordingly.

13.6.2 RESULTS AND ANALYSIS

This section provides to the readers the performance comparisons of both RSBF and SBF [12] algorithms on real as well as synthetic data sets. The real data set containing clickstream data* having around 3 million records and random data set with 1 billion records were used to evaluate the quality of membership query results generated. The clickstream data set contained a user's click history over a period. Simulating the fingerprints of URL clicks by users, the synthetic data set was uniformly randomly generated.

The two sets of experiments shown captures (a) the variation of FNR, FPR, and convergence with increasing number of records in the input and (b) the variation of FNR and FPR with increasing amounts of memory for sampling the input stream, using multiple data sets for increasing percentage of duplicates. In all the experiments, $p*$ was set to 0.03. For faster changing streams or more biased reservoir sampling method, $p*$ is set to a higher value.

---

* Obtained from http://www.sigkdd.org/kddcup/index.php?section=2000&method=data.

13.6.3 QUALITY COMPARISON

The variation of FNR and FPR along with convergence rates with increasing number of records in the input stream are now represented. The memory used for the underlying Bloom filter data structure is kept constant for both SBF and RSBF in these experiments.

Figure 13.2 presents the comparison of FPR for real data set with more than 3 M records. Initially, until the number of input stream records reaches the threshold, RSBF has better FPR (0.001) than SBF (around 0.0025). RSBF in this stage accepts all the input records in its reservoir and the available memory determines the threshold count. It can also be observed that upto the threshold point RSBF will not incur any FNR.

As the number of records increase, the FPR performance of RSBF gradually becomes comparable to that of SBF. It can be noted here that, even with a small memory of 2 KB for around 3 M elements, the FPR achieved is quite low, 0.0025. This demonstrates that both RSBF and SBF attain low FPR for large number of records with a significantly small memory space.

Figure 13.3 presents the comparison of FPR for the synthetic data set with 1B records. With 128-MB memory, as the number of records increases, the FPR for RSBF stabilizes at 0.8%, while that for SBF stabilizes around 0.7%. With larger memory, 512-MB memory, as the number of records increases, the FPR for both RSBF and SBF stabilizes at around 0.06%. Thus, both RSBF and SBF attain comparable FPR for massive number of records, with the performance becoming nearly equal at larger memory. The use of *reservoir sampling* in RSBF enables it in general to sieve out duplicates that occur in higher probability as the stream length increases, given the finite size of alphabet set of the input elements.

Figure 13.4 compares the FNR between RSBF and SBF with increase in the number of records. For around 3 M records and FPR threshold of 0.1, both RSBF and SBF show an initially increases in FNR, stabilizing as the number of records increases further. However, for both 2 KB and 4 KB memory, RSBF clearly outperforms SBF

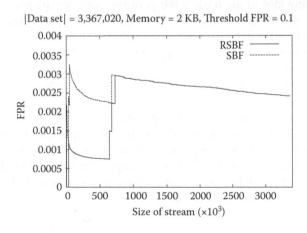

FIGURE 13.2 FPR comparison.

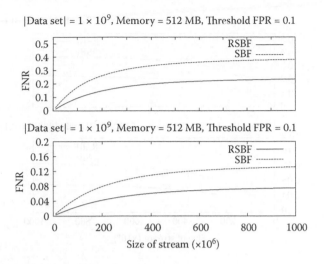

FIGURE 13.3   FPR comparison.

by a significant margin. For 2 KB memory, RSBF has a stable FNR of 10%, which is around 1.5× better as compared with SBF, which produces a stable FNR of 15%. With increase in memory the performance gap between the two further increases in favor of RSBF. Observe that for 4 KB memory, RSBF attains a stable FNR of nearly 12%, which is around 1.83× better than that of SBF with a stable FNR of 22%.

Figure 13.5 also compares the FNR between RSBF and SBF, albeit on synthetic data set having 1B records and FPR threshold of 0.1. For both RSBF and SBF, the FNR again initially increases but then stabilizes. For both 128- and 512-MB memory, RSBF similarly outperforms SBF. For 128-MB memory, RSBF has a stable FNR of 22%, which is around 1.73× better compared with SBF, which has an FNR of 38%. With 512-MB memory, RSBF attains a stable FNR of 7%, around 1.86× better

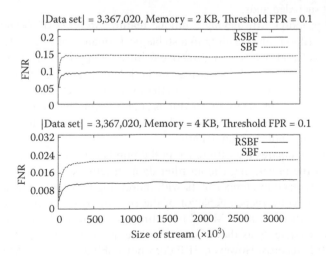

FIGURE 13.4   FNR comparison: real data set.

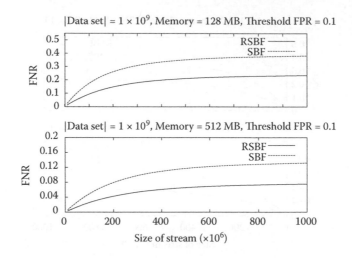

FIGURE 13.5   FNR comparison: synthetic data set.

than SBF with a stable FNR of 13%. Thus, RSBF consistently demonstrates better FNR than SBF upto to a factor of 1.86×, for different data sets.

The significant reduction in FNR obtained by RSBF is novel with respect to stable Bloom filters and extremely vital for practical applications such as search engines. This performance of RSBF can be attributed to the forced insertion of a stream element into the reservoir when the insert probability for the system falls below the threshold $p*$ as described earlier. This approach eliminates the possibility of an FNR occurring due to repeated rejection of an element from being inserted into the reservoir given the lone operation of reservoir sampling. It can also be observed that essentially it helps RSBF to adapt its reservoir in dynamic streaming environments. Hence, it partially acts as a simple bias function for RSBF. SBF, on the other hand fails to meet such demands.

Ref. [12] proposes SBF having a unique feature, *stability* of the number of 1s present in the Bloom filter leading to a stable performance of SBF in terms of FPR and FNR. This stability poses an attractive feature for applications for guaranteeing a constant performance with increasing stream lengths. However, SBF converges to its stable point at a theoretical stream length of infinity. Practically, this represents a very large input stream. RSBF also exhibits such stability but converges to a stable performance at a much earlier point. This enables applications to guarantee efficiency at a much smaller stream length.

Figure 13.6 compares the difference in the number of 1s for successive number of records, in the underlying Bloom filter data structures. By studying the variation in the difference in number of 1s with increasing number of records, one gets insights into the convergence behavior of the two algorithm. Here again, the total number of records is around 3 M and FPR threshold used is 0.1. For 2 KB memory, RSBF stabilizes quickly as the difference in the number of 1s stabilizes to nearly 0 at only 500 K records. However, SBF does not stabilize even at 3 M records. For 4 KB memory, RSBF observes stability at around 1.5 M records, but SBF fails to

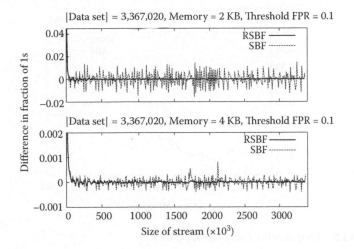

FIGURE 13.6   Convergence rate comparison: real data set.

stabilize even at 3 M records. This demonstrates that RSBF has much better convergence rate than SBF.

Figure 13.7 similarly compares the difference in the number of 1s of successive number of records for the synthetic data set. With 512 KB memory, the difference in the number of 1s stabilizes to zero faster for RSBF (shortly after 50 million records) as compared with SBF, which has not yet stabilized even at 455 million records.

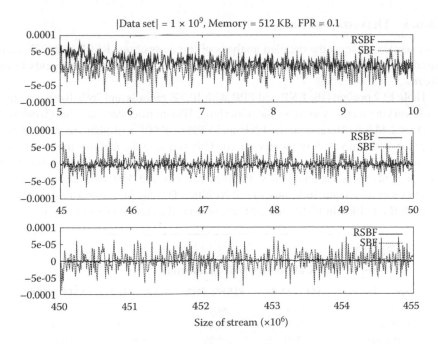

FIGURE 13.7   Convergence rate comparison: synthetic data set.

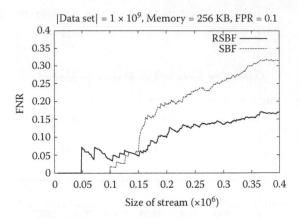

FIGURE 13.8 FNR stability rate: synthetic data set.

This exactly validates Equation 13.15 that the number of 1s in RSBF becomes nearly constant much ahead of SBF.

Figure 13.8 shows the faster convergence to stability for RSBF with increase in stream length. The increase of FNR in RSBF is around 0.1% over a stream length of 0.35 M elements, having an average deviation of 0.3×10^{-6} per element. On the other hand, SBF demonstrates an increase in FNR of around 0.3% over 0.3 M element with the average deviation as 1×10^{-6}.

13.6.4 DETAILED ANALYSIS

This section presents the detailed analysis of the algorithms, RSBF and SBF, compared against variation of memory used and percentage of distinct elements in the stream.

Table 13.2 presents the FNR and FPR with 100 K records and 76% distinct records while varying memory used for the underlying Bloom filter data structure from 16 K bits to 4.2 M bits. Here, both the FNR and FPR of RSBF and SBF are close to each other for different values of memory used. This is due to the fact that the stream size is quite small and neither of the structures have reached their stability point. Table 13.3 presents the FNR and FPR with 10 M records and 49% distinct records with varying memory from 16 K bits to 4.2 M bits. Here again, comparable results for both FNR and FPR in RSBF and SBF are observed as the number of duplicates and

TABLE 13.2

Data Set of 100 K Elements (76% Distinct)

Space (in bits)	SBF% FNR	RSBF% FNR	SBF% FPR	RSBF% FPR
16,384	85.06	84.49	10.05	11.22
65,536	74.37	74.85	8.093	8.384
4,194,304	5.51	6.29	0.00382	0.00263

TABLE 13.3
Data Set of 10 M Elements (49% Distinct)

Space (in bits)	SBF% FNR	RSBF% FNR	SBF% FPR	RSBF% FPR
16,384	88.83	87.52	11.08	12.464
262,144	88.11	86.89	10.86	12.12
4,194,304	77.33	77.73	7.822	7.914

distinct elements in the stream are roughly equal. However, with 10 M records, and percentage of distinct elements lesser than 49%, RSBF has better FNR than SBF as exhibited in other data set values given below.

Table 13.4 presents the FNR and FPR with 695 M records and 15% distinct records while varying memory used for the underlying Bloom filter data structure from 262 K bits to 4.2 B bits. Here, FNR achieved by RSBF is better than SBF, and this gap is higher when larger memory is used. At around 67 M bits, RSBF has FNR of 58.3%, while SBF has FNR of 82.48%; while at 1 B bits, RSBF has FNR of 23.12%, while SBF has FNR of 37.79%. However, the FPR values remain similar across both these algorithms.

Table 13.5 presents the FNR and FPR with 1 B records and 10% distinct records while varying memory used for the underlying Bloom filter data structure from 262 K bits to 4.2 B bits. Here again, FNR achieved by RSBF is better than SBF. At around 67 M bits, RSBF has FNR of 58%, while SBF has FNR of 82%; while at 1 B bits, RSBF has FNR of 23.47%, while SBF has FNR of 37%. The ratio of FNR between SBF and RSBF increases to 1.74x at 4.2 B bits. However, the FPR values remain similar across both these algorithms. This demonstrates that RSBF has consistent superior FNR compared with SBF, with FPR values close to SBF though sometimes higher by a small margin.

TABLE 13.4
Data Set of 695 M Elements (15% Distinct)

Space (in bits)	SBF% FNR	RSBF% FNR	SBF% FPR	RSBF% FPR
262,144	88.86	87.47	12.51	11.1
67,108,864	82.48	58.2818	8.3	8.4
1,073,741,824	37.79	23.12	0.742	0.89
4,294,967,296	12.94	7.37	0.069	0.072

TABLE 13.5
Data Set of 1 B Elements (10% Distinct)

Space (in bits)	SBF% FNR	RSBF% FNR	SBF% FPR	RSBF% FPR
67,108,864	82.58	67.66	8.262	10.262
1,073,741,824	38.17	23.47	0.7	0.83
4,294,967,296	13.163	7.53	0.0634	0.0664

13.7 CONCLUSIONS

Real-time de-duplication or data redundancy removal (DRR) for streaming data sets poses a challenging problem. This chapter has presented novel Bloom filter based algorithms to tackle the problem efficiently. The *stable Bloom filter* (SBF) uniquely proposed the *stability* condition leading to constant FP and FN rates. However, the stability is achieved at infinite stream length theoretically and SBF suffers from high FNR. The constant guarantee on error rates makes SBF an extremely efficiently and attractive data structure for DRR applications.

Using a novel combination of reservoir sampling and Bloom filters, the *reservoir sampling–based stable Bloom filter* (RSBF) obtained enhanced FNR and faster convergence to stability at comparable FPR with that of SBF. The stability property is adhered to at each element of the stream. RSBF thus eliminates the problems faced by SBF, and thus currently offers the best technique for de-duplication.

This chapter discussed at length the state-of-art structures for de-duplication along with a broad theoretical outline. Detailed discussions on SBF and RSBF and their working principles have been presented to the readers. Real-time in-memory de-duplication experiments using both real and synthetically generated data sets of up to 1 billion records have also been presented and compared. Despite such advancements and enhanced performances, the effects of other biasing and sampling functions to further decrease the FNR and FPR simultaneously along with other improved data structures and parallel algorithms remain an open direction of future work. It would also be interesting to study the effects of reservoir sampling on SBF.

REFERENCES

1. A. Adya, W.J. Bolosky, M. Castro, G. Cermak, R. Chaiken, J.R. Douceur, J. Howell, R.J. Lorch, M. Theimer, and R. Wattenhofer. Farsite: Federated, available, and reliable storage for an incompletely trusted environment. In *OSDI*, pages 1–14, 2002.
2. C. Aggarwal and P. Yu. *Data Streams: Models and Algorithms*. Springer, 2007.
3. C.C. Aggarwal. On biased reservoir sampling in the presence of stream evolution. In *VLDB*, pages 607–618, 2006.
4. N. Alon, Y. Matias, and M. Szegedy. The space complexity of approximating the frequency moments. In *STOC*, pages 20–29, 1996.
5. B. Babcock, M. Datar, and R. Motwani. Sampling from moving window over streaming data. In *SODA*, pages 633–634, 2002.
6. F. Baboescu and G. Varghese. Scalable packet classification. In *ACM SIGCOMM*, pages 199–210, 2001.
7. M. Bilenko and R.J. Mooney. Adaptive duplicate detection using learnable string similarity measures. In *Proc. SIGKDD*, pages 39–48, 2003.
8. B.H. Bloom. Space/time trade-offs in hash coding with allowable errors. *Commun. ACM*, 13(7):422–426, 1970.
9. A.Z. Broder and M. Mitzenmacher. Network applications of bloom filters: A survey. *Internet Math.*, 1(4):485–509, 2003.
10. A. Chowdhury, O. Frieder, D. Grossman, and M. McCabe. Collection statistics for fast duplicate document detection. *ACM Trans. Inform. Syst.*, 20(2):171–191, 2002.
11. J. Conrad, X. Guo, and C. Schriber. Online duplicate document detection: Signature reliability in a dynamic retrieval environment. In *CIKM*, pages 443–452, 2003.

12. F. Deng and D. Rafiei. Approximately detecting duplicates for streaming data using stable bloom filters. In *SIGMOD*, pages 25–36, 2006.
13. S. Dharmapurikar, P. Krishnamurthy, and D.E. Taylor. Longest prefix matching using bloom filters. In *ACM SIGCOMM*, pages 201–212, 2003.
14. F. Douglis, J. Lavoie, J.M. Tracey, P. Kulkarni, and P. Kulkarni. Redundancy elimination within large collections of files. In *USENIX*, pages 59–72, 2004.
15. S. Dutta, S. Bhattacherjee, and A. Narang. Towards "intelligent compression" in streams: A biased reservoir sampling based bloom filter approach. In *EDBT*, pages 228–238, 2012.
16. L. Fan, P. Cao, J. Almeida, and Z.A. Broder. Summary cache: A scalable wide area web cache sharing protocol. In *IEEE/ACM Transaction on Networking*, pages 281–293, 2000.
17. W.C. Feng, D.D. Kandlur, D. Sahu, and K.G. Shin. Stochastic fair blue: A queue management algorithm for enforcing fairness. In *IEEE INFOCOM*, pages 1520–1529, 2001.
18. P. Flajolet and G.N. Martin. Probabilistic counting algorithms for database applications. *Comput. Syst. Sci.*, 31(2):182–209, 1985.
19. H. Garcia-Molina, J.D. Ullman, and J. Widom. *Database System Implementation*. Prentice Hall, 1999.
20. V.K. Garg, A. Narang, and S. Bhattacherjee. Real-time memory efficient data redundancy removal algorithm. In *CIKM*, pages 1259–1268, 2010.
21. J. Gehrke, F. Korn, and J. Srivastava. On computing correlated aggregates over continual data streams. In *SIGMOD*, pages 13–24, 2001.
22. P. Gibbons and Y. Mattias. New sampling-based summary statistics for improving approximate query answers. In *ACM SIGMOD*, pages 331–342, 1998.
23. P. Gupta and N. McKeown. Packet classification on multiple fields. In *SIGCOMM*, pages 147–160, 1999.
24. A. Heydon and M. Najork. Mercator. A scalable, extensive web crawler. In *World Wide Web*, volume 2, 1999.
25. Y. Hua and B. Xiao. A multi-attribute data structure with parallel bloom filters for network services. In *International Conference on High Performance Computing*, pages 277–288, 2006.
26. N. Jain, M. Dahlin, and R. Tewari. Taper: Tiered approach for eliminating redundancy in replica synchronization. In *FAST*, pages 281–294, 2005.
27. A. Kumar, J. Xu, J. Wang, O. Spatschek, and L. Li. Space-code bloom filter for efficient per-flow traffic measurement. In *IEEE INFOCOM*, pages 1762–1773, 2004.
28. D. Lee and J. Hull. Duplicate detection in symbolically compressed documents. In *ICDAR*, pages 305–308, 1999.
29. M.C. Little, N.A. Speirs, and S.K. Shrivastava. Using bloom filters to speed-up name lookup in distributed systems. *Comput. J.*, 45(6):645–652, 2002.
30. A. Metwally, D. Agrawal, and A.E. Abbadi. Duplicate detection in click streams. In *WWW*, pages 12–21, 2005.
31. M. Mitzenmacher. Compressed bloom filters. In *IEEE/ACM Transaction on Networking*, pages 604–612, 2002.
32. P. Gibbons. Distinct sampling for highly accurate answers to distinct value queries and event reports. In *VLDB*, pages 541–550, 2001.
33. S. Quinlan and S. Dorward. Venti: A new approach to archival storage. In *FAST*, pages 89–101, 2002.
34. M. Reiter, V. Anupam, and A. Mayer. Detecting hit-shaving in click-through payment schemes. In *USENIX*, pages 155–166, 1998.
35. C. Saar and M. Yossi. Spectral bloom filters. In *ACM SIGMOD*, pages 241–252, 2003.
36. H. Shen and Y. Zhang. Improved approximate detection of duplicates for data streams over sliding windows. *J. Comput. Sci. Technol.*, 23(6), 2008.

37. N. Tolia, M. Kozuch, M. Satyanarayanan, B. Karp, T.C. Bressoud, and A. Perrig. Opportunistic use of content addressable storage for distributed file systems. In *USENIX*, pages 127–140, 2003.

38. J.S. Vitter. Random sampling with a reservoir. *ACM Trans. Math. Software*, 11(1):37–57, 1985.

39. M. Weis and F. Naumann. Dogmatrix tracks down duplicates in xml. In *Proc. ACM SIGMOD*, pages 431–442, 2005.

14 Large-Scale Network Traffic Analysis for Estimating the Size of IP Addresses and Detecting Traffic Anomalies

Ahmed Metwally, Fabio Soldo,
Matt Paduano, and Meenal Chhabra

CONTENTS

14.1 INTRODUCTION

Today, a large number of Internet services such as web search, web mail, maps, and other web-based applications are highly available and provided free of charge. Designing, deploying, and maintaining these services is expensive, but is only possible due to the revenue generated by Internet advertising, an industry that in 2011 generated over $31B [3] in the United States alone.

For the aforementioned reasons, detecting abusive ad clicks is a critical component for the well being of numerous Internet services. Abusive click attacks refer to the fraudulent activity of generating charges for online advertisers without a real interest in the products advertised. Abusive clicks are the biggest threat to the Internet advertising industry [9,14].

Generating abusive clicks can be classified into publishers' and advertisers' attacks. Publishers' attacks use fake traffic in an attempt to increase publishers' revenues from online advertising.* Advertisers' attacks aim at increasing the overall amount of activities, such as impressions or clicks on competitors' ads. The main objective here is throttling the competitors' exposure to the market, mainly by depleting their advertising budgets.

Abusive clicks can be generated in many ways, using different network infrastructures and levels of sophistication. Figure 14.1 depicts three publishers with different types of traffic. Ads on the publisher sites thispagemakesmoney.com and thispagetoo.com receive legitimate traffic, that is, users interested in the ads clicked on them. Ads on thispagetoo.com also receive fake traffic. For instance, the publisher may ask friends to repeatedly click on ads displayed on their site. Finally, in a more sophisticated click attack, publisher iwontmakemoney.com hires a botnet to automatically generate a large volume of fake traffic.

---

* We will use the terms "fake," "abusive," and "fraudulent" interchangeably.

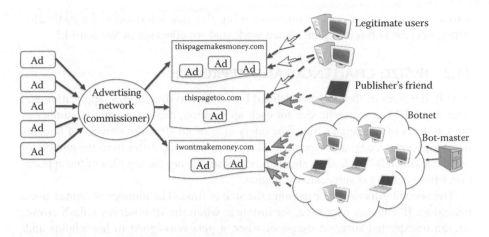

FIGURE 14.1 Three publishers contract with an advertising network to host ads for a commission for each, click on these ads and they illustrate three types of traffic: (1) ads on the publisher site thispagemakesmoney.com are clicked only by legitimate users (white pointers); (2) ads on thispagetoo.com are clicked by both legitimate users and fraudsters (gray pointers); and (3) iwontmakemoney.com uses a large botnet to generate fake traffic.

Combating abusive traffic is at the heart of analyzing large data sets because it involves building statistical models at a global scale. This chapter explains how a statistical framework was built for estimating the number of the users of a specific application that are currently sharing a public IP address, called hereinafter the size of the IP, to combat abusive traffic at Google. From a data analysis perspective, this is a very challenging problem because the range of sizes is huge; the size of any IP can change abruptly, and sizes of a significant portion of the IP space need to be estimated. The estimation techniques presented are scalable, parallelizable using the MapReduce framework [6], and provide statistically sound and timely estimates of the IP sizes that rely solely on passively mining aggregated application log data, without probing machines or deploying active content like Java applets.

The chapter also describes how IP size estimation is employed to detect traffic anomalies. The detection technology relies on the observation that various machine-generated traffic attacks share a common characteristic: they induce an anomalous deviation from the IP size distribution expected from legitimate users. The detection technology is based on a fundamental characteristic of these attacks and is thus robust (e.g., to DHCP re-assignment) and hard to evade or reverse engineer, even if the spammers are aware of its existence. Most importantly, it has low complexity and is parallelizable using MapReduce.

The methodologies presented here, while mainly motivated by combating publishers' attacks, can be applied to detect advertisers' attacks, as well as other machine-generated anomalous traffic, including combating DDoS and detecting spam on social networks.

The rest of the chapter is organized as follows. Section 14.2 discusses the challenges and the main framework. Section 14.3 discusses building statistical models for size estimation. Section 14.4 discusses predicting the size of each possible IP in a timely manner. Section 14.5 discusses using the size information for combating abuse. Section 14.6 reviews the related work, and we conclude in Section 14.7.

14.2 IP SIZE: CHALLENGES AND APPROACH

In [19], the sizes of the IPs were defined based on two dimensions: application and time. Each IP has a specific size for each application, depending on the number of human users of this application. The query size of an IP is the number of humans querying a search engine for example, Google, which may differ from the number of users clicking ads. Thus, sizes should be estimated using the log files of the application whose activity is subject to estimation.

The second dimension for defining the size is time. The number of human users behind an IP changes over time, for instance, when the IP observes a flash crowd, i.e., an unexpected surge in usage, or when it gets reassigned to households and/ or companies. The size estimates should be issued frequently enough to cope with these frequent changes. This calls for a short estimation time period. On the other hand, the estimation period should be long enough to yield enough IP coverage, and enough traffic per IP to produce statistically sound estimates.

14.2.1 ESTIMATION CHALLENGES AND METHODOLOGY

While estimating the sizes of individual IPs has ramifications on the security field, the primary concern is violating the user privacy. The work at [19] preserves the user privacy by estimating sizes of IPs using the application-level log files. First, the application users are assumed to be only temporarily identified, for example, with cookie IDs in the case of HTTP-based log files. Thus, no Personally Identifiable Information, such as the name or the email address, is revealed. Second, no individual machines are tracked. Third, the framework uses application log data aggregated at the IP level. Over 30% of dynamic IPs are reassigned every 1 to 3 days [27], and thus an IP is considered a temporary identification of a user. Finally, the majority of the users share IPs. This is illustrated in Figure 14.2, where 10M random IPs (from Google ad click log files) are shared by 26.9M total estimated users.

Estimating sizes from the log files is not straightforward. Naïve counting of distinct user identifications, for example, cookie IDs or user agents (UAs), per IP fails

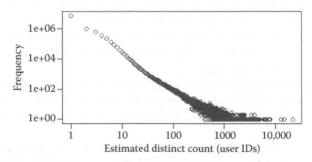

FIGURE 14.2 The estimated sizes of 10M random IPs.

to accurately estimate sizes. Corporate network address translation (NAT) devices usually have the same UA on all hosts. Similarly, an Internet cafe host is used by several users often sharing the same user ID. Meanwhile, small IPs can masquerade as large IPs by clearing or farming cookies and overwriting UAs in HTTP requests. Hence, estimating sizes by distinct counting cookies and UAs may result in overestimation or underestimation. Filtering traffic based on these inaccurate sizes yields high false-negatives and false-positives rates.

Instead, advocates [19] using the log files to build statistical models that are later used for estimating sizes. This approach poses some challenges. First, the log files do not contain only legitimate traffic. The existence of abusive traffic entries in these files degrades the quality of the models and the estimated sizes. To avoid such quality degradation, the models should be built only from the traffic of the trusted users.* This introduces a sampling bias in the traffic used to build the models. To mitigate this bias later in the estimation phase, only the trusted traffic of each IP† during a period, p, is used to estimate its size for p.

Second, the sizes of the IPs change due to legitimate reasons, such as reassignments, flash crowds and business-week cycles. For an estimation period, p, the log files cannot be finalized before the end of p. They are then analyzed to produce estimates after each IP has already made its activities during p. Hence, estimated sizes are always lagging behind real-time sizes. Meanwhile, real-time abuse detection needs the estimates when p begins. This lag reduces the filtering accuracy when an IP legitimately changes size.

Given the above challenges, [19] proposed building statistical models for size estimation in an autonomous, passive and privacy-preserving way from aggregated log files, and predicted size using time series analysis on the estimated size.

14.2.2 The Size Estimation Cycle

The cycle of size estimation and filtering is laid out in this section. The basic cycle consists of four processes that communicate via log files and size lookup tables. For period p, the inputs and outputs of the real-time traffic event logging, estimation, predictions, and real-time abuse detection processes are formalized in Equations 14.1, 14.2, 14.3, and 14.4, respectively.

$$traffic_p \xrightarrow{RT\text{-}Log(p)} log\text{-}files_p \tag{14.1}$$

$$log\text{-}files_p \bowtie_{entry} abusive\text{-}log\text{-}files_p \xrightarrow{Est(p)} estimates\text{-}table_p \tag{14.2}$$

---

* Trusted users can be defined as those with some signature of good traffic, where the definition of good traffic is application-dependent. For combating abusive ad clicks, trusted cookies can be defined as those with a relatively high conversion rate, where conversions are trusted post-click activities, like purchases from the advertisers.

† Traffic entries tagged by the abusive click detection filters are logged in abusive log files. Both trusted and untrusted traffic entries exist in the log files. Only untrusted entries exist in the abusive log files.

$$\forall_{i=p-w-1}^{p-2} \; estimates\text{-}table_i \xrightarrow{Prd(p)} predictions\text{-}table_p \qquad (14.3)$$

$$traffic_p \bowtie_{IP} predictions\text{-}table_p \xrightarrow{RT\text{-}Abuse\text{-}Dtct(p)} abusive\text{-}log\text{-}files_p \qquad (14.4)$$

Real-time logging, denoted $RT\text{-}Log(p)$ in Equation 14.1, finalizes the traffic $log\text{-}files_p$ as $p + 1$ starts. Next, the $log\text{-}files_p$ are consumed, among other input, by the estimation process, $Est(p)$, to produce the $estimates\text{-}table_p$ mapping IPs that issued traffic during p to their estimated sizes (Equation 14.2). Next, the algorithm for predicting sizes, $Prd(p + 2)$, consumes the $estimates\text{-}tables$ from a sliding window of length w periods,* $p - w + 1$ through p, to produce the $predictions\text{-}table_{p+2}$. This prediction process, $Prd(p + 2)$, is assumed to complete before $p + 2$, and produce $predictions\text{-}table_{p+2}$, mapping IPs to their predicted sizes of period $p + 2$.

The $estimates\text{-}tables$ that contributed to $predictions\text{-}table_p$ are shown in Equation 14.3. The $predictions\text{-}table_p$ is used by the real-time abuse detection process, denoted $RT\text{-}Abuse\text{-}Dtct(p)$ in Equation 14.4, to produce the $abusive\text{-}log\text{-}files_p$ for p. The $abusive\text{-}log\text{-}files_p$ contain the IDs of the traffic entries in $log\text{-}files_p$ identified as abusive. The $abusive\text{-}log\text{-}files_p$ are joined with the $log\text{-}files_p$ by $Est(p)$ to disregard the abusive traffic entries, and produce estimates based solely on legitimate traffic (Equation 14.2). While this joining makes estimation exclusively based on nonabusive traffic, care should be taken to avoid overfiltering of legitimate traffic.

This overfiltering caveat is best clarified by an example. Let IP 10.1.1.1 be stable at an estimated size of 1 for the periods $p - w$ through $p - 1$, and then suddenly observes a flash crowd during period p. $Prd(p + 1)$, which runs during period p, is agnostic to this flash crowd and predicts a size of 1 for period $p + 1$. Hence, $RT\text{-}Abuse\text{-}Dtct(p + 1)$ filters the majority of the traffic from 10.1.1.1. When the $log\text{-}files_{p+1}$ and the $abusive\text{-}log\text{-}files_{p+1}$ are joined, most of the traffic from this IP is not considered for estimation, and $Est(p + 1)$ underestimates its size. Since the $estimates\text{-}table_{p+1}$ are fed back into $Prd(p + 3)$, 10.1.1.1 continues to have a small predicted size, and to be overfiltered in $p + 3$. To mitigate overfiltering caused by this hysteresis loop, estimation only disregards the egregiously abusive traffic.†

The estimation and prediction phases have been assumed so far to run together in less than $l = |p|$, the period length. This introduced a lookahead delay of $2l$. That is,

---

* The length, w, of the estimates window should be long enough to span cycles in the activities of the IPs such that $Prd(.)$ considers legitimate cyclic size changes. Conversely, w should not be excessively large not to include very old sizes unrepresentative of future sizes. In our system, the estimates window was set to span several weekly cycles.

† Egregious traffic has been defined in as the traffic that was filtered by another fraud detection filter already deployed at Google. However, as a guideline if this is the only deployed filter, egregious traffic can be defined as the traffic filtered using a threshold h times higher than the normal threshold for the size of the source IP, where $h > 1$. Selecting h involves a tradeoff. As h increases, filtering abusive traffic is reduced, which could later contribute to overestimating sizes of abusive IPs. Building attacks slowly over time exploits this vulnerability. As h decreases, the filter becomes less vulnerable, but produces more false positives since the estimation cycle becomes less responsive to unforeseen legitimate changes in sizes.

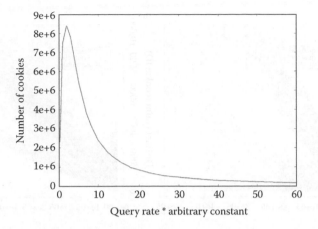

FIGURE 14.3 The query rate distribution PDF.

the output of *RT-Log(p)* is not used by *RT-Abuse-Dtct(.)* before $p + 2$. The longer the lookahead delay, the higher the chance of filtering based on inaccurate sizes.

14.3 IP SIZE ESTIMATION

A user is defined as an entity that generates the average activity of a trusted human for a specific application over a particular time period of length l. Cookie IDs in the log files temporarily identify trusted users. Models of the average activity built from cookie IDs are influenced by the noise of users sharing or frequently clearing cookies. The log entries of one cookie may show the activity of multiple users, or part of the activity of one user. This phenomenon is part of the problem and is not dealt with in the scope of this study.

A regression model is built for the numbers of trusted cookies behind IPs, i.e., the baseline of the measured sizes, as related to the following two types of features, the rate of the activity of the IP and the features diversity of the IP.

The activity rate: For any activity, if the trusted-user activity rate follows a Poisson distribution, then from the distribution properties, the size of an IP can be estimated based on its activity rate. Figure 14.3 shows the Google query rate distribution of $\approx$100M highly trusted cookies.* If the average trusted user has a query rate of λ_m, an IP with M users is expected to have a rate of $M \times \lambda_m$.

Explanatory diversity of The Observed Traffic: The *explanatory diversity* of a feature(s) can be quantified in several ways. One simple way is counting its distinct values in the IP traffic. More sophisticated ways include calculating the perplexity of the feature in the IP traffic. A feature, X (e.g., the query) in the traffic of an IP typically assumes several values, $x_1, x_2,...$ (all the possible query phrases). The perplexity of a feature is calculated as $Perp(X,b) = b^{H_b(p)}$, where b is some base and

---

* Due to the sensitive nature of the exact distribution, the rate is scaled by an arbitrary constant.

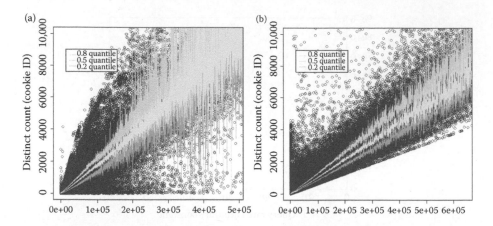

FIGURE 14.4   The scatter plots of query diversity and the number of users. (a) Distinct count (Raw queries) * Arbitrary constant (c1). (b) Perplexity (Raw queries) * Arbitrary constant (c2).

$H_b(p) = \sum_x p(x) \log_b \left(\dfrac{1}{p(x)} \right)$ is the entropy of the distribution of feature X in the IP traffic.*

A training sample of $\approx$10M IPs, was collected to build a regression model of the number of users as related to the query diversity quantified using distinct counting and perplexity. The data used to build the regression model for query sizes is plotted in Figure 14.4. In Figure 14.4, each circle represents one, or multiple overlapping sampled IP(s). Each circle shows the distinct number of trusted cookies querying Google, and the distinct count (Figure 14.4a) and perplexity (Figure 14.4b) of the queries issued by these trusted cookies.[†]

Because models are built from log files aggregated at the IP level, and the overwhelming majority of IPs have very few trusted cookies behind them, sampling noise can cause issues. If a random training sample is selected, the few IPs with large measured sizes, that is, the IPs with numerous trusted cookies, can be easily missed out. To avoid underrepresenting IPs with large measured sizes, stratified sampling is used [21]. IPs are bucketed into disjoint classes by their measured sizes. The number of samples from each class should represent this class in the global sample by the same proportion of that class in the global IPs population.

From Figures 14.4a and b, an observation can be made about the stratified sample of IPs. The relationship between the measured sizes, that is, the number of trusted cookies, and query diversity shows high heteroscedasticity. That is, the variance of the measured sizes increases with the distinct count (Figure 14.4a) and perplexity (Figure 14.4b) of queries.

---

* Perplexity was verified on several data sets to exhibit linear relationship with the numbers of trusted cookie IDs behind IPs (measured sizes). Entropy does not exhibit this quality.

[†] Due to the sensitive nature of the exact distribution, the x-axes of Figure 14.4 are scaled, and the perplexity is calculated with two bases, $b1 \neq b2$, as $Perp(X, b_1, b_2) b_1^{H_{b_2}(p)}$.

14.3.1 THE LEARNING MODELS

For each IP, estimates are calculated based on its traffic rate and diversity. A regression-based model is built using the following four below. An evaluation follows in Section 14.3.2.

Linear regression: Linear regression is one of the most widely used regression techniques and it minimizes the root mean square error.

Quantile regression: Quantile regression is more robust than linear regression toward outliers because it estimates a conditional quantile instead of mean. Median quantile is often used for estimation. Using principal components of the features instead of true features were not found to improve the results, and are hence not used.

PCA + MARS: Multivariate Adaptive regression Splines (MARS) [8] and principal component analysis (PCA) [11] is used to build regression models for IP size estimation. MARS is a nonparametric regression technique that captures nonlinear behavior by building piecewise nonlinear models. The scope of the evaluation is limited to the piecewise linear functions only to avoid overfitting. It automatically does variable selection, however, collinearity can be a problem. To reduce multicollinearity, the principal components are identified using principal component analysis. This was found to significantly improve the final results.

Percentage regression: Percentage regression [26] minimizes the relative error (ratio of absolute error and the true observed values).

14.3.2 GAUGING ESTIMATION ACCURACY

Assessing the accuracy of the estimation process is done using the estimation models on a hold out testing set. These estimates are compared against the baseline measured sizes, the number of trusted cookies behind these IPs. For the purpose of modeling and gauging accuracy, only the traffic from the trusted cookies is used to produce the size estimates, and traffic from the nontrusted cookies is ignored. However, in reality, all the traffic is used to estimate the total number of users and not only the trusted cookies users.

The estimated sizes from the four learning models and the measured sizes are plotted in Figure 14.5 with logarithmic axes, where a circle represents one, or multiple overlapping IP(s). The line passing though (1, 1) with slope 1 represents perfect estimation. For a quantile, q, let the q-quantile-curve be the set of the q-quantile points of the measured sizes across all values of the estimated sizes on the x-axis. The 0.1, 0.5, and 0.9 quantile-curves are plotted.

The median quantile-curve for quantile-regression-based and MARS-based IP estimates is almost overlapping with perfect estimation for estimates above 1. The estimation using percentage regression is less spread out for the lower values of IPs compared with the other learning methods, however, for large IPs, the other methods are better.

The different learning models are compared using the following types of error: root mean square error (RMSE), relative error (i.e., ratio of the absolute difference between the true and the estimated value, and the true value), and *bucket error*.

The bucket error increases as IPs get assigned different size buckets, where buckets are based on a function of the IP size. Minimizing the bucket error is crucial to

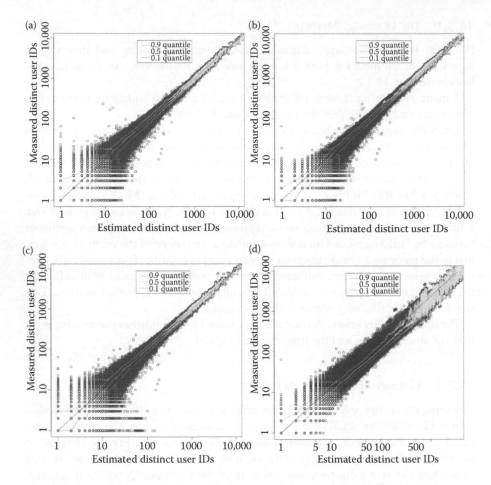

FIGURE 14.5 Comparison of the true *vs.* estimates IP sizes in various regression techniques. (a) Linear regression. (b) Quantile regression. (c) PCA + MARS. (d) Percentile regression.

applications where the rough estimate of the IP size is more important than the exact value of the size, such as the abusive traffic filtering application discussed in Section 14.5. To calculate the bucket error, each IP is bucketed based on its size. The bucket of an IP is given by *bucket*(IP) = Φ(SizeOf(IP)), for some function Φ. The bucket error of an IP is defined as the absolute difference between the true bucket of an IP and the estimated one. The average bucket error for a bucket B is the average absolute bucket deviation of the IPs with the true bucket B, and the average bucket error is the average of the bucket error for all buckets.*

The following table summarizes the error values for estimating the IPs using the four learning models (discussed in Section 14.3.1) on the clicks data set. There is no

---

* If instead of averaging over all the buckets we average over all the IPs, then all the IPs would contribute equally to the error, which disregards the relative importance of larger IPs.

clear winner, but linear regression is a clear loser. The regression technique selected is application-dependent.

	Linear Regression	Quantile Regression	PCA+MARS	Percentage Regression
RMSE	24.95	35.33	22.49	158.46
Relative error	0.261	0.22	0.387	0.169s
Average bucket error	0.256	0.231	0.284	0.841

14.4 IP SIZE PREDICTION

As discussed in Section 14.2.2, the *estimates-tables* produced by the *Est*(.) phase over a window of size w are input to the *Prd*(.) phase. To reduce the lookahead delay, the prediction algorithm was developed with high focus on efficiency.

14.4.1 THE SIZE PREDICTION ALTERNATIVE APPROACHES

Predicting the size of every possible IP based on its previous size estimates is a massive web-scale time series analysis problem. Typically, a time series prediction is carried out by doing a weighted average of the previous w values, where the weights are usually calculated offline using regression analysis. This is effective with time series with high autocorrelation where the current state is a function of previous states and white noise. This is customarily combined with smoothing, such as moving averages, to reduce noise, yielding the commonly known autoregressive moving average (ARMA) models [10]. The ARMA model is used to model time series with both autoregressive and moving average part.

There are several challenges with applying conventional time series procedures for predicting sizes of IPs. First, the time series of sizes are nonstationary. The time series of each IP does not follow the same distribution over time due to, among other factors, the reassignments of the dynamic IPs [27]. Such abrupt and unforeseen changes to sizes cause lack of stationarity, which limits the application of some techniques, like ARMA.

The second and bigger challenge is the estimates of each IP form a time series that should be analyzed to produce a prediction for this IP. Given the high heterogeneity in the behavior of IPs according to numerous factors including their assignments, time zones, and sizes, building a one-size-fits-all predictive model based on a sample of IPs becomes impracticable. Therefore, a specialized and efficient prediction algorithm is required. The *PredictSizes* algorithm employs some concepts from seasonal autoregressive integrated moving average (ARIMA) models [10]. The ARIMA model is further generalization of an ARMA model and is applied to nonstationary data with some seasonality or trend. At a high level, for each IP, *PredictSizes* predicts its size in isolation based on its latest w size estimates. For each IP, the *PredictSizes* algorithm performs three main functions. First, it analyzes the periodicity of the size estimates, since it has been consistently observed that the activity of IPs is periodic (Section 14.4.2). Second, for each periodicity, *PredictSizes* analyzes a sliding window of estimates and seeks their representative stable size by doing iterative variance reduction until the estimates lie within an acceptable confidence interval. Third, it combines the estimates of all periodicities.

14.4.2 CONSIDERING MULTIPLE SIZE PERIODICITIES

Considering the periodicity of IP activity is imperative. Periodicities of the sizes of the IPs were discovered by selecting a sample of IPs, and applying discrete Fourier transform to each. The terms with the highest coefficients correspond to the periodicities used by the *PredictSizes* algorithm [2]. The vast majority of IPs have diurnal and weekly periodicities. These periodicities are especially clear for the IPs of school districts and large institutes.

PredictSizes fetches the estimates of several periodicities, for example, diurnal and weekly, for each IP to produce its prediction. For n periodicities, $s_1 < s_2 < \cdots < s_n$, *PredictSizes* considers the most recent w_i estimates s_i periods apart, for $1 \le i \le n$. For example, to estimate the sizes of IPs in six hours with all the sliding windows having length 10, $s_1 = 1$, $s_2 = 4$, and $s_3 = 28$, *PredictSizes* considers the last 10 six-hour contiguous estimates, as well as the same-slot estimates of the last 10 days and the last 10 weeks.

14.4.3 ITERATIVE VARIANCE REDUCTION

PredictSizes deals with the sizes time series of each periodicity of each IP in isolation. It then combines the predictions from all the periodicities of an IP as discussed in Section 14.4.4.

For time series predictions, it is typical to do simple trend analysis using simple linear regression to show consistent increase or decrease over time (allowing for some white noise) [10]. The trend is then used for extrapolation. However, based on analysis of numerous IPs, time series of size periodicities almost never show strong trends within the window of estimates used for predictions. Moreover, using trend analysis hurts IPs that have drastic size change, since false trends result in erroneous predictions. Hence, *PredictSizes* assumes a stable value for each time series. The stable value, the representative statistic on the time series, is calculated using the *StableSize* function and is produced as the prediction.

For simplicity, *StableSize* deals with each periodicity time series as a set. For each time series, *StableSize* does iterative variance reduction by removing outliers that contribute the most to the variance until the ratio of the width of the confidence interval to the mean falls to a given bound. The truncated mean of the remaining sizes is declared the stable size.

At each iteration, *StableSize* calculates the standard deviation, mean of the time series, and the width of its c-confidence interval. The element that contributes the most to the variance is the farthest from the mean. This element can be identified in constant time by checking the maximum and the minimum elements. This element is deleted in each iteration. Each time an extreme element is deleted, the new mean and variance are updated in constant time. The most costly process is identifying the extreme elements, which can be done efficiently using a minmax heap. The algorithm fails if the time series exhibits little stability, due to abrupt size changes or due to the weakness of this periodicity compared with others. It bails out once the fraction of the discarded elements exceeds some threshold.

14.4.4 THE PREDICTSIZES ALGORITHM

Since *PredictSizes* deals with each periodicity of each IP separately, it can be massively parallelized using the Mapreduce framework [20], as the size estimates are stored in files sharded by the period IDs and IPs. The algorithm combines all the stable sizes of all the periodicities using a *Combiner* function that also does sanity checks on the predicted sizes.

The main factor that influences the choice of the *Combiner* is the loss function of the predictions, which is application-dependent. In its simplest form, a *Combiner* can be a simple statistic, such as the mean, truncated mean, median, max, or min. For instance, when sizes are used for service optimization, the mean statistic minimizes the expected loss under the mean squared error loss function. Another alternative for *Combiner* functions is using a weighted average of the stable sizes, where the weights are inversely proportional to the fraction of size outliers (extreme estimates) discarded by the *StableSize* function for each periodicity. More involved analysis entails doing a regression of the size estimates of a particular period (as the expected predicted size) as related to the stable sizes from individual periodicities (as explanatory sizes(s)). However, such a regression-based *Combiner* can be easily influenced by the heterogeneity of IPs discussed in Section 14.4.1, such as time zones.

The *Combiner* algorithm ensures that the predicted size agrees with the stable sizes of all the periodicities. A simple solution was implemented that does two sanity checks. First, it checks that the predicted size is within some factor of the stable size for each periodicity. Second, it checks that the predicted size is within a specific quantile range of all the stable sizes. If the predicted size does not conform to the *Combiner* sanity check, the IP is deemed unstable, and no predicted size is produced for it. In our experiments, these simple sanity checks proved to be very effective in detecting abrupt legitimate size changes early on, and hence reducing the false positives caused by overfiltering legitimate traffic.

14.4.5 EVALUATING PREDICTIONS

To evaluate the predictions algorithm, an experiment was run on three months worth of query data log files. Two metrics were measured: (i) for every period p, the agreement of the predicted sizes of the IPs with their estimated sizes during p; and (ii) the coverage (the ratio of IPs in the traffic in period p that had predictions).

14.4.5.1 Prediction Accuracy

To assess the prediction accuracy, a random sample of 10M IPs was collected. The relative ratio, *predicted size/estimated size*, is shown in Figure 14.6, where each circle represents one or multiple overlapping IP(s).

A total of 98% of the absolute errors are between -4 and 2 and 54% of the predictions are exact. The mean absolute error is -0.149. All the quantiles with a step of 0.001 were calculated. The topmost four 0.001 quantiles are 5282, 5, 4, and 3, and

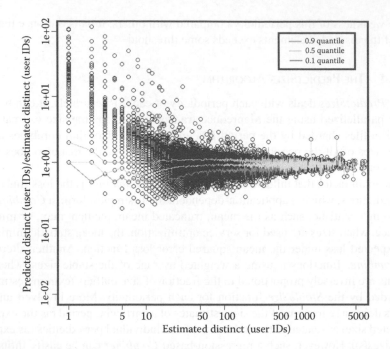

FIGURE 14.6 The relative ratio in predicting query sizes by the estimated sizes.

the bottommost quantiles are −6870, −12, −8, −7. Based on Whois databases, the IPs that caused the largest absolute errors belonged to large commercial ISPs with several netblocks and diverse customer bases. These IPs probably changed sizes due to reassignment.

From Figure 14.6, among all the predicted sizes, 98% were within a factor of 2 of the estimated size. The topmost four 0.001 quantiles of the relative ratios were 5283, 4, 4, and 3, and the bottommost quantiles were 0.2, 0.4, 0.4, and 0.44.

The relative ratio is broken down by the estimated sizes in Figure 14.6. The line that passes through the y-axis point 1 with slope 0 represents perfect predictions. Clearly, the median quantile-curve is almost overlapping with the perfect predictions line for medium and large values of estimated sizes. Moreover, the accuracy of the predictions increases as the estimated size increases, where the accuracy is more operationally desired.

14.4.5.2 Predictions Coverage

For predictions to be effective, they should have high coverage, that is, a high ratio of the IPs in the traffic has predictions. There are several factors that contribute to the predictions coverage, such as the stability of the estimated sizes of the IPs, the diversity of the IPs that visit the application provider, the length of the estimation period, and the length of the sliding windows of estimates used for prediction.

The coverage of the 3-month experiments dropped below 95% on 2 days and never dropped below 93%. The coverage of the click sizes was also examined. The click-coverage averaged around 65% and never dropped below 61%. Since the number of queries is at least one order of magnitude more than the clicks, the query traffic is expected to come from more IPs, which better cover the IP space than the click traffic. Hence, the probability any IP generates traffic on two distinct *IP-period* is higher for queries than clicks, which explains the higher query-coverage.

14.5 DETECTING MACHINE-GENERATED ATTACKS

We now describe the IP size distribution filter proposed in [22]. This filter uses the IP size estimates to detect abusive ad click traffic. It combines several desirable characteristics: it successfully detects fraudulent traffic; it has low complexity and it is easy to parallelize, making it suitable for large-scale fraud detection; it is based on a fundamental characteristic of machine-generated traffic, and is thus robust (e.g., to DHCP reassignment) and hard to evade; and finally, it does not entail profiling users individually, but leverages only aggregate statistics. This traffic filter has been deployed at Google, thanks to its high accuracy.

14.5.1 OBSERVED IP SIZE DISTRIBUTIONS

Different publishers naturally exhibit different empirical IP size distributions. Figure 14.7 shows two examples of IP size distributions that are typically seen on (1) a website that receives mainly desktop traffic and (2) a website that receives mainly mobile traffic. Websites that receive mainly desktop traffic have most of their clicks coming from IPs with small sizes. This is because typically only a handful of users share the same IP address. As such, the IP size distribution is highly skewed toward the left. However, websites receiving mainly mobile traffic have an IP size distribution exhibiting two distinct modes. This is because mobile users typically access the Internet either through WiFi IP addresses, which have relatively small sizes, or through large proxies of mobile carriers, which are shared by numerous users. In general, different publishers have different IP size distributions depending on both the type of their services and the type of traffic driven to their websites.

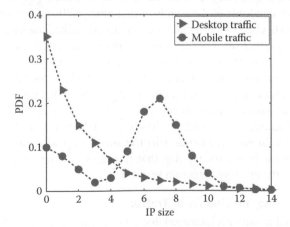

FIGURE 14.7 Two publishers with different IP size distributions.

14.5.2 MACHINE-GENERATED ATTACKS AND IP SIZE DISTRIBUTIONS

Machine-generated attacks can be performed in various ways, depending on the resources available, motivations, and skills of the attackers. For instance, if an attacker controls a large number of hosts through a botnet, the attack can be highly distributed across the available hosts to maximize the overall amount of traffic generated while maintaining a low-activity profile for each individual host. This type of attacks is referred to as *botnet-based* attacks. Conversely, if an attacker controls a few hosts but still wants to generate a large amount of traffic, she can use anonymizing proxies, such as TOR nodes, to hide the actual source IPs involved. This type of attacks is referred to as *proxy-based* attacks. Botnet- and proxy-based attacks are two diverse examples in the wide spectrum of possible attacks using machine-generated traffic, in terms of both the resources required and level of sophistication.

Figure 14.8 illustrates these two attacks and how they affect the IP size distribution associated with a publisher. Let us assume the existence of an *a priori* knowledge of the expected IP size distribution based on historical data. The curve marked as "Reference PDF" represents the expected distribution of IP sizes. Figure 14.8a depicts an example of a botnet-based attack. Bots are typically end-user machines and have a relatively small IP size. Intuitively, this is because end-user machines are easier to compromise than large well-maintained proxies. As a result, a botnet-based attack generates a higher than expected number of clicks with small size. Analogously, a proxy-based attack skews the IP size distribution toward large IP sizes because as higher than expected number of clicks comes from large proxies, as in Figure 14.8b.

The attacks in Figure 14.8 represent two opposite scenarios. However, despite their differences, they both can be revealed as a deviation from the expected IP size distribution. Most attacks induce an unexpected deviation of the IP size distribution. In fact, different deviations represent different signatures of attacks.

14.5.3 THE DATA SET

The data set used in this analysis is the advertisement click logs collected at Google from a sample of hundreds of thousands of different publisher websites. These logs were to gain insights into modern machine-generated traffic attacks, as well as to test and evaluate the performance of this anomaly detection system on real data. In this section, the data set and the specific features used in this study are briefly described.

The IPs were bucketed, and from each bucket, 100k clicks logs were sampled for a period of 90 consecutive days. Total samples vary each day but on average there were 1M IPs. The analysis and development relies on the following fields in each entry: (i) the source IP address that generated the click; (ii) the publisher ID, a unique identifier associated with each publisher; (iii) the timestamp when the click occurred; and (iv) the abusive flag: a binary flag that indicates whether or not the click was tagged by any of the existing detection systems.

14.5.3.1 Assessing the Quality of Traffic

A Google-internal classifier is leveraged that takes as input click logs of network traffic and determines the likelihood that the network traffic is fraudulent machine-generated

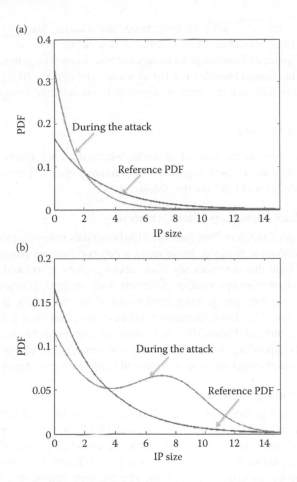

FIGURE 14.8 Types of attacks and their effect on the IP size distribution: The expected IP size distribution is marked as "Reference PDF". (a) A botnet-based attack: clicks are generated by a large number of bots. These are typically end-user machines and thus skew the distribution toward small IP sizes. (b) A proxy-based attack: the IP addresses generating the clicks are rerouted through anonymizing proxies (e.g., TOR nodes). Since many users share these proxies, this attack skews the IP size distribution toward large IP sizes.

traffic. The score obtained through this system is called the *quality score*. This classification system takes as input a variety of features that accounts for different types of user inputs and different types of anomalies. This classifier provides an estimate on the aggregate quality of a large set of clicks. Similar classifiers exist for other kinds of attacks depending on the application. For instance, in the case of email spam, a classifier can be built on several features of the email, such as the relative number of users that labeled this email as spam, or the relative number of invalid recipient addresses.

In addition, a *fraud score* is defined as a function of the ratio between the number of abusive clicks and the total number of clicks, with different weights assigned to the abusive clicks depending on the reason for tagging them as fraudulent.

Finally, two sets of blacklists were used, the Gmail Blacklist [25] and the Spamhaus Exploit Blacklist (XBL) [24], to determine whether or not the IP addresses that generate fraudulent ad events are also known to generate other types of abusive traffic. Gmail blacklist is a list of source IPs that are likely to send email spam. Spamhaus XBL is a real-time database of hosts infected by some exploits.

14.5.4 CLICK FILTERING

This section focuses on the general scenario, where the click traffic received by a publisher is a mixture of both legitimate and abusive clicks. The main goal is to automatically detect and filter out the abusive clicks.

14.5.4.1 IP Size Histogram Filter Overview

As shown in Figure 14.8, machine-generated traffic attacks naturally induce an anomalous IP size distribution. Keeping this in mind, a detection system based on the IP size histogram was built that automatically filters abusive clicks associated with any publisher. The system first groups together publishers with similar legitimate IP size distributions. Second, for each group, a statistical model of the click traffic is built based on historical data. Since the IP size distribution might change over time, a fresh estimation is periodically computed. Finally, live click traffic of each publisher is partitioned into separate buckets depending on the IP size value and sets of clicks of any publishers that violate the computed model while some statistical confidence are filtered out.*

14.5.4.2 Grouping Publishers

Identifying a proper grouping of publishers is the first fundamental step in combating machine-generated traffic. As observed in Section 14.5.1, the type of services provided by the publisher's website and the type of traffic driven to her website affect the IP size distribution of a publisher. Furthermore, this is also influenced by the geolocation of the source IP addresses visiting her website. The rationale behind this is that different countries have different IP size distributions due to various reasons, such as heavy use of proxy, population density vs. number of IP addresses available, and government policies.

For these reasons, publishers are grouped together if they provide the same type of service, receive clicks from the same type of connecting device (e.g., desktops, smartphones, tablets), and from IP addresses assigned to the same country. For instance, if a publisher receives clicks from more than one type of device, its traffic is split depending on the type of devices, and accordingly assigned to different groups. This provides a fine-grained grouping of publishers, which takes into account the various factors that affect the IP size.

14.5.4.3 Threshold Model for Legitimate Click Traffic

After grouping publishers, a statistical threshold model of the click traffic associated with each group is computed. First, the click traffic received by any publisher within the same group, over a time period τ, is aggregated. Next, a minimum quality score,

---

* Publishers that do not receive a statistically significant number of clicks in the period considered are not considered in this analysis, since this is not enough information to provide a statistically sound estimation.

q_{min}, is set that should be satisfied by a set of legitimate clicks. Different websites have different quality scores depending on various factors, such as the services provided and the ads displayed. Thus, q_{min} is computed as a fixed fraction of the average quality score associated with each publisher group.

For each group and each bucket, a percentile threshold, t, is computed. In real time, if any publisher receives more than $t\%$ of her traffic on this bucket, its traffic from this bucket gets filtered. To set t, a fine-grain scan of all the possible percentiles of this bucket is carried out. For each percentile, p, the traffic from all the publishers that received more than $p\%$ of their traffic from that bucket, with some binomial confidence threshold, is aggregated. If the quality score of this aggregated traffic is lower than q_{min}, p is set as a candidate threshold. The final threshold, t, is picked to be the candidate threshold that has the highest impact, that is, discards the most traffic. This technique takes into account the observed empirical distributions, the number of available samples (IP sizes), and the desired confidence level.

Intuitively, the filtered clicks represent regions of high probability for specific publishers, i.e., spikes in their IP size distributions, that also have a significantly lower quality than expected for the same group of publishers and set of ads.

14.5.4.4 Performance Results

In this section, the effectiveness of the IP size histogram filter is assessed. The system is implemented using a Google-built language specifically designed to handle massive data sets using a distributed MapReduce-based infrastructure. Each phase of the above filter is distributed across a few hundred machines using the MapReduce framework [6]. For the results described in this section, τ was set to 90 days to build the threshold model, and a testing period of $\tau_{live} = 30$ days was used.

Figures with the sensitive values of the quality score, the fraud scores, and the number of clicks have been anonymized by scaling the original values by arbitrary constants so as to preserve trends and relative differences while obscuring the absolute numbers.

14.5.4.5 IP Size Distributions

Figure 14.9a–d depicts two groups of publishers, named here A and B for anonymity purpose. Each figure is a four-dimensional plot. The x-axis represents the bucket of the IP size, while the y-axis represents the probability value. Each point is associated with a single publisher and represents the probability that the publisher receives a click of a certain size. In Figure 14.9a and c, the size of data points represents the number of clicks and the color represents the scaled fraud score. Figure 14.9b and d display the same points as in Figure 14.9a and c with the difference that the size represents the number of clicks fed to the quality classifier system, and the color represents the scaled quality score. Circles are plotted with different sizes to represent different levels of statistical confidence.

These figures confirm on real data the motivating intuition discussed in Figure 14.8. Figure 14.9a and b shows the results on one of the largest groups, comprising hundreds of publishers. Despite the complexity of the problem and the variety of possible attacks, Figure 14.9a shows that spikes in the IP size distribution of a publisher are reliable indicators of high fraud score. In fact, most points associated with an anomalous high probability are red, thus indicating that they are known to be abusive clicks. As an additional validation, Figure 14.9b illustrates the corresponding

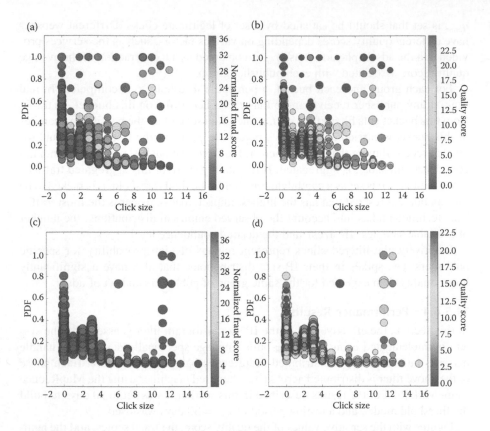

FIGURE 14.9 (a)–(d) The IP size distribution of two groups of publishers, named A and B for anonymity purpose, which include hundreds of different publishers. Each point represents the percentage of clicks, of a given size, received by a publisher. For each group of publishers, two figures are plotted. In (a) and (c), the color indicates the scaled fraud score. The volume is proportional to the number of clicks associated with the data point. In (b) and (d), the color indicates the scaled quality score.

quality score. The spikes corresponding to high fraud score also have very low, or zero, quality score. This confirms that the clicks identified by the anomaly detection system are indeed abusive clicks.

Figure 14.9c and d illustrates a sample group where the IP size distribution filter detects machine-generated traffic that would have been undetected otherwise. For instance, Figure 14.9c shows the case of a publisher that has about 70% of its clicks in bucket 6. This spike in distribution is particularly suspicious since all other publishers in the same group have 15% or less click of this size range. The quality score associated with this point confirms this intuition. In fact, the large number of clicks (large circle in Figure 14.9d) was associated with very low quality score.

14.5.4.6 Analysis of a Single Bucket

In Figure 14.10, the focus is on bucket 0 of Figure 14.9a, as this is the bucket with the largest number of data points. The variation of number of filtered clicks, the fraud

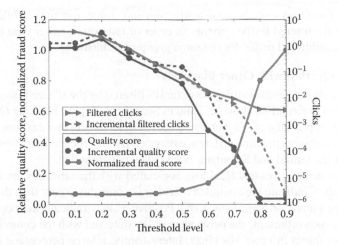

FIGURE 14.10 Single bucket analysis.

score, and the quality score with the percentile threshold set by the histogram filter for this bucket is studied. Moreover, the number of incremental abusive clicks, that is, the number of abusive clicks detected solely by the IP size histogram filter and not by other systems, as well as the incremental quality score, that is, the quality score associated with the incremental abusive clicks, are analyzed. As clear from Figure 14.10, there is a sweet spot around 0.7 that identifies a small fraction of clicks, about 1% of the total number of clicks in this buckets, which have both high fraud score and low quality score.

14.5.4.7 Performance over Time

Figure 14.11 shows the IP size histogram filter performance over a month, where the filter was run daily. The fraud score and quality score of the filtered click traffic were

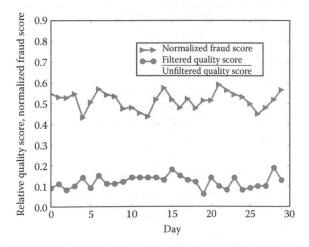

FIGURE 14.11 Fraud score and quality score for different days.

computed. The fraud score is consistently high and stable over time, while the quality score of the filtered traffic remains an order of magnitude lower than the quality score of the unfiltered traffic for the same group of publishers.

14.5.4.8 Overlap with Other Blacklists

Figure 14.12 illustrates the overlap between IPs filtered by the IP size histogram filter and IPs listed in Gmail blacklist [25] and in Spamhaus Exploit blacklist (XBL) [24]. For each day, a blacklist of IPs that sent abusive clicks during that day was compiled. The x-axis represents the time difference between the day the blacklist was compiled and the day the Gmail and Spamhaus blacklists were compiled.

A zero value indicates that blacklists associated with the same day are compared. Negative values indicate the compiled blacklist is some days older than the blacklist compiled by Gmail or Spamhaus XBL. Positive values indicate the opposite scenario. The y-axis represents the percentage of IPs detected with the compiled system that are also found in other blacklists. Interestingly, a large percentage of abusive clicks are generated by IPs that also generate other kinds of abusive traffic, such as spam emails. In particular, up to 45% of abusive clicks are generated by source IPs listed either in Gmail blacklist or in Spamhaus XBL.

14.5.5 FLAGGING ENTITIES

The IP size histogram filter described in Section 14.5.4 can distinguish between a set of legitimate and a set of abusive clicks by automatically detecting anomalous spikes in a distribution associated with low quality click traffic. To avoid detection, a fraudster may spread its clicks across various buckets to avoid generating high probability regions in few buckets. This warrants a method that examines the entire distribution.

In this section, the IP size distributions associated with entities are considered. An entity can be a user-agent, an e-mail domain, a publisher, a city, a country, and so

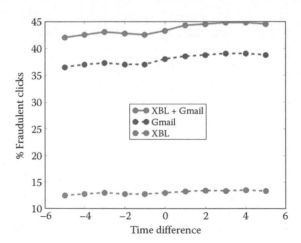

FIGURE 14.12   Percentage of abusive clicks generated by IPs listed on the Gmail blacklist or on XBL.

on. In general, an entity is any dimension that aggregates ad events. For each type of entity, a detection system based on the IP size distribution can be built. This is useful to build several complementary defense mechanisms that protect against different types of attacks.

14.5.5.1 Flagging Entities—System Overview

Figure 14.13 illustrates the workflow of the system implemented at Google. The first step is the estimation of the expected IP size distribution of each entity. Each group might have a different IP size distribution. However, entities within the same group are expected to share a similar distribution. Since the majority of abusive clicks are already filtered out by existing detection systems, the aggregate distribution of legitimate IP sizes within each group is used as an estimation of the true IP size distribution for that group. Next, multiple statistical methods are used to accurately characterize the deviation between the observed and the expected distribution. As noted in Figure 14.8, different attacks result in different deviations in the IP size distribution. Finally, an ensemble-learning model [23] is used to combine the outcome of these methods in a signature vector specific to each entity. A regression model is built that identifies and classifies signatures associated with fraudulent entities.

14.5.5.2 Combining Statistical Methods

To characterize the deviation between the observed and the expected distribution of each entity, an ensemble of different statistical methods is used. These can be

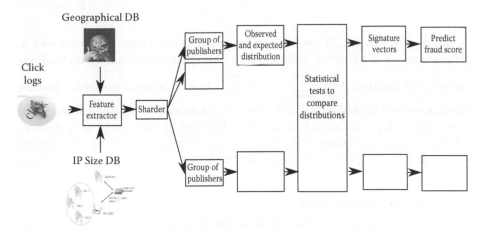

FIGURE 14.13 Flagging entities—system overview: the click logs and the information provided by Google IP size and Geographical databases are fed as input. The feature extractor module extracts only the features of interest, as discussed in Section 14.5.3. Next, the sharder partitions the data into groups based on the type of entity, the type of connecting device, and the geolocation of the source IP. For each of these groups, an expected distribution, r, is built from the historical data of legitimate clicks. For each entity, the observed distribution of IP sizes, $f = f(P)$ is computed. The observed and expected distribution are compared using several statistical methods. Finally, these results are combined in a signature vector specific to each entity. The vector is used to predict the entity's fraud score.

classified into the four categories: (i) vector-based methods: include the L_p distance, the cosine similarity; (ii) skewness-based methods: include computing skewness (sample and Bowley); (iii) entropy-based methods: include the Jensen-Shannon and the Kullback-Leibler divergence [15]; and (iv) goodness-of-fit tests include the Kolmogorov-Smirnov and the chi-square test statistic.

Different methods for comparing probability distributions provide different information as they measure different properties. For instance, if the skewness of a distribution is measured, all symmetric distributions will be considered similar to each other as they have null skewness. However, if other properties are measured, such as, the L_2 distance, two symmetric distributions will, in general, be different. Using an ensemble of statistical methods provides a more accurate characterization of the observed deviation than using a single method. This is crucial for analyzing massive data sets, comprising a wide range of different patterns.

To precisely measure the observed deviation and identify fraudulent entities, the outcomes of the different statistical methods listed above are combined in a signature vector, σ_k, specific to each publisher. Intuitively, significant deviations from the expected distribution, measured by several statistical methods, represent strong indicators of abusive click traffic. For this reason, the fraud score is modeled as a linear function of the observed deviations,

$$\phi_k = \sum_{j=1}^{p} \theta_j \sigma_{kj}, \tag{14.5}$$

where σ_{kj} indicates the jth component of σ_k and θ_j is the weight associated with it. The optimal set of weights, θ, in Equation 14.5 are determined to minimize the least-square cost function, $J(\theta) = \sum_{k \in \mathcal{K}} \left(\bar{\phi}_k - \sum_{j=1}^{p} \theta_j \sigma_{kj} \right)^2$ using a stochastic gradient descent method trained on a small subset of publishers, $\mathcal{K}$, which includes legitimate distributions and known attacks provided both by other automated systems, and by manual investigation of the logs. The model in Equation 14.5 is then applied to a large data set of entities to predict the fraud score as a function of their IP size distribution.

14.5.5.3 Performance Results

Figure 14.14 shows the accuracy of the model in Equation 14.5 in predicting the fraud score as a function of the number of statistical methods used to compare distributions. First, the accuracy of the anomaly detection system is assessed when all methods are used. Next, the features that cause the least amount of variation in the prediction accuracy are iteratively removed until a single feature is left [13]. The training set is 10% of the entities, and testing set comprises the remaining entities. Figure 14.14 shows that using multiple comparison methods that measure different type of deviations allows for reducing the prediction errors, down to a 3% error. This

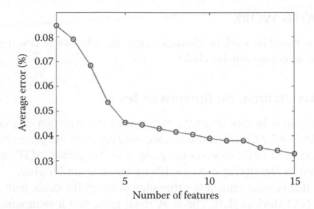

FIGURE 14.14 Prediction accuracy: number of comparison methods vs. average error in predicting the fraud score.

is about three times lower than when using a single method. Moreover, the additional methods improve the accuracy of the model but with decreasing gain.

To validate the goodness of fit of the model in Equation 14.5, the adjusted coefficient of determination, $\bar{R}^2 = 1 - \dfrac{n-1}{n-p} \dfrac{SS_{err}}{SS_{tot}}$, where $SS_{err} = \sum_k (\tilde{\phi}_k - \phi)^2$ is the sum of squares of residuals, is also computed. Figure 14.15 shows that as more statistical tests are used, the adjusted coefficient of determination increases. This demonstrates that additional features increase the explained variance of the model. When all features are used, the model in Equation 14.5 captures over 40% of the total variation in the data. This result is particularly significant in a large data set that includes a wide range of patterns of click traffic.

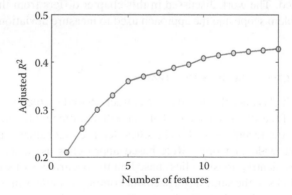

FIGURE 14.15 Prediction accuracy: number of comparison methods vs. R^2. As the number of features increases, the adjusted coefficient of determination, R^2, increases as well, and so does the explained variance.

14.6   RELATED WORK

This chapter is based on work on characterizing the behavior of IPs, traffic anomaly detection, and detecting abusive clicks.

14.6.1   CHARACTERIZING THE BEHAVIOR OF IPS

The work discussed in this chapter complements the work on characterizing the behavior of IPs [1,4,7,27,28]. The use of traceroute data and the geographic mappings of IPs were explored in [7] to study the geographic properties of IP prefixes, while [27,28] focused on identifying dynamic IPs for email spam filtering.

The work that is most related to estimating sizes of IPs deals with counting the hosts behind NAT devices [1,4]. The work in [1] presented a technique for counting the hosts behind a NAT using the `IPid` field. The technique relies on the host operating system sequentially incrementing the `IPid` field for each successive packet. However, in the modern operating systems, `IPid` is not incremented sequentially. The focus of [4] was identifying middle-boxes and classifying them as NAT devices and proxies by learning the internal IPs of the hosts using active web content. However, this technique underestimates the sizes by the ratio of users not collaborating with the research effort. It also fails if a NAT box has a hierarchy of NAT devices behind it, where collisions, and hence underestimation can happen.

14.6.2   TRAFFIC ANOMALY DETECTION

In the wide area of anomaly detection, [5] represents a recent survey on various categories of anomaly detection systems. The latter part of the work in this chapter falls in the category of statistical anomaly detection, where an anomaly can be defined as an observation that is extremely unlikely to have been generated by the probabilistic model assumed. In [12], a histogram filter similar in spirit to the IP size histogram filter is presented. The work discussed in this chapter differs from these two works in both the problem scope and the approach used to measure deviations and compare distributions.

14.6.3   DETECTING ABUSIVE CLICK TRAFFIC

The work in [17] classifies the abusive click attacks based on the resources available at the disposal of the attacker and based on her collaboration with other attackers. On the other hand, the recent work [14] classifies defense mechanisms against abusive clicks into three wide categories. Rule based approaches use a set of rules, often manually set, to identify abusive click, based on the occurrence of specific patterns. For instance, clicks to the same advertisement coming from the same IP at about the same time. Anomaly-based approaches try to identify clicks that deviated from an expected distribution. Finally, classifier-based approaches rely on machine learning methods to label clicks based on the observed features value. The work on which this chapter falls in the intersection of the last two categories. It uses anomaly-based detection to identify deviation from the norm.

A different line of research has proposed a data analysis approach to discriminate legitimate from abusive clicks. Ref. [16] focuses on the problem of finding colluding publishers. The proposed system analyzes the IP addresses generating the click traffic for each publisher to identify groups of publishers receiving clicks from roughly the same IPs. Ref. [18] addresses the scenario of a single publisher generating fraudulent traffic from several IPs. The authors propose a system to automatically detect highly correlated pairs of publisher and IP address.

14.7 CONCLUSION

This chapter describes (a) a data-driven approach that accurately estimates the sizes of IP addresses [19]; (b) the details of novel findings on employing different size estimation models, and their error analysis; and (c) the machine-generated traffic filter that uses the IP size information effectively [22]. The filter operates at the click granularity to combat attacks that use homogeneous infrastructures, and at the publisher granularity to combat sophisticated attacks that spread malicious traffic across a wide range of IP sizes.

The techniques discussed here (i) do not require any identification or authentication of the users generating the clicks; (ii) are fully automated, have low complexity (it scales linearly in the amount of data to be processed), are easy to parallelize, and are suitable for large-scale detection; (iii) are general and can be applied to a wide spectrum of fraud detection problems (e.g., distribution of UA size sending emails, or the time series distribution of plus ones on the Google social network); (iv) are robust to DHCP reassignment (clicks generated from a specific host have the same size regardless the specific IP address assigned, which is particularly useful in practice, since a large fraction of IPs are dynamically reassigned every 1 to 3 days [27]), and are hard to evade. In fact, even if the attacker knows the legitimate distribution of IP sizes for all publishers in their group, and the exact mechanisms used to estimate the IP size, they would still need to generate clicks according to the legitimate IP size distribution, which is not controlled or even accessible to them.

The main limitation is that the filter requires a statistically significant number of clicks per publisher. If this is not the case, approaches that identify colluding publishers, e.g., [16], would catch these attacks. The techniques discussed in this chapter are currently used as part of a larger detection system deployed at Google in conjunction with complementary techniques.

REFERENCES

1. S. Bellovin. A Technique for Counting NATted hosts. In *SIGCOMM IMW*, pp. 267–272, 2002.
2. P. Bloomfield. *Fourier Analysis of Time Series: An Introduction*. Wiley-IEEE, 2004.
3. I. A. Bureau. Internet Ad Revenues Hit $31 Billion in 2011, Historic High Up 22% Over 2010 Record-Breaking Numbers. http://www.iab.net/about the iab/recent press releases/press release archive/press release/pr-041812, April 18, 2012.
4. M. Casado and M. Freedman. Peering Through the shroud: The effect of edge opacity on IP-based client identification. In *NSDI*, pp. 173–186, 2007.

5. V. Chandola, A. Banerjee, and V. Kumar. Anomaly detection: A survey. *CSUR*, 41(3):1–58, 2009.

6. J. Dean and S. Ghemawat. MapReduce: Simplified data processing on large clusters. *CACM*, 51(1):107–113, 2008.

7. M. Freedman, M. Vutukuru, N. Feamster, and H. Balakrishnan. Geographic locality of IP prefixes. In *SIGCOMM IMC*, pp. 13–13, 2005.

8. J. Friedman. Multivariate adaptive regression splines. *Annals of Statistics*, 19(1), 1991.

9. B. Grow, B. Elgin, and M. Herbst. Click fraud—The dark side of online advertising. *Business Week Online*, 10(02), 2006.

10. J. Hamilton. *Time series analysis*. Princeton University Press, illustrated edition, 1994.

11. I. T. Jolliffe. *Principal component analysis*, volume 487. Springer-Verlag, New York, 1986.

12. A. Kind, M. Stoecklin, and X. Dimitropoulos. Histogram-based traffic anomaly detection. *IEEE Transactions on Network and Service Management*, 6(2):110–121, 2010.

13. K. Kira and L. Rendell. The feature selection problem: Traditional methods and a new algorithm. In *AAAI*, pages 129–129. John Wiley & Sons Ltd., 1992.

14. N. Kshetri. The economics of click fraud. *IEEE Security and Privacy*, 8(3):45–53, 2010.

15. J. Lin. Divergence measures based on the shannon entropy. *IEEE Transactions on Information Theory*, 37(1):145–151, 1991.

16. A. Metwally, D. Agrawal, and A. El Abbadi. DETECTIVES: DETEcting Coalition hiT Inflation attacks in adVertising nEtworks Streams. In *WWW*, pp. 241–250, 2007.

17. A. Metwally, D. Agrawal, A. El Abbadi, and Q. Zheng. On hit inflation techniques and detection in streams of web advertising networks. In *ICDCS*, 2007.

18. A. Metwally, F. Emekçi, D. Agrawal, and A. El Abbadi. SLEUTH: Single-pubLisher attack dEtection Using correlaTion Hunting. *Proceedings of the VLDB Endowment*, 1(2):1217–1228, 2008.

19. A. Metwally and M. Paduano. Estimating the number of users behind ip addresses for combating abusive traffic. In *SIGKDD*, pp. 249–257. ACM, 2011.

20. R. Pike, S. Dorward, R. Griesemer, and S. Quinlan. Interpreting the data: Parallel analysis with Sawzall. *Scientific Programming*, 13(4):277–298, 2005.

21. G. Snedecor and W. Cochran. *Statistical Methods*. John Wiley & Sons, 8th edition, 1991.

22. F. Soldo and A. Metwally. Traffic anomaly detection based on the ip size distribution. In *INFOCOM*, pp. 2005–2013. IEEE, 2012.

23. P. Sollich and A. Krogh. Learning with ensembles: How over-fitting can be useful. *Advances in neural information processing systems*, pp. 190–196, 1996.

24. Spamhaus XBL. http://www.spamhaus.org/xbl/.

25. B. Taylor. Sender reputation in a large webmail service. In *CEAS*, 2006.

26. C. Tofallis. Least squares percentage regression. *Journal of Modern Applied Statistical Methods*, 2009.

27. Y. Xie, F. Yu, K. Achan, E. Gillum, M. Goldszmidt, and T. Wobber. How dynamic are IP addresses? In *SIGCOMM*, pp. 301–312, 2007.

28. L. Zhuang, J. Dunagan, D. Simon, H. Wang, and J. Tygar. Characterizing botnets from email spam records. In *LEET*, pp. 1–9, 2008.

15 Recommending Environmental Big Data Using Semantically Guided Machine Learning

*Ritaban Dutta, Ahsan Morshed,
and Jagannath Aryal*

CONTENTS

15.1 INTRODUCTION

15.1.1 Environmental Big Data and Knowledge

In information technology, Big Data is a collection of data sets so large and complex that it becomes difficult to process using on-hand database management tools or traditional data-processing applications [74]. The trend to larger data sets is due to the additional information derivable from analysis of a single large set of related data, as compared with separate smaller sets with the same total amount of data [26,51,68]. Scientists regularly encounter limitations due to large data sets in many areas, including meteorology, genetics, complex physics simulations, and environmental research [9,35]. Wireless technology-based automated data gathering from the large environmental sensor networks have increased the quantity of sensor data available for analysis and sensor informatics. Next-generation environmental monitoring, natural resource management, and agricultural decision support systems are becoming heavily dependent on very large scale multiple sensor network deployments, massive-scale accumulation, harmonization, web-based Big Data integration and interpretation of Big Data. With large amount of the data availability, the complexity of data has also increased hence regular maintenance of large-scale sensor are becoming a difficult challenge. Uncertainty factors in the environmental monitoring processes are more evident than before due to current technological transparency achieved by most recent advanced communication technologies [47–49]. The other challenges include capture, storage, search, sharing, analysis, and visualization. Data availability from a particular environmental sensor web is often very limited and data quality is subsequently very poor. This practical limitation could be due to difficult geographical location of the sensor node or sensor station, extreme environmental conditions, communication network failure, and lastly technical failure of the sensor node. Data uncertainty from a sensor network makes the network unreliable and inefficient. This inefficiency leads to failure of natural resource management systems such as agricultural water resource management, weather forecast, crop management including irrigation scheduling and natural resource-based crop business model systems. The ultimate challenge in environmental forecasting and decision support systems, is to overcome the data uncertainty and make the derived output more accurate. It is evident that there is a need to capture and integrate environmental knowledge from various independent sources including sensor networks, individual sensory system, large-scale environmental simulation models, and historical environmental data [13,33,36,41,56,58] for each of the independent sources). It is not good enough to produce efficient decision support system using a single data source. So there is an urgent requirement for on demand complementary knowledge integration where different sources of environmental sensor data could be used to complement each other automatically [1,17,37,38].

15.1.2 BIG DATA SOURCES

This study considered five different environmental data sources for large-scale unified complementary knowledge integration. They are as following:

- Long Paddock SILO database operated by the Queensland Climate Change Centre of Excellence (QCCCE) within the Department of Science, Information Technology, Innovation and the Arts (DSITIA) based on all 4760 Australian Bureau of Meteorology (BOM) weather station data [67].
- Australian Water Availability Project (AWAP) database, which is developed to monitor the state and trend of the terrestrial water balance of the Australian continent, using model–data fusion methods to combine both measurements and modeling [64].
- The Australian Cosmic Ray Sensor Network (CosmOz) database, which is a near-real time soil moisture measurement network, developed through collaboration between CSIRO, Monash University, Charles Darwin University, and the University of New South Wales [65].
- The Australian Soil Resource Information System (ASRIS) database, which provides online access to the best publicly available information on soil and land resources in a consistent format across Australia [63].
- MODIS (or MODerate Resolution Imaging Spectroradiometer) database, which includes data from Terra MODIS and Aqua MODIS satellites— viewing the entire Earth's surface every 1 to 2 days, acquiring data in 36 spectral bands, or groups [66].

Table 15.1 shows the approximate dimensions of the five big environmental data sets considered for this study

TABLE 15.1
Cosmos Data Format

Data Source	Historic Time Period	Data Size
SILO-BOM	12/2010–06/2012	15 GB
AWAP	12/2010–06/2012	45 GB
COSMOZ	12/2010–06/2012	5 GB
ASRIS (static)	12/2010–06/2012	29 GB
NASA-MODIS	12/2010–06/2012	155 GB

15.1.3 Linked Open Data Approach

Next-generation recommendation systems on the web would be based around the Linked Open Data (LOD). This chapter deals with five big environmental data sources to comprehend and discover knowledge in an integrated fashion, interprets knowledge, and finally proposes a semantically guided machine learning–based architecture to recommend knowledge from that discovery. To make the knowledge widely accessible it is important to publish the interpreted recommendation on the LOD. Publishing recommendations about the Big Data integrated on the LOD will make analytical knowledge about the data machine readable and autonomously available to the machines. Prior analytical recommendations about the Big Data would provide an automatic framework that could be used to prioritize, optimize, and minimize Big Data accessibility issues. It would be interesting to capture some of the basic understanding about the LOD concept before moving toward the detailed sections about the Big Data recommendation system. Primarily web pages are built in hypertext markup languages (HTML) that make the web as a web of document. All the webs of documents are possible to navigate through the hyperlinks. In recent years, the World Wide Web is moving from the web of document to the web of data [3,4,6]. In this situation, metadata is moving from merely machine-readable toward automatic processing power, where it is essential to break the record and repositories silos to make data (especially metadata) into machine understandable pieces. These pieces could be presented using Resource Description Framework (RDF), which provides a data model for presenting metadata in a form that can be understood and process into triple statements (i.e., subject, object, predicate) automatically, by a machine [30–32,40]. LOD relies on documents containing data in the RDF format. However, rather than simply connecting these documents, linked data uses RDF to make typed statement that links arbitrary things in the world, which may be referred to as web of things. Tim Berners-Lee designed a set of rules for publishing data on the web in a way that all published data become part of a big machine readable umbrella. The rules were

- Use Universal Resource identifier (URI) as names of things
- Use HTTP URIs so that people can look up those names
- When someone looks up an URI, provides useful information, using the standards (RDF, SPARQL)
- Include links to the other URIs, so that they can discover more things

They have become known as the LOD principles and provide the basic idea for publishing and connecting data on the web. Although the idea of LOD has yet to be accepted as mainstream (like the web WWW is known to all), there are a lots of LODs already available. The so called LOD cloud covers more than an estimated 50 billion facts from many different domain like geography, media, biology, chemistry, economy, energy, etc. [3,4,6,31,32]. The data from the cloud can also be reused for building the end users applications or for the research purposes [11]. The basic idea of a semantic web is to provide cost-effective ways to publish information in a distributed environment (Figure 15.1). The LOD fulfills these ideas where organizations

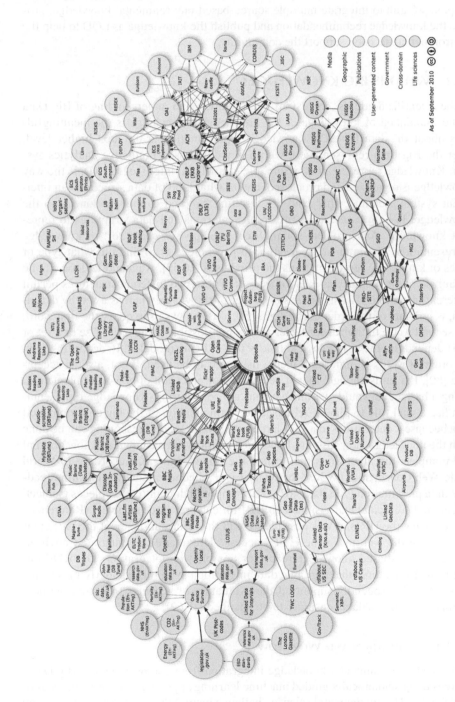

FIGURE 15.1 Representation of linked open data cloud. (From Linking Open Data cloud diagram. http://lod-cloud.net/.)

upload their data on the web for open use of their information [4,11,30,31,40]. In this chapter, we aim to integrate multiple source-based environmental knowledge, provide the knowledge recommendation and publish the knowledge as LOD to help the environmental decision support the community.

15.2   WHAT IS BIG KNOWLEDGE?

In the scientific domains, contextual interpretation and understanding of Big Data is the foundation of knowledge or big knowledge. Knowledge is the meaningfulness about the data [19]. Big knowledge representation is the next higher level, after the Big Data representation, within any data-based predictive analytics system. Knowledge representation, a subtopic of artificial intelligence (AI), is the way knowledge is organized and processed, and to what kind of data structures an intelligent system uses and what kind of reasoning can and cannot be done with the knowledge. In both cases, it requires representations and data structures to represent knowledge. Any problem-solving task presupposes some sort of knowledge representation. The interesting question in psychology is to find out what type or types of knowledge representations the mind uses [16,59]. A mental lexicon can be organized in the memory as a list or as a set. These two different structures permit different operations. A list encodes the order of the words whereas a set, by definition, is ignorant of the order of the items. So, a list allows us to query the first word, the second word, the third word, etc. This is not possible using a set. Use of a set or a list depends on the psychological theory that is being modeled. If, according to it, the order of words is important, then a list needs to be used, if not, a set is acceptable [60]. If a set is enough, then it needs further precision of how to implement it. Using a hash table would guarantee a constant search time. Knowledge representation has a vital role to play in AI-based recommendation of the big environmental data because it determines to a very large extent what kind of reasoning can be done with the knowledge, how fast it is, how much memory is consumed and how optimal and complete the algorithms that utilize the knowledge are. According to World Wide Web Consortium (W3C), the RDF was a standard model for machine readable data presentation [7,18,45,55,62]. It decomposed data into three pieces (subject, object, and predicate) and assigned an URI for each resource or object (Reference). By accessing the URIs, it was possible to read the information about the particular resource on the web using the HTTP access. This made the integrated environmental feature-based knowledge ready for flexible web integration. The RDF format provided features that facilitate data integration even if the underlying schema differed, and it specially supported the evaluation of schemas over time without requiring the entire data consumer to be changed [18,62].

15.2.1   Motivation and Workflow

Large-scale environmental knowledge integration from complementary "Big Data" sources using semantically guided machine learning approach was the main focus of this chapter. The fundamental science challenge behind this work was to design and implement dynamic data-processing architecture to process multiple environmental data sources, capture features, unify, and integrate knowledge in a meaningful way that could be used for any future application. The idea was to process the raw data, capture feature extraction-based knowledge, and also maintain the provenance information along with the extracted knowledge. Capturing available provenance information as a part of the knowledge integration was important so that knowledge from the data sources could be traced back to the origin. Figure 15.2 shows the dynamic workflow of the proposed system. The idea was to capture the knowledge from multiple environmental Big Data sources so that the large-scale cross-validation and the complementary knowledge integration could be conducted. This flow diagram explains the concept and motivation behind this chapter to recommend about the available Big Data in an autonomous way. This study considered five different large environmental data sources for large-scale unified complementary knowledge integration. The knowledge integration architecture was designed, which consisted of two different processing parts, namely "data accumulation through web integration" and "integrated knowledge recommendation-based on machine learning." For any given geographical location and a given time frame, five different data sources were acquired automatically using intelligent web data adaptors, which were developed for this purpose. All data sets were then preprocessed, integrated, and represented in a unified resource structured manner. Unified knowledge RDFs were created for all the environmental data sources based on preprocessed data, available metadata, and original provenance information. The provenance information (such as origin of data, author, and time along with all the raw data) were also captured within the integrated RDF knowledge file and stored into the triple store knowledgebase. The next part of the chapter covers a data and knowledge recommendation system based on novel mixture of unsupervised machine learning clustering algorithms, Clustering algorithms-based on principal component analysis (PCA) [43] and guided self-organizing map (g-SOM) [44] were used to process data dynamically without

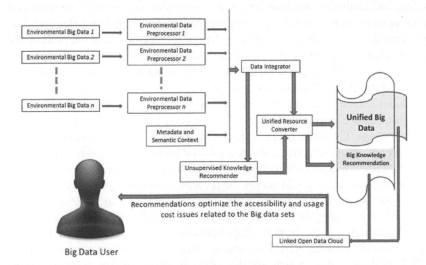

FIGURE 15.2 Motivation and work flow of this chapter.

any processing delay. The objective of this analysis was to establish a list of least correlated semantic attributes, which contribute toward most data variance. g-SOM was applied on the selected least correlated attributes from PCA to estimate natural grouping of the data. This dynamic data analysis provided ranked semantic attributes (according to their importance), which was effectively a valuable recommendation about the whole integrated data set for any future application design. g-SOM clustering on the integrated preprocessed data was quite useful as this technique provided a 2D visual map representation of the whole database and natural grouping of the data attributes. Using this knowledge map (or a region of the map) the user could design an application or make the decision about which variables to consider, so the purpose of the SOM on the database was to provide a visual knowledge recommendations system. Based on the knowledge recommendation the user could also optimize the Big Data usage by prioritizing and minimizing unwanted data download and reducing data-processing time. The recommendations from the machine learning clustering algorithms were also published into the RDF format to represent the extracted knowledge in a completely machine readable manner and to be able to interpret programmatically [42,52]. Development of this unique system based on semantic data integration and machine learning–based data recommendation was the main achievement of this study. This semantically guided machine learning–based approach provided a great deal of flexibility in terms of data, knowledge, and provenance integration. Big knowledge integration and recommendation architecture, based on complementary knowledge integration could provide a generic knowledge platform for any future environmental decision support application system [22,42].

15.3   DATA TO KNOWLEDGE ARCHITECTURE

Design of knowledge integration architecture was motivated by the fact that none of the existing data model integration architectures were capable of handling, processing, and analyzing multiple large environmental data sources simultaneously. Database on its own does not carry any weight unless data is converted into knowledge. True data integration is completely dependent on contextual integration of data sources, where the physical attribute-based parametric integration is complemented with the semantically matched metadata, information about the purpose of the data, data usability information, and knowledge recommendation based on unsupervised data analysis. Designing the architecture focus was mainly on the development of the architectural capability to get the final outcomes integrated and published with the LOD cloud. The main purpose of this architecture was to integrate knowledge from different sources, analyze, and recommend knowledge in a way that could have the highest possible accessibility on the web, so that the next-generation environmental application designer could access the recommendation, knowledge, and also the original data sources programmatically. The design of this architecture had seven different layers, namely Web Adaptors Layer, Data Harmonization Layer, Semantic Cross Validation Layer, Feature Representation Layer, SOM-Based Knowledge Recommendation Layer, RDF Conversion Triple Store implementation Layer, and LOD Publishing Layer, which are described in details in the following sections (Figure 15.3).

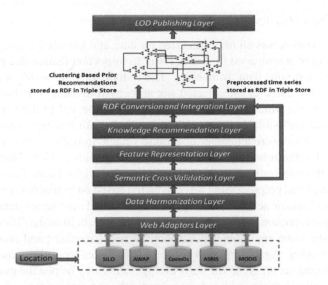

FIGURE 15.3   The architecture for Big Data to big knowledge representation.

15.3.1   WEB ADAPTORS LAYER

Dedicated data adaptors were developed to form this layer. The environmental Big Data sources used for this study were accessible through ftp web data portals, so automatically downloading the data, checking the data redundancy, and saving all the data sources dynamically was the main purpose of this layer. Individual web data adaptors were implemented as raw data sources which were available in various file formats (i.e., .txt, .csv, .nc, .shp, and .hdf), so it was essential to have dedicated data processors for the individual file formats. The other aspect of accessing the different web-based data was the data security, so web adaptors were designed in a way that it could automatically use the data agreement protocols already in place and where applicable. Publicly available data were accessed as open data sources. For any given latitude and longitude combination point and time period, the nearest BOM weather station was selected based on minimum geographical distance from that point and corresponding SILO data files were downloaded and processed. CosmOz data was also downloaded from the nearest available CosmOz cosmic ray data station. SILO and CosmOz data were available as time series data sources. The AWAP database was connected through a secured ftp server and gridded files were downloaded locally. The ASRIS database was downloaded from publicly available ASRIS website. For the given location, a pixel position was derived on the daily continental AWAP gridded map, the historical time series were extracted for all the available variables by combining individual daily pixel-based data points for the desired time period. Similarly, a pixel position was also calculated from the ASRIS gridded map to extract soil resource information for the same latitude and longitude. The NASA MODIS satellite images were downloaded and processed to extract the environmental time series data, using image processing framework.

15.3.2 DATA HARMONIZATION LAYER

Data harmonization was an important step for data and knowledge integration. The preprocessing of downloaded time series was an important feature due to the uncertainty associated with data availability. The individual time series was identified according to the name of the selected site and environmental variable. Data were available from the time of deployment. As can be expected in the real-world networks, each of the available time series had periods with missing values. For some sensor nodes, there were a number of Infinite values. Initially a filter was designed to remove all of the Infinite values, and replace them with a "Not a Number" string to keep the filtering statistically insignificant and the original time frame unaltered. Data validation and preprocessing was conducted based on available knowledge from the sensor and sensor network Ontologies. Preprocessed time series data were batch processed and represented as the daily averaged data. Data from the different sources measuring the same environmental attribute were harmonized and cross-validated against each other. Again, different measured attributes from the same node were also harmonized according to the daily average. This step helped the evaluation and data visualization processes by reducing the number of data points and also solving the issues related to different data logging frequencies. It also helped to compress the data to certain extent without losing any daily observation characteristics. The final outcome of this layer was to produce multisource-based environmental time series data harmonized, unit converted if required, and semantically integrated in a single structure on a daily scale.

15.3.3 SEMANTIC CROSS-VALIDATION LAYER

Semantics representations are usually intended as a medium for conveying the meaning about some world or environment. A knowledge representation must therefore have a semantic theory that provides an account in which a particular representation corresponds to the external world or environment. Preprocessed data were cross-validated using semantic metadata matching and statistical cross-correlation calculation. Metadata is "data about the data" and it can be provided the description of what, where, who, and how about the data [5,53,61]. For example, a sensor node metadata could describe when and where the sensor node was deployed, who deployed that node, which environmental attributes are being measured, what are the key semantic features or characteristics of that particular sensory system, and finally the valid range of measurement that could be expected. However, metadata are generally used to describe the principal aspect of data with the aim of sharing, reusing, and understanding heterogeneous data sets. In fact, different types of sensor or sensor-simulation model metadata may be considered, namely, static and dynamic sensor metadata and associated sensing information. Based on natural language processing and sensor-model ontologies, a cross-validation layer was created. Ideally, all similar environmental variables from different data sources should be able to cross-validate each other statistically, as representative similar variables for the same location for the same time frame should be statistically very similar. Variables were semantically matched according to their units, attributes they measure, context of the semantically extracted features attributes, and scientific meaningfulness, to form several variable subgroups, that is, SILO rainfall (mm/day), SILO rainfall rate (mm/hr.), AWAP rainfall (mm/day), CosmOz rainfall (mm/day), MODIS post real-time TRMM Multi-Satellite Precipitation Analysis (TMPA) product (mm/day). Combination of this kind formed a pool of similar variables, which should be able to cross-validated or complemented each other in case of missing values from a particular time series within that pool. The complementary method identified the missing value segments of a time series and replaced those segments with an average segment based on available other time series in the same pool. This was done to model missing data segment as a semantic attribute. Sensor model Ontologies were used in this processing to use the correct meaning of a time series to avoid any wrong complement. Next a "cross-correlation technique" was used to measure the similarities between two complemented time series signals representing similar scenarios (in terms of location and time period). The other purpose of this layer was to cross-validate similar time series data in the same pool to find a representative time series from that particular pool [10,28,29]. If the two signals being compared were completely identical then the cross-correlation coefficient should be equal to 1 and if there are significant similarities between the signals it should be close to 0. A scoring protocol was designed on cross-correlation results. The time series with highest score were selected from each subgroup as best representative of the associated environmental variable for that time period. The selected time series from all attribute pools were stored in an integrated structured array where columns represented different variables whereas rows represented time frames.

$$
\tilde{R} = \begin{pmatrix} x_{11}(t) & x_{12}(t) & \cdots & x_{1m}(t) \\ x_{21}(t) & x_{22} & \cdots & x_{2m}(t) \\ \vdots & \ddots & x_{ij}(t) & \vdots \\ x_{n1}(t) & x_{n2}(t) & \cdots & x_{nm}(t) \end{pmatrix} \tag{15.1}
$$

Integrated data was represented as a response matrix R where $\chi_{ij}(t)$ represents daily value of variable i on the date j, which is the jth location on the common time frame (Equation 15.1).

15.3.4 FEATURE REPRESENTATION LAYER

An important issue with multidimensional Big Data sources is optimal feature extraction to represent the knowledge within less dimensions. Data mining or unsupervised machine learning techniques are widely being used for feature extraction in physical, chemical, and environmental sciences [21,34,54,73]. Purpose of this layer was to preprocess the time series matrix, extract sets of semantic features from this matrix to create a reduced semantically enriched representation instead of the full size input, so that the relevant and most significant meaningful information from the input data would be captured to solve the multivariate problem. The general multivariate problem in large-scale environmental sensing is commonly referred to as a pattern recognition problem, which could be analyzed qualitatively, using the patterns produced by these various sensory data sources, and also quantitatively, by computing individual semantic component's knowledge variance contribution. It is envisaged that data processing and pattern analysis would provide useful and better understanding of the data generated and perhaps greater robustness. Pattern recognition algorithms have been a critical component in the implementation, development, and successful application of this knowledge processing architecture. Data normalization was used to prepare the integrated sensor response matrix for the subsequent signal preprocessing paradigms on a local or global level.

$$x_{ij} = x_{ij} \left/ \left(\sum_{i=1}^{n} x_{ij}^2 \right)^1 \right/ 2 \qquad (15.2)$$

Equation 15.2 was employed to normalize and compensate for differences in the magnitudes of the signals and to reduce the effects of noise. This normalization model was used to make the responses linear, to increase the relative contribution of the sensors and the overall dynamic range. The data produced from this layer were more linear and thus were simpler and easier to process than the original raw data. The most widely used local method is vector normalization (Equation 15.2), in which each feature vector (sample) is divided by its norm so that it is forced to lie on a hypersphere of unit radius. This has the beneficial effect of compensating for sample-to-sample variations due to signal to noise dependencies and other correlated sensor drift. It was preferable to use sensor response normalization because it ensured that sensor magnitudes were comparable, preventing signal preprocessing techniques from being overwhelmed by sensors with arbitrarily large values. The principal components analysis (PCA) is an unsupervised linear nonparametric projection method, which has been incorporated in this layer for dimension reduction and feature extraction. It is a multivariate statistical method, based on the Karhunen-Lowve expansion (Equation 15.3). The method consists of expressing the response vectors r_{ij} in terms of linear combinations of orthogonal vectors, and is sometimes referred to as vector decomposition. Each orthogonal vector, principal component (PC), accounts for a certain amount of variance in the data with a decreasing degree of importance. The scalar product of the orthogonal vectors with the response vector gives the value of the *pth* principal components:

$$X_p = \alpha_{1p} r_{1j} + \alpha_{2p} r_{2j} + \ldots + \alpha_{ip} r_{ij} + \ldots + \alpha_{np} r_{nj} \qquad (15.3)$$

The variance of each PC score, X_p, is maximized under the constraint that the sum of the coefficients of the orthogonal vectors or eigenvectors $\alpha_p = (\alpha_{1p} \alpha_{jp} \alpha_{np})$ is set to unity, and the vectors are uncorrelated. PCA was applied to extract least correlated attributes from the integrated attribute matrix to capture the maximum data variances. Output from this layer were a dynamic list of variables, which were the biggest contributors for knowledge variance in a particular instance. Variances are represented in a dynamically projected score matrix of the whole integrated data matrix [10,21,25,28,29,34,54,73].

15.3.5 SOM-Based Knowledge Recommendation Layer

Prior availability of recommendation about knowledge base could potentially optimize the accessibility and usability issues related to large data sets and minimize the overall application costs. Unsupervised machine learning–based visual knowledge recommendation was the main aspect of this knowledge recommendation layer. The guided self-organizing map (g-SOM) has the property of effectively creating spatially organized internal representations of various features of input signals and their abstractions. One aspect of this SOM is that the self-organization process that can discover semantic relationships in complex environmental attributes. The model of SOM was developed by T. Kohonen while applying neurobiology concepts for which adjacent neurons react to similar stimuli [44]. The SOM was a rough simplification and abstraction of the processes in the brain. The grid structure of the topology of the competition layer can be hypercuboid, triangles, circles, or hexagonal [22,42,52,53]. The purpose of this architectural layer was to analyze the dynamic data set using SOM clustering and provide visual knowledge recommendation about the less correlated attributes that could be selected for an application based on quick visual inspection or based on some sort of automated reasoning. The projection matrix from feature representation layer was used to design and initialize the SOM, whereas dynamically established least correlated attribute list was used to guide the g-SOM clustering in terms of initializing the weights. A SOM of $[n \times 1]$ network size was created to capture the natural grouping among the data points where selected list had n attributes. A set of data can be separated into several classes using unsupervised competitive learning; each neuron of the competition layer is responsible for the recognition of a certain class of data. The similarity measure on the data induces a similarity measure on the classes. Because the competition layer consists of a set of neurons without any architecture, the neighborhood relation among individual clusters cannot be implemented, only SOMs feature maps can. This last one relies on the modification of competitive networks, defining a topological structure on the competition layer, training the SOMs in such a way that adjacent clusters are represented by adjacent neurons of the last layer. While in competitive learning only, the weight vector of the winner neuron is shifted toward the current input vector, in contrast, SOMs change all weight vectors of neurons close to the winner. Neurons of the competition layer are organized in the shape of a straight line, of a rectangle, of a cuboid, etc. Self-organizing maps no longer use an angle measurement for the degree of similarity, but Euclidean distance between the input vector and the weight vector, thus the network input of neuron u in the competition layer is

$$net_u = \sqrt{\sum_{j=1}^{n} (W(v_j, u) - o_{vj})^2} = \left\| w^{(u)} - i \right\|$$

(15.4)

The neuron with the smallest net_{Us}, is declared the winner, and then the change in the weight vector of neuron u in the competition layer is determined by

$$W_{new}^{(u)} = W_{old}^{(u)} + v(u_s, t)\sigma(t)(i - W^{(u)})$$

(15.5)

As the learning rate decreases in competitive learning, large changes are possible at the beginning of the process. $v(u_s,t)$ indicates the neighborhood function of the neuron u_s. Later with decreasing radius r of the $r(t)$-neighborhood of the winner neuron, only neurons close to the winner are affected. Weights vectors of a SOM can gradually develop an approximately regular grid after being subjected to input patterns uniformly distributed over the unit square. SOMs are suitable for solving free learning problems, but it can also be advantageous to use it to divide the input domain of a fixed learning problem, for example, counter propagation networks. First, the input domain is partitioned, and then the mean value of the output given by the learning problem for each individual set of the partition is determined. Finally, the counter propagation provides for all inputs classified by a neuron of the competition network, and the mean value over this set as output. This kind of network can only learn piecewise constant function correctly; linear associates can be used to extend the number of applications to linear function with the help of the delta rule. The g-SOM clustering on the integrated selected preprocessed data was quite useful as this technique provided a 2D visual map representation of the whole database and natural grouping of the data attributes.

15.3.6 RDF CONVERSION AND TRIPLE STORE IMPLEMENTATION LAYER

This layer was constructed based on RDF, uniform resource identifier (URI), and triple store technologies. The aim of this layer was to present the integrated complex knowledge and associated dynamic recommendations in a more meaningful, transparent, and highly accessible way. W3C introduced the RDF format, which is now a standard model for machine readable data presentation [7,18,27,55,62]. It decomposes data into the pieces (subject, object, and predicate) and gives a URI for each resource or object. In computing, a URI is a string of characters used to identify a name or a resource. Such identification enables interaction with representations of the resource over a network (typically the WWW) using specific protocols. Schemes specifying a concrete syntax and associated protocols define each URI. Through the URIs, it is possible to read the information about the particular resource on the web using the HTTP access. A unified knowledge integration and representation model was developed using RDF format. Unified knowledge RDFs were created for all the data sources based on preprocessed data, extracted semantic features, available metadata, and original provenance information. This made the integrated environmental feature-based knowledge ready for flexible web integration. The RDF format provided semantic features sets a unique capability to facilitate data integration even if the underlying schema differed and it specially supported the evaluation of schemas over time without requiring the entire data consumption to be changed. A triple store is a framework used for storing and querying RDF data. It provides a mechanism for persistent storage and access of RDF graphs. Recently, there has been a major development initiative in query processing, access protocols and triple store technologies. The knowledge integration framework was developed using a triple called "Sesame triple store." Sesame (Figure 15.4) is an open-source framework for storage inference and querying of RDF data. Sesame matches the features of Jena with the availability of a connection API, inference support for multiple back ends like MySQL and Postgres [7,18,30,32,55,62].

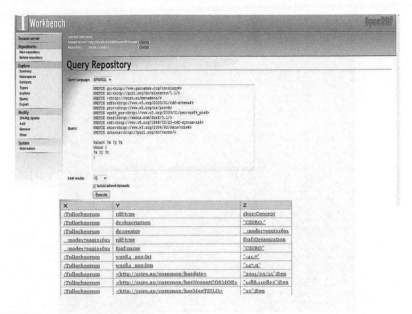

FIGURE 15.4   Sesame triplestore.

15.3.7   LOD PUBLISHING LAYER

The term Linked Open Data (LOD) was introduced by Tim Berners-Lee in his Linked Open data note and the famous lecture at Ted Talk [8,46]. The main purpose of the LOD publishing layer was to make people connected through data on the web where people can share, and reuse the knowledge very easily. In computing, linked data describes a method of publishing structured data so that it can be interlinked and become more useful. Publishing knowledge as linked open data cloud, which is the next-generation knowledge representation, was a very important aspect of this architecture. The final layer of this architecture was motivated by the philosophy that knowledge and recommendation about the knowledge should be openly accessible to the broader community. It was built upon standard web technologies such as HTTP and URIs, but rather than using them to serve web pages for human readers, it extends them to share information in a way that can be read automatically by computers. This enables data from different sources to be connected and queried. Layer wise RDF representation made this knowledge integration architecture very flexible to publish on LOD cloud. It is the best practice for exposing, sharing, and connecting pieces of data, information, and knowledge on the semantic web.

15.4   BIG KNOWLEDGE PROCESSING: TULLOCHGORUM CASE STUDY

15.4.1   TULLOCHGORUM SITE

The motivation behind this case of the study was to conduct some novel data knowledge engineering experiments associated with complexity of multiple data integration and

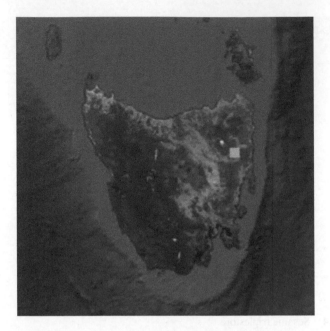

FIGURE 15.5   Tullochgorum, Tasmania, on MODIS satellite image.

to evaluate the purpose of this knowledge integration architecture. Tullochgorum, Tasmania (Figure 15.5), was selected as case study location for this chapter which was described by latitude −41.7 and longitude 147.9. All data sets for this site were automatically downloaded for the time period December 2010 to June 2012, preprocessed, analyzed, and visualized using unsupervised knowledge extraction techniques, and finally knowledge recommendations were published as LOD cloud. This was to develop and demonstrate an application of this newly developed environmental knowledge integration architecture.

15.4.2   TIME SERIES PROCESSING

15.4.2.1   Processing CosmOz Time Series

The Australian Cosmic Ray Sensor Soil Moisture Monitoring Network is a near-real-time continental scale soil moisture monitoring system being developed by the Commonwealth Scientific and Industrial Research Organization, Monash University, Charles Darwin University, and the University of New South Wales. CosmOz aims to test the utility of Hydroinnova cosmic ray soil moisture probes for water management, water information and hydrological process research applications, and test the feasibility and utility of a national near-real-time soil moisture measurement network. CosmOz also aims to support the evaluation of remote sensing products and hydrological models across Australia. The cosmic ray soil moisture probe measures the neutrons released when cosmic rays interact with hydrogen atoms in water molecules found in the soil. The neutrons are emitted into the atmosphere where they mix instantaneously at a scale of hundreds of meters and whose density is inversely correlated with the bulk soil moisture. Data from Hydroinnova CRS-1000 cosmic ray soil moisture probe [15] deployed in the Tullochgorum site in Tasmania, Australia was used for this study. The Tullochgorum CosmOz cosmic ray sensor was calibrated using ground truth soil samples collected around the probe. Soil moisture was measured using the oven-drying method and area-average bulk soil moisture was computed. The CosmOz cosmic ray probe comprising neutron detectors plus associated electronics is manufactured by Hydroinnova, LLC, of Albuquerque, New Mexico, USA. An Iridium satellite modem then transmits the data at 1-hour time intervals to the CosmOz CSIRO data server (Figure 15.6). Table 15.2 represents an example of hourly data format transmitted from the probe through the Iridium satellite communications system to a CSIRO data server. Data files were made available as .csv format. Most important and practical data attributes were atmospheric pressure, neutron pulse count, and rainfall (separately measured using a rain gauge), which have been used for this study. Time series data from the CSIRO server were downloaded, extracted, and pressure correction on the neutron counts were performed dynamically, using CosmOz web adaptor. Finally, the two time series namely "pressure corrected neutron count" and "daily rainfall" were made available for the data integration in the later stage, of the architecture.

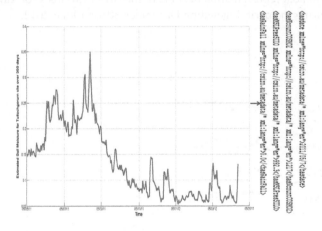

FIGURE 15.6   Time series data from Hydroinnova CRS-1000 cosmic ray soil moisture probe.

TABLE 15.2
Cosmos Data Format

Time	Atmospheric Pressure	Neutron Pulse Count	Rainfall
7/05/2011	992.3	1217	0.00

15.4.2.2 Processing BOM-SILO Time Series

The Long Paddock SILO database is operated by the Queensland Climate Change Centre of Excellence (QCCCE) within the Department of Science, Information Technology, Innovation, and the Arts (DSITIA). Data is based on all 4760 Australian Bureau of Meteorology (BOM) weather stations. SILO contains Australian climate data from "1889 to yesterday," in a number of ready-to-use formats, suitable for research and climate applications. Data files were available in .txt format. Web data adaptor were able to download data files automatically through HTTP access from the SILO server, extract all relevant text information from these files using a dedicated batch processor, and finally converted them into numeric time series. Sixteen attributes measured daily are extracted from downloaded patched point SILO file which are namely, maximum temperature (°C), minimum temperature (°C), rainfall (mm), evaporation (mm), radiation (MJ/m^2), vapor pressure (hPa), relative humidity at maximum temperature (%), relative humidity at minimum temperature (%), FAO56 potential evapotranspiration (mm), Morton evaporation over shallow lakes (mm), Morton potential evapotranspiration over land (mm), Morton actual evapotranspiration over land (mm), Morton wet environment areal evapotranspiration over land (mm), a comparison between measure class A pan evaporation, and synthetic pan evaporation (mm), class A evaporation (used post-1970) followed by synthetic pan evaporation (pre-1970) (mm), and mean sea level pressure (hPa). Figure 15.7 shows the graphical representation of some of the SILO variables for Tullochgorum, Tasmania, during the period including December 2010 to June 2012.

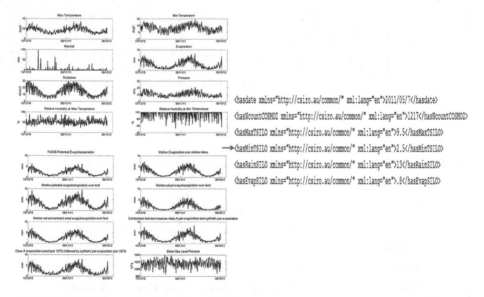

FIGURE 15.7 Time series data from SILO.

15.4.3 Gridded Data Processing

15.4.3.1 Processing ASRIS Map

The ASRIS database provides online access to the best publicly available information on soil and land resources in a consistent format across Australia. The database information is available in seven different scale levels. Seven different levels are namely (1) land division, (2) land province, (3) land zone, (4) land district, (5) land system, (6) land facet, and (7) site. The use and purpose of each level are different. These data sets provide information on the source of the data and hence indicate quality of the individual soil attribute data sets. The values of the source data sets are as follows: 2 = Digital Atlas of Australian Soils (1:2000000 scale mapping), 3 = ASRIS Level 3 (approximately 1:10,000,000 scale mapping), 4 = ASRIS Level 4 (approximately 1:2500000 scale mapping), and 5 = ASRIS Level 5 (approximately 1:100000 scale mapping). The ASRIS Level 5 data, that is, land system data is the most detailed mapping (value 5) through to the Atlas of Australian Soils, which is the broadest scale mapping (value 2). Three different soil data sets namely clay, bulk density, and plant available water capacity are taken into account in this study. Figure 15.8 shows the map for clay, bulk density, and the plant available water capacity. Associated

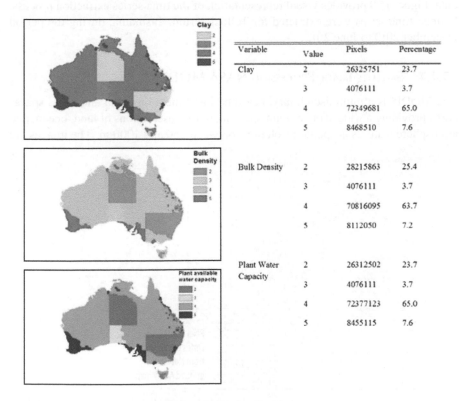

Variable	Value	Pixels	Percentage
Clay	2	26325751	23.7
	3	4076111	3.7
	4	72349681	65.0
	5	8468510	7.6
Bulk Density	2	28215863	25.4
	3	4076111	3.7
	4	70816095	63.7
	5	8112050	7.2
Plant Water Capacity	2	26312502	23.7
	3	4076111	3.7
	4	72377123	65.0
	5	8455115	7.6

FIGURE 15.8 Static Soil data from ASRIS data source.

number of pixels for each of the corresponding value in Figure 15.8 shows the quality of the soil attributes.

15.4.3.2 Processing AWAP Map

The AWAP database is developed to monitor the state and trend of the terrestrial water balance of the Australian continent, using model–data fusion methods to combine both measurements and modeling. The AWAP database provided weekly gridded map of the Australian continent on a latitude–longitude matrix (813 × 670) with 0.5 degree resolution. Data files were available as .zip folders from the AWAP server. Inside these folders multiple NetCDF files were stored, each of these .nc files was representing weekly combined Australian gridded maps for 16 environmental attributes, namely, radiation (MJ/m^2), maximum temperature (°C), minimum temperature (°C), rainfall (mm), upper layer soil moisture (fraction 0–1), lower layer soil moisture (fraction 0–1), evaporation (soil+vegetation) (mm), total transpiration (mm), soil evaporation (mm), potential evaporation (mm), local discharge (runoff + drainage) (mm), surface runoff (mm), open water evaporation ("pan" equiv) (mm), deep drainage (mm), sensible heat flux (MJ/m^2), and latent heat flux (MJ/m^2). AWAP data adaptor was developed and used to download and unzip all AWAP folders automatically, process the sequential NetCDF gridded data files to extract all time series data. Figure 15.9 provides visual representation of the time series extraction process. Sixteen time series were extracted for Tullochgorum, Tasmania, during the period December 2010 to June 2012.

15.4.4 SATELLITE IMAGE PROCESSING NASA MODIS

The MODIS is a multidisciplinary, keystone instrument on Aqua and Terra spacecraft, providing a wide array of multispectral, daily observations of land, ocean, and atmosphere features at spatial resolutions between 250 and 1000 m. The images are

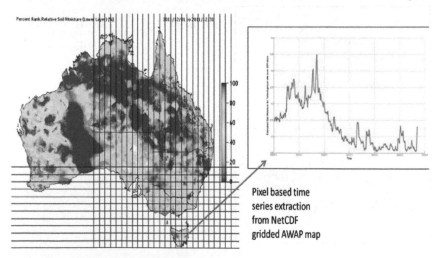

Pixel based time series extraction from NetCDF gridded AWAP map

FIGURE 15.9 AWAP data processing.

freely available in the NASA website for different products. The instrument type on-board is a medium-resolution, multispectral, cross-track scanning radiometer with daylight reflection, and day/night emission spectral imaging. The MODIS instruments acquire data in three native spatial resolutions: Bands 12 in 250 m, Bands 37 in 500 m and Bands 836 in 1000 m. The images are freely available in NASA website for different products. For this study, we have downloaded the MODIS/ Terra Land Surface Temperature and Emissivity (LST/E) 8-day L3 Global 0.05Deg CMG product (MOD11C2) version 5 for Tullochgorum, Tasmania during the period December 2010 to June 2012. This product provides per-pixel temperature and emissivity values in a sequence of swath-based global products. MOD11C2 product comprises the Science Data Set (SDS) layers for day time and night time observations: LSTs, quality control assessments, observation times, view zenith angles, clear sky coverage, and emissivity for bands, that is, 20, 22, 23, 29, 31, and 32 (Figure 15.10). This was explicitly mentioned in the Land Processes Distributed Active Archive Center (LP DAAC) portal of NASA that MOD11C2 products are ready for use in science applications. Time series were created from these downloaded image data files based on image processing techniques (Figure 15.11) [14,69–71]. Similarly, Tropical Rainfall Measuring Mission (TRMM) 3B42 satellite-based precipitation products were constructed from the post real-time TRMM Multi-Satellite Precipitation Analysis (TMPA) product, 3B42. The purpose of the 3B42 algorithm is to produce TRMM-adjusted merged-infrared (IR) precipitation and root-mean-square (RMS) precipitation-error estimates. The algorithm consists of two separate steps. The first step uses the TRMM VIRS and TMI orbit data (TRMM products 1B01 and 2A12) and the monthly TMI/TRMM Combined Instrument (TCI) calibration parameters (from TRMM product 3B31) to produce monthly IR calibration parameters. The second step uses these derived monthly IR calibration parameters to adjust the merged-IR precipitation data. These gridded estimates are on a 3-hour temporal resolution and a $0.25° \times 0.25°$ spatial resolution, which provided the adjusted merged-IR precipitation (mm/hr) and RMS precipitation error [14,39,69–71]. Figure 15.12 shows an example of MODIS production on a global scale.

15.4.5   UNSUPERVISED KNOWLEDGE RECOMMENDATION

15.4.5.1   Time Series Integration

As described in the previous section, all time series data were integrated together to form a complete list of environmental data set on a dynamic time scale. Extracted and integrated time series data were processed through the harmonization layer, semantic cross validation layer, and feature representation layer to form a representative semantic feature based. Refreshed, complemented, cross-validated, and normalized integrated time series matrix was formed, which had 40 different environmental variables from five different big environmental data sources. Semantic attribute matrix had 40 columns and n rows, where n was representing dynamic total number of days during which the integration was performed. Uniqueness of this processing was that depending on the total time of integration the whole matrix could dynamically adapt to represent most recent and most relevant data matrix (Figure 15.13).

```
MODIS Reprojection Tool (v4.1 March 2009)
Start Time: Fri Feb 22 01:16:02 2013
-------------------------------------------------------
Input image and reprojection info
-------------------------------
input_filename:    C:\Users\jaryal\Downloads\Downloaded MODIS hdf files\MOD11C2.A2010345.005.2011031210429.hdf
output_filename:   D:\Documents\Research\Collaborations\Book chapter\MODIS processed output\MOD11c2_429.hdf
input_filetype:    HDF-EOS
output_filetype:   HDF-EOS
input_projection_type:  GEO
input_datum:       No Datum (use projection parameters)
output_projection_type: GEO
output_datum:      No Datum (use projection parameters)
resampling_type:      NN
Output image info
----------------
output image extents (lat/lon):
   UL:  90.000000000000 -180.000000000000
   UR:  90.000000000000 180.000000000000
   LL: -90.000000000000 -180.000000000000
   LR: -90.000000000000 180.000000000000

output image extents (X-Y projection units):
   UL: -180.000000000000 90.000000000000
   UR:  180.000000000000 90.000000000000
   LL: -180.000000000000 -90.000000000000
   LR:  180.000000000000 -90.000000000000
```

band	type	lines	smpls	pixsiz	min	max	fill
1) QC_Day	UINT8	3600	7200	0.0500	0	255	0
2) Day_view_time	UINT8	3600	7200	0.0500	0	120	255
3) Day_view_angl	UINT8	3600	7200	0.0500	0	130	255
4) Clear_sky_days	UINT8	3600	7200	0.0500	0	255	0
5) LST_Night_CMG	UINT16	3600	7200	0.0500	7500	65535	0
6) QC_Night	UINT8	3600	7200	0.0500	0	255	0
7) Night_view_time	UINT8	3600	7200	0.0500	0	120	255
8) Night_view_angl	UINT8	3600	7200	0.0500	0	130	255
9) Clear_sky_nights	UINT8	3600	7200	0.0500	0	· 255	0
10) Emis_20	UINT8	3600	7200	0.0500	1	255	0
11) Emis_22	UINT8	3600	7200	0.0500	1	255	0
12) Emis_23	UINT8	3600	7200	0.0500	1	255	0
13) Emis_29	UINT8	3600	7200	0.0500	1	255	0
14) Emis_31	UINT8	3600	7200	0.0500	1	255	0
15) Emis_32	UINT8	3600	7200	0.0500	1	255	0
16) Percent_land_in_grid	UINT8	3600	7200	0.0500	1	100	0

```
End Time: Fri Feb 22 01:26:25 2013
Finished processing!
```

FIGURE 15.10   Modis data processing.

15.4.5.2   PCA-Based Feature Space Representation

For feature space representation, the first PCA was applied for data visualization, exploration of data clustering in multisensor space, and to establish sensor correlations. The objective of the PCA exploration was to establish whether or not simple classes exist in the feature space and to see whether the data clusters could be found by investigation, before the self organizing knowledge recommendation. The PCA method consists of expressing the response vectors in terms of a linear combination

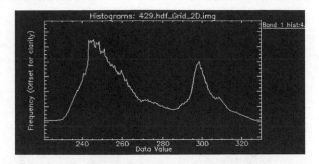

FIGURE 15.11 A representative histogram for land surface temperature.

of orthogonal vectors. Each orthogonal (principal) vector accounts for a certain amount of variance in the data, with a decreasing degree of importance. PCA-based data clustering was used to investigate how the response vectors from the different sensors are clustered into multisensor space. The main aim of this analysis was to establish a list of least correlated attributes, which contribute toward most data variance. This clustering approach was used on normalized data. Individual feature or variable data column was normalized to avoid any unnecessary data value imbalance. Based on the PCA method, all attributes were sorted according to their correlation coefficients. In this case, as the integrated time series matrix had 40 columns, coefficient matrix had 40 columns, and 40 rows, where individual column represented one PC and 40 rows of that column represented data variance contribution of all 40 variables along that particular PC. Depending on total data, variance number of PC count was automatically decided. Five principal components were kept, which accounted for 100% of the variance in data set (PC no. 1, PC no. 2, PC no. 3, PC no. 4, and PC no. 5) which accounted for 71.67%, 8.85%, 5.23%, 4.57%, and 0.41% of the variance, respectively, in this particular case study. It was very clear that the first principal component captured most of the information variance from the data set. The PCA method was used to get a better understanding of the nature of our data. For reference, all the load values for the first five PCs are included here. The loadings associated with the five least correlated variables, namely, n-count COSMOZ, Evap SILO, PotEvap AWAP, Temperature MODIS, and rain AWAP were (0.5066 0.0754 0.7806), (0.5135 0.0823 0.7808), (0.2828 0.5490 0.5490), (0.367 0.678 0.4910), and (0.4754 0.8164 0.2987), respectively. The next five criteria from the sorted list were EvSp SILO, totalTRANSP AWAP, DeepDrain AWAP, LatHeatFlux AWAP, and Temperature MODIS. Although these later five variables did not carry significant information variance, the loadings associated with them were (0.5613 0.1810 0.6947), (0.5478 0.1608 0.0663), (0.4828 0.5490 0.5490), (0.2828 0.1490 0.4490), and (0.1754 0.8164 0.2987), respectively. Findings from this dynamic PC analysis were significant as they were able to reduce the dimension significantly from a big multivariate data set, and also provided the valuable recommendation about the statistically significant attributes. These recommendations were used to form the ultimate dynamic environmental knowledge recommendation layer.

FIGURE 15.12   Density sliced land surface temperature map generated from MODIS11C2 image, the study site is bounded in red rectangle.

Index	Variable	Description	Unit
0	n-count COSMOZ	Atmospheric Pressure Corrected n-count from COSMOZ	N/A
1	maxT SILO	maximum temperature SILO	degC
2	minT SILO	minimum temperature SILO	degC
3	rain SILO	Daily rainfall from SILO	mm
4	Evap SILO	evaporation from SILO	mm
5	Rad SILO	solar radiation from SILO	MJ/m2
6	VP SILO	vapour pressure from SILO	hPa
7	RH@Tmax SILO	Humidity at maximum temperature from SILO	%
8	RH@Tmin SILO	Humidity at minimum temperature from SILO	%
9	FAO56 SILO	FAO56 Potential Evapotranspiration from SILO	mm
10	Mlake SILO	Morton evaporation over shallow lakes from SILO	mm
11	Mpotential SILO	Morton potential evapotranspiration over land from SILO	mm
12	Mactual SILO	Morton actual evapotranspiration over land fromSILO	mm
13	Mwet SILO	Morton wet environment areal evapotranspiration over land fromSILO	mm
14	Span SILO	a comparison between measure class A pan evaporation and sythetic pan evaporation from SILO	mm
15	EvSp SILO	class A evaporation (used post 1970) followed by sythetic pan evaporation (pre 1970) from SILO	mm
16	MSLPres SILO	Mean Sea Level Pressure from SILO	hPa
17	SolarMJ AWAP	solar radiation from AWAP	MJ/m^2
18	maxT AWAP	maximum temperature from AWAP	degC
19	minT AWAP	minimum temperature from AWAP	degC
20	rain AWAP	Daily rainfall from AWAP	mm
21	MsoilUL AWAP	soil moisture (upper layer) from AWAP	Fraction (0-1)
22	MsoilULagg AWAP	soil moisture (upper layer)at end of aggregation period from AWAP	Fraction (0-1)
23	MsoilLL AWAP	soil moisture (lower layer) from AWAP	Fraction (0-1)
24	MsoilLLagg AWAP	soil moisture (lower layer) at end of aggregation period from AWAP	Fraction (0-1)
25	Evap(soil+veg) AWAP	evaporation (soil+vegetation) from AWAP	mm
26	totalTRANSP AWAP	Total Transpiration from AWAP	mm
27	Evap(soil) AWAP	Soil Evaporation from AWAP	mm
28	PotEvap AWAP	Potential Evaporation from AWAP	mm
29	LocDis (Run + Drain) AWAP	Local Discharge (Runoff+Drainage) from AWAP	mm
30	SurfRun AWAP	Surface Runoff from AWAP	mm
31	OpenWaEvap AWAP	Open Water Evaporation ('pan' equiv) from AWAP	mm
32	DeepDrain AWAP	Deep Drainage from AWAP	mm
33	SeniHeatFlux AWAP	Daily Sensible Heat Flux from AWAP	W/m^2
34	LatHeatFlux AWAP	Daily Latent Heat Flux from AWAP	W/m^2
35	% Clay ASRIS	Percentage Clay content	%
36	% Bulk Density ASRIS	Percentage Bilk Density	%
37	% Plant Available Water Capacity ASRIS	Percentage Plant Available Water Capacity	%
38	Temperature MODIS	Pixel temperature from MODIS	degC
39	Rain MODIS	Daily rainfall from MODIS	mm
40	Humidity MODIS	Daily Humidity from MODIS	%

FIGURE 15.13 Integrated metadata set.

15.4.5.3 SOM-Based Big Knowledge Recommendation

SOM may be considered a nonlinear generalization of the PCA. After multiple training SOMs learn to classify input vectors according to how they are grouped in the input space. They differ from competitive layers in that neighboring neurons in the SOM learning to recognize neighboring sections of the input space. Thus, SOMs learn both the distribution (as do competitive layers), and topology of the input vectors they are trained on. There are two ways to interpret a SOM. As in the training, phase weights of the whole neighborhood are moved in the same direction, and similar items tend to excite adjacent neurons. Therefore, SOM forms a semantic map where similar samples are mapped close together and dissimilar ones mapped apart. The SOM network was applied on the selected least correlated semantic attributes from PCA to estimate and visualize the natural grouping of the data. The most significant PCs covering 99(%) of the data variance were used to design, initialize, and guide the self-organizing map network. Using 3D scatter plot-based on the first three most significant PC found that two clear clusters could be formed for the currently available integrated data matrix. This information was used to design the initial SOM. Two clear clusters were chosen based on inter-cluster distance and individual locations of the data points. The dynamically established number of the most significant PCs (in this case $p = 5$) and number of clear clusters (in this case $c = 2$) were used to define a SOM network of $[p \times c]$ dimension. This SOM was trained using the whole

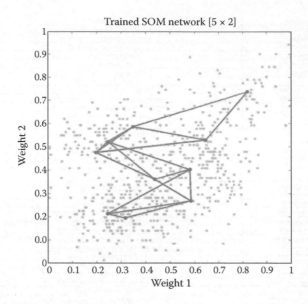

FIGURE 15.14   Trained SOM network.

integrated data set (Figure 15.14). The usage of PCA to define the design of SOM network selection is unique and completely dynamic. Depending on the data quality and variance, the size of the selected SOM is dynamically varied. This design made the SOM training completely adaptable to the dynamic nature of available integrated data. As the SOM was trained with whole data matrix containing 40 input variables, SOM had 40 internal weights that were updated iteratively. After a certain number of iterative training, the weights of the partially trained SOM could be used to visualize as 2D visual patterns or weight maps. SOM weight planes were used in the training window to obtain these maps. There was a weight plane (or visual 2D pattern map) for each element of the input vector (40, in this case). They were visualizations of the weights that connect each input to each of the neurons. This SOM-based analysis and visualization provided a unique node connection pattern representation about the input space. Lighter and darker colors represent larger and smaller weights, respectively. If the connection color patterns of two inputs are very similar, it is estimated that these two inputs are highly correlated. Highly correlated attributes are almost similar in terms of data variance contributions, so unless both of these variables are required for a specific application, one of them can easily be ignored and reduce the problem dimensionality and to increase the overall data variance. The novelty about this SOM-based approach is that it provides visual patterns about all the variables, so database customers can easily understand and decide about the most important variables with simple visual inspection without even accessing any data. The SOM-based visual representation method provides a great dynamic way to recommend knowledge about the Big Data. SOM clustering on the integrated preprocessed data is quite useful as this technique provided a 2D visual map representation of the whole database and natural grouping of the data attributes (Figure 15.15). Using this knowledge map (or a region of the map), a user could design an application, so

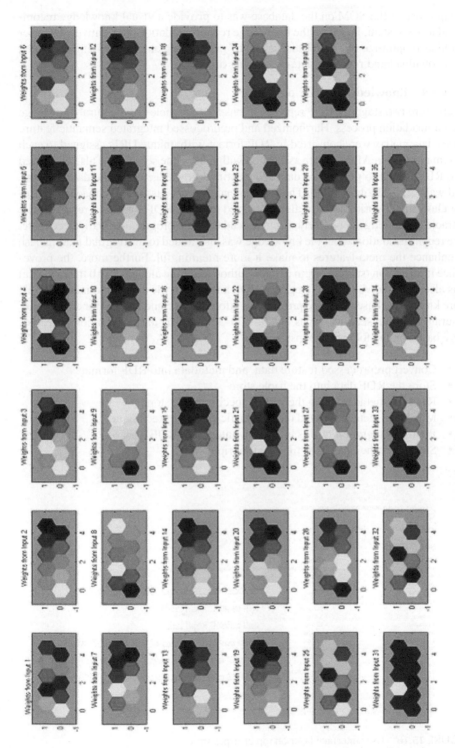

FIGURE 15.15 Weight-based 2D visual attribute map providing knowledge recommendation.

the purpose of the SOM on the database was to provide a visual knowledge recommendations system. Based on the knowledge recommendation, qualitatively one user could also optimize the "Big Data" usage by prioritizing and minimizing unwanted data download and reducing data-processing time.

15.4.5.4 Knowledge as RDF on LOD

There were two stages of RDF representations for the whole architectural knowledge recommendation process. Harmonized and preprocessed integrated semantic feature series data matrix were converted in RDF format with unique URIs assigned to each of semantic entry. All metadata associated with these time series were also converted into RDF format to present the data and existing knowledge about the data in a unified way [2,20,23,24,50,57,72]. The recommendation results from the machine learning clustering algorithms were also converted into the RDF format to represent the extracted knowledge completely machine readable and programmatically accessible. The recommendation about the knowledge was also added to the original feature base to enhance the meta-features to make it more meaningful. Furthermore, the provenance information (such as origin of data, author, and time along with all the raw data) was also captured within the integrated RDF knowledge file and stored into the triple store knowledge base. In future provenance information could be used for data quality assurance or data security issues [3,4,6,11,30–32,40]. The data integration processes were based on the following steps:

- Convert preprocessed feature data, and metadata into RDF format
- Store the RDF data into the triple store
- Read the metadata from the source specific triple store
- Match the metadata based on a syntactic matching technique
- Publish integration results into a new integrated RDF file
- Store back the final RDF file into the triple store

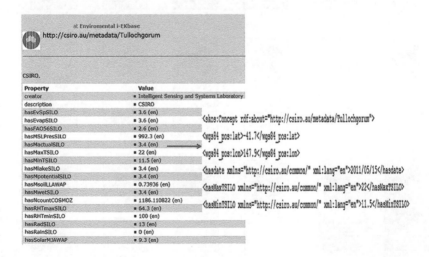

FIGURE 15.16   User interface layer on top of triple store.

Integrated knowledge RDF files were uploaded into the triple store, which provided all facilities of browsing, querying, exporting data in a different formats, etc. RDF representation of the processed knowledge and PCA-SOM-based recommendation made the knowledgebase easily interpretable to the data customers and to the application designers. A user interface layer (Figure 15.16) was developed on top of these triples to provide great flexibility to the application designers. A SPARQL endpoint was available for navigating and downloading the already analyzed data for greater usage.

15.5 CONCLUSION

Our understanding of the environment is greatly associated with the interlinked knowledge of the phenomena surrounding us. Such knowledge is a result of data and extracted information. With the availability of very high and even ultra-high-resolution sensor data there is a greater need of managing data, information, and essentially the knowledge. With the advent of technological novelties and their wider applications, the generated data is surpassing our capacities to store it. There is an urgent need for improved methods and advancement in data-intensive science to retrieve, filter, integrate, and share data. Data and meaningful information are key for the actors in every walk of life, however, how to conceive, perceive, recognize, and interpret such data in space and time is a big question and a big challenge. Taking this challenge into the perspective, we have presented an opportunity of recommending environmental Big Data using semantically guided machine learning approaches. In our approach, we were successful in integrating various data sources available in the web by developing web adaptors. For example, data from SILO, COsMOZ, AWAP, ASRIS, and MODIS were processed within the machine learning and image processing framework. The methodology resulted meaningful information, which was later captured as knowledge. The knowledge was published in the LOD cloud environment for the wider use of scientific community and policy-making authorities. Currently, the most promising approach is LOD cloud in handling the Big Data. By developing this methodology and recommending environmental big knowledge, we believe that this approach will enable us to better address complex scientific and social questions. We have a firm belief that our simple approach will contribute to the body of knowledge in the Big Data study and big knowledge management in this era of data-intensive science.

REFERENCES

1. Don't Build a Database of Ruin. http://blogs.hbr.org/cs/2012/08/.
2. Frederic Achard, Guy Vaysseix, and Emmanuel Barillot. Xml, bioinformatics and data integration. *Bioinformatics*, 17(2):115–125, 2001.
3. Sören Auer and Jens Lehmann. Creating knowledge out of interlinked data. *Semantic Web*, 1(1):97–104, 2010.
4. Tim Berners-Lee. http://www.w3.org/DesignIssues/LinkedData.html/.
5. Muhammad Bilal and Sharifullah Khan. Ontology-driven relevance reasoning architecture for data integration techniques. In *Intelligent Systems, 2008. IS'08. 4th International IEEE Conference*, volume 3, pages 22–8. IEEE, 2008.

6. Christian Bizer, Tom Heath, and Tim Berners-Lee. Linked data – the story so far. *International Journal on Semantic Web and Information Systems (IJSWIS)*, 5(3):1–22, 2009.

7. Jeen Broekstra, Arjohn Kampman, and Frank Van Harmelen. Sesame: A generic architecture for storing and querying rdf and rdf schema. *The Semantic WebISWC 2002*, pages 54–68, 2002.

8. Arne Bröring, Johannes Echterhoff, Simon Jirka, Ingo Simonis, Thomas Everding, Christoph Stasch, Steve Liang, and Rob Lemmens. New generation sensor web enablement. *Sensors*, 11(3):2652–2699, 2011.

9. Jacques Bughin, Michael Chui, and James Manyika. Clouds, big data, and smart assets: Ten tech-enabled business trends to watch. *McKinsey Quarterly*, 56, 2010.

10. Diego Calvanese, Giuseppe De Giacomo, and Maurizio Lenzerini. A framework for ontology integration. In *The Emerging Semantic WebSelected Papers from the First Semantic Web Working Symposium*, pages 201–214, 2002.

11. Anja Jentzsch, Christian Bizer, and Pablo Mendes. *Topology of the Web of Data*. Book chapter in De Virgilio, Guerra, Yannis (Eds.): Semantic Search over the Web. Springer, 2012.

12. Linking Open Data cloud diagram. http://lod-cloud.net/.

13. Michael Compton, Cory Henson, Laurent Lefort, Holger Neuhaus, and Amit Sheth. A survey of the semantic specification of sensors. *Proc. Semantic Sensor Networks*, 17, 2009.

14. Zhengming Wan, Yulin Zhang, Qincheng Zhang, and Zhao-liang Li. Quality assessment and validation of the modis global land surface temperature. *International Journal of Remote Sensing*, 25(1):261–274, 2004.

15. Hydroinnova cosmic ray soil moisture probes. http://hydroinnova.com/.

16. William Day. Zhenzhi and acknowledgment in Wang Yangming and Stanley Cavell. *Journal of Chinese Philosophy*, 39(2):174–191, 2012.

17. Big Data Definition. http://mike2.openmethodology.org/wiki/.

18. Resource describe framework. http://www.w3.org/RDF/.

19. Cora Diamond. The difficulty of reality and the difficulty of philosophy. *Partial Answers: Journal of Literature and the History of Ideas*, 1(2):1–26, 2003.

20. AnHai Doan, Pedro Domingos, and Alon Levy. Learning source descriptions for data integration. In *WebDB (Informal Proceedings)*, pages 81–86, 2000.

21. Ritaban Dutta, Aruneema Das, Nigel G Stocks, and David Morgan. Stochastic resonance-based electronic nose: A novel way to classify bacteria. *Sensors and Actuators B: Chemical*, 115(1):17–27, 2006.

22. Ritabrata Dutta and Ritaban Dutta. Maximum probability rule-based classification of mrsa infections in hospital environment: Using electronic nose. *Sensors and Actuators B: Chemical*, 120(1):156–165, 2006.

23. Dieter Fensel, Ying Ding, Borys Omelayenko, Ellen Schulten, Guy Botquin, Mike Brown, and Alan Flett. Product data integration in b2b e-commerce. *Intelligent Systems, IEEE*, 16(4):54–59, 2001.

24. Daniela Florescu, Daphne Koller, Alon Levy, and Avi Pfeffer. Using probabilistic information in data integration. In *Proceedings of the International Conference on Very Large Data Bases*, pages 216–225. Citeseer, 1997.

25. Ross Folland, Evor Hines, Ritaban Dutta, Pascal Boilot, and David Morgan. Comparison of neural network predictors in the classification of tracheal-bronchial breath sounds by respiratory auscultation. *Artificial Intelligence in Medicine*, 31(3):211–220, 2004.

26. Mary Anne M Gobble. Resources: Big data: The next big thing in innovation. *Research Technology Management*, 56(1):64–67, 2013.

27. Semantic Sensor Network Incubator Group. http://www.w3.org/2005/Incubator/ssn/wiki/.

28. Thomas R Gruber et al. Toward principles for the design of ontologies used for knowledge sharing. *International Journal of Human Computer Studies*, 43(5):907–928, 1995.

29. Michael Gruninger, Mark S Fox et al. Methodology for the design and evaluation of ontologies. In *Proceedings of the Workshop on Basic Ontological Issues in Knowledge Sharing, IJCAI*, volume 95, 1995.

30. Olaf Hartig, Christian Bizer, and Johann-Christoph Freytag. Executing SPARQL queries over the web of linked data. *The Semantic Web-ISWC 2009*, pages 293–309, 2009.

31. Olaf Hartig and Jun Zhao. Publishing and consuming provenance metadata on the web of linked data. *Provenance and Annotation of Data and Processes*, pages 78–90, 2010.

32. Tom Heath and Christian Bizer. Linked data: Evolving the web into a global data space. *Synthesis Lectures on the Semantic Web: Theory and Technology*, 1(1):1–136, 2011.

33. Cory A Henson, Josh K Pschorr, Amit P Sheth, and Krishnaprasad Thirunarayan. Semsos: Semantic sensor observation service. In *Collaborative Technologies and Systems, 2009. CTS'09. International Symposium on*, pages 44–53. IEEE, 2009.

34. Hynek Hermansky, Daniel PW Ellis, and Sangita Sharma. Tandem connectionist feature extraction for conventional hmm systems. In *Acoustics, Speech, and Signal Processing, 2000. ICASSP'00. Proceedings. 2000 IEEE International Conference on*, volume 3, pages 1635–1638. IEEE, 2000.

35. Herodotos Herodotou, Harold Lim, Gang Luo, Nedyalko Borisov, Liang Dong, Fatma Bilgen Cetin, and Shivnath Babu. Starfish: A self-tuning system for big data analytics. In *Proc. of the Fifth CIDR Conf*, 2011.

36. Pascal Hitzler, Krzysztof Janowicz, Gary Berg-Cross, Leo Obrst, Amith Sheth, Tim Finin, Isabel Cruz, Naicong Li, and Karen Stacks. Semantic aspects of earthcube. Technical report, Technical report, Semantics and Ontology Technical Committee. Available online at: http://knoesis.wright.edu/faculty/pascal/pub/EC-SO-TC-Report-V1.0.pdf, 2012.

37. What is Big Data? http://www-01.ibm.com/software/data/bigdata/.

38. What is Big Data? http://www.zdnet.com/blog/virtualization/.

39. Md Nazrul Islam and Hiroshi Uyeda. Trmm observed vertical structure and diurnal variation of precipitation in south Asia. In *Geoscience and Remote Sensing Symposium, 2006. IGARSS 2006. IEEE International Conference on*, pages 1292–1295. IEEE, 2006.

40. Prateek Jain, Pascal Hitzler, Peter Z Yeh, Kunal Verma, and Amit P Sheth. Linked data is merely more data. *Linked Data Meets Artificial Intelligence*, pages 82–86, 2010.

41. Krzysztof Janowicz and Michael Compton. The stimulus-sensor-observation ontology design pattern and its integration into the semantic sensor network ontology. In *The 3rd International Workshop on Semantic Sensor Networks*, pages 7–11, 2010.

42. Erich Jantsch. *The self organizing universe scientific and human implication: Of the emerging paradigm of evolution*. New York, 1980.

43. Ian Jolliffe. *Principal component analysis*. Wiley Online Library, 2005.

44. Teuvo Kohonen. The self-organizing map. *Proceedings of the IEEE*, 78(9):1464–1480, 1990.

45. Ora Lassila, Ralph R Swick et al. *Resource description framework (rdf) model and syntax specification*. 1998.

46. Danh Le-Phuoc, Hoan Nguyen Mau Quoc, Josiane Xavier Parreira, and Manfred Hauswirth. The linked sensor middleware-connecting the real world and the semantic web. *Proceedings of the Semantic Web Challenge*, 2011.

47. Newton Lee. *Facebook Nation*. Springer, New York.

48. Newton Lee. Generation c in the age of big data. *Facebook Nation*, pages 77–82.

49. Newton Lee. *Facebook Nation: Total Information Awareness*. Springer-Verlag New York Incorporated, 2012.

50. Maurizio Lenzerini. Data integration: A theoretical perspective. In *Symposium on Principles of Database Systems: Proceedings of the Twenty-First ACM SIGMOD-SIGACT-SIGART Symposium on Principles of Database Systems*, volume 3, pages 233–246, 2002.

51. Clifford Lynch. Big data: How do your data grow? *Nature*, 455(7209):28–29, 2008.

52. Mike Miller. The Future of Big Data. see at http://architects.dzone.com/articles/future-big-data-according.
53. Ahsan Morshed, Caterina Caracciolo, Gudrun Johannsen, and Johannes Keizer. Thesaurus alignment for linked data publishing. In *International Conference on Dublin Core and Metadata Applications*, pages 37–46, 2011.
54. Ramakant Nevatia and K Ramesh Babu. Linear feature extraction and description. *Computer Graphics and Image Processing*, 13(3):257–269, 1980.
55. Provenance. http://www.w3.org/2011/prov/wiki/.
56. Joshua Pschorr, Cory Henson, Harshal Patni, and Amit Sheth. Sensor discovery on linked data. In *Proceedings of the 7th Extended Semantic Web Conference, ESWC2010, Heraklion, Greece*, volume 30, 2010.
57. Hairong Qi, Sitharama Iyengar, and Krishnendu Chakrabarty. Multiresolution data integration using mobile agents in distributed sensor networks. *Systems, Man, and Cybernetics, Part C: Applications and Reviews, IEEE Transactions on*, 31(3):383–391, 2001.
58. Amit Sheth, Cory Henson, and Satya S Sahoo. Semantic sensor web. *Internet Computing, IEEE*, 12(4):78–83, 2008.
59. Herbert A Simon. *The sciences of the artificial*. MIT press, 1996.
60. Herbert A Simon, Werner Callebaut, and Diego Rasskin-Gutman. *Modularity: Understanding the development and evolution of natural complex systems*. MIT press, 2005.
61. Margherita Sini, Boris Lauser, Gauri Salokhe, Johannes Keizer, and Stephen Katz. The agrovoc concept server: Rationale, goals and usage. *Library Review*, 57(3):200–212, 2008.
62. SKOS. http://www.w3.org/TR/skos-reference/skos-xl.html.
63. ASRIS Data Source. www.asris.csiro.au/.
64. AWAP Data Source. www.eoc.csiro.au/awap/.
65. CosmOz Data Source. http://www.ermt.csiro.au/html/cosmoz.html/.
66. MODIS Data Source. www.modis.gsfc.nasa.gov/.
67. SILO Data Source. www.longpaddock.qld.gov.au/silo/.
68. Mitch Waldrop. Big data: Wikiomics. *Nature*, 455(7209):22, 2008.
69. Zhengming Wan. New refinements and validation of the MODIS land-surface temperature/emissivity products. *Remote Sensing of Environment*, 112(1):59–74, 2008.
70. Zhengming Wan and Jeff Dozier. A generalized split-window algorithm for retrieving land-surface temperature from space. *IEEE Transactions on Geoscience and Remote Sensing*, 34(4):892–905, 1996.
71. Zhengming Wan and Zhao-Liang Li. A physics-based algorithm for retrieving land-surface emissivity and temperature from EOS/MODIS data. *IEEE Transactions on Geoscience and Remote Sensing*, 35(4):980–996, 1997.
72. Jennifer Widom. Research problems in data warehousing. In *Proceedings of the Fourth International Conference on Information and Knowledge Management*, pages 25–30. ACM, 1995.
73. Alan L Yuille, Peter W Hallinan, and David S Cohen. Feature extraction from faces using deformable templates. *International Journal of Computer Vision*, 8(2):99–111, 1992.
74. Shufeng Zhou. Exposing relational database as rdf. In *Industrial and Information Systems (IIS), 2010 2nd International Conference on*, volume 2, pages 237–240. IEEE, 2010.

16 Virtualizing Resources for the Cloud

Mohammad Hammoud and Majd F. Sakr

CONTENTS

Virtualization is at the core of cloud computing. It lies on top of the cloud infrastructure, whereby virtual resources (e.g., virtual CPUs, memories, disks, networks) are constructed from the underlying physical resources and act as proxies to them. As is the case with the idea of cloud computing, which was first introduced in the 1960s [1], virtualization can be traced back to the 1970s [55]. Forty years ago, the mainframe computer systems were extremely large and expensive. To address expanding user needs and costly machine ownerships, the IBM 370 architecture, announced in 1970, offered complete virtual machines (virtual hardware images) to different programs running at the same computer hardware. Over time, computer hardware became less expensive and users started migrating to low-priced desktop machines. This drove the adoption of the virtualization technology to fade for a while. Today, virtualization is enjoying a resurgence in popularity with a number of research projects and commercial systems providing virtualization solutions for commodity PCs, servers, and the cloud.

In this chapter, we present various ingredients of the virtualization technology and the crucial role it plays in enabling the cloud computing paradigm. First, we identify major reasons for why virtualization is becoming important, especially for the cloud. Second, we indicate how multiple software images can run side by side on physical resources while attaining security, resource and failure isolations. Prior to delving into more details about virtualization, we present a brief background requisite for understanding how physical resources can be virtualized. In particular, we learn how system complexity can be managed in terms of levels of abstractions and well-defined interfaces. To this end, we formally define virtualization and examine two main virtual machine types: process and system virtual machines.

After introducing and motivating virtualization for the cloud, we describe in detail CPU, memory, and I/O virtualizations. Specifically, we first explore conditions for virtualizing CPUs, identify the difference between full virtualization and paravirtualization, explain emulation as a major technique for CPU virtualization, and examine virtual CPU scheduling in Xen, a popular hypervisor utilized by Amazon at its Amazon Web Services (AWS) cloud computing platform. Second, we outline the difference between conventional operating system's virtual memory and system memory virtualization, explain the multiple levels of page mapping as dictated by system memory virtualization, define memory overcommitment and illustrate memory ballooning, a reclamation technique to tackle memory overcommitment in VMware ESX, another common hypervisor. Third, we explain how CPU and I/O devices can communicate with and without virtualization, identify the three main interfaces, system call, device driver, and operation level interfaces, at which I/O virtualization can be ensued. As a practical example, we discuss Xen's approach to I/O virtualization. Finally, we close with a case study on Amazon Elastic Compute Cloud (Amazon EC2), which applies system virtualization to provide Infrastructure as a Service (IaaS) on the cloud. We investigate the underlying virtualization technology of Amazon EC2 and some of its major characteristics such as elasticity, scalability, performance, flexibility, fault tolerance, and security.

16.1 WHY VIRTUALIZATION?

Virtualization is predominantly used by programmers to ease software development and testing, by IT datacenters to consolidate dedicated servers into more cost effective hardware, and by the cloud (e.g., Amazon EC2) to isolate users sharing a single hardware layer and offer elasticity, among others. Next, we discuss seven areas that virtualization enables on the cloud.

16.1.1 ENABLING THE CLOUD COMPUTING SYSTEM MODEL

A major use case of virtualization is cloud computing. Cloud computing adopts a model whereby software, computation, and storage are offered as services. These services range from arbitrary applications (called Software as a Service, or SaaS) like Google Apps [25], through platforms (denoted as Platform as a Service, or PaaS) such as Google App Engine [26], to physical infrastructures (referred to as Infrastructure as a Service, or IaaS) such as Amazon EC2. For example, IaaS allows cloud users to provision virtual machines (VMs) for their own use. As shown in Figure 16.1, provisioning a VM entails obtaining virtual versions of every physical machine component, including CPU, memory, I/O, and storage. Virtualization

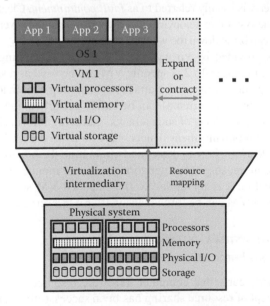

FIGURE 16.1 Provisioning a virtual machine (VM) on a physical system.

makes this possible via a virtualization intermediary known as the hypervisor or the virtual machine monitor (VMM). Examples of leading hypervisors are Xen [9,47] and VMware ESX [59]. Amazon EC2 uses Xen for provisioning user VMs.

16.1.2 ELASTICITY

A major property of the cloud is *elasticity or* the ability to respond quickly to user demands by including or excluding resources for SaaS, PaaS, and/or IaaS, either manually or automatically. As shown in Figure 16.1, virtualization enhances elasticity by allowing providers/users to expand or contract services on the cloud. For instance, Google App Engine automatically expands servers during demand spikes, and contracts them during demand lulls. On the other hand, Amazon EC2 allows users to expand and contract their own virtual clusters either manually (by default) or automatically (using Amazon Auto Scaling [2]). In short, virtualization is a key technology for attaining elasticity on the cloud.

16.1.3 RESOURCE SANDBOXING

A system VM provides a sandbox that can isolate one environment from others, ensuring a level of security that may not be applicable with conventional operating systems (OSs). First, a user running an application on a private machine might be reluctant to move her/his applications to the cloud; unless guarantees are provided that her/his applications and activities cannot be accessed and monitored by any other user on the cloud. Virtualization can greatly serve in offering a safe environment for every user, through which, it is not possible for one user to observe or alter another's data and/or activity. Second, as the cloud can also execute user applications concurrently, a software failure of one application cannot generally propagate to others, if all are running on different VMs. Such a property is usually referred to as *fault containment*. Clearly, this increases the robustness of the system. In a nonvirtualized environment, however, erratic behavior of one application can bring down the whole system.

Sandboxing as provided by virtualization opens up interesting possibilities as well. As illustrated in Figure 16.2, a specific VM can be used as a sandbox whereby security attacks (e.g., denial-of-service attacks or inserting a malicious packet into a legitimate IP communication stream) can be safely permitted and monitored. This can allow inspecting the effects of such attacks, gathering information on their specific behaviors, and replaying them if necessary so as to design a defense against future attacks (by learning how to detect and quarantine them before they can cause any harm). Furthermore, suspicious network packets or input can be sent to a clone (a specific VM) before it is forwarded to the intended VM so as to preclude any potential ill effect. A VM can be thrown away after it has served its purpose.

16.1.4 IMPROVED SYSTEM UTILIZATION AND REDUCED
COSTS AND ENERGY CONSUMPTION

It was observed very early that computer hardware resources are typically underutilized. The concept of resource sharing has been successfully applied in multiprogramming OSs to improve system utilization. Resource sharing in multiprogramming

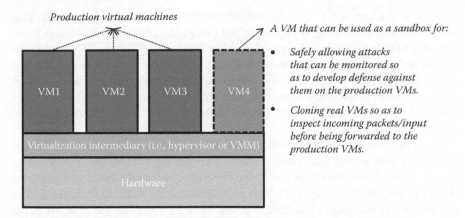

FIGURE 16.2 Using Virtual Sandboxes to develop defenses against attacks and to monitor incoming data.

OSs, however, provides only process abstractions (not systems) that can access resources in parallel. Virtualization takes this step forward by creating an illusion of complete systems, whereby multiple VMs can be supported simultaneously, each running its own system image (e.g., OS) and associated applications. For instance, in virtualized datacenters, seven or more VMs can be provisioned on a single server, providing potentially resource utilization rates of 60% to 80% [8]. In contrast, only 5% to 10% resource utilization rates are accomplished in nonvirtualized datacenters [8]. By enabling multiple VMs on a single physical server, virtualization allows consolidating physical servers into virtual servers that run on many fewer physical servers (a concept referred to as *server consolidation*). Clearly, this can lead not only to improved system utilization but also to reduced costs.

Server consolidation as provided by virtualization leads not only to improved system utilization and reduced costs but further to optimized energy consumption in cloud datacenters. Datacenters hosting cloud applications consume tremendous amounts of energy, resulting in high operational costs and carbon dioxide emissions [11]. Server consolidation is perceived as an effective way to improve the energy efficiency of datacenters via consolidating applications running on multiple physical servers into fewer virtual servers. Idle physical servers can subsequently be switched off so as to decrease energy consumption. Studies show that server consolidation can save up to 20% of datacenter energy consumption [31,53]. A large body of research work illustrates the promise of virtualization in reducing energy consumption in cloud datacenters (e.g., [11–13,31,33,57]). Indeed, mitigating the explosive energy consumption of cloud datacenters is currently deemed as one of the key challenges in cloud computing.

16.1.5 FACILITATING BIG DATA ANALYTICS

The rapidly expanding Information and Communications Technology (ICT) that is permeating all aspects of modern life has led to a massive explosion of data over the last few decades. Major advances in connectivity and digitization of information have led to the creation of ever increasing volumes of data on a daily basis. This data is also diverse, ranging from images and videos (e.g., from mobile phones being uploaded to websites such as Facebook and YouTube), to 24/7 digital TV broadcasts and surveillance footages (e.g., from hundreds of thousands of security cameras), to large scientific experiments (e.g., the Large Hadron Collider [35]), which produces many terabytes of data every single day. IDC's latest Digital Universe Study predicts a 300-fold increase in the volume of data globally, from 130 exabytes in 2012 to 30,000 exabytes in 2020 [23].

Organizations are trying to leverage or, in fact, cope with the vast and diverse volumes of data (or *Big Data*) that is seemingly growing ever so fast. For instance, Google, Yahoo!, and Facebook have gone from processing gigabytes and terabytes of data to the petabyte range [37]. This puts immense pressure on their computing and storage infrastructures that need to be available 24/7 and scale seamlessly as the amount of data produced rises exponentially. Virtualization provides a reliable and elastic environment, which ensures that computing and storage infrastructures can effectively tolerate faults, achieve higher availability and scale as needed to handle large volumes, and varied types of data; especially when the extent of data volumes are not known a priori. This allows efficient reaction to unanticipated demands of Big Data analytics, better enforcement of reliable Quality of Service (QoS) and satisfactory meeting of Service Level Agreements (SLAs). Besides, virtualization facilitates the manageability and portability of Big Data platforms by abstracting data from its underpinnings and removing the dependency from the underlying physical hardware. Lastly, virtualization provides the foundation that enables many of the cloud services to be used either as Big Data analytics or as data sources in Big Data analytics. For instance, Amazon Web Services added a new service, Amazon Elastic MapReduce (EMR), to enable businesses, researchers, data analysts, and developers to easily and cost effectively process Big Data [4]. EMR exploits virtualization and uses Hadoop [28] as an underlying framework hosted on Amazon EC2 and Amazon Simple Storage Service (Amazon S3) [5]. The state-of-the-art Hadoop MapReduce can also be used with Amazon S3, exactly as is the case with Hadoop Distributed File System (HDFS) [24,28].

16.1.6 Mixed-OS Environment

As shown in Figure 16.3 and pointed out in Section 16.1.4, a single hardware platform can support multiple OSs simultaneously. This provides great flexibility for users where they can install their own OSs, libraries, and applications. For instance, a user can install one OS for office productivity tools and another OS for application development and testing, all on a single desktop computer or on the cloud (e.g., on Amazon EC2).

16.1.7 Facilitating Research

Running an OS on a VM allows the hypervisor to instrument accesses to hardware resources and count specific event types (e.g., page faults) or even log detailed information about events' natures, events' origins, and how operations are satisfied.

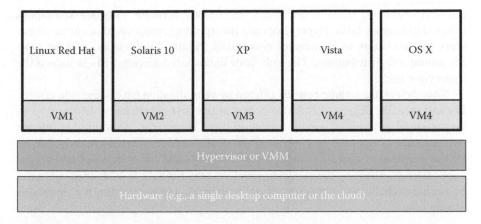

FIGURE 16.3 Mixed-OS environment offered by system virtualization.

Moreover, traces of executions and dumps of machine states at points of interests can be taken at the VM level, an action that cannot be performed on native systems. Lastly, system execution can be replayed on VMs from some saved state for analyzing system behavior under various scenarios. Indeed, the complete state of a VM can be saved, cloned, encrypted, moved, and/or restored again, actions that are not so easy to do with physical machines [15]. As such, it has become quite common for OS researchers to conduct most of their experiments using VMs rather than native hardware platforms [55].

16.2 LIMITATIONS OF GENERAL-PURPOSE OPERATING SYSTEMS

The operating system (OS) binds all hardware resources to a single entity, which is the OS. This limits the flexibility of the system, not only in terms of applications that can run concurrently and share resources but also in terms of isolation. Isolation is crucial in cloud computing with many users sharing the cloud infrastructure. A system is said to provide full isolation when it supports a combination of *fault isolation*, *resource isolation*, and *security isolation* [56]. Fault isolation reflects the ability to limit a buggy program from affecting another program. Complete fault isolation requires no sharing of code or data. Resource isolation corresponds to the ability of enforcing/controlling resource usages of programs. This requires careful allocation and scheduling of resources. Lastly, security isolation refers to the extent at which accesses to logical objects or information (e.g., files, memory addresses, and port numbers) are limited. Security isolation promotes safety where one application cannot reveal information (e.g., names of files or process IDs) to any other application. General-purpose OSs provide a weak form of isolation (only the process abstraction) and not full isolation.

On the other hand, virtualization relaxes physical constraints and enables optimized system flexibility and isolation. Hypervisors allow running multiple OSs side-by-side, yet provide full isolation (i.e., security, resource, and failure isolations). To mention a few, hypervisors can effectively authorize and multiplex accesses to physical resources. Besides, undesired interactions between VMs are sometimes referred to as cross-talks. Hypervisors can incorporate sophisticated resource schedulers and allocators to circumvent cross-talks. Finally, hypervisors offer no sharing among OS distributions. The only code/data shared among VMs is indeed the hypervisor itself.

Nonetheless, the unique benefits offered by virtualization have some side effects. For instance, the degree of isolation comes at the cost of efficiency. Efficiency can be measured in terms of overall execution time. In general, VMs provide inferior performance as opposed to equivalent physical machines. This is mainly due to: (1) the overhead of context switching between VMs and the hypervisor and (2) the duplication of efforts by the hypervisor and the OSs running in VMs (e.g., all might be running schedulers, managing virtual memories, and interpreting I/O requests), among others.

16.3 MANAGING SYSTEM COMPLEXITY

Modern computers are among the most advanced human-engineered structures. These structures are typically very complex. Such complexity stems from incorporating various silicon chips embodied as processors, memories, disks, displays, keyboards, mice, network interfaces, and others, upon which programs are operated and services are offered. The key to managing complexity in computer systems is by dividing system components into levels of abstractions separated by well-defined interfaces.

16.3.1 LEVELS OF ABSTRACTIONS

The first aspect of managing computer complexity is by abstracting computer components. For instance, gates are built on electronic circuits, binary on gates, machine languages on binary, programming languages on machine languages, and operating systems along with associated applications on programming languages. Another abstraction that almost every computer user understands and uses is the file. Files are abstractions of disks. As demonstrated in Figure 16.4, the details of a hard disk are

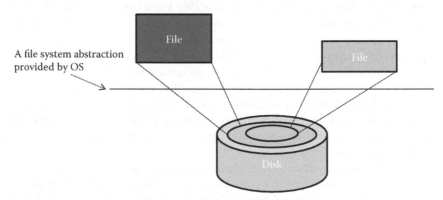

FIGURE 16.4 Files are abstractions of disks.

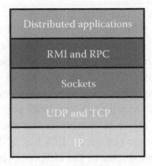

FIGURE 16.5 Abstraction layers in distributed systems.

abstracted by the OS so that disk storage appears to applications as a set of variable-size files. Consequently, programmers need not worry about locations and sizes of cylinders, sectors, and tracks or bandwidth allocations at disk controllers. They can simply create, read, and write files without knowledge of the way the hard disk is constructed or organized.

Another common example of abstraction is the process. Processes are abstractions of CPUs and memories. Hence, programmers need not worry whether their processes will monopolize CPUs or consume full memory capacities. The OS creates and manages all users processes without any involvement from users. Abstractions for displays are also delivered through drawing packages, windowing packages, and the like. Mouse clicks are abstracted as invocations to program functions. Keydown events at keyboards are abstracted as inputs of characters. Finally, abstractions for networks include layers/protocols such as IP, UDP, and TCP. As shown in Figure 16.5, distributed systems (e.g., the cloud) build upon network layers and involve extra ones such as sockets, RMIs, and RPCs, among others. In short, the ability of abstracting system components enables simplified design, programming, and use of computer systems.

To this end, we note that abstractions could be applied at the hardware or software levels. At the hardware level, components are physical (e.g., CPU, RAM). Conversely, at the software level, components are logical (e.g., RMI, RPC). In this chapter, we are most concerned with abstractions at the software or near the hardware/software levels.

16.3.2 WELL-DEFINED INTERFACES

A system (or subsystem) interface is defined as a set of function calls that allows leveraging the underlying systems functionalities without needing to know any of its details. The two most popular interfaces in systems are the Application Programming Interface (API) and the Instruction Set Architecture (ISA) interface. Another interface that is less popular, yet very important (especially in virtualization), is the Application Binary Interface (ABI). API is used by high-level language (HLL) programmers to invoke some library or OS features. An API includes data types, data structures, functions, and object classes, to mention a few. An API enables compliant applications to be ported easily (via recompilation) to any system that supports the same API. As the API deals with software source codes, the ABI is a binary interface. The ABI is essentially a compiled version of the API. Hence, it lies at the machine language level. With ABI, system functionalities are accessed through OS system calls. OS system calls provide a specific set of operations that the OS can perform on behalf of user programs. A source code compiled to a specific ABI can run unchanged only on a system with the same OS and ISA. Finally, ISA defines a set of storage resources (e.g., registers, memory) and a set of instructions that allows manipulating data held at storage resources. ISA lies at the boundary between hardware and software. As discussed later in the chapter, ABI and ISA are important in defining virtual machine types.

16.4   WHAT IS VIRTUALIZATION?

Formally, virtualization involves the construction of an isomorphism that maps a virtual guest system to a real host system [48]. Figure 16.6 illustrates the virtualization process. The function V in the figure maps guest state to host state. For a sequence of operations, e, that modifies a guest state, there is a corresponding sequence of operations, e', in the host that performs equivalent modifications. Informally, virtualization creates virtual resources and maps them to physical resources. Virtual resources are formed based on physical resources and act as proxies to them.

The concept of virtualization can be applied to either a system component or to an entire machine. Traditionally, virtualization has been applied to only the memory component in general purpose OSs, providing what is known as the *virtual memory*. In a revisit to the hard disk example in Figure 16.4, some applications might desire multiple hard drives. To satisfy such a requirement, the physical hard drive can be partitioned into multiple virtual disks as shown in Figure 16.7. Each virtual disk will be offered *logical* cylinders, sectors, and tracks. This keeps the level of detail analogous to what is offered by general-purpose OSs, yet at a different interface and actually without being abstracted. The hypervisor can map (the function V in the isomorphism) a virtual disk to a single large file on the physical disk. Afterwards, to carry a read/write operation on a virtual disk (the function e in the isomorphism), the hypervisor interprets the operation as a file read/write followed by an actual disk read/write (the function e' in the isomorphism).

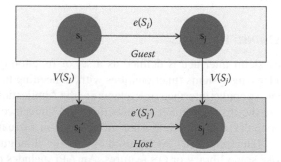

FIGURE 16.6   Virtualization isomorphism.

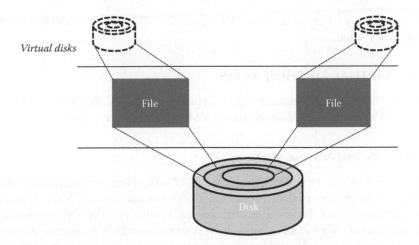

Virtual disks

FIGURE 16.7 Constructing virtual disks by mapping their contents to large files.

As opposed to a single system component, when virtualization is applied to an entire machine, it provides what is known as a *virtual machine* (VM). Specifically, a full set of hardware resources, including processors, memory, and I/O devices will be virtualized to provide the VM. As shown in Figure 16.8, an underlying hardware machine is usually referred to as *host* and an OS running on a VM is denoted as *guest OS*. A VM can only run at a single host at a time. As compared with a host, a VM can have resources different in quantity and in type. For instance, a VM can obtain more processors than what a host offers and can run an ISA that is different than that of the host. Finally, every VM can be booted, shut down, and rebooted just

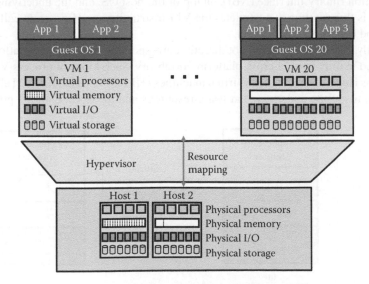

FIGURE 16.8 Virtualization as applied to an entire physical system. An OS running on a VM is referred to as a *guest OS* and every physical machine is denoted as a *host*. Compared to a host, a VM can have virtual resources different in *quantity* and *type*.

like a regular host. Further details on VMs and their different types will be provided in the next section.

16.5 VIRTUAL MACHINE TYPES

There are two main implementations of virtual machines (VMs): *process VMs* and *system VMs*. We will first discuss process VMs and then system VMs.

16.5.1 PROCESS VIRTUAL MACHINES

A process VM is a virtual machine capable of supporting an individual process as long as the process is alive. Figure 16.9a demonstrates process VMs. A process VM terminates when the hosted process ceases. From a process VM perspective, a machine consists of a virtual memory address space, user-level registers and instructions assigned to a single process so as to execute a user program. Based on this definition, a regular process in a general-purpose OS can also be deemed a machine. However, a process in an OS can only support user program binaries compiled for the ISA of the host machine. In other words, executing binaries compiled for an ISA different than that of the host machine cannot be ensued with regular processes. Conversely, a process VM allows that to happen via what is denoted as *emulation*. As shown in Figure 16.10, emulation is the process of allowing the interfaces and functionalities of one system (the source) to be employed on a system with different interfaces and functionalities (the target). Emulation will be discussed in detail in Section 16.6.3. The abstraction of the process VM is provided by a piece of a virtualizing software called the *runtime* (see Figure 16.9a). The runtime is placed at the Application Binary Interface (ABI), on top of the host OS, and the underlying hardware. It is this runtime that emulates the VM instructions and/or system calls when guest and host ISAs are different.

Finally, a process VM may not directly correspond to any physical platform but employed mainly to offer cross-platform portability. Such kinds of process VMs are known as High Level Language virtual machines (HLL VMs). An HLL VM abstracts away details of the underlying hardware resources and the OS and allows programs

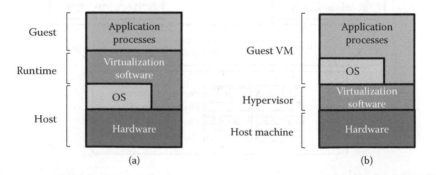

FIGURE 16.9 Virtual machine types: (a) process virtual machines and (b) system virtual machines.

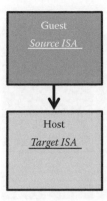

FIGURE 16.10 The emulation process.

to run in the same way on any platform. Java VM (JVM) [36] and Microsoft common language infrastructure (CLI) [42] are examples of HLL VMs. In summary, a process VM is similar to a regular process running on an OS. However, a process VM allows, through emulation, the execution of an application compiled for an ISA different than that of the host machine.

16.5.2 SYSTEM VIRTUAL MACHINES

Contrary to process VMs, a system VM is a virtual machine capable of virtualizing a full set of hardware resources including processors, memories, and IO devices, thus providing a complete system environment. A system VM can support an OS along with its associated processes as long as the system environment is alive. Figure 16.9b illustrates system VMs. As defined previously, the hypervisor (or the virtual machine monitor [VMM]) is a piece of software that provides abstraction for the system VM. It can be placed at the ISA level directly on top of the raw hardware and below system images (e.g., OSs). The hardware resources of the host platform can be shared among multiple guest VMs. The hypervisor manages the allocation of, and access to, the hardware resources to/by the guest VMs. In practice, the hypervisor provides an elegant way to logically isolate multiple guest VMs sharing a single physical infrastructure (e.g., the cloud datacenters). Each guest VM is given the illusion of acquiring the hardware resources of the underlying physical machine.

There are different classes of system VMs. Figure 16.11 exhibits three of these classes as well as traditional systems. In a conventional time-shared system, the OS runs in privileged mode (system mode) while the applications associated with it run in unprivileged mode (user mode) (more details on execution modes will be discussed in Section 16.6.1). With system virtualization, however, the guest OS(s) will run in unprivileged mode while the hypervisor can operate in privileged mode. Such a system is denoted as *native system VM*. In native system VM, every privileged instruction issued by a user program at any guest OS has to trap to the hypervisor. In addition, the hypervisor needs to specify and implement every function required for managing hardware resources. In contrary, if the hypervisor operates in unprivileged mode on top of a host OS, the guest OS(s) will also operate in unprivileged

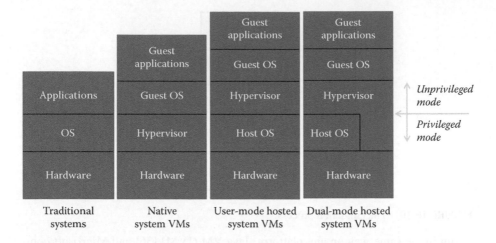

FIGURE 16.11 Different system VM classes.

mode. This system is called *user-mode hosted system VM*. In this case, privileged instructions from guest OS(s) still need to trap to the hypervisor. In return, the hypervisor needs also to trap to the host OS. Clearly, this increases the overhead by adding one more trap per every privileged instruction. Nonetheless, the hypervisor can utilize the functions already available on the host OS to manage hardware resources. Finally, the hypervisor can operate partly in privileged mode and partly in user mode in a system referred to as *dual-mode hosted system VM*. This way, the hypervisor can make use of the host OS's resource management functions and also preclude the one more trap per each privileged instruction incurred in user-mode-hosted system VMs.

16.6 CPU VIRTUALIZATION

Virtualizing a CPU entails two major steps: (1) multiplexing a physical CPU (pCPU) among virtual CPUs (vCPUs) associated with virtual machines (this is usually referred to as vCPU scheduling), and (2) virtualizing the ISA of a pCPU to make vCPUs with different ISAs run on this pCPU. First, we present some conditions for virtualizing ISAs. Second, we describe ISA virtualization. Third, we make distinction between two types of ISA virtualization, full virtualization and paravirtualization. Fourth, we discuss Emulation, a major technique for virtualizing CPUs. Fifth, we recognize between two kinds of VMs: Simultaneous Multiprocessing (SMP) and Uniprocessors (UP) VMs. Finally, we close with a discussion on vCPU scheduling. As examples, we present two popular Xen vCPU schedulers.

16.6.1 The Conditions for Virtualizing ISAs

The key to virtualize a CPU lies in the execution of both privileged and unprivileged instructions issued by guest virtual processors. The set of any processor instructions is documented and provided in the ISA. Besides, special privileges to system resources are permitted by defining modes of operations (or rings) in the ISA. Each

CPU ISA usually specifies two modes of operations, system (or supervisor/kernel/ privileged) mode and user mode (see Figure 16.12a). System mode allows a wide accessibility to system components while user mode restricts such accessibility. In an attempt to provide security and resource isolations, OSs in traditional systems are executed in system mode while associated applications are run in user mode. Some ISAs, however, support more than two rings. For instance, the Intel IA-32 ISA supports four rings (see Figure 16.12b). In traditional systems, when Linux is implemented on an IA-32 ISA, the OS is executed in ring 0 and application processes are executed in ring 3.

A privileged instruction is defined as one that traps in user mode and does not trap in system mode. A trap is a transfer of control to system mode, wherein the hypervisor (as in virtualization) or the OS (as in traditional OSs) performs some action before switching control back to the originating process. Traps occur as side effects of executing instructions. Overall, instructions can be classified into two different categories: *sensitive* and *innocuous*. Sensitive instructions can be either *control-sensitive* or *behavior-sensitive*. Control-sensitive instructions are those that attempt to modify the configuration of resources in a system such as changing the mode of operation or CPU timer. An example of control-sensitive instructions is load processor status word (LPSW) (IBM System/370). LPSW loads the processor status word from a location in memory if the CPU is in system mode and traps otherwise. LPSW contains bits that determine the state of the CPU. For instance, one of these bits is the P bit, which specifies whether the CPU is in user mode or in system mode. If executing this instruction is allowed in user mode, a malicious program can easily change the mode of operation to privileged and obtain control over the system. Hence, to protect the system, such an instruction can only be executed in system mode. Behavior-sensitive instructions are those whose behaviors are determined by the current configuration of resources in a system. An example of behavior-sensitive instructions is Pop Stack into Flags Register (POPF) (Intel IA-32). POPF pops the flag registers from a stack held in memory. One of these flags, known as the interrupt

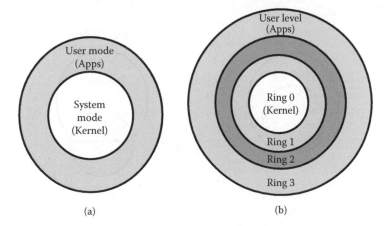

(a) (b)

FIGURE 16.12 System modes of operation (or rings): (a) simple ISAs have two modes of operation and (b) Intel's IA-32 allows four rings.

enable flag, can be altered only in system mode. If POPF is executed in user mode by a program that attempts to pop the interrupt enable flag, POPF will act as a *no-op* (i.e., no operation) instruction. Therefore, the behavior of POPF depends on the mode of operation, thus rendering behavior-sensitive. Finally, if the instruction is neither control-sensitive nor behavior-sensitive, it is innocuous.

According to Popek and Goldberg [48], a hypervisor can be constructed if it satisfies three properties, *efficiency, resource control*, and *equivalence*. Efficiency entails executing all innocuous instructions directly on hardware without any interference from the hypervisor. Resource control suggests that it is not possible for any guest software to change the configuration of resources in a system. Equivalence requires identical behavior of a program running on a VM vs. running on a traditional OS. One exception can be a difference in performance. Popek and Goldberg's proposal (or indeed theorem) implies that a hypervisor can only be constructed if the set of sensitive instructions is a subset of the set of privileged instructions. That is to say, instructions that interfere with the correct functioning of the system (i.e., sensitive instructions such as LPSW) should always trap in user mode. Figure 16.13a illustrates Popek and Goldberg's theorem.

Finally, let us discuss how a trap can be handled in a system. Specifically, we will describe traps in the context of CPU virtualization. Figure 16.14 demonstrates how a hypervisor can handle an instruction trap. The hypervisor's trap handling functions can be divided into three main parts: *dispatcher, allocator*, and a set of *interpreter routines*. First, a privileged instruction traps to the hypervisor's dispatcher. If the hypervisor recognizes that the instruction is attempting to alter system resources, it directs it to the allocator; otherwise, it sends it to a corresponding interpreter routine. The allocator decides how system resources are to be allocated in a nonconflicting manner, and satisfies the instruction's request accordingly. The interpreter routines emulate (more on emulation shortly) the effects of the instruction when operating on virtual resources. When the instruction is fully handled (i.e., done), control is passed

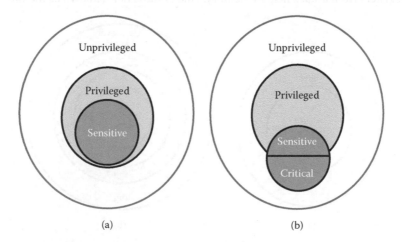

(a)   (b)

FIGURE 16.13 Demonstrating Popek and Goldberg's theorem: (a) satisfies Popek and Goldberg's theorem and (b) does not satisfy Popek and Goldberg's theorem.

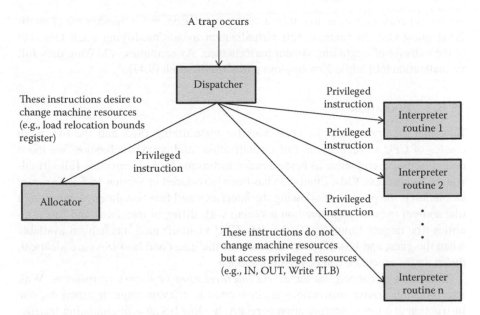

FIGURE 16.14 Demonstrating a trap to a hypervisor. The hypervisor includes three main components, the dispatcher, the allocator, and the interpreter routines.

back to the guest software at the instruction that comes immediately after the one that caused the trap.

16.6.2 Full Virtualization and Paravirtualization

A problem arises when an instruction that is sensitive but unprivileged is issued by a process running on a VM in user mode. According to Popek and Goldberg [48], sensitive instructions have to trap to the hypervisor if executed in user mode. However, as explained earlier, sensitive instructions can be privileged (e.g., LPSW) and unprivileged (e.g., POPF). Unprivileged instructions do not trap to the hypervisor. Instructions that are sensitive and unprivileged are called *critical* (see Figure 16.13b). ISAs that contain critical instructions do not satisfy Popek and Goldberg's theorem. The challenge becomes, can a hypervisor be constructed in the presence of critical instructions? The answer is yes. Nonetheless, Smith and Nair [55] distinguish between a hypervisor that complies with Popek and Goldberg's theorem and one that does not, by referring to the former as a true or efficient hypervisor and to the latter simply as a hypervisor.

A hypervisor can be typically constructed using *full virtualization* and/or *paravirtualization*. Full virtualization emulates all instructions in the ISA. Emulation degrades performance as it implies reproducing the behavior of every source instruction, by first translating it to a target instruction and then running it on a target ISA (we describe emulation in the next section). Paravirtualization deals with critical instructions by modifying guest OSs. Specifically, it entails rewriting every critical instruction as a *hypercall* that traps to the hypervisor. As such, paravirtualization improves performance due to totally avoiding emulation, but at the expense of modifying guest OSs. In contrast, full virtualization avoids modifying guest OSs, but at the expense of degrading system performance. As examples, VMWare uses full virtualization [60] while Xen employs paravirtualization [9,47].

16.6.3 EMULATION

Now that we understand the conditions for virtualizing ISAs and the two main classes of CPU virtualization, full virtualization, and paravirtualization, we move on to discussing emulation as being a major technique for implementing full virtualization and process VMs. Emulation has been introduced in Section 16.5.1. To recap, emulation is the process of allowing the interfaces and functionalities of one system (the source) to be implemented on a system with different interfaces and functionalities (the target). Emulation is the only CPU virtualization mechanism available when the guest and host ISAs are different. If the guest and host ISAs are identical, direct native execution can be possibly applied.

Emulation is carried out either via *interpretation* or *binary translation*. With interpretation, source instructions are converted to relevant target instructions, one instruction at a time. Interpretation is relatively slow because of emulating instructions one by one and not applying any optimization technique (e.g., avoiding the interpretation of an already encountered and interpreted instruction). Binary translation optimizes upon interpretation by converting blocks of source instructions to target instructions and caching generated blocks for repeated use. Typically, a block of instructions is more amenable to optimizations than a single instruction. As compared with interpretation, binary translation is much faster because of applying block caching as well as code optimizations over blocks.

There are three major interpretation schemes, *decode-and-dispatch*, *indirect-threaded*, and *direct-threaded* [55]. Basically, an interpreter should read through the source code instruction by instruction, analyze each instruction, and call relevant routines to generate the target code. This is actually what the decode-and-dispatch interpreter does. Figure 16.15 exhibits a snippet of code for a decode-and-dispatch interpreter used for interpreting the PowerPC ISA. As shown, the interpreter is structured around a central loop and a switch statement. Each instruction is first decoded (i.e., the extract () function) and subsequently dispatched to a corresponding routine, which in return performs the necessary emulation. Clearly, such a decode-and-dispatch strategy results in a number of direct and indirect branch instructions. Specifically, an indirect branch for the switch statement, a branch to an interpreter routine, and a second indirect branch to return from the interpreter routine will be incurred per each instruction. Furthermore, with decode-and-dispatch, every time the same instruction is encountered, its respective interpreter routine is invoked. This, alongside of excessive branches, tend to greatly degrade performance.

As an optimization over decode-and-dispatch, the indirect-threaded interpreter attempts to escape some of the decode-and-dispatch branches by appending (or *threading*) a portion of the dispatch code to the end of each interpreter routine [20,32,34]. This precludes most of the branches incurred in decode-and-dispatch, yet keeps invoking an interpreter routine every time the same instruction is decoded.

```
while (!halt && !interrupt) {
        inst = code [PC];
        opcode = extract(inst, 31, 6);
        switch( opcode ) {
        case LoadWordAndZero: LoadWordAndZero_Routine(inst);
        case ALU: ALU_Routine(inst);
        case Branch; Branch_Routin(inst);
        ....
        ....
        }
}

LoadWordAndZero_Routine(inst){
        RT = extract(inst, 25, 5);
        RA = extract(inst, 20, 5);
        displacement = extract(inst, 15, 16);
        if(RA == 0)
                        source = 0;
        else
                        source = regs[RA];

        address = source + displacement
        regs[RT] = (data[address] << 32) >> 32;
        PC = PC + 4;
}
.....
.....
```

FIGURE 16.15 A snippet of code for a decode-and-dispatch interpreter. Interpreter routines are all omitted except one for the brevity of the presentation. (Example from J. E. Smith and R. Nair, *Virtual Machines: Versatile Platforms for Systems and Processes*, Morgan Kaufmann, 2005.)

To address such a drawback, the direct-threaded interpreter capitalizes on the indirect-threaded one and seeks to interpret a repeated operation only once [10]. This is achieved by saving away the extracted information of instructions in an intermediate form for future references [39]. Although the direct-threaded interpreter improves upon the indirect-threaded one, it limits portability because of the dependency of the intermediate form on the exact locations of the interpreter routines (the addresses of the interpreter routines are saved in the intermediate form). Moreover, the size of the intermediate form is proportional to the original source code, thus resulting in vast memory requirements.

Finally, it has been observed that performance can be significantly enhanced by mapping each individual source binary instruction to its own customized target code [55]. This process of converting the source binary program into a target binary program is referred to as *binary translation* [54]. As pointed out earlier, binary translation suggests improving upon the direct-threaded interpreter by (1) translating a block of source binary instructions to a block of target binary instructions, one at a time, and (2) caching the translated blocks for future use. It is possible to binary translate a program in its entirety before execution. Such a scheme is called *static binary translation* [55]. However, a more general approach is to translate the binary

TABLE 16.1

Qualitative Comparison of Different Emulation Techniques

	Memory Requirements	Start-Up Performance	Steady-State Performance	Code Portability
Decode-and-dispatch interpreter	Low	Fast	Slow	Good
Indirect-threaded interpreter	Low	Fast	Slow	Good
Direct-threaded interpreter	High	Slow	Medium	Medium
Binary translation	High	Very slow	Fast	Poor

instructions during the program execution and interpret new sections of code incrementally as encountered by the program. This mechanism is denoted as *dynamic binary translation* [27,55].

To this end, Table 16.1 qualitatively compares binary translation, decode-and-dispatch, indirect-threaded, and direct-threaded emulation techniques in terms of four metrics, memory requirements, start-up performance, steady-state performance, and code portability (a quantitative performance evaluation can be found in [52]). To exemplify, the decode-and-dispatch interpreter row reads as follows. First, with decode-and-dispatch, memory requirements remain low. This is because of having only one interpreter routine per each instruction type in the target ISA. Alongside, the decode-and-dispatch interpreter averts threading the dispatch code to the end of each routine, thus inherently reduces the pressure on the memory capacity. Second, start-up performance is fast because neither using intermediate forms nor caching translated blocks are adopted. Third, steady-state performance (i.e., the performance after starting up the interpreter) is slow because of (1) the high number of branches and (2) the interpretation of every instruction upon every appearance. Finally, code portability is good since saving addresses of interpreter routines (as is the case with direct-threaded interpreters) and caching ISA-dependent translated binary code are totally avoided.

16.6.4 UNIPROCESSOR AND MULTIPROCESSOR VMs

As described earlier in the chapter, a virtual CPU (vCPU) acts as a proxy to a physical CPU (pCPU). In other words, a vCPU is a representation of a pCPU to a guest OS. A vCPU can be initiated within a VM and mapped to an underlying pCPU by the hypervisor. In principle, a VM can have one or many vCPUs. For instance, a VM in VMWare ESX 4 can have up to 8 vCPUs [61]. This is usually referred to as the *width* of a VM. A VM with a width greater than 1 is denoted as *Symmetric Multiprocessing* (SMP) VM. In contrary, a VM with a width equal to 1 is referred to as *Uniprocessor* (UP) VM. Figure 16.16 demonstrates an SMP native system VM with a width of 4 and a UP native system VM, both running on the same hardware.

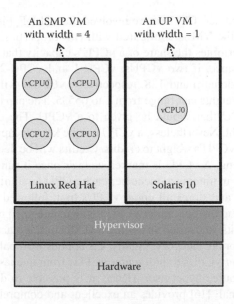

FIGURE 16.16 SMP and UP VMs. A VM is defined whether it is SMP or UP by its width. Width is the number of vCPUs in a VM. If the width of a VM = 1, the VM is UP, otherwise, it is SMP.

Similar to a process on a general-purpose OS, a vCPU can be in different states such as running, ready, and wait states. At a certain point in time, a vCPU can be scheduled by the hypervisor at only a single core (akin to scheduling an OS process at a core). For instance, a UP VM running on a host machine equipped with 2 × Xeon 5405 (i.e., total of 8 pCPUs) will run on only 1 of the 8 available cores at a time. Inherently parallel workloads, such as MapReduce applications, prefer SMP VMs. We next discuss how the hypervisor schedules vCPUs on pCPUs.

16.6.5 VIRTUAL CPU SCHEDULING AND XEN'S SCHEDULERS

General-purpose OSs support two levels of scheduling, process and thread scheduling. With a hypervisor, one extra level of scheduling is added, that is, vCPU scheduling. The hypervisor schedules vCPUs on the underlying pCPU(s), thereby providing each guest VM with a portion of the underlying physical processing capacity.

We *briefly* discuss two popular schedulers from Xen, *Simple Earliest Deadline First* (SEDF) and *Credit Scheduler* (CS) [16,18]. As its name suggests, SEDF is simple, whereby only two parameters, n (the slice) and m (the period), are involved. A VM(or domain U_i in Xen's parlance) can request n every m. SEDF specifies a deadline for each vCPU computed in terms of n and m. The deadline is defined as the *latest time* a vCPU should be scheduled within the period m. For instance, a domain U_i can request $n = 10$ ms and $m = 100$ ms. Accordingly, a vCPU at this domain can be scheduled by SEDF as late as 90 ms into the 100-ms period, yet still meet its deadline. SEDF operates by searching across the set of all runnable vCPUs, held in a queue, and selecting the one with the earliest deadline.

Xen's Credit Scheduler (CS) is more involved than SEDF. First, when creating a VM, each vCPU in the VM is configured with two properties, the *weight* and the *cap*. The weight determines the share of a pCPU's capacity that should be provided to a vCPU. For instance, if two vCPUs, vCPU-1 and vCPU-2 are specified with weights of 256 (the default) and 128, respectively, vCPU-1 will obtain double the shares of vCPU-2. Weights can range from 1 to 65535. The cap determines the total percentage of a pCPU that should be given to a vCPU. The cap can modify the behavior of the weight. Nevertheless, a vCPU can be kept uncapped.

CS converts each vCPU's weight to credits. Credits will be deducted from a vCPU as long as it is running. A vCPU is marked as *over* once it runs out of credits and *under* otherwise. CS maintains a queue per each pCPU (assuming a chip multiprocessors architecture) and stores all *under* vCPUs first, followed by all *over* vCPUs. CS operates by picking the first *under* vCPU in the queue to go next. CS keeps track of each vCPU's credits, and when switching a vCPU out, it places it in the queue at the end of the appropriate category. Finally, CS applies load balancing by allowing a pCPU with no *under* vCPUs to pull *under* vCPUs from queues of other pCPUs.

Xen is an open-source hypervisor. Hence, it is possible to devise and add your own scheduler. Chisnall [16] provides an excellent and comprehensive coverage of Xen's internals as well as step-by-step instructions for adding a new scheduler to Xen.

16.7   MEMORY VIRTUALIZATION

In essence, a VM can be deemed as a generalization of the classical virtual memory concept. Memory virtualization in a system VM is simply an extension to that concept. Virtual memory in traditional systems distinguishes between the virtual (or logical) view of memory as seen by a user program and the actual (or physical) memory as managed by the OS. We next provide a brief overview of virtual memory then delve into memory virtualization in system VMs.

16.7.1   ONE-LEVEL PAGE MAPPING

Virtual memory is a well-known virtualization technique supported in most general-purpose OSs. The basic idea of virtual memory is that each process is provided with its own virtual address space, broken up into chunks called virtual pages. A page is a contiguous range of addresses. As shown in Figure 16.17, virtual memory maps virtual pages to physical pages in what is denoted as a page table. We refer to this as *one-level page mapping* between two types of addresses, the virtual and the physical addresses. Each process in the OS has its own page table. A main observation pertaining to page tables is that not all virtual pages of a process need to be mapped to respective physical pages in order for the process to execute. When a process references a page that exists in the physical memory (i.e., there is a mapping between the requested virtual page and the corresponding physical page), a page hit is said to be attained. Upon a page hit, the requested physical page is fetched from the main memory with no further actions. In contrary, when a process references a page that does not exist in the physical memory, a page miss is said to be incurred. Upon a

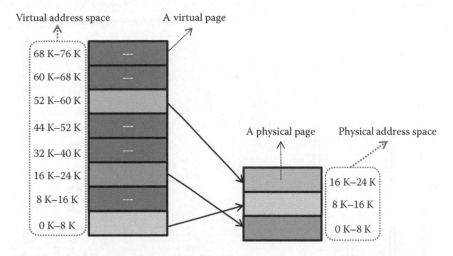

FIGURE 16.17 Mapping a process virtual address space to physical address space. This is captured in what is referred to as a page table. Each process has its own page table.

page miss, the OS is alerted to handle the miss. Subsequently, the OS fetches the missed page from disk storage and updates the relevant entry in the page table.

16.7.2 TWO-LEVEL PAGE MAPPING

Contrary to OSs in traditional systems, with system virtualization, the hypervisor allocates a contiguous addressable memory space for each created VM (not process). This memory space per a VM is usually referred to as *real memory*. In return, each guest OS running in a VM allocates a contiguous addressable memory space for each process within its real memory. This memory space per a process is denoted as *virtual memory* (same name as in traditional systems). Each guest OS maps the virtual memories of its processes to the real memory of the underlying VM, while the hypervisor maps the real memories of its VMs to the system physical memory. Clearly, in contrast to traditional OSs, this entails two levels of mappings between three types of addresses, virtual, real, and physical addresses. In fact, these virtual-to-real and real-to-physical mappings define what is known as system memory virtualization.

Like any general-purpose OS, a guest OS in a system VM would still own its set of page tables. In addition, the hypervisor would own another set of page tables for mapping real to physical addresses. The page tables in the hypervisor are usually referred to as *real map tables*. Figure 16.18 demonstrates system memory virtualization in a native system VM. It shows page tables maintained by guest VMs and real map tables maintained by the hypervisor. Each entry in a page table maps a virtual page of a program to a real page in the respective VM. Likewise, each entry in a real map table maps a real page in a VM to a physical page in the physical memory. When a guest OS attempts to establish a valid mapping entry in its page table, it traps to the hypervisor. Subsequently, the hypervisor establishes a corresponding mapping in the relevant VM's real map table.

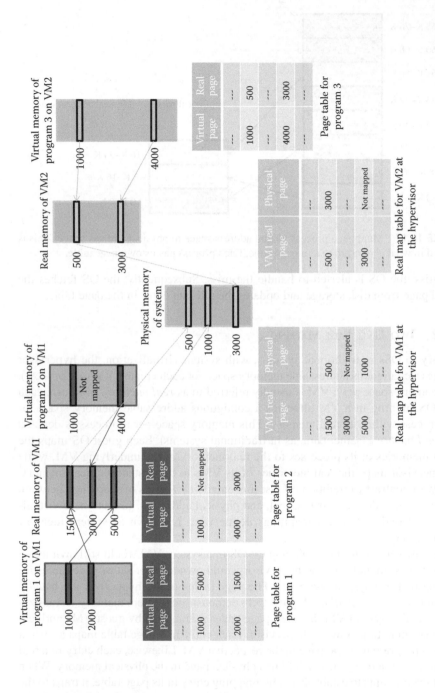

FIGURE 16.18 Memory virtualization in a native system VM. (Example from J. E. Smith and R. Nair, *Virtual Machines: Versatile Platforms for Systems and Processes*, Morgan Kaufmann, 2005.)

16.7.3 MEMORY OVER-COMMITMENT

In system memory virtualization, the combined total size of real memories can grow beyond the actual size of physical memory. This concept is typically referred to as *memory overcommitment* [62]. Memory overcommitment ensures that physical memory is highly utilized by active real memories (assuming multiple VMs running simultaneously). Indeed, without memory overcommitment, the hypervisor can only run VMs with a total size of real memories that is less than that of the physical memory. For instance, Figure 16.19 shows a hypervisor with 4-GB physical memory and 3 VMs, each with 2-GB real memory. Without memory overcommitment, the hypervisor can only run 1 VM, for the fact of not having enough physical memory to assign to 2 VMs at once. Although each VM would require only 2 GB of memory and the hypervisor has 4 GB of physical memory, this cannot be afforded because the hypervisor generally requires overhead memories (e.g., to maintain various virtualization data structures).

To this end, in practical situations, some VMs might be lightly loaded while others might be heavily loaded. Lightly loaded VMs can cause some pages to sit idle, while heavily loaded VMs can result in memory page thrashing. To deal with such situations, the hypervisor can take (or steal) the inactive physical memory pages away from idle VMs and provide them to heavily loaded VMs. As a side note, hypervisors usually write zeros to the stolen/reclaimed inactive physical memory pages to avert information leaking among VMs.

16.7.4 RECLAMATION TECHNIQUES AND VMWARE MEMORY BALLOONING

To maintain full isolation, guest OSs are kept unaware that they are running inside VMs. VMs are also kept unaware of the states of other VMs running on the same physical host. Furthermore, with multiple levels of page mapping, VMs remain oblivious of any physical memory shortage. Therefore, when the hypervisor runs

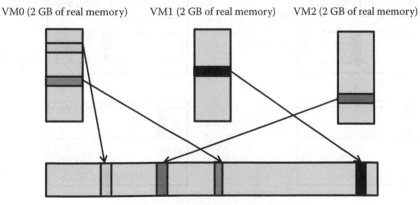

FIGURE 16.19 A hypervisor with 4 GB of physical memory enabling 3 VMs at once with a total of 6 GB of real memory.

multiple VMs at a physical host and the physical memory turns stressed, none of the VMs can automatically help in freeing up memory. The hypervisor deals with the situation by applying a *reclamation technique*. As its name suggests, a reclamation technique attempts to reclaim inactive real memory pages at VMs and make them available for the hypervisor upon experiencing a memory shortage. One popular reclamation technique is *the ballooning process* incorporated in VMWare ESX [62].

In VMWare ESX, a balloon driver must be installed and enabled in each guest OS as a pseudodevice driver. The balloon driver regularly polls the hypervisor through a private channel to obtain a target balloon size. As illustrated in Figure 16.20, when the hypervisor experiences memory shortage, it inflates the balloon by setting a proper target balloon size. Figure 16.20a shows 4 real memory pages mapped to 4 physical pages, out of which only 2 pages are actually active (the red and the yellow ones). Without involving the ballooning process, the hypervisor is unaware of the other 2 inactive pages (the green and the dark blue ones) since they are still mapped to physical pages. Consequently, the hypervisor will not be able to reclaim inactive pages unless getting informed. With memory ballooning, however, the hypervisor can set the balloon target size to an integer number (say 2 or 3). When recognized by the balloon driver at the guest OS, the driver checks out the pages, locates the 2 inactive ones, and pins them (see Figure 16.20b). The pinning process is carried out by the guest OS via ensuring that the pinned pages cannot be read/written by any process during memory reclamation. After pinning the inactive pages, the balloon driver transmits to the hypervisor the addresses of the pinned pages. Subsequently, the hypervisor proceeds safely with reclaiming the respective physical pages and allocating them to needy VMs. Finally, to unpin pinned pages, the hypervisor deflates the balloon by setting a smaller target balloon size, and communicates that to the balloon driver. When received by the balloon driver, it unpins the pinned pages so as the guest OS can utilize them.

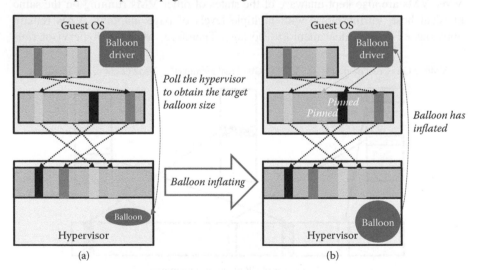

FIGURE 16.20   The ballooning process in VMWare ESX. (a) Two inactive memory pages at the guest OS which can be reclaimed by the hypervisor via inflating the balloon. (b) The guest OS pins the inactive pages (for the hypervisor to reclaim) after recognizing a balloon inflation.

16.8 I/O VIRTUALIZATION

The virtualization strategy for a given I/O device type consists of (1) constructing a virtual version of that device and (2) virtualizing the I/O activity routed to the device. Typical I/O devices include disks, network cards, displays, and keyboards, among others. As discussed previously, the hypervisor might create a virtual display as a window on a physical display. In addition, a virtual disk can be created by assigning to it a fraction of the physical disk's storage capacity. After constructing virtual devices, the hypervisor ensures that each I/O operation is carried out within the bounds of the requested virtual device. For instance, if a virtual disk is allocated 100 cylinders from among 1000 cylinders provided by a physical disk, the hypervisor guarantees that no I/O request intended for that virtual disk can access any cylinder other than the 100 assigned to it. More precisely, the disk location in the issued I/O request will be mapped by the hypervisor to only the area where the virtual disk has been allocated on the physical disk. Next, we will cover some I/O basics and then move on to the details of I/O virtualization.

16.8.1 I/O BASICS

To start with, each I/O device has a device controller. A device controller can be typically signaled either by a *privileged I/O instruction* or *memory-mapped I/O*. I/O instructions are provided by ISAs. Intel-32 is an example of a processor that provides I/O instructions within its ISA. Many recent processors, however, allow performing I/O between the CPU and the device controllers through memory-mapped I/O (e.g., RISC processors). As shown in Figure 16.21, with memory-mapped I/O, a specific region of the physical memory address space is reserved for accessing I/O

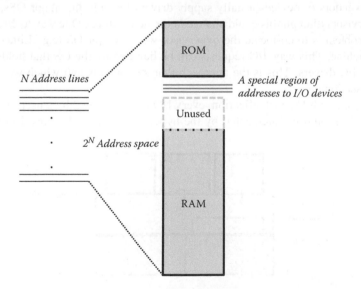

FIGURE 16.21 Memory-mapped I/O with a specific region in the RAM address space for accessing I/O devices.

devices. These addresses are recognized by the memory controller as commands to I/O devices and do not correspond to memory physical locations. Different memory-mapped addresses are used for different I/O devices. Lastly, to protect I/O devices, both I/O instructions and memory-mapped addresses are handled in system mode, thus becoming privileged.

Because I/O operations are executed in system mode, user programs can only invoke them through OS system calls (assuming traditional systems). The OS abstracts most of the details of I/O devices and makes them accessible through only well-defined interfaces. Figure 16.22 shows the three major interfaces that come into play when a user program places an I/O request. These are the *system call interface*, the *device driver interface*, and the *operation level interface*. Starting an I/O operation, a user I/O request causes an OS system call that transfers control to the OS. Next, the OS calls device drivers (a set of software routines) via the device driver interface. A relevant device driver routine converts the I/O request to an operation specific to the requested physical device. The converted operation is subsequently carried through the operation level interface to the corresponding physical device.

16.8.2 VIRTUALIZING I/O DEVICES

I/O virtualization allows a single physical I/O device to be shared by more than one guest OS. Figure 16.23 demonstrates multiple guest OSs in native system VMs sharing a single hardware machine. As shown, the hypervisor constructs virtual devices from physical devices. A main observation is that both the guest OSs and the hypervisor must have device drivers encapsulating the interfaces to the devices. This means that with virtualization, two different device drivers must be supported per each device, versus only one without virtualization [21]. In reality, this is a problem because vendors of devices usually supply drivers for only the major OSs, but not for hypervisors (though this could change in the near future). One way to circumvent such a problem is to co-locate the hypervisor with a major OS (e.g., Linux) on the same machine. This way, I/O requests can be handled by the OS that holds all the requisite I/O drivers. This is the approach that Xen adopts and which we detail in the next section.

Moreover, with I/O virtualization, every I/O request issued by a user program at a guest VM should be intercepted by the hypervisor. This is because I/O requests

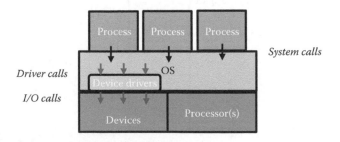

FIGURE 16.22 The three major interfaces involved in I/O operations, system call, device driver, and operation-level interfaces.

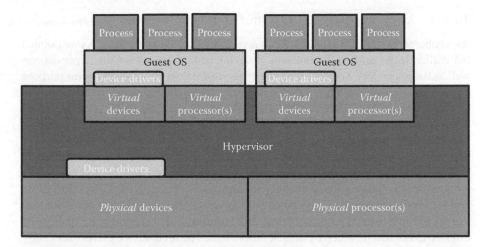

FIGURE 16.23 Logical locations of device drivers within multiple guest OSs in native system VMs sharing a single hardware machine.

are all sensitive, thus need to be controlled by the hypervisor. Clearly, this would necessitate a trap to the hypervisor per every I/O request. I/O requests are all privileged, whether issued using I/O instructions or memory-mapped I/O, hence, they are not critical instructions and can naturally trap to the hypervisor. In principle, the hypervisor can intercept I/O requests at any of the three interfaces: the system call interface, the device driver interface, or the operation level interface.

If the hypervisor intercepts an I/O request at the operation level interface, some essential information about the I/O action might be lost. In particular, when an I/O request arrives at the device driver interface, it might get transformed into a sequence of instructions. For instance, a disk write is usually transformed into multiple store instructions, thus when received at the operation level interface, it becomes difficult on the hypervisor to identify the instructions as belonging to a single write request. As such, intercepting I/O requests at the operation level interface is typically avoided. In contrast, intercepting an I/O request at the device driver interface allows the hypervisor to efficiently map the request to the respective physical device and transmit it via the operation level interface. Clearly, this is a natural point to virtualize I/O devices; yet would oblige hypervisor developers to learn about all the device driver interfaces of various guest OSs so as to encode the approach. Finally, intercepting I/O requests at the system call interface (i.e., the ABI), might theoretically make the I/O virtualization process easier, whereby every I/O request can be entirely handled by the hypervisor (the solo controller in this case). To achieve that, however, the hypervisor has to emulate the ABI routines of every guest OS (different OSs have different ABI routines). Consequently, hypervisor developers need again to learn about the internals of every potential guest OS. Alongside, emulating ABI routines can degrade system performance due to the overhead imposed by the emulation process. To this end, intercepting I/O requests at the device driver interface is usually the most efficient approach, thus normally followed.

16.8.3   XEN'S APPROACH TO I/O VIRTUALIZATION

As a concrete example, we discuss Xen's approach to I/O virtualization. As we pointed out earlier, to get around the problem of having device drivers for the hypervisor as well as the guest OSs, Xen co-locates its hypervisor with a traditional general-purpose OS. Figure 16.24 shows a host OS and the Xen hypervisor executing in full privileges at ring 0. In contrary, guest OSs run unprivileged at ring 1, while all processes at all domains (i.e., virtual machines) run unprivileged at ring 3, assuming a system with four rings (e.g., Intel-32). On systems with only two levels of privileges, the hypervisor and the host OS can execute in system mode, while domains and processes can execute in user mode. As illustrated in the figure, Xen eliminates the device drivers entirely from guest OSs and provides a direct communication between guest OSs at domain U_i and the host OS at domain 0 [21]. More precisely, every domain U_i in Xen will exclude virtual I/O devices and relevant drivers. I/O requests will accordingly be transferred directly to domain 0, which by default hosts all the required device drivers necessary to satisfy any I/O request. For instance, rather than using a device driver to control a virtual Network Card Interface (vNIC), with Xen, network frames/packets are transmitted back and forth via event channels between domain U_i and domain 0, using NIC front-end and back-end interfaces, respectively (see Figure 16.24). Likewise, no virtual disk is exposed to any guest OS and all disk data blocks incurred by file reads and writes are delegated by the Xen hypervisor to domain 0.

16.8.4   A TAXONOMY OF VIRTUALIZATION SUITES

To this end, we briefly survey some of the current and common virtualization software suites. We distinguish between virtualization suites and hypervisors; many vendors often use these terms interchangeably. As discussed throughout this chapter, a hypervisor is mainly responsible for running multiple virtual machines (VMs) on a single physical host. On the other hand, a virtualization suite comprises of various software components and individual hypervisors that enable the management of many physical hosts and VMs. A management component typically issues commands to the hypervisor to create, destroy, manage, and migrate VMs across multiple physical hosts. Table 16.2 shows our taxonomy of four virtualization suites, vSphere 5.1 [59], Hyper-V [43], XenServer 6 [17], and RHEV 3 [50]. We compare the suites in terms of multiple features including the involved hypervisor, the virtualization type, the allowable maximum number of vCPUs per a VM, the allowable maximum memory size per a VM, and whether memory overcommitment, page sharing, and live migration are supported. In addition, we indicate whether the involved hypervisors contain device drivers, and list some of the popular cloud vendors that utilize such hypervisors. To elaborate on some of the features, live migration allows VMs to be seamlessly shifted from one VM to another. It enables many management features like maintenance, power-efficient dynamic server consolidation, and workload balancing, among others. Page Sharing refers to sharing identical memory pages across VMs. This renders effective when VMs use similar OS instances. Lastly, some hypervisors eliminate entirely device drivers at guest OSs and provide direct communications between guest OSs and host OSs co-located with hypervisors (similar to what we discussed in Section 16.8.3 about the Xen hypervisor).

TABLE 16.2

Comparison between Different Virtualization Suites

Feature	vSphere 5.1	Hyper-V 2012	XenServer 6	RHEV 3
Hypervisor name	ESXi	Hyper-V	Xen	KVM
CPU virtualization support	Full virtualization	Para-virtualization	Para-virtualization	Full virtualization
Maximum vCPUs per VM	160	320	64	160
Maximum memory per VM	1 TB	1 TB	128 GB	2 TB
Memory overcommitment support	Yes	Yes	Yes	Yes
Page sharing support	Yes	No	No	No
Live migration support	Yes	Yes	Yes	Yes
Contains device drivers	Yes	No	No	Yes
Common cloud vendors(s)	vCloud Hybrid Service [58]	Microsoft Azure [41]	Amazon EC2 [3] and Rackspace [49]	IBM SmartCloud [29]

16.9   CASE STUDY: AMAZON ELASTIC COMPUTE CLOUD

Amazon Elastic Compute Cloud (Amazon EC2) is a vital part of Amazon's cloud computing platform, Amazon Web Services (AWS). On August 25, 2006 Amazon launched EC2, which together with Amazon Simple Storage Service (Amazon S3), marked the change in the way IT was done. Amazon EC2 is a highly reliable and scalable Infrastructure as a Service (IaaS) with a utility payment model. It allows users to rent virtual machines (VMs) and pay for the resources that they actually consume. Users can set up and configure everything in their VMs, ranging from the operating system up to any application. Specifically, a user can boot an Amazon Machine Image (AMI) to create a VM, referred in Amazon's parlance as an *instance*. AMI is a virtual appliance (or a VM image) that contains user's operating system, applications, libraries, data, and associated configuration settings.

Users can create EC2 instances either via using default AMIs prepackaged by Amazon or via developing their own AMIs using Amazon's bundling tools. Default AMIs are preconfigured with an ever-growing list of operating systems including Red Hat Enterprise Linux, Windows Server, and Ubuntu, among others. A wide selection of free software provided by Amazon can also be directly incorporated within AMIs and executed over EC2 instances. For example, Amazon provides software for databases (e.g., Microsoft SQL [44]), application servers (e.g., Tomcat JavaWeb Application [7]), content management (e.g., MediaWiki [40]), and business intelligence (e.g., Jasper Reports [30]). Added to the wide assortment of free software, Amazon services (e.g., Amazon Relational Database Service, which supports

MySQL [45], Oracle [46], and Microsoft SQL databases) can be further employed in conjunction with EC2 instances. Finally, users can always configure, install, and run at any time any compatible software on EC2 instances, exactly as is the case with regular physical machines. We next discuss the virtualization technology that Amazon underlies EC2.

16.9.1 AMAZON EC2 VIRTUALIZATION TECHNOLOGY

Amazon EC2 demonstrates the power of cloud computing. Under the hood, it is a marvel of technology. As of March 2012, it presumably hosts around 7100 server racks with a total of 454,400 blade servers, assuming 64 blade servers per rack [38]. Above its datacenters, Amazon EC2 presents a true virtualization environment using the Xen hypervisor. Xen is a leading example of system virtualization, initially developed as part of the Xenoserver project at the Computer Laboratory, Cambridge University [18]. Currently, Xen is maintained by an open-source community [63]. The goal of Xen is to provide IaaS with full isolation and minimal performance overhead on conventional hardware. As discussed previously in the chapter, Xen is a native hypervisor that runs on bare metal at the most privileged CPU state. Amazon EC2 utilizes a *highly customized version of Xen* [6], supposedly to provision and isolate user instances rapidly, consolidate instances so as to improve system utilization, tolerate software and hardware failures by saving and migrating instances, and apply system load balancing through live and seamless migration of instances, to mention a few.

Amazon EC2 instances can be created, launched, stopped, and terminated as needed. Such instances are system VMs composed of virtualized (or paravirtualized) sets of physical resources including CPU, memory, and I/O components. To create instances, Xen starts a highly privileged instance (*domain 0*) at a host OS out of which other user instances (*domain U_i*) can be instantiated with guest OSs (see Figure 16.24). As host OSs, Novell's SUSE Linux Enterprise Server, Solaris and OpenSolaris, NetBSD, Debian, and Ubuntu, among others, can be used. It is not known, however, which among these host OSs Amazon EC2 supports. On the other hand, Linux, Solaris and OpenSolaris, FreeBSD, and NetBSD can be employed as guest OSs, to mention a few. Among the guest OSs that Amazon EC2 supports are Linux, OpenSolaris, andWindows Server 2003 [66]. Amazon EC2's guest OSs are run at a lesser privileged ring as opposed to the host OS and the hypervisor. Clearly, this helps isolating the hypervisor from guest OSs and guest OSs from each other, a key requirement on Amazon AWS's cloud platform. Nonetheless, running guest OSs in unprivileged mode violates the usual assumption that OSs must run in system mode. To circumvent consequent ramifications, Xen applies a paravirtualized approach, where guest OSs are modified to run at a downgraded privileged level. As a result, sensitive instructions are enforced to trap to the hypervisor for verification and execution. Linux instances (and most likely OpenSolaris) on Amazon EC2 use Xen's paravirtualized mode, and it is conjectured also that Windows instances do so [14,66]. Upon provisioning instances, Xen provides each instance with its own vCPU(s) and associated ISA. As discussed in Section 16.6, the complexity of this step depends entirely on the architecture of the underlying pCPU(s). To this end, it is

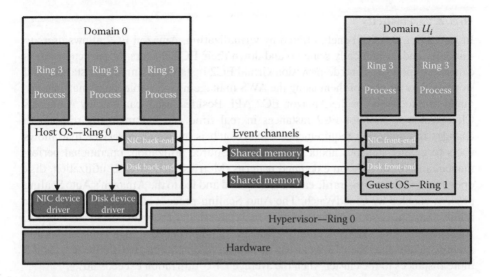

FIGURE 16.24 Xen's approach to I/O virtualization assuming a system with four rings (e.g., Intel-32). Xen co-locates the hypervisor with a host OS on the physical platform to borrow the host OS's device drivers and avoid coding them within the hypervisor. This makes the hypervisor thinner and accordingly more reliable. Besides, it makes it easier on the hypervisor developers.

not clear what vCPU scheduler Amazon EC2 applies, but Xen's default scheduler is the Credit Scheduler (see Section 16.6.5). It is suspected though that Amazon EC2 has a modified version of the Credit Scheduler [66].

Memory and I/O resources are virtualized in Xen in a way similar to what is described in Sections 16.7.2 and 1.8.3, respectively. First, Xen uses a two-level page mapping method. Second, the hardware page tables are allocated and managed by guest OSs, with a minimal involvement from the hypervisor [9]. Specifically, guest OSs can read directly from hardware page tables, but writes are intercepted and validated by the Xen hypervisor to ensure safety and isolation. For performance reasons, however, guest OSs can batch write requests to amortize the overhead of passing by the hypervisor per every write request. Finally, with Xen, existing hardware I/O devices are not emulated as is typically done in fully virtualized environments. In contrast, I/O requests are always transferred from user instances to domain 0 and vice versa, using a shared memory communication paradigm as demonstrated in Figure 16.24. At domain 0, device drivers of the host OS are borrowed to handle the I/O requests.

16.9.2 AMAZON EC2 PROPERTIES

Amazon EC2 is characterized with multiple effective properties, some that are stemmed naturally from its underlying virtualization technology and others that are employed specifically for the AWS cloud computing platform to meet certain performance, scalability, flexibility, security, and reliability criteria. We next concisely discuss some of these properties.

16.9.2.1 Elasticity

In leveraging a major benefit offered by virtualization, Amazon EC2 allows users to statically and dynamically scale up and down their EC2 clusters. In particular, users can always provision and de-provision virtual EC2 instances by manually starting and stopping any number of them using the AWS management console, the Amazon command line tools and/or the Amazon EC2 API. Besides, users can employ Amazon's CloudWatch to monitor EC2 instances in real time and automatically respond to changes in computing requirements. CloudWatch is an Amazon service that allows users to collect statistics about their cluster resource utilization, operational performance, and overall resource demand patterns. Metrics such as CPU utilization, disk operations, and network traffic can be aggregated and fed to the Amazon's Auto Scaling process enabled by CloudWatch. The Auto Scaling process can subsequently add or remove instances so as performance is maintained and costs are saved. In essence, Auto Scaling allows users to closely follow the demand curve of their applications and synergistically alter their EC2 clusters according to conditions they define (e.g., add 3 more instances to the cluster when the average CPU utilization exceeds 80%).

16.9.2.2 Scalability and Performance

Amazon EC2 instances can scale to more than 255 pCPUs per host [65], 128 vCPUs per guest, 1 TB of RAM per host, up to 1 TB of RAM per unmodified guest and 512 GB of RAM per paravirtualized guest [64]. In addition, Amazon EC2 reduces the time needed to boot a fresh instance to seconds, thus expediting scalability as the needs for computing varies. To optimize performance, Amazon EC2 instances are provided in various resource capacities that can suit different application types, including CPU-intensive, memory-intensive and I/O-intensive applications (see Table 16.3). The vCPU capacity of an instance is expressed in terms of Elastic Compute Units (ECU). Amazon EC2 uses ECU as an abstraction of vCPU capacity whereby one ECU provides the equivalence of a 1.0–1.2 GHz 2007 Opteron or 2007 Xeon processor [3]. Different instances with different ECUs provide different application runtimes. The performances of instances with identical type and ECUs may also vary as a result of what is denoted in cloud computing as performance variation [22,51].

16.9.2.3 Flexibility

Amazon EC2 users are provided with complete control over EC2 instances, with a root access to each instance. They can create AMIs with software of their choice and apply many of Amazon services, including Amazon Simple Storage Service (Amazon S3), Amazon Relational Database Service (Amazon RDS), Amazon SimpleDB, and Amazon Simple Queue Service (Amazon SQS), among others. These services and the various available Amazon EC2 instance types can jointly deliver effective solutions for computing, query processing and storage across a wide range of applications. For example, users running I/O-intensive applications like data warehousing and Hadoop MapReduce [19,28] can exploit High Storage instances. On the other hand, for tightly coupled, network-intensive applications users can utilize high-performance computing (HPC) clusters.

In addition, users have the flexibility to choose among multiple storage types that can be associated with their EC2 instances. First, users can rent EC2 instances

TABLE 16.3

Amazon EC2 Instance Types as of March 4, 2013

Instance Type	Instance Name	CPU Capacity	Memory Size	Storage Size and Type	Platform
Standard	M1 Small	1 vCPU with 1 ECU	1.7 GB	160-GB local storage	32-bit or 64-bit
	M1 Medium	1 vCPU with 2 ECUs	3.75 GB	410-GB local storage	32-bit or 64-bit
	M1 Large	2 vCPUs, each with 2 ECUs	7.5 GB	850-GB local storage	64-bit
	M1 Extra large	4 vCPUs, each with 2 ECUs	15 GB	1690-GB local storage	64-bit
	M3 Extra large	4 vCPUs, each with 3.25 ECUs	15 GB	EBS storage only	64-bit
	M3 Double extra large	8 vCPUs, each with 3.25 ECUs	30 GB	EBS storage only	64-bit
Micro	Micro	Up to 2 ECUs	613 MB	EBS storage only	32-bit or 64-bit
High memory	Extra large	2 vCPUs, each with 3.25 ECUs	17.1 GB	420-GB local storage	64-bit
	Double extra large	4 vCPUs, each with 3.25 ECUs	34.2 GB	850-GB local storage	64-bit
	Quadruple extra large	8 vCPUs, each with 3.25 ECUs	68.4 GB	1690-GB local storage	64-bit
High CPU	Medium	2 vCPUs, each with 2.5 ECUs	1.7 GB	350-GB local storage	32-bit or 64-bit
	Extra large	8 vCPUs, each with 2.5 ECUs	7 GB	1690-GB local storage	64-bit
Cluster compute	Eight extra large	88 ECUs	60.5 GB	3370-GB local storage	64-bit and 10-Gb Ethernet
High memory cluster	Eight extra large	88 ECUs	244 GB	240-GB local storage	64-bit and 10-Gb Ethernet
Cluster GPU	Quadruple extra large	33.5 ECUs 2 × NVIDIA Tesla Fermi M2050 GPUs	22 GB	1690-GB local storage	64-bit and 10-Gb Ethernet
High I/O	Quadruple extra large	35 ECUs	60.5 GB	2 × 1024 GB SSD-based local storage	64-bit and 10-Gb Ethernet
High storage	Eight extra large	35 ECUs	117 GB	24 × 2 TB hard disk drive local storage	64-bit and 10-Gb Ethernet

with *local instance-store disks* as root devices. Instance-store volumes are volatile storages and cannot survive stops and terminations. Second, EC2 instances can be attached to Elastic Block Storages (EBS), which provide raw block devices. The block devices can then be formatted and mounted with any file system at EC2 instances. EBS volumes are persistent storages and can survive stops and terminations. EBS volumes of sizes from 1 GB to 1 TB can be defined and RAID arrays can be created by combining two or more volumes. EBS volumes can even be attached or detached from instances while they are running. They can also be moved from one instance to another, thus rendering independent of any instance. Finally, applications running on EC2 instances can access Amazon S3 through a defined API. Amazon S3 is a storage that makes web-scale computing easier for developers, whereby any amount of data can be stored and retrieved at any time and from anywhere on the web [5].

To this end, Amazon EC2 users do not only have the flexibility of choosing among many instance and storage types, but further have the capability of mapping elastic IP addresses to EC2 instances, without a network administrator's help or the need to wait for DNS to propagate new bindings. Elastic IP addresses are static IP addresses, but tailored for the dynamicity of the cloud. For example, unlike a traditional static IP address, an Elastic IP address enables tolerating an instance failure by program-matically remapping the address to any other healthy instance under the same user account. Thus, Elastic IP addresses are associated with user accounts and not EC2 instances. Elastic IP addresses exist until explicitly removed and persist even while accounts have no current running instances.

16.9.2.4 Fault Tolerance

Amazon EC2 users are capable of placing instances and storing data at multiple locations represented as *regions* and *availability zones*. As shown in Figure 16.25, a region can consist of one or many availability zones and an availability zone can consist of typically many blade servers. Regions are independent collections of AWS resources that are geographically dispersed to avoid catastrophic disasters. An

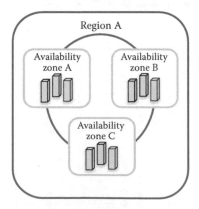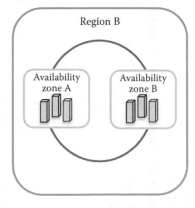

FIGURE 16.25 Regions and availability zones in AWS cloud platform. Regions are geographically dispersed to avoid disasters. Availability zones are engineered as autonomous failure zones within regions.

availability zone is a distinct location in a region designed to act as an autonomous failure zone. Specifically, an availability zone does not share a physical infrastructure with other availability zones, thus limiting failures from transcending its own boundaries. Furthermore, when a failure occurs, automated AWS processes start moving customer application traffic away from the affected zone [6]. Consequently, applications that run in more than one availability zone across regions can inherently achieve higher availability and minimize downtime. Amazon EC2 guarantees 99.95% availability per each Region [3].

Lastly, EC2 instances that are attached to Amazon EBS volumes can attain improved durability over EC2 instances with local stores (or the so-called ephemeral storage). Amazon EBS volumes are automatically replicated in the backend of a single Availability Zone. Moreover, with Amazon EBS, point-in-time consistent snapshots of EBS volumes can be created and reserved in Amazon S3. Amazon S3 storage is automatically replicated across multiple availability zones and not only in a single availability zone. Amazon S3 helps maintain the durability of users' data by quickly detecting and repairing losses. Amazon S3 is designed to provide 99.999999999% durability and 99.99% availability of data over a given year [6]. A snapshot of an EBS volume can also serve as the starting point for a new EBS volume in case the current one fails. Therefore, with the availability of regions and availability zones, the virtualized environment provided by Xen, and the Amazon's EBS and S3 services, Amazon EC2 users can achieve long-term protection, failure isolation, and reliability.

16.9.2.5 Security

Security within Amazon EC2 is provided at multiple levels. First, as pointed out earlier, EC2 instances are completely controlled by users. Users have full root access or administrative control over their instances, accounts, services, and applications. AWS does not have any access rights to user instances and cannot log into their guest OSs [6]. Second, Amazon EC2 provides a complete firewall solution, whereby the default state is to deny all incoming traffic to any user instance. Users must explicitly open ports for specific inbound traffic. Third, API calls to start/stop/terminate instances, alter firewall configurations and perform other related functions are all signed by the user's Amazon Secret Access Key. Without the Amazon Secret Access Key, API calls on Amazon EC2 instances cannot be made. Fourth, the virtualized environment provided by Xen provides a clear security separation between EC2 instances and the hypervisor as they run at different privileged modes. Fifth, the AWS firewall is placed within the hypervisor, between the physical network interface and the virtual interfaces of instances. Hence, as packet requests are all privileged, they must trap to the hypervisor and accordingly pass through the AWS firewall. Consequently, any two communicating instances will be treated as separate virtual machines on the Internet, even if they are placed on the same physical machine. Finally, as Amazon EBS volumes can be associated with EC2 instances, their accesses are restricted to the AWS accounts that created the volumes. This indirectly denies all other AWS accounts (and corresponding users) from viewing and accessing the volumes. We note, however, that this does not impact the flexibility of sharing data on the AWS cloud platform. In particular, users can still create Amazon S3 snapshots of their Amazon EBS volumes and share them with other AWS accounts/users. Nevertheless, only the users who own the volumes will be allowed to delete or alter EBS snapshots.

16.10 SUMMARY

In this chapter, we first motivated the case of why virtualization is important in cloud computing. We discussed various key properties required by the cloud and offered by virtualization such as elasticity, resource sandboxing, enhanced system utilization, reduced costs, optimized energy consumption, facilitated Big Data analytics, and mixed-OS environment. Next, we discussed the limitations of general-purpose OSs for acting as sole enablers for cloud computing. Specifically, we described OS limitations pertaining to flexibility, fault isolation, resource isolation and security isolation. Before delving into further details about virtualization, we introduced two major strategies for managing complexity in computer systems (which are necessary for virtualizing cloud resources), abstracting the system stack, and specifying well-defined interfaces. Afterwards, we formally defined virtualization and presented two main implementations of virtual machines (VMs), process VMs, and system VMs.

To this end, we started describing how various physical components can be virtualized and encompassed within VMs. We began with the CPU component whereby we discussed the conditions for virtualizing CPUs and investigated different techniques for virtualizing CPUs such as paravirtualization and emulation. We closed the discussion on CPU virtualization with a real example from Xen, a popular virtualization hypervisor employed by Amazon's cloud computing platform, Amazon Web Services (AWS). Subsequently, we introduced system memory virtualization and detailed how virtual memory in the contexts of OSs and hypervisors can be constructed. In particular, we examined the one-level and the two-level page mapping techniques for creating virtual memories in OSs and hypervisors, respectively. As a side effect of virtual memory, we identified the memory overcommitment problem and presented a solution from VMWare ESX, the memory ballooning reclamation technique. Next we explored I/O virtualization. We commenced with a brief introduction on some I/O basics and debated on the pros and cons of virtualizing I/O operations at the system call, device driver, and operation level interfaces. As a practical example, Xen's approach to I/O virtualization was described. Finally, we wrapped up our discussion on virtualizing resources for the cloud with a case study, Amazon Elastic Compute Cloud (Amazon EC2), a vital part of Amazon's AWS. Specifically, we discussed the underlying virtualization technology of Amazon EC2 and some of its major characteristics including elasticity, scalability, performance, flexibility, fault tolerance, and security.

REFERENCES

1. A History of Cloud Computing, http://www.cloudtweaks.com/2011/02/a-history-of-cloud-computing/.
2. Amazon Auto Scaling, http://aws.amazon.com/autoscaling/.
3. Amazon Elastic Compute Cloud, http://aws.amazon.com/ec2/.
4. Amazon Elastic MapReduce, http://aws.amazon.com/elasticmapreduce/.

5. Amazon Simple Storage Service, http://aws.amazon.com/s3/.
6. Amazon, Amazon Web Services: Overview of Security Processes, *Amazon Whitepaper*, 2011.
7. Apache Tomcat, http://tomcat.apache.org/.
8. M. Bailey, The Economics of Virtualization: Moving Toward an Application-Based Cost Model, *VMware Sponsored Whitepaper*, 2009.
9. P. Barham, B. Dragovic, K. Fraser, S. Hand, T. Harris, A. Ho, R. Neugebauer, I. Pratt and A. Warfield, Xen and the Art of Virtualization, *SOSP*, 2003.
10. J. R. Bell, Threaded Code, *Communications of the ACM*, 1973.
11. A. Beloglazov and R. Buyya, Energy Efficient Allocation of Virtual Machines in Cloud Data Centers, *CCGrid*, 2010.
12. A. Beloglazov, J. Abawajy and R. Buyya, Energy-Aware Resource Allocation Heuristics for Efficient Management of Data Centers for Cloud Computing, *Future Generation Computer Systems*, 2012.
13. A. Berl, E. Gelenbe, M. Di Girolamo, G. Giuliani, H. De Meer, M. Q. Dang and K. Pentikousis, Energy-Efficient Cloud Computing, *The Computer Journal*, 2010.
14. C. Boulton, Novell, Microsoft Outline Virtual Collaboration, *Serverwatch*, 2007.
15. P. M. Chen and B. D. Nobel, When Virtual Is Better Than Real, *HOTOS*, 2001.
16. D. Chisnall, *The Definitive Guide to the Xen Hypervisor*, 1st Edition, Prentice Hall, 2007.
17. Citrix XenServer 6 Platinum Edition, http://support.citrix.com/product/xens/v6.0/.
18. G. Coulouris, J. Dollimore, T. Kindberg and G. Blair, *Distributed Systems: Concepts and Design*, 5 Edition, Addison-Wesley, 2011.
19. J. Dean and S. Ghemawat, MapReduce: Simplified Data Processing On Large Clusters, *OSDI*, 2004.
20. R. B. K. Dewar, Indirect Threaded Code, *Communications of the ACM*, 1975.
21. T. W. Doeppner, *Operating Systems In Depth: Design and Programming*, 1st Edition, Wiley, 2010.
22. B. Farley, V. Varadarajan, K. Bowers, A. Juels, T. Ristenpart and M. Swift, More for Your Money: Exploiting Performance Heterogeneity in Public Clouds, *SOCC*, 2012.
23. J. Gantz and D. Reinsel, The Digital Universe in 2020, *IDC Whitepaper*, 2012.
24. S. Ghemawat, H. Gobioff and S. T. Leung, The Google File System, *SOSP*, October 2003.
25. Google Apps. https://developers.google.com/google-apps/.
26. Google App Engine. https://developers.google.com/appengine/.
27. M. Gschwind, E. R. Altman, S. Sathaye, P. Ledak and D. Appenzeller, Dynamic and Transparent Binary Translation, *IEEE Computer*, 2000.
28. Hadoop, http://hadoop.apache.org/.
29. IBM SmartCloud, http://www.ibm.com/cloud-computing/us/en/.
30. Jasper Reports, http://community.jaspersoft.com/project/jasperreports-library.
31. Y. Jin, Y. Wen and Q. Chen, Energy Efficiency and Server Virtualization in Data Centers: An Empirical Investigation, *Computer Communications Workshops (INFOCOM WKSHPS)*, 2012.
32. P. Klint, *Interpretation Techniques, Software Practice and Experience*, 1981.
33. D. Kusic, J. O. Kephart, J. E. Hanson, N. Kandasamy and G. Jiang, Power and Performance Management of Virtualized Computing Environments via Lookahead Control, *Cluster Computing*, 2009.
34. P. M. Kogge, An Architecture Trail to Threaded-Code Systems, *IEEE Computer*, 1982.
35. Large Hadron Collider, http://www.lhc.ac.uk/.
36. Learn About Java Technology, http://www.java.com/en/about/.
37. P. Li, Cloud Computing: Big Data is the Future of IT, http://assets.accel.com/5174affa160bd cloud computing big data.pdf, 2009.

38. H. Liu, Amazon Data Center Size, http://huanliu.wordpress.com/2012/03/13/amazon-data-center-size/, 2012.
39. P. Magnusson and D. Samuelsson, A Compact Intermediate Format for SIMICS, Swedish Institute of Computer Science, Tech. Report R94:17 1994.
40. MediaWiki, http://www.mediawiki.org/wiki/MediaWiki.
41. Microsoft Azure, http://www.windowsazure.com/en-us/.
42. Microsoft Corporation, ECMA C# and Common Language Infrastructure Standards, 2009.
43. Microsoft Hyper-V Server 2012, http://www.microsoft.com/en-us/server-cloud/hyper-v-server/.
44. Microsoft SQL Server, http://www.microsoft.com/en-us/sqlserver/default.aspx.
45. MySQL, http://www.mysql.com/.
46. Oracle SQL, http://www.oracle.com/technetwork/developer-tools/sql-developer/overview/index.html.
47. I. Pratt, K. Fraser, S. Hand, Limpach, A. Warfield, Magenheimer, Nakajima and Mallick, Xen 3.0 and the Art of Virtualization, *Proceedings of the Linux Symposium (Volume Two)*, 2005.
48. G. J. Popek and R. P. Goldberg, Formal Requirements for Virtualizable Third Generation Architectures, *Communications of the ACM*, 1974.
49. Rackspace, http://www.rackspace.com/.
50. Red Hat Enterprise Virtualization (RHEV) 3 for Servers, http://www.redhat.com/promo/rhev3/.
51. M. S. Rehman and M. F. Sakr, Initial Findings for Provisioning Variation in Cloud Computing, *CloudCom*, 2010.
52. T. H. Romer, D. Lee, G. M. Voelker, A. Wolman, W. A. Wong, J.-L. Baer, B. N. Bershad and H. M. Levy, The Structure and Performance of Interpreters, *ASPLOS*, 1996.
53. Silicon Valley Leadership Group, Accenture, Data Centre Energy Forecast Report, Final Report, 2008.
54. R. L. Sites, A. Chernoff, M. B. Kirk, M. P. Marks and S. G. Robinson, Binary Translation, *Communications of the ACM*, 1993.
55. J. E. Smith and R. Nair, *Virtual Machines: Versatile Platforms for Systems and Processes*, Morgan Kaufmann, 2005.
56. S. Soltesz, H. Potz, M. E. Fiuczynski, A. Bavier and L. Peterson, Container-Based Operating System Virtualization: A Scalable, High-Performance Alternative to Hypervisors, *EuroSys*, 2007.
57. S. Srikantaiah, A. Kansal and F. Zhao, Energy Aware Consolidation for Cloud Computing, *Cluster Computing*, 2009.
58. vCloud Hybrid Service, http://www.vmware.com/products/datacenter-virtualization/vCloud-hybridservice/overview.html.
59. VMWare, http://www.vmware.com.
60. VMWare, Understanding Full Virtualization, Paravirtualization, and Hardware Assist, *VMware Whitepaper*, 2007.
61. VMWare, VMware vSphere: The CPU Scheduler in VMware ESX 4.1, *VMware Whitepaper*, 2010.
62. VMWare, Understanding Memory Resource Management in VMware ESX Server, *VMware Whitepaper*, 2009.
63. Xen Open Source Community, http://www.xen.org.
64. Xen 4.0 Release Notes, http://wiki.xen.org/wiki/Xen 4.0 Release Notes.
65. Xen 4.1 Release Notes, http://wiki.xen.org/wiki/Xen 4.1 Release Notes.
66. F. Zhou, M. Goel, P. Desnoyers and R. Sundaram, Scheduler Vulnerabilities and Attacks in Cloud Computing, *arXiv:1103.0759v1 [cs.DC]*, 2011.

17 Toward Optimal Resource Provisioning for Economical and Green MapReduce Computing in the Cloud

Keke Chen, Shumin Guo, James Powers, and Fengguang Tian

CONTENTS

Running MapReduce programs in the cloud introduces the important problem: how to optimize resource provisioning to minimize the financial charge or job finish time for a specific job. An important step toward this ultimate goal is modeling the cost of MapReduce program. In this chapter, we study the whole process of MapReduce processing and build up a cost function that explicitly models the relationship among the amount of input data, the available system resources (map and reduce slots), and the complexity of the reduce program for the target MapReduce job. The model parameters can be learned from test runs. Based on this cost model, we can solve a number of decision problems, such as the optimal amount of resources that minimize the financial cost with a job finish deadline, minimize the time under certain financial budget, or find the optimal tradeoffs between time and financial cost. With appropriate modeling of energy consumption of the resources, the optimization problems can be extended to address energy-efficient MapReduce computing. Experimental results show that the proposed modeling approach performs well on a number of tested MapReduce programs in both the in-house cluster and Amazon EC2.

17.1 INTRODUCTION

With the deployment of web applications, scientific computing, and sensor networks, a large amount of data can be collected from users, applications, and the environment. For example, user clickthrough data has been an important data source for improving web search relevance [9] and for understanding online user behaviors [20]. Such data sets can be easily in terabyte scale; they are also continuously produced. Thus, an urgent task is to efficiently analyze these large data sets so that the important information in the data can be promptly captured and understood. As a flexible and scalable parallel programming and processing model, recently, MapReduce [5] (and its open-source implementation Hadoop) has been widely used for processing and analyzing such large-scale data sets [4,8,11,15,17,18].

On the other hand, data analysts in most companies, research institutes, and government agencies have no luxury to access large private Hadoop/MapReduce clouds. Therefore, running Hadoop/MapReduce on top of a public cloud has become a realistic option for most users. In view of this requirement, Amazon has developed Elastic MapReduce* that runs on-demand Hadoop/MapReduce clusters on top of Amazon EC2 nodes. There are also scripts† for users to manually setup Hadoop/MapReduce on EC2 nodes.

---

* aws.amazon.com/elasticmapreduce/.
† wiki.apache.org/hadoop/AmazonEC2.

However, running a Hadoop cluster on top of the public cloud has different requirements from running a private Hadoop cluster. First, for each job normally a dedicated Hadoop cluster will be started on a number of virtual nodes to take advantage of the "pay-as-you-use" economical cloud model. Because users' data-processing requests normally come in intermittently, it is not economical to maintain a constant Hadoop cluster like private Hadoop clusters do. Instead, on-demand clusters are more appropriate to most users. Therefore, there is no multiuser or multijob resource competition happening within such a Hadoop cluster. Second, it is now the user's responsibility to set the appropriate number of virtual nodes for the Hadoop cluster. The optimal setting may differ from application to application and depend on the amount of input data. An effective method is needed to help the user make this decision.

The problem of optimizing resource provisioning for MapReduce programs involves two intertwined factors: the cost of provisioning the virtual nodes and the time to finish the job. Intuitively, with a larger amount of resources, the job can take a shorter time to finish. However, resources are provisioned at cost, which are also related to the amount of time for using the resources. Thus, it is tricky to find the best setting that minimizes the financial cost. With other constraints such as a deadline or a financial budget to finish the job, this problem appears more complicated. More generally, energy consumption of a MapReduce program can also be modeled in a similar way, which is critical to energy efficient cloud computing [2].

We propose a method to help users make the decision of resource provisioning for running MapReduce programs in public clouds. This method is based on the proposed specialized MapReduce cost model that has a number of model parameters to be determined for a specific application. The model parameters can be learned with test runs on a small scale of virtual nodes and small test data. Based on the cost model and the estimated parameters, the user can find the optimal setting for resources by solving certain optimization problems.

Our approach has several unique contributions.

- Different from existing work on the performance analysis of MapReduce program, our approach focuses on the relationship among the critical variables: the number of Map/Reduce slots, the amount of input data, and the complexity of application-specific components. The resulting cost model can be represented as a weighted linear combination of a set of nonlinearly functions of these variables. Linear models provide robust generalization power that allows one to determine the weights with the data collected on small-scale tests.
- Based on this cost model, we formulate the important decision problems as several optimization problems. The resource requirement is mapped to the number of map/reduce slots; the financial cost of provisioning resources is the product of the cost function and the acquired map/reduce slots. With the explicit cost model, the resultant optimization problems are easy to formulate and solve.
- We have conducted a set of experiments on both the local Hadoop cluster and Amazon EC2 to validate the cost model. The experiments show that this cost model fits the data collected from four tested MapReduce programs very well. The experiment on model prediction also shows low error rates.

The entire paper is organized as follows. In Section 17.2, we introduce the MapReduce Programming model and the normal setting for running Hadoop on the public cloud. In Section 17.3, we analyze the execution of MapReduce program and propose the cost model. In Section 17.4, we describe the statistical method to learn the model for a specific MapReduce program. In Section 17.5, we formulate several problems on resource provisioning as optimization problems based on the cost model. In Section 17.6, we present the experimental results that validate the cost model and analyze the modeling errors. In Section 17.7, the related work on MapReduce performance analysis is briefly discussed.

17.2 PRELIMINARY

MapReduce programming for large-scale parallel data processing was recently developed by Google [5] and has become popular for big-data processing. MapReduce is more than a programming model—it also includes the system support for processing MapReduce jobs in parallel in a large-scale cluster. Apache Hadoop is the most popular open-source implementation of the MapReduce framework. Thus, our discussions, in particular the experiments, will be based on Apache Hadoop, although the analysis and modeling approach should also fit other MapReduce implementations.

It is better to understand how MapReduce programming works with an example—the famous WordCount program. WordCount counts the frequency of word in a large document collection. Its map program partitions the input lines into words and emits tuples $\langle w, 1 \rangle$ for aggregation, where "w" represents a word and "1" means the occurrence of the word. In the reduce program, the tuples with the same word are grouped together and their occurrences are summed up to get the final result.

Algorithm 17.1: The WordCount MapReduce Program

1: **map**(*file*)
2: **for** each line in the file **do**
3:     **for** each word w in the line **do**
4:         Emit($\langle w, 1 \rangle$)
5:     **end for**
6: **end for**

1: **reduce**(w, v)
2: w: word, v: list of counts.
3: $d \leftarrow 0$;
4: **for** each v_i in v **do**
5:     $d \leftarrow d + v_i$;
6: **end for**
7: Emit($\langle w, d \rangle$);

When deploying a Hadoop cluster in a public cloud, users need to request a number of virtual machines from the cloud and then start them with a system image that has the Hadoop package preinstalled. Because users' data may reside in the cloud storage system, for example, Amazon S3, the Hadoop cluster needs to load the data from the storage system or to be appropriately configured to directly use the storage system. The configuration files are passed to the corresponding master and slave nodes, and the Hadoop cluster can then be started. Here comes the difficult decision problem for the user: how many nodes would be appropriate for a specific job, which will minimize the financial charge and guarantee the job to be finished on time? We start exploring this problem with an analysis on the cost model of MapReduce processing.

17.3   RESOURCE-TIME COST MODEL FOR MapReduce

In this section, we analyze the components in the whole MapReduce execution process and derive a cost model in terms of the input data, the application-specific complexity, and the available system resources. The goal of developing this cost model is to identify the relationships (functions) between the resources and time complexity for a specific application. We will see that with this cost model, solving the resource prediction and optimization problems becomes easy.

Due to the complex multi-tenant run-time environment and uncertain factors such as network traffic and disk I/O performance, it is impossible to precisely model the cost of a MapReduce program. Instead, we will introduce a statistical modeling approach to minimize the possible modeling error. We will give the basic idea of modeling. Let the amount of system resources be S, which can be the number of virtual machines of certain type in a public cloud. Let the amount of input data be D, and the MapReduce setting be C, for example, the number of reduce tasks in our discussion. We want to find a cost function—the total time cost of the MapReduce job $T = T(S, D, C)$. There are a number of special features with this modeling task.

1. Because Map/Reduce tasks have very different logic and time complexity for different applications, this cost function should be different from application to application.
2. Ideally, this cost function should be learned from small-scale instances that have small amounts of resources and input data and still be robust for large-scale instances. It can certainly provide better models for repetitively running jobs.
3. We expect to learn a closed-form function, which can be nicely incorporated in optimization tasks. Some machine learning methods [6] result in special forms of function such as decision trees, which are not easy to handle in optimization and will not serve our purpose well.

Because of these special requirements, we aim to design a modeling method that gives a closed form function with good generalization power. There are two general ways to do cost modeling. First, we can carefully analyze all the components of the system in detail and then try to precisely model the cost functions. As we already know, this approach is impractical because of the uncertain environment and the diversity of program logic. The other approach is solely depending on learning algorithms to find the cost function. However, due to the limited features (e.g., only four features as we will show), this approach tends to overfit the cost model [6].

We take a combined approach instead. This method depends on the best-effort analysis of the whole process of MapReduce processing framework, which will result in the following cost function:

$$T(S, D, C) = \sum_{i=1}^{k} \beta_i h_i(S, D, C) + \beta_0, \qquad (17.1)$$

where $h_i(S, D, C)$ are possibly some nonlinear transformations of the input factors S, D, and C, which are the time complexity of sequential processing components in the system, and β_i are the component weights, different from application to application. $h_i(S, D, C)$ are obtained through the analysis of the MapReduce processing components, while β_i will be learned for a specific application based on sample runs of that application. With this modeling idea in mind, in the following subsections, we will conduct the modeling analysis, give a concrete formulation of the cost functions of map task and reduce task to find $h_i(S, D, C)$, and finally integrate these components into the whole cost function.

17.3.1 ANALYZING THE PROCESS OF MAPREDUCE

MapReduce processing is a mix of sequential and parallel processing. The map phase is executed before the reduce phase,* as Figure 17.1 shows. However, in each phase many map or reduce processes are executed in parallel. To clearly describe the MapReduce execution, we would like to distinguish the concepts of *Map/Reduce slot* and *Map/Reduce process*. Each map (or reduce) process is executed in a map (or reduce) slot. A slot is a unit of computing resources allocated for the corresponding process. According to the system capacity, a computing node can only accommodate a fixed number of slots so that the parallel processes can be run in the slots without serious competition. In Hadoop, the Tasktracker running in each slave node has to set the number of map slots and the number of reduce slots. A common setting for a multicore computer is to have two map and reduce slots per core. Without loss of generality, let us assume there are m map slots and r reduce slots in total over all slave nodes.

We define a map/reduce process as a map/reduce task running on a specific slot. By default, in Hadoop each map process handles one chunk of data (e.g., 64 MB). Therefore, if there are M chunks of data, M map processes in total will be scheduled and assigned to the m slots. In the ideal case, m map processes can run in parallel in the m slots—we call it one round of map processes. If $M > m$, which is normal for large data sets, $[M/m]$ map rounds are needed.

Different from the total number of map processes, the number of reduce processes, denoted as R, can be set by the user or determined by specific application requirements. The map outputs, that is, the key-value pairs, are organized by the keys and then distributed evenly by the keys to the R reduce processes.† Similarly, if $R > r$, more than one round of reduce processes are scheduled. It is probably not very

---

* The copy operation in the reduce phase overlaps the map phase—when a map's result is ready, copy may start immediately.
† Thus, it is not meaningful to set R greater than the number of output keys of map.

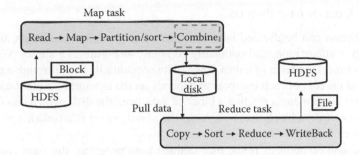

FIGURE 17.1 Components in map and reduce tasks and the sequence of execution.

helpful to set R greater than r because there is no restriction on the amount of data a reduce process can handle. As a rule of thumb, when the number of map output keys is much large than r, R is often set close to the number of all available reduce slots for an in-house cluster, for example, 95% of all reduce slots [22]. When it comes to public clouds, we will set $R = r$ and choose an appropriate number of reduce slots, r, to find the best tradeoff between the time and the financial cost.

Figure 17.2 illustrates the scheduling of map and reduce processes to the map and reduce slots in the ideal situation. In practice, map processes in the same round may not finish exactly at the same time—some may finish earlier or later than others due to the system configuration, the disk I/O, the network traffic, and the data distribution. However, we can use the total number of rounds to roughly estimate the total time spent in the map phase. The variance caused by all these factors will be considered in modeling. Intuitively, the more available slots, the faster the whole MapReduce job can be finished. However, in the pay-as-you-go setting, there is a tradeoff between the amount of resources and the amount of time to finish the MapReduce job. Thus, we cannot simply increase the amount of resources.

In addition to the cost of map and reduce processes, the system has some additional cost for managing and scheduling the M map processes and the R reduce processes, which will also be considered in modeling. Based on this understanding, we will first analyze the cost of each map process and reduce process, respectively, and then derive the overall cost model.

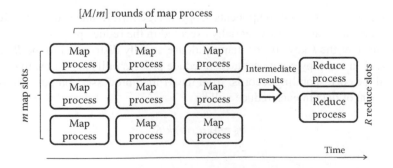

FIGURE 17.2 Illustration of parallel and sequential execution in the ideal situation.

17.3.2 Cost of Map Process

A map process can be divided into a number of sequential components, including read, map, sort/partition, and optionally combine, as Figure 17.1 shows. We understand this process in term of a data flow—data sequentially flow through each component and the cost of each component depends on the amount of input data.

The first component is reading a block of data from the disk, which can be either local or remote data block. Let us assume the *average cost* is a function of the size of data block b: $i(b)$.

The second component is the user defined map program, the time complexity of which is determined by the input data size b, denoted as $f(b)$. The map program may output data in size of $o_m(b)$ that might vary depending on the specific data. The output will be a list of ⟨*key, value*⟩ pairs.

The result will be partitioned and sorted by the key into R shares for the R reduce processes. We denote the cost of partitioning and sorting with $s(o_m(b), R)$. If the partitioning process uses a hash function to map the keys, the partitioning cost is independent of R. However, the sorting phase is still affected by R. Let us skip the combiner component temporarily and we will revisit the combiner component later.

In summary, the overall cost of a map process is the sum of the costs (without the combiner component):

$$\Phi_m = i(b) + f(b) + s(o_m(b), R) + \epsilon_m. \tag{17.2}$$

$i(b)$ and $f(b)$ are only related to the size of the data block b and the complexity of the map program, independent of the parameters m and M. ϵ_m has a mean zero and some variance σ_m^2, which needs to be calibrated by experiments. We also observed that $s(o_m(b), R)$ is slightly linear to R. In practice, we can model it with parameters m, M, r, R as

$$\Phi_m(m, M, r, R) = \mu_1 + \mu_2 + \epsilon_m, \tag{17.3}$$

where μ_1, μ_2, and the distribution of ϵ_m are constants and specific to each application.

17.3.3 Cost of Reduce Process

The reduce process has the components: Copy, MergeSort, Reduce, and WriteResult. These components are also sequentially executed in the reduce process.

Assume that the k keys of the map result are equally distributed to the R reduce processes.* In the copy component, each reduce process pulls its shares, that is, k/R keys and the corresponding records, from the M map processes' outputs. Thus, the total amount of data in each reduce will be

$$b_R = M \, o_m(b) \, k/R \tag{17.4}$$

---

* For this reason, the user normally selects R to satisfy $k \geq R$. If $R > k$, only k reduces are actually used.

Here, we simplify the analysis by assuming the amount of data is proportional to the number of keys assigned to the reduce. In practice, many applications have skewed data distributions, that is, some keys may have more records while other may have less, which may affect the quality of modeling.

The copy cost is linear to b_R, denoted as $c(b_R)$. However, most of the time is overlapped with the map phase. Normally only the last few rounds of map processing may contribute to the overall time cost. We thus approximate the cost as $c(b_R) \sim m\, o_m(b)\, k/R$.

A merge process follows to merge the M shares from the map results. Because the records are already sorted by the key, this process simply merges the shares by the key in multiple rounds. Assume the buffer size is B, the merge round i will generate M/B^i files, and its cost is proportional to b_R. The total number of rounds is $\lceil \log_B M\ rceil \rceil$. Thus, the total merge cost $ms(b_R)$ is proportional to $b_R \lceil \log_B M \rceil$.

The reduce program will process the data with some complexity $g(b_R)$ that depends on the specific application. Assume the output data of the reduce program has an amount $o_r(b_R)$, which is often less than b_R. Finally, the result is duplicated and written back to multiple nodes, with the complexity linear to $o_r(b_R)$, denoted as $wr(o_r(b_R))$.

In summary, the cost of the reduce process is the sum of the component costs,

$$\Phi_r = c(b_R) + ms(b_R) + g(b_R) + wr(o_r(b_R)) + \epsilon_r \tag{17.5}$$

Both the Copy and the WriteResult costs may vary because of the varying network I/O performance, which are modeled with the random variable ϵ_r. Similar to ϵ_m for the map phase, ϵ_r has a mean zero and some variance σ_r^2. These variances should be captured in modeling.

If we model Φ_r with m, M, r, R, and keep the relevant components for each phase, we have

$$\Phi_r(m, M, r, R) = \lambda_1(m/R) + \lambda_2(M \log M/R) + g(M/R) + \lambda_3(M/R) + \epsilon_r, \tag{17.6}$$

where λ_1 and the distribution of ϵ_r are application-specific constants.

17.3.4 PUTTING IT ALL TOGETHER

According to the parallel execution model we described in Figure 17.2, the overall time complexity T depends on the number of map rounds and reduce rounds. The cost of managing and scheduling the map and reduce processes $\Theta(M, R) = \xi_1 M + \xi_2 R$ is linear to M and R, as stated in the documentation [22]. By assuming all the processes in each map (or reduce) round finish around the same time, we can represent the overall cost as

$$T = \left\lceil \frac{M}{m} \right\rceil \Phi_m + \left\lceil \frac{R}{r} \right\rceil \Phi_r + \Theta(M, R). \tag{17.7}$$

We are more interested in the relationship among the total time T, the input data size $M \times b$, the user defined number of reduce processes R, and the number of map and reduce slots, m and r.

This general representation can be slightly simplified with a number of settings. As we discussed, it is safe to assume $R = r$, as running Reduces in multiple rounds might be unnecessary. Thus, $\left\lceil \dfrac{R}{r} \right\rceil \Phi_r = \Phi_r$. To make it more convenient to manipulate the equation, we also remove $\lceil\rceil$ from $\lceil M/m \rceil$ by assuming $M \geq m$ and M/m is an integer. After plugging in Equations 17.3 and 17.6 and keeping only the variables M, R, and m in the cost model, we get the detailed model

$$
\begin{aligned}
T_1(M, m, R) = \beta_0 &+ \beta_1 \frac{M}{m} + \beta_2 \frac{MR}{m} + \beta_3 \frac{m}{R} + \beta_4 \frac{M \log M}{R} \\
&+ \beta_5 M/R + \beta_6 M + \beta_7 R + \beta_8 g\left(\frac{M}{R}\right) + \epsilon,
\end{aligned}
\tag{17.8}
$$

where β_i are the positive constants specific to each application. Note that $T_1(M, m, R)$ is not linear to its variables, but it is linear to the transformed components: M/m, MR/m, m/R, $M \log M/R$, M/R, M, R, and $g(M/R)$. The parameter β_i defines the contribution of each components in the model. β_0 represents some constant cost invariant to the parameters. β_i are the weights of each components derived in the component-wise cost analysis. Finally, ϵ represents the overall noise. We leave the discussion on the item $g(M/R)$ later.

17.3.4.1   With Combiner

In the map process, the combiner program is used to aggregate the results by the key. If there are k keys in the map output, the combiner program reduces the map result to k records. The cost of the combiner is only subject to the output of the map program. Thus, it can be incorporated into the parameter β_1. However, the combiner function reduces the output data of the map process and thus affects the cost of the reduce phase. With the combiner, the amount of data that a reduce process needs to pull from the map is changed to

$$
b_R = Mk/R.
\tag{17.9}
$$

Since the item M/R is still there, the cost model (Equation 17.8) applies without any change.

17.3.4.2   Function $g()$

The complexity of reduce program has to be estimated with the specific application. There are some special cases that the $g()$ item can be removed from Equation 17.8. If $g()$ is linear to the size of the input data, then its contribution can be merged to the factor β_4, because $g(M/R) \sim M/R$. For other cases that cannot be merged, a new item should be created and in the cost model. In the linear case, which is common as we have observed, the cost model can be further simplified to

$$T_2(M, m, R) = \beta_0 + \beta_1 \frac{M}{m} + \beta_2 \frac{MR}{m} + \beta_3 \frac{m}{R}$$

$$+ \beta_4 \frac{M \log M}{R} + \beta_5 M/R + \beta_6 M + \beta_7 R + \epsilon, \tag{17.10}$$

17.4 LEARNING THE MODEL

With the formulation of the cost function in terms of input variables M, m, and R, we need to learn the parameters β_i. Note that β_i should be different from application to application. We design a learning procedure as follows.

First, for a specific MapReduce program, we randomly choose the variables M, m, and R from certain ranges. For example, m and R (i.e., r) are chosen within 50; M is chosen so that at least two rounds of map processes are available for testing. Second, we collect the time cost of the test run of the MapReduce job for each setting of (M, m, R), which forms the training data set. Third, regression modeling [14] is applied to learn the model from the training data with the transformed variables

$$x_1 = M/m, \; x_2 = MR/m, \; x_3 = m/R, \; x_4 = (M \log M)/R, \; x_5 = M/R, \; x_6 = M, \; x_7 = R. \quad (17.11)$$

Because β_i has practical meaning, that is, the weights of the components in the total cost, we have $\beta_i \geq 0$, $i = 0...r$, which requires non-negative linear regression [14] to solve the learning problem. The cross-validation method [6] is then used to validate the performance of the learned model. We will show more details in experiments.

17.5 OPTIMIZATION OF RESOURCE PROVISIONING

With the cost model we are now ready to find the optimal settings for different decision problems. We try to find the best resource allocation for three typical situations: (1) with a certain limited amount of financial budget; (2) with a time constraint; and (3) the optimal tradeoff curve without any constraint. In the following, we formulate these problems as optimization problems based on the cost model.

In all the scenarios we consider, we assume the model parameters β_i have been learned with sample runs in small scale settings. For the simplicity of presentation, we assume the simplified model T_2 (Equation 17.10) is applied. Cost models with other reduce complexity do not change the optimization algorithm. Since the input data is fixed for a specific MapReduce job, M is a constant. We also consider all general MapReduce system configurations have been optimized via other methods [1,7,8] and fixed for both small- and large-scale settings. With this setup, the time cost function becomes

$$T_3(m, R) = \alpha_0 + \frac{\alpha_1}{m} + \frac{\alpha_2 R}{m} + \frac{\alpha_3 m}{R} + \frac{\alpha_4}{R} + \alpha_5 R \qquad (17.12)$$

where

$$\alpha_0 = \beta_0 + \beta_6 M,$$

$$\alpha_1 = \beta_1 M,$$

$$\alpha_2 = \beta_2 M,$$

$$\alpha_3 = \beta_3,$$

$$\alpha_4 = \beta_4 M \log M + \beta_5 M,$$

$$\alpha_5 = \beta_7.$$

In the virtual machine (VM) based cloud infrastructure (e.g., Amazon EC2), the cost of cloud resources is calculated based on the number of VM instances used in time units (typically in hours). Let us consider the same type of VM instances are used in the deployment. According to the capacity of a virtual machine (CPU cores, memory, disk, and network bandwidth), a virtual node can only have a fixed number of map/reduce slots. Let us denote the number of slots per node as γ, which are also fixed for learning and applying the model. Thus, the total number of slots $m + r$ required by an on-demand Hadoop cluster can be roughly transformed to the number of VMs, v, as

$$v = (m + r)/\gamma. \qquad (17.13)$$

If the price of renting one VM instance for an hour is u, the total financial cost is determined by the result $uvT_3(m, R)$. Since we usually set R to r, it follows that the total financial cost for renting the Hadoop cluster is

$$uvT_3(m, R) = u(m + R)T_3(m, R)/\gamma. \qquad (17.14)$$

Now we are ready to formulate the optimization problems.

- Given a financial budget ϕ, the problem of finding the best resource allocation to minimize the job time can be formulated as

$$\begin{aligned} &\text{minimize } T_3(m, R) \\ &\text{subject to } u(m + R)T_3(m, R) / \gamma \le \phi, \\ &m > 0, \text{ and } R > 0. \end{aligned} \qquad (17.15)$$

- If the constraint is about the deadline τ for finishing the job, the problem of minimizing the financial cost can be formulated as

$$\text{minimize } u(m + R)T_3(m, R)/\gamma$$
$$\text{subject to } T_3(m, R) \leq \tau, m > 0, \text{ and } R > 0.$$
(17.16)

- The above optimization problem can also be slightly changed to describe the problem that the user simply wants to find the most economical solution for the job without the deadline, that is, the constraint $T_3(m, R) \leq \tau$ is removed.

Note that the T_3 model parameters might be specific for a particular type of VM instance that determines the parameters u and γ. Therefore, by testing different types of VM instance, and applying this optimization repeatedly on each instance type, we can also find which instance type is the best.

These optimization problems do not involve complicated parameters except for the T_3 function. Once we learn the concrete setting of the T_3 model parameters, these optimization problems can be nicely solved since they are all in the category of well-studied optimization problems. There are plenty of papers and books discussing how to solve these optimization problems. In particular, the search space of m and R is quite limited, for many medium-scale MapReduce jobs, they are normally integers less than 10,000. In this case, a brute-force search over the entire space to find the optimal result will not cost much time. Therefore, we will skip the details of solving these problems.

17.6 EXPERIMENTS

As we have shown, as long as the cost model is accurate, the optimization problems are easy to solve. Therefore, our focus of experiments will be validating the formulated cost model. We first describe the setup of the experiments, including the experimental environment and the data sets. Four programs are presented: WordCount, TeraSort, PageRank, and Join, which are used in evaluating the cost model. Finally, a restrict evaluation on both the in-house cluster and Amazon cloud will be conducted to show the model goodness of fit and the prediction accuracy.

17.6.1 EXPERIMENTAL SETUP

The experiments are conducted in our in-house 16-node Hadoop cluster and Amazon EC2. We describe the setup of the environments and the data sets used for experiments as follows.

17.6.1.1 In-House Hardware and Hadoop Configuration

Each node in the in-house cluster has four quad-core 2.3-MHz AMD Opteron 2376, 16-GB memory, and two 500-GB hard drives, connected to other nodes with a gigabit switch. Hadoop 1.0.3 is installed in the cluster. One node serves as the master node and 15 nodes as the slave nodes. The single master node runs the *JobTracker* and the *NameNode*, while each slave node runs both the *TaskTracker* and the *DataNode*. Each slave node is configured with eight map slots and six reduce slots (about one process per core). Each map/reduce process uses 400 MB memory. The data block size is set to 64 MB. We use the Hadoop fair scheduler* to control the total number of map/reduce slots available for different testing jobs.

17.6.1.2   Amazon EC2 Configuration

We also used the on-demand clusters provisioned from Amazon EC2 for experiments. Only the small instances (1EC2 compute unit, 1.7 GB memory, and 160 GB hard drive) are used to setup the on-demand clouds. For the simplicity of configuration, one map slot and one reduce slot share one instance. Therefore, a cluster that needs m map slots and r reduce slots will need $\max\{m, r\} + 1$ small instances in total, with the additional instance as the master node. The existing script[†] in the Hadoop package is used to automatically setup the required Hadoop cluster (with proper node configurations) in EC2.

17.6.1.3   Data Sets

We use a number of generators to generate three types of testing data sets for the testing programs. (1) We revise the RandomWriter tool in the Hadoop package to generate random float numbers. This type of data is used by the Sort program. (2) We also revise the RandomTextWriter tool to generate text data based on a list of 1000 words randomly sampled from the system dictionary /usr/share/dict/words. This type of data is used by the WordCount program and the TableJoin program. (3) The third data set is a synthetic random graph data set, which is generated for the PageRank program. Each line of the data set starts with a node ID and its initial PageRank, followed by a list of node IDs representing the node's outlinks. Both the node ID and the outlinks are randomly generated integers.

Each type of data consists of 150 1 GB files. For a specific testing task with the predefined size of input data (the parameter M), we will randomly choose the required number of files from the pool to simulate input data.

17.6.1.4   Modeling Tool

As we mentioned, we will need a regression modeling method that works on the constraints $\beta_i \geq 0$. In experiments, we use the MATLAB® function lsqnonneg[‡] to learn the model, which squarely fits our goal.

17.6.2   TESTING PROGRAMS

In this section, we describe the MapReduce programs used in testing and give the complexity of each one's reduce program, that is, the $g()$ function. If $g()$ is in one of the two special cases, the simplified cost model Equation 17.10 is used.

---

* http: //hadoop.apache.org/docs/r1.1.1/fair_scheduler.html.
† wiki.apache.org/hadoop/AmazonEC2.
‡ http://www.mathworks.com/help/techdoc/ref/lsqnonneg.html.

17.6.2.1 WordCount

WordCount is a sample MapReduce program in the Hadoop package. The map program splits the input text into words and the result is locally aggregated by word with a combiner; the reduce program sums up the local aggregation results ⟨*word, count*⟩ by words and output the final word counts. Since the number of words is limited, the amount of output data to the reduce stage and the cost of reduce stage are small, compared with the data and the processing cost for the map stage. The complexity of the reduce program, $g()$, is linear to reduce's input data.

17.6.2.2 Sort

Sort is also a sample MapReduce program in the Hadoop package. It depends on a custom partitioner that uses a sorted list of $N-1$ sampled keys to define the key range for each reduce process. All keys such that sample[$i-1$] <= key < sample[i] are sent to reduce i. Then, the inherent MergeSort in the Shuffle stage sorts the input data to the reduce. This guarantees that the output of reduce i are all less than the output of reduce $i + 1$. Both the map program and the reduce program do nothing but simply pass the input to the output. Therefore, the function $g()$ is also linear to the size of the input of reduce.

17.6.2.3 PageRank

PageRank is a MapReduce implementation of the well-known Google's PageRank algorithm [3]. PageRank can be implemented with an iterative algorithm and applied to a graph data set. Assume each node p_i in the graph has a PageRank $PR(p_i)$. $M(p_i)$ represents the set of neighboring nodes of p_i that have outlinks pointing to p_i. $L(p_j)$ is the total number of outlinks the node p_j has. d is the damping factor and N is the total number of nodes. The following equation calculates the PageRank for each node p_i.

$$PR(p_i) = (1 - d)/N + d \sum_{p_j \in M(p_i)} \frac{PR(p_j)}{L(p_j)} \tag{17.17}$$

PageRank values are updated in multiple rounds until they converge. In one round of PageRank MapReduce program, all nodes' PageRank values are updated in parallel based on the above equation. Concretely, the map program distributes a share of each node's PageRank, that is, $PR(p_j)/L(p_j)$, to all its outlink neighbors. The reduce program collects the shares from its neighbors and applies the equation to update the PageRank. The complexity function $g()$ is also linear to the size of the input of reduce.

17.6.2.4 Join

Join is a MapReduce program that joins a large file with a small file based on a designated key attribute, which mimics the Join operation in relational database. The large files are the text files randomly generated with RandomTextWriter. The small file consists of 50 randomly generated lines using the same method for generating the large text data set. The first word of each line in both types of file serves as the join key. The map program emits the lines of the input large and small files. Each line of the small file is labeled so that they can be distinguished from the map output. In the reduce, the lines are checked to find those with matched keys. If the lines from both files are found to be matched, a Cartesian product is applied between the two sets of lines with the same key to generate the output. Depending on the key distribution, the size of output data may vary. In the reduce program, assume there is λ lines from the large file and μ lines from the small file. The result of Cartesian product is $\lambda\mu$ lines. Since $\mu \leq 50$ is very small, the complexity function $g()$ is approximately linear to the input $\lambda + \mu$ lines.

17.6.3 MODEL ANALYSIS

We run a set of experiments to estimate the model parameters β_i for the four programs. We randomly select the values for the three parameters M, m, and R. The number of data chunks M is calculated by the number of selected 1 GB files (one file has $1024/64 = 16$ blocks). For the in-house cluster, because all available map slots will be used in executing the MapReduce job, we control the number of map slots m by setting the maximum number of map slots in the *fair scheduler*. R is randomly set to a number smaller than the total number of reduce Slots in the system. For on-demand EC2 clusters, it is straightforward to allocate m nodes as the map slots and R nodes for the reduce slots.

For each tested program, we generate tens of random settings of (M, m, R). M is randomly selected from the integers $[1...150] \times 16$, that is, the number of 1 GB files $\times$ 16 blocks/file. R is randomly selected from the integers $[1...50]$. Since changing m will need to update the scheduler setting, we limit the choices of m to 30, 60, 90, and 120. For each setting, we record the time (seconds) used to finish the program. The examples are ordered by the time cost for further analysis.

17.6.3.1 Regression Analysis

With the transformed variables (Equation 17.11), we can conduct a linear regression on the transformed cost model

$$T(x_1,x_2,x_3,x_4,x_5,x_6,x_7) = \beta_0 + \sum_{i=1}^{7}\beta_1 x_1. \tag{17.18}$$

Table 17.1 shows the result of regression analysis with the constraints $\beta_i \geq 0$ for programs running in the in-house cluster. R^2 is a measure for evaluating the goodness of fit in regression modeling. $R^2 = 1$ means a perfect fit, while $R^2 > 90\%$ indicates a very good fit. Note that the MATLAB function lsqnonneg also demotes the insignificant β_i and sets them to 0.

Table 17.1 shows most models have very high R^2 values, except for TableJoin on AWS. The reason of lower-quality models might be caused by either the dynamic run-time environment or the special characteristics of the program (or data) that the model does not capture. However, the TableJoin model in the local cluster shows

TABLE 17.1

Results of Regression Analysis for the In-House Cluster and AWS Clusters

	WordCount		Sort		PageRank		TableJoin	
	Local	AWS	Local	AWS	Local	AWS	Local	AWS
β_0	51.82	0	20.55	0	25.89	37.73	47.53	3.61
β_1	28.32	54.30	0.72	21.74	12.24	10.37	12.27	20.07
β_2	0.01	0	0	0	0	0.18	0	0
β_3	9.24	0	0	0	0	0	0	14.75
β_4	0	0	4.09	3.58	6.58	0	1.60	3.01
β_5	0	0	0	0	0	26.79	0	0
β_6	0.10	0	0.59	0.05	0.51	0	0.19	0
β_7	0.38	0	0	0	0	0	0	0
R^2	0.9751	0.9524	0.9692	0.9253	0.9847	0.9733	0.9647	0.8432

Note: R^2 values higher than 0.90 indicate good fit of the proposed model.

good accuracy, which may imply the run-time environment is the main reason. The cause of the problem will be further studied in our future work.

17.6.3.2   Prediction Accuracy

We also conduct a careful analysis on the prediction accuracy of the models. The leave-one-out [6] cross-validation is used to identify the average prediction accuracy and also the outliers that have low accuracy. Concretely the leave-one-out cross-validation runs in n rounds if there are n training samples. In each round, one of the n samples is used for testing, while the other $n - 1$ samples for training.

Figures 17.3 and 17.4 show the comparison between the actual running time and the predicted running time for each sample case. The x-axis represents the actual running time, and the y-axis the predicted time. In ideal cases, all the points will be distributed on the line $y = x$, which is shown as the solid line. These figures show that the points are very close to the ideal line, indicating excellent prediction accuracy.

We define the average accuracy as the average relative errors (ARE) over the n rounds of testing in the cross-validation. Let C_i be the real cost and $\hat{C}_i$ be the estimated cost by the trained model in the round i. We calculate ARE with the following equation.

$$ARE = \frac{1}{n}\sum_{i=1}^{n}\frac{\left|C_1 - \hat{C}\right|}{C_i} \tag{17.19}$$

Intuitively, this represents the percentage of prediction error in terms of the actual execution time. Table 17.2 shows the AREs in leave-one-out cross-validation. The result confirms most models are robust and perform well. However, certain models such as PageRank in the local cluster perform less effectively than others. A further detailed study will be performed to understand the factors affecting the modeling.

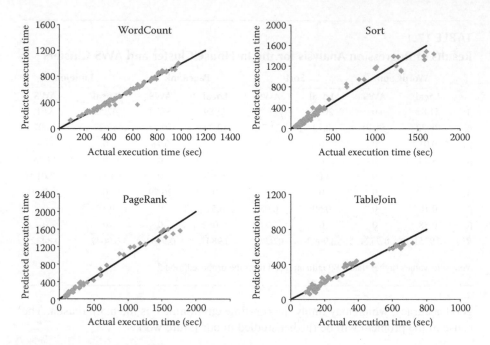

FIGURE 17.3 Model accuracy in local cluster.

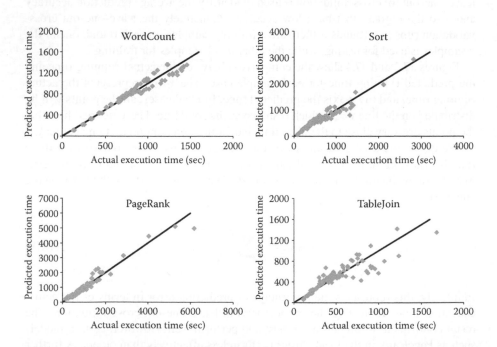

FIGURE 17.4 Model accuracy in Amazon EC2.

TABLE 17.2

Average Relative Error Rates of the Leave-One-Out Cross-Validation and of the Testing Result on Training Data for the Four Programs

	WordCount	Sort	PageRank	TableJoin
Local	5.49%	15.23%	12.18%	13.57%
AWS	6.46%	15.61%	7.92%	14.62%

17.7 RELATED WORK

The recent research on MapReduce has been focused on understanding and improving the performance of MapReduce processing in a dedicated private Hadoop cluster. The configuration parameters of Hadoop cluster are investigated in [1,7,8] to find the optimal configuration for different types of job. In [21], the authors simulate the steps in MapReduce processing and explore the effect of network topology, data layout, and the application I/O characteristics to the performance. Job scheduling algorithms in the multiuser multijob environment are also studied in [19,23,24]. These studies have different goals from our work, but an optimal configuration of Hadoop will reduce the amount of required resources and time for jobs running in the public cloud as well. A theoretical study on the MapReduce programming model [12] characterizes the features of mixed sequential and parallel processing in MapReduce, which justifies our analysis in Section 17.3.

MapReduce performance prediction has been another important topic. Kambatla et al. [10] studied the effect of the setting of map and reduce slots to the performance and observed different MapReduce programs may have different CPU and I/O patterns. A fingerprint-based method is used to predict the performance of a new MapReduce program based on the studied programs. Historical execution traces of MapReduce programs are also used for program profiling and performance prediction in [13]. For long MapReduce jobs, accurate progress indication is important, which is also studied in [16]. A strategy used by [10,13], and shared by our approach, is to use test runs on small scale settings to characterize the behaviors of large-scale settings. However, these approaches do not study an explicit cost function that can be used in optimization problems.

17.8 CONCLUSION

Running MapReduce programs in the public cloud raises an important problem: how to optimize resource provisioning to minimize the financial cost for a specific job? To answer this question, we believe a fundamental problem is to understand the relationship between the amount of resources and the job characteristics (e.g., input data, processing algorithm). In this paper, we study the components in MapReduce processing and build a cost function that explicitly models the relationship between the amount of data, the available system resources (map and reduce slots), and the complexity of the reduce program for the target MapReduce program. The model parameters can be learned from test runs. Based on this cost model, we can solve a number of decision problems, such as the optimal amount of resources that can minimize the financial cost with the constraints of financial budget or time deadline. We have also conducted a set of experiments on both an in-house Hadoop cluster and on-demand Hadoop clusters in Amazon EC2 to validate the model. The result shows that this cost model fits well on four tested programs. Note this modeling and optimization framework also aligns with the goal of energy efficient computing by reducing the unnecessary possession and use of cloud resources. If we can model the energy consumption profiles of the resources, we can also precisely optimize the overall energy consumption with the proposed framework.

Some future studies include (1) understand the model prediction errors to improve the modeling process, which might include sample selection and model adjustment, (2) conduct more experiments on different MapReduce programs and different types of EC2 instances, and (3) extend the study to energy efficient MapReduce computing.

ACKNOWLEDGMENTS

This project is partly supported by the Ohio Board of Regents and Amazon Web Services.

REFERENCES

1. Shivnath Babu. Towards automatic optimization of mapreduce programs. In *Proceedings of the 1st ACM Symposium on Cloud Computing*, pages 137–142, New York, USA, 2010. ACM.
2. Jayant Baliga, Robert W. A. Ayre, Kerry Hinton, and Rodney S. Tucker. Green cloud computing: Balancing energy in processing, storage and transport. *Proceedings of the IEEE*, 99(1): 149–167, January 2011.
3. Sergey Brin and Lawrence Page. The anatomy of a large-scale hypertextual web search engine. In *International Conference on World Wide Web*, 1998.
4. Abhinandan S. Das, Mayur Datar, Ashutosh Garg, and Shyam Rajaram. Google news personalization: Scalable online collaborative filtering. In *International Conference on World Wide Web*, pages 271–280, New York, USA, 2007. ACM.
5. Jeffrey Dean and Sanjay Ghemawat. MapReduce: Simplified data processing on large clusters. In *OSDI*, pages 137–150, 2004.
6. Trevor Hastie, Robert Tibshirani, and Jerome Friedman. *The Elements of Statistical Learning*. Springer-Verlag, 2001.
7. Herodotos Herodotou and Shivnath Babu. Profiling, what-if analysis, and cost-based optimization of MapReduce programs. *PVLDB*, 4(11):1111–1122, 2011.
8. Dawei Jiang, Beng Chin Ooi, Lei Shi, and Sai Wu. The performance of MapReduce: An in-depth study. In *Proceedings of Very Large Databases Conference (VLDB)*, 2010.
9. Thorsten Joachims, Laura Granka, Bing Pan, and Geri Gay. Accurately interpreting click-through data as implicit feedback. In *Proceedings of ACM SIGIR Conference*, 2005.
10. Karthik Kambatla, Abhinav Pathak, and Himabindu Pucha. Towards optimizing hadoop provisioning in the cloud. In *USENIX Workshop on Hot Topics in Cloud Computing (HotCloud09)*, 2009.
11. U Kang, Charalampos E. Tsourakakis, and Christos Faloutsos. Pegasus: Mining peta-scale graphs. *Knowledge and Information Systems (KAIS)*, 2010.

12. Howard Karloff, Siddharth Suri, and Sergei Vassilvitskii. A model of computation for MapReduce. In *Symposium on Discrete Algorithms (SODA) (2010)*, 2010.
13. Soila Kavulya, Jiaqi Tan, Rajeev Gandhi, and Priya Narasimhan. An analysis of traces from a production mapreduce cluster. In *IEEE/ACM International Conference on Cluster Cloud and Grid Computing*, pages 94–103, 2010.
14. Charles L. Lawson and Richard J. Hanson. *Solving Least Squares Problems*. Society for Industrial Mathematics, 1987.
15. Jimmy Lin and Chris Dyer. *Data-Intensive Text Processing with MapReduce*. Morgan and Claypool Publishers, 2010.
16. Kristi Morton, Abram Friesen, Magdalena Balazinska, and Dan Grossman. Estimating the progress of MapReduce pipelines. In *Proceedings of IEEE International Conference on Data Engineering (ICDE)*, 2010.
17. Biswanath Panda, Joshua S. Herbach, Sugato Basu, and Roberto J. Bayardo. Planet: Massively parallel learning of tree ensembles with MapReduce. In *Proceedings of Very Large Databases Conference (VLDB)*, 2009.
18. Andrew Pavlo, Erik Paulson, Alexander Rasin, Daniel J. Abadi, David J. DeWitt, Samuel Madden, and Michael Stonebraker. A comparison of approaches to large-scale data analysis. In *Proceedings of ACM SIGMOD Conference*, 2009.
19. Thomas Sandholm and Kevin Lai. MapReduce optimization using regulated dynamic prioritization. In *SIGMETRICS/Performance09*, 2009.
20. Ashish Thusoo, Zheng Shao, Suresh Anthony, Dhruba Borthakur, Namit Jain, Joydeep Sen Sarma, Raghotham Murthy, and Hao Liu. Data warehousing and analytics infrastructure at Facebook. In *Proceedings of ACM SIGMOD Conference*, pages 1013–1020. ACM, 2010.
21. Guanying Wang, Ali Butt, Prashant Pandey, and Karan Gupta. A simulation approach to evaluating design decisions in MapReduce setups. In *IEEE/ACM Intl. Symposium on Modelling, Analysis and Simulation of Computer and Telecommunications Systems*, 2009.
22. Tom White. *Hadoop: The Definitive Guide*. O'Reilly Media, 2009.
23. Matei Zaharia, Dhruba Borthakur, Joydeep Sen Sarma, Khaled Elmeleegy, Scott Shenker, and Ion Stoica. Job scheduling for multi-user MapReduce clusters. Technical Report UCB/EECS-2009-55, University of California at Berkeley, 2009.
24. Matei Zaharia, Andy Konwinski, Anthony D. Joseph, Randy Katz, and Ion Stoica. Improving MapReduce performance in heterogeneous environments. In *8th USENIX Symposium on Operating Systems Design and Implementation (OSDI08)*, 2008.

18 Performance Analysis for Large IaaS Clouds

Rahul Ghosh, Francesco Longo,
and Kishor S. Trivedi

CONTENTS

18.1 INTRODUCTION

IaaS clouds are major enablers of data-intensive cloud applications because they provide necessary computing capacity for managing Big Data environments. In a typical IaaS cloud, virtual machine (VM) instances deployed on physical machines (PM) are provided to the users for their computing needs. Recently, IaaS cloud providers are realizing that merely providing the basic functionalities for Big Data processing is not sufficient to survive intense business competitions. Rather, the performance of the cloud provided service is an equally important factor when a user signs up for the service contract. We observe that, to date, most of the IaaS cloud providers offer SLAs only in terms of guaranteed availability. With increasing demand and popularity of cloud services, we believe that performance SLAs will also be necessary in the near future. However, performance analysis of a cloud infrastructure is difficult due to a variety of reasons. Hardware (e.g., CPU speed, disk properties), software (e.g., nature of hypervisor), workload (e.g., arrival rate), and many other management characteristics (e.g., placement policy) can impact the overall cloud performance.

To evaluate the performance of a cloud, broadly three choices can be made. First, one can carry out experimentation for measurement based performance quantification. Unfortunately, scale of cloud becomes prohibitive in terms of time and cost of such measurement-based analysis. Second, discrete event simulation can be used as another alternative [1]. Still, such simulation can take a long time to get statistically significant results. Third, stochastic models can be used as a low-cost option where the model solution time is much less compared with simulation and experimentation. However, stochastic models may not scale given the size and complexity of a cloud system. For cloud environments processing large data sets, the state space of the developed Markov model tends to be very large as the model takes into account many details of the system. This well-known largeness problem of stochastic model arises because of a growing number of model states as the number of system component increases. As the model size becomes prohibitively large, the generation and solution of such a model become a tedious task, if not impossible. Simplifying a model to reduce complexity may turn out to be fatal as the model might diverge from the realistic scenario. Hence, a scalable modeling approach that can preserve accuracy is of interest.

In this chapter, we describe the principle of scalable stochastic modeling approach with an example of performance analysis for an IaaS cloud that are large scale and well-suited for Big Data environments. The proposed approach is based on interactions among several submodels, where the overall solution is composed by iteration over individual submodel solutions. Scalability and tractability are two key features of our approach when compared with a one-level monolithic modeling approach [8]. Thus, interacting submodels can provide results for large clouds within reasonable solution time. A comparison of analytic–numeric results between the two approaches also show the accuracy of the proposed interacting submodels approach. An additional benefit of the proposed approach is that submodels often become simple enough to obtain a closed-form solution. Stochastic modeling software packages such as SHARPE [20] and SPNP [11] can be complemented using such closed-form expressions when the system becomes too large.

Key contributions of this chapter are the following: (1) We demonstrate that scalable stochastic models can be developed and solved for large-scale performance analysis of IaaS clouds. (2) Interested readers can extend submodels shown in the chapter by modifying the provided SHARPE codes. (3) Such modeling approaches can help in what-if analysis of overall cloud performance. Especially, we show how bottlenecks in provisioning delay can shift with varying cloud capacity and job service characteristics.

The rest of the chapter is organized as follows. A three-pool cloud architecture is described in Section 18.2. Our performance analysis approach will be based on the system described in Section 18.2. The main idea of interacting submodels approach is presented in Section 18.3. Analytic–numeric solutions of the interacting submodels and comparison with monolithic model solutions are presented in Section 18.4. Section 18.5.2 presents discussions on the proposed approach, possible extensions and some highlights on related research. Finally, this chapter is concluded in Section 18.6.

18.2 A THREE-POOL CLOUD ARCHITECTURE

We consider an IaaS cloud where PMs are grouped into multiple pools based on power consumption and response time characteristics. Specifically we consider three pools: hot, warm, and cold. Figure 18.1 shows the overall architecture and request provisioning steps. In the hot pool, all PMs are running and VMs need to be configured and deployed as per user request. In contrast, PMs in the warm pool are turned on but not running. Warm PMs initially remain in a power-saving/sleep mode and they are turned on whenever a deployment request comes. Thus, provisioning a VM in the warm pool requires additional delay compared with PMs in the hot pool. PMs in the cold pool are initially turned off. Hence, provisioning a VM in the cold pool requires additional delay. Notice that, power consumption of a hot PM is maximum, whereas the power consumption of a cold PM is minimum. Grouping the PMs in multiple pools helps the provider to maintain a tradeoff in service offering, based on power consumption and response time characteristics [9].

We assume that the service requests are homogeneous and each request is for one VM instance with specific CPU, RAM, and disk capacity. Throughout this chapter, we use the term *job* to denote a service request. When a request arrives, Resource Provisioning Decision Engine (RPDE) tries to find a PM from the hot pool that can accept the request. If all the PMs in hot pool are already busy in running jobs, RPDE tries to find a PM from the warm pool. If no such PMs are available in the warm pool, RPDE tries to find a cold PM that can accept the job. A request is rejected if none of the PMs in the hot/warm/cold pool can accept the request. The elapsed time

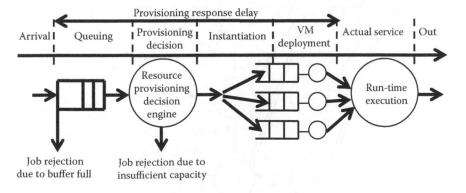

FIGURE 18.1   Request provisioning steps in a three-pool cloud architecture.

duration between the submission of a request to cloud and the VM made available to the user is called response delay. We use job rejection probability and response delay as the two performance metrics for our analysis.

18.3   INTERACTING SUBMODELS FOR PERFORMANCE ANALYSIS

18.3.1   CTMC Submodel for RPDE

Figure 18.2 shows the CTMC model for RPDE. The input parameters for this submodel are: (i) job arrival rate (λ), (ii) mean searching delays to find a PM in a hot/warm/cold pool that can be used for resource provisioning ($1/\delta_h$, $1/\delta_w$, and $1/\delta_c$, respectively), (iii) probabilities that a hot/warm/cold PM can accept a job for resource provisioning (P_h, P_w, and P_c, respectively), and (iv) maximum number of jobs in RPDE (N). All the input parameters can be measured directly except the probabilities P_h, P_w, and P_c. These probabilities are computed from the outputs of the VM provisioning submodel as described later.

We briefly describe the CTMC submodel here. Detailed description of the submodel can be found in [8]. The state index of the CTMC in Figure 18.2 is denoted by (j, x), where j denotes the number of jobs in the queue and x denotes the type of pool where the job is undergoing provisioning decision. In state $(0, 0)$, there is no job in the system. When RPDE is trying to find a PM from the hot pool, x is set to h. Similarly, x is set to "w" (or "c"), when RPDE is deciding if any warm (or cold) PM can accept the job. With the arrival of a job, model moves from state $(0, 0)$ to state $(0, h)$ with rate λ. Three possible events can occur in state $(0, h)$: (a) a job is accepted in hot pool with probability P_h, (b) with probability $(1 - P_h)$, the submodel goes to state $(0, w)$, (c) the submodel goes to state $(1, h)$ with the arrival of a new job. The rest of the submodel can be followed in the similar manner.

It is possible to derive a closed form solution for the state probabilities on the model shown in Figure 18.2. Assume that $\pi_{(j,x)}$ denotes steady-state probability of state (j, x), where $0 \le j \le (N-1)$ and $x \in \{0, h, w, c\}$.

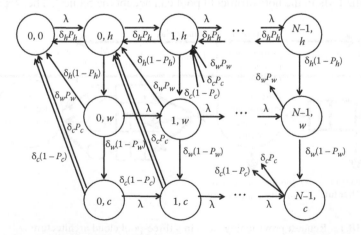

FIGURE 18.2   Resource provisioning decision engine submodel.

The general forms of steady-state probabilities to be in states (k,h), (k,w), and (k,c) are given by

$$\pi_{(k,h)} = A_{(k,h)}\pi_{(0,0)} \tag{18.1}$$

$$\pi_{(k,w)} = A_{(k,w)}\pi_{(0,0)} \tag{18.2}$$

$$\pi_{(k,c)} = A_{(k,c)}\pi_{(0,0)} \tag{18.3}$$

where $1 \le k \le (N-2)$,

$$A_{(k,h)} = XYA_{(k,c)} - YZA_{(k-1,c)} - WA_{(k-1,w)} = YA_{(k,w)} - WA_{(k-1,w)} \tag{18.4}$$

$$A_{(k,w)} = X A_{(k,c)} - Z A_{(k-1,c)} \tag{18.5}$$

$$A_{(k,c)} = \frac{(\lambda+\delta_h)A_{(k-1,h)}}{\delta_h P_h XY + \delta_w P_w X + \delta_c} + \frac{\delta_h P_h YZA_{(k-1,c)} + \delta_h P_h WA_{(k-1,w)}}{\delta_h P_h XY + \delta_w P_w X + \delta_c}$$
$$+ \frac{\delta_w P_w ZA_{(k-1,c)} - \lambda A_{(k-2,h)}}{\delta_h P_h XY + \delta_w P_w X + \delta_c} \tag{18.6}$$

$$A_{(-1,h)} = 1 \tag{18.7}$$

$$W = \frac{\lambda}{\delta_h(1-P_h)} \tag{18.8}$$

$$X = \frac{\lambda+\delta_c}{\delta_w(1-P_w)} \tag{18.9}$$

$$Y = \frac{\lambda+\delta_w}{\delta_h(1-P_h)} \tag{18.10}$$

$$Z = \frac{\lambda}{\delta_w(1-P_w)} \tag{18.11}$$

Steady-state probabilities of states $(N{-}1,h)$, $(N{-}1,w)$, and $(N{-}1,c)$ are given by

$$\pi_{(N-1,h)} = \lambda/\delta_h \pi_{(N-2,h)} = \lambda/\delta_h A_{(N-2,h)} \pi_{(0,0)} \tag{18.12}$$

$$\pi_{(N-1,w)} = \lambda/\delta_w \pi_{(N-2,w)} + \frac{\delta_h(1-P_h)}{\delta_w} \pi_{(N-1,h)} \tag{18.13}$$

$$= \lambda/\delta_w A_{(N-2,w)} \pi_{(0,0)} + \frac{\delta_h(1-P_h)}{\delta_w} \lambda/\delta_h A_{(N-2,h)} \pi_{(0,0)} \tag{18.14}$$

$$\pi_{(N-1,c)} = \lambda/\delta_c \pi_{(N-2,c)} + \frac{\delta_w(1-P_w)}{\delta_c} \pi_{(N-1,w)}$$

$$= \lambda/\delta_c A_{(N-2,c)} + \frac{\delta_w(1-P_w)}{\delta_c} \left(\lambda/\delta_w A_{(N-2,w)} \right.$$

$$\left. + \frac{\delta_h(1-Ph)}{\delta_w} \lambda/\delta_h A_{(N-2,h)} \right) \pi_{(0,0)} \tag{18.15}$$

Observe that steady-state probabilities of all states in the CTMC of Figure 18.2 can be expressed as a function of the steady-state probability of state (0,0). Using normalization,

$$\pi_{(0,0)} + \sum_{i=0}^{N-1} (\pi_{(i,h)} + \pi_{(i,w)} + \pi_{(i,c)}) = 1, \tag{18.16}$$

we can compute the steady-state probability of state (0,0) and all other states.

18.3.1.1   Submodel Outputs

(i) **Job rejection probability** (P_{reject}). Job rejection probability due to buffer full is given by

$$P_{block} = \pi_{(N-1,h)} + \pi_{(N-1,w)} + \pi_{(N-1,c)} \tag{18.17}$$

Jobs can also be rejected if during the provisioning decision steps, all (hot, warm, and cold) PMs are fully occupied. Thus, job rejection probability due to insufficient PM capacity is given by

$$\sum_{i=0}^{(N-1)} \left(\frac{\delta_c(1-P_c)\pi_{(i,c)}}{\lambda} \right) \tag{18.18}$$

Equation 18.18 can be explained in the following way. In states, $\pi_{(i,c)}$, jobs can be rejected if there is no cold PM is available for provisioning. To compute the job rejection probability, we use a Markov reward approach [19]. A reward rate of $\delta_c(1 - P_c)/\lambda$ is assigned to each state and the overall probability is computed as expected steady-state reward rate.

(ii) **Mean number of jobs in the RPDE queue** $(E[N_{R^{PDE}}])$. We can compute the RPDE queue length as

$$E\left[N_{R^{PDE}}\right] = \sum_{i=0}^{N-1} i(\pi_{(i,h)} + \pi_{(i,w)} + \pi_{(i,c)}) \tag{18.19}$$

(iii) **Mean queuing delay** $(E[T_{q\_dec}])$. Conditioned upon the job not being rejected, we can compute mean queuing delay using Little's law [21]:

$$E\left[T_{q\_dec}\right] = \frac{\sum_{i=0}^{N-1} i(\pi_{(i,h)} + \pi_{(i,w)} + \pi_{(i,c)})}{\lambda(1 - P_{block} - P_{drop})} \tag{18.20}$$

(iv) **Mean decision delay** $(E[T_{decision}])$. Conditioned upon the job not being rejected, this is given by

$$E\left[T_{decision}\right] = \frac{1/\delta_h + (1 - P_h)(1/\delta_w + (1 - P_w)/\delta_c)}{\left(1 - P_{block} - P_{drop}\right)} \tag{18.21}$$

18.3.2 SHARPE CODE FOR THE RPDE SUBMODEL

The RPDE submodel can be implemented using SHARPE software package, as shown below.

```
format 8
* Markov model for RPDE; all rates are in jobs/hr
bind
lambda          1000
delta_h         20*60
delta_w         20*60
delta_c         20*60
N               100
* Dummy values for P_h, P_w, and P_c
* These values will be computed from VM provisioning sub-model
P_h             0.8
P_w             0.9
P_c             1.0
end
```

```
markov provision_decision
0_0      0_H      lambda
0_H      0_0      delta_h*P_h
0_W      0_0      delta_w*P_w
0_C      0_0      delta_c
loop     i,0,N-2
         $(i)_H       $(i+1)_H    lambda
         $(i)_W       $(i+1)_W    lambda
         $(i)_C       $(i+1)_C    lambda
end
loop     i,1,N-1
         $(i)_H       $(i-1)_H    delta_h*P_h
         $(i)_W       $(i-1)_H    delta_w*P_w
         $(i)_C       $(i-1)_H    delta_c
end
loop     i,0,N-1
         $(i)_H       $(i)_W      delta_h*(1-P_h)
         $(i)_W       $(i)_C      delta_w*(1-P_w)
end
end
end
* Blocking probability
bind   P_block        (prob(provision_decision,$(N-1)_H)+prob
(provision_decision,$(N-1)_W)+prob(provision_decision,$(N-1)_C))
* Dropping probability
bind   P_drop (delta_c*(1-P_c)/(lambda)) * (sum(p, 0, (N-1),
prob(provision_decision, $(p)_C)))
* Overall job rejection probability
bind   P_reject       (P_block + P_drop)
* Mean number of jobs in RPDE
bind   mean_num_RPDE  sum(p, 0, (N-1), (p+1)*(prob(provision_
decision, $(p)_H)+prob(provision_decision, $(p)_W)+prob
(provision_decision, $(p)_C)))
expr   P_block
expr   P_drop
expr   P_reject
expr   mean_num_RPDE
end
```

The above SHARPE code shows how states and transitions can be specified in a SHARPE input file. For example, the first line within the Markov model *provision_decision* shows that the model moves from state *0_0* to state *0_H* with rate λ. Also, notice the use of loop statements to describe the structure of the CTMC. Input parameters P_h, P_w, and P_c are originally computed from VM provisioning submodels. However, we use some dummy values in the above code to demonstrate the working of the SHARPE input file to the readers. Detailed SHARPE input file for the interacting submodels can be found in [7]. Detailed tutorials on SHARPE can be found in [1].

18.3.3 CTMC FOR VM PROVISIONING

We construct one CTMC submodel for a hot, warm, and cold PM respectively. Overall VM provisioning submodel of a pool is modeled by a set of independent submodels that represent each PM in the pool. These submodels keep track of number of VMs running on a PM.

18.3.3.1 Hot PM CTMC

Figure 18.3 shows the VM provisioning submodel for a hot PM. State index of this model is denoted by (i, j, k), where, i denotes the number of jobs in queue, j denotes number of provisioning VMs, and k denotes number of deployed VMs. The model input parameters are: (i) effective job arrival rate (λ_h), (ii) VM provisioning rate (β_h), (iii) service rate (μ), (iv) size of buffer (L_h), and (v) maximum number of VMs that can run in parallel (m). The value of j is 0 or 1, since we assume that the VMs are provisioned one at a time. With n_h PMs in the hot pool, λ_h is given by

$$\lambda_h = \frac{\lambda(1 - P_{block})}{n_h} \tag{18.22}$$

Notice that P_{block} in Equation 18.22 is computed from RPDE submodel. All other input parameters can be measured. As shown in Figure 18.3, after a job arrival submodel moves from state $(0,0,0)$ to state $(0,1,0)$, with rate λ_h, mMean VM provisioning time on a hot PM is $1/\beta_h$. Submodel moves from state $(0,1,0)$ to state $(0,0,1)$ with rate β_h. The mean service completion time is $1/\mu$. When the service finishes, VM instance is removed and the submodel moves from state $(0,0,1)$ to state $(0,0,0)$ with rate μ. The rest of the submodel can be described in a similar manner. Notice that by using a

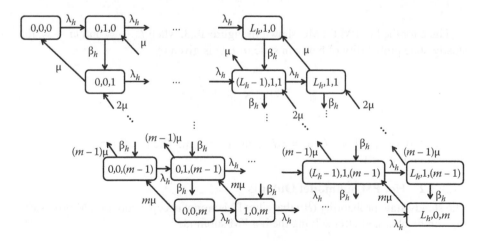

FIGURE 18.3 VM provisioning submodel for each hot PM. λ_h is an effective job arrival rate to each hot PM, β_h is rate of VM provisioning on hot PM, μ is job service rate, L_h is buffer size, m is the maximum number of VMs on each PM.

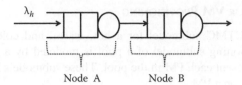

Node A   Node B

FIGURE 18.4 Hot PM modeled as a two-stage tandem network of queues. The queuing system consists of two nodes: (i) node A is a M/M/1 queue, with service rate β_h and (ii) node B is a M/M/∞ queue, with service rate of each server being μ.

state-dependent multiplier to the VM provisioning rate β_h, our submodel can easily be extended for parallel deployments of multiple VMs.

It is possible to derive closed-form solutions of the state probabilities when $L_h \to \infty$, and $m \to \infty$. In such a case, it can be shown that the CTMC can be represented as a two-stage tandem network of queues as shown in Figure 18.4. Observe that node A is an M/M/1 queue with server utilization $\rho_A = \lambda_h/\beta_h$, while node B is an M/M/∞ queue with server utilization $\rho_B = \lambda_h/\mu$. For node A, steady-state probability mass function (pmf) of i jobs ($i > 0$) waiting in the queue and j VMs ($j \in \{0,1\}$) being provisioned is given by

$$p_A(i,j) = (1-\rho_A)\rho_A^{i+j} \quad \text{where, } \rho_A < 1 \tag{18.23}$$

For node B, steady-state pmf of k VMs ($k > 0$) running, is given by

$$p_B(k) = \frac{\rho_B^k}{k!}e^{-\rho_B} \tag{18.24}$$

Thus, for the hot PM CTMC shown in Figure 18.3, when $L_h \to \infty$ and $m \to \infty$, the steady-state probability of being in state (i, j, k) is given by

$$\phi_{(i,j,k)}^{(h)} = (1-\rho_A)\rho_A^{i+j}\frac{\rho_B^k}{k!}e^{-\rho_B} \tag{18.25}$$

where $i \geq 0$, $j \in \{0,1\}$, $k \geq 0$, $\rho_A = \lambda_h/\beta_h$, and $\rho_B = \lambda_h/\mu$. The condition for stability of the system is $\rho_A < 1$.

18.3.3.2 Hot PM Submodel Outputs

The steady-state probability (B_h) that a hot PM cannot accept a job for VM provisioning can be obtained after solving the hot PM submodel:

$$B_h = \sum_{i=0}^{m-1}\phi_{(L_h,1,i)}^{(h)} + \phi_{(L_h,0,m)}^{(h)} \tag{18.26}$$

Probability (P_h) that a hot pool can accept a job for provisioning is given by

$$P_h = 1 - (B_h)^{n_h} \tag{18.27}$$

Observe that P_h is used as an input parameter in the RPDE submodel (Figure 18.2).

18.3.4 SHARPE Code for Hot PM Submodel

We present the SHARPE code for hot PM submodel below.

```
format 8
bind
* Dummy value of P_block
P_block         0.01
P_not_blocked   1-P_block
lambda          1000
beta_h          12
m               4
Lh              2
mu              1
n_h             10
epsilon_zero    0.000001
end
* Function to compute effective arrival rate for each hot PM
func lambda_h(i)
if (i==0)
        0
else
        lambda*P_not_blocked/i
end
end
* Markov model to describe VM provisioning model for hot PM
markov hot(num_hot)
loop    i,0,m-1
        0_0_$(i)        0_1_$(i)        lambda_h(num_hot)
end
loop    j,0,m-1
        loop    i,0,Lh-1
                $(i)_1_$(j)     $(i+1)_1_$(j)   lambda_h(num_hot)
        end
end
loop    i,0,Lh-1
        $(i)_0_$(m)     $(i+1)_0_$(m)   lambda_h(num_hot)
end
loop    i,0,m-1
        0_1_$(i)        0_0_$(i+1)      beta_h
end
loop    j,0,m-2
```

```
         loop    i,1,Lh
                 $(i)_1_$(j)    $(i-1)_1_$(j+1) beta_h
         end
end
loop    i,1,Lh
         $(i)_1_$(m-1)    $(i)_0_$(m)          beta_h
end
loop i,1,m
         0_0_$(i)    0_0_$(i-1)          i*mu
end
loop    j,1,m-1
         loop    i,0,Lh
                 $(i)_1_$(j)    $(i)_1_$(j-1) j*mu
         end
end
loop    i,1,Lh
         $(i)_0_$(m)                  $(i-1)_1_$(m-1) m*mu
end
end
end
* hot_full(i) computes value of 1-Ph with `i' hot PMs
func hot_full(i)
if (i==0)
         1
else
         ^(i*ln(sum(p, 0, m-1, prob(hot,$(Lh)_1_$(p);i)) +
prob(hot,$(Lh)_0_$(m);i))))
end
end
func    compute_Ph(i)
if(i == 0)
         0
else
         if(lambda_h(i) > epsilon_zero)
                 (1-hot_full(i))
         else
                 1
         end
end
end
bind    P_h    compute_Ph(n_h)
expr    P_h
end
```

Observe the use of functions to compute the values of different input parameter and output measures. Input parameter effective job arrival rate is computed using the function *lambda_h(.)*. Steady-state probability that a PM cannot accept a job for provisioning is given by the function *hot_full(.)*, while P_h is computed using the function *compute_Ph(.)*. Further, the value of P_{block} is obtained as an output from the RPDE submodel, but we use a dummy value to describe the working of the code.

18.3.4.1 Warm PM CTMC

Warm PM CTMC is shown in Figure 18.5. Although warm PM CTMC is similar to hot PM CTMC, there are few differences that set them apart. Jobs arrive to the warm PM pool only if they are not provisioned on any of the hot PMs. Thus, effective arrival rate (λ_w) to each warm PM is

$$\lambda_w = \frac{\lambda(1 - P_{block})(1 - P_h)}{n_w} \tag{18.28}$$

Initially, (state (0,0,0) in Figure 18.5), it is turned on but not ready for use. When a job arrives, the warm PM requires some additional startup delay to be able to start provisioning and the CTMC submodel goes from state (0,0,0) to state (0,1*,0). We assume that (i) time to make a warm PM ready for use is exponentially distributed with mean $1/\gamma_w$, (ii) provisioning delay of the first VM on a warm PM is $1/\beta_w$, and (iii) provisioning delay for subsequent VMs is the same as that for a hot PM, that is, $1/\beta_h$. The buffer length of each warm PM is assumed to be L_w.

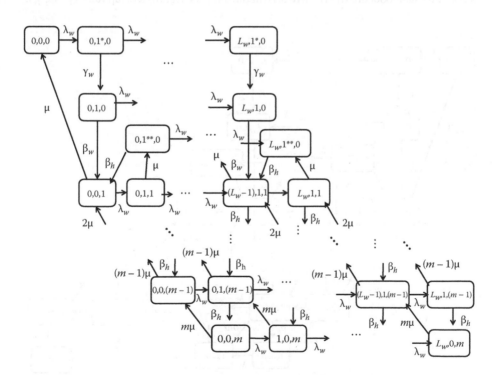

FIGURE 18.5 VM provisioning submodel for each warm PM.

18.3.4.2   Warm PM Submodel Outputs

Steady-state probability (B_w) that a warm PM cannot accept a job for VM provisioning is given by

$$B_w = \phi_{(L_w,1^*,0)}^{(w)} + \phi_{(L_w,1,0)}^{(w)} + \phi_{(L_w,1^{**},0)}^{(w)} + \sum_{i=1}^{m-1} \phi_{(L_w,1,i)}^{(w)} + \phi_{(L_w,0,m)}^{(w)} \qquad (18.29)$$

Assuming n_w as independent warm PM submodels for the whole pool, the probability (P_w) that warm PM can accept a job for provisioning is computed as

$$P_w = 1 - (B_w)^{n_w} \qquad (18.30)$$

18.3.4.3   Cold PM CTMC

Cold PM CTMC submodel is shown in Figure 18.6. The overall cold pool submodel is the set of n_c independent cold PM submodels. Key differences between a warm and a cold PM submodel are (i) effective arrival rates (λ_w vs. λ_c), (ii) startup rates (γ_w vs. γ_c),

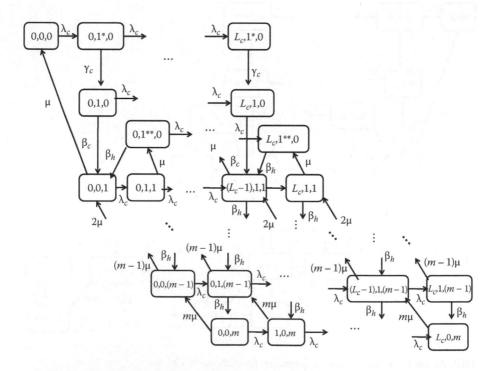

FIGURE 18.6   VM provisioning submodel for each cold PM.

(iii) initial VM provisioning rates (β_w vs. β_c) and buffer sizes (L_w vs. L_c). Effective arrival rate (λ_c) to each cold PM is given by

$$\lambda_c = \frac{\lambda(1 - P_{block})(1 - P_h)(1 - P_w)}{n_c} \tag{18.31}$$

18.3.4.4 Cold PM Submodel Outputs

The steady-state probability (B_c) that a cold PM cannot accept a job is given by

$$B_c = \phi_{(L_c,1^*,0)}^{(c)} + \phi_{(L_c,1,0)}^{(c)} + \phi_{(L_c,1^{**},0)}^{(c)} + \sum_{i=1}^{m-1} \phi_{(L_c,1,i)}^{(c)} + \phi_{(L_c,0,m)}^{(c)} \tag{18.32}$$

Thus, the probability (P_c) that at least one PM in a cold pool can accept a job is given by

$$P_c = 1 - (B_c)^{n_c} \tag{18.33}$$

SHARPE codes for the warm and cold PM submodels can be developed in a similar manner [7] as shown in Section 18.3.4. From the VM provisioning submodels, we can also compute mean queuing delay ($E[T_{q\_vm}]$) and conditional mean provisioning delay ($E[T_{prov}]$) [8]. The mean response delay is then given by

$$E[T_{resp}] = E[T_{q\_dec}] + E[T_{decision}] + E[T_{q\_vm}] + E[T_{prov}] \tag{18.34}$$

18.3.5 Submodel Interactions

Figure 18.7 shows the interactions among the submodels as an import graph [5]. Steady-state probabilities (P_h, P_w, and P_c) that at least one PM in a pool (hot, warm,

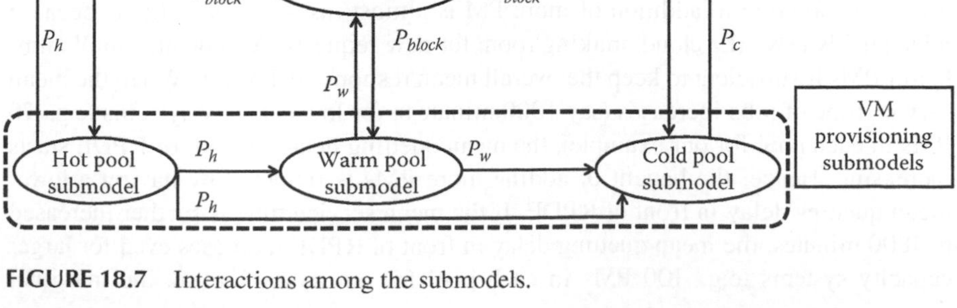

FIGURE 18.7 Interactions among the submodels.

and cold, respectively) can accept a job is computed by VM provisioning sub-models. The RPDE submodel uses these probabilities as input parameters. Output measures such as rejection probability due to buffer full (P_{block}), rejection probability due to insufficient capacity (P_{drop}), and their sum (P_{reject}) are obtained from the RPDE submodel. Observe that P_{block} computed in the RPDE submodel is used as an input parameter in VM provisioning submodels. Also, outputs from VM provisioning submodels (P_h, P_w, P_c) are needed as input parameters to solve the RPDE submodel. Hence, there is a cyclic dependency among the submodels. Such dependency is resolved using fixed-point iteration [14,17]. Proof of existence of a solution can be shown for such fixed-point iteration [8]. Apart from existence, two other important issues with fixed-point iteration are uniqueness of solution and rate convergence. By trying different initial guesses, we have never found multiple solutions, that is, the final solution remains unique. Also, in all the scenarios investigated, the maximum number of iterations required was 4, which indicates reasonably fast convergence.

18.4   ANALYTIC–NUMERIC RESULTS

Using SHARPE [20] software package, we solve the interacting submodels to compute: (1) job rejection probability and (2) mean response delay. As shown in Figure 18.8a, for a fixed arrival rate (1000 jobs/hour) and given number of PMs in each pool (e.g., 80 PMs in each pool), job rejection probability increases with longer mean service time. Also, at a given value of mean service time, if the PM capacity in each pool is increased, job rejection probability reduces. Similar effects on mean response delay is shown in Figure 18.8b. With increasing mean service time, mean response delay increases for a fixed number of PMs in each pool. To explain these effects we define a term called marginal gain. When all other input parameter values are kept unchanged, marginal gain is the amount of reduction in job rejection probability or mean response delay with increasing PM capacity. Notice that the marginal gains in Figure 18.8b, change with increasing mean service time. Marginal gain increases for gradual increase in PM capacity from 70 to 100 in each pool. In the example scenario investigated, marginal gain is maximum when the mean service time is around 1000 minutes. We provide the following arguments to explain this behavior. For a given number of PMs, mean response delay has three components: (i) mean queuing delay in front of RPDE, (ii) mean decision delay, and (iii) conditional mean provisioning delay. With increasing mean service time, marginal gain changes depending upon a dominant component of the overall delay. For a low mean service time (100–300 minutes), gain due to addition of more PM is almost insignificant. This is because jobs quickly leave the cloud, making room for new requests. As a result, small number of PMs is sufficient to keep the overall mean response delay low. When the mean service time of jobs increases (say 1000 minutes), for low capacity systems (e.g., 70 PMs in each pool for our example), the mean queuing delay in front of RPDE starts increasing. Hence, the benefit of adding more PMs is reflected by having a lower mean queuing delay in front of RPDE. If the mean service time is further increased to 1800 minutes, the mean queuing delay in front of RPDE increases even for larger capacity systems (e.g., 100 PMs in each pool for our example). So, the marginal

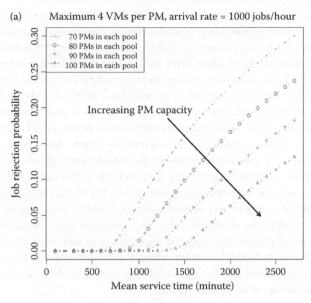

(a) Maximum 4 VMs per PM, arrival rate = 1000 jobs/hour

- --- 70 PMs in each pool
- -○- 80 PMs in each pool
- -+- 90 PMs in each pool
- -△- 100 PMs in each pool

Increasing PM capacity

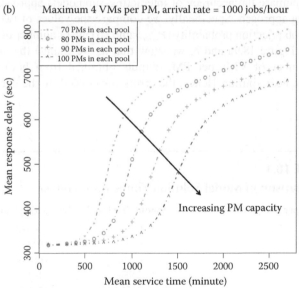

(b) Maximum 4 VMs per PM, arrival rate = 1000 jobs/hour

- --- 70 PMs in each pool
- -○- 80 PMs in each pool
- -+- 90 PMs in each pool
- -△- 100 PMs in each pool

Increasing PM capacity

FIGURE 18.8 (a) Job rejection probability vs. mean job service time and (b) mean response delay vs. mean job service time at a different number of PMs.

gain diminishes once again. This result demonstrates that using the developed performance model, one can do what-if analysis for the overall system. Specifically, we show that in overall mean response delay, bottleneck component (mean queuing delay in this case) shifts as the job characteristics (mean service time in this example) and cloud capacity (PMs in each pool) are changed.

We compare the scalability and accuracy of our approach w.r.t. a one-level monolithic model [8]. Such a monolithic model is constructed using a variant of stochastic Petri net called stochastic reward net (SRN). Stochastic Petri Net Package (SPNP) [11] is used to solve the monolithic SRN model. In Table 18.1, we compare the solution times for both the monolithic model and interacting submodels. When the number of PMs in each pool increases beyond 3 and the number of VMs per PM increases beyond 38, monolithic model runs into a memory overflow problem. Even for a small number of PMs and VMs, state space size of the monolithic model increases quickly and becomes too large to construct the reachability graph. Also, for a given number of PMs and VMs, the nonzero elements in the infinitesimal generator matrix of the underlying CTMC of monolithic model, are hundreds to thousands of orders of magnitude larger compared with interacting submodels [8]. In the interacting submodels, a reduced number of states and nonzero entries leads to concomitant reduction in solution time needed. As shown in Table 18.1, solution time for monolithic model increases almost exponentially with the increase in model size, while the solution time for interacting submodels remains almost constant with the increase in model size. This analysis shows that the proposed approach is scalable and tractable compared with the one-level monolithic model.

Next, we compare the accuracy of interacting submodels approach w.r.t. monolithic modeling approach. Specifically, we compare the values of two performance measures: (i) job rejection probability (P_{reject}) and (ii) mean number of jobs in RPDE ($E[N_{RPDE}]$). In Figure 18.9a and b, we show that as we change the arrival rate and maximum number of VMs per PM, outputs obtained from both the modeling approaches are near similar. Hence, the errors introduced by the decomposition of

TABLE 18.1
Comparison of Model Solution Times (in seconds)

(#PMs per pool, #VMs per PM)	Monolithic Model	Interacting Submodels
(1, 1)	0.124	0.066 (n.i. = 4)
(1, 2)	0.196	0.074 (n.i. = 4)
(1, 4)	0.556	0.088 (n.i. = 3)
(1, 8)	2.998	0.141 (n.i. = 3)
(1, 16)	79.563	0.208 (n.i. = 3)
(1, 32)	188.174	0.346 (n.i. = 3)
(1, 38)	293.672	0.399 (n.i. = 3)
(1, 39)	m.o.	0.406 (n.i. = 3)
(2, 1)	2.024	0.063 (n.i. = 3)
(3, 1)	166.704	0.062 (n.i. = 3)
(4, 1)	m.o.	0.060 (n.i. = 2)
(500, 64)	m.o.	0.055 (n.i. = 1)

Note: m.o., memory overflow; n.i., number of iterations.

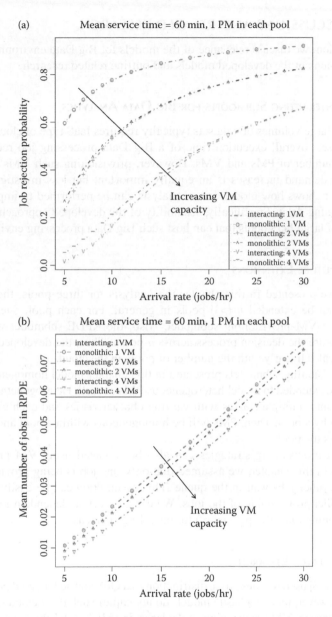

FIGURE 18.9 (a) Job rejection probability vs. arrival rate and (b) mean number of jobs in RPDE vs. arrival rate.

the monolithic model are negligible and interacting submodels approach preserves accuracy while being scalable. Such errors stem from the fact that we solve only one model for all the PMs in each pool, and aggregate the obtained results to approximate the behavior of the pool as a whole. As a result, values of the probabilities (e.g., P_h, P_w, P_c) that at least one PM is able to accept a job in a pool are different in monolithic (exact) model and interacting (approximate) submodels.

18.5 DISCUSSIONS AND RELATED RESEARCH

In this section, we discuss relevance of the models for Big Data environments, possible extensions of the developed models and outline related research.

18.5.1 INTERACTING SUBMODELS FOR BIG DATA ANALYTICS

Processing large volumes of data sets typically requires IaaS type of cloud services. In most cases, overall execution time of a Big Data processing job reduces with larger the number of PMs and VMs. However, provisioning such VMs quickly as the service demand increases is an equally important but less investigated issue. This chapter shows how model-driven analysis can be performed to improve overall provisioning delay. Specifically, scalability of the developed approach facilitates modeling of large IaaS pools that can host such Big Data processing environments.

18.5.2 FUTURE EXTENSIONS

Although we presented in this chapter the analysis for three pools, the proposed approach can be extended n (>3) pools in general. For each pool, one CTMC is needed for a VM provisioning submodel. Also, the RPDE submodel will have n rows to capture the decision process across n pools. Thus, the developed modeling approach scales linearly with the number of pools in the cloud.

VM provisioning submodels presented in this chapter model homogeneous PMs. They can be extended to model heterogeneous PMs as well. Heterogeneous PMs can be divided into multiple classes with varying characteristics and each class can be represented by a pool. Then, PMs will be homogeneous within a pool and heterogeneous across the pools.

Different provisioning strategies can also be modeled using VM provisioning submodels. In this chapter, we assumed that only one job is being provisioned at a time, while other jobs wait in the queue. This assumption can be easily relaxed to model parallel provisioning of the jobs. We can use a state dependent multiplier to the provisioning rates (β_h, β_w, and β_c) for modeling such cases.

18.5.3 RELATED RESEARCH

Xiong et al. [23] used response time distribution as a QoS metric for cloud performance analysis. However, their stochastic models do not capture details of cloud service provisioning decision, VM provisioning, and release. In [23], Varalakshmi et al. addressed workflow scheduling in cloud to meet user-requested QoS parameters. The authors analyzed the PM performance behaviors using Generalized Processor Sharing queues.

Mills et al. [16] used sensitivity analysis methods to identify important input parameters that can affect cloud placement algorithms. Mi et al. [17] developed an approach to detect performance bottlenecks in large cloud services. Using hierarchical structure, the authors constructed an execution path graph of user request. Such an approach can be combined with our performance model to optimize the request placement decisions.

In [6], Genaud et al. used simulations to evaluate scheduling strategies in cloud. The authors primarily focused on minimizing the wait time of jobs and the monetary cost of the rented resources. Our numeric–analytic models can complement such studies. Goudarzi et al. [10] studied optimization problems for multitier cloud applications by taking into account requests with different CPU, memory, and network resource requirements. Performance models developed in this paper can be extended for such heterogeneous requests. Yigitbasi et al. [24] performed an experimental analysis for the resource acquisition and release times in Amazon EC2. Our stochastic models can complement these studies and analyze root-causes behind the major results. Performance analysis of VM live migration and its impacts on SLAs was studied by Voorsluys et al. [22]. Examples of other measurement based performance evaluation of cloud services include [2,4,12,13,18].

18.6 CONCLUSIONS

With increasing popularity of IaaS cloud-based services, data-intensive applications will find a natural home in such shared and virtualized environments. While a variety of cloud providers offer similar services, performance will be a key differentiator among the delivered services. This chapter presents how model driven stochastic performance analysis can scale for large sized clouds. The main idea is to develop interacting submodels so that the overall model becomes scalable and tractable. Once developed, such scalable models can be used for what-if analysis, bottleneck detection, and capacity planning. Tools and software packages can be developed based on such models to assist a cloud administrator overseeing Big Data applications.

REFERENCES

1. Tutorial on the Sharpe interface, June 2013. http://sharpe.pratt.duke.edu/node/4.
2. A. Bhadani and S. Chaudhary. Performance evaluation of web servers using central load balancing policy over virtual machines on cloud. In *COMPUTE '10: Proceedings of the Third Annual ACM Bangalore Conference*, pp. 16:1–16:4, Bangalore, India, 2010.
3. R. Buyya, R. Ranjan, and R. N. Calheiros. Modeling and simulation of scalable cloud computing environments and the cloudsim toolkit: Challenges and opportunities. In *IEEE International Conference on High Performance Computing and Simulation (HPCS)*, pp. 1–11, Leipzig, Germany, 2009.
4. J. Che, Q. He, K. Ye, and D. Huang. Performance Combinative Evaluation of Typical Virtual Machine Monitors. In *Second International Conference on High Performance Computing and Applications (HPCA)*, pp. 96–101, Shanghai, China, 2009.
5. G. Ciardo and K. S. Trivedi. A decomposition approach for stochastic reward net models. *Elsevier Performance Evaluation*, 18(1):37–59, 1993.
6. S. Genaud and J. Gossa. Cost-wait trade-offs in client-side resource provisioning with elastic clouds. In *IEEE International Conference on Cloud Computing (CLOUD)*, pp. 1–8, Washington, DC, July 2011.
7. R. Ghosh. Scalable stochastic models for cloud services. *PhD Thesis, Duke University*, 2012.
8. R. Ghosh, F. Longo, V. K. Naik, and K. S. Trivedi. Modeling and performance analysis of large scale IaaS clouds. *Elsevier Future Generation Computer Systems*, 2012. Available online: http://dx.doi.org/10.1016/j.future.2012.06.005.

9. R. Ghosh, V. K. Naik, and K. S. Trivedi. Power-performance trade-offs in IaaS cloud: A scalable analytic approach. In *IEEE/IFIP International Conference on Dependable Systems and Networks (DSN), Workshop on Dependability of Clouds, Data Centers and Virtual Computing Environments (DCDV)*, pp. 152–157, Hong Kong, China, 2011.

10. H. Goudarzi and M. Pedram. Multi-dimensional SLA-based resource allocation for multitier cloud computing systems. In *IEEE International Conference on Cloud Computing (CLOUD)*, pp. 324–331, Washington, DC, July 2011.

11. C. Hirel, B. Tuffin, and K. S. Trivedi. SPNP: Stochastic Petri Nets. Version 6. In *International Conference on Computer Performance Evaluation: Modelling Techniques and Tools (TOOLS 2000)*, B. Haverkort, H. Bohnenkamp (eds.), Lecture Notes in Computer Science 1786, Springer Verlag, pp. 354–357, Schaumburg, IL, 2000.

12. A. Iosup, N. Yigitbasi, and D. Epema. On the performance variability of production cloud services. In *IEEE/ACM International Symposium on Cluster, Cloud and Grid Computing (CCGrid)*, pp. 104–113, Newport Beach, CA, 2011.

13. H. Liu and S. Wee. Web server farm in the cloud: Performance evaluation and dynamic architecture. In *International Conference on Cloud Computing (CloudCom)*, pp. 369–380, Beijing, China, 2009.

14. V. Mainkar and K. S. Trivedi. Sufficient conditions for existence of a fixed point in stochastic reward net-based iterative models. *IEEE Transaction on Software Engineering*, 22(9):640–653, 1996.

15. H. Mi, H. Wang, G. Yin, H. Cai, Q. Zhou, T. Sun, and Y. Zhou. Magnifier: Online detection of performance problems in large-scale cloud computing systems. In *IEEE International Conference on Services Computing (SCC)*, pp. 418–425, Washington, DC, July 2011.

16. K. Mills, J. Filliben, and C. Dabrowski. An efficient sensitivity analysis method for large cloud simulations. In *IEEE International Conference on Cloud Computing (CLOUD)*, pp. 724–731, Washington, DC, July 2011.

17. L. Tomek and K. Trivedi. Fixed-point iteration in availability modeling. In *M. Dal Cin, editor, Informatik-fachberichte, Vol. 91: Fehlertolerierende Rechensysteme*, pp. 229–240. Springer-Verlag, Berlin, 1991.

18. S. Toyoshima, S. Yamaguchi, and M. Oguchi. Storage access optimization with virtual machine migration and basic performance analysis of amazon EC2. In *IEEE International Conference on Advanced Information Networking and Applications Workshops (WAINA)*, pp. 905–910, Perth, WA, 2010.

19. K. S. Trivedi. *Probability and Statistics with Reliability, Queuing and Computer Science Applications, second edition*. Wiley, 2001.

20. K. S. Trivedi and R. Sahner. SHARPE at the age of twenty two. *ACM Sigmetrics Performance Evaluation Review*, 36(4):52–57, March 2009.

21. P. Varalakshmi, A. Ramaswamy, A. Balasubramanian, and P. Vijaykumar. An optimal workflow based scheduling and resource allocation in cloud. In A. Abraham, J. L. Mauri, J. F. Buford, J. Suzuki, and S. M. Thampi, (eds.), *ACC (1)*, volume 190 of *Communications in Computer and Information Science*, pp. 411–420. Springer, 2011.

22. W. Voorsluys, J. Broberg, S. Venugopal, and R. Buyya. Cost of virtual machine live migration in clouds: A performance evaluation. In *International Conference on Cloud Computing (CloudCom)*, pp. 254–265, Beijing, China, 2009.

23. K. Xiong and H. Perros. Service performance and analysis in cloud computing. In *World Conference on Services*, pp. 693–700, Los Angeles, 2009.

24. N. Yigitbasi, A. Iosup, D. Epema, and S. Ostermann. C-meter: A framework for performance analysis of computing clouds. In *IEEE/ACM International Symposium on Cluster Computing and the Grid (CCGrid)*, pp. 472–477, Shanghai, China, 2009.

19 Security in Big Data and Cloud Computing

Challenges, Solutions, and Open Problems

Ragib Hasan

CONTENTS

19.1   INTRODUCTION

The age of Big Data has begun, and our computing needs and technology are at a crossroads. Cloud computing has become the dominant computing model for processing Big Data in recent years. The flexibility and cost savings made possible through migration to a cloud have encouraged many companies to use clouds for their critical applications. Unfortunately, today's clouds have major security issues related to the confidentiality, integrity, availability, and privacy of the data and applications outsourced to the cloud. Multi-tenancy and other inherent properties of the cloud computing model have introduced novel attack surfaces and threats. Clouds and their clients are also the target of new types of attacks that threaten their trustworthiness, reliability, and economic sustainability. Unless these issues are resolved, clouds cannot and should not be used for sensitive Big Data applications such as defense-related data and intelligence, financial transactions, or medical records.

In this chapter, we will discuss the major security issues related to Big Data in cloud computing, and present an overview of open problems. By systematically exploring the state of the art in Big Data and cloud computing security, we formulate the key security research questions that we need to resolve before cloud computing can become mainstream. Finally, we will highlight some unexplored research areas in cloud security and also discuss some fundamental shortcomings of current approaches to cloud security research.

19.1.1   MOTIVATION

Applications of cloud computing technology have increased greatly since 2006, for both enterprises and individuals seeking additional computing power and more storage at a low cost. Small- and medium-scale industries find cloud computing highly cost effective, as it replaces the need for costly physical and administrative infrastructure and offers the flexible pay-as-you-go structure for payment. Khajeh-Hosseini et al. found that an organization could save 37% cost if they could migrate their IT infrastructure from an outsourced data center to the Amazon's cloud [21]. A recent research by Market Research Media states that the global cloud computing market is expected to grow at a 30% Compound Annual Growth Rate (CAGR) reaching $270 billion in 2020 [24]. According to Gartner Inc., the strong growth of cloud computing will bring $148.8 billion revenue by 2014 [14]. Cloud computing is getting popular not only in the private industry, but also in the government sector. According to a research from INPUT, the US Federal government's spending on the cloud will reach $792 million by 2013 [19].

Clouds use the multitenant usage model and virtualization to ensure better utilization of resources. However, these fundamental characteristics of cloud computing are actually a double-edged sword—the same properties also make cloud-based crimes and attacks on clouds and their users difficult to prevent and investigate. According to a recent IDCI survey, 74% of IT executives and CIOs referred security as the main reason to prevent their migration to the cloud services model [11]. Some recent attacks on cloud computing platforms strengthen the security concern.

For example, a botnet attack on Amazon's cloud infrastructure was reported in 2009 [1]. Besides attacking cloud infrastructure, adversaries can use the cloud to launch attack on other systems. For example, an adversary can rent hundreds of virtual machines (VM) to launch a distributed denial of service (DDoS) attack. After a successful attack, they can erase all the traces of the attack by turning off the VMs. A criminal can also keep their secret files (e.g., child pornography, terrorist documents) in cloud storage and can destroy all evidence from their local storage to remain clean. In light of the above, it is important to examine and understand the critical security issues in cloud computing and Big Data. The goal of this chapter is to motivate and educate researchers about the various security threats in cloud computing and Big Data and provide them with a guideline toward solving the security challenges.

19.1.2 TOPICS COVERED

Big Data and cloud security problems may be roughly grouped into categories involving data integrity, computation integrity, data confidentiality and privacy, misuse detection, and novel attacks. We point out that to properly address open problems in the security of Big Data and clouds, it is vital to understand what makes cloud security different from traditional distributed systems security.

The main security and privacy issues in Big Data and cloud computing in form of the following research questions:

- **Exploitation of Co-tenancy**: How can we prevent attackers from exploiting cotenancy in attacking the infrastructure and/or other clients [27]?
- **Secure Architecture for the Cloud**: How do we design cloud computing architectures that are semitransparent and provide clients with some accountability and control over security [30]?
- **Accountability for Outsourced Data**: How can clients get assurance/proofs that the cloud provider is actually storing data, is not tampering with data, and can make the data available on demand [3,20]?
- **Confidentiality of Data and Computation**: How can we ensure confidentiality of data and computations in a cloud?
- **Privacy**: How do we perform outsourced computation while guaranteeing user privacy [28]?
- **Verifying Outsourced Computation**: How can we (efficiently) verify the accuracy of outsourced computation [12]?
- **Verifying Capability**: How can a client remotely verify the capability and resource capacity of a cloud provider [8]?
- **Cloud Forensics**: How can we augment cloud infrastructures to allow forensic investigations [23]?
- **Misuse Detection**: How can we rapidly detect misbehavior of clients in a cloud [18]?
- **Resource Accounting and Economic Attacks**: How do we ensure proper, verifiable accounting, and prevent attackers from exploiting the pay as you go model of clouds [32]?

19.1.3 Organization

The rest of this chapter will be organized as follows: In Section 19.2, we will present background information about various cloud models and explain what is new in cloud security and what characteristics of clouds make security more difficult than traditional distributed systems. In Section 19.3, we will introduce the main research questions and challenges in cloud security and elaborately discuss each of them in a set of subsections. For each subsection covering a research question, we will examine the issue at stake, explore the challenges, discuss existing solution approaches, and analyze the pros and cons of existing solutions. Next, in Section 19.4, we will present a list of open research problems, which will provide the readers with a list of potential research problems that remain unsolved. Finally, we will summarize the chapter and conclude in Section 19.5.

19.2 BACKGROUND

To understand the security challenges in cloud computing and Big Data, we need to look into the unique operational and architectural models of clouds and the properties of Big Data. In this section, we discuss the definition and various service models used in cloud computing. We then present the properties of Big Data and finally discuss why securing a cloud poses new challenges in addition to traditional distributed system security issues.

19.2.1 Cloud Computing

Cloud computing is a relatively new business model for outsourced services. However, the technology behind cloud computing is not entirely new. While virtualization, data outsourcing, and remote computation have been developed over the last 40 years, cloud computing provides a streamlined way of provisioning and delivering such services to customers. In this regard, cloud computing is best described as a business paradigm or computing model than any specific technology.

The U.S. National Institute of Standards and Technology (NIST) has defined cloud computing as "a model which provides a convenient way of on-demand network access to a shared pool of configurable computing resources (e.g., networks, servers, storage, applications, and services), that can be rapidly provisioned and released with minimal management effort or service provider interaction" [25]. The Open Cloud Manifesto Consortium defines cloud computing as "the ability to control the computing power dynamically in a cost-efficient way and the ability of the end user, organization, and IT staff to utilize the most of that power without having to manage the underlying complexity of the technology" [26].

A key characteristic of cloud computing according to the above definitions is that, a cloud is by nature a shared resource. Therefore, the same physical hardware can be shared by multiple users.

Based on which services are provided and how the services are delivered to customers, cloud computing can be divided into three categories: software as a service (SaaS), platform as a service (PaaS), and infrastructure as a service (IaaS) [25]. Figure 19.1 shows the three cloud service models.

In *software as a service* (*SaaS*), clients access software applications hosted on the cloud infrastructure, using their web browsers, through the Internet. In this model, customers do not have any control over the network, servers, operating systems, storage, or even on the application, except some access control management for multi-user application. Some of the examples of SaaS are Salesforce [29], Google Drive [16], and Google calender [15].

In *platform as a service* (*PaaS*), clients can build their own application on top of a configurable software platform deployed in a cloud. Clients do not manage or control the underlying cloud infrastructure including network, servers, operating systems, or storage, but have control over the deployed applications and some application hosting environment configurations. Customers can only use the application development environments, which are supported by the PaaS providers. Two examples of PaaS are Google App Engine (GAE) [13] and Windows Azure [4].

In the *infrastructure as a service* (*IaaS*) model, a customer rents processing power and storage to launch his own virtual machine and/or outsource data to the cloud. Here, customers have a lot of flexibility in configuring, running, and managing their

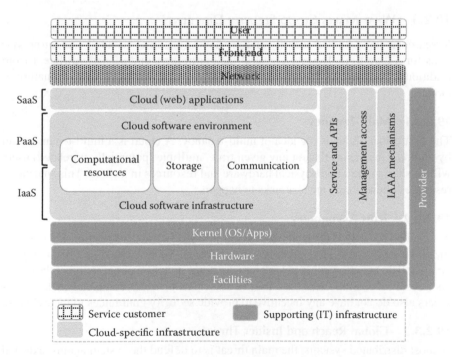

FIGURE 19.1 Three service models of cloud computing. (From B. Grobauer and T. Schreck, Towards incident handling in the cloud: Challenges and approaches, in *Proceedings of the 2010 ACM Workshop on Cloud Computing Security Workshop*, CCSW'10, pages 77–86, ACM, New York, 2010.)

own applications and software stack. The customers have full control over operating systems, storage, deployed applications, and possibly limited control of selecting networking components (e.g., host firewalls). An example of IaaS is Amazon EC2 [2]. EC2 provides users with access to virtual machines (VM) running on its servers. Customers can install any operating system and can run any application in that VM.

19.2.2   BIG DATA

With the advance of data storage and processing infrastructure, it is now possible to store and analyze huge amounts of data. This has ushered the age of Big Data, where large-scale and high-volume collections of data objects require complex data collection, processing, analysis, and storage mechanisms.

According to Gartner [6], "Big data are high volume, high velocity, and/or high variety information assets that require new forms of processing to enable enhanced decision making, insight discovery and process optimization."

Existing database technology as well as localized data-processing techniques often do not scale high enough to handle Big Data. Therefore, most Big Data-processing techniques require the use of cloud computing to process the data.

19.2.3   WHAT MAKES CLOUD SECURITY DIFFERENT?

Researchers have studied security and privacy issues in distributed computing systems for a long time. However, several factors make cloud security different from traditional distributed systems security. This is related to the fundamental nature of clouds.

19.2.3.1   Multi-Tenancy

The first critical issue is the idea of multi-tenancy. A cloud is a multi-tenant model by nature. This means that, at any given time, multiple (potentially unrelated) users will be sharing the same physical hardware and resources in a cloud. This sharing of resources allows many novel attacks to happen.

19.2.3.2   Trust Asymmetry

Next, cloud security is difficult because of the asymmetric trust relationship between the cloud service provider and the customers/users. Today's clouds act like big black boxes and do not allow users to look into the inner structure or operation of the cloud. As a result, the cloud users have to trust the cloud provider completely. Cloud providers also do not have any incentive to provide security guarantees to their clients.

19.2.3.3   Global Reach and Insider Threats

In most distributed systems, the main threat is to defend the system against external attack. Therefore, a lot of effort is directed toward keeping the malicious attackers outside the system perimeter. However, in a cloud, the attackers can legitimately be inside the system. All they need to do is to pay for the use of cloud resources. In most clouds, anyone possessing a valid credit card is given access to the cloud. Using this, attackers can get inside a cloud without actually violating any law or even cloud provider's usage policy. This access to a cloud's system has increased the vulnerabilities to user data and applications in a cloud. In addition, the global nature of clouds mean that the attackers from all over the world can target a victim just by accessing a cloud. Since clouds are shared resources, often there is the risk of collateral damage when other users sharing the same resources with a victim, will also face the effects of an attack.

19.3 RESEARCH QUESTIONS IN CLOUD SECURITY

In this section, we discuss the main research questions in cloud security. For each question, we will examine the background of the issue and look at potential research approaches.

19.3.1 EXPLOITATION OF CO-TENANCY

Research Question 1: How can we prevent attackers from exploiting co-tenancy in attacking the infrastructure and/or other clients?

As mentioned earlier, a cloud is a multi-tenant architecture. However, this fundamental property of clouds has been manipulated by many attackers to attack clouds. The attacks can exploit multi-tenancy in several ways. First, the multi-tenancy feature allows attackers to get inside a cloud legitimately, without violating any laws or bypassing any security measures. Once inside the cloud infrastructure, the attacker can then start gathering information about the cloud itself. Next, the attacker can gather information about other users using the same cloud and sharing resources with the attacker. Finally, co-tenancy also exposes cloud users from active internal attacks launched by co-resident attackers.

An example of the above was presented by Ristenpart et al. in [27]. Here, the authors show that it is possible to reverse engineer the IP address allocation scheme of Amazon.com's Amazon Web Services. Once the allocation strategy was discovered, the authors showed that attackers can exploit this knowledge to place their virtual machines in the same physical machine as their target virtual machine. Finally, the authors showed how the malicious virtual machines can gather information about their target virtual machines by exploiting CPU cache-based side channels. A follow-up work shows that the attackers can actually steal encryption keys using this attack [34].

While the attack described in [27] could easily be prevented by obfuscating the IP address allocation scheme in Amazon AWS, key features of the attack on co-resident users still remain. Solution approaches suggested in [27] include using specially designed caches that will prevent cache-based side channels and cache-wiping schemes. However, such schemes are expensive due to the specialized nature of the cache hardware needed.

19.3.2 SECURE ARCHITECTURE FOR THE CLOUD

Research Question 2: How do we design cloud computing architectures that are semi-transparent, and provide clients with some accountability and control over security?

Today's cloud computing models are designed to hide most of the inner workings of the cloud from the users. From the cloud provider's point of view, this is designed to protect the cloud infrastructure as well as the privacy of the users. However, this comes at a cost – the users of a cloud get no information beyond whatever is provided by the cloud service provider. The users do not usually have control over the operation of their virtual machines or applications running on the cloud other than through the limited interface provided by the cloud service provider.

To resolve this, researchers have proposed architectures that provide security guarantees to the users. Santos et al. designed a secure cloud infrastructure by leveraging trusted platform module or TPM chips to build a chain of trust [30]. This was used to ensure that virtual machines or applications were always loaded on a trustworthy machine with trusted configuration.

Alternatively, there have been proposals in which part of the security decision and capabilities are extended to the client's domain [22]. In this approach, a virtual management infrastructure is used for control of the cloud's operations, and the clients are allowed to have control over their own applications and virtual machines.

There are several other research approaches for securing cloud architectures [7]. For example, Zhang et al. proposed hardening the hypervisor to enforce security [33]. Excalibur [31] is another system that uses remote attestations and leverages TPMs to ensure security of the cloud architecture.

19.3.3 ACCOUNTABILITY FOR OUTSOURCED BIG DATA SETS

Research Question 3: How can clients get assurance/proofs that the cloud provider is actually storing data, is not tampering with data, and can make the data available on demand [3,20]?

Data outsourcing is a major role of clouds. Big Data is by nature large in scale and beyond the capacity of most local data storage systems. Therefore, users use clouds to store their data sets. Another reason for using clouds is to ensure the reliability and survivability of data stored in an off-site cloud.

However, today's cloud service providers do not provide any technical assurance for ensuring the integrity of outsourced data. As clouds do not allow users to examine or observe their inner workings, users have no idea where their data is being stored, how it is stored, and whether the integrity of the data set is preserved. While encryption can ensure confidentiality of outsourced data, ensuring integrity is difficult. The clients do not, most likely, have a copy of data, so comparing the stored version to the local copy is not a realistic assumption. A naive solution is to download the data completely to determine whether it was stored without any tampering. However, for large data sets, the network bandwidth costs simply prohibit this approach.

A better approach has been to perform spot checks on small chunks of data blocks. Provable Data Possession (PDP) [3] further improves this by first adding redundancy to files, which prevents small bit errors, and then preprocessing the files to add cryptographic tags. Later, the client periodically sends challenges for a small and random set of blocks. Upon getting a challenge, the cloud server needs to compute the response by reading the actual file blocks. PDP ensures that the server will be able to respond correctly only if it has the actual file blocks. The small size of the challenge and responses makes the protocol efficient. However, PDP in its original form does not work efficiently for dynamic data.

Another similar approach is based on insertion of sentinels or special markers inside the stored file. In this Proof of Retrievability (POR) approach [20], clients can send small challenges for file blocks and the presence of unmodified sentinels provide a probabilistic guarantee about the integrity of files.

19.3.4 CONFIDENTIALITY OF DATA AND COMPUTATION

Research Question 4: How can we ensure confidentiality of data and computations in a cloud?

Many users need to store sensitive data items in the cloud. For example, healthcare and business data needs extra protection mandated by many government regulations. But storing sensitive and confidential data in an untrusted third-party cloud provider expose the data to both the cloud and malicious intruders who have compromised the cloud.

Encryption can be a simple solution for ensuring confidentiality of data sent to a cloud. However, encryption comes at a cost—searching and sorting encrypted data is expensive and reduces performance. A potential solution is to use homomorphic encryption for computation on encrypted data in a cloud. However, homomorphic encryption is very inefficient, and to this day, no practical homomorphic encryption schemes have been developed.

19.3.5 PRIVACY

Research Question 5: How do we perform outsourced computation while guaranteeing user privacy [28]?

For Big Data sets of very large scale, often clients or one-time users of such data sets do not have the capability to download the data to their own systems. A very common technique is to divide the system into data provider (which has the data objects), computation provider (which provides the code), and a computational platform (such as a MapReduce framework where the code will be run on the data). However, for data sets containing personal information, a big challenge is to prevent unauthorized leaks of private information back to the clients.

As an example, suppose that a researcher wants to run an analysis on the medical records of 100,000 patients of a hospital. The hospital cannot release the data to the researcher due to privacy issues, but it can make the data accessible to a trusted third-party computational platform, where the code supplied by the researcher (computation provider) is run on the data, with the results being sent back to the researcher.

However, this model has risks—if the researcher is malicious, he can write a code that will leak private information from the medical records directly through the result data or via indirect means. To prevent such privacy violations, researchers have proposed techniques that use the notion of differential privacy. For example, the Airavat framework [28] modifies the MapReduce framework to incorporate differential privacy, thereby preventing the leakage of private information. However, the current state-of-the-art in this area is very inefficient in terms of performance, often causing more than 30% in overheads for privacy protection.

19.3.6   Verifying Outsourced Computation

Research Question 6: How can we (efficiently) verify the accuracy of outsourced computation [12]?

Users of clouds often outsource large and complex computations to a cloud. However, doing so exposes the cloud user to a new issue: what guarantees that the cloud provider will accurately execute the program and provide a correct value as a result?

Users have several options: first, clients can redo the computation. However, for costly computations, the clients often would lack the capability to do so (and which is precisely why they outsource the computations). Next, users can do redundant computation by sending the computation to multiple clouds and later take majority voting or other consensus schemes to determine correctness. For large computations, this also may not be practical.

A slightly different approach was developed by Du et al. [12], who used run-time attestation. In their scheme, the same data in a DataFlow programming system is routed via multiple paths, and results are compared in each pair of cloud nodes performing the same computation on the same data. Based on agreements between the results from the two nodes, an attestation graph is created. From that graph, the maximal clique of nodes is computed. If that clique has more than half of the nodes, then it is assumed to be trustworthy, and results coming from the nodes belonging to the maximal clique are also considered trustworthy.

19.3.7   Verifying Capability

Research Question 7: How can a client remotely verify the capability and resource capacity of a cloud provider [8]?

Verifying capability of a service provider is difficult, and even more so when the service provider does not allow inspection of its infrastructure. Therefore, verifying the capability of a cloud to store data or run applications is a complex problem. Researchers have only recently developed techniques for verifying the storage capability of cloud service providers. Bowers et al. [8] developed a strategy to determine whether a cloud is indeed storing multiple replicas of a file, and therefore is capable of recovering from crashes. In this approach, file read latencies are used to determine the presence of multiple physical replicas. Similar research has also looked into verifying the capability of storing files in geographically separate data centers [5].

19.3.8   Cloud Forensics

Research Question 8: How can we augment cloud infrastructures to allow forensic investigations [23]?

Cloud forensics is the application of computer forensic principles and procedures in a cloud computing environment. Traditional digital forensics strategies and practices often fail when the suspect uses a cloud. As an example, a suspect using a traditional file storage to store his incriminating documents would be easy to convict and prosecute—the law enforcement investigators can make an image of his hard drives and run forensic analysis tools there.

However, when the suspect stores the files in a cloud, many complications occur. For example, since the suspect does not have any files stored locally, seizing and imaging his drives do not yield any evidence. The law enforcement agents can raid the cloud provider and seize the disks from there. However, that brings on more complications—since a cloud is a shared resource, many other unrelated people would have their data stored in those drives. Thus, seizure or imaging of such drives will compromise the privacy and availability of many users of the cloud.

The cloud service providers can provide access to all data belonging to a client on request from law enforcement. However, the defense attorneys can claim that the prosecution and the cloud provider have planted evidence to frame the suspect. Since clouds intentionally hide their inner workings, this cannot be disproved using the current cloud models. Maintaining a proper chain of custody for digital evidence is also difficult.

19.3.9 MISUSE DETECTION

Research Question 9: How can we rapidly detect misbehavior of clients in a cloud [18]?

Besides being used by legitimate users, clouds can be misused for malicious purposes. For example, an attacker can rent thousands of machines in a cloud for a relatively cheap price and then send spam or host temporary phishing sites or simply create a botnet to launch denial of service attacks. In [10], Chen et al. discussed the threat of using clouds for running brute forcers, spammer, or botnets.

Another usage of clouds is for password cracking. In fact, there are commercial password cracking services such as WPACracker.com, which leverages cloud computing to crack WPA passwords in less than 20 minutes using a rainbow table approach.

19.3.10 RESOURCE ACCOUNTING AND ECONOMIC ATTACKS

Research Question 10: How do we ensure proper, verifiable accounting and prevent attackers from exploiting the pay as you go model of clouds?

From the cloud user's point of view, accounting is also a critical issue. It is vital to ensure that cloud users are only billed for resources they have consumed and also that the consumption is what they were supposed to require given their application requirements. Sekar et al. [32] proposed a model for verifiable accounting in clouds where clients get a cryptographic proof of resource usage. Clouds are also subject to economic attacks where attackers launch variations of denial of service attacks to cause their victims to consume more cloud resources than needed and thereby cause economic loss.

19.4 OPEN PROBLEMS

Many open problems remain in cloud and Big Data security. In this section, we discuss a few of these areas and the associated challenges.

19.4.1 DETACHMENT FROM REALITY

A big limitation of existing research is the failure to look at reality. Many security schemes impose unrealistic overheads (e.g., >35%). In practice, users are unlikely to use such inefficient systems. Another issue facing current research efforts is the failure to consider economy—many security schemes would cause significant changes to existing cloud infrastructures, which are not economically feasible. Finally, many attacks are based on flawed or impractical threat models and simply do not make any economic sense. For example, in most cases, a multibillion dollar cloud service provider has little incentive to act dishonestly, but many solutions are designed with a cloud provider as the main adversary. Designing a realistic and practical threat model for cloud computing, and Big Data is vital toward creating solutions to real-life problems.

19.4.2 REGULATORY COMPLIANCE

While a lot of research has been conducted on many areas of cloud security involving data confidentiality, integrity, and privacy, very little research has been done in the areas of regulatory compliance [9]. Sensitive data such as patient medical records and business information are highly regulated through government regulations worldwide. For example, in the United States, the Sarbanes-Oxley Act regulates financial data while the Health Insurance Portability and Accountability Act of 1996 regulates patient information. Such regulations require strict integrity and confidentiality guarantees for sensitive information. Although extensive work has been done for complying with these regulations for local storage systems, it is not very clear whether any cloud based system complies with the regulations, given the fundamental nature and architecture of clouds.

19.4.3 LEGAL ISSUES

Another murky legal issue is that of jurisdiction: in many cases, clouds span the whole world. For example, Amazon's clouds are located in North and South America, Europe, and Asia. It is not very clear whether a client's data is subject to, say, the European Union regulations if the subject is based in the United States, but his data is replicated in one of Amazon's data centers located in, say, Europe. The legal foundations for forensic investigations as well as other cybercrime prosecution involving a cloud are yet to be decided.

19.5 CONCLUSION

Cloud computing and Big Data represent the massive changes occurring in our data processing and computational infrastructures. With the significant benefits in terms of greater flexibility, performance, scalability, clouds are here to stay. Similarly, advances in Big Data-processing technology will reap numerous benefits. However, as many of our everyday computing services move to the cloud, we do need to ensure that the data and computation will be secure and trustworthy. In this chapter, we have outlined the major research questions and challenges in cloud and big security and privacy.

The fundamental nature of clouds introduce new security challenges. Today's clouds are not secure, accountable, or trustworthy. Many open problems need to be resolved before major users will adopt clouds for sensitive data and computations. For wider adoption of clouds and Big Data technology in critical areas such as business and healthcare, it is vital to solve these problems. Solving the security issues will popularize clouds further, which in turn, will lower costs and have a broader impact on our society as a whole.

AUTHOR BIOGRAPHY

Dr. Ragib Hasan is a tenure-track assistant professor at the Department of Computer and Information Sciences at the University of Alabama at Birmingham (UAB). With a key focus on practical computer security problems, Hasan explores research on Big Data, cloud security, mobile malware security, secure provenance, and database security. Hasan is the founder of the SECuRE and Trustworthy Computing Lab (SECRETLab, http://secret.cis.uab.edu) at UAB. He is also a member of the UAB Center for Information Assurance and Joint Forensics Research. Before joining UAB in the Fall of 2011, Hasan was an NSF/CRA Computing Innovation Fellow and assistant research scientist at the Department of Computer Science, Johns Hopkins University. He received his PhD and MS degrees in computer science from the University of Illinois at Urbana Champaign in October 2009 and December 2005, respectively. Before that, he received a BSc in computer science and engineering and graduated summa cum laude from Bangladesh University of Engineering and Technology in 2003. He is a recipient of a 2013 Google RISE Award, a 2011 Google Faculty Research Award, the 2009 NSF Computing Innovation Fellowship, and the 2003 Chancellor Award and Gold Medal from Bangladesh University of Engineering and Technology. Dr. Hasan's research is funded by the Department of Homeland Security, the Office of Naval Research, and Google. He is also the founder of The Shikkhok Project (http://www.shikkhok.com)—an award-winning grassroots movement and platform for open content and localized e-learning in South Asia, which has won the 2013 Google RISE Award and 2013 Information Society Innovation Fund Award.

REFERENCES

1. Amazon. Zeus botnet controller. http://aws.amazon.com/security/security-bulletins/zeus-botnet-controller/. [Accessed July 5, 2012.]
2. Amazon EC2. Amazon elastic compute cloud (amazon ec2). http://aws.amazon.com/ec2/. [Accessed July 5, 2012.]
3. Giuseppe Ateniese, Randal Burns, Reza Curtmola, Joseph Herring, Lea Kissner, Zachary Peterson, and Dawn Song. Provable data possession at untrusted stores. In *Proceedings of the 14th ACM Conference on Computer and Communications Security*, CCS'07, pages 598–609, New York, 2007. ACM.
4. Azure. Windows Azure. http://www.windowsazure.com. [Accessed July 5, 2012.]
5. Karyn Benson, Rafael Dowsley, and Hovav Shacham. Do you know where your cloud files are? In *Proceedings of the 3rd ACM Workshop on Cloud Computing Security Workshop*, pages 73–82. ACM, 2011.

6. Mark A. Beyer and Douglas Laney. The importance of "big data": A Definition. Gartner, Available online at http://www.gartner.com/DisplayDocument?ref=clientFriendly Url&id=2057415, 2012.

7. Sara Bouchenak, Gregory Chockler, Hana Chockler, Gabriela Gheorghe, Nuno Santos, and Alexander Shraer. Verifying cloud services: Present and future. *Operating Systems Review*, 48, 2013.

8. Kevin D. Bowers, Marten van Dijk, Ari Juels, Alina Oprea, and Ronald L. Rivest. How to tell if your cloud files are vulnerable to drive crashes. In *Proceedings of the 18th ACM Conference on Computer and Communications Security*, CCS'11, pages 501–514, New York, 2011. ACM.

9. Jon Brodkin. Seven cloud-computing security risks. Report by Gartner, 2008.

10. Yanpei Chen, Vern Paxson, and Randy H. Katz. What's new about cloud computing security. *University of California, Berkeley Report No. UCB/EECS-2010-5 January*, 20(2010):2010–5, 2010.

11. Clavister. Security in the cloud. http://www.clavister.com/documents/resources/white papers/clavister-whp-security-in-the-cloud-gb.pdf. [Accessed July 5, 2012.]

12. Juan Du, Wei Wei, Xiaohui Gu, and Ting Yu. Runtest: Assuring integrity of dataflow processing in cloud computing infrastructures. In *Proceedings of the 5th ACM Symposium on Information, Computer and Communications Security*, ASIACCS'10, pages 293–304, New York, 2010. ACM.

13. GAE. Google app engine. http://appengine.google.com. [Accessed July 5, 2012.]

14. Gartner. Worldwide cloud services market to surpass $68 billion in 2010. http://www.gartner.com/it/page.jsp?id=1389313, 2010. [Accessed July 5, 2012.]

15. Google. Google calendar. https://www.google.com/calendar/. [Accessed July 5, 2012.]

16. Google. Google drive. https://drive.google.com/start#home. [Accessed July 5, 2012.]

17. Bernd Grobauer and Thomas Schreck. Towards incident handling in the cloud: Challenges and approaches. In *Proceedings of the 2010 ACM Workshop on Cloud Computing Security Workshop*, CCSW'10, pages 77–86, New York, 2010. ACM.

18. Joseph Idziorek, Mark Tannian, and Doug Jacobson. Detecting fraudulent use of cloud resources. In *Proceedings of the 3rd ACM Workshop on Cloud Computing Security Workshop*, CCSW'11, pages 61–72, New York, 2011. ACM.

19. INPUT. Evolution of the cloud: The future of cloud computing in government. http://iq.govwin.com/corp/library/detail.cfm?ItemID=8448&cmp=OTC-cloudcomputing ma042009, 2009. [Accessed July 5, 2012.]

20. Ari Juels and Burton S. Kaliski. Pors: Proofs of retrievability for large files. In *Proceedings of the 14th ACM Conference on Computer and Communications Security*, pages 584–597. ACM, 2007.

21. Ali Khajeh-Hosseini, David Greenwood, and Ian Sommerville. Cloud migration: A case study of migrating an enterprise it system to iaas. In *Proceedings of the 3rd International Conference on Cloud Computing (CLOUD)*, pages 450–457. IEEE, 2010.

22. F. John Krautheim. Private virtual infrastructure for cloud computing. In *Proceedings of the 2009 Conference on Hot Topics in Cloud Computing*, pages 1–5. USENIX Association, 2009.

23. Rongxing Lu, Xiaodong Lin, Xiaohui Liang, and Xuemin (Sherman) Shen. Secure provenance: The essential of bread and butter of data forensics in cloud computing. In *Proceedings of the 5th ACM Symposium on Information, Computer and Communications Security*, ASIACCS'10, pages 282–292, New York, 2010. ACM.

24. Market Research Media. Global cloud computing market forecast 2015–2020. http://www.marketresearchmedia.com/2012/01/08/global-cloud-computing-market/. [Accessed July 5, 2012.]

25. Peter Mell and Timothy Grance. Draft NIST working definition of cloud computing-v15. 21 Aug 2009, 2009.

26. Open Cloud Consortium. Open cloud manifesto. *The Open Cloud Manifesto Consortium*, 2009.

27. Thomas Ristenpart, Eran Tromer, Hovav Shacham, and Stefan Savage. Hey, you, get off of my cloud: Exploring information leakage in third-party compute clouds. In *Proceedings of the 16th ACM Conference on Computer and Communications Security*, ACM CCS'09, pages 199–212, New York, 2009. ACM.

28. Indrajit Roy, Srinath T. V. Setty, Ann Kilzer, Vitaly Shmatikov, and Emmett Witchel. Airavat: Security and privacy for MapReduce. In *Proceedings of the 7th USENIX Conference on Networked Systems Design and Implementation*, NSDI'10, pages 297–312, Berkeley, CA, 2010. USENIX Association.

29. Salesforce. Social Enterprise and CRM in the cloud—salesforce.com. http://www.sales force.com/, 2012. [Accessed July 5, 2012.]

30. Nuno Santos, Krishna P. Gummadi, and Rodrigo Rodrigues. Towards trusted cloud computing. In *Proceedings of the 2009 Conference on Hot Topics in Cloud Computing*, Hotcloud'09, Berkeley, CA, USA, 2009. USENIX Association.

31. Nuno Santos, Rodrigo Rodrigues, Krishna P Gummadi, and Stefan Saroiu. Policy-sealed data: A new abstraction for building trusted cloud services. In *Usenix Security*, 2012.

32. Vyas Sekar and Petros Maniatis. Verifiable resource accounting for cloud computing services. In *Proceedings of the 3rd ACM Workshop on Cloud Computing Security Workshop*, CCSW'11, pages 21–26, New York, 2011. ACM.

33. Fengzhe Zhang, Jin Chen, Haibo Chen, and Binyu Zang. Cloudvisor: Retrofitting protection of virtual machines in multi-tenant cloud with nested virtualization. In *Proceedings of the Twenty-Third ACM Symposium on Operating Systems Principles*, pages 203–216. ACM, 2011.

34. Yinqian Zhang, Ari Juels, Michael K. Reiter, and Thomas Ristenpart. Cross-vm side channels and their use to extract private keys. In *ACM Conference on Computer and Communications Security*, pages 305–316, 2012.

Index

Page numbers followed by f and t indicate figures and tables, respectively.

T - #0217 - 101024 - C0 - 234/156/34 [36] - CB - 9781466581500 - Gloss Lamination